Archaeology of the IROQUOIS

The Iroquois and Their Neighbors
Christopher Vecsey, *Series Editor*

Other titles in The Iroquois and Their Neighbors

The Ceremonial of Midwinter
    Elisabeth Tooker

The Collected Speeches of Sagoyewatha, or Red Jacket
    Granville Ganter, ed.

Cornplanter: Chief Warrior of the Allegheny Senecas
    Thomas S. Abler

Iroquoia: The Development of a Native World
    William E. Engelbrecht

Joseph Brant, 1743–1807: Man of Two Worlds
    Isabel Thompson Kelsay

A Journey into Mohawk and Oneida Country, 1634–1635: The Journal of Harmen Meyndertsz van den Bogaert
    Charles T. Gehring & William A. Starna, trans. & ed.

King of the Delawares: Teedyuscung, 1700–1763
    Anthony F. C. Wallace

Mohawk Baronet: A Biography of Sir William Johnson
    James Thomas Flexner

The Montaukett Indians of Eastern Long Island
    John A. Strong

A Narrative of the Life of Mrs. Mary Jemison
    James E. Seaver

Oneida Iroquois, Folklore, Myth, and History: New York Oral Narrative from the Notes of H. E. Allen and Others
    Anthony Wonderley

Red Jacket: Iroquois Diplomat and Orator
    Christopher Densmore

Samson Occom and the Christian Indians of New England
    W. DeLoss Love

Archaeology of the
IROQUOIS

Selected Readings and Research Sources

• • •

Edited by Jordan E. Kerber

With a Foreword by Dean R. Snow

SYRACUSE UNIVERSITY PRESS

Copyright © 2007 by Syracuse University Press
Syracuse, New York 13244–5290

All Rights Reserved

First Edition 2007
14 15 16 17 18 19   6 5 4 3 2

∞ The paper used in this publication meets the minimum requirements
of the American National Standard for Information Sciences—Permanence
of Paper for Printed Library Materials, ANSI Z39.48-1992.

For a listing of books published and distributed by Syracuse University Press,
visit www.SyracuseUniversityPress.syr.edu.

ISBN-13: 978–0–8156–3139–2
ISBN-10: 0–8156–3139–1

Library of Congress Cataloging-in-Publication Data

Archaeology of the Iroquois : selected readings and research sources /
edited by Jordan E. Kerber ; with a foreword by Dean R. Snow.—1st ed.
    p. cm.—(The Iroquois and their neighbors)
Includes bibliographical references and index.
ISBN 978–0–8156–3139–2 (pbk. : alk. paper)
1. Iroquois Indians—Antiquities. 2. Iroquois Indians—History.
3. Archaeology—Northeastern States. 4. Archaeology—Canada, Eastern.
5. Northeastern States—Antiquities. 6. Canada, Eastern—Antiquities.
I. Kerber, Jordan E., 1957–

E99.I7A73 2007
970.004'9755—dc22   2007001244

Manufactured in the United States of America

*For Aunt Jayne
and her Native spirit and open mind*

Contents

Illustrations   *xi*

Foreword, DEAN R. SNOW   *xvii*

Preface   *xxi*

Introduction   *xxiii*

Contributors   *xxix*

PART ONE | **Origins**

Overview
 JORDAN E. KERBER   3

1. Migration in Prehistory: *The Northern Iroquoian Case*
 DEAN R. SNOW   6

2. Migration in Prehistory: *Princess Point and the Northern Iroquoian Case*
 GARY W. CRAWFORD AND DAVID G. SMITH   30

3. More on Migration in Prehistory: *Accommodating New Evidence in the Northern Iroquoian Case*
 DEAN R. SNOW   41

4. New Dates for Owasco Pots
 JANET K. SCHULENBERG   48

5. The Death of Owasco
 JOHN P. HART AND HETTY JO BRUMBACH   67

PART TWO | **Precolumbian Dynamics**

Overview
JORDAN E. KERBER   91

6. Phytolith Evidence for Early Maize *(Zea mays)* in the Northern Finger Lakes Region of New York
JOHN P. HART, ROBERT G. THOMPSON
AND HETTY JO BRUMBACH   93

7. The Precontact Iroquoian Occupation of Southern Ontario
GARY A. WARRICK   124

8. Aboriginal Settlement Patterns in Late Woodland Upper New York State
ROBERT J. HASENSTAB   164

9. The Iroquoian Longhouse: *Architectural and Cultural Identity*
MIMA KAPCHES   174

PART THREE | **Postcolumbian Dynamics**

Overview
JORDAN E. KERBER   191

10. Early Historic Exchange between the Seneca and the Susquehannock
MARTHA L. SEMPOWSKI   194

11. New York Iroquois Political Development
WILLIAM E. ENGELBRECHT   219

12. An Eighteenth-Century Seneca Iroquois Short Longhouse from the Townley-Read Site, ca. A.D. 1715–1754
KURT A. JORDAN   234

13. Contact, Neutral Iroquoian Transformation, and the Little Ice Age
WILLIAM R. FITZGERALD   251

14. European Infectious Disease and Depopulation of the Wendat-Tionontate (Huron-Petun)
GARY A. WARRICK   269

PART FOUR | Material Culture Studies

Overview
JORDAN E. KERBER   287

15. Basque Earrings and Panther's Tails: *The Form of Cross-Cultural Contact in Sixteenth-Century Iroquoia*
JAMES W. BRADLEY AND S. TERRY CHILDS   290

16. The Iroquois and the World's Rim: *Speculations on Color, Culture, and Contact*
GEORGE R. HAMELL   306

17. Reconstructing Patterns of Interaction and Warfare Between the Mohawk and Northern Iroquoians During the A.D. 1400–1700 Period
ROBERT D. KUHN   321

18. Oneida Ceramic Effigies: A Question of Meaning
ANTHONY WONDERLEY   343

19. The Mandeville Site: *A Small Iroquoian Village and a Large Smoking-Pipe Collection—An Interpretation*
CLAUDE CHAPDELAINE   370

PART FIVE | Contemporary Iroquois Perspectives, Repatriation, and Collaborative Archaeology

Overview
JORDAN E. KERBER   387

20. Iroquois Roots
DOUG GEORGE-KANENTIIO   391

21. Who Owns the Past?
G. PETER JEMISON   403

22. Regenerating Identity: *Repatriation and the Indian Frame of Mind*
RICHARD W. HILL, SR.   410

23. Made in Akwesasne
SALLI M. KAWENNOTAKIE BENEDICT   422

24. Case Studies in Collaborative Archaeology
The Oneida Indian Nation of New York and Colgate University
JORDAN E. KERBER   442

PART SIX | Research Sources

25. Research Sources   *457*

   Works Cited   *497*

   Index   *545*

Illustrations

Figures

I.1. Location of Northern Iroquoian nations in the sixteenth century   *xxiv*
I.2. Location of modern Northern Iroquoian nations   *xxiv*
1.1. Late Iroquoian cultures, A.D. 1450–1650   *9*
1.2. A simplified chronology of the archaeological and historical cultures mentioned in the text   *11*
1.3. Generalized distributions of sites pertaining to early Iroquoian cultures, A.D. 900–1300, and principal geological features of the region   *12*
2.1. The Princess Point region   *32*
4.1. Location of the Kipp Island, Hunter's Home, and Levanna sites   *54*
4.2. Residue encrusted on interior of sherd no. 13   *58*
4.3. Point Peninsula sherds nos. 1, 12, and 15, untyped sherd no. 13   *60*
4.4. Owasco sherds nos. 4, 6, 7, 137   *60*
4.5. Owasco sherds nos. 99, 40, 107, 23   *61*
4.6. 2–σ calibrated AMS dates and intercepts from encrusted residues   *63*
5.1. Ritchie's (1936) culture-historic scheme for New York   *72*
5.2. Ritchie's (1969) final late prehistoric culture-historic scheme for New York   *83*
6.1. Approximate locations of archaeological sites from which samples were used for this study   *96*
6.2. Photograph of sherd 41119–5 interior showing cooking residue and area where residue has been removed   *99*
6.3. Entire decorated rondel   *109*
6.4. Indented rondel   *109*
6.5. Variety of rondel forms   *110*
6.6. Rondel forms more typical of maize and wild rice   *110*
6.7. Detrended correspondence analysis using morphology and size data   *112*
6.8. Squash phytolith from residue sample 40525–1   *114*

6.9. Sedge phytolith from sample 40525–1   115
6.10. Distribution of *Zizania aquatica* in New York State   119
6.11. Distribution of the sedge *Cyperus odoratus* in New York State   120
7.1. Southern Ontario   125
7.2. Princess Point vessel from Varden site, Long Point   132
7.3. Princess Point site clusters   135
7.4. Holmedale site plan, Brantford   138
7.5. Early Iroquoian site clusters   142
7.6. Ireland site plan, Burlington   143
7.7. Uren site plan, Norwich   147
7.8. Middle Iroquoian site clusters   148
7.9. Decorated pipe bowls from Winking Bull site, Mountsberg   152
7.10. Precontact Neutral, Huron-Petun, and St. Lawrence Iroquoian site clusters   153
7.11. Ivan Elliot site, house 1   154
7.12. Draper village reconstruction   155
7.13. Occupational history of Draper site   156
7.14. Lawson site excavation and reconstruction, London   157
7.15. Pottery rim sherds, Draper site   159
7.16. St. Lawrence Iroquoian vessel   160
8.1. The study area showing the homelands of the Five Nations and the three physiographic zones in upper New York State   165
8.2. Changes in village locations in the central valley zone with respect to five environmental variables   167
9.1. Map of Iroquoia   175
9.2. Two plans of house 7, Nodwell site   179
9.3. House 12 at Draper site, house 4 at Draper site, house 2 at Hamilton site   182
9.4. House 16 and house 37 from Ball site; house 5 from Mackenzie Woodbridge site   184
10.1. Map of region showing locations of Seneca Cameron and Dutch Hollow sites and Susquehannock Schultz site   199
10.2. Most common glass-bead varieties in each of nine groupings used in this study   206
10.3. Frequencies of glass-bead groups in Seneca and Susquehannock sites under study   208
10.4. Rounded brass beads from the Cameron site   210
10.5. Rolled brass spiral from the Cameron site   210
10.6. Corrugated brass bracelet from the Schultz site   211
11.1. Sixteenth- and seventeenth-century Seneca and Onondaga sites   221

11.2. Model of Iroquois political development and population
distribution   222
11.3. Ceramic vessels from the Adams site   225
11.4. Ceramic vessels from the Adams site   226
12.1. Topographic map of the Townley-Read site occupied
ca. A.D. 1715–54   235
12.2. Structure 1 post molds and features from the Townley-Read site,
area D, domestic refuse cluster 1   238
12.3. Interpretation of size and internal features of structure 1 at the
Townley-Read site, area D, domestic refuse cluster 1   239
13.1. Neutral territory in the fifteenth century and by the
mid-sixteenth century   253
13.2. Plan of the MacPherson site, showing expansion of the
palisaded village   255
13.3. Carbon isotope trends   256
13.4. Ceramic vessel rims from the fifteenth-century Ivan Elliot site   259
13.5. Houses 5 and 6 from the sixteenth-century MacPherson site   260
13.6. Ceramic vessel rims from the sixteenth-century MacPherson site   261
13.7. Corn heat unit values for southern Ontario   265
14.1. Distribution of Iroquoian groups in northeastern North America
ca. A.D. 1615   271
14.2. Population growth curve for the Wendat-Tionontate A.D. 800–1650   278
15.1. Spiral #76/94 from the Seneca Adams site   291
15.2. Hoop #526/94 from the Seneca Adams site   291
15.3. Distribution of spirals and hoops on sixteenth-century
sites before 1575   293
15.4. Distribution of spirals and hoops on sixteenth-century
sites after 1575   294
15.5. Occurrence of spirals and hoops on Seneca sites   295
15.6. Occurrence of spirals and hoops on Susquehannock sites   295
15.7. Annealed structure in the cross-section of spiral #76/94   298
15.8. Spiral #178/94 from the Seneca Adams site   298
15.9. Annealed structure at one bend in the cross-section
of hoop #526/94   299
15.10. Spiral from the Onondaga Dwyer site   299
15.11. Annealed structure in the cross-section of the Dwyer spiral   300
17.1. Frequency of Northern Iroquoian pottery in Mohawk
ceramic assemblages   327
17.2. Exotic pottery from the Garoga site   330
17.3. St. Lawrence Iroquoian-like low collar stamped rim sherd from
the Martin site   331

xiv · Illustrations

17.4. Huron-like Seed Incised variant rim from the Martin site   *331*
17.5. Huron Incised rim sherds with basal notching from the Martin site   *332*
17.6. Topographic maps showing location of the Mohawk Getman, Elwood, Otstungo, and Garoga sites   *339*
18.1. Locations of Oneida and other ceramic effigy traditions mentioned in text   *347*
18.2. Iroquois effigies   *349*
18.3. Iroquois effigies possibly depicting females   *349*
18.4. Oneida effigies (ca. 1450–1500) from the Buyea and Goff sites   *351*
18.5. Oneida effigies (ca. 1500–1525) from the Olcott site   *352*
18.6. Oneida effigies (ca. 1500–1525) from the Vaillancourt site   *353*
18.7. Oneida effigy vessel (ca. 1500–1525), ca. 28 cm high, from the Vaillancourt site   *354*
18.8. Oneida effigies (ca. 1525–70) from the Diable and Bach sites   *355*
18.9. Oneida effigies (ca. 1570–95) from the Cameron site   *356*
18.10. Oneida effigies from the Beecher/Blowers and Thurston sites   *357*
18.11. Oneida effigy vessel (ca. 1595–1625) from the Beecher/Blowers site   *358*
18.12. Oneida effigy vessel (ca. 1625–37), ca. 16 cm high, from the Thurston site   *358*
18.13. Oneida effigy forms and the "corn ear" rim design   *359*
18.14. Effigy faces and incised designs characteristic of Munsee Incised pottery, Minisink Culture of the upper Delaware River   *365*
18.15. Sacred drumsticks used in the Delaware Big House Ceremony   *367*
19.1. Variability of the human effigy pipes from the Mandeville site   *373*
19.2. Variability of the animal effigy pipes from the Mandeville site   *375*
19.3. Human or human/animal effigy pipes from the Mandeville site   *376*
19.4. This smoking pipe is a double human face effigy pipe found on the occupation floor of a longhouse at the Mandeville site, Tracy, Quebec   *381*
23.1. Akwesasne Wolf Belt   *428*
23.2. Two-Row Wampum   *430*
24.1. New York State map, showing the location of Colgate University and the Sterling, Dungey, and Wilson sites   *443*
24.2. Oneida Youth Work/Learn Program participant rejoices at finding a seventeenth-century glass trade bead during the archaeological workshop at the Wilson site in August 2003   *448*

Tables

I.1. Woodland Period Chronology and Approximate Dates   *xxvi*
1.1. Calibrated Radiocarbon Age Determinations for the Earliest Owasco, Glen Meyer, and Pickering Sites   *14*

2.1. AMS Radiocarbon Dates on Maize from Two Princess Point Sites   33
4.1. Key Components of the Three Models of Iroquoian Development   52
4.2. Ceramic Sherds AMS Dated   53
4.3. Radiocarbon Dates from Kipp Island   54
4.4. Carpenter Brook Phase Houses in Central New York   57
4.5. Physical Characteristics of Sherds Selected for Dating   59
4.6. AMS Dates and Calibrated Two-Sigma Ranges on Sherd Residues   62
5.1. Late Point Peninsula and Early Owasco Types   77
5.2. AMS Dates on Charred Cooking Residue from Three New York Sites   79
5.3. Pottery Types and Corresponding Dates on Cooking Residues   80
6.1. AMS Dates on Charred Cooking Residue from Three New York Sites   100
6.2. AMS Dates on Cooking Residue from the Hunter's Home Site   101
6.3. AMS Dates on Cooking Residue from the Kipp Island Site   102
6.4. Archaeological and Comparative Sample Proveniences   105
6.5. Data on Prehistoric Maize Cobs Subjected to Phytolith Analysis   106
6.6. Rondel Phytolith Taxonomy   108
6.7. Squared-Chord Distance Values Using Morphology and Size Data   111
6.8. Squared-Chord Distance Matrix for Comparative Maize Samples Using Morphology Data Only   113
6.9. Squared-Chord Distance Values for Maize Samples Using Morphology Data Only   114
6.10. $\delta^{13}C$ Values for Experimental Cooking Residues   117
6.11. Residue $\delta^{13}C$ Enrichment above Value for a Prehistoric Wild Rice Seed   117
6.12. Summary of Results   118
10.1. Comparison of Glass Beads from Early Historic Seneca and Susquehannock Sites   202
11.1. Coefficients of Agreement as Measured by Ceramic Similarity among Seneca Sites   223
11.2. Coefficients of Homogeneity for Seneca Sites   224
11.3. Coefficients of Homogeneity for Oneida Sites   232
12.1. Post Mold Diameter Figures (cm) for Selected Iroquoian Sites   243
12.2. Iron Nail Density per Square Meter of Excavated Area at Selected Iroquois Sites   244
13.1. Frequencies of Deer and Woodchuck Remains at Neutral Iroquoian Settlements   256
13.2. Trends in Neutral Iroquoian Longhouse Lengths   257
14.1. Archaeological Estimates of Wendat-Tionontate Population   277
15.1. Chronological Distribution of Spirals and Hoops   292

15.2. Mortuary Associations for Spirals and Hoops   296
15.3. Chemical Analysis by Atomic Absorption   301
17.1. Mohawk Site Chronology and Ceramic Assemblage Sizes   326
17.2. Ceramic Samples Used in the Trace Element Analysis   334
17.3. List of Northern Iroquoian Pipes in Mohawk Assemblages by Time Period   335
19.1. The Mandeville Site Smoking-Pipes Collection   372
19.2. Mandeville Pipe-Type Frequencies   374
19.3. Mandeville Pipe-Bowl Capacity   376
19.4. Effigy Pipes on St. Lawrence Iroquoian Sites   380

Foreword
DEAN R. SNOW

THIS BOOK IS A SAMPLING of recent key articles that reflect the current state of Northern Iroquoian studies. Apart from one article that was published in 1985, none of them predates the last decade of the twentieth century. They are drawn mostly, but not entirely, from the scientific literature, books and journals that are subject to rigorous peer review and thereby represent what are currently regarded as the most reliable conclusions available.

Iroquoian studies have come a long way since the pen of Lewis Henry Morgan propelled them to international notoriety in 1851. The downward curve of Native American populations, which did not reach its nadir until the end of that century, caused anthropologists to scramble to salvage what remained of their cultures, caused bureaucrats to call for assimilation, and caused many Iroquois to turn over cultural patrimony to collectors and museums. There Iroquoian objects took their places near mastodon skeletons, stuffed bison, and other things extinct or nearly so.

No one predicted the resurgence of Iroquois culture that gathered momentum through the twentieth century. This revival was largely because both popular and scientific models tended to regard Native American cultures as static and brittle things that could experience change only in the form of irreversible loss. William Fenton's 1948 position paper on the current status of anthropology in the region was typical of the time, being entirely historical in outlook. His own research focused on recording and thereby preserving the rich heritage of Iroquois language and ritual, which was commanded by an ever-shrinking pool of elders. Later, when younger Iroquois began asserting themselves, Fenton gave them little notice, for they did not share that wealth of traditional knowledge. Not surprisingly this disregard was perceived by many Iroquois as condescension and returned in kind.

The annual Conference on Iroquois Research began informally after the Second World War. At first it was usually attended by a small number of scholars and a few traditional Iroquois elders. By the end of the century the meeting had grown considerably, and it is now attended by dozens of academics, students, Iroquois, and others, individual participants often fitting into more than one of those categories. At the same time the American Indian Program at Cornell University, the Iroquois Indian Museum, and many other similar programs and institutions have broadened both interest in Iroquois topics and the array of techniques used to address them.

Iroquois culture, like any other, is dynamic and constantly changing. Modern Iroquois are no less Iroquois than their ancestors even though they might not speak anything but English. Yet rapid change and the homogenizing ubiquity of modern America have unsettled even the most self-assured modern American Indians. The new Museum of the American Indian in Washington is one result. It is a forward-looking institution that for all its value to American Indian pride disappoints non-Indians for its relative disinterest in their rich heritage of 14,000 years.

By the end of the twentieth century it was fashionable in academic circles generally and cultural anthropology in particular to approach topics of interest more subjectively, and to give greater credence to alternative points of view. This shift was abetted by the writings of postmodernist philosophers, a failed movement that has now largely disappeared from disciplines other than cultural anthropology. The notions that all assertions are equal by definition, that there is no such thing as objectivity, that science is inherently evil, and that all arguments are political were unsustainable, for they contained the seeds of their own chaotic demise.

There is never a last word in the world of archaeological (or any other) science, only the latest one. With that in mind, this volume is of great value to students learning the scientific method and the techniques of source criticism. Has a given paper cited all the relevant sources or just some of them? Has it represented the sources fairly? What data are presented to support conclusions? Was the paper published after rigorous peer review? Are conclusions based on hypotheses that have been tested or are they merely the ones currently favored for other reasons? Is there new evidence that invalidates what might have been the best hypothesis when the paper was written? That is how these papers were read when first published and their republication here does not exempt them from continued criticism, especially because new data are always emerging.

The sometimes intemperate free-for-all that temporarily afflicted scholarship in the late twentieth century occasionally drove debates to polar extremes. Vine Deloria, the late Dakota author, was able to get away with saying that the hypothesis that "Indians came first via the Bering Strait" is "a myth with little to recommend it." To him oral tradition, whatever the specifics, trumped archaeological science. Archaeologists for their part often dismissed oral tradition as worthless because it is so easily reworked for contemporary political purposes. But both extreme views are wrong. It does not matter at all where a hypothesis comes from, so long as it is testable and so long as it is tested in good faith. In my own work, I have used hypotheses derived from archaeological theory, archaeological finds, Iroquois oral tradition, and historical documents, letting the chips fall where they may. I have learned much more than would have been the case had I dismissed one or another of these sources beforehand.

Astute readers will detect from these chapters where current research is taking Iroquoian archaeology. The in situ hypothesis, which was a controlling model used by Iroquoian archaeologists for half a century, has acquired such a load of contradictory evidence that it can no longer be sustained except by selective disregard of relevant data. Even the basic units of archaeological analysis that were useful, even indispensable, a few decades ago have been made obsolete by modern radiocarbon dating and other techniques. Thus we have the obituary announcing the unlamented "death of Owasco."

There are also persisting uncertainties that should inform any critical reading of these papers. Did maize (corn) spread to the region independent of population movement or did it arrive with Iroquoian-speaking peoples? Can phytolith specialists consistently and reliably distinguish maize pollen from cattail pollen? Is current oral tradition contradicted by oral tradition recorded two centuries ago? How do epidemics behave in populations that live in small scattered towns and villages? These are just a sampling of the questions that cannot be fully answered as of this writing, and they are part of the reason for the dynamic state of Iroquois archaeology today.

Iroquoian archaeology is covered by a very large number of books and journal articles. As a consequence, Jordan Kerber's task has been much more daunting than it would have been a half-century ago. No two scholars would winnow this vast literature to the same set of 24 articles that are reprinted in this volume. Any of us could criticize any other for not including something we consider indispensable, and I suppose that our own writings would in each case rise near to the top of each list of glaring omissions. But what the reader has here is a good start, a portal into a subject that appears esoteric only until one gets to know it a little. Whatever you do, do not stop reading here.

| Preface

I INITIATED THIS PROJECT with the idea to assemble a reader on the archaeology of the Iroquois, a selection of relatively recent articles well-suited for teaching college and graduate courses in archaeology and Native American Studies. Despite a voluminous body of literature on the subject, I was struck by the absence of a collection of selected contemporary readings. As I began to list and then to peruse key sources for possible inclusion, I created a bibliography of suggested further readings. I envisioned incorporating a short listing of such references within each section of the reader, a common occurrence with similar collections. The more articles I read, however, the larger the bibliography grew, and the more difficult it became to decide which sources to list and which to exclude. As a result, the "suggested further readings" evolved into a significantly larger and broader listing of relevant publications (and Ph.D. dissertations) on Iroquoian archaeology. The topical sections are the same as those used to organize the selected readings. Although not exhaustive, the research sources section forming part 6 is much more useful to specialists and nonspecialists than lists of suggested further readings.

Because Iroquoian archaeological sites exist on both sides of the border between Canada and the United States (principally in Ontario, Quebec, New York, and Pennsylvania), there is a parochial tendency among many Canadian Iroquoian scholars to work in their country and among American ones to work in theirs. Most researchers in Iroquoian archaeology, therefore, likely are not familiar with all the references in the extensive list of research sources forming part 6 of this volume. As a result, the bibliography enables archaeologists studying the Iroquois in the United States to increase their awareness of the published record of their colleagues in Canada and vice versa. I am hopeful that such knowledge will lead to a more unified and integrated approach to understanding the Iroquois in the past.

I have several people to thank for their contributions to this volume. Colgate University librarians, especially Ann Ackerson, were especially helpful in obtaining numerous publications through interlibrary loan, no small feat when the university's Case Library was "closed" for months during renovation. I am grateful for permission from the respective publishers, authors, and editors to republish the articles in this volume, and for the copies of articles and illustrations that many people kindly sent me. I thank Dean Snow for writing the foreword and, along with Mary Moran, Jack Rossen, and Kurt Jordan, for constructively commenting on drafts of the manuscript. I am also grateful for the support of Glenn Wright, Acquisitions Editor, and Christopher Vecsey, Series Editor. A special thanks goes to Lindsey Guerin for scanning and formatting most of the articles; to Mary Peterson Moore, Manager of Design and Production, and her staff for scanning nearly all of the illustrations; to Jill Root for copyediting the manuscript; to Scott Smiley for indexing the book; to the Colgate University Research Council for providing funds to assist in the completion of this book; and to Lourdes Rojas-Paiewonsky and Marilyn Thie, Division Directors of University Studies at Colgate University, Michael Johnston, Division Director of Social Sciences at Colgate University, Lyle Roelofs, Provost and Dean of the Faculty at Colgate University, and Christopher Vecsey, Director of the Native American Studies Program at Colgate University, for subsidizing a portion of the reprint fees and other costs. I am also indebted to the authors of the selected readings and of the research sources listed in part 6, for without their scholarship this volume would not be possible.

My family remains a lasting source of encouragement. They contributed to the completion of this project in ways that are less obvious to others. In particular, I thank my wife, Mary Moran, and my children, Pearl and John, for their patience and understanding while I worked on the volume. I also wish to acknowledge my aunt, Jayne Lesser, to whom this book is dedicated. She nurtured a sense of curiosity and wonder in me at a young age that continues still.

| Introduction

THERE EXISTS A VAST, ever-increasing body of literature on the archaeology of the Iroquois that spans more than 100 years of work by scholars, students, avocational archaeologists, and others. The Research Sources section forming part 6 of this book includes more than 500 sources on Iroquoian archaeology. Such a listing not only makes a valuable contribution to the study of past Iroquois cultures, but also is useful for specialists and nonspecialists alike in their pursuit of knowledge and research, as well as in their preparation of papers and publications on the archaeology of this group of Native Americans from the northeastern United States and Canada. In addition to the extensive Research Sources section, this book contains 24 contemporary articles, originally published in regional and international journals, edited volumes, and conference proceedings. They cover a wide range of current topics in Iroquoian archaeology.

For hundreds of years, the Iroquois have settled much of northeastern North America before and after Europeans arrived in the sixteenth century. During this time, they were surrounded by Algonquian-speaking Native peoples, from whom they differed in numerous ways beyond language. The term *Iroquois* was coined by the French based on a word pronounced as "Hirokoa" and meaning "killer people," which the Algonquians and early European Basque fishermen used to describe their Iroquois neighbors (Bakker 1990). For the purposes of this book, the term *Iroquois* refers to northern groups of indigenous people who spoke Iroquoian languages and resided in present-day New York, Pennsylvania, northern Maryland, southern Ontario, and southern Quebec during the sixteenth and seventeenth centuries (fig. I.1). Of course, Iroquois still live in their homelands (see fig. I.2) and in other regions, and some continue to speak their native languages. Although Southern Iroquoian groups (including the Cherokee) have long roots in what is now southern Virginia and northern North Carolina, the Northern Iroquoians are the focus of this volume, because the vast majority of archaeological research pertains to these communities.

Northern Iroquoians consist of the following nations, most of which settled in the vicinity of Lake Ontario, Lake Erie, Lake Huron, and the St. Lawrence River:

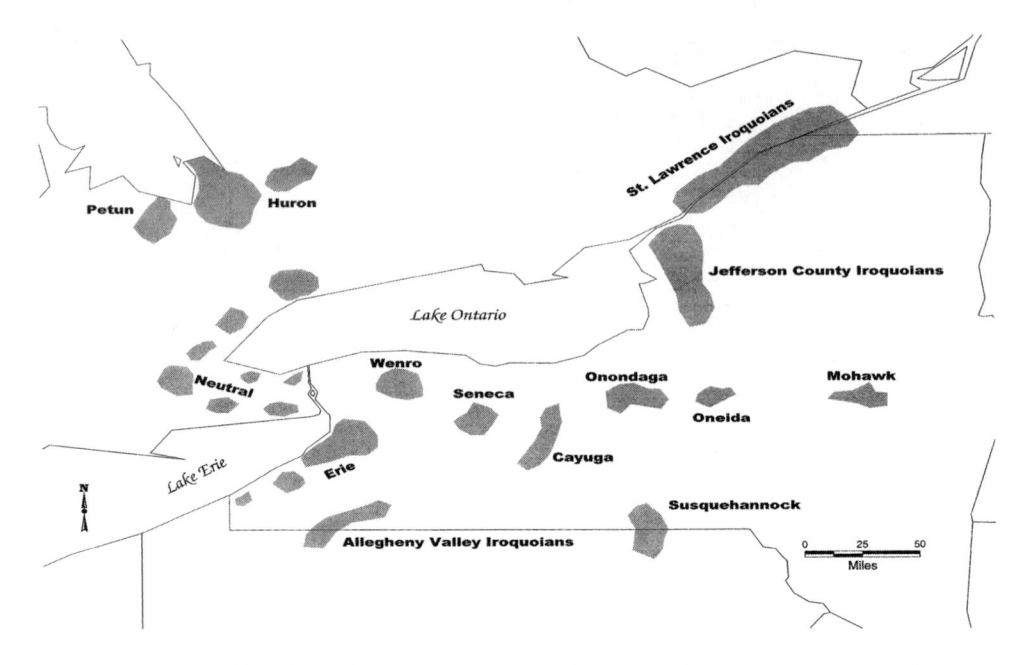

Fig. I.1. Location of Northern Iroquoian nations in the sixteenth century (from Engelbrecht 2003, 2). Printed with permission of William E. Engelbrecht.

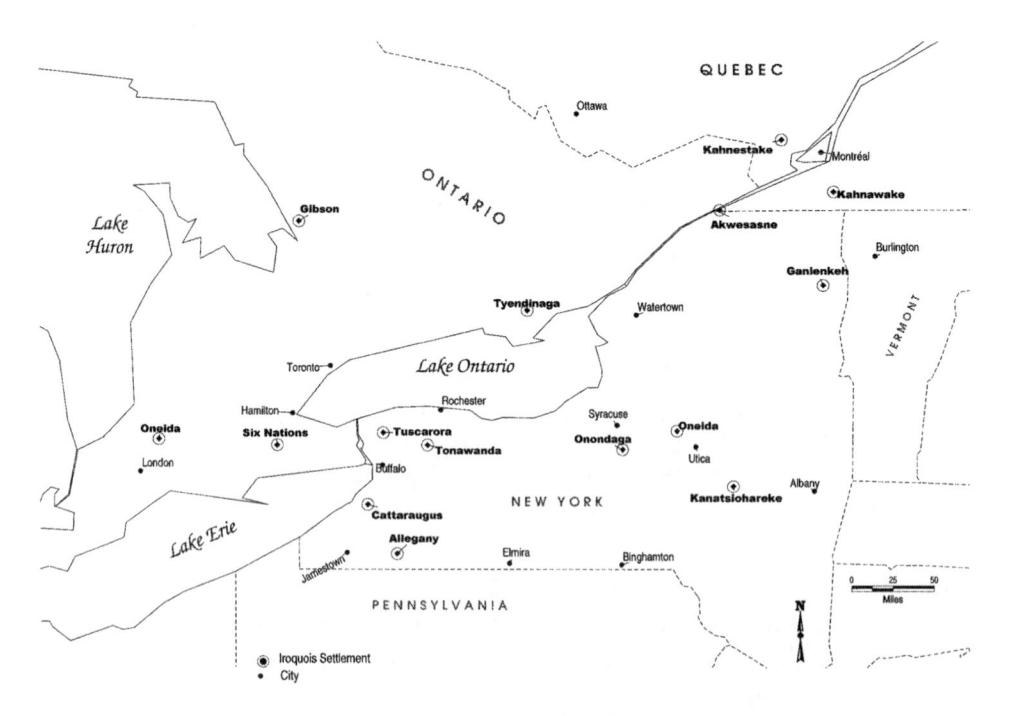

Fig. I.2. Location of modern Northern Iroquoian nations (from Engelbrecht 2003, 172). Printed with permission of William E. Engelbrecht.

Mohawk, Oneida, Onondaga, Cayuga, and Seneca across central New York State from east to west, respectively (which together comprise the League of the Iroquois or Five Nations Iroquois Confederacy—the Tuscarora were added as the sixth nation by 1713); Jefferson County Iroquoians, Wenro, and Erie of Western New York; Susquehannock of southern New York, Pennsylvania, and northern Maryland; Allegheny Valley Iroquoians of western New York and Pennsylvania; St. Lawrence Iroquoians (or Laurentian Iroquoians) of southern Quebec and southern Ontario; and Huron (or Wyandot, Wendat consisting of a confederacy of five nations), Neutral (also consisting of a five-nation confederacy), and Petun (or Tobacco) of southern Ontario. Other unnamed Northern Iroquoian communities, also studied by archaeologists, were absorbed by neighboring Iroquois or disappeared from the archaeological record along with the Susquehannock, Erie, Neutral, and St. Lawrence Iroquoians, among others. At their height, just before European contact, the Northern Iroquoians totaled more than 90,000 individuals, with the Five Nations Iroquois probably accounting for just under 22,000.

Many authors use the term *Iroquois* to refer to the Five Nations Iroquois (or later, after the Tuscarora joined, Six Nations Iroquois) of New York and *Iroquoians* to refer to the other populations of Iroquoian speakers in the northeastern United States and Canada. Nevertheless, all of these groups tend to be called *Northern Iroquoians*, despite some differences among their individual cultures. They are also known by other names in their separate, but related, Iroquoian languages. Similarly, members of the League of the Iroquois often call themselves the *Haudenosaunee*, an indigenous term meaning "People of the Longhouse."

As the readings and references in this volume discuss, the Iroquois (i.e., Northern Iroquoians) are typically identified in the archaeological record on the basis of several common traits. They planted maize, beans, and squash (the "three sisters") for their subsistence, in addition to hunting, gathering, and fishing. They lived in longhouses within villages often defended by fences or palisades. Many of their artifacts, such as pottery vessels, smoking pipes, and carved bone objects, were decorated with distinctive styles. They also highly valued wampum, the small beads made of marine shell used for trade and for commemorating important events, as well as glass beads and items modified from brass obtained from Europeans during contact. Although other Native groups possessed some of these archaeological traits, only the Iroquois maintained the entire set. Unfortunately, because of partial preservation, biases, and other problems, archaeology is unable to provide a complete picture of the Iroquois past. Additional aspects of early Iroquois cultures, including language, belief systems, marriage, kinship, and other customs, are more aptly reconstructed from oral history and documentary information following initial European contact than they are from archaeological remains. These sources, however, have their own limitations in depicting entirely accurate accounts.

Perhaps more than any other Native group, the Iroquois have long been studied by archaeologists, cultural anthropologists, historians, and linguists. One of the first anthropological accounts of the Iroquois, especially the Seneca, was written by Lewis Henry Morgan in 1851. Completed in the late nineteenth and early twentieth centuries, the works of Arthur Parker, a member of the Seneca Nation; William Beauchamp; David Boyle; and William Wintemberg are among the earliest writings on Iroquoian archaeology in New York and Ontario. Several of these publications are listed in the Research Sources section. A substantially greater number of references on Iroquois history and ethnography, however, are excluded because they are not archaeological. The bibliographical sources are limited to those focusing on archaeological research or material evidence in the form of artifacts, food residue, structures, and features (including hearths, refuse and storage pits, and burials), in addition to other cultural remains. This restriction means that references based entirely on historical records and documentary sources, although relevant to archaeology, are not included. For instance, only one of the publications by the prolific Iroquois cultural anthropologist William Fenton is listed.

The Research Sources section primarily contains archaeological references commonly cited in the literature, although others that are somewhat obscure have also been included. It is not intended to represent an exhaustive coverage of Iroquoian archaeology. Such a goal is impossible to achieve given the enormity of extant sources, many with restricted circulation. Perusal of the following publications will locate innumerable relevant articles, some of which are listed in the Research Sources: *Pennsylvania Archaeologist, The Bulletin: Journal of the New York State Archaeological Association, Ontario Archaeology, Annual Archaeological Report for Ontario, London Museum of Archaeology (Museum of Indian Archaeology) Bulletin, Canadian Journal of Archaeology, Canadian Journal of Anthropology, Canadian Archaeological Association Bulletin,* and *Archaeological Survey of Canada* (National Museum of Man, Mercury Series). The Research Sources section does not include works in French, and, with the exception of Ph.D. dissertations, all listings are publications. Thus, numerous unpublished sources of considerable relevant material from M.A. theses,

Table I.1

Woodland Period Chronology and Approximate Dates

Chronology	*Approximate Dates*
Early Woodland Period	1000 B.C.–A.D. 300
Middle Woodland Period	A.D. 300–900
Princess Point Complex	A.D. 500–1000
Point Peninsula Tradition	A.D. 100–900
Late Woodland Period	A.D. 900–1550
Owasco Tradition	A.D. 900–1300
Pickering Tradition	A.D. 900–1300
Glen Meyer Tradition	A.D. 900–1300

cultural resource management reports, conference papers, and articles in archaeological society chapter bulletins and newsletters are excluded, as limited copies are available. Interested readers should check issues of the following chapter bulletins and newsletters in particular: *Bulletin of the Chenango Chapter of the New York State Archaeological Association* (Norwich, N.Y.); *Bulletin of the William M. Beauchamp Chapter of the New York State Archaeological Association* (Syracuse, N.Y.); *Kewa* (Newsletter of the London Chapter, Ontario Archaeological Society); and *Arch Notes* (Newsletter of the Ontario Archaeological Society). The diligent researcher is also referred to Paul Weinman's (1969) bibliography of the Iroquoian literature, specifically pages 3–47, for several archaeological references, principally on the Five Nations Iroquois, that are not listed in this book. Likewise, relevant material in abundance may be found in the texts and bibliographies of assorted recent syntheses, such as Bamann et al. (1992), Bekerman and Warrick (1995), Ellis and Ferris (1990), Engelbrecht (2003), and Pendergast and Chapdelaine (1993), to name just a few.

After combing through countless sources and their bibliographies, as well as scouring various publication databases, in amassing this volume's listing of references, deciding on an organization for the Research Sources was the next obstacle to overcome. In light of the large number and diversity of sources I determined that, instead of simply listing all items, a more useful format would be to organize the more than 500 entries under a few headings. I have therefore chosen five headings, based on a combination of major topics and time periods (though one could arrange the works using other categories). These are: Origins (focusing on the origins of the Iroquois and the Iroquois Confederacy); Precolumbian Dynamics (focusing on subsistence, settlement pattern, sociopolitical organization, and demography); Postcolumbian Dynamics; Material Culture Studies; and Contemporary Iroquois Perspectives, Repatriation, and Collaborative Archaeology. These categories cover the myriad subjects addressed in the literature on Iroquoian archaeology.

The task of assigning each reference (and many selected readings) to a particular section was often difficult. Numerous sources contain material pertinent to more than one part. Instead of listing the same reference in multiple sections, I placed each in the most relevant part, a subjective call at best. Similarly, a decision was needed as to whether to list an entire edited volume or its individual chapters. If an edited book contains several pertinent papers, as opposed to only a few, the edited book as a whole is cited; otherwise, the chapters are listed separately rather than the entire volume—again a subjective choice.

The readings are organized into the same five parts as the Research Sources. Choosing the particular articles was no easy task. I sought a variety, ranging from site-specific studies to broad synthetic overviews of diverse topics on Iroquoian archaeology in the northeastern United States and Canada. I also selected these particular articles for their usefulness in teaching undergraduate and graduate classes in the archaeology of North America, of the Northeast, and of the Iroquois. They are not intended to be the "classics" (though some may now or eventually will be so regarded), nor should they be viewed as representing the "best" articles or the "definitive" word on the subject. Put simply, they reflect the wide spectrum of contemporary publications in the field. A number of other sources by different authors could effectively substitute for those presented here.

At the beginning of each of the five parts that follow, I provide a brief overview to introduce and to contextualize the articles. For readers who are unfamiliar with the Woodland Period chronology discussed in the reprints, see table I.1 for approximate dates. Some of the dates in this table, however, as well as the Owasco Tradition construct itself, have been called into question, as demonstrated by the essays in part 1. As research on Iroquoian archaeology continues, and new discoveries and interpretations are made, I hope that a subsequent edition of readings and research sources will replace this one.

| Contributors

Salli M. Kawennotakie Benedict is research manager for the Aboriginal Rights and Research Office of the Mohawk Council of Akwesasne in Rooseveltown, New York. A member of the Mohawk Nation (Akwesasne), she is also a professional writer whose work has been published in anthologies such as *New Voices from the Longhouse* (1989) and *Reinventing the Enemy's Language: Contemporary Native Women's Writing of North America* (1997).

James W. Bradley is the founder and president of ArchLink, a nonprofit organization linking archaeology with education and preservation and located in Charlestown, Massachusetts.

Hetty Jo Brumbach holds the position of associate curator of anthropology in the University of Albany's Department of Anthropology, and is also a museum associate of the New York State Museum in Albany, New York. Her research focuses on the northeastern United States, especially the prehistory of the Iroquois and Algonquian-speaking peoples and their predecessors of central New York and the Hudson River Valley.

Claude Chapdelaine is professor of anthropology in the Department of Anthropology of the University of Montreal, in Montreal, Canada. His research interests include prehistoric archaeology in the American Northeast and the northern coast of Peru.

S. Terry Childs is an archaeologist with the Archaeology and Ethnography Program of the National Park Service in Washington, D.C., and a research collaborator at the Conservation Analytical Laboratory, Smithsonian Institution. Her research interests include African iron and copper production and North American native copper. Among other work, she has edited *Our Collective Responsibility: The Ethics and Practice of Archaeological Collections Stewardship* (2004).

Gary W. Crawford is chairman and professor of the Department of Anthropology of the University of Toronto at Mississauga. He is an anthropological archaeologist specializing in archaeological botany and environmental archaeology.

William E. Engelbrecht is emeritus professor of anthropology in Buffalo State College's Department of Anthropology in Buffalo, New York, and president of the New York State Archaeological Association. In 2002 he published *Iroquoia: The Development of a Native World* with Syracuse University Press.

William R. Fitzgerald is a curator for the Bruce County Museum and Cultural Centre in Southampton, Ontario.

Doug George-Kanentiio, a member of the Mohawk Nation (Akwesasne), is chairman of Round Dance Productions of Oneida, New York, a nonprofit, Native-operated educational foundation dedicated to preserving Iroquois culture. He is also a journalist and former editor of *Akwesasne Notes*.

George R. Hamell is the ethnology collections manager of the Research and Collections Division of the New York State Museum in Albany, New York. He has written extensively on his research specialties of ethnohistory, ethnology, and the Iroquois.

John P. Hart is the director and chief scientist for archaeology of the Research and Collections Division of the New York State Museum in Albany, New York, with a research specialty in the evolution of prehistoric agriculture. He is currently heading a project to establish the history of the three principal agricultural crops used by Native Americans in New York, maize, bean, and squash, and explore the development of the polycropping system that included these crops.

Robert J. Hasenstab is clinical assistant professor and director of the GIS (Geographic Information Systems) Laboratory of the Department of Anthropology and Program in Geography at the University of Illinois at Chicago. His research interests include archaeology, geographic information systems, remote sensing, economic anthropology; the northeastern United States, and Iroquois.

Richard W. Hill, Sr., a member of the Tuscarora Nation at Six Nations in Ontario, is the director of the Haudenosaunee Resource Center of the Tonawanda Seneca Nation and the chair of the Haudenosaunee Standing Committee on Burial Rules and Regulations. He has held several museum posts, including the directorship of the American Indian Arts Museum in Santa Fe, and is a consultant for the Smithsonian's National Museum of the American Indian in Washington, D.C.

G. Peter Jemison, a member of the Seneca Nation of Indians, is site manager for the Ganondagan State Historic Site in Victor, New York. An artist whose work has been acquired by numerous museums and private collectors worldwide, he has also served as board member at large for the Association of American Museums. In 2005 President Bush appointed him to a three-year term as the Native American member to the Federal Advisory Council on Historic Preservation.

Kurt A. Jordan is assistant professor of anthropology and American Indian studies in Cornell University's Department of Anthropology in Ithaca, New York. His research interests include Iroquoian archaeology and history, historical archaeology of indigenous peoples, colonialism and cultural entanglement, and archaeology and present-day indigenous communities.

Mima Kapches is senior curator of Ontario archaeology and deputy head of the Department of World Cultures in the Royal Ontario Museum, Toronto, specializing in southern Ontario's Iroquoian-speaking peoples. She has also served as president of the Ontario Archaeological Society and the Canadian Archaeological Association.

Jordan E. Kerber is associate professor of anthropology and Native American studies in Colgate University's Department of Sociology and Anthropology at Hamilton, New York, and also serves as curator of archaeological collections, in the university's Longyear Museum of Anthropology. He has published widely on his research specialties, which include archaeology of the Iroquois, hunter-gatherer adaptations, and coastal archaeology. In 2006 he was volume editor of *Cross-Cultural Collaboration: Native Peoples and Archaeology in the Northeastern United States*, a project reflecting his interest in collaboration with Native Americans in archaeological projects.

Robert D. Kuhn is regional director of the New York State Office of Parks, Recreation, and Historic Preservation in Saratoga Springs, New York. He previously served as a faculty member in the Department of Geography and Planning of the State University of New York at Albany. His research interests include cultural resource management, historic preservation, and northeastern North America.

Janet K. Schulenberg is adjunct assistant professor of anthropology in the Department of Anthropology of the State University of New York College at Potsdam in Potsdam, New York. Her research interests include the archaeology of New

York, the Iroquois, archaeological method and theory, and transition to food production.

Martha L. Sempowski is a research fellow in archaeology at the Rochester Museum and Science Center in Rochester, New York. She has contributed articles to a variety of scholarly journals.

David G. Smith is associate professor of anthropology in the Department of Anthropology of the University of Toronto at Mississauga. He has published widely in his research specialties of prehistoric cultures in northeastern North America and the Caribbean, particularly regarding the origins of agriculture in the Northeast Woodlands, stylistic change in Northeast Woodland ceramics, environmental archaeology in tropical and continental regions, and archaeological method and theory.

Dean R. Snow is professor of anthropology in Pennsylvania State University's Department of Anthropology, in University Park, Pennsylvania, specializing in ethnohistoric and demographic problems, particularly in Mexico and northeastern North America. He has written and edited numerous books and articles and is currently president-elect of the Society for American Archaeology.

Robert G. Thompson is a doctoral candidate in the University of Minnesota's Department of Anthropology, in Minneapolis.

Gary A. Warrick is an associate professor of contemporary studies and indigenous studies at Wilfrid Laurier University in Brantford, Ontario. He has contributed many scholarly articles in the areas of his research interests, which include Iroquoian archaeology and history, Ontario archaeology, colonialism and indigenous peoples, history of the Grand River watershed, and indigenous archaeology.

Anthony Wonderley is an historian in the Legal Department of the Oneida Indian Nation in Oneida, New York. His book *Oneida Iroquois Folklore, Myth, and History: New York Oral Narrative from the Notes of H. E. Allen and Others* was published by Syracuse University Press in 2004.

PART ONE

| *Origins*

| Overview

IT IS APPROPRIATE to begin the selected readings section of this volume with the topic of origins of the Iroquois. For more than a century, many have pondered when the Iroquois first appeared in the Northeast and whether they have always lived in their historic homelands, or whether they arrived from other regions, and if so, when? Based on archaeological remains, the answers are far from definitive. In contrast, the Iroquois themselves rely on their oral tradition to answer questions regarding from whence they came, as Native authors elaborate in a few papers in part 5. Ironically, the first archaeologist to write on the issue of Iroquois origins is Arthur C. Parker, a Seneca, who proposed a migration hypothesis in 1916. He suggests that the Iroquois originated around the mouth of the Ohio River and later moved to their historic locations in the Northeast, overpowering the local Algonquian speakers who had been occupying these lands.

Arguing for ceramic stylistic continuity between Owasco (ancestral Iroquois) and Iroquois culture, Richard S. MacNeish (1952) counters Parker with the hypothesis that the Iroquois of New York and Canada developed gradually in place instead of having migrated from distant areas. This model is known as the "in situ" hypothesis and has dominated the interpretation of Iroquoian archaeology. It stresses that the hallmarks of Iroquois culture (e.g., matrilineal kinship, matrilocal residence in large multifamily dwellings, villages, and maize-beans-squash horticulture) evolved from local hunter-gatherer groups of the Point Peninsula Tradition toward the end of the Middle Woodland Period (before A.D. 1000). Archaeologists had long thought that the Iroquois cultural transformation began by about A.D. 1000 (near the beginning of the Late Woodland Period) with the assumed introduction of maize horticulture during the Owasco Tradition in New York and the contemporaneous Glen Meyer and Pickering Traditions in Ontario. Current evidence, however, indicates an earlier date for the advent of maize horticulture, as discussed in readings in parts 1 and 2.

The first three essays in this section focus on the ongoing debate over Iroquois development. The lead article by Dean R. Snow identifies weaknesses in the in situ model. He introduces a revised migration hypothesis to accommodate "major anomalies" and discontinuities in ceramic styles and subsistence and settlement patterns at the end of Point Peninsula and the beginning of Owasco around 1000 B.P. (years before present). According to Snow, shortly after A.D. 900, at the end of the Middle Woodland Period, ancestral Iroquoians (pre-Owasco) began to spread northward from their origins in Clemson's Island culture situated in central Pennsylvania, bringing with them their longhouse settlements, maize horticulture, and ceramics. Over a number of years, they continued to migrate along the upper tributaries of the Susquehanna River in central New York and ultimately dispersed throughout their historic territories. He contends that along the way these powerful early Iroquoians displaced resident Algonquian hunters and gatherers of the Point Peninsula Tradition and the Princess Point Complex and incorporated many of the foreign women into their own intrusive societies in the course of sporadic warfare. A warming trend around A.D. 1000 that lengthened the growing season likely triggered this northern move, as climates and soils in New York and southern Ontario became better able to support crops to feed increasing Iroquois populations.

In the second reading in this trilogy, Gary W. Crawford and David G. Smith offer newly recovered data on the Princess Point Complex in Canada to refute Snow's revised model as it applies specifically to the period from A.D. 500 to 1000 in south-central Ontario. Although the authors do not reject migration per se to explain Iroquoian cultural evolution, they disagree with a number of Snow's assumptions concerning the Princess Point Complex: namely, that it is a variant of Point Peninsula; that it is a Middle Woodland Culture; that Princess Point people were Algonquians; that they were not horticulturalists; and that they were replaced by ancestral Iroquois populations invading from the south sometime after A.D. 900. In Snow's response piece, he concedes that a clarification of the Princess Point Complex and of the introduction of maize horticulture in Ontario necessitates a revision of his hypothesis. He admits that Princess Point and later Iroquoian manifestations cannot be derived from Clemson's Island. His new version maintains that the migration from Pennsylvania occurred about 300 years earlier than he had proposed (ca. A.D. 600). Although this debate continues, "the story of Iroquois origins involves more than a choice between migration and the in situ hypothesis" (Engelbrecht 2003, 112).

The next two papers examine aspects of the Point Peninsula and Owasco Traditions in relation to Iroquois origins. Janet K. Schulenberg compares the competing in situ and migration models and their different implications for social complexity, subsistence, and settlement patterns. A common problem with the models is that they are based on ceramic typologies developed in the 1940s and on untested culture history, both in need of revision. In an attempt to reevaluate the ceramic and cultural chronology of Iroquois development in the Finger Lakes region of central New York, Schulenberg presents the results of direct AMS (accelerator mass spectrometry) dating of encrusted carbonized food residues on the interior wall of 11 Point Peninsula and Owasco type ceramic sherds from the Kipp Island and Hunter's Home sites. Both sites date to the critical period of transition, A.D. 600–1200, between these two traditions. The study revealed discrepancies between the expected and actual dates of the Owasco sherds. Five of the eight Owasco pottery types yielded AMS dates surprisingly associated with the earlier Point Peninsula time frame. She concludes that these and other early dates from Owasco sites push the appearance of Owasco ceramics in particular and Iroquois culture in general several hundred years earlier than expected, well before A.D. 900. Although foragers and farmers likely overlapped in Iroquois country, the in situ versus migration debate remains unresolved.

In the last chapter of part 1, John P. Hart and Hetty Jo Brumbach call into question the use of the Owasco construct altogether, introduced more than a half-century ago by William A. Ritchie (1936). The term was intended to refer to both a proto-Iroquoian culture and a period when archaeologically identifiable Iroquoian traits first appear, especially in New York sites. Hence, one conventionally speaks of the Owasco people and the Owasco Tradition, believed to date around A.D. 900–1300 within the Late Woodland Period, as precursors to the Iroquois. The authors urge that this culture-historic taxon be discontinued (no replacement is proposed) as it lacks theoretical and empirical support in light of recent data. Although the data are somewhat limited and AMS dating is not infallible, such a recommendation has important implications for the search for Iroquois origins and the migration versus in situ debate, particularly in New York where the term is most commonly applied. It is too soon to know whether the Owasco construct will be rejected, modified, or remain unchanged by the archaeological community of Iroquoian researchers.

1 | Migration in Prehistory
The Northern Iroquoian Case
DEAN R. SNOW

> But too often, indeed I would say usually, theories act as straitjackets to channel observations toward their support and to forestall data that might refute them. Such theories cannot be rejected from within, for we will not conceptualize the potentially refuting observations.
> —Stephen J. Gould, "Dinosaurs in the Haystack"

ONE PURPOSE OF THIS PAPER is to explore the argument in favor of migration in the development of Northern Iroquoian culture in northeastern North America. A second purpose is to examine the history of the controlling model that has dominated regional archaeological interpretation for a half-century. I argue that the recognition of anomalies has created a new situation in Iroquoian archaeology that requires a major revision in the working model. It should also entail a reexamination of the ways in which societies propagate through time and space.

The fragmentary distributions of sets of linguistically related societies in North America at the time of first European contact strongly suggest that societal fissioning and migration were demographic processes no less important here than in other parts of the world (Coe et al. 1986, 42–45). In recent years, glottochronological estimates of the time depths of splits leading to the fragmentary distributions of surviving languages have tended to become shorter, suggesting that, for the most part, the languages developed over the course of only the last few millennia (Fiedel 1987; 1991). It follows that attempts to correlate archaeological and linguistic lines of evidence for periods before recent millennia are specious. Few historical linguists now speculate about deep connections between North American Indian lan-

Previously published in *American Antiquity* 60, no. 1 (1995): 59–79. Reproduced by permission of the Society for American Archaeology.

guage phyla (Campbell and Mithun 1979), and fewer archaeologists attempt to correlate such speculations with data from the Archaic (or even earlier), as for example Gordon R. Willey (1966, 266) once did. Thus not only was population movement a feature of societal development in prehistoric North America, the complex patterns still observable in the ethnographic record must have unfolded almost entirely in recent millennia.

The current standard interpretation of Northern Iroquoian societies is of particular interest because it emphasizes long-term development in place despite evidence that they were comparatively recent migrants into the Northeast. I argue here that the elaboration of simplistic migration scenarios in the writings of early professional archaeologists led skeptical scholars to advocate in-place development of the Northern Iroquois by the middle of this century. By halting credulous speculation the skeptics redirected research agendas into more productive avenues, but they also oversimplified presumed demographic processes by in effect outlawing one of them, namely migration. In recent decades the in situ model of Northern Iroquoian development has become an almost universally accepted controlling model in the Northeast. Minor contrary evidence has been ignored or summarily dismissed. However, in the last decade major anomalies have been recognized and Northeast regional archaeology faces a situation that I argue must lead to a revision of the standard working hypothesis.

The Iroquois Case

The Iroquois have long been recognized as unusual in the Northeast region, because, at the time of their first European contact, the Algonquian speakers that nearly surrounded them did not share with them strongly matrilineal organization, matrilocal residence in large multifamily dwellings, large compact settlements, and heavy dependence upon maize-beans-squash horticulture. The origins of the Iroquois have thus been a focus of archaeological interest for a century and a half.

The historical distribution of Northern Iroquoian in what would otherwise have been an exclusively Algonquian region, their strongly matrilineal social systems, their maize horticulture, and their linguistic connections with both the Cherokee and Iroquois resident in the southern Appalachians and the Carolina lowlands—all suggest northward expansion. However, for half a century nearly everyone has assumed that the expansion took place 2,000 to 3,000 years ago, and that the features of Northern Iroquoian culture just mentioned developed gradually in situ after that early initial movement (Snow 1984).

Earlier speculation on the origins of the Northern Iroquois usually assumed that they had come from somewhere else shortly before European contact. Before the 1940s migration was not merely a frequently referenced process in the study of culture change; it was often considered to be in itself an explanation. Dissatisfaction with migration as explanation grew partly because critics saw no objective means to choose between equally plausible (or implausible) scenarios, partly because they realized that the scenarios masked a variety of other possible processes (e.g., Grayson 1970).

Migration scenarios were also consistent with earlier prevailing ethnographic concepts. American Indian cultures were seen as static and immutable; acculturation theory treated post-Columbian change in terms of disintegration and loss. The processes by which so many different cultures came to exist and persist were left largely unexplored. Archaeologists who did not yet appreciate the temporal depth of American prehistory were usually content to move these unchanging pieces about the map, explaining change over time as the displacement or absorption of one piece by another.

One example will serve to illustrate the early migration scenarios proposed for the distribution of the Northern Iroquois shown in figure 1.1. In 1916 Arthur C. Parker proposed that the Iroquois had originated within the milieu of the Mississippian developments around the mouth of the Ohio River. He imagined an elaborate scenario that led to some groups crossing the Detroit River and pushing northeastward through southern Ontario. Those that moved farthest east to the vicinity of Montreal were the Mohawk. Ancestral Onondaga soon moved across the Saint Lawrence to take up residence in Jefferson County, New York. The remainder became the ancestors of the Huron, Petun, and Neutral nations. He supposed that at the same time the ancestors of the Erie, Seneca, Cayuga, and Susquehannock had moved along the southern shore of Lake Erie to their historic locations.

Parker (1916a, 479–80) ignored older archaeological evidence of Iroquoian settlements in the Mohawk Valley so that he could claim that this part of Iroquoia was not occupied until the Mohawk left the Saint Lawrence Valley late in the sixteenth century. This claim provided him with a convenient explanation for the disappearance of the Saint Lawrence Iroquois after Cartier visited them between 1534 and 1541. Similarly, while his ideas about Onondaga origins conveniently explained abandoned Iroquoian sites in Jefferson County, they denied a local development of Onondaga culture around Syracuse. James A. Tuck's (1971) work later showed that the Onondaga were not simply transplanted northerners; that of William A. Ritchie and Robert E. Funk (1973) clearly showed the same for the Mohawk.

Parker's hypotheses might seem almost foolish in retrospect, but it is important to realize that the scenario he concocted was consistent with European American concepts of cultural development, and with at least some of the details of documented Indian migrations and Iroquois folklore. Contemporary reconstructions of European history were replete with examples of migration and waves of mounted nomadic invaders. Although American Indians lacked horses in many cases, the movements of refugee American Indian nations seemed also to conform

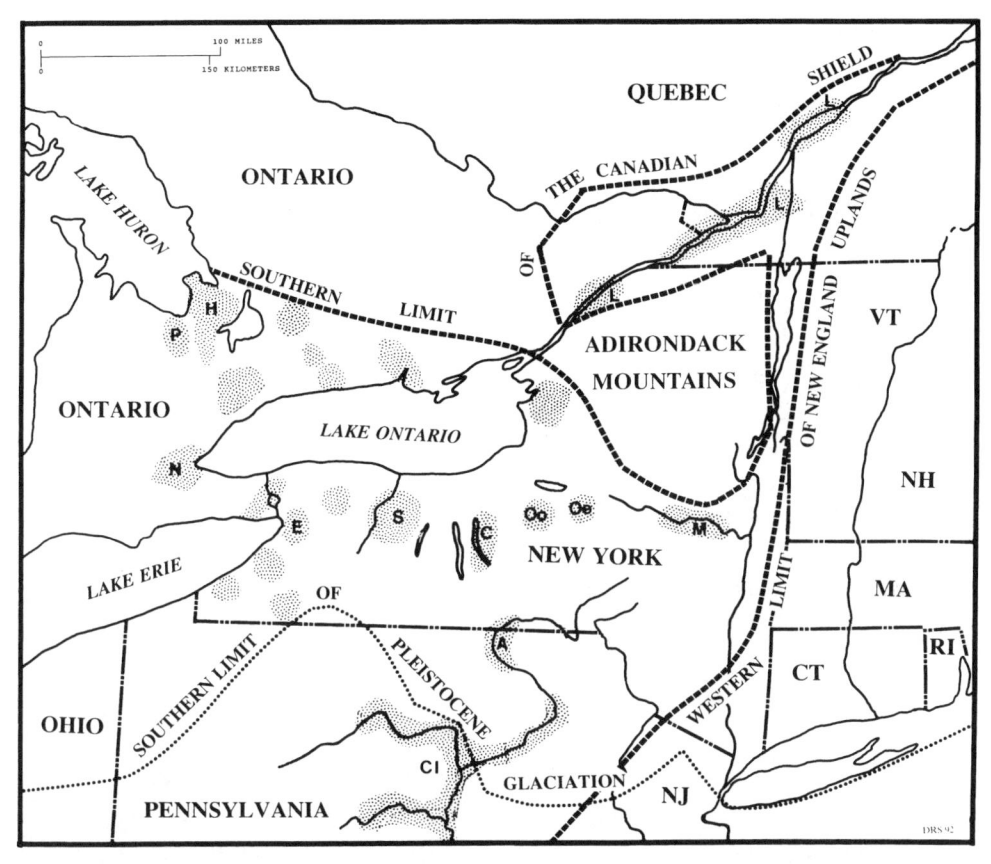

Fig. 1.1. Late Iroquoian cultures, A.D. 1450–1650. Clusters that became postcontact nations and confederacies include the Mohawk (M), Oneida (Oe), Onondaga (Oo), Cayuga (C), Seneca (S), Susquehannock (A), Erie (E), Neutral (N), Petun (P), Huron (H), and Saint Lawrence Iroquoians (L).

to this pattern. If the seventeenth-century Huron were defeated and driven westward (some eventually to Oklahoma), it was not unreasonable to imagine that they had made long journeys prehistorically as well.

Parker's error was to assume that he could work backward in time from the perceived realities of recorded history to accurately portray prehistory. Today, few anthropologists cling to the implicit notion that sixteenth-century Indian cultures were pristine static societies that changed mainly through erosion by acculturative processes into later debased forms. Nor is it assumed that the earliest documented forms of those societies necessarily bore close resemblance to ancestral forms only a century or two earlier. Thus many modern students of the Northern Iroquois, including this one, are reluctant even to use national terms such as *Seneca* or *Mohawk* for periods before A.D. 1500, when it is uncertain that such groups existed even in incipient forms.

Archaeological explanation that depended upon cartographically precise but processually unspecified migration was already bothersome to some archaeologists a half century ago. James B. Griffin (1944) was one of the first to argue against the uncritical use of such scenarios as explanations of prehistoric change. It was largely this kind of criticism that led archaeologists to focus the burden of proof on migration hypotheses, leaving presumed immobility (rather than simple uncertainty) as the default hypothesis. That approach has prevailed during the decades in which regional sequences have been constructed by archaeologists working in the Northeast.

Interior Northeast Sequence

Northern Iroquoia is the interior portion of the Northeast that was used and occupied by speakers of Northern Iroquoian languages, which include but are not limited to the languages of the nations that constitute the Iroquois proper (fig. 1.1). This definition of Northern Iroquoia applies primarily to the centuries following A.D. 900, when it was a well-defined culture area. It does not necessarily apply before that date, when the region was successively occupied by various Archaic and Woodland complexes.

The region is also geologically distinct, for it is underlaid by sedimentary (often carbonate) bedrocks of Paleozoic age (Rickard 1973). This bedrock province covers most of New York, southern Ontario, southwestern Quebec, northern Pennsylvania, and the northwestern edge of New England (fig. 1.1). The Adirondack Mountains of New York are more ancient igneous rocks that protrude high enough to exclude the later sedimentary beds from their area. They were thinly and sporadically populated throughout prehistory. The Adirondacks are linked to the geologically similar Canadian Shield by way of the Thousand Islands portion of the Saint Lawrence River valley, a threshold called the "Frontenac Axis" (Chapman and Putnam 1984). The northern edge of Northern Iroquoia thus is defined by the southern limit of the Canadian Shield. It is bounded on the east by the Taconic and Green mountains, the western edge of the New England Uplands. In the south it extends to the southern boundary of Ice Age glaciation on the Allegheny Plateau. Some prehistoric Iroquois moved northeast of the Adirondack Mountains and spread into the lower Saint Lawrence Valley, but for the most part, Northern Iroquois preferred glaciated landscapes underlaid by sedimentary bedrocks.

Point Peninsula Culture

Figure 1.2 shows a very simplified chronology of the archaeological cultures described here. Ritchie defined Point Peninsula as a tradition in 1944, based on its type site near the Canadian border on the eastern shore of Lake Ontario. After several revisions, Ritchie settled on using the name to cover a variety of mainly New

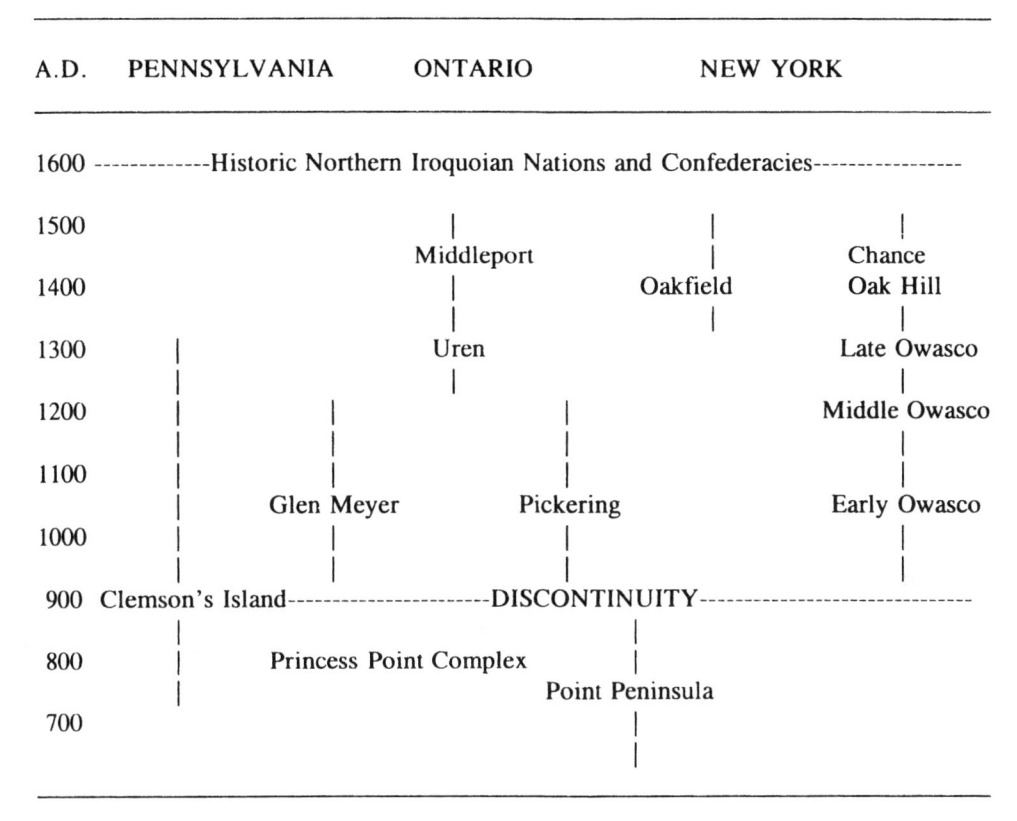

A.D.	PENNSYLVANIA	ONTARIO		NEW YORK
1600	------------Historic Northern Iroquoian Nations and Confederacies----------------
1500				
		Middleport		Chance
1400			Oakfield	Oak Hill
1300		Uren		Late Owasco
1200				Middle Owasco
1100				
		Glen Meyer	Pickering	Early Owasco
1000				
900	Clemson's Island-------------------------DISCONTINUITY--------------------------
800		Princess Point Complex		
			Point Peninsula	
700				

Fig. 1.2. A simplified chronology of the archaeological and historical cultures mentioned in the text.

York phases that he dated to the period A.D. 100 to 1000 (Ritchie 1969, 205–8). Although he initially included them, in his 1969 and later formulations he left out the Early Woodland period phases that would have taken the beginnings of the tradition back to at least 1000 B.C.

Canadian archaeologists view Point Peninsula as a prehistoric culture. They have tended to include Early Woodland period evidence. Some infer that the Point Peninsula culture of Ontario and Quebec began around 700 B.C. and extended through the Early and Middle Woodland periods to A.D. 1150 (J. Wright 1972, 44–51; 1979, 55–59). Other syntheses set the earlier evidence apart (Spence et al. 1990). In any case, it seems clear that Point Peninsula appeared earlier in Ontario than in New York, but that it ended at about the same time in both (J. Wright 1990, 496).

The Point Peninsula tradition covered all of the territory shown in figure 1.3 except for southwestern Ontario, Ohio, Pennsylvania, and New Jersey. It also covered quite a bit more to the north and east of the area shown, although its poorly defined boundary resists precise definition. It is found west of Lake Ontario, but the

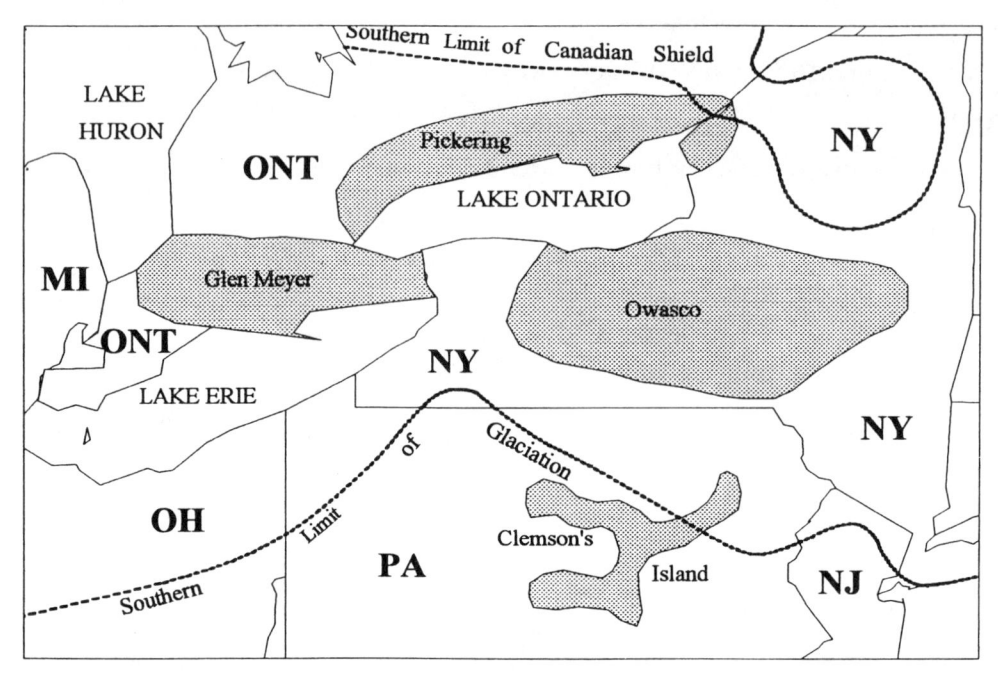

Fig. 1.3. Generalized distributions of sites pertaining to early Iroquoian cultures, A.D. 900–1300, and principal geological features of the region.

related Saugeen culture is found instead farther west around Lake Huron (Spence et al. 1990, 157–58).

In New York, earlier Point Peninsula pottery is characterized by what Ritchie (1969, 206) terms the Vinette 2 series. Ceramics in this series exhibit pseudo-scallop shell, dentate, and rocker stamp decorative techniques. They mark the onset of the Middle Woodland period in New York (Ritchie and MacNeish 1949, 100–107). Later Point Peninsula pottery in New York differs from earlier forms in several ways. Later vessels are larger, and lips are more rounded to slightly flattened. Most later vessels have cord-malleated surfaces, and corded decorations predominate. Dentate stamping, pseudo-scallop shell decoration, and rocker stamping all disappear. There are some appliquéd collars, but although they are superficially similar to the collars that appear on later Owasco and Iroquois vessels, these are technologically different (Ritchie 1969, 230).

If Point Peninsula resulted from the expansion of a hunter-gatherer population across the region and the culture continued residence there for several centuries, increasing regional diversity in archaeological assemblages should be expected. Thus it is not surprising that decorative trends in Ontario differ from those in New York. However, basic technological features having to do with the way in which Point Peninsula vessels were constructed are consistent throughout its geographic range. All Point Peninsula vessels tend to be elongated, with bases that are paraboloid rather than rounded in cross section. Interior surfaces are often channeled. Sherds often show fracture planes, indicating that the vessels were constructed from coils and fillets (Ritchie and MacNeish 1949, 100).

The subsistence practices of the people responsible for Point Peninsula appear to have been broadly based on hunting, foraging, and fishing. Point Peninsula sites are usually small camps that were sited at strategic places near where fish runs, waterfowl, passenger pigeons, or other naturally abundant resources would have been concentrated. Scheduled movements probably took community members to a succession of regularly used camps, mainly on the shores of lakes and streams. Although we still lack the detailed direct evidence for the cultivation of local plants cited by Bruce D. Smith (1989) for the central Eastern Woodlands in the same period, some tending of locally native food plants seems likely. This early and weakly developed form of plant manipulation has been called the "cultivating ecosystem type" (Stoltman and Baerreis 1983) or "early horticultural" (Snow 1980, 261).

Later New York Sequence

Ritchie's New York chronology sets the beginning of a "Late Woodland Stage" at A.D. 1000, defined by the first appearance of the "Owasco Tradition" (Ritchie 1969, 272–300), which is generally agreed to have been carried by Northern Iroquois. The three-century tradition is in turn divided into three one-century-long phases named Carpenter Brook, Canandaigua, and Castle Creek, in that order. This framework has been generally accepted and used to classify A.D. 1000 to 1300 remains in New York, except for those found near the southeastern and western margins of the state.

Calibration of radiocarbon age determinations (Stuiver and Reimer 1993) published by Ritchie and Funk (1973, iv) and by Williamson (1990, 309–10) indicates that the calendar dates of Owasco and later phases will have to be adjusted somewhat. This adjustment is important because dating methods other than radiocarbon are beginning to have some use in the Northeast, and because key global climatological trends are tied to calendrical rather than radiocarbon dates. The calibrated calendrical date for the beginning of the Early Owasco or Carpenter Brook phase as defined by Ritchie appears to be around A.D. 1150 rather than A.D. 1000. This produces a gap between the dates associated with the last phase of the Point Peninsula tradition and the first Owasco dates; there are four plausible alterative explanations. First, standard error in the small number of available radiocarbon dates might have created an apparent gap where none really exists. Second, Early Owasco might have been established later than expected. Third, our small sample of Owasco dates might simply lack any from the period A.D. 900 to 1150, during which the first Owasco villages were established. Fourth (and I have argued elsewhere [Snow 1991] for this possibility), the poorly dated Hunter's Home phase, the last of the Point Peninsula tradition, might in fact be an artificial hybrid phase based on mixed assemblages. Its components are probably a mix of early Owasco village sites containing a few Point Peninsula sherds and late Point Peninsula camp sites having the remains of still later Owasco camp sites superimposed. Some dates that have been attributed to the Hunter's Home phase should apply to Early Owasco. These include a date of 1045 ± 250 B.P. (M-176) for the White site and 955 ± 250 B.P. (M-177) for the Willow Tree site. The first of these calibrates to cal A.D. 1010 and the second calibrates to cal A.D. 1040 (Stuiver and Reimer 1993). The calibrated date of cal A.D. 1180 for Roundtop is still the earliest dated evidence of maize, beans, and squash in New York. These dates, which are shown in table 1.1, push the beginnings of Owasco in New York back once again to at least A.D. 1000.

Calibration of dates from Middle Owasco (Canandaigua) sites suggests that it grew out of Early Owasco by A.D. 1200. Middle Owasco was succeeded quickly, for Late Owasco (Castle Creek) sites have produced calibrated dates that cluster in the period A.D. 1275 to 1350. Thus, calibration indicates that the whole tradition came and went between A.D. 1000 and 1350. However, few new radiocarbon dates have been secured for samples from Owasco sites in recent years, and it is likely this sim-

Table 1.1
Calibrated Radiocarbon Age Determinations for the Earliest Owasco, Glen Meyer, and Pickering Sites

Site	Lab Number	B.P. Date	Calibrated Date[a]
OWASCO			
White	M-176	1045 ± 250	699 (1010) 1258 A.D.
Roundtop	Y-1534	880 ± 60	1045 (1180) 1229 A.D.
Willow Tree	M-177	955 ± 250	828 (1040) 1292 A.D.
GLEN MEYER			
Van Besien	I-6167	1005 ± 90	975 (1020) 1161 A.D.
Van Besien	I-6847	1010 ± 90	972 (1020) 1159 A.D.
Van Besien	I-6848	1175 ± 140	682 (880) 1012 A.D.
Porteous	I-4972	1130 ± 100	785 (900, 910, 960) 1014 A.D.
Porteous	I-5820	1370 ± 90	617 (660) 766 A.D.[b]
PICKERING			
Boys	I-7322	975 ± 120	975 (1030) 1216 A.D.
Auda	S-1948	1065 ± 110	884 (990) 1039 A.D.

Source: Information presented in this table taken from Kapches (1987, 168), Noble (1975b), Noble and Kenyon (1972, 29), Ritchie and Funk (1973, iv), and Williamson (1990, 309–10).

[a] Calibration after Stuiver and Reimer (1993). Calibrations follow the convention in which one or more intercepts are placed in parentheses between the 1-sigma ranges.

[b] An aberrant date probably derived from an improperly associated or contaminated sample.

ple picture will be changed by additional research. Parallel developments in Ontario (discussed below), which are much better dated than Owasco, suggest that we should expect some early Owasco sites to date to as early as A.D. 900.

Ritchie (1969, 272) based his definition of Owasco on the type site at Auburn, New York, and 23 others across the state. These and a few more recently discovered Owasco sites are distributed broadly in the area identified in figure 1.3. Ritchie (1969, 273) considered scattered Owasco artifacts in western New York sites to indicate contact with but not permanent residence of Owasco people there. During A.D. 1150 to 1350 the Niagara frontier and the adjacent portions of both Ontario and New York appear to have been generally devoid of Owasco occupation, although not altogether empty (White 1966, 11). It is possible that contemporaneous sites there would be classified as late Middle Woodland in age except for the presence of a little Owasco pottery and pipes (White 1976, 119–20). Ritchie noticed the same pattern in the Hudson Valley, where what he assumed were resident Algonquian speakers picked up a few Owasco ceramics, perhaps by means of capturing the women who manufactured them (Ritchie 1969, 274).

Owasco sites include relatively large hilltop village sites as well as waterside camps, whereas Point Peninsula sites are found only in the latter context. There appears to be considerable variation in Owasco house form (Ritchie 1969, 281; Ritchie and Funk 1973, 166), but it is not inconsistent over time. Seven houses were found at Maxon-Derby, and they were already consistent with multifamily residence. The smallest of them was 6 x 7 meters (m) and squarish, containing partitions and four hearths. Another was an 8 x 18 m oblong structure with end doors and a line of hearths, a multifamily form that presaged later larger matrilocal longhouses. The traces of a 27-m-long longhouse at the Roundtop site is even more convincing. The variation noted by Ritchie and Funk suggests that the form was new and still unstandardized, but multifamily residences were present from the beginning of Owasco. Similar multifamily houses are not documented for Point Peninsula sites. Supposedly contrary evidence from the White site, which Ritchie and Funk (1973, 119) thought belonged to Point Peninsula because of its early radiocarbon date, actually documents an early Owasco village containing some Point Peninsula pottery (Snow 1991).

The earthen ring at the later Owasco Sackett site enclosed a 62 x 74 m area of well over 1 hectare (ha). Ritchie and Funk (1973, 215 16) interpret the post-mold patterns at the Sackett site to indicate small round houses, but both Trigger (1981a, 12) and I (Snow 1980, 313) independently concluded that their data could be better interpreted as partially uncovered longhouses. The pattern of lengthening longhouses at the Bates site (Ritchie and Funk 1973, 227) was probably generally found on all Middle Owasco village and hamlet sites. Overlapping patterns of post molds also suggest that these communities rebuilt houses in place over long occupation periods as compared to the frequent moves of larger historic Iroquois villages.

The analysis by Robert J. Whallon (1968, 236) of Owasco ceramics led him to say that Owasco population grew rapidly but that contacts between Owasco villages decreased over time. By Late Owasco times (A.D. 1275–1350) most Owasco villages were palisaded. The Chamberlain site had an earthen ring that was still visible in the nineteenth century. Two houses excavated here by Tuck (1971) were about 7 m wide and 15 m and 26 m long, respectively. Clearly the standard Iroquoian longhouse, which varied in length depending upon the sizes of the matrilocal lineages that lived in them, but which was uniform in most other dimensions, reached its classic form by this time.

The Ontario Sequence

Much as Ritchie's work in New York established a chronological framework that is still with us, James V. Wright's (1966) synthesis of the Ontario Iroquoian tradition established an enduring framework north and west of Lake Ontario. With some adjustments, this chronological framework remains quite useful.

The Princess Point Complex remains a poorly understood contemporary of Point Peninsula in southern Ontario, appearing sometime after A.D. 650. Stothers (1976, 137) saw no local antecedents for Princess Point, and there has been a general tendency to interpret it as intrusive. Inasmuch as Princess Point culture was, when first recognized, thought to have brought maize horticulture to Ontario, many archaeologists have also interpreted it as being directly ancestral to the later Iroquoian communities of Ontario (J. Wright and Fecteau 1987; Snow 1984). However, all of the evidence of charred corn that was once attributed to three Princess Point sites is now regarded by at least some Canadian archaeologists as having come from later Ontario Iroquoian strata (Fox 1990a, 178). The Porteous site, a village yielding carbonized corn and considered by Stothers (1977, 308) to be a key Princess Point site, is now generally regarded as an Early Iroquoian site (Noble and Kenyon 1972; Williamson 1990, 308). Noble (1975a) links it specifically to early Glen Meyer culture, one of two main lines of early Iroquoian development in southern Ontario. Princess Point also lacks the relatively large and distinctively compact settlements of Northern Iroquois (Fox 1990a, 179). Princess Point sites are often on the shores of large rivers or bays of the Great Lakes. These are largely warm-season camps that are similar in siting to those of Point Peninsula. Winter camps are not well known, but all people in the region during the periods leading up to A.D. 900 might have dispersed to very small family hunting camps in the coldest months.

None of this constitutes a strong argument for the development of Ontario Iroquoian cultures out of Princess Point culture. The situation is parallel to the general lack of continuity between Point Peninsula and Owasco in New York. As can be seen in figure 1.3, there is little continuity at the regional level between the distributions of Glen Meyer and Pickering sites on the one hand and the distributions of earlier Point Peninsula and Princess Point sites from which they presumably derive on the other. Yet that is the derivation that has been central to the major controlling model in regional archaeology for four decades.

In Wright's chronology, there were two branches of the Ontario Iroquois tradition during its early period, Glen Meyer and Pickering. Major village sites of the Glen Meyer and Pickering branches are distributed north of Lake Erie and north of Lake Ontario, respectively (fig. 1.3). A radiocarbon date from the Porteous site suggests that Early Glen Meyer might have been in place by A.D. 900, but not earlier (Noble and Kenyon 1972). A second date (table 1.1, I-5820) is clearly aberrant when compared to all others from Early Glen Meyer sites, and should be omitted from consideration. Radiocarbon dates from Pickering sites indicate that it too developed after A.D. 900 (Fox 1980a), and it is possible that this branch was derived from the same source as Early Glen Meyer. Some investigators have argued that the inceptions of both Glen Meyer and Pickering date to as early as A.D. 500 to 800. Kapches (1987, 168), for example, subtracts a one-sigma error of 110 years from an uncalibrated date of A.D. 885 to propose a date of A.D. 775 for the Auda site. One of three dates from the Van Besien site can be construed to indicate a similarly early date (Noble 1975b), as can the aberrant date from the Porteous site. However, the majority of the earliest dates shown in table 1.1 and the much larger number of later dates reported by Williamson (1990, 309–10) do not support such a construction. Neither David G. Smith (1990, 287) nor Williamson (1990, 308–10) finds support in the available radiocarbon data for dating either Pickering or Glen Meyer to before A.D. 900 in their critical evaluation.

In general, Ontario Iroquoian ceramics parallel those of Owasco and later New York Iroquois types. "In contrast to earlier times where vessels were made by coiling or by building up the vessel using a relatively thin rope of clay, Early Iroquoian vessels are made largely by 'modelling' in which the potter begins with a large lump of clay rather than a thin coil and models this lump into the vessel shape" (Williamson 1990, 297–98). Thus as in New York, a sharp technological discontinuity exists between Iroquoian ceramics and earlier ones from which they presumably derive.

Glen Meyer villages were palisaded and usually situated on hills away from major streams. Like Owasco villages, they were sited on defensible locations, often flanked by ravines. Residents built multifamily longhouses, presumably occupied by matrilocal lineages, in a clearly Iroquoian style. Initially the houses had only two or three hearths, but they were clearly forerunners of later Northern Iroquoian longhouses (Noble and Kenyon 1972, 30). The evidence for both chronic external warfare and matrilocality is strong, and contrasts sharply with the lack of such evidence for Princess Point or Point Peninsula culture (J. Wright 1966; 1972).

Pickering sites are similar to Glen Meyer sites in most respects, but the two branches of Early Ontario Iroquoian culture are clearly distinct regional variants.

Differences between the Pickering and Glen Meyer branches disappeared during the Middle period, and Wright (1966, 52–55) inferred that this was the consequence of a "conquest" of Glen Meyer by Pickering. This interpretation, which does not conform to the expected pattern of prestate warfare, is no longer generally accepted (Williamson 1990, 311). However, Wright's Uren and Middleport cultures remain useful to researchers as period designations (Dodd et al. 1990, 323–24). Finally, the Late Ontario Iroquoian period saw the emergence of a Neutral-Erie branch near the Niagara frontier and a Huron-Petun branch north of Lake Ontario. These two groupings echo the earlier distinction between Glen Meyer and Pickering in roughly the same areas of southern Ontario.

Wright divided the Ontario Iroquois tradition into three main periods. Radiocarbon calibration has changed their dates slightly, as has been the case in New York. The Early Ontario Iroquoian period, which is equivalent to Early and Middle Owasco, now appears to span the years A.D. 900 to 1275. The Middle Ontario Iroquoian, which after calibration coincides with the Late Owasco and Oak Hill phases in New York, dates to A.D. 1275 to 1400. The Late Ontario Iroquoian, which covers the emergence and dispersal of the historically known Iroquoian nations in Ontario, dates to A.D. 1400 to 1650.

In Situ Hypothesis

Most archaeologists currently assume that Ontario Iroquoian culture grew out of Point Peninsula and/or the Princess Point complex in a process that paralleled an emergence of Owasco from Point Peninsula in New York. In both cases archaeologists have assumed that there were rapid shifts in ceramic technology and settlement pattern, but that there was continuity over time. An in situ development of Northern Iroquoians has been generally assumed as a working model.

Ritchie pointed out in 1965 that "until rather recently it has been customary to regard the Iroquois people and their culture as intrusive into the Northeast from a center or centers situated south or southwest of our area" (Ritchie 1965, 300). He cited Parker (1916a) as the principal advocate of this interpretation of Iroquoian prehistory. He then cited his own paper discussing the failure of archaeologists to find evidence of the population movement, as well as the steady accumulation of evidence from within the Northeast pointing to a long slow evolution toward historic Northern Iroquoian nations (Ritchie 1961). Indeed, much of the evidence to refute hypothetical sixteenth-century migrations had been accumulated by Ritchie himself over a quarter of a century. Nevertheless, he credited Richard S. MacNeish (1952) with propounding the in situ hypothesis of Iroquois origins. MacNeish (1976, 80), in turn, gives much of the credit to James B. Griffin.[1]

---

1. MacNeish (1976, 80) credits Griffin's 1946 article for the inspiration, but it is clear that it must have come from Griffin's 1944 article on the Iroquois.

MacNeish had been inspired by Griffin to reinvestigate the question of Iroquois origins using a combination of archaeological data from Ritchie's work, a direct historical approach to Iroquois prehistory from historically known nations, and the ceramic collections of several institutions and avocational archaeologists. His work assumed two things that were commonly (if silently) assumed by most archaeologists of the day. First, MacNeish assumed that ceramics alone were a suitable data set for working out chronology and cultural affiliations. He had little choice given that ceramic data were about the only data available to him at the time. Second, he assumed that the historically known Northern Iroquoian nations were appropriate cultural units for discussing archaeological evidence well back into prehistory. Neither of these assumptions is generally accepted today.

MacNeish looked at about 500 collections, and used 15,000 sherds from about 50 sites to define 59 Iroquois pottery types (MacNeish 1952; 1976, 83–84). He grouped them into nine sets named according to historically known nations. These were the Neutral-Wenro, Erie, Huron, Seneca, Cayuga, Susquehannock, Onondaga, Oneida, and Mohawk nations. When temporal information was added, this framework became the basis for the Iroquois tradition (A.D. 1300–1700) of Ritchie (1965, 300–324) and others.

MacNeish, working with Ritchie, also used about 5,000 sherds from a dozen sites to define pre-Iroquoian types. Fifteen of these were types assigned to the Owasco tradition (Ritchie and MacNeish 1949). While not typologically "Iroquois culture" in Ritchie's (1969, xxx-xxxi) chronology, the Owasco tradition has also been generally assumed to have been directly ancestral to it. This mixture of linguistic and archaeological terminology has been confusing, but it cannot now be easily replaced.

Ritchie and MacNeish (1949) also defined 16 types from the Point Peninsula tradition and assumed continuity from Point Peninsula, through Owasco, to Iroquois. Indeed MacNeish (1952, 87) was explicit about the development of Late Woodland (Owasco and Iroquois) ceramics from a Middle Woodland Point Peninsula base. He has remained convinced of this development over the years, asserting that more recent archaeological evidence has tended to confirm the long branching derivation from Point Peninsula that he had proposed in 1952 (MacNeish 1976, 85–95).

Ritchie did not initially push ceramic genealogy back that far, and he went beyond ceramics when assessing cultural systems. He later followed the consensus in regarding Hunter's Home phase of the Point Peninsula tradition as "ancestral" to Owasco, with the two having close affinities around an A.D. 1000 transition (Ritchie 1969, 272–73). However, he saw the "essential elements of Iroquois maize economy and settlement patterns in the Owasco and Pickering phases" (Ritchie 1969, 301). He saw continuity from Glen Meyer and Pickering cultures to the historic Neutral-Erie and Huron-Petun, respectively, of Ontario. In New York he saw parallel continuity from the beginnings of Owasco to the historic Five Nations. A careful reading of his assessment of the in situ hypothesis reveals that despite opting for continuity over time, he still did not push the essential characteristics of Iroquois culture back into Point Peninsula times in his last major discussion of it (Ritchie 1969, 301).

However, Ritchie's last major joint publication with Robert Funk reflected the shift in general archaeological opinion toward MacNeish's view. "The unbroken continuity of material culture and settlement patterns, from Early Point Peninsula into the earliest Owasco expressions, persisted into the early historic period" (Ritchie and Funk 1973, 359). At that time I also assumed continuity over two millennia. Based on a glottochronological estimate of the timing of a split between Northern and Southern Iroquoian, I looked for a discontinuity in the archaeological record at some time in the period 2000 to 1000 B.C., but not later (Snow 1984).

Early archaeologists working in Ontario implicitly accepted migration hypotheses with the same enthusiasm as their colleagues in the United States. Although W. J. Wintemberg's own analyses in the first half of this century often showed greater sophistication, he did not question migration hypotheses (Dodd et al. 1990; Trigger 1978b). But as in New York, MacNeish's (1952) research changed the generally held view from one favoring frequent large-scale migrations to one favoring in-place development.

Recognition of Anomalies

The in situ model has dominated interpretation of Northern Iroquoian development for half a century. Anomalies, however, have accumulated in recent years, which must be addressed, either by refuting them or by constructing an alternate hypothesis that accommodates them, along with other generally accepted evidence that has until now supported the prior hypothesis.

Anomalies in Linguistic History

Many linguists now regard the breakup of Northern Iroquoian languages from a single proto-Northern Iroquoian language to have begun only a millennium ago (Crowe 1994). This breakup does not include the Tuscarora and Nottoway, whose ancestors probably broke off and moved to what is now North Carolina perhaps 1,500 years ago, moving north to rejoin the Northern Iroquoian in the eighteenth century (Foster 1987). It also does not necessarily affect a much earlier date for the split with ancestral Cherokee. It remains the case, however, that the Northern Iroquoian languages, apart from the Tuscarora/Nottoway branch, show too little diversity to support inference of a breakup earlier than around a millennium ago. Archaeologists are often quick to dismiss dates derived from glottochronology, and I am not necessarily suggesting here that much reliance be put on the technique. Even if the age of the proto-Northern Iroquoian speech community is older than a millennium by several centuries, it is not possible to correlate it with the initial spread of Point Peninsula. The origins of Point Peninsula are too early and its ultimate distribution too wide to be matched to proto-Northern Iroquoian.

No horticultural terms have been reconstructed for proto-Iroquoian, but some can be reconstructed for proto-Northern Iroquoian, including Tuscarora (Mithun 1984, 271–74). These terms include *maize* and *corn husk*. The languages of the Five Nations Iroquois share terms for *corn silk, corn cob,* and *bread*. This similarity indicates that Northern Iroquoians all probably had maize horticulture when they began to break up into separate languages a millennium ago. Thus horticulture was not acquired by the Northern Iroquoians gradually or separately later on. Moreover, proto-language reconstruction assumes that compared to descendant languages there was once a relatively small speech community, both in terms of the number of speakers and their regional distribution. This is to some extent a limitation of the linguistic model, but it is nonetheless reasonable to argue that proto-Northern Iroquoian could never have been spoken over an area as large as the distribution of Point Peninsula sites. None of this is consistent with the idea of a gradual evolution of Iroquoian societies out of a Point Peninsula base. Fiedel (1987) argues that glottochronological dates and lexical items in the reconstructed proto-Algonquian vocabulary both indicate that Point Peninsula is an archaeological manifestation of proto-Algonquian expansion. The evidence internal to Northern Iroquoian is entirely consistent with that interpretation.

Anomalies in Culture Theory

William Divale's (1984) work on matrilocal residence and its origins suggests another anomaly. He argues that matrilocality always arises in dominant societies that expand into territories at the expense of hostile but subordinate societies already there. It does not develop slowly in place along with the slow elaboration of horticulture in societies in which women are gradually expanding their economic roles. Curiously, although several cultural anthropologists have expressed serious doubts to me privately, I have been unable to locate any negative criticism of Divale's hypothesis in print. The most notable reference to it that I have been able to find uses it to explain the otherwise inexplicable appearance of matrilocality among northern Athapaskans (Perry 1989).

Divale took as a point of departure Sahlins's (1961, 323) argument that "a segmentary lineage system is a social means of intrusion and competition in an already occupied ecological niche. . . . [It] is a successful predatory organization in conflicts with other tribes, although perhaps unnecessary against bands and ineffective against chiefdoms and states; it develops specifically in a tribal society which is moving against other tribes, in a tribal intercultural environment."

Leaving aside nineteenth-century notions of primitive matriarchy, it is generally true that anthropologists have traditionally tended to assume gradual development of matrilocal residence and to attribute it to the advent of dependence on female activities in subsistence. Trigger's (1978a) essay on Iroquoian matriliny has this hypothesis as its central theme. Archaeologists have also tended to assume that it was a gradual process that paralleled the gradual development of plant domesticates and the role of women in food production. Consequently, attempts to discover archaeological evidence of the emergence of matrilocality have usually focused on long-term trends in ceramic attributes or settlement patterns (e.g., Deetz 1965; Whallon 1968). However, the underlying hypothesis has not been supported by archaeological evidence. Whallon's (1968, 235–36, 240) analysis indicates increasing village endogamy and a shift in New York from smaller extended families to larger matrilineages from Owasco times on. But there is no evidence for gradual in-place development of matrilocality from some earlier custom. Multifamily residences and charred maize appear in early Owasco, Glen Meyer, and Pickering sites. Although patrilocal multifamily residences are known for horticultural contexts elsewhere in the world (Coult and Habenstein 1965, 301, 358, 392), they are unknown historically in northeastern North America. Moreover, there is no evidence of residential discontinuity in the archaeological record in this region. The archaeological evidence indicates that multifamily (probably matrilocal) residence, horticulture, and compact villages appeared suddenly, not gradually, in Iroquoia. The arguments put forward by Sahlins and Divale constitute a significant anomaly that cannot be explained by the in situ hypothesis.

Anomalies in Ceramic Manufacture

As described above, Owasco, Glen Meyer, and Pickering vessels are technologically similar to each other but contrast strikingly with earlier Point Peninsula ceramics. The contrast between coil construction and paddle-and-anvil modeling, basic construction techniques, indicates very different sets of motor habits between the potters of these two ceramic traditions. The two fundamental techniques are very different for they involve quite different manufacturing steps as well as contrasting procedures for preparing the clay. Modeling requires greater plasticity of the clay and is often regarded as a less advanced technique than coiling (Shepard 1956, 57–59). Yet modeling was still preferred by Iroquoian potters in the seventeenth century, as attested by what is virtually our only written source on the matter (Sagard-Théodat 1939 [1632], 109). One should not expect to find rapid shifts of such a profound nature in basic motor habits within a slowly evolving technology. Yet the dominance of the in situ hypothesis has led most of us to ignore this striking anomaly in a search for continuity over time.

Anomalies in Site Distributions

It must also be admitted that the mechanisms through which a broad and generally even distribution of earlier (presumably patrilocal) Point Peninsula communities could have evolved into the spatially more restricted and very spotty distribution of later (presumably matrilocal) Iroquoian communities have never been specified. Peter G. Ramsden (1993) has pointed out the spatially restricted nature of Pickering sites as compared to Point Peninsula sites in the same part of Ontario (fig. 1.3), noting that the in situ hypothesis does not explain this discontinuity. The same observation applies in the cases of Glen Meyer and Owasco (fig. 1.3). The in-place evolution of a widespread diverse culture into a less widespread uniform culture is anomalous against the background of what we know about cultural evolution.

An Alternative Hypothesis of Incursion

The disjunction between the in situ hypothesis and evidence derived from linguistics, cultural anthropology, and archaeology suggests that ancestral Northern Iroquoians arrived in the region with their matrilineages and their subsistence practices already developed. Further, they must have arrived on the order of a thousand years ago, not earlier.

Trigger (1970) raised several questions regarding the implications of the in situ hypothesis over three decades ago. Starna and Funk (1994) made their own critique more recently. Despite these criticisms, the in situ hypothesis has survived as an untested working hypothesis. However, the working hypothesis has become a controlling model of such strength that criticisms have not been generally accepted as identifying legitimate anomalies. By failing to articulate a compelling explanation within a new conceptual framework, we have allowed the natural conservatism of science to dismiss the criticisms (Lightman and Gingerich 1992).

One of the most enduring of archaeological problems has been the detection, confirmation, and explanation of human migration. Migration presents a problem that is in part theoretical and in part technical. On the theoretical level, we have chosen to essentially ignore migration as a demographic process in recent decades, leaving our understanding of it largely undeveloped. This general disregard has produced the artificial benefit of simplifying interpretation, but as Anthony (1990) has pointed out, it has done so at the cost of discarding the baby with the bathwater.

On the technical level, the issue of migration is underlain by various other problems that also remain difficult and incompletely resolved. These problems include issues such as the detection of age, contemporaneity, site duration, ethnicity, and the other lower-level problems that archaeologists must either solve or evade before getting on to other goals. Furthermore, *migration* is often used to cover a range of several distinct demographic processes, and people using the term seem often to silently assume either that only one of these processes was at work, or that they were all at work in some impenetrably chaotic way. Migration can progress at various speeds, over broad fronts or as focused thrusts. The sizes of migrating units and the mobility provided by available technology might vary greatly. Colonization might involve long leaps over intermediate space, and be complicated by processes of return migration, continuing political dependence, and a continuing need for supplies from the donor population. A migrating group might encounter no earlier inhabitants, meet fierce resistance, or experience something between these two extremes. The consequence of interaction between a resident population and an intrusive one might be annihilation, tolerance, or absorption of one by the other. More likely in specific cases, all of these processes and more occurred together, perhaps changing in proportion over time.

Despite these complications, objective consideration of the evidence suggests that Northern Iroquoian matrilocal residence was probably an adaptive response to the stresses experienced by communities migrating into a region that was already inhabited. Such migrations are usually stimulated by the realization of some adaptive advantage, typically an economic one, that prompts the migrating population to expand into new territory. The development is rapid because its immediate stimulus is warfare, which virtually always accompanies this kind of population displacement (Otterbein 1968). Matrilocal societies like the Iroquois are relatively successful at suppressing both feuding and internal warfare, while patrilocal societies engage in both more feuding and more internal warfare. Their residence pattern breaks up groups of fraternal males and suppresses both feuding and internal warfare. At the same time, it facilitates the organization of external warfare, allowing the intrusive society to deal effectively with any resistance from the people being displaced.

The Case for Migration

All of the above leads one to expect that we should find archaeological evidence of a swift appearance of Northern Iroquoians in the Northeast after A.D. 900. However, additional archaeological support is still required of any migration hypothesis. Following Rouse (1958), there should be (1) clear evidence of discontinuity with respect to earlier culture(s) in such things as ceramic styles and settlement patterns; (2) we should be able to identify a source (homeland) for the intruders; (3) independent dating should consistently show that the source culture was earlier than the derivative culture(s); and (4) there should be evidence of the nature of the adaptive advantage that allowed the Iroquoians to displace the previous residents of the region.

There is clear evidence of discontinuity with respect to earlier culture(s) in such things as ceramic styles and settlement patterns, both already described. Owasco pottery types have occasionally been found together with supposedly earlier Point Peninsula and Clemson's Island types. There has been a tendency to interpret these instances as evidence of a gradual replacement of earlier types by Owasco types. However, both Ritchie (1969, xxv) and Turnbaugh (1977, 227) describe dissimilar assemblages that are intermixed, sometimes in the same refuse pits. Although such evidence might have resulted from mixture on multicomponent sites, at least some of these instances are probably evidence of captive Owasco females being incorporated into non-Owasco communities. It is also possible that Owasco females were being incorporated by some peaceful means. In either case, Point Peninsula ceramics appearing on Owasco sites may well have a similar origin.

There is a major discontinuity in site location, settlement size, and house form between Point Peninsula and Owasco. As discussed above, recent findings have tended to sharpen that discontinuity. An additional test of discontinuity might be a new comparative examination of Point Peninsula and Owasco skeletal remains (Starna and Funk 1994). Although Ritchie gives some indications that there might have been significant differences between the Point Peninsula and Owasco populations, the detailed analysis necessary to resolve the question remains to be done. However, it should be remembered that the absorption of non-Iroquoian women into intrusive Iroquoian communities, a practice predicted by what is known of tribal warfare (Otterbein 1968), could blur evidence of biological discontinuity. Wright (1972, 67) asserts that "basically the same local racial stock of the Archaic period carried through the Initial Woodland period to the Pickering culture and later Iroquois peoples." This statement is based in part on work carried out by Wright and Anderson (1969, 131) at the Bennett site. A more detailed examination of morphogenetic evidence has been provided by Joseph Eldon Molto. He was unable to find any biological discontinuities between the Middle and Late Woodland populations of southern Ontario, although he also suggests that the lack of large skeletal samples means that the inference of continuity is still speculative (Molto 1983, 252–53). What is required is a new osteological study using modern techniques to directly test a hypothesis favoring discontinuity. This study has not yet been done.

Any migration hypothesis should be able to specify a source for the migrating population. Marianne Mithun (1984) has reconstructed proto-Northern Iroquoian vocabulary that suggests very general Appalachian origins. Milton William Wykoff (1988) has advanced a more specific argument for a homeland on the unglaciated portion of the Allegheny Plateau. I propose more specifically that the Northern Iroquoians derived from Clemson's Island culture, which flourished in central Pennsylvania after A.D. 775. That date is based on calibration of 30 radiocarbon dates published by Michael Stewart (1990, 81). Although Clemson's Island culture appears to have lasted through the thirteenth century, there is little basis on which to deny that it was in existence by A.D. 800, and a strong suggestion that some occupations began even earlier. The derivation is not entirely new, for Ritchie (1969, 275) derived Owasco "from its roots in late Middle Woodland, Point Penin[s]ula and perhaps other cultures, including the Clemson's Island."

The origins of Clemson's Island culture remain obscure, but that is an issue for further work. Sites first appear over a century before derivative Iroquoian sites begin to appear farther north in New York. Maize, squash, and other cultigens are present from the beginning. Clemson's Island ceramics are very similar to Owasco ceramics. The same is true of burial practices and bone technology (Stewart 1990, 84, 89). Moreover, the collared rims that are so characteristic of most later Iroquoian ceramic types could have easily been developed out of increasingly everted Clemson's Island rim styles (Stewart 1990, 91).

Clemson's Island settlements were horticultural hamlets that were occupied during at least the summer and fall seasons. Some hamlets are apparently associated with burial mounds. Derivative Owasco burials are similar, but mound construction did not move north with migrating communities. Their hamlets were not palisaded, and Clemson's Island disappeared in Pennsylvania with the spread of palisading after A.D. 1300.

Glen Meyer sites sprang up first in southern Ontario, between Lakes Erie and Huron, while Owasco sites appeared across central and eastern New York as far east as the Mohawk Valley. The distance from the junction of the West and North branches of the Susquehanna River to the Grand River is about 370 kilometers (km) (230 miles). The distance from the same junction in central Pennsylvania to the Mohawk is about 310 km (193 miles). In all cases, migrating communities would have covered most of the distance by moving northward along the upper tributaries of the Susquehanna.

The expansion and spread of Iroquoian villages across the Northeast were probably dissimilar to those proposed by Albert J. Ammerman and Luigi L. Cavalli-Sforza (1973; 1979) for the spread of Bankeramik sites across Europe or other common models of wave-front expansion. We know that later Northern Iroquoians sometimes leaped much greater distances in single moves. Samuel de Champlain (1907, 314) noted that while villages only moved 1 to 3 leagues in a normal relocation, moves of 40 to 50 leagues (over 200 km) were sometimes made when warfare forced relocation. This movement is consistent with the spotty distribution of clusters of Iroquoian villages across the region (fig. 1.1). Iroquoian sites are not scattered randomly, nor do they necessarily cluster according to environmental factors. The pattern probably results from a small number of major relocations followed by many smaller village relocations by communities that moved every generation or two. Displacement of smaller non-Iroquoian hunter-gatherer populations would not have presented much of an impediment.

A combination of related cultural and environmental factors produced the conditions favorable to the Northern Iroquoian expansion. They cultivated maize and lived in compact hamlets by at least A.D. 900 and perhaps as early as A.D. 750. This preadaptation made them dominant over the smaller, less compact, and less sedentary Point Peninsula communities that they were about to displace. By adopting an aggressive matrilocal settlement system, they would have been equipped to settle anywhere in the thinly populated region to the north, even if they were initially outnumbered on a regional scale.

It is probably not merely coincidental that the northward incursion occurred around the beginning of the Medieval warm epoch (Ingram et al. 1981). Longer growing seasons and the availability of maize that was adapted to the region would have made the loamy soils of what are now New York and southern Ontario very attractive to farmers. Once established on rich soils along an east-west axis south of Lake Ontario, the Iroquoians were positioned for later expansion around the lake, down the St. Lawrence, and along the eastern shore of Lake Huron. I have discussed ecological factors at greater length elsewhere (Snow 1994a).

Norman Clermont (1980) has argued that Iroquoian population growth could not have been rapid enough to generate from a small founding population the aggregate size of at least 95,000 individuals living in A.D. 1600. Population decline did not begin in the region until after that date (Snow and Starna 1989). Clermont concluded that the Iroquoians must have developed in situ out of a Point Peninsula base, because that was the only way to postulate a sufficiently large founding population. However, I have been able to show that even if the time for growth is minimized, the ultimate population size is maximized, and William E. Engelbrecht's (1987) findings regarding slow growth are stipulated, there was more than enough time for the Iroquoians to multiply from a small founding population, even if it numbered only 500 (Snow 1992a). The Iroquoians did not have to exceed the modest birth rates observed by later Europeans to multiply beyond 100,000 in only 19 generations (less than 500 years). Growth potential was therefore a favorable condition, not an unfavorable one.

Dena F. Dincauze and Robert J. Hasenstab (1989) have attempted to explain the Iroquois in terms of a "core-periphery hypothesis," which assumes a chain reaction from Cahokia. This hypothesis suffers from the assumption that Iroquois origins postdate A.D. 1300, too late to account for well-dated Early Iroquoian sites in the region. Hasenstab (1990) later developed a second alternative "predatory expansion hypothesis," which is closer to the new hypothesis presented here. Hasenstab does not discuss demographic implications, but this hypothesis might be consistent with Clemson's Island origins and a migration scenario, adding only an initial stimulus from somewhere to the southwest. I have criticized these hypotheses elsewhere (Snow 1994a).

Conclusions

The in situ hypothesis remains alive and well with archaeologists who are comfortable with the assumptions that (1) historical linguists do not have the ability to judge the time depth of proto-Northern Iroquoian; (2) matrilineality and horticulture developed together slowly over the course of centuries; and (3) the archaeological record shows no evidence of discontinuity around A.D. 900. Only when the anomalies discussed above become generally accepted as valid will the controlling in situ model cease to be the straitjacket it has become. It may be that either more evidence for these anomalies or evidence of additional anomalies will be required before this acceptance will happen.

There are many implications for future research embedded in the new working hypothesis I have proposed here, and they are not all archaeological. The Susquehannock communities of northern Pennsylvania were very near the Clemson's Island homeland in the early sixteenth century. Cayuga is linguistically unusual among Northern Iroquoian languages, exhibiting a complex history of contacts with Susquehannock and (possibly) an early split from the others in this group. Perhaps the origins of both the Cayuga and the Susquehannock are linked to the disappearance of Clemson's Island culture from central Pennsylvania around A.D. 1300.

The Iroquoian incursion was probably not a single migration, but several branching and sequential ones. The first groups moved northward around A.D. 900, and the last ones to depart might not have done so until later. Major migratory leaps by communities hiving off from older ones continued within Northern Iroquoia, as village clusters were established in areas like the St. Lawrence Valley and Jefferson County, New York. With each new major migration, a group of Iroquoians established itself in a new area, displacing any older population and perhaps absorbing largely female portions of it in the course of sporadic warfare. This absorption would account for the appearance of some Point Peninsula ceramics in early Owasco sites. It also leads to the prediction that efforts to distinguish Iroquoian from Algonquian skeletal populations will be difficult.

Some of the major moves failed. The Nodwell site (J. Wright 1974) on the shore of Lake Huron was not followed up by a subsequent proliferation of later sites in the area. The villagers found by Cartier around the modern city of Quebec could be viewed as the victims of a similar overextension.

Some of the areas were abandoned by the seventeenth century as certain groups used renewed major migrations to join others. Figure 1.1 names the principal clusters that survived by absorbing others to become the Northern Iroquoian nations and confederacies known to seventeenth-century Europeans. Unnamed clusters are those that were abandoned before contact. The descendants of them all survive in the Northeast and elsewhere today, surrounded but still not absorbed by later immigrants.

Acknowledgments

An earlier version of this paper was read and commented on by several colleagues. They include Penelope Drooker, Stuart Fiedel, Michael Foster, William

Fox, Robert Funk, Robert Kuhn, James Molnar, and James Pendergast. William Engelbrecht, Kathleen Allen, and Michael Graves provided very constructive comments on later drafts. James Wright and an anonymous reviewer both took the time to provide very lengthy remarks and some useful criticisms. They all have my sincere thanks and the customary assurance that they will be held harmless in the event of further retrorecognition of anomalies. María Nieves Zedeño prepared the Spanish version of the abstract.

2 | Migration in Prehistory
Princess Point and the Northern Iroquoian Case
GARY W. CRAWFORD AND DAVID G. SMITH

THE PREVAILING IN SITU explanation for the development of Northern Iroquoian culture has recently come under question. Dean R. Snow, in chapter 1 of this volume and in a series of other papers, proposes that Iroquoian-speaking peoples migrated into the Northeast between A.D. 900 and 1000, bringing with them maize horticulture and matrilineal/matrilocal social organization and displacing indigenous groups of Algonquian hunter-gatherers (Snow 1992a; 1994a; 1995a; 1995b; 1995c). An important component of Snow's model is his interpretation of the archaeological record for the Princess Point Complex in southern Ontario. In brief, Snow argues that Princess Point was one of many Algonquian-speaking foraging societies displaced by invading Iroquois. The model has been debated to some extent, but the recent discussions suffer from a lack of informed reference to the Princess Point Complex (Chapdelaine 1992). We contend that evidence resulting from research we have conducted on Princess Point since 1993 does not support this aspect of the migration model for Northern Iroquoian development as Snow articulates it. We do, however, agree with Snow's assertion that existing theoretical constructs may act as "straitjackets" (chap. 1, 6). In fact, we wholeheartedly support rigorous and systematic questioning and review of hypotheses by examining the inferential reasoning involved and testing with new data.

We are not criticizing migration hypotheses per se and we commend Snow for reopening discussion on this sensitive topic and calling for a continued examination of the propagation of societies in time and space (chap. 1). We point out, however, that contrary to Snow's assertion (chap. 1, 7), migration as a demographic process was not "outlawed" by researchers investigating Northern Iroquois over the last 50 years; indeed, scenarios involving movements of people, albeit within

Previously published in *American Antiquity* 61, no. 4 (1996): 782–90. Reproduced by permission of the Society for American Archaeology.

the Northeast, are common in the work of several influential archaeologists. For example, Richard S. MacNeish's *Iroquois Pottery Types* (MacNeish 1952), in which the in situ hypothesis of Northern Iroquoian origins was formally proposed, includes relocations of various Iroquoian groups. Both J. Norman Emerson (1961) and James V. Wright (1966) argued for the movement of Iroquoian societies within Ontario. Thus, Snow's argument for a migration of an Iroquoian group from one part of the Northeast to another is not as radical a departure from traditional approaches to Northern Iroquoian demography as it might first appear. Unfortunately, the revitalized migration model depends on either negative or inconclusive evidence as it applies to Ontario. In this essay we introduce the new Princess Point data from Ontario pertinent to the in situ hypothesis critique and show why the recent results cast serious doubts on the migration model as Snow has presented it.

Recent Research on Princess Point in Southern Ontario

The Princess Point Complex has undergone some revision since it was first identified and defined by David M. Stothers in the late 1960s and early 1970s. Stothers used the term *complex* because he viewed Princess Point as a relatively widely distributed archaeological "manifestation" found in all of southwestern and south-central Ontario (Stothers 1977). He recognized three regional "foci" (Point Pelee, Ausable, and Grand River) and three "phases" (Early, A.D. 600–750; Middle, A.D. 750–850; and Late, A.D. 850–900). More recently, Fox (1990a) revised both the spatial and temporal parameters of Princess Point. He excluded the Ausable focus as too poorly known to classify; reassigned the Point Pelee focus to the Riviere au Vase phase of the Western Basin tradition; and shortened the time period by dropping the Late phase. The Grand River focus inherited the label "Princess Point Complex." Although the rationale for using the term *complex* appears to have been eliminated, the designation *Princess Point Complex* remains in general use. Princess Point has never been incorporated within a more general classificatory framework such as the Ontario Iroquoian tradition (J. Wright 1966), and redefinition is beyond the scope of this paper. We will continue to use the designation *Princess Point Complex* for now.

The redefined Princess Point Complex is restricted geographically to south-central Ontario, extending from Long Point to the Niagara River along the north shore of Lake Erie and around the western end of Lake Ontario to the Credit River (fig. 2.1). Fox's revised chronology dated Princess Point roughly from A.D. 650 to 900, but recent accelerator mass spectrometry (AMS) dates on maize indicate a longer duration, from A.D. 500 to 1000 (Crawford et al. 1997). The Princess Point settlement pattern is distinctive in that most of the known sites are closely associated with lacustrine, riverine, and wetland environments. The material culture is distinguished by pottery decoration dominated by cord-wrapped stick impressions and

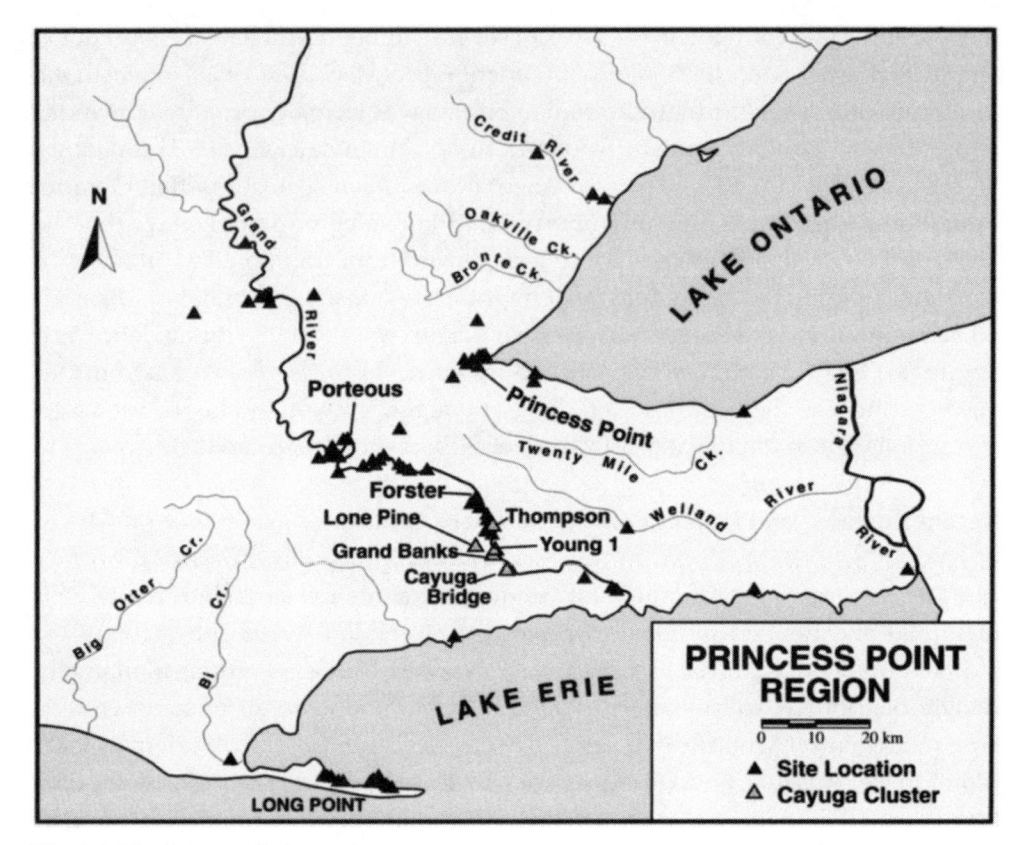

Fig. 2.1. The Princess Point region.

by a flake-based lithic assemblage that includes Levanna-type projectile points. Snow is correct, however, when he points out that, as of 1992, the Princess Point Complex remained very poorly understood (chap. 1, 16).

Three years ago [1993] we launched a multidisciplinary research program to investigate Princess Point and the origins of food production in southern Ontario (Smith and Crawford 1995). This program incorporates both archaeological and geomorphological research. We are investigating regional settlement patterns, chronology, environmental history, and several other aspects of the Princess Point Complex. We have also recompiled the data on site locations for known Princess Point sites, which number about 80 at present. In particular, Crawford is examining palaeoethnobotanical remains from throughout the region, and Smith is analyzing pottery assemblages from a number of Princess Point sites.

We have concentrated our efforts to date on the Lower Grand River valley, where clusters of Princess Point sites have been identified (fig. 2.1). For three field seasons (1993–95), we have conducted excavations at one of these clusters near the village of Cayuga (fig. 2.1). This cluster includes three probable settlement types: first, two large occupations situated on alluvial bars of the Grand River (Grand

Banks, AfGx-3, and Cayuga Bridge, AfGx-1); second, a small locality on the first terrace of the Grand River (the Young 1 site, AfGx-6); and third, a 0.5-hectare (ha) site situated in an upland environment on Roger's Creek, a tributary of the Grand River (the Lone Pine site, AfGx-113). We cannot fully detail the results of our research here; however, we can shed light on earlier interpretations of Princess Point critical to the debate.

First, at the outset of our project we shared Snow's and others' concerns about the validity of the Princess Point corn associations. Only one kernel had been recovered from the Grand Banks site from what, at the time, appeared to be an unequivocal Princess Point context (Stothers 1977). The other two sites with corn of potential Princess Point affiliation were Princess Point and Porteous. The Princess Point site has a later Iroquoian occupation so the corn could be intrusive to the Princess Point component, and Porteous, which is interpreted to be transitional between Princess Point and the later Glen Meyer branch of the Early Ontario Iroquois tradition (Noble and Kenyon 1972; Stothers 1977), is considered too late to be relevant to the discussion of the earliest corn in Ontario. Radiocarbon dates from Porteous are too wide-ranging to allow a clear dating of the occupation, although one interpretation places the occupation at A.D. 900 (Fox 1995, 147).

Our palaeoethnobotanical research has resulted in a confirmation of corn associated with Princess Point. So far, the sample resulting from flotation of 419 liters of soil from the 1993 field season at Grand Banks and Lone Pine has been analyzed, and roughly one gram (about 180 fragments) of carbonized corn kernel and cupule remains has been identified, with about one-quarter of these coming from Grand Banks (Bowyer 1995). Six samples of corn from the two sites have been AMS dated so far (table 2.1). The dated samples from the Grand Banks site come from separate locations that could represent different occupations of the site. The calibrated (cal) A.D. 540, 570, and 780 dates are from a paleosol containing a high density of

Table 2.1
AMS Radiocarbon Dates on Maize from Two Princess Point Sites

Site Name	Material	^{14}C Years (B.P.)	Calibrated Date (A.D.)	Lab Number
Grand Banks	kernel	1250 ± 80	650 (780) 980	TO-4585
Grand Banks	kernel	1060 ± 60	880 (1000) 1150	TO-4584
Grand Banks	cupules	1570 ± 90	410 (540) 610	TO-5307
Grand Banks	cupules	1500 ± 150	420 (570, 600) 670	TO-5308
Lone Pine	kernel	1040 ± 60	890 (1010) 1160	TO-4586
Lone Pine	cupule	800 ± 50	1210 (1250) 1280	TO-4083

Note: Calibrated at 2-sigma with the program CALIB 3.0 (Stuiver and Reimer 1993). Calibrations are rounded to the nearest ten years. One or more intercepts are presented between the 2-sigma ranges; dates are corrected for isotopic fractionation.

Princess Point pottery fragments (Crawford et al. 1997). The cal A.D. 1000 date is from a pit located in an area of the site with no obvious paleosol and some 25 meters (m) north of the area from which the earlier dates were obtained. The pit contains a grinding stone (metate) and two large Princess Point pottery rim sections. The two Lone Pine dates are both associated with the same hearth floor. We consider the cal A.D. 1250 date to be too late for Princess Point. The implications of these dates for Snow's migration hypothesis will be discussed below.

Our second area of major concern was the interpretation of Princess Point settlement patterns. The working model, first formulated by Stothers (1977), envisages short-term seasonal occupations, with large spring-summer encampments located in riverine-lacustrine situations and small fall-winter camps in upland settings. This is essentially the settlement system interpreted for earlier Point Peninsula and Saugeen (Middle Woodland) cultures extended to Princess Point. Stothers argued that Grand Banks was an example of a spring-summer site on a riverine bar. Lone Pine, found only recently, is located in an upland environment 2 kilometers (km) from the Grand River, and in Stothers's model would be interpreted to be a winter camp. Our recent research, however, has not recovered any data to indicate that Lone Pine and Grand Banks must have been short-term seasonally occupied sites. Lone Pine is about 0.5 ha in area with substantial artifact densities in a clearly defined area on a flattened knoll. In our testing at Lone Pine we have identified two large hearth areas containing pipes similar to those from Glen Meyer sites.

At Grand Banks, artifacts are distributed over most of a lateral bar of the Grand River. Many of these artifacts may have been redeposited because our geomorphological research details a complex history of deposition and channeling around the area we are excavating (Desloges and Walker 1995). The actual area of occupation is likely much smaller than the floodplain itself, probably confined to the higher areas around which the channeling took place. Nevertheless, we interpret the floodplain locality where we are excavating as having been a stable, rarely flooded locality for centuries (Desloges and Walker 1995). This explanation is contrary to previous interpretations of the Grand Banks site as having been seasonally flooded, thereby forcing people away from the floodplain for parts of the year. We feel that there are no grounds to call for short-term seasonal encampments there, although claiming a year-round occupation at Grand Banks is still premature. We feel that it is important to explore alternatives to the short-term seasonal occupation scenario for Princess Point, and it is still too early to offer a conclusive scheduling interpretation for the sites we have been examining. For now, the evidence suggests that both Lone Pine and Grand Banks are relatively large and distinctively compact, similar to later Northern Iroquoian sites (as described by Fox 1990a, 179). We have no evidence to support the scheduling patterns proposed for Princess Point by earlier investigators (Stothers 1977).

Princess Point and the New Migration Model

Snow (chap. 1, 7) argues that the in situ theory for Northern Iroquoian origins has become an "almost universally accepted controlling model," thereby precluding serious consideration of alternatives. For Northern Iroquoian origins, Snow claims that uncritical adherence to the in situ paradigm has led researchers to overlook evidence that supports a migration explanation. In the following, we examine the anomalies that Snow proposes as departures from the expectations of the in situ model along with our evaluation of his arguments within the context of Princess Point in Ontario. Although Snow has recently stated that "the situation in Ontario is less clear" (1995c, 7), an important connotation of his arguments is that Princess Point was a variant of Point Peninsula, a Middle Woodland culture in the Northeast, replaced by invading Clemson's Island people.

In the new model, Proto-Northern-Iroquoian is the common ancestor for Northern Iroquoian languages spoken by a relatively small and homogeneous group occupying a spatially limited homeland until about A.D. 900. The Clemson's Island culture of central Pennsylvania is the proposed archaeological manifestation of this group. The rest of the Northeast was supposedly occupied by groups speaking Algonquian languages. Snow argues that Clemson's Island people expanded out of their homeland shortly after A.D. 900 and displaced Algonquian-speaking groups in New York State and south-central Ontario. Separate Northern Iroquoian languages began to differentiate at this time (chapter 1, 20). By implication, Princess Point would have been an Algonquian society with no ethnic or linguistic relationship with (1) contemporary Clemson's Island in Pennsylvania, or (2) the subsequent Glen Meyer in the same region of southern Ontario. If such was the case, this distinction should be reflected in a broad array of characteristics, including material culture and settlement-subsistence patterns from which we may also infer aspects of social organization.

Snow argues that matrilocality and matriliny, distinguishing features of Northern Iroquoian social organization, can be inferred from the combination of horticulture, villages, and longhouses, and that these features appeared suddenly and coterminously in the Northeast about A.D. 900. The in situ model cannot explain this rapid appearance, according to Snow. He cites William Divale's (1984) arguments that matrilocal segmentary lineage systems develop from patrilineal band-level social organization only within the context of aggressive and hostile expansion. The new migration model proposes that Clemson's Island is the likely group that expanded to the north. Members of this group adopted corn horticulture and lived in compact hamlets (proto-villages?) by A.D. 775. Their expansion into New York State and southern Ontario after A.D. 900 was made possible by the development of a matrilocal and matrilineal social organization, which gave them an advantage over the resident patrilineal hunter-gatherer bands. The evidence for this social transformation is horticultural villages characterized by palisades and longhouses that appear relatively suddenly in the early Late Woodland of both areas (i.e., after A.D. 1000). Furthermore, the appearance of corn and related evidence for horticulture in the archaeological record must postdate A.D. 900 in Ontario. The changes depicted by the revised migration model should have taken place after Princess Point, the implication being that Princess Point social organization would have been band-level patriliny with patrilocality in a non-village setting.

Snow uses the equation between village horticulture and matriliny-matrilocality to argue that absence of the former will mean absence of the latter. Despite the strength of the association between social organization and subsistence pattern, we feel that the argument does not apply to Princess Point. In particular, to make this connection, Snow must build a case for the absence of corn horticulture in the Northeast before the putative migration. When he formulated his model, the affinity between corn and Princess Point was weak. We now have collected enough corn kernels and cupules from clear Princess Point contexts to argue that Princess Point people were at least incipient horticulturalists by A.D. 800, well before the Roundtop site (New York) date of cal A.D. 1010 (1180) 1230, and as early as the sixth century A.D. (Crawford et al. 1997). Five of the calibrated dates from the Cayuga cluster are significantly older than the date cited for Roundtop. In particular, two Grand Banks AMS dates are 300–400 years earlier than the proposed A.D. 900 migration date. Although it appears that corn is earlier in Ontario than it is in Clemson's Island, this is probably an artifact of research intensity in Ontario. Besides the Roundtop site cultigens in New York, corn from the Chenango Point Binghamton Mall site is associated with a radiocarbon date of cal A.D. 970 (1050, 1150) 1280 (Gardner 1992). Corn in Pennsylvania dates to cal A.D. 920 ± 80 at the Gnagey site (Blake and Cutler 1983, 83). Evidence for corn from southeastern Michigan and from the Dawson Creek site in Ontario is as early as the seventh century A.D. (Crawford et al. 1997; Jackson 1983; Stothers and Yarnell 1977). The evidence from these locations, however, is weak because the dates are all on associated wood charcoal. Isotopic analysis of human bone has not been particularly helpful in resolving the question of when corn was introduced to the Northeast, although it gives some indication of when corn became a significant dietary component there (Crawford et al. 1997; Katzenberg et al. 1995). With the new AMS dates, the timing of the appearance of corn in the Northeast changes substantially from what Snow described (chap. 1). Evidence of corn dating before A.D. 900 in the Northeast is strong, although only confirmed by AMS dating at the Grand Banks site, Ontario. In part, the reason for this is the lack of attention being paid to this important period in the Northeast.

Migration need not be the only mechanism whereby cultigens are introduced to a region, of course. The "availability" model for secondary agricultural origins proposes an initial period during which cultigens may be transferred across a frontier between hunter-gatherers and farmers (Zvelebil 1986). But besides the presence of cultigens in this model, nothing else in the archaeological record differentiates the cultures receiving cultigens from their predecessors or hunter-gatherer neighbors. One of us has examined this phenomenon in northern Japan, where unequivocal evidence of migration is found in the archaeological record (Crawford 1992; Crawford and Takamiya 1990). In the Northern Iroquoian case, however, the context of the corn, particularly in Ontario Princess Point sites, is instructive in that Princess Point is not simply Point Peninsula with the addition of cultigens.

The migration model argues that the change in settlement distribution represents the requirements of the invading horticulturalists living in villages as opposed to the displaced foragers who engaged in seasonal movements of campsites. Snow claims that the distribution of late Middle Woodland sites can be characterized as widespread and even, whereas that of early Late Woodland sites is restricted and spotty. This change occurs suddenly at about A.D. 900, a discontinuity that cannot be explained by the in situ model. More specifically, Snow states that "there is little continuity at the regional level between the distributions of Glen Meyer and Pickering sites on the one hand and the distributions of earlier Point Peninsula and Princess Point sites from which they presumably derive on the other" (chap. 1, 37). The settlement system of patrilineal Princess Point foragers, following Snow's argument, would have been characterized by a widespread and even distribution of camp sites. For Princess Point and Glen Meyer distributions this disparity is more apparent than real. We are just beginning settlement pattern studies for Princess Point, but, despite some differences in site distribution, we are beginning to see overlap in Glen Meyer and Princess Point locations. Indeed, the recent discovery of the Forster (AgGx-134) and Thompson (AgGx-208) sites, the first Glen Meyer villages to be documented in the Lower Grand Valley, reinforces the spatial continuity between Princess Point and Glen Meyer. Furthermore, several Iroquoian communities in our research area are underlaid with earlier Princess Point components, including the Princess Point type site (AhGx-1) and the fourteenth-century Middle Ontario Iroquois tradition Middleport site (AgHa-2). In addition, the distribution of Princess Point sites in general (fig. 2.1) shows that it is not widespread and evenly distributed, but concentrated in clusters.

Also, in the new migration model, there would be no evidence for the villages of later horticultural Iroquoian communities nor the "compact" hamlets of contemporaneous Clemson's Island. We have already discussed above whether Grand Banks and Lone Pine are compact hamlets. Our interpretations of site type and season of occupation for the Cayuga cluster suggest that the Princess Point settlement pattern was more complex than that inferred for the southern Ontario Middle Woodland. The current interpretation of Middle Woodland seasonality and scheduling in southern Ontario encompasses a seasonal pattern of large spring-summer macrobands and small fall-winter microbands (Spence et al. 1990). This interpretation has not been adequately tested, so care must be exercised when attempting to base Princess Point scheduling patterns on preceding ones. Grand Banks may not have been simply a spring-summer macroband camp, but may have been occupied for all or most of the year. In fact, the attraction of the Grand Banks location seems to have been the stable flats that seldom severely flooded. The Lone Pine site, if it is a village or "proto-village," suggests that the transition to more centered communities was occurring before the Glen Meyer in south-central Ontario. As far as the ethnic and linguistic character of Princess Point is concerned, we suggest that the broad-based distinctions between Princess Point and either Clemson's Island or Glen Meyer that might reflect a fundamental difference in identity are not evidenced. Snow himself notes (chap. 1, 20) that glottochronology cannot supply dates precise enough to support linguistic replacement in the absence of supporting data, and such data are lacking in this case (see also Fox 1995, 144–45). The argument that the divergence among the Northern Iroquoian languages has no great temporal depth is, of course, of great interest, but by itself sheds little light on the relationship between Princess Point and Clemson's Island cultures.

Next, Snow points out that the coil method of manufacture typical of Middle Woodland Point Peninsula pottery is very different from the modeling method employed by Late Woodland potters (chap. 1, 22). He argues that the change from coil to modeling in the Northeast occurred rapidly at about A.D. 900. The in situ model predicts that such a profound change in ceramic technology would occur gradually. The migration model, on the other hand, has Clemson's Island potters adopting the paddle-and-anvil technique before their expansion after A.D. 900. The rapid replacement of the coil method by modeling is, therefore, simply a by-product of the displacement of Algonquian foragers by Iroquoian horticulturalists. Princess Point pottery would have been manufactured using the coil method in this scenario. In addition, pottery form and decoration should more closely resemble Point Peninsula styles than either Clemson's Island or Glen Meyer pottery.

Unfortunately, Snow's characterization of Princess Point pottery manufacture is incorrect. He states that in Ontario "a sharp technological discontinuity exists between Iroquoian ceramics and earlier ones from which they presumably derive" (chap. 1, 17), and "Owasco, Glen Meyer, and Pickering vessels are technologically similar to each other but contrast strikingly with earlier Point Peninsula ceramics" (chap. 1, 22). Snow supports these assertions by quoting a very general statement by Ronald F. Williamson contrasting Early Iroquoian vessels to pottery made in "earlier times" (Williamson 1990, 295–98). Most Princess Point pottery we have examined is made by modeling (also referred to as *paddle-and-anvil* or *paddled* construction) (D. Smith 1995), although the coil production typical of Point Peninsula pottery is still evidenced. Other researchers have observed this as well (Fox 1990a, 172; 1995, 145; Stothers 1977, 58).

Three other aspects of early Late Woodland material culture are not taken into account in the revitalized migration scenario. First, differences between Princess Point and Point Peninsula in both ceramic manufacture and style are, in fact, rather striking. Second, as we have argued elsewhere, there is substantial evidence for continuity between Princess Point and Glen Meyer material culture in general, not just in ceramics (Smith and Crawford 1995). Finally, the diagnostic cord-wrapped stick decoration of Princess Point pottery is ignored entirely. Cord-wrapped stick decoration is found in the pottery assemblages of cultures throughout the Northeast during the time period from ca. A.D. 650 to 1000, including Clemson's Island (Smith 1995).

Conclusions

The exploration of evidence for anomalies in the early Late Woodland period may ultimately prove useful in understanding Northern Iroquoian development. The strength of the case for these apparent anomalies is weakened by the lack of up-to-date interdisciplinary research on this important period. We undertook our recent reinvestigation of the Princess Point Complex to address a number of outstanding concerns that directly impact on understanding Northern Iroquoian development. Our current evidence indicates Princess Point was not an Algonquian-speaking group of patrilineal foragers displaced by predatory matrilocal horticulturalists entering Ontario from the south. Princess Point is not, in fact, a Middle Woodland culture at all, but should be considered to be early Late Woodland, or at least "Transitional Woodland" (see Spence and Pihl 1984). We can find little or no evidence for discontinuity between Princess Point and Glen Meyer but, rather, a great deal of support for direct continuity (Smith and Crawford 1995). The controversy over the cultural affiliation of the Porteous site (chap. 1, 16) is a case in point. The problem arises because the material culture at Porteous is clearly derived from Princess Point, not because there is evidence of discontinuity. Porteous could be considered either late Princess Point or early Glen Meyer; the confusion is a reflection of the limitations (if not abuse) of current cultural classification.

Establishing an accurate chronology within the period from A.D. 500 to 1000 in the Northeast is critical to resolving the issues raised by Snow and the present writers. For the time being, without many more AMS dates on cultigens in the area we will still be in the dark. Our dates from the Cayuga cluster of Princess Point sites are beginning to clarify the Ontario situation. We urge a concerted effort to resolve these chronological issues.

Contrary to being a *cultura madre* of all other Northern Iroquoian societies, we view Clemson's Island as simply one group participating in more general changes and developments that affected communities throughout the Northeast between A.D. 500 and 1000; another of these groups is Princess Point. Although our understanding is generally limited for all regions of the Northeast for this important time period, and downright abysmal in some cases, we can identify a number of cultures that appear to be transitional between Middle and Late Woodland.

Although we do not reject migration as a possible factor during the transitional period between Middle and Late Woodland, we do not find Snow's model as it is presently articulated to be valid for explaining Princess Point and the origins of food production in southern Ontario. With further research, we may learn that substantial migrations occurred several centuries earlier. Perhaps the most important result of Snow's and our examinations is a realization of how poorly we understand this crucial and highly complex period of Northeast prehistory. We hope this discourse stimulates the investigations that this issue so much deserves.

Acknowledgments

This research is being supported by a Social Sciences and Humanities Research Council of Canada research grant (410–93–1095), the Ontario Heritage Foundation, and Earthwatch. We wish to thank the three reviewers and Dean Snow for their useful comments on a draft of this paper. Hugo de Burgos prepared the Spanish abstract.

3 | More on Migration in Prehistory
Accommodating New Evidence in the Northern Iroquoian Case
DEAN R. SNOW

I VERY MUCH APPRECIATE the opportunity to comment on the article written by Gary W. Crawford and David G. Smith (chap. 2). They have undertaken some much-needed research in their effort to clarify the Princess Point Complex, and their recent findings necessarily force a major rethinking of the evidence for Iroquoian origins and the advent of maize horticulture in the Lower Great Lakes region. That said, while the new findings necessitate a revision in the specifics of the migration hypothesis I proposed in 1995 (see chapter 1), I conclude that they provide additional support for a migration hypothesis of some kind. The following discussion includes a revised hypothesis.

The Princess Point Complex is currently a very different construct from that initially defined by David M. Stothers (1976; 1977) two decades ago. As currently used, the complex is comprised of sites found along the Lower Grand River of southern Ontario and the nearby shorelines of western Lake Ontario and northeastern Lake Erie. Stothers initially referred to this complex as only one of three "foci" of Princess Point culture, the other two lying westward in two areas between Lake Huron and Lake Erie. He estimated the age of the complex to be in the A.D. 800–1000 period. Later researchers reassigned the two western expressions to other traditions and extended the age of the remaining Grand River expression of Princess Point to A.D. 600 or 650 (Fox 1990a). Furthermore, while Stothers (1976, 139, 158) made the Porteous site on the Grand River a component of the Princess Point Complex, William C. Noble and Ian T. Kenyon (1972) argued that it was probably an early Glen Meyer village site. So far as I am aware, everyone agrees that Glen Meyer is an archaeological construct found in roughly the same area as

---

Previously published in *American Antiquity* 61, no. 4 (1996): 791–96. Reproduced by permission of the Society for American Archaeology.

Princess Point, that it is later than Princess Point, and that it was associated with Northern Iroquoian people.

My main problem in applying the migration hypothesis to the Ontario evidence was in deciding whether Princess Point was part of the developmental continuum begun by Iroquoian immigrants and evolving into Glen Meyer and later phases, or (alternatively) that it was an independent Middle Woodland period development that was not directly ancestral to Glen Meyer. I was influenced by evidence that charred maize kernels once attributed to Princess Point occupations at key sites were by 1990 thought by at least some investigators to have come from later occupations (Fox 1990a, 178). Although Princess Point seemed to have appeared suddenly and without predecessors in the Grand River area (Stothers 1977, 155–58), from published accounts there seemed also to be a discontinuity between Princess Point and Glen Meyer. Given that Princess Point sites did not include the large compact village sites usually associated with early Iroquoians, that their ages often predated A.D. 900, and that doubt had been cast on the association of charred maize with Princess Point components, I decided that Princess Point was probably outside the continuum of Iroquoian development, not inside it. Crawford and Smith are quite right in saying that this conclusion depended on either negative or inconclusive evidence at the time I came to it.

Crawford and Smith's new data have changed matters considerably. They have shown with as much certainty as one can expect from archaeology that charred maize is indeed associated with Princess Point sites and that AMS dates carried out on the maize kernels indicate that the sites were occupied by at least A.D. 600, perhaps earlier. Furthermore, their recent work has shown that at least the Lone Pine and Grand Banks sites are the large compact village sites that we previously thought were missing from the Princess Point Complex.

The findings of Crawford and Smith put Princess Point within and at the beginning of the long continuum leading to the historic Ontario Iroquois. Furthermore, they indicate that Princess Point is at least as old as, and perhaps older than, Clemson's Island culture in central Pennsylvania. If Michael Stewart's dating of Clemson's Island sites is correct, the later Owasco sites in New York could be derivative from Clemson's Island, but Princess Point cannot be. Thus the specific hypothesis that Owasco, Glen Meyer, Pickering, and other later Iroquoian expressions all derived from Clemson's Island must be modified.

Although the 1995 version of the migration hypothesis must be modified, the anomalies that I cited in 1995 still persist. Matrilocality and matrilineality do not develop slowly over time; they usually appear suddenly and as a feature of migrating communities having means of subsistence that allow for relatively large compact permanent villages. The communities are typically large relative to those of the population(s) being displaced by the migrating one. Anomalies also still persist in Iroquoian historical linguistics. The speakers of proto-Northern Iroquoian knew about maize and had a vocabulary that strongly suggests origins in the Appalachian uplands. Moreover the site distribution data and ceramic data that I argued pointed to discontinuity in the sequence have also not gone away. The difference in the latter is that David Smith's reanalysis of Princess Point ceramics indicates that they are similar in basic construction to later Iroquoian ceramics and not fundamentally similar to Point Peninsula ceramics (D. Smith 1995). I inferred too much from Ronald F. Williamson's (1990, 295–98) statements contrasting Princess Point and Early Iroquoian vessels. The discontinuity is now clearly at the boundary between Princess Point and Point Peninsula, around A.D. 600 or earlier.

Where I must continue to disagree with Crawford and Smith is on the nature of the association of horticulture, matrilocality, migration, and compact villages. Horticulture need not be associated with matrilocality, as cases from interior Alaska attest. However, matrilocality and migration are often associated with compact villages, and the latter must be supported by means of subsistence that are productive enough to allow their persistence over the long term. Thus, while matrilocality is often associated with horticulture, horticulture does not in itself produce matrilocality (Divale 1984). This conclusion is contrary to assumptions in much earlier literature (e.g., Trigger 1978a). I do not now conclude that Princess Point was just another Middle Woodland complex with a little maize added. What I do conclude is that the new Princess Point evidence puts the Iroquoian intrusion into Ontario about three centuries earlier than I had previously thought. The new data have not erased the discontinuity in the sequence, they have pushed it back. Migration is still necessary to explain discontinuity in the archaeological record.

I am grateful that migration is no longer a taboo subject. It is one of a small number of essential demographic processes, and its denial does not facilitate realistic archaeological inference in the long run (Anthony 1990). Peter Bogucki's very recent synthesis of the evidence for the spread of agriculture into Europe is additional evidence of the new appreciation for a realistic assessment of paleodemography. If farming entered Europe from Anatolia by way of Greece, then a major issue becomes whether the process involved colonization or the spread of domesticated plants and animals to indigenous foraging groups. The answer appears to be that both processes were going on, and that archaeologists can often detect which one characterized any particular case. Colonizing farmers moved into floodplain habitats not much used by indigenous foragers, and their sites appear without precedent in the seventh millennium B.C. Elsewhere in Greece there is evidence for continuity on forager sites in terms of most of their artifactual inventories, with the addition of domesticated plants and animals. In the former case there is archaeological discontinuity; in the latter there is continuity, and the two can be distinguished (Bogucki 1996).

Returning to the Iroquoian case, there is additional evidence from the Eastern Woodlands that deserves mention. It is clear from maps published by David G. Anderson (1991) that the spatial distribution of archaeological phases in the Eastern Woodlands was very spotty over the last thousand years of prehistory. A recent revision of those maps confirms that there were large buffer zones in the region and that core areas defined by site clusters shifted in space over time (Milner et al. 1992). Anderson's (1994) examination of Savannah River chiefdoms reveals cycles of subregional florescence and abandonment that can only be explained in terms of dynamic demographic processes that must have included migration. The signatures of those processes are repeated many times over in the region. Of specific interest to the Iroquoian case is the sudden appearance of the Cashie phase in North Carolina sometime around A.D. 800 (D. G. Anderson 1991, 12; Phelps 1983, 43). This phase persists in modified form and without discontinuity into the seventeenth century, and is identified with the historic Tuscarora, Meherrin, and Nottoway, all of them Northern Iroquoian speakers. This branch of Northern Iroquoians represents, on linguistic grounds, the oldest divergence from proto-Northern Iroquoian. All other differentiation of Northern Iroquoian languages must have taken place after the separation of ancestral Tuscarora, Meherrin, and Nottoway. The associated archaeological evidence (i.e., the Cashie phase) indicates that this separation must have taken place by at least A.D. 800, perhaps a century or two earlier. Northern Iroquoian glottochronology, such as it is, supports this inference.

Glottochronology continues to be alternately used and condemned by archaeologists and linguists. Although it has worked in specific cases, it has failed spectacularly in others. One problem appears to be that the persistence of linguistic homogeneity over large areas is density dependent (Shaul 1986). A thin population of foragers might maintain a widespread common language for centuries, and in this kind of situation one should expect glottochronology to fail. While linguistic diversification may be maladaptive for low-density populations, it may characterize locally dense populations of horticulturalists. Unfortunately, historical linguists have typically given up on glottochronology rather than make an attempt to refine it by finding ways to control for the density effect and other possible variables. Based on archaeological tests, glottochronology does appear to work reasonably well for the last millennium of prehistory in the portion of the Eastern Woodlands lying south of the subarctic (Fiedel 1987; 1991). My hope is that historical linguists will take a fresh look at demographic factors and attempt to refine a technique that in my judgment is not hopelessly flawed.

The new evidence from Princess Point sites suggests that the breakup of Northern Iroquoian languages must have begun at least three centuries earlier than I previously thought. In other words, it now appears likely that Princess Point, Clemson's Island, and Cashie all represent early Northern Iroquoian speech communities. On the basis of current evidence, Owasco still looks like it is derivative from Clemson's Island, for the accepted dates for Early Owasco sites in south-central New York average around A.D. 900. However, there are at least four radiocarbon dates from Owasco occupations in that area that calibrate to earlier than A.D. 900 (Funk 1993, 158–71; Wurst and Versaggi 1993). The earliest of these is a date of 1425 ± 150 B.P. (QC-1001), which calibrates to 644 cal A.D. with the program CALIB 3.0.3 (Stuiver and Reimer 1993). Robert E. Funk, LouAnn Wurst, and Nina M. Versaggi discount this very early date as well as three dates calibrating to the eighth century A.D. However, this rationalization of early dates might have more to do with expectations arising from the generally accepted orthodox New York sequence than with a critical appraisal of the age determinations, the samples from which they derived, and their associations. I have argued elsewhere (chap. 1, 13–14) that the Hunter's Home phase, the last in the Point Peninsula tradition, is a spurious construct. If that phase never existed and it is actually based on an archaeological amalgam of earlier Point Peninsula and intrusive Early Owasco remains as I have argued, then perhaps the growing number of radiocarbon dates calibrating to the period A.D. 644–900 should be taken at face value rather than dismissed. If the Hunter's Home phase never existed, then Owasco sites in south-central New York dating to the eighth century or even earlier should not be unacceptable. Indeed, the early dates are consistent with dates for early Clemson's Island sites and (thanks to Crawford and Smith) what we now know to be similar dates for Princess Point sites.

If Owasco eventually proves to be as old as Clemson's Island and Princess Point, then it too cannot be derivative from Clemson's Island. My hypothesis will have to be modified again, and I will do it without regret. Either way, a more basic question remains: where did all of these complexes (including Cashie) come from? What persists from my original hypothesis is the argument that they cannot have come from the Point Peninsula tradition. What is new is that some and perhaps all of them arrived earlier than we had realized.

What is thus also new is that the Princess Point evidence makes it likely that the initial spread of horticulture (and horticulturalists) into southern Ontario was not simply a consequence of the onset of the Medieval warm epoch, for this climatic episode did not begin until ca. A.D. 1000 (Ingram et al. 1981). If Owasco proves to be similarly older than currently thought, then we have additional evidence leading to the same observation.

I remain mindful that general acceptance of the migration hypothesis, or some further revision of it that might be made necessary by still more new data, depends on prior acceptance in principle of some important demographic processes. The spottiness of Middle and Late Woodland populations and their mobility over the long term are necessary assumptions. So too is the assumption that there was linguistic and other cultural continuity over time within the shifting clusters mapped by Anderson (1991) and others (Milner et al. 1992). That said, it is worth noting that the historic Cheyenne case provides both a supportive example and a cautionary tale. In the seventeenth century the Cheyenne were wild-rice gatherers living in temporary camps in what is now northern Minnesota. By the middle of the eighteenth century they were sedentary maize horticulturalists living in southern Minnesota and the Dakotas. By the early nineteenth century they were mounted buffalo hunters living in nomadic tipi dwellings on the Plains. Archaeologists have pretended for too long that this kind of movement over time and space was a special and generally unprecedented consequence of the rapid displacements, population declines, and technological changes brought on by contact with Europeans. It may be that normal demographic processes were accelerated and/or magnified by European contact, but they were surely not created by it without precedent. The same criticism can be leveled at traditional archaeological inferences regarding the presumed lack of demographic dynamics in northern Europe before contact with the Roman armies that supposedly both set them in motion and documented the process. I argue that paleodemography is not exempt from uniformitarian principles.

The cautionary part of the Cheyenne case has to do with the rapid, perhaps even revolutionary, transformation that Cheyenne culture went through at least twice in only two centuries. One could not hope to track such an evolution archaeologically without the assistance of documentary sources. There are at least two great discontinuities in the Cheyenne archaeological record despite documented cultural continuity over time (Moore 1987, 82–87). Moreover, the transformations they experienced each involved pervasive cultural reconstruction from elements derived from two or more antecedent societies, a rhizotic form of ethnogenesis that is very different from the cladistic model often used to describe the inferred development and diversification of cultures over time (Moore 1994). We would not necessarily be able to assume continuity in various Northern Iroquoian sequences after A.D. 600 were it not present in the archaeological record. Fortunately for us, that continuity is present. More important, perhaps, is that we cannot necessarily expect to find a clear common archaeological ancestor for the related Princess Point, Clemson's Island, Owasco, and Cashie complexes. Lexical items in proto-Northern Iroquoian and the deeper relationship between Northern Iroquoian languages and the sole surviving Southern Iroquoian language (Cherokee) all point to origins in the Appalachians. Proto-Northern Iroquoian has words for red oak, hickory, maple, elm, basswood, and pine, but words for northern species like birch, hemlock, fir, and tamarack were added later to descendant languages. Even the historic distribution of those languages points to origins in the central Appalachians. Unfortunately, their adaptive radiation out of their homeland might have involved speed and transformational change like that of the historic Cheyenne, leaving us at least for now with no means to identify their common archaeological origins with reasonable certainty. We may search for them, and we might even find them, but we should not be surprised if we do not.

I suspect and hope that Crawford and Smith will find much to agree with in all of this. They have made an important empirical contribution to Iroquoian archaeology. What seems to me to be most needed now is further refinement of the theoretical issues I have raised and new empirical studies to better define the beginnings of Owasco in New York. If the prehistoric Iroquoians force us to deal with those issues more productively, they too will have done another service for archaeology.

4 | New Dates for Owasco Pots

JANET K. SCHULENBERG

Introduction

THE IDEA THAT THE IROQUOIAN TRADITION is deeply rooted in a long sequence of continuous cultural development in the northeastern United States and southern Ontario has dominated reconstruction of Iroquoian prehistory for the past 50 years. The Iroquois were considered relative newcomers to the Northeast until the mid-1940s, when James B. Griffin (1944) suggested that archaeologists consider the possibility that the Iroquois were indigenous to the Northeast. Following a typological study of pottery from a number of supposed Iroquoian and pre-Iroquoian sites in Pennsylvania, New York, and Ontario, Richard S. MacNeish (1952) argued that the ceramic stylistic continuity he saw from pre-Iroquoian to Iroquoian periods indicated that the Iroquois culture developed in place, forming the core of the in situ model. According to the model, Iroquoian prehistory spans over 1,500 years (Starna and Funk 1994, 47). MacNeish (1952) put the temporal boundary between pre-Iroquoian and Iroquoian at about A.D. 1000, between the older Point Peninsula (pre-Iroquoian, foraging) tradition and the more recent Owasco (earliest Iroquoian, farming) tradition, but argued that there was ceramic continuity across this temporal boundary. Despite the fact that the cultural implications of the in situ model were never tested, the model has dominated the interpretation of archaeological remains in the Iroquoian region (Snow 1995a, 59 [chap. 1 in this volume]).

The issue of chronology is central to any discussion of Iroquoian origins and the development of social complexity in the Northeast. The competing scenarios of Iroquoian development have radically different implications for the social circumstances underlying the development of maize horticulture, village settlements, and

Previously published in *Northeast Subsistence-Settlement Change, A.D. 700–1300*, New York State Museum Bulletin 496, ed. J. P. Hart and C. B. Rieth (Albany: Univ. of the State of New York, State Education Department, 2002), 153–65. Printed with permission by the New York State Museum, Albany, New York 12230.

matrilocality among the Iroquois. One obstacle to differentiating the models is the untested culture history underlying each model. The culture history of the Iroquoian region is in large part based on inferences made from the ceramic chronology developed in the 1940s. The basic chronology has not been substantially revised or tested either through excavation or direct dating of organic artifacts in unequivocal association with typed ceramics.

A reevaluation of radiocarbon dates from sites in Ontario has produced evidence for a 300-year overlap between Middle Woodland stage foragers and Late Woodland stage (Iroquoian) farmers (D. Smith 1997a). A similar overlap that is masked by the current confusion of cultural stages and temporal periods could have existed in New York. Many sites from the critical transitional period were excavated in the mid-twentieth century and have museum collections that may provide additional information about the Point Peninsula to Owasco transition. Absolute dates are not readily and reliably available from ceramic sherds themselves, but AMS dating is particularly useful for dating the encrusted food residues in direct association with the sherds. This method provides absolute dates in unequivocal association with ceramic sherds, thereby allowing a test of the absolute chronology assigned to ceramic typologies. A limited series of AMS dates from food residues encrusted on ceramic sherds belonging to Point Peninsula and Owasco types from the Kipp Island, Hunter's Home, and Levanna sites have offered an opportunity to reevaluate the ceramic and cultural chronology for the central region of New York.

Models of Iroquoian Development

Models of the development of the Iroquois have alternated between models of incursions and models of in situ development. Several of those models have been adequately refuted. Other models, however, play a major role in modern interpretations of Iroquoian and pre-Iroquoian archaeological remains. There are currently three models of the transition from Point Peninsula to Owasco cultures under debate. These are the punctuated in situ model (Ritchie 1969), the gradual in situ model (Chapdelaine 1993), and the incursion model (Snow 1995a [chap. 1]; 1996a [chap. 3]).

As discussed above, the original in situ model was developed by MacNeish as an explanation for the perceived continuity in ceramics from the Iroquoian region across the ca. A.D. 1000 Point Peninsula to Owasco transition. In his summary of the prehistory of New York State, William A. Ritchie (1969, 301–2) explicitly adopted the in situ model as an explanatory framework for culture change in the Iroquoian region, and attempted to place a mechanism for change into the in situ model. Based on the ceramic chronology, he suggested changes began around A.D. 1000 with the introduction of maize cultivation (Ritchie 1969, 301; Ritchie and Funk

1973, 165). Ritchie (1969, 276) believed that once maize was introduced its benefits were immediately recognized and exploited by the indigenous hunting-gathering-fishing peoples. Ritchie suggested that changes in subsistence, community organization, household organization, and political organization accompanied the shift from Point Peninsula to Owasco periods (Ritchie 1969, 272–81). The changes in ceramics from Point Peninsula to Owasco styles presumably correspond with the general social changes taking place as village life and matrilocal residence brought female potters together.

During the mid-twentieth century, models of the inherent superiority of agriculture were prevalent. Archaeologists often assumed that maize horticulture would be adopted unless there was some obstacle to it, such as too few frost-free days (Hart 2001, 155). Horticulture was equated with formal village life and vice versa (e.g., Braidwood 1964; Childe 1951; MacNeish 1964; Sears 1971; Struever 1971). It was not until the mid-1970s—after Ritchie published his revisions to the in situ model—that Robert J. Braidwood (1974) published his work from Jarmo, MacNeish (1971) published the results of his Tehuacan Valley project, and archaeologists began to realize that domesticates were not necessarily adopted rapidly and completely.

In considering archaeological sites in Ontario, Claude Chapdelaine (1993) offered an alternative to Ritchie's punctuated model of in situ development, where he suggested that changes in settlement and social organization were taking place before the introduction of maize horticulture and that populations were gradually becoming increasingly sedentary. Because of the lack of evidence for a pre-maize horticultural system, he suggested the transition to maize horticulture required a period of experimentation. The introduction of maize augmented changes in settlement pattern and social organization, but these changes were part of a gradual continuum of change (Chapdelaine 1993, 201). Drawing on regional similarities in ceramic styles, Chapdelaine suggested matrilineages were developing before the adoption of maize horticulture, perhaps through the development of female work groups on seasonally reoccupied sites (Chapdelaine 1993, 198). He went further with this idea, suggesting that the development of these incipient matrilineages was a precondition for the successful adoption of the food-producing economy (Chapdelaine 1993, 198).

This model is similar to the archaeological pattern of settlement and subsistence change observed for Midwestern and Southeastern North America, although neither of these regions appears to have required the development of matrilocal residence to accommodate maize horticulture. Chapdelaine (1993, 174) specifically asserts that this process happened without the influx of new populations; however, a similar pattern of change could have resulted from the influx of enclaves of farming populations.

Dean R. Snow (Snow 1992a; 1994a; 1994b; 1995a [chap. 1]; 1996a [chap. 3]) offered an alternative to the in situ models where, rather than developing out of indigenous populations, the Iroquoian culture was initiated by Iroquoian migrants.

Snow perceived a sharp discontinuity between Point Peninsula and Owasco patterns of subsistence, settlement, and social organization (Snow 1995a, 70–72 [chap. 1]). In this model, the Iroquois intruded into southern Ontario and New York, carried maize horticulture and village settlement patterns with them, and eventually displaced, absorbed, or annihilated the indigenous Point Peninsula populations (Snow 1995a, 76 [chap. 1]). Based on Divale's (1984) work on matrilocal residence, matrilineal social structure is suggested as one of the outcomes of the migration process (Snow 1995a, 71 [chap. 1]).

Snow did not believe this incursion happened in a single migration or a wave of advance like that proposed by Albert J. Ammerman and Luigi L. Cavalli-Sforza for Europe (1973; 1979). Rather, he suggested the incursion happened as a result of several "branching and sequential" migrations in a fashion similar to the hiving off of communities seen in later Iroquoian times (Snow 1995a, 75 [chap. 1]). Immigrants interacting with the surrounding indigenous population initiated pockets of Owasco settlement in the Finger Lakes and Upper Susquehanna regions. Given evidence that the Iroquoian pattern appeared in Ontario as early as A.D. 500 (Crawford and Smith 1996), Snow (1996a [chap. 3]) revised his model to allow for enclaves of horticultural Iroquoians to coexist with indigenous foragers from at least A.D. 600–900 before the Iroquoian culture began to dominate the region.

The basic premise of the incursion model is consistent with the adoption of domesticated plants and animals in other parts of the world. Most notably, the Iroquoian incursion model is similar to the adoption of domesticates throughout Europe at the beginning of the Neolithic. In Europe, the transition from an economy based on foraging to one based primarily on domesticates was not sudden (Bogucki 1995, 113). The transition began with the establishment of enclaves of farming communities in areas already thinly occupied by foraging populations (Bogucki and Grygiel 1993, 402). The coexistence of these two groups in close proximity continued for more than a millennium (Bogucki 1995, 113). Peter Bogucki suggests that foraging and farming populations in Europe at first interacted through the adoption of escaped livestock, followed by exchange of domesticated plants. At some point, the indigenous foragers adopted economies based on domestic plants and animals, but only after a millennium of interaction with intrusive farmers and their domesticates (Bogucki 1995, 108).

The gradual in situ model implies that changes in settlement, subsistence, and social organization are disjointed, and are occurring at different rates (table 4.1). Changes in settlement pattern begin before the introduction of maize horticulture, and the shifting of social organization begins after its introduction. The punctuated in situ model suggests that changes in subsistence, social organization, and settlement are happening roughly in concert, but that maize is clearly the trigger for those changes. This model predicts the appearance of maize before the changes in social organization evident by multifamily longhouses appear. Finally, the migration model predicts that there is a tight correspondence between maize horticul-

Table 4.1

Key Components of the Three Models of Iroquoian Development

Model	Ceramics	Chronology	Subsistence	Social Organization	Settlement
Ritchie	Changes show continuity	Oswego follows Point Peninsula; no coexistence	Owasco people are farmers	Matrilocal residence accompanies adoption of maize (Owasco period)	Villages develop with adoption of maize (Owasco period)
Chapdelaine	Changes show continuity	Owasco and Point Peninsula are not readily differentiated	Both Owasco and Point Peninsula people are experimenting with maize	Matrilocal residence precedes adoption of maize (begins in Owasco or Point Peninsula period)	Villages develop with the adoption of maize (Iroquoian period)
Snow	Changes show discontinuity	Owasco and Point Peninsula are different and may coexist	Owasco people are farmers	Matrilocal residence accompanies Owasco people as a result of incursion	Villages accompany Owasco people

ture, nucleated sedentary villages, and longhouse dwellings. According to the migration model, on any Iroquoian site, all these characteristics should co-occur.

The ceramic chronology becomes critical in this argument. The chronology developed for ceramics in New York State was created under a model of continuity. Recently, Snow (1994b, 16–19; 1995a, 65 [chap. 1]) has argued that this continuity is an artifact of the grouping of archaeological components, and the chronology does not reflect real historical continuity. It is not clear if the current ceramic chronology holds up to this separation. Empirical dates that would test whether or not Owasco types postdate Point Peninsula types have not been available. It is also not clear if Owasco ceramics are associated with Early Iroquoian style settlements and with evidence of maize horticulture as the incursion model suggests. The first step toward resolving these problems is to directly date typable ceramic sherds.

Sample Selection

As part of a larger project designed to address subsistence issues from the Point Peninsula-Owasco transition, a series of 12 AMS dates on carbonized food residues

Table 4.2
Ceramic Sherds AMS Dated

Cultural Affiliation	Number of Sherds	Ceramic Type	Site Name	Approximate Date Based on Ceramic Chronology (Ritchie and MacNeish 1949)
Point Peninsula	1	Wickham Incised	Kipp Island	A.D. 400–800
	2	Point Peninsula Corded	Kipp Island	A.D. 700–900
	1	Carpenter Brook Cord-on-Cord	Kipp Island	A.D. 950–1200
	1	Carpenter Brook Cord-on-Cord	Hunter's Home	A.D. 950–1200
Owasco	1	Levanna Cord-on-Cord	Hunter's Home	A.D. 950–1200
	1	Levanna Cord-on-Cord	Levanna	A.D. 950–1200
	1	Owasco Herringbone	Kipp Island	A.D. 1200–1350
	1	Owasco Corded Oblique	Kipp Island	A.D. 1200–1350
	1	Owasco Corded Horizontal	Kipp Island	A.D. 1200–1350
	1	Owasco Corded Horizontal	Hunter's Home	A.D. 1200–1350
Unaffiliated	1	Cordmarked	Kipp Island	

was obtained from the interior wall of ceramic sherds from the Kipp Island, Hunter's Home, and Levanna sites (table 4.2). These sites are located at the northern end of Cayuga Lake near the Montezuma marshlands, and represent the critical period from A.D. 600 to 1200 (fig. 4.1).

Kipp Island Site

Kipp Island is located in a marshy area at the confluence of the Seneca and Clyde Rivers near the Montezuma wetlands. The island is a drumlin near the old shore of the wetlands, which were drained in the last century for canal and road construction. During floods, the marsh fills to become a shallow extension of Cayuga Lake, replicating predrainage water levels.

Ritchie identified several components on Kipp Island (Ritchie and Funk 1973, 155). Kipp Island No. 1 is a small Middlesex cemetery, No. 2 is a small Hopewellian burial mound dating to the fourth century A.D., No. 3 is a major habitation component dated to the seventh century A.D., and No. 4 is a Late Point Peninsula/Hunter's Home habitation and cemetery component. Based on three radiocarbon dates from Ritchie's excavations at Kipp Island, the occupation of this drumlin spans about 600 years (table 4.3) (Ritchie and Funk 1973, 155).

Ritchie spent several weeks during the summer of 1963 excavating Kipp Island No. 4 (NYSM 2084), which includes a cemetery of over 125 individuals and a habitation area. The excavators found a small number of carbonized seeds in the habi-

54 • Origins

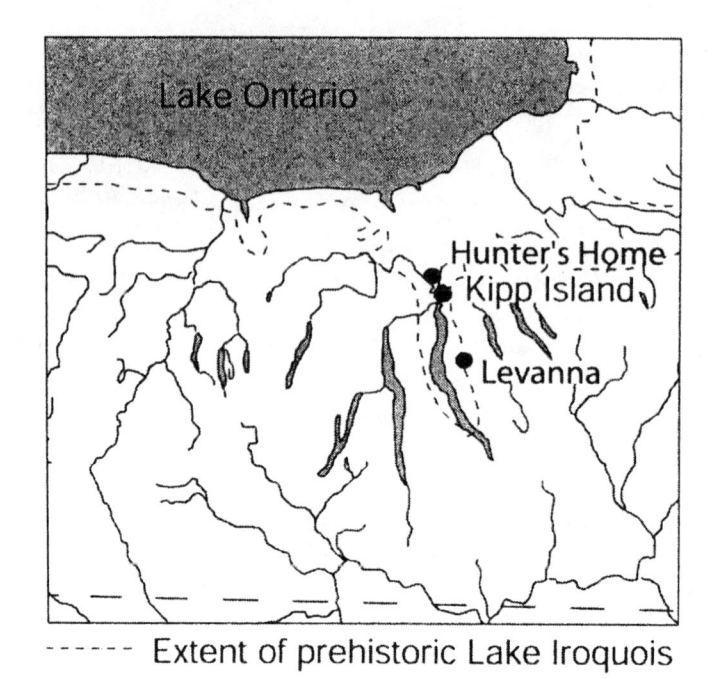

Fig. 4.1. Location of the Kipp Island, Hunter's Home, and Levanna sites.

– – – – – Extent of prehistoric Lake Iroquois

tation area, some of which Ritchie tentatively identified as *Chenopodium* (Ritchie 1969, 241; Ritchie and Funk 1973, 161). Based on the evidence for Hopewell corn production, Ritchie expected that the Hunter's Home people might also have corn, although he did not find evidence of maize at the site (Ritchie 1969, 241). According to Ritchie's publications (Ritchie 1969, 243) and the field notes kept by D. Barber (Rochester Museum and Science Center [RMSC] files), there is good evidence for use of aquatic foods such as mollusks, fish, turtles, and waterfowl. At Kipp Island the animal bone was found in refuse pits and middens that appear to have been formed over some period of time (Ritchie 1969, 242).

Table 4.3

Radiocarbon Dates from Kipp Island

Component	Radiocarbon Date	2–σ Calibrated Date[a]	Context
Kipp Island No. 2	A.D. 310 ± 100	cal A.D. 134 (417) 638	Hearth with Point Peninsula Rocker Stamped pottery
Kipp Island No. 3	A.D. 630 ± 100	cal A.D. 542 (683) 959	Earth oven with Kipp Island phase pottery
Kipp Island No. 4	A.D. 895 ± 100	cal A.D. 725 (995) 1211	Cremated burial

Source: Ritchie 1973, 155.
[a]Calibrated with CALIB 4.3.

The excavations of the habitation component at Kipp Island No. 4 exposed 3,000 square feet (sq. ft.) of the habitation area. The excavators identified hundreds of post molds, and numerous pits and hearths. The ceramics found in the trash pits and hearths are both Point Peninsula and Owasco, leading Ritchie to suggest the site was occupied by a Point Peninsula-Hunter's Home continuum (Ritchie and Funk 1973, 161). The post molds are dense, obscuring house outlines and indicating much reuse of the site. Ritchie tentatively identified three houses (Ritchie and Funk 1973, 160). None of the structures outlined by Ritchie is obvious from the published map. It is possible that the field-identified structures have post molds consistent in width and depth, but this information has not been preserved. Ritchie identifies a round house about 6 meters (m) in diameter and suggests this structure resembles dome-shaped wigwam-type dwellings found in Algonquian areas of the Northeast. He considers it a Point Peninsula phase structure (Ritchie and Funk 1973, 160). Another possible house outline is rectanguloid, with rounded corners and a doorway on a short side of the house. This structure encloses about 20 sq. m. Ritchie proposes it is a prototype to the larger Owasco longhouses in the region (Ritchie and Funk 1973, 160). This house has a width:length ratio of 1:>2.0, a proportion seen in later Iroquoian houses (see Kapches 1984). Finally, the most tenuous structure is one wall of a longhouse at least 12 m long. Ritchie interprets these houses as evidence for a continuum of development from Point Peninsula through Hunter's Home to Early Owasco (Ritchie and Funk 1973, 160). Based on the questionable nature of the Hunter's Home phase as a true transitional phase (Snow 1995a, 65 [chap. 1]) and the presence of substantial amounts of Early Owasco pottery, it appears that this site was also used by both Point Peninsula and Early Owasco people in some fashion.

The northern two-thirds of the Kipp Island drumlin was removed for gravel use during construction of the New York State Thruway, destroying all but Kipp Island No. 4. Kipp Island No. 4 lies along the southern margin of the drumlin, where there is an extensive refuse deposit that has been known to collectors for decades. A number of sherds in this study are from Charles "Bill" Breen's collection from this area of the Kipp Island site. Breen has been collecting the southern midden area of the Kipp Island drumlin for over 50 years. Artifacts from Ritchie's excavations are housed at the RMSC.

Hunter's Home Site

Hunter's Home A (NYSM 1538) is one component located on an archaeologically rich terrace overlooking Montezuma Marsh in Wayne County, New York. In published literature, Hunter's Home is often described as a specific site, whereas in reality it is an area encompassing four or five adjoining farms and several archaeological sites from different periods. The richest occupation appears to be on the Hunter's Home Farm and the adjoining Rogers Farm.

Hunter's Home A is located on Hunter's Home Farm and was first excavated in 1948 by Harold Secor and Arthur Seeley (RMSC files). Their excavations indicated that the area contained two strata, one with remnants of Point Peninsula occupations and one of Owasco occupations. Based on Secor and Seeley's excavations, Ritchie initiated investigations at several locations on Hunter's Home Farm in 1960. Ritchie concentrated his 268 sq. ft (25 sq. m) trench over a refuse midden, which was named Hunter's Home A. This midden is located at the edge of a terrace that overlooked prehistoric Lake Iroquois (Ritchie 1969, 258). Ritchie's excavations at Hunter's Home A produced archaeological remains that he attributed to both the late Point Peninsula and the early Owasco periods. Ritchie used these remains to argue that the Hunter's Home A site indicated a smooth transition between Point Peninsula and Owasco occupations. However, his proposed continuity is based more on interpretations of ceramic stylistic change than on real stratigraphic continuity. Ritchie (1969, 258) describes the stratigraphy of the excavation unit as an 8-inch layer of sand containing Owasco-style sherds and decorated pipes, and a layer of darker sand containing Point Peninsula pottery with similarities to the later Owasco styles separated by a 20- to 40-inch-thick sterile deposit. A barn now covers Hunter's Home A, prohibiting new excavations at the exact location.

Levanna Site

Levanna (NYSM 2092) is a village and cemetery located on a hill overlooking Cayuga Lake in Cayuga County, New York. Arthur C. Parker conducted preliminary excavations at Levanna during 1923 (RMSC files). Based on the preliminary results, Parker returned to Levanna in 1927 with a junior assistant (Ritchie) to conduct formal excavations.

The habitation area is approximately 150 m long by 30 m wide, and is situated on a triangular, naturally fortified location (Ritchie 1928). Steep embankments protect the north and south sides of the site. The gullies on the north and south converge on the western edge of the site, forming a constricted neck facing the lake. The eastern edge of the site is bounded by a shallow gully, which was probably filled with water before modern land drainage. The site is located over a mile away from the lake. Water for the site was available from the springs located at the base of the gullies. The site is located on well-drained sandy soil.

The excavations exposed middens along the northern, eastern, and southern margins of the site, some approaching 30 m in length (Ritchie 1928). The most substantial midden was located on the southeastern margin of the site. The midden contained Owasco pottery, stone mortars, pipe fragments, and bone from deer, birds, and fish (Ritchie 1928).

Twenty-two possible structures, or "lodge sites," were identified by the excavations (Ritchie 1928). Unfortunately, it is not clear what evidence was used to identify these locations. Based on Ritchie's description of these houses, it seems that the basis was a concentration of darker soil and an increase in artifact density. No mention is made of post molds in any of the records of the excavations. The unpublished field map (RMSC files) shows "lodge sites" where there are multiple fire pits, so perhaps their locations are based on the location of hearths. The "lodges" appear to vary from 4 to 6 m in length, and would have encompassed roughly 30 sq. m. These structures are small compared to other early Owasco houses (table 4.4).

From 1932 to 1948, H. C. Follet and G. B. Selden, members of the original excavation party, continued excavating at Levanna and charged admission. Eventually they found several animal effigies, including a thunderbird. Parker campaigned against these excavations with little success. The RMSC file contains extensive correspondence by Parker concerning these excavations. The work destroyed the portion of the site not excavated by Parker.

AMS Testing

Seven food residues from sherds from Kipp Island, three from Hunter's Home, and one from Levanna were submitted to Geochron Laboratory for AMS dating (table 4.2). The sherds included in this analysis are housed in two collections. The sherds from Hunter's Home and Levanna are housed in the Rochester Museum and Science Center collection. The sherds from Kipp Island are from Breen's private collection of Kipp Island materials. The Breen collection is ideal for this project because the sherds were never cleaned and have retained substantial amounts of carbonized food residue (fig. 4.2). Because of the extraordinary condition of the Breen collection, the AMS dating focuses heavily on sherds from Kipp Island. The physical characteristics of each sherd are summarized in table 4.5.

Table 4.4
Carpenter Brook Phase Houses in Central New York

Site	House Dimensions (m)	House Area (m^2)	Reference
Levanna	5 x 4–6	20–30	(Ritchie 1928)
White	6.9 x 11.4	78	(Prezzano 1992)
Port Dickinson	ca. 3–4 diameter	ca. 7–12.5	(Prezzano 1992)
Maxon-Derby	7 x 9–11	63–77	(Hart 2000a)
Boland	6 x ca. 14	ca. 84–85	(Prezzano 1992)
	5.5 x ca. 15.5		
Bates	6.7 x 11.6	78	(Hart 2000a)

Source: Adapted from Hart 2000a, 19; 2001, 175.

58 · Origins

Fig. 4.2. Residue encrusted on interior of sherd no. 13.

Point Peninsula Sherds

Three sherds, all from Kipp Island, are Point Peninsula pottery types. These sherds represent ceramic types spanning the period from A.D. 400 to 900. One sherd is from a Wickham Incised vessel (No. 1, table 4.5; fig. 4.3), a Middle Point Peninsula type (Ritchie and MacNeish 1949, 104). The other two sherds (Nos. 12, 15, table 4.5; fig. 4.3) are Point Peninsula Corded-rim sherds. Point Peninsula Corded-type ceramics are common throughout the Point Peninsula period, but increase in frequency later in the period (Ritchie and MacNeish 1949, 102).

Early Owasco Sherds

Of the eight Owasco-type sherds, four are from Kipp Island, three are from Hunter's Home, and one is from Levanna. These sherds are from types common throughout all three phases of the Owasco period. The Owasco Herringbone rim sherd from the Kipp Island site (No. 6, table 4.5; fig. 4.4) is the only Owasco type that Ritchie and MacNeish (1949, 111) thought might also be present during the Late Point Peninsula period. According to the typology, this type increases in popularity until the Middle Owasco period (Ritchie and MacNeish 1949, 111). Two sherds—one from Kipp Island, the other from Hunter's Home—are Carpenter Brook Cord-on-Cord (Nos. 4, 137, table 4.5; fig. 4.4). Carpenter Brook Cord-on-Cord is common during the Early Owasco period (Ritchie and MacNeish 1949, 108). Levanna Cord-on-Cord is also an early Owasco-type ceramic (Ritchie and MacNeish 1949, 110). Residues from two Levanna Cord-on-Cord sherds (Nos. 40, 99, table 4.5; fig. 4.5) were collected from Hunter's Home and Levanna. An Owasco Corded Oblique rim sherd from Kipp Island (No. 7, table 4.5; fig. 4.4) is a type that was common throughout the Owasco period, but peaked in popularity during the Middle

Table 4.5
Physical Characteristics of Sherds Selected for Dating

Sherd No.	Ceramic Type	Temper	Thickness (mm)	Body Treatment	Decoration	Rim Diameter (cm)
1	Wickham Incised	Quartz (2 mm)	8	Smoothed over cordmarking	Incised horizontal lines, crossed with incised lines at a 45° angle	42
4	Carpenter Brook Cord-on-Cord	Grit (1 mm)	6	Cordmarked	Horizontal cord impressed lines around neck	NA
6	Owasco Herringbone	Grit (1 mm)	9	Smooth	Herringbone of cord impressions, oblique cord impressions on rim interior	16
7	Owasco Corded Oblique	Grit (1–2 mm)	8	Smoothed over cordmarked	Plats of oblique cord impressions, which continue over rim to interior	12
12	Point Peninsula Corded	Grit (1 mm)	9	Smooth	Cordwrapped stick impressions in horizontal lines around rim and neck	16
13	Untyped	Quartz (4 mm)	11	Cordmarked	NA	NA
15	Point Peninsula Corded	Grit (1 mm)	7	Cordmarked	Horizontal lines of cordwrapped stick impressions, series of vertical impressions along rim	22
23	Owasco Corded Horizontal	Grit (1 mm)	8	Smooth	Horizontal cord impressions, short oblique impressions around neck	20
40	Levanna Cord-on-Cord	Grit (4 mm)	7	Cordmarked	NA	16
99	Levanna Cord-on-Cord	Grit (2–4 mm)	8	Cordmarked	NA	28
107	Owasco Corded Horizontal	Grit (2–4 mm)	7	Cordmarked	Horizontal cord impressions around neck, continuing over rim to interior	14
137	Carpenter Brook Cord-on-Cord	Grit (1–2 mm)	11	Cordmarked	Horizontal lines of cord impressions along neck and rim	20

60 · *Origins*

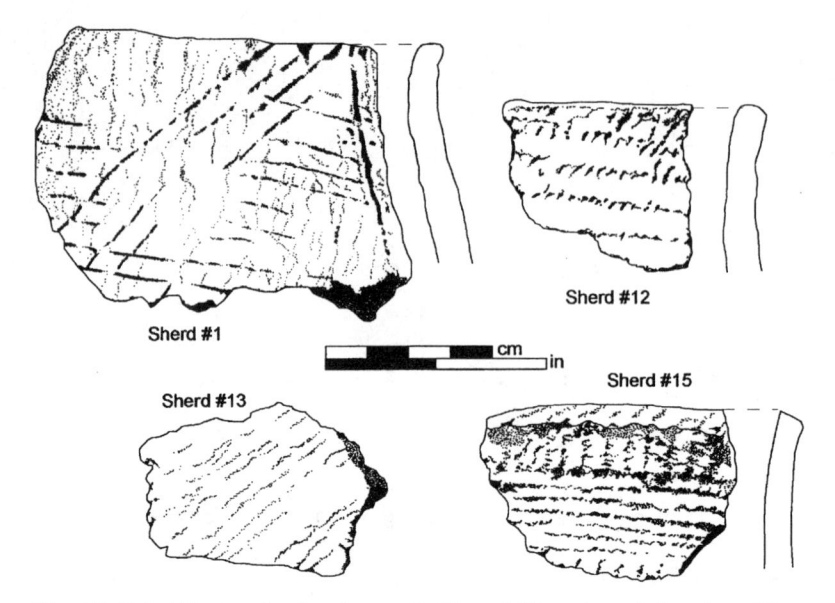

Fig. 4.3. Point Peninsula sherds nos. 1, 12, and 15; untyped sherd no. 13.

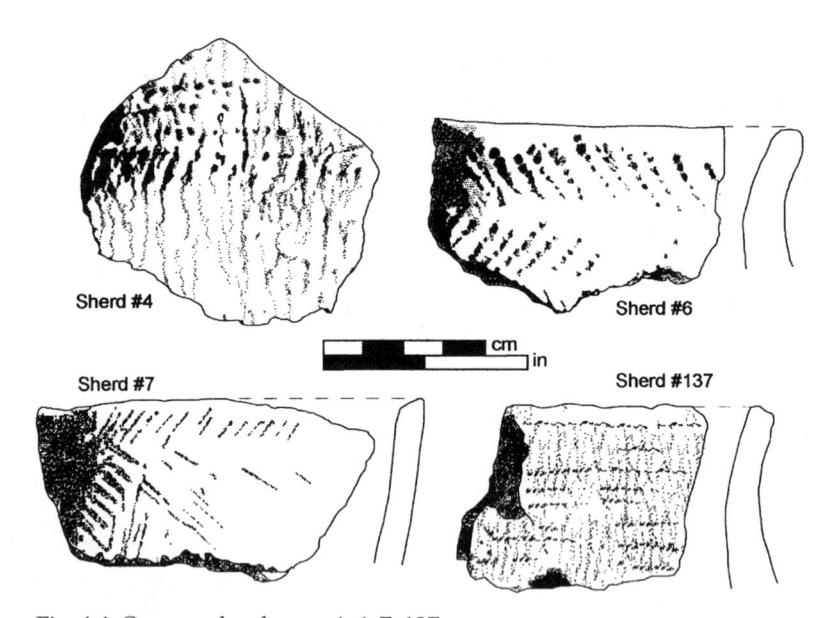

Fig. 4.4. Owasco sherds nos. 4, 6, 7, 137.

Owasco period (Ritchie and MacNeish 1949, 112). Two sherds are from Owasco Corded Horizontal vessels (Nos. 23, 107, table 4.5; fig. 4.5). Owasco Corded Horizontal appears during Early Owasco times and increases in popularity throughout the Owasco period (Ritchie and MacNeish 1949, 112).

Finally, the cordmarked body sherd is from Kipp Island and is not typable to any period or ceramic type (No. 13, table 4.5; fig. 4.3). It has a coil break, suggesting that it belonged to a Point Peninsula phase.

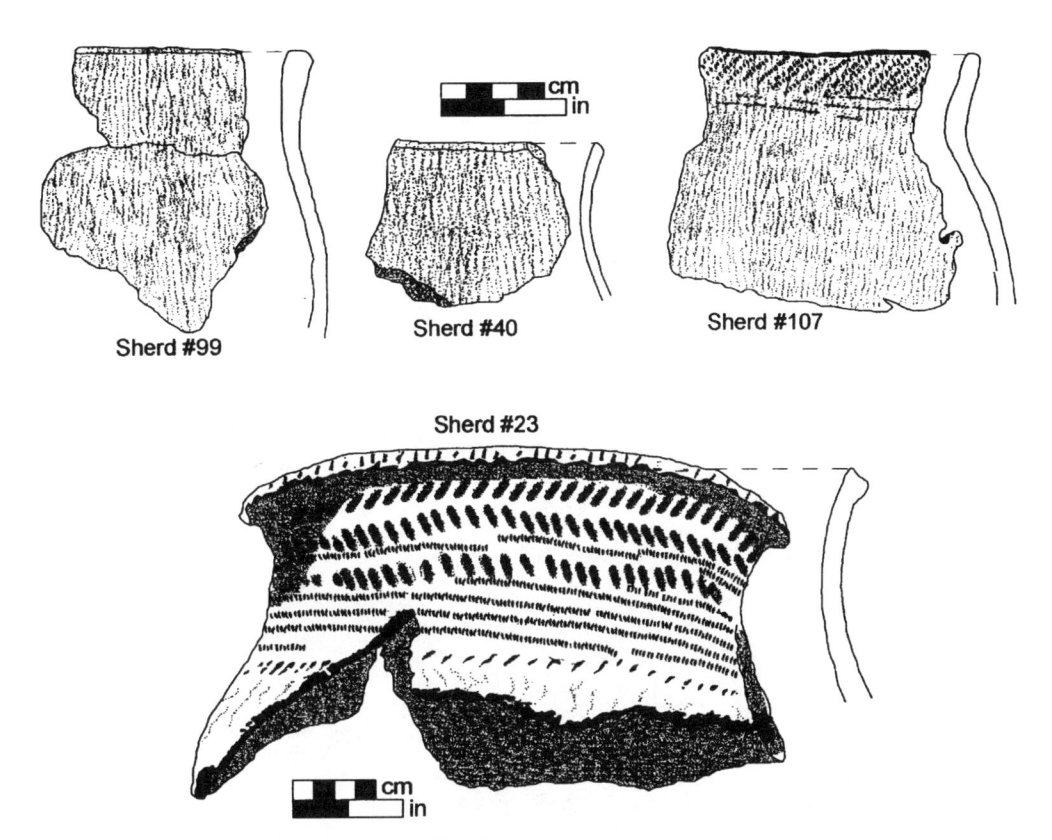

Fig. 4.5. Owasco sherds nos. 99, 40, 107, 23.

The residues encrusted on these sherds were removed under magnification with a stainless steel scalpel. Each sample of residue was wrapped in aluminum foil and sent to Geochron Laboratories, Inc., in Cambridge, Massachusetts, for AMS dating.

Results

The AMS radiocarbon dates returned on the residue samples are summarized in table 4.6 and fig. 4.6. The results bear importantly on the three models of Iroquoian development.

Point Peninsula Sherds

According to the classic typology, all three Point Peninsula sherds were expected to predate A.D. 950. The Wickham Incised sherd (No. 1) was expected to have an absolute date in the range of Middle Point Peninsula (ca. A.D. 400–800). The lab returned a date of 1280 ± 40 B.P., or a calibrated date in the seventh or eighth century A.D. (table 4.6; fig. 4.6). I expected the residues from the Point Peninsula

Table 4.6
AMS Dates and Calibrated Two-Sigma Ranges on Sherd Residues

Sherd No.	Site Name	Type	Lab Number	Uncalibrated Date B.P.	Calibrated Dates A.D. Two (intercepts) Sigma[a]
1	Kipp Island	Wickham Incised	GX-26448-AMS	1280 ± 40	660 (693, 699, 715, 749, 764) 863
4	Kipp Island	Carpenter Brook Cord-on-Cord	GX-26449-AMS	960 ± 40	999 (1034) 1186
6	Kipp Island	Owasco Herringbone	GX-26450-AMS	1410 ± 40	563 (646) 681
7	Kipp Island	Owasco Corded Oblique	GX-27558-AMS	1360 ± 40	619 (662) 766
12	Kipp Island	Point Peninsula Corded	GX-26451-AMS	1240 ± 40	676 (776) 891
13	Kipp Island	Cordmarked body	GX-26452-AMS	1170 ± 40	729 (887) 980
15	Kipp Island	Point Peninsula Corded	GX-27559-AMS	1210 ± 40	689 (781, 793, 802) 956
23	Kipp Island	Owasco Corded Horizontal	GX-26453-AMS	1220 ± 40	687 (779) 939
40	Levanna	Levanna Cord-on-Cord	GX-28193-AMS	1090 ± 40	886 (979) 1020
99	Hunter's Home	Levanna Cord-on-Cord	GX-27484-AMS	1180 ± 40	722 (885) 977
107	Hunter's Home	Owasco Corded Horizontal	GX-27485-AMS	1280 ± 40	660 (693, 699, 715, 749, 764) 863
137	Hunter's Home	Carpenter Brook Cord-on-Cord	GX-27486-AMS	1130 ± 40	780 (897, 922, 942) 998

[a] Calibrated with CALIB 4.3.

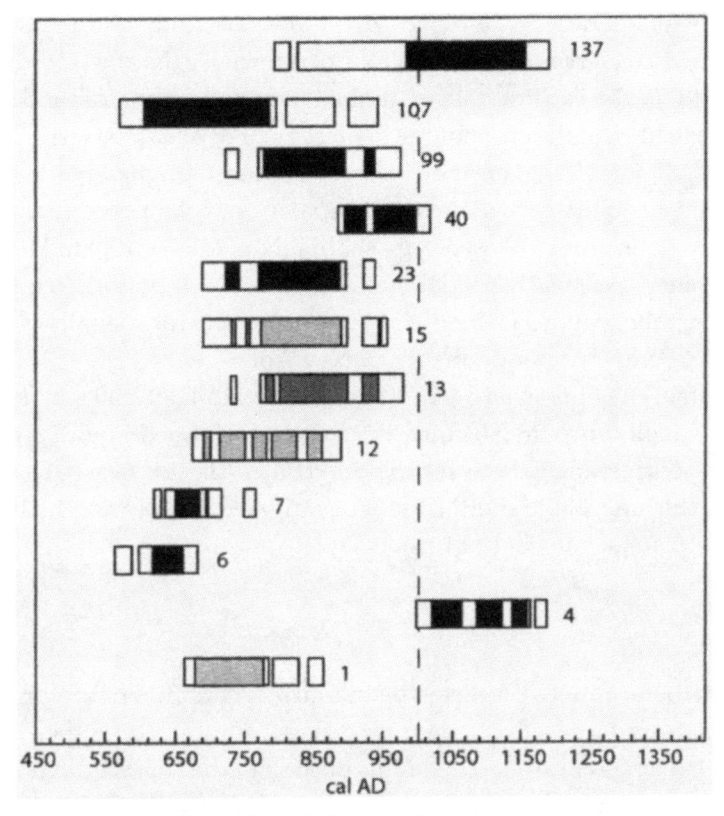

Fig. 4.6. 2–σ calibrated AMS dates and intercepts from encrusted residues. Owasco type sherds (nos. 137, 107, 99, 40, 23, 7, 6, 4) are shaded in black, Point Peninsula (nos. 15, 12, 1) in light gray. The dashed line delineates the classically defined break between the Point Peninsula and Owasco periods.

Corded sherds to date in the Middle to Late Point Peninsula periods (ca. A.D. 400–950). The Point Peninsula Corded sherds had dates of 1240 ± 40 B.P. or cal A.D. 776 (No. 12) and 1210 ± 40 B.P., which calibrates to the late eighth century A.D. (No. 15). All three of these calibrated dates are consistent with the expected results; each produced a solid Late Point Peninsula date.

Owasco Sherds

All of the Owasco-type sherds were expected to postdate A.D. 950 because this is the beginning of the Owasco period. As expected, the Carpenter Brook Cord-on-Cord sherds produced dates of 960 ± 40 B.P. or cal A.D. 1034 (No. 4) and 1130 ± 40 B.P. or the early tenth century A.D. (No. 137), and the Levanna Cord-on-Cord sherd from Levanna produced a date of 1090 ± 40 B.P. or cal A.D. 979 (No. 40). However, these were the only Owasco sherds to date in the classically defined Owasco time range. The Owasco Herringbone sherd (No. 6) returned a date of 1410 ± 40 B.P. or cal A.D. 646. This was the earliest date of all the Owasco-type sherds, and can be considered consistent with the chronological placement of Owasco Herringbone in the ceramic chronology. However, the Owasco Corded Oblique sherd (No. 7) produced an almost equally early date of 1360 ± 40 B.P. or cal A.D. 662 (fig. 4.6). The remaining three dates from Owasco-type sherds (Nos. 23, 99, 107) fall between A.D. 660 and 977, and consistently predate the Late Woodland period. In all, five of the eight Owasco pottery types yielded AMS dates that are traditionally considered to be in the Point Peninsula period in central New York.

The cordmarked body sherd (No. 13) was dated to 1170 ± 40 B.P. or cal A.D. 877 (fig. 4.6). Although this date falls into the classically defined Point Peninsula periods, given the discrepancies between expected dates for the Owasco sherds and the actual dates, this untypable sherd cannot be affiliated with either the Point Peninsula or Owasco archaeological culture.

Discussion

Contrary to the pattern predicted by the current ceramic chronology, the oldest absolute date from these sites came from a classic Owasco-type sherd. While this was considered a possible outcome of this portion of the study, I did not expect the dates to be so drastically different from the accepted chronology. This is not the first study to produce absolute dates associated with Owasco material that date to the Middle Woodland period. Several dates from other Owasco components have been disregarded as too early (Snow 1996a, 793 [chap. 3]). These dates are from sites whose artifact assemblage and settlement characteristics place them within the Owasco tradition. Radiocarbon dates from Street, Chenango Point, and Boland calibrate to the seventh and eighth centuries A.D. (Funk 1993; Snow 1996a [chap. 3]; Wurst and Versaggi 1993), as do the dates from Kipp Island and Hunter's Home presented here. The existence of several dates in this early range from other sites suggests that the AMS dates on the Owasco ceramics from Kipp Island and Hunter's Home should be taken at face value. It is clear that the early dates are not the result of a systematic bias; none of the dates from Point Peninsula sherds is earlier than expected.

While the dates from Kipp Island and Hunter's Home suggest culture occupations that are traditionally considered Owasco during a Point Peninsula time range, the single AMS date from Levanna corresponds to the expected range of occupation. Unlike Kipp Island and Hunter's Home, Levanna appears to be an Owasco village with no Point Peninsula occupation.

Although the absolute dates push the appearance of Owasco-style ceramics several hundred years earlier than expected, they do not resolve the issue of how the dates are interpreted, that is, how the ceramic styles relate to ethnic groups. Does the overlap of Point Peninsula and Owasco ceramics at the two campsites indicate cultures in contact, or an emerging Owasco culture? It appears that the ceramic chronology developed in the 1940s and the cultural affiliations made on the basis of the ceramic chronology need revisions. The three latest dates, however, are all from Owasco ceramics, and Owasco-style ceramics are the only ceramics at Levanna, a village site. These dates seem to suggest that Point Peninsula styles, and therefore Point Peninsula culture, had declined by the late tenth century A.D., and that by this time Owasco populations were establishing fairly substantial villages on higher ground.

The primary difference between these sites is the probable subsistence system being practiced at each site. The Levanna site is well situated for maize farming, and is occupied during a cultural period in which maize horticulture is supposed to have been practiced. Kipp Island and Hunter's Home, on the other hand, are not located on soils conducive for maize farming (although they are near good agricultural land). In addition, the Kipp Island and Hunter's Home sites are occupied during a period of cultural transition. Owasco ceramics have traditionally been interpreted as indicating the presence of Iroquoians. However, at these two sites, the Iroquoian and pre-Iroquoian populations appear to coexist. Consequently, the validity of considering Point Peninsula and Owasco ceramics as indicators of different ethnic groups is questionable.

Conclusion

These 12 dates in combination with other known early dates from Owasco sites suggest that the Owasco culture may have its origins well before A.D. 900. If ceramic types indeed indicate different cultures, these dates also suggest that Point Peninsula and Owasco cultures overlapped in central New York, perhaps much like Middle and Late Woodland cultures overlapped in southern Ontario (D. Smith 1997a). Both Chapdelaine's in situ model and Snow's incursion model allow for an overlap between Point Peninsula and Owasco cultural traditions, while Ritchie's in situ model does not. The in situ models suggest that the Iroquoian pattern developed either gradually or rapidly from a Point Peninsula base. While the overlap in Point Peninsula-type and Owasco-type ceramics seems to support the gradual in situ model, that model remains unsatisfactory in several ways not addressed in this project. Neither of the in situ models explains why the Iroquoian language, a unique language in the Northeast, became dominant (Fiedel 1991), or why the Iroquois are genetically different from their Algonquian-speaking neighbors (Langdon 1995). Snow's (1996a [chap. 3]) revised incursion model allows for an overlap in Point Peninsula and Owasco ceramics and explains the appearance of a unique linguistic and biological population in the Northeast.

The transition from a primarily foraging economy to one dominated by food production in other parts of the world may shed some light on these new data. Theoretical contributions made by Susan A. Gregg (1988; 1991) and Bogucki (1995) suggest that the transition to farming in Europe was often a long, multilayered process of interaction between foragers and farmers. With intensive radiocarbon dating, we now know that foragers and farmers in Europe coexisted for over 1,000 years (Bogucki 1995). A recent review of radiocarbon dates from Ontario also shows Middle Woodland foraging cultures overlapping with Late Woodland farming cultures for at least 300 years (D. Smith 1997a). It is likely that overlapping of subsistence adaptations also occurred in the Finger Lakes region. The possibility of this situation does not resolve the in situ versus migration debate, but it does suggest that the Iroquoian area of New York shares developmental similarities with other parts of the world.

Regardless of which model of Iroquoian origins one accepts, the AMS dates presented here indicate that the ceramic chronology developed in the 1940s and the cultural affiliations made on the basis of the ceramic chronology need revisions. Ceramic studies in the future need to address the issue of how strong the linkage is between ceramic types and ethnic groups or cultures. Given the data presented here, it appears the Iroquoian adaptation may have roots several hundred years earlier than is generally accepted.

Acknowledgments

Funding for this research was provided by the Wenner Gren Foundation (grant #6606) and the Hill Foundation. This project was made possible by the help of Bob Gorall and Betty Prisch. I would especially like to thank Bill Breen for allowing me to use his extraordinary collection. I would also like to thank John Hart and Christina Rieth for inviting me to participate in the conference on Northeast Subsistence-Settlement Change.

5 | The Death of Owasco

JOHN P. HART AND HETTY JO BRUMBACH

ARCHAEOLOGY IS A HISTORICAL SCIENCE. As a result, its activities are guided by key concepts and words rather than laws or law-like statements (Hart and Terrell 2002; cf. Mayr 1982). These concepts and words guide the kinds of questions asked about the past and characterize the discipline to the outside world. One of the most influential guiding and characterizing words in archaeology is *origin*. In fact, much of what many archaeologists do can be characterized as origins research, whether it be, for example, the search for the origins of agriculture (see Terrell et al. 2003) or the New York northern Iroquoians (e.g., Parker 1922; Snow 1995a [chap. 1]).[1] As a corollary to this interest in origins research, archaeologists and their audiences are fascinated by the earliest evidence for various phenomena. For example, there is a continuing search for the earliest maize in eastern North America, in part because it represents the "origin" of the agricultural systems that dominated the fields of Native American agriculturists at the time of European contact (Hart 1999a). In New York the search is for the earliest evidence of specific clusters of traits associated with historic northern Iroquoian speakers to pinpoint their "origin" as recognizable ethnic groups.

Origins research is fostered by the use of culture-historic taxa as units of analysis under their mistaken identification as ethnic groups (Trigger 1989). Reliance on culture-historic taxa as units of analysis has been a long-standing problem in archaeological research in North America generally (e.g., Binford 1965; J. Brown 1965; Moore 1994) and New York specifically (e.g., Engelbrecht 1999; 2003; Starna and Funk 1994). Culture-historic taxa have been a straightjacket, serving to define research agenda and restrict the questions asked about the past. These taxa are theory bound (Dunnell 1971); using them as units of analysis under varying theoretical

---

Previously published in *American Antiquity* 68, no. 4 (2003): 737–52. Reproduced by permission of the Society for American Archaeology.

1. In this article we use the term *Iroquois* to refer to historic speakers of Iroquoian languages in New York. We use the term *Iroquoian* to refer to other historic speakers of Iroquoian languages throughout the Northeast and to prehistoric constructs.

constructs without justification, we argue, has hindered the development of North American archaeology (Taylor 1948).

In this article we review as a case study the historical development of the key culture-historic taxon in New York associated with the origin of northern Iroquois groups from its beginnings with Arthur C. Parker (1922) and its subsequent adoption and refinement by William A. Ritchie (1944; 1969; Ritchie and Funk 1973) over the next half-century. We show that Owasco is a subjectively, extensionally defined culture-historic taxon based primarily on the thoughts of two men, Parker and Ritchie. We then review the current evidence for the various traits that Ritchie (1969; Ritchie and Funk 1973) used in his final statements on Owasco, including the results of a recent program of direct dating of cooking residues adhering to diagnostic pottery sherds (also see Hart et al. 2003; Schulenberg 2002a; 2002b [chap. 4]). The results of this research, using analytical techniques not available to Ritchie and Parker, indicate that the key traits used by Ritchie have very different chronologies than he thought. The definition of Owasco does not hold up under empirical test and we argue that the taxon should be abandoned for that reason alone. Because Owasco was originally extensionally defined, it would be possible to redefine it based on current data. But we argue on theoretical grounds that such a redefinition is unwarranted. The search for the origin of New York Iroquoians within a culture-historic framework can no longer be considered a viable research agenda.

Origin

Origin is one of a legion of vernacular words widely used in archaeology that reflects the broader context of the discipline. According to the *Oxford English Dictionary* (online second edition 1989), *origin* means "The act or fact of arising or springing from something: derivation, rise; beginning of existence in reference to its source or cause." The use of this word in archaeology, then, means that the search for the first evidence of a phenomenon is a search for the point of change from one state or condition to another—the beginning of something new, something different, something important. This definition is consistent with the commonsense notion that things remain the same until something causes them to change, thereby creating something new.

Of particular importance in the definition of *origin* are the notions of "arising or springing from something" and the "beginning of existence in reference to its source." Both of these notions require the existence of a recognizable source of the new phenomenon and by extension the existence of a state different from that of the new phenomenon. So, in the case of the northern Iroquoians, there must have been a specific source or a prior state from which this group sprang or arose.

The idea of origins in archaeology is perpetuated by, or in fact helps to perpetuate, the continued reliance on culture-historic taxa as units of analysis. These are formally, temporally, and spatially bounded units that are extensionally defined so as to minimize internal variation (Dunnell 1971; Willey and Phillips 1958). These units were more or less successful in controlling spatial and temporal variation under the culture-historic paradigm. In present-day archaeology they are frequently used as units of analysis for purposes that were never intended (Hart 1999b; Starna and Funk 1994). Following from precedents established in the early twentieth century (e.g., Parker 1922), they are frequently conceived of as the equivalent of ethnic groups or ethnographic cultures (Trigger 1989). In other words, they are thought to have had some reality in the past rather than just in the present under specific definitional contexts (Dunnell 1971).

Within that conceptual context, because the rules for definition require a temporally bounded, internal homogeneity of traits, change only occurs at the temporal boundaries of taxa. The origin of a taxon must be a preceding one in the same or from another location. Because change can only be sudden or saltational, the notion of "arising or springing from something" fits this conception of the past almost without thought.

The search for the origin of the northern Iroquois is pursued within the culture-historic constructs of the early to mid-twentieth century. In New York, that construct was developed by Ritchie (e.g., 1936; 1944; 1969), building on earlier work by Parker (1922). Following the advent of radiocarbon dating, Ritchie (1969) defined his Late Woodland stage and its Owasco culture both as beginning at ca. A.D. 1000.[2] While he saw a continuum of development from his preceding Middle Woodland stage through the historic northern Iroquois in his final version of the scheme, he divided the continuum based on limited series of traits that he felt characterized particular periods of time. The key characteristics of the Late Woodland stage and Owasco culture, setting them off from earlier manifestations, were ultimately to Ritchie (1969; Ritchie and Funk 1973) the advent of maize-bean-squash agriculture, nucleated villages, and longhouses with inferred matrilocal residence, along with a series of pottery types (also see Snow 1995a [chap. 1]; compare to Parker's 1922 "Third Algonkian Period").[3] Ritchie saw each of these characteristics as occurring for the first time during the Carpenter Brook phase dating from A.D. 1000 to A.D. 1100, effectively originating the recognizable development of the New York Iroquoians. It is the onset of Owasco at A.D. 1000, or as is more widely accepted now

---

2. In this article dates denoted by B.P. are in radiocarbon years before present. Those denoted with A.D. are calibrated with CALIB 4.3 (Stuiver et al. 1998), except for those with "ca.," which are estimates used by Ritchie in defining his culture history.

3. Parker and Ritchie used spellings of *Algonkian* and/or *Algonkin* to refer to the language family and its speakers. In this article we follow this usage when discussing Parker's and Ritchie's work, but otherwise favor the alternative spelling, *Algonquian*, which came into common usage about 15 years ago.

A.D. 900 (see Funk 1993; Snow 1995a [chap. 1]), that is typically accepted as the origin of northern Iroquoian groups in New York, whether an in situ or migration hypothesis for that origin is postulated. Owasco is the source from which the northern Iroquoians arose or sprang, whether researchers accept the A.D. 1000 date or not (Snow 1995a [chap. 1]; 1996a [chap. 3]). However, the continued use of Ritchie's scheme and its concomitant identification with the search for the origins of New York Iroquois now can be challenged on evidential and theoretical grounds.

A Short History of Owasco

The major focus of William A. Ritchie's career as the foremost archaeologist in New York was the construction of a culture history of the state. The ultimate expression of this effort is *The Archaeology of New York State* (1965; 1969), with some elaboration in his later volume with Robert E. Funk, *Aboriginal Settlement Patterns in the Northeast* (1973). Within these final statements of Ritchie's culture history, the origin of recognizable Iroquoian traits in New York begins with the onset of the Late Woodland stage (or period) and the Owasco culture at ca. A.D. 1000. This culture history continues to dominate archaeological research in New York, framing and defining research issues (e.g., Gates St-Pierre 2001; Snow 1995a [chap. 1]; 1996a [chap. 3]; 2001) and regional summaries (e.g., Funk 1993; Prezzano and Rieth 2001). In order to understand what Owasco represents, it is necessary to briefly summarize the history of the taxon.

Culture-historic units in North American archaeology are extensionally defined (Dunnell 1971; Lyman and O'Brien 2002; Lyman et al. 1997). According to Dunnell (1971, 15) extensional definitions are "accomplished by listing all objects to which the term is applicable, or doing this within some specified and restricted set of boundaries." Extensional definitions "cannot convey why a thing is that thing, but only that it is" (Dunnell 1971, 16). The extensional definition of units is subjective, being based on the person doing the defining, and historically contingent because the definitions are based on objects available for enumeration. "The procedure is murky because what one analyst chooses to perceive may be different from the choices of another analyst" (Lyman and O'Brien 2002, 81). As we will show in the following brief history of the Owasco culture, it has always been extensionally defined; Ritchie accepted a previously defined taxon (Parker 1922) and spent the remainder of his career extensionally defining the unit's content and adjusting its boundaries (see Ritchie 1969, xxxii).

The first time Ritchie used the term *Owasco* as a culture-historic taxon was in his 1936 monograph *A Prehistoric Fortified Village Site at Canandaigua, Ontario County, New York*. In the foreword to that volume, Ritchie (1936, 3) stated that the Owasco aspect was a replacement for Parker's (1922) Third Algonkian period. The change from the Third Algonkian period to the Owasco aspect followed the adoption of the Midwest Taxonomic Method. As clearly stated in his later publications, for Ritchie it was a simple replacement of terms:

> The Owasco culture takes its name from the first reported site, located in Lakeside (now Emerson) Park on the outlet of Owasco Lake, at Auburn, Cayuga County.... The distinctiveness of the assemblage from other cultures known at that time was recognized by Parker, who attributed the site to his "Third Algonkian Period" (Parker 1922, 49).... following the writer's exploration in 1934 of the Sackett site ... and the formulation and adoption of the Midwestern Taxonomic Method of classification in 1935, the cultural designation was changed to the "Owasco Aspect." (Ritchie 1969, 272–73)

As related by Ritchie and Funk (1973, 165), "At that time (1936) the earlier designation of 'Third Algonkian Period' (Parker 1922, 49) was changed to 'Owasco Aspect,' in line with the general adoption by American archaeologists of the Midwestern Taxonomic System."

Parker's definition of the Third Algonkian period is as follows:

> The later [third] Algonkian occupation is more definite in character and covers almost the entire area of the State. It is characterized by numerous flints, by steatite pottery, clay pottery, notched choppers, grooved axes, celts, adzes, hoes, some copper implements, gouges, gorgets, birdstones, banner stones, cord-marked and pattern-stamped clay pottery, mediocre clay pipes, roller pestles, numerous net sinkers, and a considerable amount of bone implements, as awls, harpoons, needles and beads. The sites are generally on lowlands near streams and lakes, none of importance being on hilltops. The later Algonkian peoples were agricultural as is proved by the numerous instances in which maize and beans have been found in refuse pits. The later Algonkian tribes were more sedentary than their predecessors and their settlements presumably larger. This seems to be indicated by the presence of deposits of refuse, by refuse pits and heaps and large areas of ground filled with carbonized matter, fire-burned stone and calcined bone. (Parker 1922, 48–49)

Parker, of course, had no idea of the time depth of human occupation of the Western Hemisphere. He conceived the precontact history of New York in terms of its historic Native occupants and contact with outside groups such as the Eskimo. As a result his nomenclature was based on historic language groups and ethnographic analogies. He envisioned the Algonquian occupations as "wave after wave of these peoples, coming in band after band to hunt over the territory or make settlements" before the arrival of "the Iroquoian tribes" (Parker 1922, 46). Following the adoption of the Midwest Taxonomic Method, Ritchie worked with Parker to place Parker's 1922 taxonomy within the new nomenclature (Ritchie 1936, 3), resulting in the terminology switch to Owasco aspect (fig. 5.1). Per the Midwest Taxonomic Method (McKern 1939), one goal was to eliminate reference to historic language and ethnic groups and base taxonomies purely on archaeological data,

72 • *Origins*

BASE	PATTERN	PHASE	ASPECT (Period)	FOCUS (Phase)	COMPONENT (Site)
	Mississippi	Upper	Iroquois (Iroquois)	Huron, Neutral, Erie, Seneca, Cayuga, Onondaga, Oneida, Mohawk, Tuscarora, Andaste	
		Hopewellian	Elemental (Mound Intrusion)	New York	Squawkie Hill
	Woodland	Northeastern	Owasco (Third Algonkian)	Castle Creek	Castle Creek, Bainbridge
				Canandaigua (Owasco)	Owasco Lake, Levanna, Canandaigua, Hilltop, Wilber Lake, White's Pond, Willow Point
			Vine Valley (Second Algonkian)	Pt. Peninsula	Pt. Peninsula, Long Point, Northrop, Dundee, Wray
				Middlesex (Vine Valley)	Vine Valley, Palatine Bridge, Hoffmans
				Coastal	Sites on Long Island, etc.
				Orient	Sites on Eastern Long Island, etc.
		Ground Slate	(Eskimo-like)		
	Archaic		(Archaic Algonkian)	Lamoka	Lamoka Lake, Geneva, Scottsville

Ritchie's 1936 "Classification of Aboriginal Cultures of New York State"

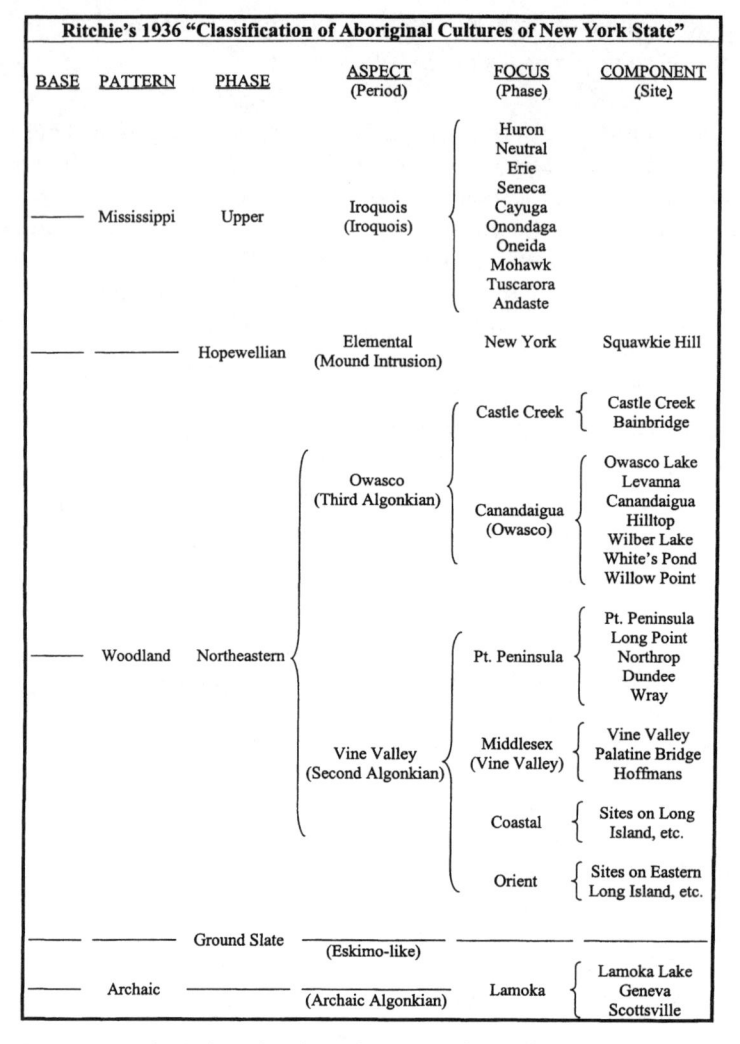

Fig. 5.1. Ritchie's (1936) culture-historic scheme for New York (after Ritchie 1936, 4). Terms in parentheses are Parker's (1922) corresponding taxa.

but Ritchie (1936, 3) stated that "[i]t must not consequently be concluded that the ultimate recognition of the Vine Valley or Owasco aspects as products of an Algonkin people has been abandoned. The line of evidence now being followed seems to be tending toward the coincidence of the latter with a well known Algonkin group." Thus the foundations of Owasco are in Parker's initial attempt to define taxa related to historically recorded language groups in New York. Parker provided the boundaries, while Ritchie's later work revised the content.

In his first major synthesis of New York prehistory, *The Pre-Iroquoian Occupations of New York State,* Ritchie (1944) elaborated the list of attributes defining the

Owasco aspect, and defined two Owasco foci. At this early time, like Parker, Ritchie had no conception of the time depth of human occupations in New York, projecting the entire sequence back only 1,600 years (Ritchie 1944, 10; also see Ritchie 1969, xxviii), with the Owasco aspect originating at approximately A.D. 1200, extending to A.D. 1650, and overlapping with and being influenced by the Iroquois aspect for some 300 years after the latter's origination from elsewhere at approximately A.D. 1350. Along with an extensive description and illustration of Owasco pottery, and a brief discussion of settlement traits, Ritchie (1944, 46) identified 288 traits for the Owasco aspect, based on excavations at 30 sites. The enumerated traits expanded with the number of sites excavated as part of the continuing extensional definition of the taxon. Ritchie summarized the aspect as follows: "Clearly the Owasco culture was the product of a rather numerous agricultural people, having a well-developed ceramic complex in which Woodland pipes and pottery attained their apogee" (Ritchie 1944, 52). Reflecting the fact that extensional definitions change as additional sites are excavated, Ritchie (1944, 29) contra Parker (1922) indicated that Owasco sites are "often situated on hilltops a mile or more from navigable water."

The fact that Ritchie accepted this taxon as viable and only in need of refinement is clear in his 1949 publication with Richard S. MacNeish on "The Pre-Iroquoian Pottery of New York State." The stated goal of that paper was to refine an already accepted taxon and cultural sequence:

> The establishment of ceramic type categories for the pre-Iroquoian horizons of New York state . . . was undertaken for a number of reasons. Primarily, it was believed that such an analysis, breaking down the existing ware divisions into finer type inventories, would prove useful in obtaining a more minute chronological differentiation of the Owasco and Point Peninsula cultures than would be possible on any other basis, and in so doing, would aid in clarifying their possible relationships as well as their conceivable affinities with other major ceramic manifestations in the New York area. It was also hoped that our survey might reveal significant areal subdivisions which eventually might be referred to historic tribal units. Finally, the achievement of a pottery typology for New York would elucidate problems of prehistoric culture diffusion and development over the Northeastern area and might, indeed, contribute to broader interpretations of cultural dynamics and processes of acculturation involved in the complex interconnections of sequential archaeological components. (Ritchie and MacNeish 1949, 97–98)

Following his work with Ritchie on pre-Iroquoian pottery, MacNeish (1952) undertook a study of Iroquoian pottery, which led him to conclude that Iroquois pottery developed from Owasco. He observed that while there are significant differences in decorative motif, surface finish, and location of decoration, these changes occurred gradually and there was significant overlap in attributes. MacNeish also observed that Owasco ceramic types appear on early Iroquois sites, and that there are "transitional" types with features distinctive of both Owasco and Iroquois (MacNeish 1952, 82). MacNeish (1952, 82–83) also pointed out that Iroquois is in many cases stratigraphically later than Owasco, "and that no culture of the same time period as Owasco, and with as many connections with the Iroquois has been found in the areas which surround the Iroquois." MacNeish's work convinced the majority of New York archaeologists that Iroquois developed from Owasco.

By the mid to late 1960s Ritchie had had two decades to further compile traits for the Owasco taxon. As with the earlier change from Third Algonkian period to Owasco aspect with the adoption of the Midwest Taxonomic Method, Ritchie (1969, xxvii-xxviii) now adopted the terminology of Willey and Phillips' (1958) systematics, trading the terms *aspect* and *focus* for *culture* and *phase*. Although he claimed to have adopted Taylor's (1948) conjunctive approach, Ritchie's primary focus remained on defining boundaries and enumerating the traits of the Owasco culture, as is demonstrated by the list of subheadings for his section on the taxon: Geographic Range, Site Locations, Chronology, The Owasco People, Subsistence Bases, Hunting and Fishing Equipment, Vegetable Foods and Their Storage, Food Preparation, Settlement Pattern, Clothing and Personal Decoration, Tools, Textiles and Basketry, Pottery, Travel and Trade, Warfare, Games, Smoking Pipes, Burial Customs, Social and Political Organization, Religious Concepts, and Linguistic Affiliations.

While no longer using an exhaustive list of traits, expanded with each excavated site, what is more than clear here is that Ritchie accepted Owasco as a taxon without formal definition or justification other than that it ultimately derived from Parker's Third Algonkian period. What Ritchie did was place the traditional discussion and listing of traits into a descriptive narrative, reflecting his interpretation of Taylor's approach: "The emphasis has thus been shifted from a primary concern with taxonomy, chronology, culture content and relationships, to the examination of whole cultures, within the relatively narrow limits afforded by their archaeological survivals" (Ritchie 1969, xxvii).

Two important changes in the conceptualization of Owasco were the refinement of chronology based on radiocarbon dating and the association of Owasco with the origin of Iroquoian groups in New York state. Ritchie noted there were 12 radiocarbon dates from 8 Owasco sites. These dates were used by Ritchie to formulate a 300-year time span for Owasco, from A.D. 1000 to 1300, with each of the three phases (Carpenter Brook, Canandaigua, and Castle Creek) accounting for 100 years, respectively. This formulation established the chronology for Owasco that remains largely accepted today (e.g., Funk 1993; Prezzano and Rieth 2001; Snow 1995a [chap. 1]). As a major departure from earlier conceptualizations, while still accepting Owasco as ancestral to some historic Algonquian groups, following MacNeish (1952), Ritchie (1969, 273, 300–301) now saw Owasco as ancestral to the historic northern Iroquois of New York. He summarized the key developments defining Owasco as follows:

> A principal distinction setting off Late from Middle Woodland cultures is the now obvious fact of the importance of cultigens—corn, beans and squash demonstra-

bly—in the economy. This change accompanied, *pari passu*, a major alteration in settlement pattern, with large villages, the later ones protected by palisades, containing a sessile or semisedentary, augmenting population, dwelling communally in longhouses. (Ritchie 1969, 180)

In his last major summary of New York archaeology, focused on settlement pattern data and interpretations (Ritchie and Funk 1973), Ritchie continued the extensional definition of Owasco with narrative discussions of traits in two sections (Ritchie and Funk 1973, 165–67, 359–61). The volume's focus on settlement patterns resulted in this final summary statement on Owasco:

Throughout the Owasco period, there was a continuing trend toward larger settlements—now describable as villages—with correspondingly greater sessility. Agricultural products were the prime subsistence basis, as shown by consistent recoveries of charred corn and other cultigens and indirectly by a steady decline in the frequency of hunting and fishing gear and associated tools. In eastern and south-central New York, Late Woodland groups made use of increasingly larger and more numerous pits for storing plant foods. The average size of houses, now obviously prototypical longhouses, also tended to increase. Evidence for internecine warfare, in the form of palisaded villages, arrow-riddled corpses, evidence for cannibalism, etc., first appeared in Middle Owasco times. All of these trends, accompanied by gradual modifications in ceramics and projectile point styles, persisted through the period occupied by archaeological entities which, by A.D. 1400, were distinctly Iroquoian. (Ritchie and Funk 1973, 369)

In the end, Owasco is simply an extensionally defined culture-historic taxon. It originated subjectively under a different name with Parker (1922) based initially on the contents of a single site. It was firmly established in the literature and continually refined by Parker's protégé Ritchie (1936; 1944; 1969; Ritchie and Funk 1973). In his publications, Ritchie followed a set pattern in defining Owasco, consistent with expectations for extensional definitions (Dunnell 1971): (1) assertion of existence based on authority—on its long-standing recognition by Parker and himself; (2) establishment of time and space boundaries, refined with each publication based on additional site finds and advances in chronological control; (3) a narrative and/or list of traits, dominated by pottery descriptions, refined with each site excavated; and (4) narrative descriptions of representative sites that illustrated certain traits.

An interesting thought experiment, given all of the effort expended on distinguishing Owasco and Clemson Island pottery (see Hart 1999b; Hay et al. 1987; Rieth 2002a; Stewart 1990), is whether these taxa would have been separately identified by Parker and Ritchie had New York extended south to encompass the West Branch of the Susquehanna River basin. Would they have been recognized as a single archaeological culture, and how would that have affected the history of thought on New York Iroquoian origins?

Owasco is the creation of two men, Ritchie and Parker. There has never been an explicit justification of this taxon other than authoritative recognition of its existence by Parker and Ritchie. Ritchie never questioned Parker's identification of the taxon; he simply recast it in new terms as suited to contemporary trends in the literature, and refined its temporal, spatial, and formal properties. It has now been three decades since Ritchie's final statement on Owasco (Ritchie and Funk 1973). It remains firmly established in the literature. With the exception of temporal position, the taxon has been largely unquestionably accepted as a valid construct, an appropriate unit of analysis, and the origination of recognizable Iroquoian traits in New York State (see Snow 1995a [chap. 1]). As a result of recent empirical and theoretical research (e.g., Hart 1999c; 2000a; 2001; Hart and Scarry 1999; Hart et al. 2002; 2003; Schulenberg 2002a; 2002b [chap. 4]), the major traits identified as defining the taxon and its Iroquoian connections in Ritchie's final formulations (Ritchie 1969; Ritchie and Funk 1973) have been shown to have histories that are very different from those stated by Ritchie. These findings demonstrate that the taxon's definition can no longer stand.

Current Evidence for Key Owasco Traits

The archaeological origin of the northern Iroquoians in New York is recognized with the onset of the Owasco tradition under Ritchie's final refinement of his culture-history scheme. Specifically, the origin of Owasco is recognized by the appearance of four traits: (1) specific ceramic types, (2) longhouses and inferred matrilocal residence, (3) nucleated villages, and (4) maize-bean-squash agriculture. Recent empirical research has demonstrated that these traits have histories divergent from those accepted by archaeologists using Ritchie's taxonomy (Hart 1999c; 2000a; Hart and Scarry 1999; Hart et al. 2002; 2003; Schulenberg 2002a; 2002b [chap. 4]). In the following pages we present additional evidence that contradicts the widely accepted ceramic chronology relative to the origin of Owasco and complements data recently published by Schulenberg (2002a; 2002b [chap. 4]), and summarize the results of previously published research on the timing of subsistence and settlement traits.

Pottery Type Chronology

An important component of the extensional definition of Owasco and that of its three phases is a series of pottery types initially defined by Ritchie and MacNeish (1949). These types were used in seriations to help establish the relative chronology of Owasco's subtaxa (see, e.g., Ritchie 1969; Ritchie and MacNeish 1949; Ritchie et al. 1953). Ritchie and MacNeish (1949) ascribed relative chronological positions to the various types (table 5.1); following the advent of radiocarbon dating those same types later came to be associated with specific time ranges (see

Table 5.1
Late Point Peninsula and Early Owasco Types

Type	Relative Age
Point Peninsula Rocker-Stamped	Early to Late Point Peninsula
Kipp Island Crisscross	Late Point Peninsula
Jack's Reef Dentate Collar	Late Point Peninsula
Jack's Reef Corded	Late Point Peninsula
Jack's Reef Corded Collar	Late Point Peninsula
Jack's Reef Corded Punctate	Late Point Peninsula
Wickham Corded Punctate	Early Owasco
Carpenter Brook Cord-on-Cord	Early Owasco
Levanna Corded Collar	Early Owasco
Levanna Cord-on-Cord	Early to Late Owasco
Owasco Herringbone	Late Point Peninsula to Late Owasco
Owasco Platted	Early to Late Owasco
Owasco Corded Horizontal	Early to Late Owasco
Owasco Corded Oblique	Early to Late Owasco

Source: After Ritchie and MacNeish 1949.

especially Prezzano 1992; Schulenberg 2002a). Like Owasco itself, the pottery types are extensionally defined, and, therefore, historically contingent.

Ritchie (1969) subsequently defined the Hunter's Home phase dating to ca. A.D. 900–1000, which formed a transition between the end of the Point Peninsula culture and the beginning of the Owasco culture:

> [I]t must be emphasized that as the culture [Owasco] represents a developmental continuum through time and space, it becomes exceedingly difficult, if not impossible, narrowly and specifically to define and characterize separable and distinctive phases. One might more readily and validly discern earlier, intermediate and later stages, based mainly upon ceramic criteria, the first having closest affinities with the Hunter's Home phase, which we regard as terminal Point Peninsula, the last hardly distinguishable from the Oak Hill phase, arbitrarily assumed to represent inchoate Iroquoian culture in the New York area. (Ritchie 1969, 273)

Accordingly to this formulation, some early Owasco types occurred in late Point Peninsula times. Snow (1995a [chap. 1]) has argued that the presence of these types represents mixed Point Peninsula and Owasco deposits, that Hunter's Home is not a valid taxon, and that Owasco extends to ca. A.D. 900 (compare to Gates St-Pierre 2001).

In order to understand the Owasco types on sites assigned by Ritchie to this transitional phase, we AMS-dated charred food residues adhering to the interior surface of 13 late Point Peninsula-type and early Owasco-type pottery sherds from the Hunter's Home, Kipp Island, and Wickham sites in the New York State Museum's collections (see Gates St-Pierre 2001 for a detailed description of pottery in the Hunter's Home and Kipp Island collections). This work adds to the dates obtained by Schulenberg (2002a; 2002b [chap. 4]) on 11 sherds in different collections from the Hunter's Home and Kipp Island sites.

The results of our dating program are presented in table 5.2 along with the type ascriptions for the sherds based on Ritchie and MacNeish (1949). As described in Hart et al. (2003), these and Schulenberg's dates define several components at Kipp Island and Hunter's Home: two at Kipp Island with mean, pooled 2σ ranges and intercepts of A.D. 601 (642) 659 and A.D. 693 (778) 880 and one at Hunter's Home A.D. 774 (781, 793, 801) 888. The four dates at Wickham were widely dispersed, although two have a mean pooled 2σ range and intercept of A.D. 683 (778) 936. The Owasco and Point Peninsula types associated with each component at the three sites are listed in table 5.3. What is apparent is that sherds assigned to Early Owasco types, with a putative origination no earlier than A.D. 900–1000, date much earlier. Early Owasco and Late Point Peninsula types are unquestionably contemporaneous at and among these three sites.

Longhouses

Ritchie (1969) used the longhouses he defined at Roundtop to argue that this northern Iroquoian trait (and inferred matrilocal residence patterns) was present in New York by the eleventh century A.D. (also see Ritchie and Funk 1973). A recent series of radiocarbon dates has resulted in a reinterpretation of the ages of the two longhouses Ritchie defined at this site (Hart 2000a). The earliest longhouse dates to approximately A.D. 1350 while the second house dates to approximately A.D. 1600. New radiocarbon dates from other key New York sites (Maxon-Derby, Sackett, Bates, and Kelso; see Ritchie and Funk 1973), and a review of the literature, indicate that on present evidence large longhouses such as those at Roundtop were not present in New York until the thirteenth century A.D. and were not common until the fourteenth century A.D. (Hart 2000a). There is also no basis on which to infer a sudden appearance of matrilocality with the arrival of agriculture in the region as explained in Hart (2001; compare to Snow 1995a [chap. 1]).

Nucleated Villages

When defined as settlements having more than two households (see Hart and Means 2002), the evidence for early villages in New York is questionable. The eleventh-century Port Dickinson and White sites have only one documented structure each (Prezzano 1992) and may represent temporary camps or hamlets (Funk

Table 5.2
AMS Dates on Charred Cooking Residue from Three New York Sites

Site	Cat. No.	ISGS No.	RCY B.P.	A.D. 2σ (intercept)	Pottery Type
Wickham	40525-1	A0190	1425 ± 45	542 (642) 677	Wickham Corded Punctate
Wickham	40525-8	A0191	1228 ± 42	683 (778) 936	Wickham Corded Punctate
Wickham	40170	A0194	1648 ± 47	259 (413) 536	Point Peninsula Corded
Wickham	40194	A0195	1450 ± 43	538 (620, 634, 636) 662	Point Peninsula Corded
Hunter's Home	48580-110	A0192	1231 ± 44	678 (778) 936	Wickham Corded Punctate
Hunter's Home	48580-115	A0193	1286 ± 40	659 (692, 702, 711, 752, 760) 855	Wickham Corded Punctate
Hunter's Home	41797	A0196	1138 ± 40	779 (895, 924, 937) 996	Owasco Platted
Hunter's Home	41356-6	A0197	1247 ± 48	664 (775) 893	Carp. Brook Cord-on-Cord
Hunter's Home	48584-1	A0198	1211 ± 46	687 (781, 793, 801) 960	Owasco Corded Horizontal
Kipp Island	41119-2	A0226	1461 ± 43	535 (604, 612, 615) 660	Kipp Island Crisscross
Kipp Island	41119-5	A0225	1470 ± 43	553 (604, 612, 615) 660	Carp. Brook Cord-on-Cord
Kipp Island	41119-8	A0227	1428 ± 41	543 (641) 668	Jack's Reef Corded
Kipp Island	42729-5	A0228	1260 ± 39	664 (723, 740, 771) 886	Wickham Corded Punctate

Table 5.3
Pottery Types and Corresponding Dates on Cooking Residues

Site	A.D. 2σ (intercept)	Point Peninsula Types	Owasco Types
Kipp Island	601 (642) 659[a]	Kipp Island Crisscross Jack's Reef Corded	Carpenter Brook Cord-on-Cord Owasco Herringbone Owasco Corded Oblique
Wickham	545 (624, 627, 638) 660[a]	Point Peninsula Corded	Wickham Corded Punctate
Kipp Island	693 (778) 880[a]	Wickham Incised	Wickham Corded Punctate
		Point Peninsula Corded	Owasco Corded Horizontal
Hunter's Home	774 (781, 793, 801) 888[a]		Wickham Corded Punctate Owasco Platted Carpenter Brook Cord-on-Cord Owasco Corded Horizontal Levanna Cord-on-Cord
Wickham	683 (778) 936		Wickham Corded Punctate

Note: Data from this study and Schulenberg (2002a, 2002b [chap.4]).
[a] Pooled mean (see Hart et al. 2003, for explanation).

1993; Prezzano and Rieth 2001). At Roundtop, only one house can be identified each for the fourteenth- and sixteenth-century occupations. Maxon-Derby's eleventh-century A.D. occupation has only one associated structure, while at most two contemporaneous structures are evident for the early thirteenth-century-A.D. occupation (Hart 2000a). At the Boland site, only two structures are identified with the twelfth-century A.D. occupation (Prezzano 1992). These sites have been identified as early villages in the literature (see Prezzano and Rieth 2001). The two best documented early villages are Sackett and Kelso, which date to the thirteenth century A.D. (Hart 2000a). Thus, on current data, there is no evidence for villages appearing suddenly in New York around A.D. 1000.

Maize-Bean-Squash Agriculture

Until a few years ago it was widely accepted that maize *(Zea mays)*, the common bean *(Phaseolus vulgaris)*, and squash *(Cucurbita pepo)* entered northern Iroquoia around A.D. 900–1000, helping to define the origin of Owasco and New York Iroquoian subsistence economy (e.g., Snow 1995a [chap. 1]). The known history of these crops now suggests a very different scenario.

The earliest evidence for squash in northern Iroquoia had been A.D. 1000–1100 at the Roundtop site in New York (Ritchie 1969; Ritchie and Funk 1973). While squash rind from the Memorial Park site in the West Branch of the Susquehanna River valley in Pennsylvania had been directly dated to 1635 ± 45 B.P. (Hart and Asch Sidell 1997), no pre-A.D. 1000 evidence for this crop has been found to the north. In fact, new dates on Roundtop indicate that the squash seeds recovered there date to around A.D. 1350 (Hart 1999c; 2000a). However, squash phytoliths, probably representing *Cucurbita pepo*, were recovered from the directly dated cooking residues adhering to pottery rim sherds from the seventh- and eighth-century A.D. Kipp Island, Hunter's Home, and Wickham sites (Hart et al. 2003).

The history of maize in northern Iroquoia underwent major revision in the 1990s with substantiation of this crop's presence in southern Ontario by the sixth century A.D. (Crawford et al. 1997). Despite intensive flotation and identification efforts at numerous sites in New York (e.g., Asch Sidell 2002; Cassedy and Webb 1999; Knapp 2002), the earliest direct date on maize was A.D. 1000 (Cassedy and Webb 1999). However, maize phytoliths were recovered from the seventh-century-A.D. cooking residues from the Kipp Island and Wickham sites, as well as from residues from the later Kipp Island and Hunter's Home components (Hart et al. 2003). These results substantiate a much longer history for this crop in New York and thus throughout northern Iroquoia than previous evidence suggested.

Direct AMS dating of common bean remains from Roundtop indicated that contra Ritchie (1969; Ritchie and Funk 1973), this crop was not archaeologically visible at the site before A.D. 1300 (Hart 1999c). Subsequent dates on bean remains from the Connecticut River valley to the Illinois River valley indicate that the results at Roundtop reflect an overall pattern in the greater Northeast (Hart et al. 2002; Hart and Scarry 1999). Common bean, and by extension maize-bean-squash, agriculture is not evident across the region until approximately A.D. 1300.

Summary

What is evident from the new data on the timing of traits Ritchie used to define the origin of Owasco and thus New York northern Iroquoians is that those traits do not appear together at ca. A.D. 900–1000. Pottery types assigned to Early Owasco by Ritchie and MacNeish (1949) are present several centuries earlier. Maize and squash are similarly early, while beans, maize-bean-squash agriculture, longhouses and associated matrilocality, and villages are later.

On evidential grounds, then, Ritchie's culture-historic scheme does not hold up. The clustering of traits that he used to define the onset of the Late Woodland stage and the Owasco culture, and thus the origin of recognizable northern Iroquoian antecedents, does not come together until much later than he thought and others have accepted. Individual traits are present at least several centuries earlier than Ritchie thought or was able to identify given the methods and techniques available at the time. As a result, it is no longer possible to search for the origin of New York northern Iroquois within that construct. Because the taxonomic units are extensionally defined (Dunnell 1971), it would be possible to redefine Owasco formally and temporally to take into account the revised ages of the key traits. But that would be a questionable practice given current theoretical orientations.

Discussion

Classification systems are theory bound, whether that theory is discipline specific or drawn from common sense (Dunnell 1971). The taxonomic system used by Ritchie, while specifically originating with Parker, was developed using methods devised under the culture-historic paradigm, a primary goal of which was simply temporal and spatial control of artifact diversity (Lyman et al. 1997). Following the lead of Parker, Ritchie conflated the resulting subjectively defined units with ethnic groups. He initially believed, like Parker, that Owasco represented prehistoric Algonquian groups that were influenced and later replaced by Iroquoian groups that migrated into New York. Following the work of MacNeish (1952), Ritchie revised his opinion and saw Owasco as directly ancestral to Iroquois, part of a long continuum leading to the northern Iroquoian groups that were present in New York during historic times (fig. 5.2). Following Parker with his Third Algonkian period, Ritchie saw Owasco as covering much of New York state.

The cultural sequence followed a set pattern across the area: *Point Peninsula*

Stage	Culture	Phase	Beginning Date (A.D.)
Late Woodland	Iroquois	Five Nations	
		Garoga	1500
		Chance	1400
		Oak Hill	1300
	Owasco	Castle Creek	1200
		Canandaigua	1100
		Carpenter Brook	1000
Middle Woodland	Point Peninsula	Hunter's Home	900
		Kipp Island	600

Fig. 5.2. Ritchie's (1969) final late prehistoric culture-historic scheme for New York.

(Kipp Island → Hunter's Home) → *Owasco* (Carpenter Brook → Canandaigua → Castle Creek) → *Iroquois* (Oak Hill → Chance → Garoga → Five Nations) (see Tuck 1978 for a particularly strong interpretation of northern Iroquoian prehistory based on this sequence). The transitions from stage to stage and culture to culture were denoted by major trait changes, while those from phase to phase were defined primarily on the basis of changes in pottery type frequencies. Change was envisioned as the steady progression from one state to another, as climbing the rungs of a ladder, leading to the historic New York northern Iroquois in teleological fashion (Ritchie 1969, 273).

We have demonstrated on current evidence that the transition to Owasco from Point Peninsula and thus recognizable New York Iroquoian antecedents breaks down. In keeping with the long-standing tradition of extensional definition, we could redefine Owasco to account for the changed evidence, perhaps beginning as early as A.D. 600. However, we would only do that if we accepted the general, transitional, step-by-step progressive concept of change that goes hand-in-hand with culture history. To do so would be to accept that traits were routinely shared in consistent packages on the same time horizon over large geographical scales. We would need to accept that change occurred only at precise temporal boundaries marking shifts from one state to another. In essence, we would have to accept the reality of the taxonomic units in the past and conceive of them as long-established ethnic groups at least partially isolated from other such ethnic groups, responding to forces as a unit with little or no variation in the manners in which their members responded. The search for a specific origin of the New York Iroquoians is possible only under this framework. Migration hypotheses (e.g., Parker 1922; Ritchie 1944; Snow 1995a [chap. 1]) simply replace the transition from one unit to another with the influx of new ethnic groups, after which a new series of step-like progressive transitions occur on the way to the historic New York Iroquois. By using culture-historic taxa as units of analysis, we have limited ourselves in the kinds of questions asked and in the possible scales of analysis when investigating long-term change. The search for the origins of New York Iroquoians is enmeshed in and predestined by the continued use of Ritchie's taxonomy with its step-like, progressive conceptualization of change.

If we accept that human behavior varies at any scale imaginable, and that change occurs as the result of differential persistence of this variation (Terrell and Hart 2002), then the use of culture-historic taxa as units of analysis becomes even more suspect. If we also accept that individual aspects of human behavior and their associated artifacts have separate histories and that those histories are reticulate, then we must also accept that human behavioral evolution consists of what can be thought of as an entangled bank, with endless divergences and anastomoses of traits (Terrell 1986; also see Hart 1999b). Configurations of traits are visible at any particular slice of time at any particular place (e.g., Dunnell 1982, 10–11), but these configurations are transient, with each trait having its own history (Terrell and Hart 2002). While there have been strong statements on the ability to track not only northern Iroquoian but also specific historic Iroquois nations well back in time (e.g., Niemczycki 1984; Tuck 1978), we wonder how much this signal is predetermined by the conceptual framework of Ritchie's taxonomy and geographical positioning.

While both ethnographic and archaeological taxa are assemblages of traits, those of the former may comprise functioning, interrelated, and ongoing systems of behaviors and beliefs, while those of the latter are parts of individual, not necessarily related, systems (such as craft production, subsistence, and settlement, among others) accessed indirectly through their residues. Cultural traits include factors relating to a social community's activities to meet basic needs, including the acquisition of food and shelter, access to territory and necessary resources, and the reproduction of the community itself through child bearing and socialization, among other processes. Ethnographically defined systems may include both material traits and the values and worldviews that guide and influence actions. By contrast, archaeologically defined units usually are too fragmentary and poorly known to be equated with ethnographic cultures, quite often being composed of little more than ceramic and/or lithic assemblages (e.g., Moore 1994). The notion that an assemblage of traits represents a "culture" leads us to believe that populations that share those traits also share other characteristics in common, such as language, worldview, ethnicity, and social structure, among others.

Confusing material culture and social identity would not appear to be a problem, but it has been, as discussed by William E. Engelbrecht (1999; 2003). For example, both Ritchie and MacNeish acted under the premise that ceramics were an ethnic marker, even when their own research and that of others clearly seem to argue the contrary. When MacNeish (1952, 85) began his study of Late Woodland ceramics, the prevailing hypothesis of Northeast prehistory interpreted Owasco, Point Peninsula, and earlier taxa as that of Algonquians who were displaced and eventually pushed out of upper New York State by the incoming Iroquois. However, excavations at sites of historic Algonquians in Pennsylvania recovered ceramics very similar to Mohawk Iroquois types. Other excavations at sites in eastern New York and Long Island, all believed to have been occupied by ancestral Algonquians, also produced Mohawk types, although some of these sites did not develop out of an Owasco base (MacNeish 1952, 86–87). MacNeish (1952) concluded that many of the Algonquian groups east and south of the Iroquois had pottery more similar to the Iroquois than to Owasco, which is contrary to what would be expected if Owasco were the archaeological culture of the Algonquians. Despite their own observations that members of various language groups manufactured Iroquois-style pottery, both Ritchie and MacNeish continued to operate under the assumption that these ceramics rigidly reflected some cultural entity and termed this style "Iroquois." In other words, the ceramic types became more than associated attributes of craft production and decoration; they were treated as cultural and ethnic markers.

Similarly, ethnic and linguistic attributions were made for both Owasco and Point Peninsula. This error arose because Point Peninsula ceramics were found in areas of the Northeast not occupied by historic northern Iroquoians. According to Ritchie and MacNeish (1949, 102), some Point Peninsula ceramic types were found along the Atlantic from Nova Scotia to New York including New England, and west into parts of Ontario, Michigan, Wisconsin, and Minnesota, areas occupied in historic times almost exclusively by Algonquian-speakers. Point Peninsula became associated with speakers of an Algonquian language, fishing and foraging economies, and small-scale societies with preferential patrilocal residence and patrilineal descent, with some of these ideas representing a misapplication of Julian H. Steward's "patrilineal band" model (Steward 1955). These traits contrasted with the agricultural economy, matrilineal descent, and residence in large matrilocal longhouse villages of historic northern Iroquois.

Ritchie, MacNeish, and others, by complicating issues of style and ethnicity, even assuming that the ethnic landscape of the past was similar to that of the early historic period, which is unlikely, were operating under the assumption that ethnic groups are identifiable in the archaeological record and that upstreaming is a viable activity (Starna and Funk 1994). Instead, we argue that material culture is not necessarily equivalent with or reflective of ethnic identity, and that culture-historic taxa should not be used uncritically in historical reconstruction, in upstreaming, and in variations of the direct historical approach. This is not to say that such approaches are never productive, but only that they can be seductive and often misleading.

These problems in interpretation derive in part from a misuse or conflation of the concepts of race, language, and culture. While anthropology as a discipline strongly argues that race, language, and culture do not necessarily co-vary, and that none can be assumed to be a predictor of the others (Boas 1940), the practice of the discipline, especially by some archaeologists, has not heeded this wisdom. That race, language, and culture do not co-vary has been demonstrated in many case studies (see e.g., papers in Terrell 2001). Ethnographic studies reveal that different linguistic and ethnic groups often share the same elements of material culture (e.g., Brumbach 1975; 1995). Individuals can change both ethnic group identity and language. In separate research carried out by Hetty Jo Brumbach and Robert Jarvenpa (1989), study of nineteenth- and twentieth-century genealogical and historical records, as well as ethnographic study of kinship and ethnicity, revealed cases where language use among several Native American communities shifted dramatically over three generations and where individuals and whole families shifted ethnic and cultural affiliation in the course of two or three generations. Rather than dismissing such transformations as artifacts of modern political economy, they should be viewed as case studies of the ways individuals and groups make strategic use of language, culture, and ethnicity. Neither language nor race is a barrier to cultural exchange, as was clearly demonstrated by the recovery of Iroquois-style ceramics on sites occupied by presumed Algonquian-speakers. Despite these observations, Ritchie and MacNeish seemed uncomfortable with the idea that speakers of different language families could share a pottery tradition, or similarly that language was not a barrier to the exchange of cultural ideas.

Conclusions

Snow (1995a [chap. 1]) argues that the in situ model has been a straightjacket on our perceptions of northern Iroquoian origins. We suggest that the straightjacket is actually the continued use of a culture history that forces us to think in terms of origins. In fact, the in situ vs. migration debate is only possible within the culture-historic construct that predicates step-like, progressive developments. We have shown that the key taxon in Ritchie's culture history does not stand up to empirical scrutiny.

Reliance on culture-historic taxa as units of analysis is ubiquitous in North American archaeology. The analysis we have done on Owasco is a case study that has broader implications for the use of culture-historic taxonomies in North America. We think it important that the following points be considered before extending that reliance:

1. The history of culture-historic taxa definitions must be understood. It is important to know how and why they were defined and how and why those definitions have changed.

2. Culture-historic taxa are modern constructs; their only reality is within specific definitional contexts, which are theory bound. Consideration must be given to the appropriateness of those units under the theory being used to interpret the past.

3. Culture-historic taxa are constructed so as to minimize internal variation that may be of explanatory interest if recognized.

4. Culture-historic taxonomies foster interpretations of change that are step-like and progressive.

5. Culture-historic taxa can foster the conflation of ethnicity, language, and culture, and can foster a view of static ethnic and linguistic landscapes contrary to numerous case studies.

6. The use of culture-historic units can limit research to the search for additional, defining traits and to analysis oriented toward fitting components and artifacts into their "correct" place in existing taxa and/or typologies.

Culture-historic taxa, whether or not they "facilitate communication" among archaeologists, should be regarded with caution because they tend to affect the way we view the past and the people who occupied the past. Culture-historic taxa are not the direct correlates of ethnic groups, language groups, or cultures, nor should it be assumed that they bore any social or cultural reality in the past. These taxonomic units are modern constructs and, as such, exist only in the present as heuristic tools. We recommend abandoning assumptions that the ethnic and linguistic landscape observed at the time of the European entrada represented anything other than a temporary accommodation. We do not know enough about the prehistory of the Iroquoian and Algonquian languages to be able to substitute language history for empirical archaeological research. It is a mistake to assume that these language families can be extended backwards in time unchanged for several or more millennia, or that the speakers of these languages remained unchanged and stationary in their original homelands. Likewise, the ethnic divisions observed at the time of contact were unlikely to be those that existed in the past. Ethnicity is related to a dynamic complex of interacting social, economic, and political factors, which themselves should be subjects of research. For archaeologists to believe they can hold variables of ethnicity and language constant in order to study change in settlement or subsistence patterns or ceramic technology and decoration is untenable.

The demise of Owasco leaves a void that presents an opportunity to reevaluate the manners in which the past of New York is visualized. There are numerous hints at the variation that is present in the record that has not been well dealt with under Ritchie's culture-historic construct, including the broad patterning of pottery styles that cross-cut traditional culture-historic space and time boundaries (e.g., Brumbach 1975; 1995; Graybill 1989; Prezzano 1992; Rieth 1997; 2002a; Schulenberg 2002a; 2002b [chap. 4]), and variations in settlement pattern traits including the first evidence of villages, persistence of different site categories, and house sizes (e.g., Hart 2000a; Knapp 2002; Miroff 2002; Niemczycki 1984; Rieth 2002b; Ritchie and Funk 1973). By breaking the pattern of trying to fit variation into existing culture-historic constructs, we will probably find that the past is a much more complicated place than previously imagined.

Acknowledgments

We thank Bernard Means, Penelope Drooker, Christina Rieth, Janet Schulenberg, and John Terrell for comments and suggestions on earlier versions of this article. William Engelbrecht, Mima Kapches, and an anonymous reviewer provided many useful suggestions for improving the article. We thank Penelope Drooker for suggesting to Hart that he use cooking residues to directly date pottery sherds. Martin Solano and Miguel Aguilera translated the abstract into Spanish. The New York State Museum and State University of New York at Albany provided funds to date the residues.

PART TWO

| *Precolumbian Dynamics*

Overview

THE READINGS IN THIS SECTION address the most commonly studied group of topics in Iroquoian archaeology, as reflected by the sheer size of the Research Sources section for part 2: subsistence, settlement pattern, sociopolitical organization, and demography. All four chapters pertain to the period preceding European interaction, though information from Postcolumbian times is presented in a few.

The first one, by John P. Hart, Robert G. Thompson, and Hetty Jo Brumbach, focuses on subsistence remains central to the discussion of Iroquois origins raised in part 1. Before this study, the earliest reported evidence for maize in New York dated to around A.D. 1000, approximately when Iroquois longhouses and villages were thought by many to appear. Analyzing the cooking residues adhering to the inner surface of pottery sherds excavated several years ago from three sites in the northern Finger Lakes region of central New York, the authors identify the remains of maize and squash, as well as wild rice and sedge, dating to as early as ca. A.D. 600. These results push back the known history of maize in the region some 350 years and of squash about 650 years. Although the sample is small and temporally restricted, and Hart, Thompson, and Brumbach cannot state when maize was adopted successfully in the northern Finger Lakes area, the results illustrate that maize adoption was not the catalyst for settled village life. It should be pointed out that new microbotanical evidence, reported recently by Thompson et al. (2004), indicates the occurrence of maize in New York 500 to 600 years earlier (by ca. A.D. 100) than the age of the remains from the three Finger Lakes sites, meaning that this crop was utilized within the region at least 1,000 years before the onset of large multifamily villages. Thus it appears that the adoption of maize did not happen suddenly nor was it an impetus for the development of Iroquoian subsistence-settlement traits, in contrast to what some of the origin hypotheses propose in the previous section.

In the next article, Gary A. Warrick synthesizes a copious archaeological database, mostly recovered since the 1980s, to reconstruct various aspects of Iroquoian occupation of southern Ontario before European contact in A.D. 1534. Southern Ontario, the historic heartland of the St. Lawrence Iroquoians, Huron, Petun, and Neutral, contains an enormous amount of Iroquois remains, perhaps more so than that of any other area. Of great use to researchers, a newly modified regional chronology is presented: Princess Point (A.D. 500–1000); Early Iroquoian (A.D. 1000–1300); Middle Iroquoian (Uren phase: A.D. 1300–1330, Middleport phase: A.D. 1330–1420); and Late Precontact (A.D. 1420–1534). In his summary, Warrick points out that the Iroquoians became identifiable in the region's archaeological record around A.D. 500 with the appearance of Princess Point sites and maize remains. Longhouse villages were constructed after A.D. 1000 in the interior, north of Lake Erie, Lake Ontario, and the St. Lawrence River. This thorough overview provides an excellent basis for comparison with syntheses of other regions in Northern Iroquoia.

The third chapter shifts the focus to changing macrosettlement patterns in the historic homeland of the Five Nations Iroquois during the Late Woodland Period. Robert J. Hasenstab traces the location and movement of some 350 Iroquois villages across New York. He notes that over time the most significant settlement trend is village relocation from valley bottoms and canoeable waterways to upland hilltops, surrounded by steep slopes and fortified with palisades. This widespread movement to higher elevations, as his study contends, is owing principally to defensive responses to heightened hostilities; that is to say, changes in the social/cultural, not the physical, environment. Hasenstab hypothesizes that the root of such tension is conflict over expanding hunting territories resulting from an influx of Ontario Iroquoian populations before contact.

Perhaps the trait most often associated with the Iroquois is the longhouse, the large rectangular multifamily dwelling made almost entirely of wooden posts, saplings, and bark; some smaller longhouses were not residences, but rather special-purpose structures for storing or healing. Despite the enormity of the buildings, their remains, surprisingly, can be difficult to detect, as they consist of rather small underground post molds, or circular soil stains indicating the holes in which support posts once stood before decomposing. Archaeological evidence of longhouse interiors usually consists of centrally aligned features in the form of cooking hearths, storage and refuse pits associated with food and artifactual debris, and a few large post molds, along with another row of smaller, more numerous post molds along both sides (the remnants of support posts for side-wall benches and sleeping platforms). In the final essay of this section, Mima Kapches examines information on diverse and abundant Ontario Iroquoian longhouses, particularly those of the Huron and Neutral. Drawing on both ethnohistorical records and archaeological remains, she pieces together a wealth of architectural, cultural, and social details of this house form from Precolumbian and Postcolumbian times, ca. A.D. 1350–1640. One of the goals of her paper is to define aspects of Ontario Iroquoian longhouse variability in terms of their construction, layout, symbolism, and tribal affiliation. Despite such variation, sufficient standard features persist across time and space to convince Kapches that this type of structure is uniquely Iroquoian.

6 | Phytolith Evidence for Early Maize *(Zea mays)* in the Northern Finger Lakes Region of New York

JOHN P. HART, ROBERT G. THOMPSON, AND HETTY JO BRUMBACH

AS IN MANY PORTIONS of eastern North America, archaeologists working in New York have long been interested in the timing of agricultural crop introductions. This interest has been especially true of maize *(Zea mays)*, which is often viewed as an enabler, if not *the* catalyst, for the development of settled village life (Hart and Means 2002). Direct dates on maize macrobotanical remains have firmly established a long history for this crop west of New York. The first archaeological visibility is as early as the first century B.C.[1] in Illinois (Riley et al. 1994) to the sixth century A.D. in southern Ontario (Crawford et al. 1997), well before the first evidence for nucleated villages. The earliest direct date in New York is much later at A.D. 1000 (Cassedy and Webb 1999), near the time when longhouses and villages were thought by many to first occur (e.g., Ritchie and Funk 1973; Snow 1995a [chap. 1 in this volume]; but see Hart 2000a; 2001; Hart and Means 2002). Throughout much of the East, maize becomes ubiquitous at sites dating to between the eighth and tenth centuries A.D. (B. Smith 1992), but not until the eleventh to twelfth century A.D. in New York (Hart and Means 2002).

The published pre-A.D. 1000 macrobotanical record in New York remains meager despite intensive flotation carried out at a number of sites (e.g., Asch Sidell 2002; Cassedy and Webb 1999). A number of key archaeological sites for the A.D. 500–1000 period of interest here were excavated before the advent of flotation pro-

---

Previously published in *American Antiquity* 68, no. 4 (2003): 619–40. Reproduced by permission of the Society for American Archaeology.

1. In this article, years B.P. dates are radiocarbon years before present, while B.C./A.D. dates are calibrated unless denoted by *ca.*, which are estimated dates used by Ritchie in his culture history. All calibrations were done with CALIB 4.3 (Stuiver et al. 1998).

cessing for the recovery of macrobotanical remains (Ritchie 1969; Ritchie and Funk 1973). The collections from many professional and avocational excavations at these sites are curated in museums such as the New York State Museum. The fortuitous recovery of macrobotanical crop remains from post-A.D. 1000 sites during early excavations has been used with modern dating techniques to provide new information on crop histories (Hart 1999c; Hart and Scarry 1999). However, the lack of such remains from the earlier sites has until now prevented use of these collections for investigation of plant-based subsistence.

In this article we present the results of a pilot study on the use of cooking residues adhering to the interior of cooking pot rim sherds to obtain critical information on plant-based subsistence several centuries before A.D. 1000. The results of phytolith analysis, accelerator mass spectrometry (AMS) dating, and stable carbon isotope assays of cooking residues provide important new evidence on plants consumed in the northern Finger Lakes region of New York during the seventh and eighth centuries A.D. Evidence is reported for the cooking of maize, squash *(Cucurbita* sp.), wild rice *(Zizania aquatica),* and sedge *(Cyperus* sp.). These results highlight the continued importance of old museum collections for current research (also see Fritz and Smith 1988; Hart 2000b; Lovis 1990).

Culture History and Early Agriculture in New York

The culture history accepted by many archaeologists working in New York was developed by William A. Ritchie (e.g., 1944; 1965) during the mid-twentieth century (see Hart and Brumbach 2003 [chap. 5]). In Ritchie's scheme, the period of interest for this article is the mid– and late-Middle Woodland stage (ca. A.D. 500–1000), which encompasses the late Point Peninsula culture. This stage in turn encompasses the Kipp Island (ca. A.D. 500–800/900) and Hunter's Home (ca. A.D.800/900–1000) phases in the northern Finger Lakes region, which itself falls within Ritchie's Central New York subdivision. Ritchie's subsequent early Late Woodland stage (ca. A.D. 1000–1300) encompasses his Owasco culture, which he divided into the Carpenter Brook (ca. A.D. 1000–1100), Canandaigua (ca. A.D. 1100–1200), and Castle Creek (ca. A.D. 1200–1300) phases. This sequence was developed initially on the basis of pottery seriations (e.g., Ritchie 1944; Ritchie and MacNeish 1949) with later modifications based on a very limited number of radiocarbon dates (Ritchie 1965; 1969; Ritchie and Funk 1973). While the archaeological taxa and their relative chronology are still widely accepted, the calibration of radiocarbon dates has confused the radiocarbon-based chronology (see Snow 1995a [chap. 1]).

One of the defining attributes used by Ritchie to separate his Middle and Late Woodland stages was maize-bean-squash agriculture: "A principal distinction setting off Late from Middle Woodland cultures is the now obvious fact of the importance of cultigens—corn, beans and squash demonstrably—in the economy" (Ritchie 1969, 180). It was the combination of maize with beans and squash and the intensity of agricultural production that set the Late Woodland economy apart from that of the Middle Woodland, not the presence of maize. In fact, the timing of the introduction and subsequent intensification of maize use in New York was the subject of speculation during much of the second half of the twentieth century. In the absence of confirmed macrobotanical remains Ritchie (1944; 1965) and Ritchie and Funk (1973) suggested that maize was present during the late Middle Woodland stage on the basis of changes in settlement pattern traits:

> Trends toward increasing site size, thicker refuse deposits, more traces of dwellings, and growing reliance on deep storage pits are evident. Although these Middle Woodland groups were highly proficient in utilizing natural food resources, we have hypothesized that the trends noted above, which connote expanding populations, may be explained as the result of the introduction and subsequent development of maize horticulture in the Kipp Island phase. (Ritchie and Funk 1973, 369)

Others took the absence of maize at ca. pre-A.D. 1000 sites at face value. W. C. Galinat (1967, 4), for example, argued that there was an absence of early maize in the Northeast because of "the late arrival of an adaptable race of corn." More recently Snow (1995a, 71 [chap. 1]) argued that maize appeared in New York around A.D. 900–1000 as a result of the migration of agriculturists into the area from the south (compare to Snow 1996a [chap. 3]).

The migration issue aside, timing of the first archaeologically visible maize in New York has become increasingly puzzling in recent years given its earlier appearance in adjacent regions. In southern Ontario, maize has been directly dated to as early as the sixth century A.D. (Crawford et al. 1997). In the West Branch of the Susquehanna River basin in Pennsylvania, maize has been recovered from contexts dated to as early as the eighth century A.D. (Hatch 1980) and is regularly found in contexts dating to the ninth century A.D. (Hart and Asch Sidell 1996). However, despite the increased use of flotation recovery in New York, the earliest direct-dated maize macrobotanical remains occur no earlier than A.D. 1000 (Cassedy and Webb 1999).

While there has been little change in the physical evidence for the timing of maize in New York since Ritchie's time, the chronologies of bean and squash have changed considerably. Recent research has demonstrated that common bean is not visible archaeologically throughout the northern Eastern Woodlands until the late thirteenth century A.D. (Hart et al. 2002; Hart and Scarry 1999). *C. pepo* gourds, on the other hand, are now known to have been present in the West Branch of the Susquehanna River basin of Pennsylvania as early as the third millennium B.C., while probably edible *C. pepo* squash was present there by the ninth century B.C.

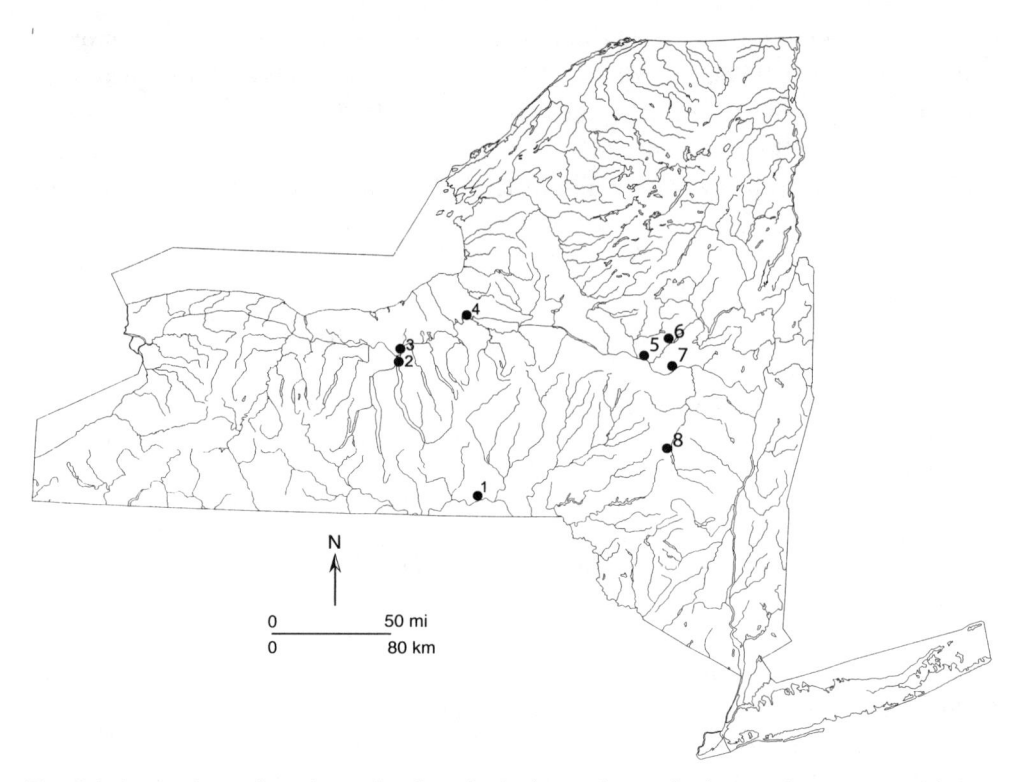

Fig. 6.1. Approximate locations of archaeological sites from which samples were used for this study: (1) Roundtop, (2) Kipp Island, (3) Hunter's Home, (4) Wickham, (5) Snell, (6) Klock, (7) Briggs Run, (8) Parslow Field.

(Hart and Asch Sidell 1997). The earliest confirmed date associated with squash in New York is in the fourteenth century A.D. at the Roundtop site in the upper Susquehanna River valley (fig. 6.1)—the earliest site with evidence for use of maize, bean, and squash together in New York (Hart 1999c).

Dating and Subsistence Analyses of Cooking Residues

The use of museum collections for the investigation of crop histories in the Northeast is not new (e.g., Ceci 1979). Most of the research done on crop histories with museum collections has used macrobotanical remains with the application of AMS dating. This technique has been used successfully in New York to refine our understanding of the history of maize-bean-squash intercropping (Hart 1999c; Hart and Scarry 1999). This refinement was enabled by (1) the fortuitous recovery of macrobotanical remains from post-A.D. 1000 sites before the widespread employment of flotation processing and (2) curation of those remains over a period of several decades (Hart 1999c; 2000b). With a few unsubstantiated exceptions, crop remains were not found in pre-Late Woodland contexts on the sites excavated by

Ritchie and his colleagues during the mid-twentieth century (Funk 1993; Ritchie 1944; 1969; Ritchie and Funk 1973). As a result, the collections generated during these excavations and housed at the New York State Museum have not been useful for the investigation of crop histories.

However, the results of a handful of studies conducted during the last two decades have demonstrated the potential importance of charred cooking residues adhering to the inside of pottery sherds in pursuing this line of research. Robert G. Thompson and associates (Staller and Thompson 2002; Thompson and Dogan 1987; Thompson et al. 1995; Thompson and Mulholland 1994) have shown that opal phytoliths can be extracted from cooking residues, allowing the identification of plants that were cooked in specific pots. Christine A. Hastorf and Michael J. DeNiro (1985), William A. Lovis (1990), and Janet K. Schulenberg (2002a), for example, have used carbon isotope measures on charred cooking residue to infer whether or not maize was cooked in vessels. Lovis (1990) and Schulenburg (2002b [chap. 4]), for example, have shown the importance of AMS dating of cooking residues to determine the age of pottery sherds. The combined employment of these techniques on charred cooking residues has the potential to refine our knowledge of crop histories using museum collections that do not contain macrobotanical remains.

Sites

Collections curated at the New York State Museum from three sites thought to date two to three centuries before A.D. 1000 had diagnostic rim sherds with residue deposits on the inner surface. These were the Hunter's Home, Kipp Island, and Wickham sites, all of which are located in the northern Finger Lakes region (fig. 6.1).

The Hunter's Home and Kipp Island sites are located along the Seneca River on landforms above Montezuma's Marsh north of Cayuga Lake. The Hunter's Home site is the type site for Ritchie's Hunter's Home phase, which he (Ritchie 1969) believed dated to ca. A.D. 800/900–1000 (but see Gates St-Pierre 2001; Snow 1995a [chap. 1]). As will be discussed later in this article, Schulenberg (2002a; 2002b [chap. 4]) has published three AMS dates on cooking residues from pottery sherds recovered from this site.

The Kipp Island site is the type site for Ritchie's Kipp Island phase (Ritchie 1969; Ritchie and Funk 1973; also see Funk 1993, 206). Ritchie (1973) obtained three dates from the Kipp Island site, which he believed related to three of four distinct occupational episodes at the site. Two of the dates are pertinent to the present study. A date of 1320 ± 100 B.P. (Y-1379) (2σ A.D. 542 [683] 959) was thought to be associated with the Kipp Island 3 occupation, which Ritchie (1973, 155) considered to be "the fully developed Kipp Island phase." A date of 1055 ± 100 B.P. (I-3441) (2σ

A.D. 725 [995] 1211) was thought by Ritchie (1973, 155) to represent a Hunter's Home phase occupation of the site. Christian Gates St-Pierre (2001, 37) has recently argued on the basis of pottery assemblages that "both components are roughly contemporaneous." Schulenberg (2002a; 2002b [chap. 4]) has published several AMS dates on cooking residues from pottery sherds recovered from this site, which will be discussed below.

The Wickham site is located at the west end of Oneida Lake (Ritchie 1946). This site was believed to have stratigraphically separated Middle Woodland (Wickham 2) and early Late Woodland (Wickham 3) components (Ritchie 1946; 1969; Ritchie and MacNeish 1949). Ritchie (1969, 254–55, plate 85) later implied that the Middle Woodland occupation belonged to the Kipp Island phase, and that the Late Woodland occupation belonged to the Carpenter Brook phase. A radiocarbon date of 1210 ± 100 B.P. (Y-1172) (2σ A.D. 645 [781, 793, 802] 1020) was published by Ritchie (1969, xxxi-xxxii) for the Middle Woodland component.

AMS Dates

Samples for this project were selected with the primary goal of refining the chronology for the end of Ritchie's Middle-to-Late-Woodland transition in the northern Finger Lakes region of New York. The goals for this aspect of the project are described in detail in Hart and Brumbach (2003 [chap. 5]). The protocol developed by Lovis (1990, 384) was used in selecting samples for dating:

> To minimize the possibilities of sampling fire soot and included charcoal, with potential for imparting later and earlier sample errors, several conventions were employed as laboratory protocol: (1) only rim/neck/shoulder sherds were inspected, (2) only interior residues were examined, (3) interior residues had to be linear accretions parallel with the vessel orifice, (4) residues composed of soil matrix were rejected, and (5) identifiable ceramic types received preference.

Using this protocol, with the desire to use residue on sherds that were of types reflecting Ritchie's Carpenter Brook, Hunter's Home, Kipp Island phases, 13 sherds were selected for sampling, 4 each from Wickham and Kipp Island, and 5 from Hunter's Home. Residue samples were removed by Hart from the interior surfaces of the sherds using a dissection probe under low magnification (fig. 6.2). Care was taken not to remove any of the pottery sherd fabric with the residue. In all cases, the residue readily separated from the pottery surface. The residue samples were submitted for AMS dating to the Illinois State Geological Survey (ISGS). Chemical pretreatment was done at ISGS and dating was done at the Oxford Radiocarbon Accelerator Unit. Important for future applications, carbon yield of the residue samples used in this study ranged between 26 percent and 61 percent. This

Fig. 6.2. Photograph of sherd 41119–5 interior showing cooking residue on the left and area where residue has been removed on the right (white bar = 2.5 mm).

means that only small samples of residue are needed for AMS dating, potentially expanding the number of samples available for dating in other collections. The results of AMS dating for this project are presented in table 6.1. They indicate these sites had occupations during the seventh and eighth to early ninth centuries A.D. and support Schulenberg's (2002a; 2002b [chap. 4]) results for the Hunter's Home and Kipp Island sites.

Hunter's Home Site. Four of the dates from Hunter's Home fall in the eighth century A.D., and one in the tenth century A.D. (table 6.1). The five dates are not significantly different from one another at the 95 percent level of confidence (Ward and Wilson 1978) and have a mean pooled age of 1221 ± 19 B.P. with a 2σ range and intercept of A.D. 694 (779) 887. Schulenberg (2002a; 2002b [chap. 4]) obtained three AMS dates on cooking residues in a different collection from this site (table 6.2), one of which falls in the eighth century A.D. and two in the ninth to early tenth centuries A.D. These dates are not significantly different from those obtained for the present study. The eight dates have a mean, pooled age of 1211 ± 16 B.P. with a 2σ range and intercepts of A.D. 774 (781, 793, 801) 888 (table 6.2).

Kipp Island Site. Three of the Kipp Island dates obtained for the current study fall in the seventh century A.D., while the fourth falls in the eighth century (table 6.1). This later date is significantly different from the three earlier dates. The mean pooled age of the three early dates is 1452 ± 24 B.P., with a 2σ range and intercept of A.D. 544 (619) 655. Schulenburg (2002a; 2002b[chap. 4]) obtained eight AMS dates on cooking residues in a different collection from this site (table 6.3), of which two fall in the seventh century A.D., four in the eighth century A.D., and one each in the ninth and eleventh centuries A.D. The five seventh-century dates obtained in the

Table 6.1
AMS Dates on Charred Cooking Residue from Three New York Sites

Site and Cat. No.	ISGS No.	$\delta^{13}C$	$\delta^{13}C$	RCY B.P.	2σ (intercept) A.D.	Pottery Type
HUNTER'S HOME						
48580–110	A0192	-26.7	-26.9	1231 ± 44	678 (778) 936	Wickham Corded Punctate
48580–115	A0193	-27.2	-26.9	1286 ± 40	659 (692, 702, 711, 752, 760) 855	Wickham Corded Punctate
41797	A0196	-24.9	-25.3	1138 ± 40	779 (895, 924, 937) 996	Owasco Platted
41356–6	A0197	-27.5	-27.5	1247 ± 48	664 (775) 893	Carp. Brook Cord-on-Cord
48584–1	A0198	-27.8	-28.6	1211 ± 46	687 (781, 793, 801) 960	Owasco Corded Horizontal
KIPP ISLAND						
41119–2	A0226	-26.5	-26.4	1461 ± 43	535 (604, 612, 615) 660	Kipp Island Crisscross
41119–5	A0225	-26.4	-26.3	1470 ± 43	553 (604, 612, 615) 660	Carp. Brook Cord-on-Cord
41119–8	A0227	-27.0	-26.9	1428 ± 41	543 (641) 668	Jack's Reef Corded
42729–5	A0228	-26.1	-25.8	1260 ± 39	664 (723, 740, 771) 886	Wickham Corded Punctate
WICKHAM						
40525–1	A0190	-28.1	-27.6	1425 ± 45	542 (642) 677	Wickham Corded Punctate
40525–8	A0191	-25.8	-25.8	1228 ± 42	683 (778) 936	Wickham Corded Punctate
40170	A0194	-29.0	-29.0	1648 ± 47	259 (413) 536	Point Peninsula Corded
40194	A0195	-29.7	-29.6	1450 ± 43	538 (620, 634, 636) 662	Point Peninsula Corded

Note: Two $\delta^{13}C$ assays were run independently for each residue. A paired T-test indicates that the results are not significantly different ($t = -.084, df = 12, p = .934$). See text for explanation.

Table 6.2
AMS Dates on Cooking Residue from the Hunter's Home Site

Lab Number	RCY B.P.	2σ (intercept) A.D.	Pottery Type	Source
A0192	1231 ± 44	678 (778) 936	Wickham Corded Punctate	This study
A0193	1286 ± 40	659 (692, 702, 711, 752, 760) 855	Wickham Corded Punctate	This study
A0196	1138 ± 40	779 (895, 924, 937) 996	Owasco Platted	This study
A0197	1247 ± 48	664 (775) 893	Carp. Brook Cord-on-Cord	This study
A0198	1211 ± 46	687 (781, 793, 801) 960	Owasco Corded Horizontal	This study
GX-27484	1180 ± 40	722 (885) 977	Levanna Cord-on-Cord	Schulenberg (2002a, b)
GX-27485	1280 ± 40	660 (693, 699, 715, 749, 764) 863	Owasco Corded Horizontal	Schulenberg (2002a, b)
GX-27486	1130 ± 40	780 (897, 922, 942) 998	Carp. Brook Cord-on-Cord	Schulenberg (2002a, b)
Pooled mean	1211 ± 16	774 (781, 793, 801) 888		

Table 6.3
AMS Dates on Cooking Residue from the Kipp Island Site

Lab Number	RCY B.P.	2σ (intercept) A.D.	Pottery Type	Source
A0226	1461 ± 43	535 (604, 612, 615) 660	Kipp Island Crisscross	This study
A0225	1470 ± 43	553 (604, 612, 615) 660	Carpenter Brook Cord-on-Cord	This study
A0227	1428 ± 41	543 (641) 668	Jack's Reef Corded	This study
GX-26450	1410 ± 10	563 (646) 681	Owasco Herringbone	Schulenberg (2002a, b)
GX-27558	1360 ± 40	619 (662) 766	Owasco Corded Oblique	Schulenberg (2002a, b)
Pooled mean	1423 ± 20	610 (642) 659		
A0228	1260 ± 39	664 (723, 740, 771) 886	Wickham Corded Punctate	This study
GX-26448	1280 ± 40	660 (693, 699, 715, 749, 764) 863	Wickham Incised	Schulenberg (2002a, b)
GX-26451	1240 ± 40	676 (776) 891	Point Peninsula Corded	Schulenberg (2002a, b)
GX-26452	1170 ± 40	729 (887) 980	Untyped body sherd	Schulenberg (2002a, b)
GX-27559	1210 ± 40	689 (781, 793, 802) 956	Point Peninsula Corded	Schulenberg (2002a, b)
GX-26453	1220 ± 40	687 (779) 939	Owasco Corded Horizontal	Schulenberg (2002a, b)
Pooled mean	1230 ± 17	693 (778) 880		

two studies are not significantly different from one another, but are significantly different from each of the eighth-century dates. The mean pooled age for the earlier dates is 1423 ± 20 B.P. with a 2σ range and intercept of A.D. 601 (642) 659 (table 6.3), suggesting an occupation in the first half of the seventh century A.D. The six eighth-century and one ninth-century dates from the two projects are not significantly different from one another. They have a mean pooled age of 1230 ± 17 B.P., with a 2σ range and intercept of A.D. 693 (778) 880 (table 6.3), suggesting an occupation contemporaneous with that at Hunter's Home. The one eleventh-century A.D. date is significantly different from the other dates. These results support Ritchie's (1973) contention that the Kipp Island components are chronologically discrete (compare to Gates St-Pierre 2001).

Wickham Site. The four Wickham dates obtained for this study are widely dispersed, with one in the fifth century A.D., two in the seventh century, and one in the eighth century (table 6.1). The two seventh-century dates have a mean pooled age of 1438 ± 31, with a 2σ range and intercepts of A.D. 545 (624, 627, 638) 660. These dates are significantly different from the other dates obtained for this site. Our results support Ritchie's contention that Wickham is a multicomponent site.

As a whole, the dates indicate seventh-century occupations at Kipp Island and Wickham and late eighth- or ninth-century occupations at Hunter's Home and Kipp Island. The results in turn support Snow's (1996a [chap. 3]) and Schulenberg's (2002a; 2002b [chap. 4]) suggestions that types traditionally associated with the early part of Ritchie's Late Woodland period (in these cases Carpenter Brook Cord on Cord, Owasco Herringbone, Owasco Corded Oblique, and Wickham Corded Punctate) occur as early as the seventh century A.D. (see Hart and Brumbach 2003 [chap. 5]; Schulenberg 2002b [chap. 4] for discussions of the implications of these results).

Phytolith Analysis

Food residues, even those recovered from long-curated pottery sherds, can provide significant data through the plant microfossils embedded in the organic matrix during food preparation. Phytoliths have been successfully extracted from cooking residues from a number of sites (Staller and Thompson 2002; Thompson 1993; 2000; Thompson and Mulholland 1994). These phytoliths, diagnostic to specific plant taxa, have been used to determine the plants that were cooked in specific vessels. Some plants, such as cucurbits and sedges, produce phytoliths sufficiently distinct to be diagnostic as individual finds (Bozarth 1987; Ollendorf 1992; Piperno et al. 2000). The two most important American grasses, maize and wild rice, produce abundant rondel phytoliths in their chaff, as do some other grasses. We follow the definition of rondel provided by Susan C. Mulholland and George Rapp Jr. (1992), a short cylinder with a round to oval base. Irwin Rovner (1983) has discussed the difficulty in attributing individual forms produced in the grasses to specific taxa. Different approaches have been taken to address this problem.

Deborah M. Pearsall and Dolores R. Piperno (1993), Thompson (1993), and Thompson and Mulholland (1994) note that maize cob chaff produces suites of phytoliths dominated by rondel forms. Pearsall and Piperno, searching mainly for ways to identify maize in sediments, examine phytoliths thought to be unique to maize cob chaff. A problem with this technique is the fact that rondel forms are produced by many grasses, and not only in the chaff. Thompson, on the other hand, has focused on food residues, where assemblages created by plants consumed would be concentrated. This focus allows the refinement of methods for identifying cob chaff assemblages first developed by Mulholland (1993), bypassing the determination of the origin of each phytolith. This method compares the entire assemblage recovered from residues with assemblages from maize cob chaff. The establishment of the role of a specific regulatory gene, *tga1*, in the deposition of silica in the cupule and glume of maize (Dorweiler and Doebley 1997) has demonstrated that silica deposition in maize is controlled at a subspecific level.

Samples. Two residue samples from each site were processed for phytolith analysis (Hunter's Home: 48580–110, 48584–1; Kipp Island: 41119–5, 41119–8: Wickham: 40525–1, 40525–8) (table 6.4). These samples were chosen to represent the components defined by the AMS dates from the three sites. The phytolith assemblages recovered from the residues were statistically compared to assemblages recovered from modern maize cob samples from the east and Midwest (table 6.4). Maize samples used to obtain comparative chaff phytolith assemblages are all from a group of related lineages known as Northern Flint Corn. This complex of lineages is derived from maize in the Southwest. The Northern Flint Corns share a strong genetic divergence from other lineages (Doebley et al. 1986; Matsuoka et al. 2002) and are indigenous to the northern half of the United States, from the Great Plains eastward. This complex of varieties includes maizes described as flint, flour, and sweet corns. The samples of maize from North Dakota include those used in a previous study (Thompson and Mulholland 1994), augmented by further samples. Samples of maize from the Northeast, both modern and archaeological, were included to expand the geographic extent of the Northern Flint Corn comparative samples. The archaeological samples come from four sites in New York (tables 6.4 and 6.5). The Northern Flint Corn Complex includes many varieties, and the comparative collection used contains only a few. A single member of the Southern Dent complex (probably shoepeg) was sampled. A modern wild rice *(Zizania aquatica)* sample was obtained from the Lake George region of New York. Previous examination of the most commonly used wild rice *(Zizania palustris)* phytolith assemblages (Thompson et al. 1995) rules this species out as a possible source of any of the residue phytolith assemblages.

Methods and Techniques. Each residue and comparative sample was placed in

Table 6.4
Archaeological and Comparative Sample Proveniences

Samples	Provenience	Provided By
	COOKING RESIDUES	
41119-8	Kipp Island Site	New York State Museum
41119-5	Kipp Island Site	New York State Museum
48580-110	Hunter's Home Site	New York State Museum
48584-1	Hunter's Home Site	New York State Museum
40525-1	Wickham Site	New York State Museum
40525-8	Wickham Site	New York State Museum
	MODERN ZEA MAYS	
Northern Flint	Harvard University Herbarium	Nora Reber
Iroquois Flour	New York State	Jane Mt. Pleasant, grown in 2001
Mandan Yellow Flour	North Dakota	Fred Schneider, grown in 1993
Mandan Sweet Corn, Samples A, B, C	North Dakota	Fred Schneider, grown in 1988, 1993
Devil's Lake Sioux Flint	North Dakota	Fred Schneider, grown in 1993
Mandan Red Flour, Mandan Red Flour B	North Dakota	Fred Schneider, grown in 1993
Arikara Flint	North Dakota	Fred Schneider, grown in 1993
Shoepeg Dent	University of Minnesota Herbarium	
	ARCHAEOLOGICAL ZEA MAYS COBS	
Briggs Run (1 and 2)	Briggs Run Site	New York State Museum
Klock Site (1 and 2)	Klock Site	New York State Museum
Roundtop Site	Roundtop Site	New York State Museum
Snell Site	Snell Site	New York State Museum
	MODERN ZIZANIA AQUATICA	
Zizania aquatica	Lake George, New York	University of Minnesota Herbarium

Table 6.5
Data on Prehistoric Maize Cobs Subjected to Phytolith Analysis

Site	Row No.	Mean Cupule Width (mm)[a]	Mean Kernel Thickness (mm)[a]	AMS Lab No.[b]	$\delta^{13}C$	RCY B.P.	A.D. 2σ (intercepts)
Briggs Run 1	8	8.27	3.86	A0328	-9.7	401 ± 38	1443 (1467) 1629
Briggs Run 2	8	10.64	4.20				
Klock 1	8	8.40	3.49	A0326	-9.0	317 ± 38	1492 (1527, 1553, 1632) 1656
Klock 2	10	10.60	4.80				
Roundtop	8	8.32	3.49	AA21979[c]	-8.7	675 ± 55	1260 (1297) 1403
Snell	8	6.89	3.10	A0327	-9.4	691 ± 39	1266 (1293) 1390

[a] Following G. Wagner (1987).
[b] A = Illinois State Geological Survey; AA = NSF Arizona AMS Facility.
[c] On maize kernel from the same feature deposit, originally published in Hart (1999c).

heated nitric acid to dissolve all organic material. The time required varied, but was at least 24 hours for all residue samples. The remaining material was then placed in centrifuge tubes, and centrifuged at 3,000 RPM for 15 minutes. The supernatant nitric acid was pipetted off and replaced with distilled water. After centrifuging and rinsing with distilled water five times, the samples were rinsed in alcohol. Ten drops of each sample were pipetted onto slides, mounted in Permount, and allowed to set until the phytoliths were fixed in position. The phytoliths were categorized and measured using a research-grade Leica Laborlux microscope. One hundred rondels in each sample (residues and comparative) were classified using the taxonomic system developed by Thompson (table 6.6). The results obtained from this technique are comparable with those using a greater number of morphometric traits from fewer forms (see A. Berlin et al. 2003).

The classification system used here is a refinement of that developed by Mulholland and Rapp (1992). Using this system, phytoliths are classified according to the planar view of their faces. A-2-B, for instance, represents a phytolith with an entire outline for the thin face, a thick face of different size than the thin face, and an entire thick face with small decorations (small silica projections from phytolith faces). Figure 6.3 illustrates this type of phytolith. Note that one side of the B face is flattened, but not indented. In the lower right of the figure is a rondel tilted on its side. This clearly shows the constriction in the middle of the phytolith, and the decorations from one face. Figure 6.4 illustrates a rondel with an indented face, slightly tilted on its side. Figure 6.5 has four rondels in planar view, and several tilted forms. Rondel A has two indentations in each face, directly across from each other, and the thick face has multiple small decorations. The classification of this form would be C-3-D-3. Rondel B has entire faces of approximately the same size, and the thick face has multiple decorations. The form of this rondel would be described as A-1-B. Phytolith C has entire faces (one side of each face is flattened, but not indented). This phytolith would be described as A-1-A. Phytolith D has two entire faces of similar size, each of them decorated, and would be described as B-1-B.

Results. Each of the six food residue samples contained abundant biogenic silica. All of the samples contained some rods and diatoms. Rods are ubiquitous in many plants, and diatoms are found in shallow-water sources. The research potential of diatoms as indicators of water source or climatic data is still largely unexplored (Battarbee 1988). Each of the six samples produced phytolith assemblages dominated by rondel forms, consistent with the recovery from the chaff of grasses. All of the samples suggested the presence of both maize and wild rice. Four of the samples, one from Wickham (40525–1), one from Hunter's Home (48580–110), and both from Kipp Island (41119–5, 41119–8), were dominated by rondel forms characteristic of maize cobs. The remaining samples from Wickham (40525–8) and Hunter's Home (48584–1) were dominated by indented rondel forms similar to those of wild rice chaff. Figure 6.6 shows two rondels typical of an assemblage cre-

Table 6.6

Rondel Phytolith Taxonomy

Phytoliths with an Entire Thin Face
    A. Thin face is a complete circle or oval outline, without decorations.
    B. Thin face is a complete circular or oval outline, with decorations present.

Relation of Thin Face to Thick Face
    A-1. Thin face is approximately the same size as the thick face.
    B-1. Thin face is approximately the same size as the thick face, with decorations present.
    A-2. Thin face is substantially different in size from the thick face.
    B-2. Thin face is substantially different in size from the thick face, with decorations present.

Phytoliths with an Indented Thin Face
    C-(1,2,3 . . .) Thin face has one to several indentations.
        1. Thin face has one indentation.
        2. Thin face has two indentations.
        3. Thin face has two indentations directly across from each other.
        4. Thin face has three indentations.
    D-(1,2,3 . . .) Thin face has one to several indentations, and decorations are present.
        1. Thin face has one indentation.
        2. Thin face has two indentations.
        3. Thin face has two indentations directly across from each other.
        4. Thin face has three indentations.

Phytoliths with an Entire Thick Face
    A. Thick face is a complete circle or oval outline, without decorations.
    B. Thick face is a complete circular or oval outline, with decorations present.

Phytoliths with an Indented Thick Face
    C-(1,2,3 . . .) Thick face has one to several indentations.
        1. Thick face has one indentation.
        2. Thick face has two indentations.
        3. Thick face has two indentations directly across from each other.
        4. Thick face has three indentations.
    D-(1,2,3 . . .) Thick face has 1 to several indentations, and decorations are present.
        1. Thick face has one indentation.
        2. Thick face has two indentations.
        3. Thick face has two indentations directly across from each other.
        4. Thick face has three indentations.

Rondel Phytolith Face Shapes
        1. Rondel face is circular.
        2. Rondel face is shaped like a square with rounded corners.
        3. Rondel face is shaped like an oval.
        4. Rondel face is shaped like an oval with squared corners on the ends.
        5. Rondel face is a rounded triangular form.
        6. Rondel face is a triangular form.
        7. Rondel face is irregular, and does not fit in a category above.

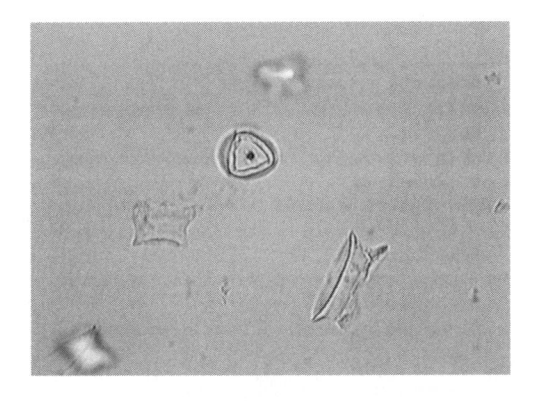

Fig. 6.3. Entire decorated rondel. Tilted rondel form to lower right. Original magnification 1000×.

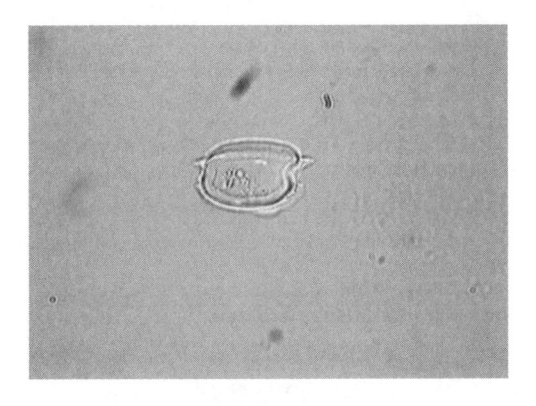

Fig. 6.4. Indented rondel. Original magnification 1000×.

ated by maize and two rondels typical of wild rice. Squared-chord distance values support this interpretation (table 6.7). Samples 40525–1, 48580–110, 41119–5, and 41119–8 are most similar to maize, while 40525–8 and 48584–1 are most similar to wild rice. The two residue samples most similar to wild rice provided the critical value (Overpeck et al. 1985) for this matrix, with values less than 0.175 from wild rice. Detrended correspondence analysis (Hammer et al. 2001) parallels these findings (fig. 6.7). Samples 41119–5, 41119–8, 48580–110, and 40525–1 fall close to maize, while 48584–1 and 40525–8 plot closer to wild rice.

Terry D. Ball and Jack D. Brotherson (1992) have shown that morphology of grass phytoliths is under tighter genetic control than is size, which is more subject to environmental effects. Examination of the phytolith assemblages from the maize samples has shown that when samples of maize are compared without the length and width data (categories based only on size), the assemblage distances are more similar to that expected based on genetics. A distance matrix of the maize samples used as a comparative database is shown in table 6.8. The shaded squares show groups of maize that are closely related. The Midwestern maize assemblages are all much more similar to each other than to the two modern maize samples from the Northeast, or to the Southern Dent sample. The archaeological cob samples display a great similarity to one another, and are also more similar to the cob samples from

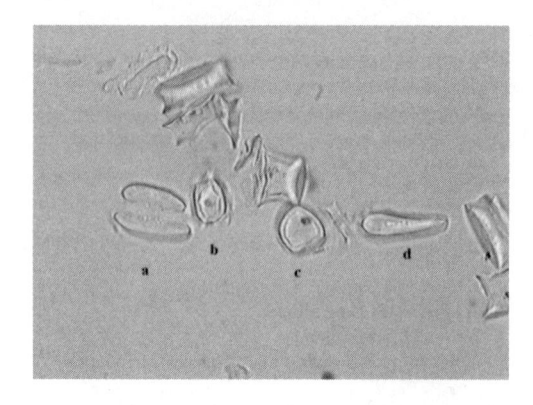

Fig. 6.5. Variety of rondel forms. Original magnification 1000×. See text for explanation.

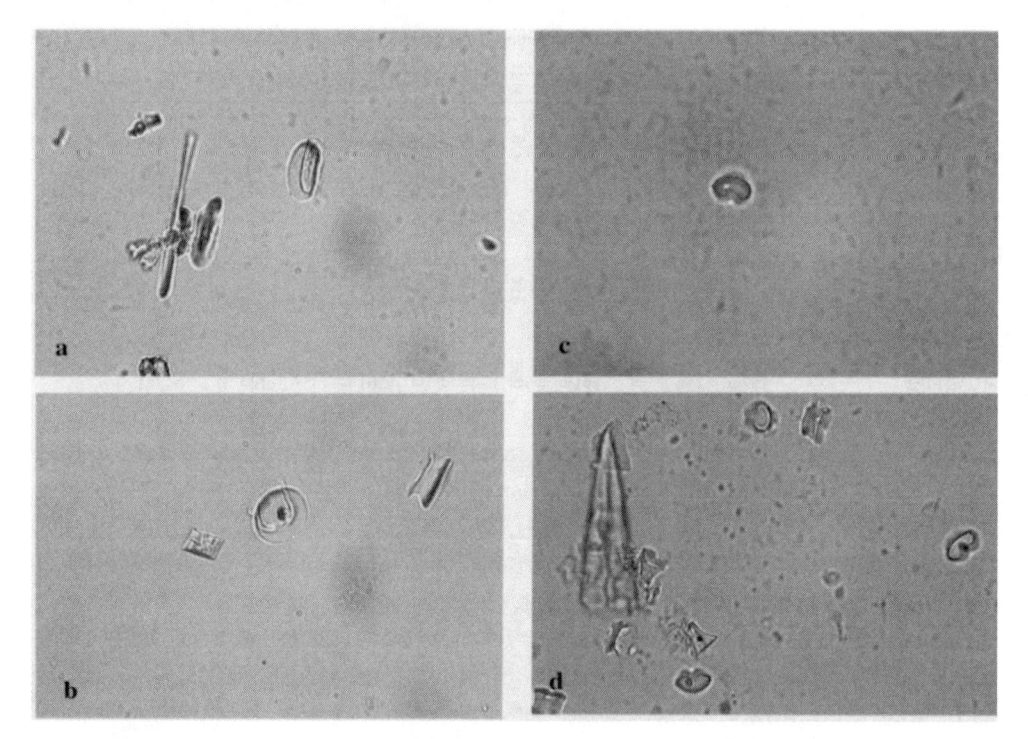

Fig. 6.6. Rondel forms more typical of maize (A, B) and wild rice (C, D). Original magnification 400×. See text for information.

the Midwest than those from the Northeast. The Mandan Sweet Corn samples are genetically nearly identical, and show a great similarity in phytolith production. Within the modern Midwestern maize sample groups 0.059 is the highest squared-chord distance value (Mandan Red Flour/Arikara Flint). Using 0.059 as the critical value (Overpeck et al. 1985), the New York archaeological cob samples have the greatest similarity with the Midwest maizes.

The four residue samples indicating the presence of maize were reexamined excluding length and width data. The squared-chord distance values for the residues and the comparative maize samples are presented as table 6.9. Using the

Table 6.7
Squared-Chord Distance Values Using Morphology and Size Data

Samples	41119–8	41119–5	40525–1	40525–8	48580–110	48584–1
Northern Flint	**.164**	**.161**	**.145**	.239	**.113**	.264
Wild Rice	.199	.184	.206	**.169**	.223	**.155**
Mandan Yellow Flour	**.093**	**.124**	**.116**	.192	**.090**	.214
Iroquois Flour	.253	.277	.223	.332	.200	.374
Mandan Sweet Corn A	**.157**	**.160**	**.151**	.241	**.121**	.285
Mandan Sweet Corn C	.268	.240	.250	.343	.211	.376
Mandan Sweet Corn B	.248	.226	.224	.306	.201	.348
Dent	.274	.266	.253	.345	.216	.401
Devil's Lake Sioux Flint	**.112**	**.153**	**.114**	.216	**.098**	.245
Mandan Red Flour	.213	.233	.197	.314	.165	.360
Mandan Red Flour B	.282	.258	.256	.336	.224	.387
Arikara Flint	**.156**	.191	**.154**	.261	**.127**	.281
Briggs Run 2	.196	.201	.203	.283	**.157**	.348
Roundtop	**.126**	**.162**	**.141**	.236	**.121**	.288
Klock 2	**.141**	.171	**.133**	.238	**.115**	.281
Snell	.204	.203	.192	.287	**.168**	.343
Klock 1	.287	.257	.261	.332	.227	.397
Briggs Run 1	.308	.294	.280	.370	.241	.416

Note: Bolded values are lowest values for each sample.

same critical value of 0.059, each of the residue samples showed affinity with the Northern Flint Corn complex, and not with the Southern Dent. With the exception of sample 41119–5, the residue samples also show affinities with the archaeological cobs. This affinity suggests that the lineages represented by those cobs were present in New York by at least the first half of the seventh century A.D. Only one sample, 48580–110, showed a strong affinity with the modern lineages from the Northeast, suggesting that these lineages developed in place after the introduction of maize from the Midwest.

Only one modern sample of wild rice (*Zizania aquatica*) chaff was available for this study. The identification of wild rice must carry the caveat that only this single comparative sample was available, and other wild grasses were not examined.

Cucurbit phytoliths, which are scalloped ovals to spheres, were in the residue samples from all three sites. Figure 6.8 shows a scalloped form typical of those recovered. Squashes produce phytoliths in the rind, and these have been located by Steven R. Bozarth (1987) in hearth deposits from the Central Plains. Some of the squash phytoliths recovered from the residues are similar to those described as representative of *Cucurbita pepo*, although this similarity cannot be statistically confirmed because of the small sample sizes.

Sedge (*Cyperus* sp.) is represented at Wickham and Kipp Island by dimpled

Fig. 6.7. Detrended correspondence analysis using morphology and size data. The Eigenvalue for axis 1 is 0.3143 and for axis 2 is 0.1051.

plates. A typical form is shown in figure 6.9. *Cyperus* forms recovered could represent a number of different aquatic forms. The weedy form *Cyperus esculentus* was a common food source in Manitoba (Shay 1980). As discussed below, in the northern Finger Lakes region the closely related *Cyperus odoratus* is a more likely source of the phytoliths.

Stable Carbon Isotopes

There has been limited use of carbon isotope ratios of charred cooking residues recovered from prehistoric pottery sherds to determine if maize was cooked in a pottery vessel (e.g., Hastorf and DeNiro 1985; Lovis 1990; Schulenberg 2002b [chap. 4]; also see Staller and Thompson 2002). Hastorf and DeNiro (1985, 490) established that isotope ratios of modern plants do not change substantially when the plants are cooked and charred. They ran stable carbon isotope assays on identifiable charred plant remains from prehistoric archaeological sites in the Peruvian Andes to establish $\delta^{13}C$ ranges for C3 (-26 $^0/_{00}$ to -22 $^0/_{00}$) and C4 (-11 $^0/_{00}$ to -9 $^0/_{00}$) plants. Hastorf and DeNiro then obtained $\delta^{13}C$ values for cooking residues removed from the interior of prehistoric pot sherds from the same sites and plotted them against

Table 6.8

Squared-Chord Distance Matrix for Comparative Maize Samples Using Morphology Data Only

	Dent	Northern Flint	Iroquois Flour	Mandan Sweet Corn A	Mandan Sweet Corn C	Mandan Sweet Corn B	Mandan Yellow Flour	Devil's Lake Sioux Flint	Mandan Red Flour	Mandan Red Flour B	Arikara Flint	Briggs Run 2	Roundtop	Klock 2	Snell	Klock 1	Briggs Run 1
Dent	.000	.127	.125	.119	.130	.118	.107	.111	.114	.108	.109	.088	.103	.096	.100	.096	.102
Northern Flint	.127	.000	.068	.073	.099	.097	.069	.072	.078	.082	.077	.112	.097	.078	.099	.088	.088
Iroquois Flour	.125	.068	.000	.096	.130	.112	.080	.047	.062	.079	.057	.107	.095	.074	.098	.088	.079
Mandan SCA	.119	.073	.096	.000	.031	.040	.040	.059	.064	.038	.083	.063	.030	.049	.046	.041	.071
Mandan SCC	.130	.099	.130	.031	.000	.038	.045	.091	.079	.050	.100	.072	.045	.068	.061	.049	.076
Mandan SCB	.118	.097	.112	.040	.038	.000	.052	.087	.062	.053	.098	.075	.045	.067	.057	.049	.068
Mandan Y Flour	.107	.069	.080	.040	.045	.052	.000	.054	.051	.043	.073	.057	.037	.046	.056	.039	.057
Devil's Lake SF	.111	.072	.047	.059	.091	.087	.054	.000	.043	.041	.052	.063	.056	.039	.064	.044	.061
Mandan RF	.114	.078	.062	.064	.079	.062	.051	.043	.000	.040	.055	.066	.050	.065	.050	.059	.048
Mandan RFB	.108	.082	.079	.038	.050	.053	.043	.041	.040	.000	.059	.053	.032	.043	.029	.034	.052
Arikara Flint	.109	.077	.057	.083	.100	.098	.073	.052	.055	.059	.000	.093	.086	.068	.075	.077	.074
Briggs Run 2	.088	.112	.107	.063	.072	.075	.057	.063	.066	.053	.093	.000	.038	.047	.037	.036	.058
Roundtop	.103	.097	.095	.030	.045	.045	.037	.056	.050	.032	.086	.038	.000	.041	.023	.026	.055
Klock 2	.096	.078	.074	.049	.068	.067	.046	.039	.065	.043	.068	.047	.041	.000	.040	.033	.064
Snell	.100	.099	.098	.046	.061	.057	.056	.064	.050	.029	.075	.037	.023	.040	.000	.037	.058
Klock 1	.096	.088	.088	.041	.049	.049	.039	.044	.059	.034	.077	.036	.026	.033	.037	.000	.037
Briggs Run 1	.102	.088	.079	.071	.076	.068	.057	.061	.048	.052	.074	.058	.055	.064	.058	.037	.000

Note: Shaded areas are genetically related maize lineages. Bold indicates values at or below the critical value of .059.

Table 6.9
Squared-Chord Distance Values for Maize Samples Using Morphology Data Only

Samples	40525–1	41119–8	41119–5	48580–110
Northern Flint	**.052**	.068	.067	**.048**
Mandan Yellow Flour	.061	**.044**	.062	**.048**
Iroquois Flour	.070	.080	.124	.068
Mandan Sweet Corn A	**.051**	**.048**	**.054**	**.046**
Mandan Sweet Corn C	.080	.076	.071	.068
Mandan Sweet Corn B	.071	.074	.073	.074
Dent	.119	.113	.124	.104
Devil's Lake Sioux Flint	**.049**	**.045**	.075	**.049**
Mandan Red Flour	.068	.065	.091	**.055**
Mandan Red Flour B	**.059**	**.054**	.071	**.053**
Arikara Flint	.084	.085	.105	.074
Briggs Run 2	.079	.060	.080	.060
Roundtop	.060	**.050**	.069	**.059**
Klock 2	**.041**	**.041**	.069	**.047**
Snell	.069	.064	.075	.070
Klock 1	.061	**.056**	.072	**.056**
Briggs Run 1	.086	.081	.107	.073

Note: Bold indicates values at or below the critical value of .059.

Fig. 6.8. Squash phytolith from residue sample 40525–1. Original magnification 400×.

the formerly established ranges. Ratios obtained for residues falling within the -26 $^0/_{00}$ to -22 $^0/_{00}$ range were interpreted to represent the cooking of C3 plants, while values above -22 $^0/_{00}$ yet below -11 $^0/_{00}$ were interpreted to represent the cooking of C3 and C4 plants together or in sequence. Lovis (1990, 384) obtained low $\delta^{13}C$ values (-31.99 $^0/_{00}$ to -29.63 $^0/_{00}$) on cooking residues from five prehistoric pot sherds recovered from the Fletcher site in Michigan. He argued that the values reflected the cooking of C3 plants or the flesh of C3 plant consumers.

The $\delta^{13}C$ values of residues dated for the present project range from -29.7 $^0/_{00}$ to -24.9 $^0/_{00}$ (table 6.1); values for residues from which phytoliths were extracted are

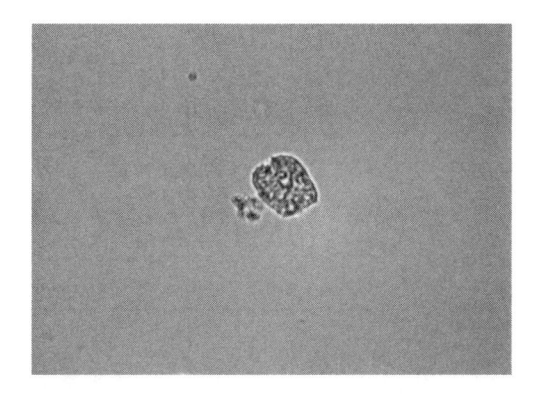

Fig. 6.9. Sedge phytolith from sample 40525–1. Original magnification 400×.

-28.1 ⁰/₀₀ to -25.8 ⁰/₀₀. Because these values are so low a second set of assays on these residues was also obtained from ISGS after maize was identified in the phytolith assemblages. The paired values of the two runs are not significantly different from one another (table 6.1). These low values may lead some to question the results of the phytolith analysis. If maize was cooked in the pots, why are the isotopic values so low? To address this question, we created experimental residues to determine if cooking maize in a pot will necessarily result in high isotopic values.

Isotopic Composition of Experimental Residues. High-powered optical and scanning electron microscopic examination of cooking residues have failed to identify any structures indicative of the foods that produced the residues (Hastorf and DeNiro 1985; Lovis 1990). Hastorf and DeNiro (1985, 490) suggested that this lack of structure resulted from the food's being mashed before charring. Lovis (1990, 384) suggested that the residues probably represented plant and animal fats "being burned onto the interior of vessel necks, where they accumulated during simmering or some other slow cooking process." Given the location of the residues used in the present study—the upper rim interior—we believe that a scenario like Lovis's best accounts for their origins; the residues probably represent fats, carbohydrates, fiber, and other fine particulate matter released by the food during slow cooking, suspended in liquid, deposited on the rim interior, and subsequently burned onto the pot's surface. Under this scenario, carbon isotope values do not reflect the proportions of C3 and C4 plants cooked in a pot, but the proportion of suspended material from C3 and C4 plants deposited and burned on the pot's rim interior.

To determine the implications of this scenario for isotopic values on cooking residues, an experiment was done using mixtures of maize and wild rice. Hand-harvested wild rice seeds purchased from a commercial vendor in Minnesota and Iroquois White Flour maize kernels from plants grown in New York obtained from Jane Mt. Pleasant of Cornell University were each ground into fine powder. The powders were each sieved through 1-mm mesh to remove coarse material. Eleven dry 12.5-liter mixtures of the two powders were then prepared in 10 percent increments ranging from 100 percent wild rice to 100 percent maize. Each mixture was placed in 100 ml of water, thoroughly stirred, brought to a boil, and allowed to simmer for 20 minutes with occasional stirring. Each sample was then decanted into a bimetal can, which was placed on a wood fire where the water evaporated and the mixture was allowed to burn. The resulting materials were submitted to the ISGS for $\delta^{13}C$ assays.

The results are presented in table 6.10. The sample consisting of 100 percent maize yielded a value of -11.84 ⁰/₀₀ and the sample consisting of 100 percent wild rice a value -26.3 ⁰/₀₀. The results show that maize in the residues is detectable at volumes as low as 10 percent, enriching the $\delta^{13}C$ value by 16.04 percent of the difference between 100 percent wild rice and 100 percent maize. The percent increase in $\delta^{13}C$ values does not exceed 30 percent until maize comprises 70 percent of dry volume, at which point the $\delta^{13}C$ value increases to 52.28 percent. This result suggests that maize can contribute a substantial amount to a residue and not substantially enrich the $\delta^{13}C$ value above that of the C3 plant components. These results are very similar to those obtained under different experimental condition by Schulenberg (2002b [chap. 4]) using maize and *Chenopodium*.[2]

Implications of the Experimental Results. With the exception of maize, $\delta^{13}C$ values for prehistoric macrobotanical remains of the plants identified in the phytolith assemblages are rare or nonexistent in the Northeast, reflecting the lack of direct AMS dates reported in the literature. Because of the burning of fossil fuels, modern carbon values are depleted by about 1.5 ⁰/₀₀, and $\delta^{13}C$ values of modern plants cannot be taken as representative of those for prehistoric plants (Tieszen and Fagre 1993, 122). No $\delta^{13}C$ values for prehistoric wild rice seeds were found in the literature. A prehistoric wild rice seed fragment from eastern New York on which we obtained an AMS date (see below) had a $\delta^{13}C$ value -29.7 ⁰/₀₀. One $\delta^{13}C$ value is available for squash in the Northeast, -24.8 ⁰/₀₀ obtained on a rind fragment recovered from the Memorial Park site in north central Pennsylvania (Hart and Asch Sidell 1997, 531). Values for maize kernels in New York range from -9.8 ⁰/₀₀ at the Goldkrest site in the Hudson River valley (Little 1999, 82) to -8.5 ⁰/₀₀ at the Thomas/Luckey site in the Chenango River valley (Knapp 2002).

While low, the $\delta^{13}C$ values for the cooking residues from which maize phytoliths were identified are 9.0 percent to 18.9 percent of the difference of the -29.7 ⁰/₀₀ value for the prehistoric wild rice seed and the mean (-9.15 ⁰/₀₀) of the range of prehistoric maize values. Based on the results of the experiments, these values can be taken to reflect the influence of maize on the $\delta^{13}C$ values (table 6.11). What is clear from this and other projects (Schulenberg 2002b [chap. 4]; Staller and Thompson 2002; Thompson and Mulholland 1994) is that low $\delta^{13}C$ values from cooking residues cannot be used as evidence that maize was not cooked in a pot.

The most logical inference that can be made at this time based on the low $\delta^{13}C$ values of the residues is that maize was not the major contributor to the material

---

2. The experiment reported here was carried out by Hart in the winter of 2002, before he became aware of Schulenberg's experiment reported in her 2002 Ph.D. dissertation.

Table 6.10
δ¹³C Values for Experimental Cooking Residues

% Maize Dry Volume	% Maize Dry Weight	δ¹³C	% Enrichment above 100% Wild Rice
0	0.0	-26.3	0.00
10	7.8	-23.98	16.04
20	15.9	-24.16	14.80
30	24.5	-23.31	20.68
40	33.6	-22.80	24.20
50	43.1	-22.32	27.52
60	53.2	-22.51[a]	26.20
70	63.9	-18.74	52.28
80	75.2	-16.31	69.09
90	87.2	-14.73	80.00
100	100.0	-11.84	100.00

[a] Mean of two assays

Table 6.11
Residue δ¹³C Enrichment above Value for a Prehistoric Wild Rice Seed

Sample	% δ¹³C Enrichment above Wild Rice Seed
40525–1	9.0
40525–8	18.9
48580–110	14.1
41119–5	16.3
41119–8	13.3
48584–1	7.3

that burned to form the residues (Staller and Thompson 2002, 43; also see Schulenberg 2002b [chap. 4]). The isotopic and phytolith data are complementary. A small amount of maize may produce a strong phytolith signature while being masked in the isotopic signature.

Discussion

The results of this study (table 6.12) provide new information on the age of maize and squash in New York and on the use of native plant species in conjunction with those crops at a period of time for which there has been a distinct lack of evidence for the plant components of subsistence economies.

Table 6.12
Summary of Results

Site	A.D. 2σ (intercept)	Phytoliths
Wickham	545 (624, 627, 638) 660	Maize, wild rice, squash, sedge
Kipp Island	601 (642) 659	Maize, wild rice, squash, sedge
Wickham	683 (778) 936	Wild rice, maize?, squash
Hunter's Home	693 (778) 880	Maize, wild rice, squash

Maize

Before this study the earliest evidence for maize in New York was in the southeastern portion of the state with a direct AMS date on a maize kernel of 1050 ± 50 B.P. (2σ A.D. 891 [997] 1149) (Cassedy and Webb 1999). The results of the present study demonstrate its presence and consumption in the northern Finger Lakes region by the early seventh century A.D. Given this crop's presence in southern Ontario by the sixth century A.D. (Crawford et al. 1997), our results should not be surprising. Comparison with phytoliths extracted from modern and archaeological cobs suggests that the Northern Flint Complex was in New York by at least the first half of the seventh century A.D. Further, this preliminary study suggests that maize entered New York from the Midwest. We cannot state that we now know when maize was adopted successfully in the northern Finger Lakes region (see Hart 1999a). Additional cooking-residue samples from contemporary and earlier sites need to be analyzed. In combination with intensive sampling for macrobotanical remains, this analysis will help us gain a better understanding of the history of maize in the northern Finger Lakes region.

Squash

The presence of seventh-century A.D. squash in the northern Finger Lakes should also not be surprising given its much earlier presence to the south and west in the Susquehanna and Ohio river basins (Hart and Asch Sidell 1997). Our results push back the known history of squash in New York some 650 years given that the oldest previously confirmed date was A.D. 1300 at the Roundtop site in the Susquehanna River valley (Hart 1999c). While it was not possible to identify a specific species of squash based on the phytolith assemblages, the phytoliths most likely originated from *Cucurbita pepo* spp. *ovifera*, which thus far is the only cultivated squash identified this early in the Eastern Woodlands (Yarnell 1993). A significant aspect of our results is that they establish that maize and squash were probably being eaten and potentially grown together at this early date, well before the time that the common bean becomes archaeologically visible across the northern Eastern Woodlands (Hart et al. 2002). This result means that bean was adopted into agricultural systems in the northern Finger Lakes in which maize and squash had evolved together for several centuries.

Wild Rice

Evidence for wild rice harvesting has been found in several areas of the Great Lakes (e.g., Arzigian 2000; Crawford and Smith 2003; Lofstrom 1987; Moffat and Arzigian 2000). *Zizania aquatica* is a native species in New York (Mitchell and Tucker 1997). Figure 6.10 shows the locations reported to the New York State Museum's herbarium for this species in New York during the nineteenth and twentieth centuries. To confirm its prehistoric presence, we submitted to ISGS for AMS dating a wild rice seed fragment recovered in 1999 during New York State Museum excavations at the Parslow Field site in the Schoharie River valley (fig. 6.1) and identified by Asch Sidell (2000). The resulting date of 2386 ± 48 B.P. (A-0286) (2σ 759 [405] 385 B.C.) firmly establishes the presence of wild rice in New York well before the seventh century A.D. to which the earliest residues used in this study date.

Wild rice has been recovered from later prehistoric contexts in the Susque-

Fig. 6.10. Distribution of *Zizania aquatica* in New York State.

hanna River basin (Hart and Asch Sidell 1996; King 1992). Neal Ferris (1999, 27, 32) has suggested that wild rice may have been an important resource for contemporary groups living along the Grand River in southern Ontario and that maize was consumed with this native resource (Ferris 1999, 28). The phytolith assemblages extracted from cooking residues for this study suggest the consumption of maize with wild rice in the northern Finger Lakes of New York during the seventh and eighth centuries A.D.

Sedge

The sedge *Cyperus esculentus* L. was a common food source ethnographically in Manitoba (Shay 1980). This species is closely related to *Cyperus odoratus* L., which is more common in the northern Finger Lakes region of New York. Figure 6.11 shows the distribution of observations reported to the New York State Museum's herbarium of *C. odoratus* during the nineteenth and twentieth centuries in New York. This tuberous sedge grows in moist settings such as the banks and shores of streams, lakes, ponds, and marshes (Mitchell 2003), and may well have been consumed by the inhabitants of the Kipp Island and Wickham sites during the seventh century

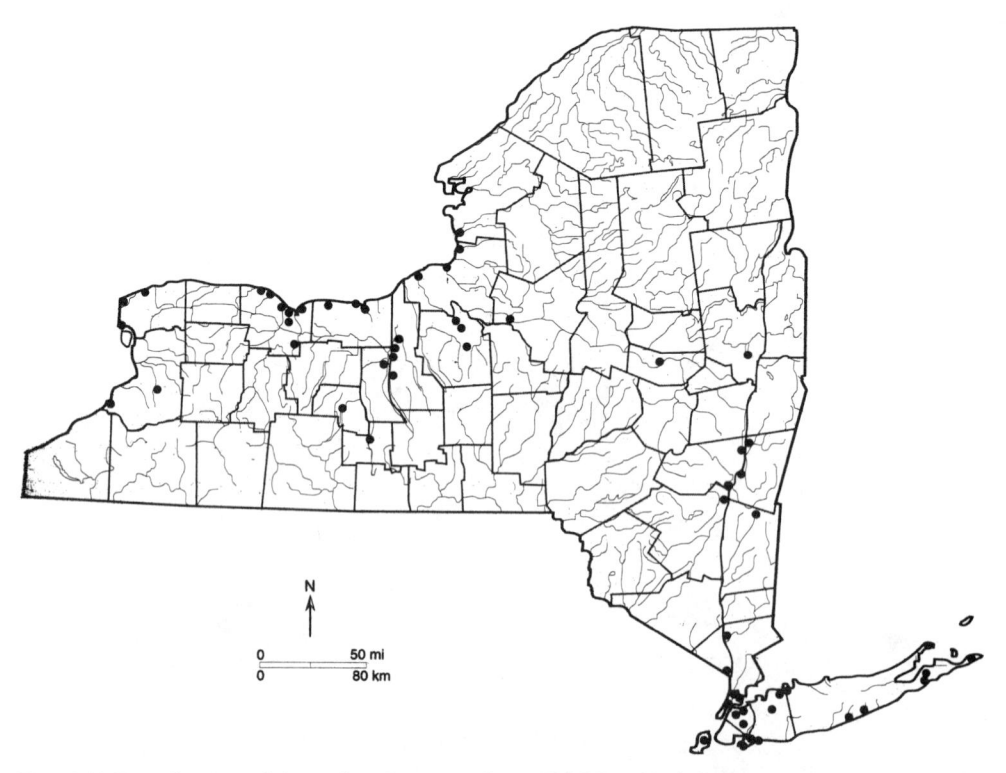

Fig. 6.11. Distribution of the sedge *Cyperus odoratus* in New York State.

A.D. Although not as common in the area today, *C. esculentus* is widely consumed (Mitchell 2003) and could be the source of the phytoliths.

Conclusions

The results of this study demonstrate that maize and squash were utilized in the northern Finger Lakes region well before macrobotanical evidence suggested, but consistent with Ritchie and Funk's (1973) inference based on other lines of evidence. It further illustrates the fact that the adoption of maize was not an immediate catalyst for settled village life (Hart 2001; Hart and Means 2002) and that the Northern Flint complex was present in New York early on. Given our small, temporally restricted sample, it is not possible to draw conclusions about the ultimate age of the two crops in this region. The study expands the known prehistoric distribution of wild rice into eastern New York and the number of locations where its exploitation by prehistoric human populations has been demonstrated. The study also demonstrates the prehistoric use of what was probably a tuberous sedge.

One hypothesis for the apparent widespread intensification of maize agriculture in the east around A.D. 1000 is that the adoption of the common bean provided the amino acids lycine and trytophane, which are missing in maize. Consuming maize and beans together would have provided a complete set of amino acids, allowing greater reliance on maize as a staple food (e.g., Stoltman 1978; Stoltman and Baerreis 1983). Hart et al. (2002) have shown that this hypothesis must be rejected given that common bean does not become archaeologically visible across the northern Eastern Woodlands until the late thirteenth to fourteenth centuries A.D. based on current recovery. The demonstrated use of maize and wild rice together at a much earlier date provides another reason to reject this hypothesis.

Cooked wild rice has higher levels of lycine and trytophene than cooked common bean, which indicates that consuming maize with wild rice together provides the amino acids that would be missed if maize were consumed alone (U.S. Department of Agriculture 2002). Like the common bean, wild rice is storable, potentially providing food for winter and spring consumption (Ferris 1999). Wild rice can be highly productive, with hand-harvested yields ranging between 40 and 100 pounds per acre (Arzigian 2000; Lofstrom 1987). Wild rice is native to the Eastern Woodlands and could be intentionally introduced by humans into new locations with the correct environmental conditions (Vennum 1988). Given that there is a lack of evidence for widespread agricultural intensification before A.D. 1000, the adoption of plant foods, such as wild rice and the common bean, that have complementary amino acids with maize cannot be considered a catalyst for the intensification of maize agriculture. This is additional evidence that the intensification of maize agriculture was not tied to the alleviation of some interfering force, in this case the lack of a full complement of amino acids, that prevented it from reaching a natural state of effective, high-yield production (Hart 1999a).

Why has macrobotanical evidence for maize, squash,[3] and wild rice use at this time not been found in the northern Finger Lakes region? None of the sites whose collections were used in this study was subjected to flotation recovery and any recovery of macrobotanical remains would have been fortuitous. Since the time of their excavation no large sites of comparable age have been excavated in the northern Finger Lakes area and intensively sampled with flotation (Kuhn 2001; New York Archaeological Council 1993–2001). As a result, no large systematically collected macrobotanical assemblages exist for the time period in question.

During the mid-1990s unexpected documentation of macrobotanical evidence for early crops was reported from extensively sampled and intensively analyzed sites in the Northeast (Hart and Asch Sidell 1996; 1997; Petersen and Asch Sidell 1996). As a result, it is possible that extensive flotation sampling and intensive identification efforts by paleoethnobotanists will result in the recovery of at least contemporaneous macrobotanical maize and squash remains in the northern Finger Lakes region as in adjacent Ontario (Crawford et al. 1997). However, the results of the present study suggest that multiple lines of evidence, including phytoliths extracted from cooking residues, will provide the best information on early agriculture in this region and in the wider Northeast.

This study shows the value of museum collections in the investigation of current research issues. It also demonstrates the value of cooking residues for the investigation of plant-based subsistence. The use of phytoliths to address issues of crop histories has been used extensively elsewhere in the Western Hemisphere, but has concentrated on the recovery of phytolith assemblages from soils at archaeological sites (Pearsall and Piperno 1993). The extraction of phytoliths from cooking residues (1) allows the direct dating of those assemblages through AMS residue dating and (2) negates the possibility that the phytoliths resulted from anything other than plants being cooked (Staller and Thompson 2002). We follow Lovis (1990) in emphasizing the importance of cooking residues in museum collections and the need to conserve them in old and new collections.

Acknowledgments

Many thanks go to Penelope Drooker, who first suggested to Hart that he consider using cooking residues to directly date pottery sherds. Without that, none of the work presented in this paper would have taken place. Thanks to Susan Mulhol-

---

3. Two small cucurbit rind fragments were recovered from non-feature Woodland Period contexts at the Zinselmeier No. 1 site in the northern Finger Lakes region (Egan 2001, 7–18). The cucurbit rind fragments were not directly dated.

land and George Rapp for years of labor in developing a viable taxonomy allowing examination of the use of grasses. Thanks to Diana Greenlee for providing many useful comments and suggestions on an earlier draft of the paper and to Antonio Curet for translating the abstract. Thanks also to Irwin Rovner and three anonymous reviewers for their many useful suggestions on how to improve the article. The AMS dating and phytolith analysis were supported by the New York State Museum and the State University of New York at Albany.

7 | The Precontact Iroquoian Occupation of Southern Ontario

GARY A. WARRICK

Introduction

BEFORE DIRECT EUROPEAN CONTACT that occurred in late July 1534 in the Gaspé region, the Iroquoian-speaking people of southern Ontario and the St. Lawrence Valley numbered about 60,000 and lived in 50–60 villages distributed south of the granite bedrock of the Precambrian Shield. Jacques Cartier's visit to Hochelaga (present-day Montreal) in the fall of 1535 provides the first eyewitness description by a European of a palisaded Iroquoian longhouse village, occupied by 1,500 St. Lawrence Iroquoians (Trigger 1972, 15). Cartier and his men were offered a feast of maize bread and soup and dried fish (Biggar 1924, 167), the mainstays of a sixteenth-century Iroquoian diet. Unbeknownst to Cartier, the *kanata* (village) of Hochelaga represented less than 2 percent of the 100,000 Northern Iroquoians who occupied Pennsylvania, New York State, Quebec, and southern Ontario (Clermont 1992; Snow 1992a). Archaeological work of the twentieth century has compiled sufficient data to permit one to trace the history of the Iroquoian occupation of southern Ontario from its origins ca. A.D. 500 to 1534. This paper will focus on settlement patterns (house, village, region), population, subsistence, and sociopolitical organization, and how these changed over time. It will draw heavily upon the recent work of both research archaeologists and cultural resource management archaeologists in Ontario. Land development in Ontario has required the partial or complete excavation of 50 Iroquoian villages over the last 20 years. This paper is an attempt to synthesize this vast body of data in the context of writing the Iroquoian history of southern Ontario before European contact.

Previously published (with modification) in *Journal of World Prehistory* 14, no. 4 (2000): 415–66. Springer and Plenum Publishing Corporation. Reproduced with kind permission from Springer Science and Business Media.

Before we deal with the precontact Iroquoian occupation of southern Ontario, there are a few terms that require definition. First of all, *southern Ontario* is generally defined as the land south of a line connecting Ottawa on the east to the Bruce Peninsula on the west, north of Lake Erie, Lake Ontario, and the St. Lawrence River (fig. 7.1). Southern Ontario is underlain by two major types of bedrock—the granite of the Precambrian Shield and the limestone/dolomite/shale of Devonian and Silurian age. Iroquoian village sites are not found on the Shield. In fact, the Frontenac Axis, dividing the Shield from the Paleozoic bedrock, demarcates the zone of Iroquoian occupation in the central and western portion of southern Ontario. In southeastern Ontario, Iroquoian villages are distributed on the Paleozoic limestone plains south of Ottawa, along the north shore of the St. Lawrence River. Iroquoian village site distribution is associated with the Wisconsin glacial and glaciolacustrine deposits that blanket much of the Paleozoic bedrock (Karrow and Warner 1990). Iroquoian subsistence revolved around the cultivation of maize grown in clearings cut out of the broad-leafed oak-hickory/maple-beech forests of southern Ontario. Thus it is no accident that the distribution of Iroquoian village sites is concentrated in those areas with the best agricultural soils (well drained and light textured) and highest number of frost-free days (Campbell and Campbell 1992).

The term *precontact* is used in place of *prehistoric* in this paper. *Prehistory* is a

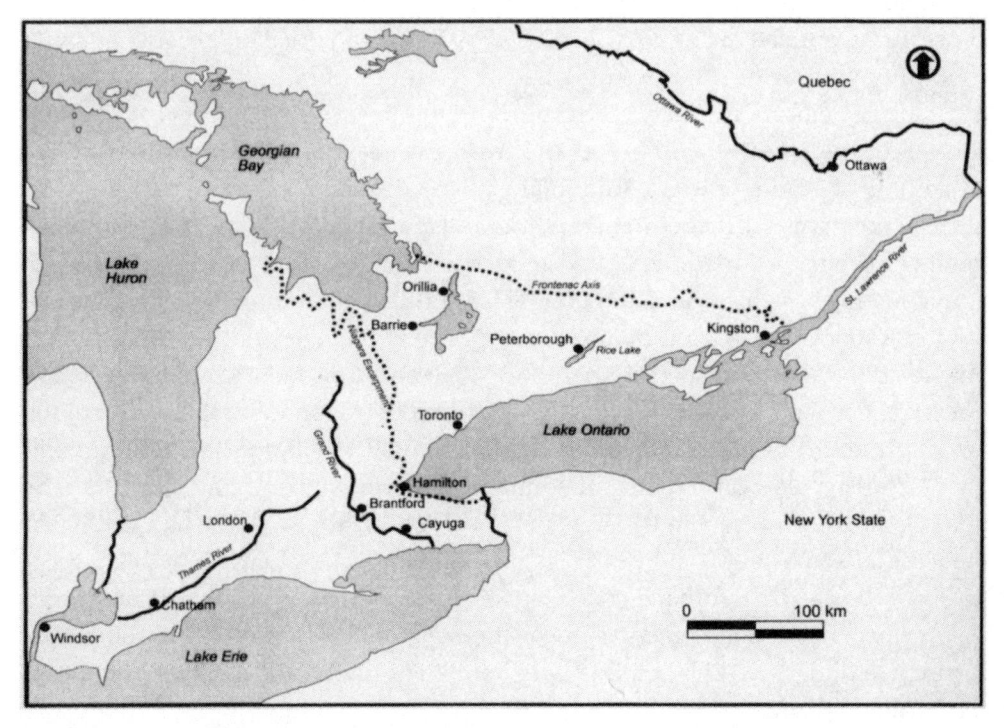

Fig. 7.1. Southern Ontario.

term that many Native Americans find pejorative (McGhee 1997). In certain parts of the world, such as Europe and the Middle East, prehistory has no derogatory connotations—it is used simply to refer to those periods of human history before written documentation. In colonized parts of the world, like the Americas, indigenous peoples dislike the concept of prehistory because it denies their oral histories and "reflects the degree to which twentieth-century archaeology has displaced Native American oral traditions as the source of valid knowledge about ancient human circumstances" (Echo-Hawk 2000, 285). The term *ancient history* has been recommended as a replacement term for *prehistory* (Echo-Hawk 2000; McGhee 1997). *Precontact history* is another term that is seeing increasing use in the archaeological literature by North American archaeologists (e.g., Milner and Katzenberg 1999). *Precontact* simply refers to the time before direct face-to-face European contact for a particular area and group. Precontact history for the St. Lawrence valley—lower Great Lakes Iroquoians—refers to events that happened before A.D. 1534.

Iroquoian is both a linguistic and a cultural term. The very word *Iroquois* may have a Basque origin that translates as "Killer People" (Bakker 1990). While it is impossible for archaeologists to dig up a language, it is possible to dig up the remains of a cultural group. Iroquoian archaeology in Ontario deals with the material remains of several Iroquoian peoples or nations who were documented by seventeenth-century French explorers and missionaries: Neutral, Petun, Huron, and St. Lawrence Iroquoian. For those sites in southern Ontario dating after A.D. 1000, it is generally accepted that they were occupied by Iroquoian speakers because of direct continuity with Iroquoian sites of the seventeenth century in the same region. In fact, village relocation sequences from A.D. 1100 to A.D. 1550 have been demonstrated for the Huron-Petun in the Pickering area, east of Toronto (Warrick 1990, 239–42). In southern Ontario, Iroquoian sites are defined by a distinctive assemblage of pottery vessels, pipes, chert points and tools, bone/antler/shell objects, remains of cabins or longhouses, and evidence of maize agriculture. Problems of ethnic identity occur beyond the bounds of southern Ontario. Sites yielding Iroquoian artifacts—primarily pottery—have been discovered on the Precambrian Shield (MacNeish 1952: von Gernet 1993; Coté and Inksetter 2000; Ridley 1954). These are normally interpreted as trade pots used by Algonquian speakers, not the actual presence of Iroquoian people. Before A.D. 1000, the linguistic/cultural affiliation of archaeological remains in southern Ontario is problematic, but there is demonstrated continuity in the archaeological record from A.D. 500 to A.D. 1000 in the Grand River valley. While there is no clear evidence for longhouse villages before A.D. 1000, all of the other archaeological indices that are identified in later times as Iroquoian have been found in Princess Point sites of the Grand River valley (i.e., distinctive pottery vessels, pipes, chert points and tools, and maize agriculture) (Smith and Crawford 1997).

In this paper, *Huron* and *Petun* are used as a conjoined term: *Huron-Petun*. The

Neutral occupied the western end of Lake Ontario and the Niagara Peninsula and were given this name by Samuel de Chaplain in 1615 because they remained neutral in the conflict between the Huron-Petun and Five Nations Iroquois (Biggar 1922–36, 3:99, 100). It is fully recognized that these names are non-Native in origin and have derogatory connotations that may offend some Native readers. Georges Sioui (1992a, 16), a Wendat (Huron) historian, prefers to use the Iroquoian name *Wendats-Tionontates* to refer to the Huron-Petun. *Huron* is from the Old French word *hure*, which means either "a wild boar" (perhaps ridiculing Huron hairstyles) or "rustic, ruffian, lout, or hillbilly" (referring to the unacculturated ways of the early seventeenth-century Huron) (Heidenreich 1971, 20, 21; Sioui 1992a, 16; Trigger 1976, 27). Neither meaning is particularly flattering to the Wendat. Champlain and Gabriel Sagard were the first ones to use the name *Huron* in print in 1623 (Biggar 1922–36, 5:100; Sagard-Théodat 1939 [1632]). The name *Petun* has a Brazilian origin, meaning "Tobacco People" and was applied by Champlain in 1632 (Biggar 1922–36, 6:248) because this group grew and traded tobacco. The term *St. Lawrence Iroquoian* is an archaeological construct and was coined by Bruce G. Trigger (1972). Georges Sioui (1992a, 82, 83) calls the St. Lawrence Iroquoians by the term *Laurentian Nadoueks*—many Algonquian groups referred to their Iroquoian neighbors as *Nadoueks* or *Naudoways*. While it seems that ethnohistorians and archaeologists should review the European-derived names for Iroquoian groups and, in consultation with living members of the various tribes or nations, assign names that are in harmony with current Native usage and self-image, for the sake of consistency and to avoid confusing the nonspecialist reader, this paper uses the conventional English names for the Huron: *Petun, Neutral, Five Nations Iroquois,* and *St. Lawrence Iroquoians.*

Iroquoian Archaeology in Ontario

Iroquoian archaeology in Ontario holds many advantages for serious researchers. First, sites are relatively well-preserved—they were occupied within the last 1,500 years and contain most materials left by the inhabitant, except for the obvious perishable organics. Even post molds and pit feature outlines are extremely clear. Second, most Iroquoian village sites were occupied for 10–50 years (Timmins 1997a, 83–87; Warrick 1990, 294), with minimal reoccupation of the same site—most sites are veritable "snapshots" or "time capsules" of a couple of decades of activity, a rare situation in world archaeology. Furthermore, the short occupation span of villages has resulted in an astonishing number of sites—there are an estimated 750 village sites for south-central Ontario alone (Warrick 1990, 157–59), a figure that can be doubled when including southwestern Ontario. In fact, the density of Iroquoian village sites (measured as number of sites/1,000 km^2/millennium) exceeds that of the Valley of Mexico and Neolithic Britain (P. Ramsden 1996, 102–4). Another advantage to Iroquoian archaeology in Ontario is the relative lack of urbanization and associated destruction of sites. Most Iroquoian sites are situated in rural settings, either in agricultural fields or woodlots. These locations do not mean, however, that Iroquoian sites have not been threatened with destruction from land development. It has been estimated, for example, that 2,500 archaeological sites of all time periods (650 deserving of full excavation) were unknowingly destroyed between 1951 and 1991 in Greater Metropolitan Toronto and surrounding York region as a result of urban sprawl (Coleman and Williamson 1994, 67–69). These totals would have included several Iroquoian village sites. Nevertheless, despite the last 200 years of European settlement and land clearance in southern Ontario, it has been estimated that few Iroquoian village sites have been destroyed before documentation (Warrick 1990, 147–67).

Before 1980, the majority of Iroquoian site excavations occurred in the context of museum or university research (e.g., Dodd et al. 1990; Lennox and Fitzgerald 1990; P. Ramsden 1977; Williamson 1990). Following passage of the *Ontario Heritage Act* in 1974, the *Environmental Assessment Act* in 1975, and the *Planning Act* in 1983, archaeological sites in Ontario became protected and subject to conservation in the face of development. Cultural resource management archaeology, both private and government-sponsored, blossomed over the last 20 years and is today a $3–5 million dollar industry in Ontario, accounting for 90 percent of all new archaeological site discoveries in the province (Ferris 1998, 236, 237). Iroquoian sites are encountered by consulting archaeologists, particularly on the outskirts of cities such as London, Brantford, Kitchener-Waterloo, Hamilton, Oakville, Mississauga, Toronto, and Barrie. Iroquoian village sites are conspicuous on the landscape because 95 percent are subject to periodic plowing, have high artifact densities, and are relatively large—thus they are difficult to overlook in cultural resource management assessments of land proposed for development. Complete excavation of an Iroquoian village site is expensive because of relatively large site size, the need for heavy machinery to expose settlement pattern during excavation, and the processing of literally tens or hundreds of thousands of recovered artifacts and ecofacts. Despite efforts to avoid and build around Iroquoian sites, land development in Ontario has required the partial or complete excavation of 50 Iroquoian villages over the last 20 years, predominantly in the City of Toronto and York region and Barrie, which are experiencing galloping urban sprawl. The data from these sites have and will contribute to a better understanding of the Iroquoian occupation of southern Ontario.

Chronology

Radiocarbon dating and serialization of decoration on pottery rim sherds or ceramic seriation form the foundation of the chronological framework for the Iroquoians of southern Ontario. Richard S. MacNeish (1952) and James V. Wright

(1966) established the Ontario Iroquoian chronological framework, based on ceramic serialization and the direct historic approach. Despite the lack of absolute dates (just four radiocarbon dates were available for Wright's study in 1966), the original Iroquoian chronology is a remarkable approximation of reality. Refinements over the last 30 years, primarily the calibration of radiocarbon dates (Pendergast 1993a; Timmins 1985; D. Smith 1997a), have modified the chronology only slightly from Early Iroquoian to Late Precontact times. The most widely accepted chronology is: Princess Point (A.D. 500–1000), Early Iroquoian (A.D. 1000–1300), Middle Iroquoian (Uren phase: A.D. 1300–1330; Middleport phase: A.D. 1330–1420), and Late Precontact (A.D. 1420–1534) (Dodd et al. 1990; Ferris and Spence 1995; Fox 1990a, D. Smith 1997a; Timmins 1985; Warrick 1990, 170–90). St. Lawrence Iroquoian chronology, despite a relatively large number of radiocarbon dates from sites in Ontario, remains problematic because of discrepancies between calibrated radiocarbon age estimates and ceramic serialization age estimates for sites (Chapdelaine 1989, 239–48; J. Jamieson 1990a; Pendergast 1993a; 1993b). Nevertheless, St. Lawrence Iroquoian occupation of southern Ontario appears to have occurred between A.D. 1300 and A.D. 1550 (J. Jamieson 1990a).

The precontact Iroquoian period of occupation is also known as the Late Woodland period in Ontario. It is generally accepted that it begins with the appearance of Iroquoian longhouse villages in the archaeological record—sometime after A.D. 900. Recent work by Gary W. Crawford and David G. Smith (Crawford et al. 1998; Smith and Crawford 1997) in the Grand River valley have acquired the earliest AMS dates for maize in the Northeast, in association with Princess Point artifacts— cal. A.D. 260–660 (uncalibrated AMS date of 1570 B.P. ± 90 [TO-5307]), from the Grand Banks site (Crawford et al. 1997). (The reader should note that all radiocarbon dates cited in the paper have been calibrated with CALIB 3.0, following Minze Stuiver and Paula J. Reimer [1993].) The latest radiocarbon dates for identifiable Princess Point occupations fall around A.D. 1000 (D. Smith 1997a). Because no clear evidence of longhouse village life has yet come to light for Princess Point, some archaeologists refer to the entire Princess Point period as Transitional Woodland, falling between Middle Woodland and Late Woodland (Ferris and Spence 1995, 103; Fox 1990a; Pihl and Williamson 1999; Spence and Pihl 1984). While it is recognized that Princess Point is indeed transitional between an earlier Middle Woodland hunting-gathering lifestyle and a Late Woodland Iroquoian farming lifestyle, this paper will ignore the Transitional and Late Woodland appellations and instead will use the names for the various time periods mentioned earlier. As Smith and Crawford (1997, 24) point out, the transition between Princess Point and Early Iroquoian, exemplified by sites such as Porteous and Lone Pine, was not sudden but gradual. This paper adopts an A.D. 1000 date for the beginning of Early Iroquoian times, following the work of Smith and Crawford (1997).

A recent challenge to the Ontario Iroquoian chronology has been proposed by

William D. Finlayson (1998). Based on radiocarbon dates; varve dates from meromictic Crawford Lake, near Milton, Ontario; and site relocation sequences in the Crawford Lake region, Finlayson (1998, 371–75) suggests that the Middle Iroquoian period began A.D. 1330 and ended A.D. 1504. The main problem with Finlayson's chronological revision is that it runs counter to the established radiocarbon chronology and site relocation sequences for all other regions of southern Ontario. Finalyson's scheme also places far too much emphasis on the varve dates from Crawford Lake, which are difficult to associate with radiocarbon-dated village sites (Dodd et al. 1990, 329).

Iroquoian Origins

The origin of Iroquoian peoples of southern Ontario can be explained by two competing hypotheses: in situ development or migration. The in situ hypothesis was formulated by Richard MacNeish (1952). Using about 15,000 pottery rim sherds from 50 sites in Ontario and New York State, MacNeish constructed a developmental sequence for Northern Iroquoians that documented an in situ origin from Middle Woodland (Point Peninsula) antecedents. James Wright (1966) entrenched the in situ hypothesis in his classic work on the Ontario Iroquois Tradition and extended Iroquoian continuity in the Northeast back several thousand years into Laurentian Archaic times (J. Wright 1984). The in situ development of southern Ontario Iroquoians has become close to an accepted fact and forms the working model of many prominent Iroquoian archaeologists (e.g., Chapdelaine 1993; Ferris and Spence 1995; Finlayson 1998; Smith and Crawford 1997; Trigger 1999; Williamson 1990).

There are some archaeologists, however, who have questioned the in situ hypothesis. David M. Stothers's (1977) seminal study of Princess Point suggests that the origins for it were outside Ontario, either in Ohio or in Illinois. Stothers (1977, 152, 153) considers Princess Point to have been ancestral Iroquoian, related to Owasco in New York State. Most recently, Dean R. Snow (1992a; 1994a; 1995a [chap. 1 in this volume]; 1996a [chap. 3 in this volume]) has argued that Northern Iroquoians migrated into their historic homelands ca. A.D. 600, from the Appalachian area of Pennsylvania or further south. According to Snow (1995a [chap. 1]; 1996a [chap. 3]), the immigrant Iroquoian speakers, represented by Princess Point sites in the Grand River valley, displaced or absorbed indigenous Middle Woodland (Algonquian speakers) peoples, and arrived with a full-blown repertoire of Iroquoian cultural traits: maize agriculture, palisaded longhouse villages, and matrilocal residence/matrilineal descent systems. (The term *matrilocal residence* is entrenched in Iroquoian studies and is used in this paper to actually refer to the more technically correct term *uxorilocal residence,* where a husband lives with his wife's relatives). Dean Snow (1992a; 1995a; 1996a) and others (Bursey 1995; Fiedel 1991; 1999) support an Iroquoian migration on the basis of archaeological, demographic, linguistic, and anthropological evidence.

Proponents of the migration hypothesis point to discontinuities or anomalies in the archaeological record between Middle Woodland (Point Peninsula) and Princess Point, primarily in ceramics, chipped lithics, site distribution, and dating. Pottery (Snow 1995a [chap. 1]) and chipped lithic assemblages (Bursey 1995) show striking dissimilarities from Middle Woodland to Princess Point, more than can be accounted for by transitional change over a generation or two. Middle Woodland pots are characterized by coil manufacture and dentate-stamped, rocker-stamped, pseudo-scallop shell or simple corded decoration (Spence et al. 1990, 144–58), whereas Princess Point pots were made by slab/paddle-and-anvil construction and decorated with cord-wrapped stick and exterior punctates (fig. 7.2) (Bursey 1995, 46, 47; Smith and Crawford 1997, 24; Snow 1995a, 71 [chap. 1]). Middle Woodland chipped lithic assemblages typically display thick side-notched points made on a variety of local and exotic cherts (Spence et al. 1990, 144–58); Princess Point chipped lithics display a preference for dark Onondaga chert from the north shore of Lake Erie and thin, triangular Levanna projectile points (Bursey 1995, 47; Smith and Crawford 1997, 25. It should be noted that the appearance of thin, triangular points occurred throughout the Northeast between A.D. 500 and A.D. 1000 [Justice 1987]).

Middle Woodland and Princess Point site distributions are quite dissimilar as well. Peter G. Ramsden (1996, 107) has noted that dense concentrations of Middle Woodland sites in south-central Ontario in the Rice Lake region are not mirrored by a similar concentration of later Iroquoian sites. Similarly, Princess Point sites in the lower Grand River valley contain little evidence of earlier Middle Woodland occupation of the same location (Crawford and Smith 1996).

Radiocarbon dating indicates that southern Ontario was occupied simultaneously (A.D. 500–800) by Middle Woodland hunter-gatherers and Princess Point agriculturalists (D. Smith 1997a). For example, the HH site, situated in the city of Hamilton at the western end of Lake Ontario and just a few kilometers from Princess Point sites at Cootes Paradise to the west, was occupied by Middle Woodland peoples as late as A.D. 550–760 (uncalibrated AMS date of 1410 B.P. ± 60 [TO-4270])(Woodley 1996). No sites have been found in southern Ontario bearing archaeological evidence of a transition between Middle Woodland and Princess Point or Early Iroquoian. (Mima Kapches's [1987, 173] claims that the Auda site radiocarbon date [calibrated to A.D. 680–1190 (D. Smith 1997a)] and that certain traits of ceramic decoration suggest a Middle Woodland ancestry are questioned by the site's close ceramic similarity to the thirteenth-century A.D. Hibou site [MacDonald and Williamson 1995, 20, 21].)

Demographic, linguistic, and anthropological arguments have been used by supporters of the migration hypothesis for Iroquoian origins. Dean Snow (1992a;

Fig. 7.2. Princess Point vessel from Varden site, Long Point (courtesy of David G. Smith, Department of Anthropology, Univ. of Toronto at Mississauga).

1995a [chap. 1]) has argued that a ca. A.D. 900 founding population of Northern Iroquoians in both New York State and Ontario need never have exceeded 500, with an average annual growth rate of 0.7 percent in order to attain a population of 95,000 by A.D. 1625. Snow's demographic inferences have been criticized (Clermont 1992; Engelbrecht 1992; Warrick 1992b) and, if the migration actually occurred, a founding population of at least 6,250 at A.D. 900 (1,560 at A.D. 540), at a more realistic but still high average growth rate of 0–4 percent per annum (Warrick 1992b), would have been required to attain seventeenth-century population levels.

Linguistic evidence in the form of glottochronology has been used to support a migration of Northern Iroquoians into New York State and Ontario (Fiedel 1991;

1999; Snow 1995a [chap. 1]). The proto-Northern Iroquoian language community was relatively small and divided into separate language groups sometime between A.D. 500 and A.D. 1000 (Fiedel 1991, 25). Snow (1995a, 70 [chap. 1]) claims that proto-Northern Iroquoian could not possibly have been represented by the wide geographical distribution of Middle Woodland peoples in southern Ontario and New York State. In addition, Stuart J. Fiedel (1991; 1999) believes that Middle Woodland sites in southern Ontario were occupied by proto-Algonquian speakers, best represented by Point Peninsula in Ontario. This belief is based on glottochronology, which indicates a separation between Eastern and Central Algonquian languages sometime between 550 B.C. and A.D. 1000 (Fiedel 1999, 198, 199). However, there are problems with the linguistic evidence for an Iroquoian migration. Both Bill (William E.) Engelbrecht (1999, 58) and Bruce Trigger (1985, 82; 1999, 317, 318) caution that language and material culture are separate entities and can diffuse independently and must only be associated in cases of clear demographic/ethnic continuity—that is, there are insufficient data to determine if Point Peninsula Middle Woodland spoke Algonquian or Iroquoian (Trigger 1999, 318).

Anthropological theory about the origins of matrilocal residence patterns has been used by Snow (1995a [chap. 1]; 1996a [chap. 3]) to support his migration hypothesis for Iroquoian origins. Citing William Divale (1984), Snow (1995a, 70, 71 [chap. 1]) argues that matrilocal residence arrived with the Princess Point immigrants and did not develop gradually in response to increased dependency on maize agriculture (cf. Trigger 1978a). Matrilocal residence is seen as a successful adaptive strategy by groups, like migratory Iroquoians, who move into a previously occupied area with the aim to dominate the hostile indigenous groups (Snow 1995a [chap. 1]). The Iroquoian origin of matrilocal residence is very difficult to reconstruct from the archaeological record, but work with ceramics from Princess Point sites (Horvath 1977) and longhouse floor patterns from Early Iroquoian sites (Kapches 1990) suggest that matrilocal residence may have been practiced in Ontario by A.D. 1000—exemplified by the Porteous village site (Stothers 1977)—but not earlier. The appearance of true longhouses after A.D. 1000 in Early Iroquoian villages may signal the onset of matrilocality (Trigger 1985, 89), but some archaeologists feel that Ontario Iroquoian matrilocal residence may not have developed until the thirteenth or early fourteenth century A.D. (Williamson 1990, 318, 319). Both Middle Woodland (Warrick 1996, 14) and Princess Point house floor areas (Smith and Crawford 1997, 21; Pihl and Williamson 1999) fall below the anthropological threshold for matrilocal households (Kapches 1990, 60). Furthermore, discontinuous cranial morphological traits of Rice Lake Middle Woodland burial populations are consistent with a patrilocal residence pattern (Spence et al. 1984, 126) and do not indicate a significantly different physical population from later Iroquoian ones (Molto 1983, 253), implying no population replacement during the Middle Woodland–Early Iroquoian transition and probably a slow development of matrilocal residence.

Most archaeologists feel that there is insufficient evidence for an Iroquoian migration and recommend a cautious interpretation of the linguistic and archaeological evidence (Engelbrecht 1999, 56–58; Ferris and Spence 1995, 105, 106; Trigger 1999, 314–16; Williamson 1992; J. Wright 1992a). In addition to the criticisms of specific arguments mentioned earlier, there are archaeological data that demonstrate continuity from Middle Woodland to Princess Point and Early Iroquoian, supporting the in situ hypothesis. As mentioned previously, skeletal biology (i.e., nonmetric cranial morphology) for Middle Woodland and Iroquoian populations in Ontario supports demographic continuity (Molto 1983, 236–41). Corded and cord-wrapped stick pottery does occur in late Middle Woodland assemblages (Ferris and Spence 1995, 97; Fox 1990a, 186; Spence et al. 1990, 156, 157) and is not exclusively a Princess Point ceramic trait. There is no appreciable difference in house size for Middle Woodland and Princess Point. Middle Woodland houses have dimensions that average 4 meters (m) wide and 6 m long (Warrick 1996, 12); Princess Point houses average 3 m wide and 5 m long (Smith and Crawford 1997; Pihl and Williamson 1999). Lastly, interpretation of the Princess Point settlement-subsistence regime of year-round occupations, based on recent archaeological data from the Grand River and Cootes Paradise (Crawford et al. 1998; Smith and Crawford 1995, 64, 65; 1997), is consistent with models for Middle Woodland settlement-subsistence on the Thames River—that is, year-round macroband villages on the river floodplains (Wilson 1991) and special-purpose microband camps in the interior (Timmins 1989). Throughout Ontario and along the St. Lawrence River, both late Middle Woodland and Princess Point show increased sedentism from earlier Archaic and Early Woodland hunter-gatherers and a strong tethering to major river systems (Chapdelaine 1993). The main difference between Middle Woodland and Princess Point is the adoption of maize agriculture by the latter group.

Princess Point and Maize Agriculture

The earliest evidence of maize in northeastern North America is in association with Princess Point artifacts, A.D. 260–660 (uncalibrated AMS date of 1570 B.P. ± 90 [TO-5307]), from the Grand Banks site, near Cayuga, Ontario (Crawford et al. 1997). Princess Point sites contain evidence of maize and a distinctive assemblage of artifacts and are considered directly ancestral to Early Iroquoian sites in Ontario (Fox 1990a; Smith and Crawford 1995; Stothers 1977; Williamson 1990). Princess Point people occupied select regions of Ontario from approximately A.D. 500 to A.D. 1000 (D. Smith 1997a). The transition to Early Iroquoian, between A.D. 900 and A.D. 1000, is marked by the appearance of upland, semipermanent longhouse villages, such as the Porteous and Holmedale sites, in Brantford, Ontario (Pihl and Williamson 1999; Smith and Crawford 1997, 24). The Princess Point-Early Iroquoian transition appears to have been gradual, marked by a persistence of distinctive Princess Point pottery on upland "Iroquoian" village sites, such as Porteous and Lone Pine (Smith and Crawford 1997, 24). The latest site in the Princess Point sequence is Lone Pine, which has been interpreted as a transitional Princess Point–Early Iroquoian village, with a calibrated date of A.D. 890–1160 (D. Smith 1997a; uncalibrated date of 1040 B.P. ± 60 [TO-4586]).

Princess Point was defined by David Stothers (1977) and originally encompassed sites from the Grand River, Ausable River, and Point Pelee in southwestern Ontario. Subsequent research has determined that Princess Point sites are restricted to the drainages around the western end of Lake Ontario, Grand River, and the north shore of Lake Erie (fig. 7.3) (Crawford and Smith 1996; Smith and Crawford 1997). The Ausable and Point Pelee sites contain slightly different artifact assemblages from Princess Point, are called Riviere au Vase, and are considered part of the Western Basin Tradition, central Algonquians who occupied extreme southwestern Ontario, eastern Michigan, and northwestern Ohio (Murphy and Ferris 1990, 189, 195–99). Cord-wrapped stick pottery, similar to Princess Point, has been found in sites at the eastern end of Lake Ontario, on the Canadian Shield, and along the St. Lawrence River. These eastern Ontario "Princess Point"-like sites have been labeled the Sandbanks Tradition (Daechsel and Wright 1988). The only radiocarbon date from a Sandbanks site, Lakeshore Lodge, on the shore of Lake Ontario in Prince Edward County, has been calibrated by Smith (1997a) to A.D. 790–1030

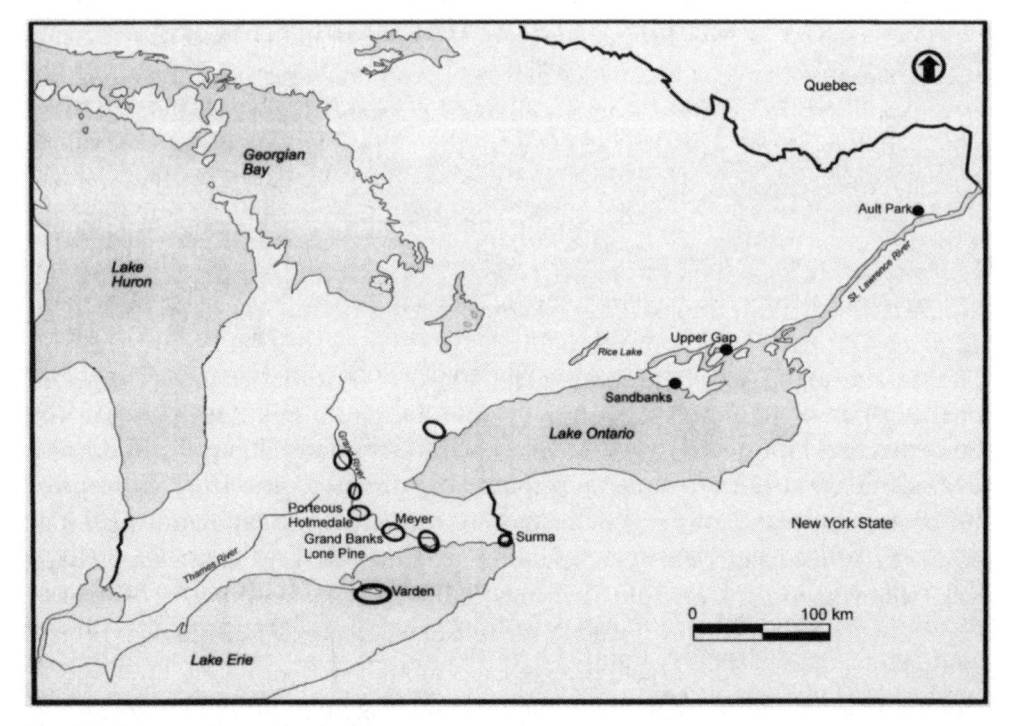

Fig. 7.3. Princess Point site clusters.

(uncalibrated date of 1110 B.P. ± 70 [S-2194]). Sandbanks pottery has surfaced from several sites, such as Upper Gap (Carl Murphy, personal communication, 1998), Ault Park, South Lake, Blogget Point, Foster, Plainfield Rapids, Red Horse Lake Portage, and Jackson's Point (Daechsel and Wright 1988; Fox 1990a) (fig. 7.3). It is quite possible that these sites were occupied by Algonquian speakers, particularly those sites on the Canadian Shield north of the St. Lawrence River (Fox 1990a, 183–85). Interpretation of Iroquoian-type ceramics on later sites in this region have been interpreted as Algonquian sites (von Gernet 1993). For the purposes of this paper, Sandbanks is too ill-defined archaeologically to be considered ancestral Iroquoian and will not be dealt with further in this paper.

The focus of Princess Point occupation was the Lower Grand River valley, a 50-kilometer (km) distance from Brantford to Lake Erie. Approximately 40 of the 80 documented Princess Point sites in Ontario are situated on the Lower Grand River, either on extensive floodplain flats or adjacent terraces (Crawford et al. 1998, 125; 1999; Smith and Crawford 1997, 13). The Lower Grand River valley is characterized by a gentle slope, sinuous to straight channel, clay loam soils, and upland areas occupied by Carolinian forests and fauna (Crawford et al. 1998, 126). Recent geoarchaeological research has determined that the floodplains of the Lower Grand River that were inhabited by Princess Point people were relatively stable and were not inundated by spring floods between A.D. 500 and 1000, spanning the entire Princess Point time period (Crawford et al. 1998, 129–32). Thus it was possible for Princess Point sites to have been occupied year-round. Both the floodplain and terrace sites are extensive, covering several hectares (Crawford et al. 1999). At the Grand Bank site, for example, Princess Point artifacts and deposits extend for 1,000 m along the river's edge (Smith and Crawford 1997, 15). Gary Crawford and David Smith have been investigating Princess Point sites since 1993 (Crawford et al. 1998; 1999; Smith and Crawford 1995; Smith and Crawford 1997). Deep "telephone-booth" excavations of floodplain sites, like Grand Banks and Cayuga Bridge, have revealed stratigraphy and have encountered buried, sealed deposits containing artifacts and maize remains (Crawford et al. 1998; Smith and Crawford 1997). Terrace sites have received more extensive excavation designed to recover household and community pattern data. Areal excavations of the Meyer site from 1997 to 1999, conducted by both research teams and field schools from the University of Toronto at Mississauga, have uncovered a complicated palimpsest pattern of pit features and post molds and thousands of artifacts per square meter, all indicating long-term or more likely successive occupation of certain preferred locations, perhaps over several centuries (Crawford et al. 1999; Smith and Crawford 1997, 24). In addition to the site clusters on the Grand River, two other clusters of Princess Point sites with lacustrine orientation have received recent archaeological attention: Cootes Paradise at the western end of Lake Ontario and Long Point on Lake Erie. A number of Princess Point special-purpose sites ring the shallow waters of Cootes Paradise and appear to have been occupied during the spring-fall by small family groups (D. Smith 1997b). Sites on Long Point, such as the Varden site, were used as spring-fall fishing stations by Princess Point people (J. MacDonald 1986).

Princess Point artifact assemblages characteristically contain pottery vessel fragments with cord-malleated body surfaces and bands of cord-wrapped stick decoration and exterior punctuates on the neck and rim sections, undecorated clay pipes, abundant Onondaga chert debitage and simple flake tools, and triangular Levanna points on Onondaga chert (Smith and Crawford 1997, 24, 25).

The size and distribution of Princess Point sites along the Grand River can be used to estimate population numbers. With reference to figure 7.3, there are five major clusters of Princess Point sites on the Grand River: Dunnville, Cayuga-Caledonia, Middleport, Brantford, and Waterloo. Not much is known about sites in the Dunnville or Waterloo clusters, but the sites appear to be less extensive than those in the Brantford-Cayuga stretch of river (Smith and Crawford 1997). Data do not exist at present to isolate individual village plans in the large floodplain/terrace sites but these sites can occupy 3.0–10.0 hectares (ha) (Crawford et al. 1999; Smith and Crawford 1997). Late Princess Point "villages," such as Porteous, Holmedale, and Lone Pine, are defined by artifact scatters less than 0.5 ha in size (Smith and Crawford 1997; Pihl et al. 1998; Pihl and Williamson 1999). For excavated sites, "settled" areas containing house structures occupy less than 0.3 ha (e.g., Porteous occupies only 0.1 ha [Stothers 1977, 126] and the Holmedale core village occupies 0.3 ha [Pihl et al. 1998]). Princess Point house structures are generally poorly preserved, but examples from Bull's Point (D. Smith 1997b), Forster (Bursey and Smith 1999), Porteous (Stothers 1977), and Holmedale (Pihl et al. 1998; Pihl and Williamson 1999) indicate both incipient longhouses and circular or square houses, averaging 3–4 m wide and 5–6 m long and containing only one or two hearths. Community patterns (e.g., Holmedale) show overlapped houses and a maximum of five contemporaneous house structures, encircled by a "fence" or rudimentary palisade (fig. 7.4). Assuming 10–20 people per house, the population of an average Princess Point village would have been about 75 people. Judging from artifact density and overlapped structures, Princess Point villages appear to have had lengthy occupations, perhaps 40–50 years like Early Iroquoian villages (Timmins 1997a; 1997b; Warrick 1990, 292). Using the 3.0 ha Meyer site as a test case, Crawford et al. (1999) proposed that the incredibly high density of artifacts and features at Meyer indicates that it was occupied by Princess Point people for at least 300 years. Thus it could have witnessed at least six sequential Princess Point village occupations before its abandonment, perhaps never housing more than 100 people at one time. The largest Princess Point sites, such as Grand Banks and Cayuga Bridge, each may have been occupied simultaneously by two communities, for a total population of 200 people. In summary, the 40 Princess Point sites of the Lower Grand River valley may have housed a maximum of 3,000–4,000 people, assuming that all sites were

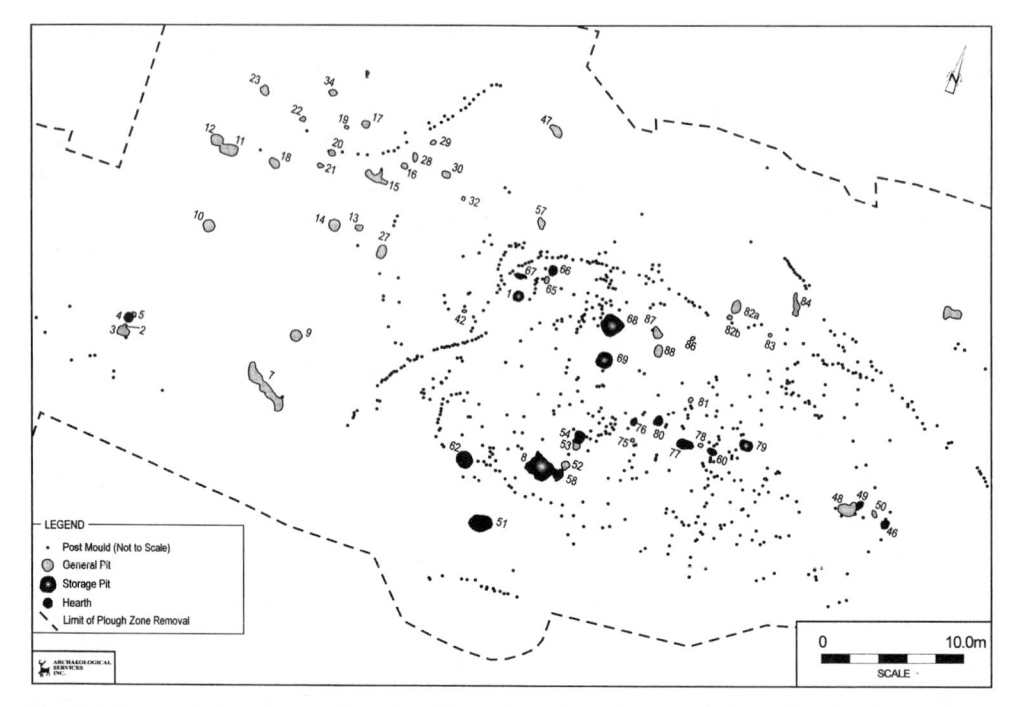

Fig. 7.4. Holmedale site plan, Brantford (courtesy of Archaeological Services Inc.).

contemporaneous and that each site held an individual community of 75–100 people. More realistically, it is likely that only 20 of the 40 sites were occupied contemporaneously, suggesting a maximum population of 2,000 at ca. A.D. 900 in the Lower Grand River valley (calculated by assuming only five sites each for the four Lower Grand River site clusters and a macroband population per a cluster of 450–500 people).

Princess Point settlement-subsistence appears to have been based on year-round village occupation and experimentation with maize agriculture on the floodplains and terraces of the Grand River, with warm-season forays inland (hunting, nut harvesting) and to lakeshores (fishing, wild rice harvesting, chert procurement) (Fox 1990a; Crawford and Smith 1996; Crawford et al. 1997; 1998; Smith and Crawford 1997).

Princess Point appears to have pioneered the adoption of maize *(Zea mays)* agriculture in northeastern North America. (The term *agriculture* is used here instead of *horticulture* because, in agreement with Bennett Bronson [1975, 55, 56], differentiating between agriculture and horticulture is ethnocentric and arbitrary.) As mentioned earlier, the first directly dated evidence of maize in the Northeast is from the Grand Banks site from a sixth-century A.D. Princess Point context. Carbonized maize remains have been found in all excavated Princess Point sites and are identified as Eastern Eight-Row variety (Crawford et al. 1997, 117). Based on

AMS-dated maize remains from other contexts in Illinois, Ohio, and Tennessee, maize entered Ontario from the south and west where it appears at least two centuries earlier (Crawford et al. 1997). As previously discussed, it is uncertain whether maize agriculture diffused to in situ Middle Woodland populations in southern Ontario or was carried to Ontario by migrating Princess Point people. Human behavior and history are complex and, judging from the discovery of maize from an A.D. 550–760 (Crawford et al. 1997, 114—uncalibrated date of 1405 B.P. ±60 [S-2207]) Middle Woodland occupation on Rice Lake, south of Peteborough (Jackson 1983), maize probably entered Ontario by both diffusion and migration. The only other cultigen recovered from a Princess Point site is tobacco, from the Holmedale site (Pihl and Williamson 1999). No beans or squash have been found in a Princess Point context, but this absence is not surprising considering that there is no directly dated archaeological evidence of beans in the Northeast before A.D. 1300 (Hart and Scarry 1999).

The actual cultivation of maize by Princess Point people evolved gradually over time, beginning with floodplain agriculture. Eight-Row Eastern maize *(Zea mays indurata)* has certain advantages as a food over wild rice, one of the carbohydrate mainstays of the Middle Woodland diet (Spence and Pihl 1984; Spence et al. 1984; 1990; Ferris and Spence 1995). Although wild rice is a more nutritious form of carbohydrate compared to maize (C. Adams 1975), wild rice is very sensitive to fluctuations in water levels and requires considerable time and effort to harvest and process (Aiken et al. 1988). Unlike wild rice, maize can be buffered from unexpected crashes in productivity, it is easily and efficiently harvested because it can be grown immediately adjacent to settlements, and it can be stored in a dried, shelled state for up to 2 years (Fecteau 1985, 20–22). Assuming that the productivity of early maize agriculture in Ontario was probably considerably less than 10 bushels/acre or 627.2 kilograms/ha and that maize comprised only 10 percent of the annual Princess Point diet, a Princess Point village of 75 people would have required only 3 ha of garden space (Schroeder 1999). Field clearance by Princess Point agriculturalists on floodplains of the Grand River is indicated by palaeoenvironmental data, suggesting that settlements and gardens were in close proximity (Crawford et al. 1998).

Stable carbon and nitrogen isotope studies of human skeletal remains demonstrate that Princess Point populations, represented by the Surma site burials in Fort Erie and Varden burials at Long Point (fig. 7.3), incorporated maize in their diet but at levels well below Early Iroquoian populations—that is, less than 20 percent of the diet (Katzenberg et al. 1995, 341–45; Schwarcz et al. 1985). Nitrogen isotope values for the Varden site skeletal population indicate a heavy reliance on terrestrial game (e.g., deer and beaver) (Katzenberg et al. 1995, 347).

What prompted Princess Point communities to adopt maize agriculture? As mentioned earlier, new interpretations of Middle Woodland sedentism have emerged, particularly in association with riverine floodplain environments (Ferris and Spence 1995; Wilson 1991). For the Lower Grand River, Middle Woodland occupation was most intense in the Dunnville area, where thick stands of wild rice were observed as recently as 1936 (Pringle 1936). Ignoring for the moment the possibility of a Princess Point migration, it is conceivable that, like the Thames River, Middle Woodland bands occupied portions of the Lower Grand River in year-round settlements. Middle Woodland sedentism and the desire to both ensure the long-term maintenance of winter communities and at the same time eliminate the spectre of occasional winter starvation episodes (as a result of the coincidence between periodic crashes in two or more critical wild foods, such as deer and wild rice) (Warrick 1990, 331–36) would have provided an ideal context for the adoption of a predictable, storable, famine-preventative food—maize. Similar explanations have been offered for the adoption of maize agriculture by Middle Woodland people living on the St. Lawrence River (Chapdelaine 1993; Clermont 1990). It is important to note here that maize agriculture seems to have been adopted by southern Ontario Natives ca. A.D. 500, in the absence of appreciable population growth and population pressure. While it is recognized that there is good relative evidence for an increase in population from Early to Middle Woodland times and increased "packing" of territorial bands (Spence et al. 1990, 161, 168), it is not until Early Iroquoian times, ca. A.D. 1000–1300, that there is definite evidence of a significant increase in population that would have stressed local deer populations (Warrick 1990). In short, maize agriculture in Ontario appears to have been a cause and not a consequence of population growth.

Princess Point subsistence can be considered a Middle Woodland pattern with the simple addition of maize. Preservation of animal bone is poor on the Lower Grand River sites, but fish seems to have been a significant dietary staple (Smith and Crawford 1997, 25). Archaeobotanical analysis of flotation samples from the Grand Banks site has yielded maize and other edible plants, including acorn, butternut, bramble, chenopod, ground cherry, strawberry, and sumac (Crawford et al. 1997, 116). The Holmedale site, excavated in 1996 by Archaeological Services Inc. (Pihl et al. 1998; Pihl and Williamson 1999), produced an exceptional array of plant and animal remains enabling a detailed study of late Princess Point subsistence. In addition to the ubiquitous maize remains, remains of collected nuts, bramble, strawberry, and chenopod were identified. Zooarchaeological identification revealed a wide array of species, fish being the most abundant (including sunfish, sucker, perch, bullhead, lake trout, whitefish, and eel). Deer, passenger pigeon, and grouse were well represented (as well as beaver, muskrat, raccoon, bear, grey squirrel, and various bird species) (Pihl and Williamson 1999, 8). Evidence for a heavy reliance on fishing, deer hunting, and edible plant collecting at Holmedale provides a strong link from earlier Middle Woodland to later Iroquoian subsistence patterns—maize agriculture being the only difference.

Sociopolitical organization of Princess Point communities is difficult to reconstruct. Contrary to Snow's (1996a [chap. 3]) arguments for matrilocality's being a core feature of Princess Point life, house floor areas (Kapches 1990) and inferred house populations seem too small to require or support a matrilocal residence system, and heterogeneity in pottery decoration within Princess Point villages, for example Porteous, does not indicate a core of related women, assuming women were the potters (Warrick 1996, 15). It has been argued (Trigger 1985, 88, 89; Warrick 1996, 15; Williamson 1990, 317) that matrilocal residence emerged in Early Iroquoian times in response to an increased reliance on maize agriculture, burgeoning population, increased need for child care, and increased house and village size. It is quite conceivable that Princess Point villages were essentially the vestiges of patrilocal/patrilineal Middle Woodland bands.

Early Iroquoians and Village Life

There is little doubt that Princess Point is ancestral to Early Iroquoian in southwestern Ontario. The coincidence and overlap of Princess Point and later Iroquoian village sites in the Lower Grand River valley is remarkable (Crawford and Smith 1996, 787), demonstrating cultural and demographic continuity and an identical land-use pattern. In south-central and southeastern Ontario, there is no demonstrable continuity between late Middle Woodland and Early Iroquoian occupations (Warrick 1990), contrary to earlier claims (Kapches 1987; 1990). The earliest village sites that are transitional between Princess Point and Early Iroquoian periods are Porteous and Lone Pine, both dating to the late tenth-early eleventh century (D. Smith 1997a; 1997b; 1997c; Smith and Crawford 1997).

An Early Iroquoian site typically dates ca. A.D. 1000–1300, covers about an acre or 0.4 ha (Pearce and Warrick 1999; Warrick 1990), has an upland location away from a major river or lake, contains four or five short (10–15 m long) longhouses (with interior central hearths and large pit features for storage and refuse) surrounded by a single- or double-row palisade, and produces a large number of pottery vessel sherds (rims decorated with bands of linear-impressed obliques), clay pipe fragments, chipped and ground stone lithics, and antler and bone tools and ornaments (Timmins 1997a; Williamson 1990).

Early Iroquoian village sites occur across southern Ontario, from the eastern end of Lake Ontario to Lake Huron (fig. 7.5) and are usually found in tight clusters on the sand plains north of Lake Erie and Lake Ontario. Site clusters are separated by 20 or 30 km of unoccupied land (Williamson 1990). Within each cluster, sites are often within 300–1000 m of one another (Pearce and Warrick 1999). Early Iroquoian sites in southwestern (i.e., west of Lake Ontario) and south-central Ontario are known respectively as Glen Meyer and Pickering sites, as defined by Jim Wright's landmark Ph.D. dissertation (J. Wright 1966). In addition to their geographical sep-

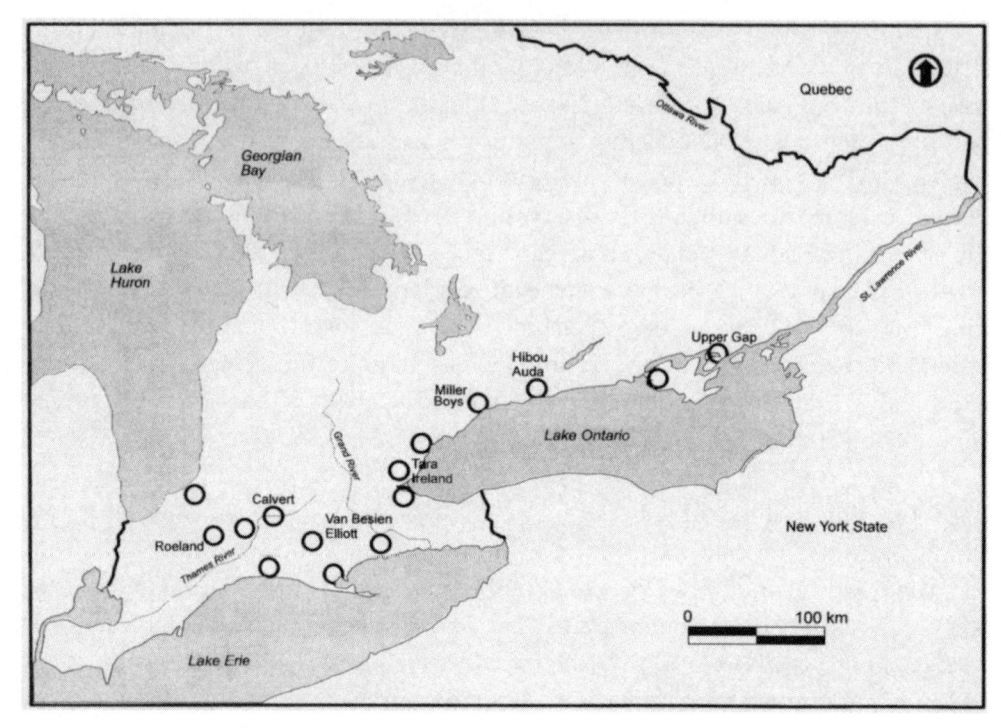

Fig. 7.5. Early Iroquoian site clusters.

aration, Wright (1966; 1992b) differentiates sites in the two regions on the basis of burial habits, house form, attributes of pottery decoration, and presence/absence of other artifact classes, such as deer toe cup-and-pin pieces. The last 30 years of archaeological research have resulted in either the elimination or blending of these earlier distinctions and recognition of clinal changes and ceramic differences between adjacent Early Iroquoian site clusters within one region, not just ceramic differences between regions (Ferris and Spence 1995; Williamson 1990; Williamson and Robertson 1994; Spence 1994; Timmins 1997a). No further distinction will be made between Glen Meyer and Pickering in this paper.

There are approximately 15 clusters of Early Iroquoian sites in southern Ontario. Each cluster contains one or two distinct villages. Village sites average 0.4 ha in size (completely excavated village plans, however, are often less than 0.3 ha) (Pearce and Warrick 1999; Timmins 1997a, 215–18; Warrick 1990, 337; Williamson 1990), were palisaded (usually only single row), and often exhibit overlapped longhouses (e.g., Miller site [W. Kenyon 1968] and Ireland site [fig. 7.6] [Warrick 1992a]) or entirely superimposed village plans (e.g., Elliott site [Fox 1986], Tara site [Warrick 1992a]). Despite earlier interpretations that overlapped houses suggested disorganization in Early Iroquoian community planning (Warrick 1984), recent analysis of the Calvert site, a thirteenth-century village just east of London, revealed three well-organized community plans with a total occupation span of 50

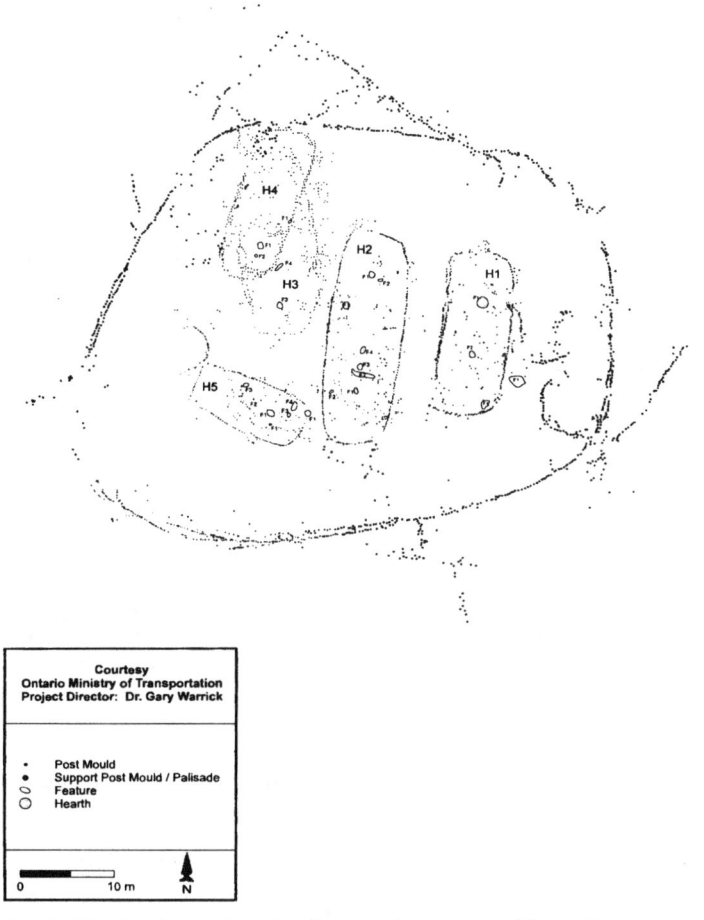

Fig. 7.6. Ireland site plan, Burlington (courtesy of Ontario Ministry of Transportation and reproduced with permission from Museum of Ontario Archaeology).

years (Timmins 1997a). Early Iroquoian longhouses average 12.4 m long (Dodd et al. 1990, 349) and contained two or three central hearths. Large storage pits inside and outside houses are a prominent feature of Early Iroquoian villages, suggesting that underground storage of maize and other foodstuffs was important (Timmins 1997a, 165). Similar longhouse and village patterns exist in Owasco sites in New York State, dating between A.D. 950 and 1350 (Snow 1996b, 27).

Population growth is demonstrated throughout the Early Iroquoian period. Based on estimates of total site area and hearth density per ha of site area, in south-central Ontario, population grew steadily from approximately 2,000 to 8,000 persons (assuming demographic continuity with Middle Woodland populations) between A.D. 900 and A.D. 1300 (Warrick 1990). This represents a mean annual growth rate of 0.35 percent and a doubling time of 200 years. This is an overall rate, however; from A.D. 900 to A.D. 1125, population increased at a slower pace of 0.18 percent per annum. Population growth occurred between A.D. 1125 and A.D. 1300 at a rapid rate of 0.55 percent per annum (Warrick 1990, 342, 343). (However, if the recent proposal of an Early Iroquoian colonization of south-central Ontario ca. A.D. 1100–1150 [Pearce and Warrick 1999] is correct, then population growth would have been very rapid in both southwestern and south-central Ontario, essentially 0.35 percent per annum between A.D. 900 and A.D. 1125.) Reasons for the observed increases could be improved maternal health, closer birth spacing, and fewer winter famine deaths (Warrick 1990, 345, 346).

Early Iroquoian subsistence was based on hunting, fishing, and gathering, supplemented heavily by maize agriculture. Stable carbon isotope analysis of human remains indicates that maize consumption was significant, perhaps 20 percent to 30 percent of the diet (Schwarcz et al. 1985; Katzenberg et al. 1995). Maize, beans, squash, and sunflower were all recovered from the ca. A.D. 1200–1280 Calvert village (Timmins 1997a, 100; 1997b, 5). Nevertheless, hunting, fishing, and gathering contributed the majority of the diet, with a particular reliance on deer (in excess of 80 percent of identifiable animal bone at Calvert [e.g., Timmins 1997a, 94]). Careful village siting and special-purpose camps and hamlets of one or two houses both were used to maximize access to a diversity of food and other important resources and were essential elements of Early Iroquoian subsistence and ecology (Pearce and Warrick 1999; Timmins 1997a, 37–59; Williamson 1990). In fact, if it were not for pest infestation, physical deterioration of the houses and palisades, and overall pollution of the village, Early Iroquoian villages could have been occupied indefinitely (Fecteau et al. 1994). Most village relocations were within one kilometer of the old village, but occasionally Early Iroquoian villages migrated tens of kilometers to colonize new areas (Pearce and Warrick 1999).

Recent recalibration of Early Iroquoian radiocarbon dates (D. Smith 1997a) has revealed an interesting pattern: most dates calibrate to the twelfth or thirteenth century. For those sites with more than one date, the characteristic pattern is a spread of thirteenth-century dates and an eleventh-century date or earlier (e.g., Boys, Elliott, Force, Grafton, Richardson: all have calibrated dates in the thirteenth century, in coherence with ceramic seriation dates [Warrick 1990, 176–80], but they also have one or more anomalous dates in the ninth-century to eleventh-century range). In addition, there are some sites, such as Auda, that have only one date calibrated to the late tenth century but whose ceramic assemblage seriates close to an acceptable thirteenth-century site—Hibou, both in the Port Hope cluster and separated by 500 m (an acceptable relocation distance) (MacDonald and Williamson 1995). The anomalous "early" radiocarbon dates for all these sites could be explained by the "old wood" problem—that is, Early Iroquoians were gathering firewood from 200- to 300-year-old trees. If this explanation is correct, then the implication is that most Early Iroquoian site clusters were established sometime between A.D. 1100 and

1150. In agreement with Peter A. Timmins (1997a, 218, 219), it would appear that Early Iroquoians migrated to their respective homelands (i.e., site clusters) from the Grand River valley (and perhaps New York State [MacDonald and Williamson 1995]) because there is no evidence in any of the site clusters for ancestral Middle Woodland or Princess Point sites (Pearce and Warrick 1999). In summary, archaeological data support an Early Iroquoian colonization and clearance of southern Ontario's primeval hardwood forest ca. A.D. 1100–1150. Spacing between Early Iroquoian site clusters (often 25–30 km) matches the required buffer zone for deer hunting, given Early Iroquoian population, deer herd density, 50 percent cull rate, and a requirement of 3.6 deer hides per person (Gramly 1977; Pearce and Warrick 1999). Population growth and resulting village fission presumably were the main causes of Early Iroquoian migration and colonization, much like they were in Middle Iroquoian times (Niemczycki 1984, 99; Sutton 1996; Warrick 1990, 348–61).

Based on site size and hearth counts, Early Iroquoian communities comprised approximately 75–200 people (Pearce and Warrick 1999; Timmins 1997a, 199), suggesting that they were reminiscent of the late Middle Woodland and Princess Point year-round aggregations of territorial bands of 50–150 people (Ferris 1989; Trigger 1976, 134; 1985, 86). As already mentioned, Princess Point communities were probably not matrilocal and may not have had any formal village government. In contrast, it is felt that Early Iroquoian communities were autonomous, highly organized, and perhaps governed by a village council of matrilineages, with each matrilineage contained within a longhouse (Timmins 1997a). Timmins (1997a, 227, 228) proposes that two or more Early Iroquoian communities, represented as a site cluster, may have shared a deer hunting territory that "may have been tenaciously protected against incursions from outsiders" (Timmins 1997a, 227). Exchange of marriage partners and other familial interaction would have been most pronounced between villages within each cluster and with villages from neighboring clusters (MacDonald and Williamson 1995; Williamson and Robertson 1994; Timmins 1997a).

Uren and Village Amalgamation

Early Iroquoian material culture underwent rapid transformation between A.D. 1300 and A.D. 1330, the Uren phase of Ontario Iroquoian precontact history (Dodd et al. 1990; J. Wright 1966, 54–59; M. Wright 1986). In particular, pottery decorated with rows of horizontal lines became universal among Iroquoian groups in southern Ontario (Dodd et al. 1990; Wright 1966, 57) and the average size of both houses and villages increased dramatically (Dodd et al. 1990). Data on Uren village sites (e.g., Bennett [Wright and Anderson 1969], Gunby [Rozel 1979], and Uren [M. Wright 1986]) indicate a mean longhouse length of 28 m (range of 6–45 m) (Dodd et al. 1990, 349). Uren villages covered 1.0 ha and display little evidence for refuse deposition in middens, unlike later Middleport villages (Dodd et al. 1990, 343; Warrick 1990, 347). In less than half a century, late Early Iroquoian settlements and houses doubled in size (the late thirteenth-century Roeland village, an Early Iroquoian site in the Caradoc cluster west of London, covers 1.5 ha and shows evidence that it expanded from an original size of 0.6 ha [Williamson 1985, 177], suggesting that village amalgamation was underway in late Early Iroquoian times). In south-central Ontario, by A.D. 1330, the Uren population numbered almost 11,000 people, representing an increase of 0.80 percent per year from A.D. 1250 totals (Warrick 1990). Population growth alone, however, does not account for the doubling of settlement and house size. Instead, the archaeological reconstruction of regional site sequences in southwestern Ontario suggests that increased house and village size during the Uren period occurred primarily as a result of the accretion of two or more smaller villages (Pearce 1996; Timmins 1997a, 215–29; Williamson 1990), supplemented by the addition of new family units owing to natural increase.

Archaeological plans of Uren villages reveal a transformation in sociopolitical organization. Unlike Early Iroquoian sites, which often display several longhouses overlapped by other houses and palisade lines, and sometimes the superimposition of entire village occupations (e.g., Calvert [Timmins 1997a] and Elliott [Fox 1986]), Uren village sites are single-component, appear to have shorter occupation spans than Early Iroquoian sites (20–30 years as opposed to 50 years or more [Warrick 1990, 292]), and contain a number of nonoverlapping longhouses of highly variable length arranged in two or more clusters with parallel alignment, exemplified by the Uren site (fig. 7.7) (e.g., M. Wright 1986). The relatively large size and aligned longhouses of early fourteenth-century Iroquoian villages have been interpreted as the crystallization of formal matrilineages and the beginnings of clan organization in both Ontario (Pearce 1996; Trigger 1985, 92–94; Warrick 1984, 66; M. Wright 1986, 63) and New York State (Engelbrecht 1985, 16; Niemczycki 1984, 85–89).

Community size during the Uren phase would have averaged 400–500 people and begun to strain the sociopolitical mechanisms that govern egalitarian communities below a normative size of 350–450 people (Forge 1972, 370–75). Village fission, a common occurrence among tribal societies experiencing growth, now appears to have been the safety valve used by the precontact Ontario Iroquoians to relieve the pressure of oversized communities, beginning about A.D. 1300 in south-central Ontario. Because of geographical constraints imposed by Lake Ontario and the poor agricultural soils of the Oak Ridges Moraine (Chapman and Putnam 1984; see fig. 7.1 for location), sociopolitical constraints imposed by the hunting territories of neighboring Iroquoian groups to the east and west, and ecological constraints imposed by deer densities (assuming deer hides were the primary source of winter clothing [Gramly 1977]), newly created Uren communities were forced to hop over the Oak Ridges Moraine and to colonize climax forest in the sandy up-

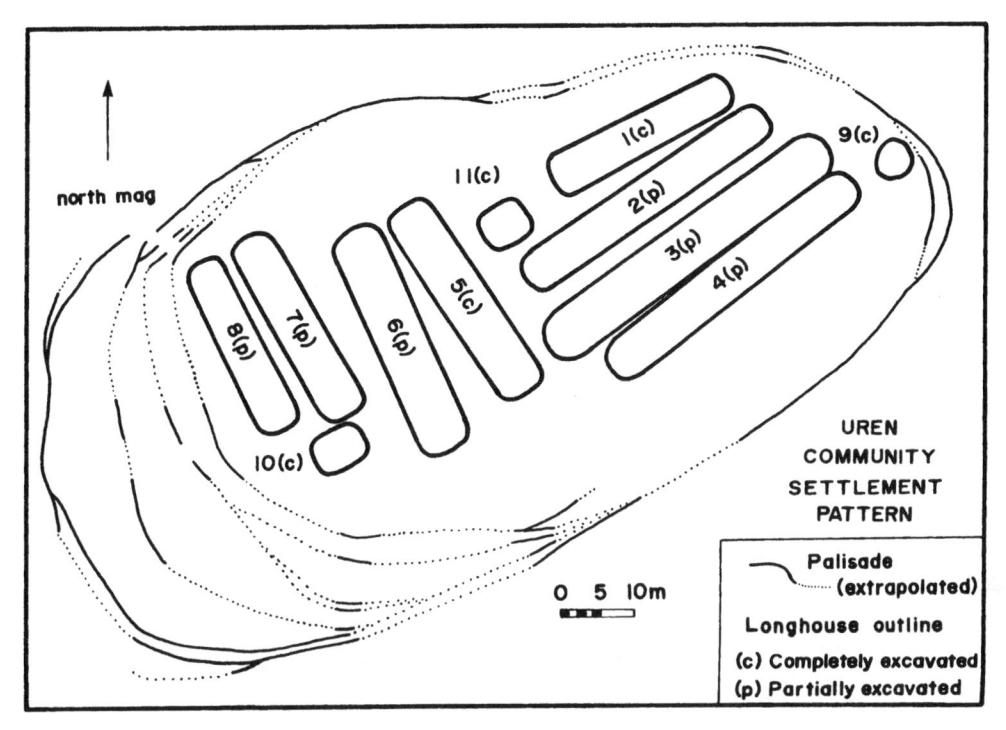

Fig. 7.7. Uren site plan, Norwich (reproduced with permission from Ontario Archaeological Society).

lands of southern Simcoe County (Warrick and Molnar 1986). It has been estimated that there were enough deer for only 3,300–6,300 people dependent on the herds for clothing (Warrick 1990, 350), assuming a 50 percent cull rate and a demand for 3.6 hides/person (Gramly 1977). Sometime between A.D. 1250 and A.D. 1300, the Uren population of south-central Ontario exceeded this critical threshold (access to deer herds does not appear to have been an issue in southwestern Ontario in Uren times). Deer comprised only 10 percent of all identified animal bone in Uren sites east of Toronto (Kapches 1981), indicating that deer were becoming locally scarce in the Toronto region by the early fourteenth century. Local extirpation of deer herds would have exacerbated this situation, forcing certain communities to hunt for deer at great distance from their settlements or to relocate farther north. The Wilcox Lake site, an early fourteenth-century 1.2-ha village that was partially excavated between 1988 and 1990, is located on the southern edge of the Oak Ridges Moraine and is probably one of the Uren communities that was moving north to Simcoe County (Austin 1994). Only after A.D. 1300, however, did Uren-phase communities relocate beyond the Oak Ridges Moraine. Over a century of archaeological research has failed to discover any *village* site in Simcoe County dating earlier than A.D. 1275. In fact, the Barrie site, a 1.0-ha village situated at the terminus of Kempenfelt Bay, is the only documented Uren-phase village north of the Oak Ridges Moraine (Sutton

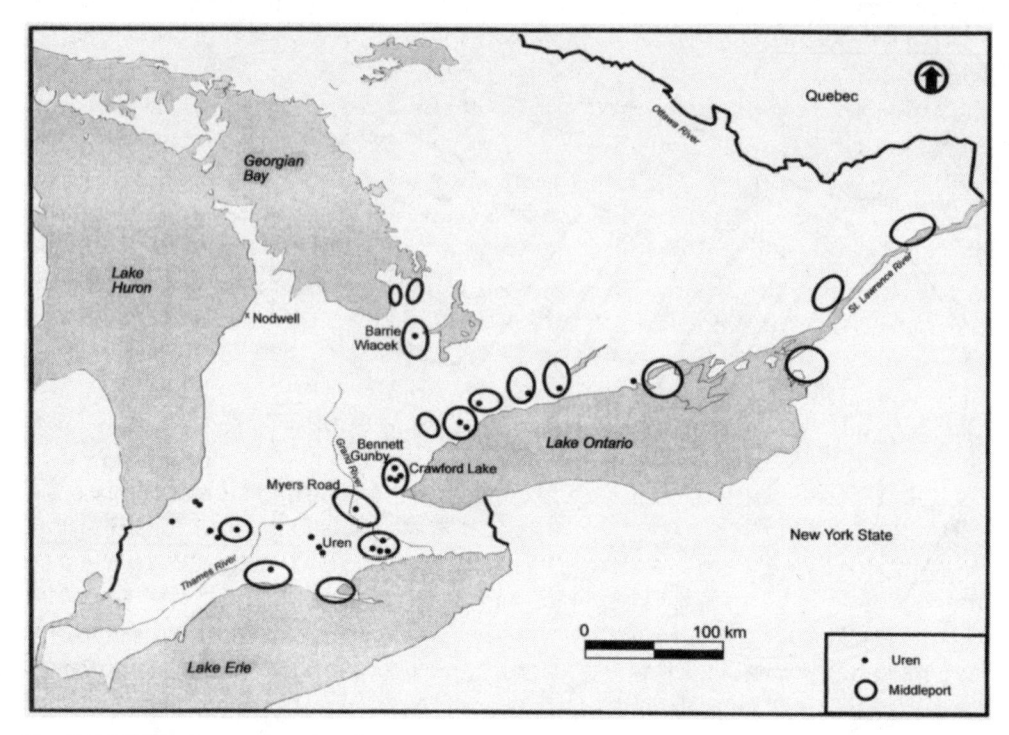

Fig. 7.8. Middle Iroquoian site clusters.

1996) (fig. 7.8). Thus the historic heartland of the Huron-Petun, Simcoe County, was not permanently settled by Iroquoians until the early fourteenth century, 800 years after the initial adoption of maize agriculture.

The long-distance movement of Uren villages (Sutton 1996), trade in Onondaga chert (Dodd et al. 1990, 357), village amalgamation (Pearce 1996), and the emergence of segmented matrilineage villages practicing village exogamy and a heightened degree of interregional interaction (MacDonald and Williamson 1995; Warrick 1984; 1996; Williamson and Robertson 1994) operated in concert to produce a relatively homogeneous Iroquoian culture in southern Ontario in the early fourteenth century. This interpretation is at odds with the "Pickering Conquest" hypothesis formulated by Jim Wright (1966; 1992a; 1992b; Wright and Anderson 1969) and tenaciously supported by Bill Finlayson (1998). In an attempt to explain the apparent sudden appearance of a homogeneous Iroquoian culture ca. A.D. 1300, Wright (1966) focused on certain traits, mostly pottery decoration, to infer a bloody conquest of the southwestern Early Iroquoians (Glen Meyer) by the southeastern groups (Pickering), the aftermath captured in the material culture of the Bennett site, north of Hamilton (Wright and Anderson 1969). Evidence is mounting that, rather than the result of a conquest of Glen Meyer by Pickering peoples (Wright and Anderson 1969), the Uren phase transition appears to have occurred peacefully (Pearce 1996; M. Wright 1986). There is no convincing archaeological evidence of village destruction and vast military alliances of Early Iroquoian communities. Second, Early Iroquoian burial practices vary widely within and between individual site clusters, ranging from individual primary interments to small ossuaries (Spence 1994). The universal adoption of pottery decorated with horizontal lines appears to have begun in late Early Iroquoian times, perhaps as a result of innovations by young potters (Kapches 1995; Timmins 1997b). The late thirteenth-century occupations of the Calvert site exhibit a clear difference in horizontal decorative motifs between juvenile and adult pottery—24 percent of juvenile pots are decorated with horizontal lines, whereas only 4.5 percent of adult pots display horizontal decoration (Timmins 1997b, 6). The rapid adoption of horizontal motif pottery is indicated by the abundance of horizontals (73 percent of all pottery vessels) at the nearby and later Dorchester site—a Uren village thought to be an amalgamation community of several Early Iroquoian sites, including the Calvert village (Keron 2000). An in situ development of Uren horizontal motif pottery and village growth by peaceful amalgamation is best exemplified by the Calvert and Dorchester sites and suggests that the Uren transition may have happened first in southwestern Ontario (i.e., Glen Meyer territory) and spread east (Dodd et al. 1990; Keron 2000; Timmins 1985; 1997a), seriously questioning the validity of a "Pickering Conquest."

Alternative explanations for the emergence of Uren culture cite Mississippi influences, through direct or indirect exchange of exotic trade items and ideology (Dincauze and Hasenstab 1989; S. Jamieson 1991; 1992; 1999). However, archaeological data for Early Iroquoian-Middle Iroquoian times in Ontario indicate little participation in long-distance exchange of exotics or Mississippian influence (Ferris and Spence 1995, 110, 111; Timmins 1997a; 1997b, 208–10; Williamson and Robertson 1994).

Uren was a period of rapid culture change, marked by population growth, village amalgamation, the appearance of large longhouses containing semisubterranean sweat lodges (MacDonald 1988), ossuary burial (e.g., Tabor Hill ossuary in the Toronto region containing the remains of over 500 individuals [Warrick 1990, 352]), and the ubiquity of horizontal decorations on pottery. It has been argued (Kapches 1995; Warrick 1984; 1996) that all of these features, but primarily sweat lodges and ossuaries, functioned to integrate socially diverse longhouses and villages, with the formalization of matriliny and matrilocality. Sweat lodges appear in Uren houses and exhibit standard characteristics: 2–3 meters square in plan dimension, relatively shallow pit profile, fire-cracked rock content, a projection at one end and post molds encircling the base of the lodge pit (MacDonald 1988; C. Ramsden et al. 1998). Their occurrence in most longhouses within a village argues that they were used by the unrelated male residents of an individual longhouse (Ferris and Spence 1995, 113; Kapches 1995). Ossuary burials contain the disarticulated remains of hundreds of people, interpreted as the accumulated dead of a single village occupation that were buried together in a ceremony similar to the "Feast of the

Dead" witnessed in 1636 by Jesuit missionary Jean de Brebeuf outside the Huron village of Ossosane (Thwaites 1896–1901, 10:279–303). Communal sweatbathing and ossuary burial bound together respectively the unrelated males of longhouses and the fictive kin of distinct Early Iroquoian villages in the recently amalgamated Uren communities of the early fourteenth century.

Despite sweatbaths and ossuaries, Uren communities were highly dynamic and sociopolitically volatile. The dynamics of village life during Uren times is best illustrated by the Myers Road site, excavated in 1987–88 to make way for a housing subdivision in Cambridge, Ontario. The entire village plan was exposed, revealing a complex occupational history, suggesting successive occupation from A.D. 1280 to A.D. 1340. Not all longhouses were contemporaneous at Myers Road and some had actually been abandoned for years before others were even constructed (Williamson and Ramsden 1998). Similar occupational complexity has been observed at large precontact Huron sites such as Draper, Coulter, and Benson (Fogt and Ramsden 1996). The coming and going of village members is a hallmark of precontact Iroquoian life that has its beginnings in Uren times. It was during Uren times that village membership was no longer entirely dependent on direct lineal relationship—the beginnings of fictive kin-based clan barrios or neighborhoods may be reflected in groups of longhouses with different orientations, evident at the Uren-type site (M. Wright 1986).

Middleport and Population Growth

The Middleport people occupied almost every habitable niche of southern Ontario, except for extreme southwestern Ontario and areas east of Lake Simcoe and the historic Petun region (fig. 7.8). Only 53 percent of Middleport village sites are situated on sandy loam soils; the remainder occupy heavier loams (Dodd et al. 1990). The average village covered an area of 1.2 ha (range 0.3–3.0 ha [Warrick 1990, 353]) and contained several artifact-rich midden deposits interspersed with the longhouses. The average house was 33 m long (range 12–45 m [Dodd et al. 1990]). Thus Middleport houses were only 5 m longer than those of Uren times, implying that burgeoning matrilineages were accommodated in a greater number of houses, not in increasingly larger ones. Likewise, Middleport and Uren community size is roughly equivalent, except that a few sites exceed 2.0 ha, particularly in the Late Middleport phase (Warrick 1990).

The Middleport phase of Ontario Iroquoian history, A.D. 1330–1420 (Dodd et al. 1990; Warrick 1990), witnessed a veritable population explosion; based on estimates of total site area and hearth counts per ha of site area, in south-central Ontario population jumped from 11,000 to 29,000 persons, representing a growth rate of 1.07 percent per annum, which has rarely been equaled for early agricultural societies (Warrick 1990, 353). Earlier researchers (Noble 1975a; Trigger 1976, 143; Warrick 1984, 62, 63; J. Wright 1966, 59), based on disparate types of data, had suspected that the Ontario Iroquoian population grew in the fourteenth century but no one had anticipated such *rapid* growth. Moreover, suggested economic causes of Middleport population growth, such as increased reliance on maize (J. Wright 1966) or the introduction of beans (Noble 1975a) are not borne out by palaeodietary (Katzenberg et al. 1995; Schwarcz et al. 1985) or archaeobotanical data (Fecteau 1985; Timmins 1997a; 1997b, 100). Palaeodemographic data from ossuary burial populations suggest that high fertility and declining infant and juvenile mortality were responsible for the Middleport population explosion (Warrick 1990, 361, 362).

Colonization contributed substantially to Middleport population increase. The potential of small groups of young, healthy humans to rapidly colonize virgin land is well known to demographers and archaeologists (Hassan 1981, 193–208). In frontier areas, continual immigration and natural increase can result in phenomenal population growth—it has been estimated that the Iroquoian population of Simcoe County increased by an incredible 5.7 percent per annum between A.D. 1330 and A.D. 1355 (Sutton 1996, 173–76). Middleport colonization occurred primarily in the Barrie region, Simcoe County (Sutton 1996), Waterloo County, Prince Edward County, and the St. Lawrence River valley (J. Jamieson 1990a) and followed a "leapfrog" pattern designed to target areas sometimes located 50 km or more from the parent settlement but offering optimal access to a diverse set of resources (Sutton 1996). (The famous Nodwell site, located on Lake Huron and over 130 km from the nearest cluster of Middleport village sites [fig. 7.8], has been considered the showcase Middleport colony [G. Wright 1974]. However, Lisa K. Rankin's (2000) reanalysis of the Nodwell site presents a compelling argument that the site was actually occupied by Algonquians for 200–300 years.) There is even the possibility of a Middleport colonization of western New York State by Ontario Iroquoians (Niemczycki 1984). Reasons for Iroquoian colonization in the fourteenth century are unclear but may include perceived population pressure, village fissioning, access to productive fishing grounds, and opportunities for trade with Algonquian neighbors (Sutton 1996, 117–43). In most cases, Middleport colonies were established on land previously unoccupied by Iroquoians. For example, Simcoe County displays a marked hiatus in human occupation between A.D. 500 and A.D. 1300. While short-term exploitation by local Algonquian hunter-gatherers or by seasonal long-distance forays to the interior and lakeshores of Simcoe County by Early Iroquoian hunters and fishermen from the sixth to fourteenth centuries A.D. is not ruled out, palaeoenvironmental evidence from the Wiacek site, a late Middleport village in Barrie, indicates that Middleport pioneers established clearings in mature maple-beech forest (Lennox et al. 1986; Robertson et al. 1995).

In addition to rapid population growth, fourteenth-century Ontario was a time of sociopolitical change. The persistence from Uren times of ossuary burial, sweatbaths (MacDonald 1988), large longhouses clustered in aligned groups in large

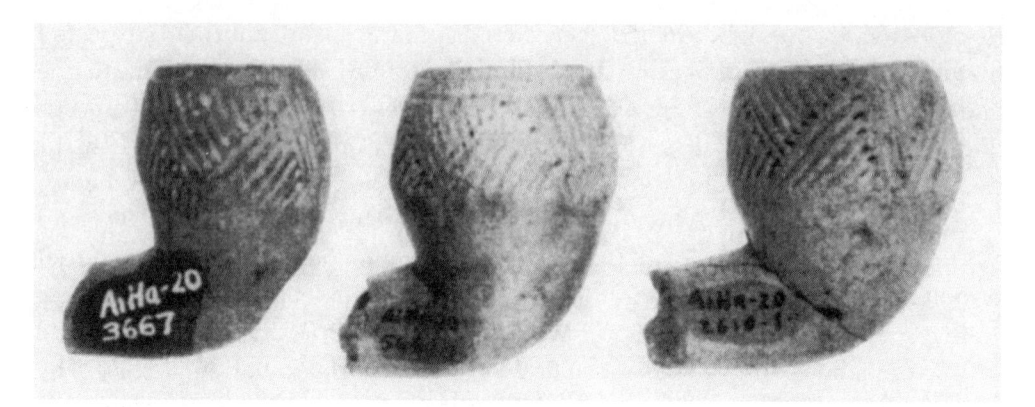

Fig. 7.9. Decorated pipe bowls from Winking Bull site, Mountsberg (courtesy of Museum of Ontario Archaeology).

communities, horizontal decorative motifs on pottery, the addition of high-collared feasting pots (Finlayson 1998) and elaborate smoking pipe decorations unique to certain villages (D. Smith 1997c) (fig. 7.9) suggest that fourteenth-century Middle Iroquoians were developing more complex sociopolitical units, such as clans, in an effort to integrate large unwieldy communities (Engelbrecht 1985; Trigger 1985, 93, 94). Considering that average village population was over 600 people, late Middleport communities must have been governed by a council composed of representative leaders from constituent clan segments (Trigger 1985, 93).

Precontact Neutral and Huron-Petun

While it is dangerous to designate collections of Ontario Iroquoian sites and artifacts as Neutral or Huron-Petun in the absence of demonstrated and direct continuity with seventeenth-century sites situated in the respective homelands of these groups (P. Ramsden 1996), the geographical distribution of mid-fifteenth-century Iroquoian sites, except for the Credit River valley, describes two major groups west and east of the Niagara Escarpment. The western sites are identified here as ancestral Neutral and the eastern as ancestral Huron-Petun (fig. 7.10).

By A.D. 1450, the fourteenth-century surge in population had slowed to a trickle (annual growth rate of less than 0.4 percent per annum), and by A.D. 1475 it had stopped altogether. Huron-Petun population peaked and stabilized at 30,000 people in the late fifteenth century (Warrick 1990, 362), and Neutral population peaked at 20,000 (Fitzgerald 1990a, 378) sometime in the early sixteenth century (based on site size data in the Crawford Lake sequence [Finlayson 1998]). Demographic stability among the precontact Huron-Petun and Neutral was accompanied by a series of interrelated historical events: unprecedented settlement nucleation at both the community and regional level, spread of density-dependent diseases such as tuberculosis, development of trade networks with Shield Algon-

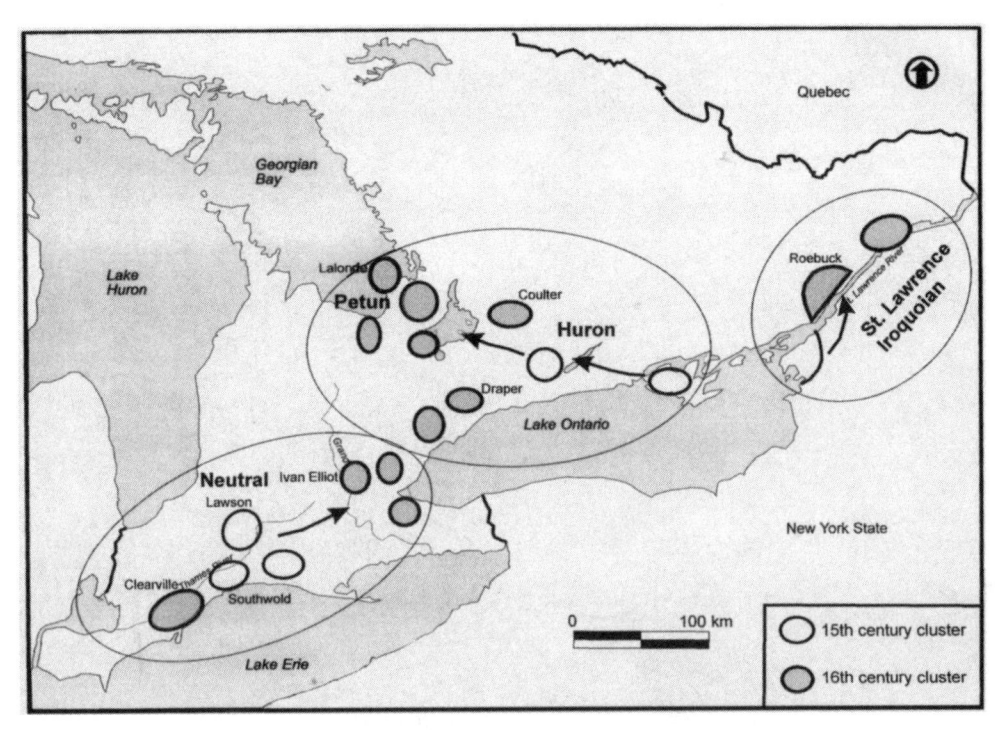

Fig. 7.10. Precontact Neutral, Huron-Petun, and St. Lawrence Iroquoian site clusters.

quians and warfare with Central Algonquians, formation of tribes, chronic intertribal warfare, and the immigration of refugee St. Lawrence Iroquoian communities (Warrick 1990).

Precontact communities were substantially larger than Middle Iroquoian ones. On average, precontact Huron-Petun and Neutral villages covered 1.7 ha (range 0.4–5.4 ha). The largest villages, such as Lalonde at a remarkable 5.4 ha and Cleary at 4.6 ha (Warrick 1990), would have held close to 2,500 people apiece! Precontact longhouses attained incredible sizes too—early to mid-fifteenth-century Neutral longhouses commonly exceeded 50 m in length (average 62 m [Lennox and Fitzgerald 1990, 445]), and some reached monstrous proportions, such as the 90-m Slack-Caswell house (S. Jamieson 1986), a 93-m dwelling at the Moyer site (Wagner et al. 1973), a 108-m house at Ivan Elliot (Fitzgerald 1990b) (fig. 7.11), and a 124-m longhouse at the Coleman site (MacDonald 1986). Extremely large houses appear to have grown over time by periodic extensions of one or both ends accommodating two to four new nuclear families per expansion (MacDonald 1986, 60–63). In certain cases, such as House 1 of the Coleman village site in southwestern Ontario, house extensions doubled original house size (MacDonald 1986, 32). Over 30 percent of all fifteenth-century houses show at least one extension, adding an extra 18 m; in contrast only 8 percent of Early Iroquoian longhouses exhibit extensions, which added only 3 m to house length (Dodd 1984, 358).

Longhouse growth and large longhouses can be explained by simple architec-

154 · *Precolumbian Dynamics*

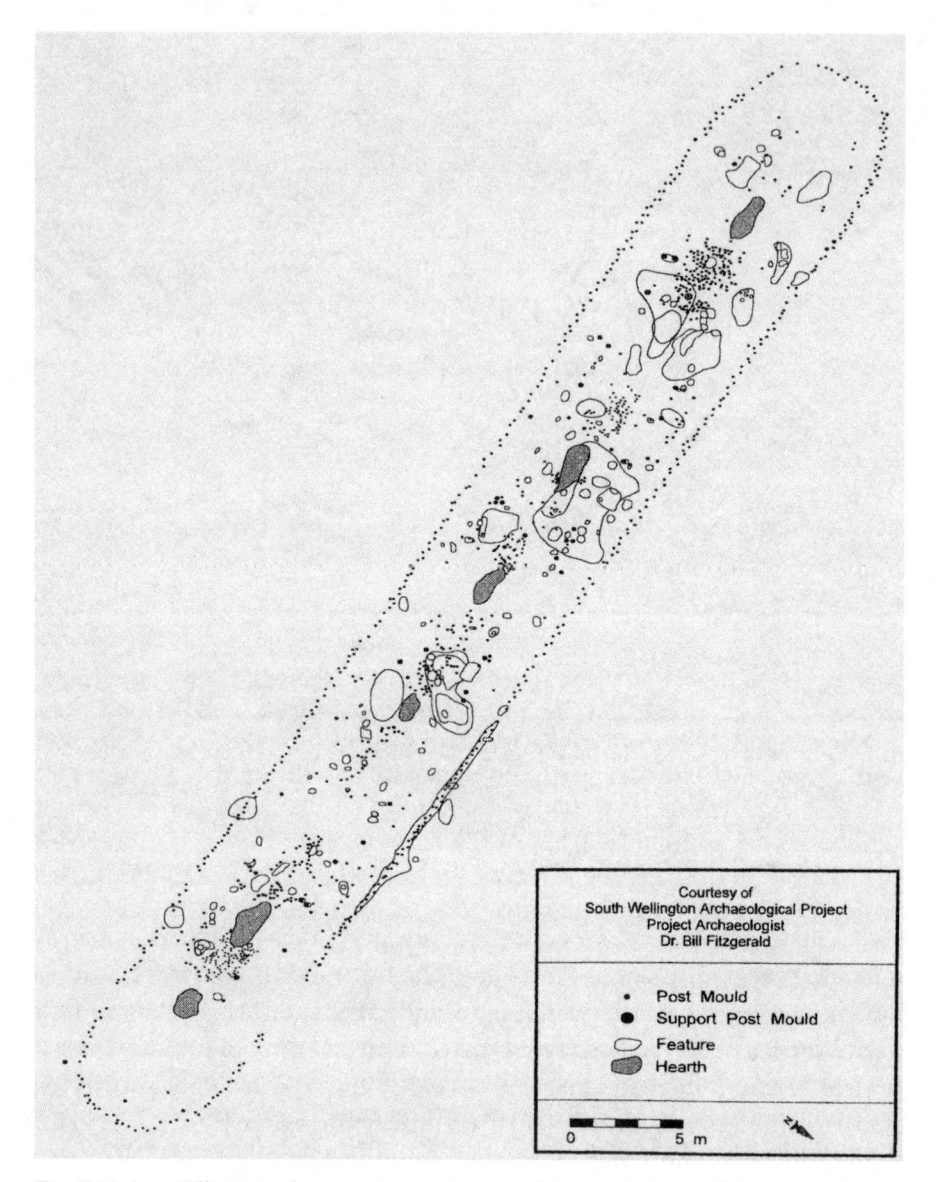

Fig. 7.11. Ivan Elliot site, house 1 (reproduced with permission of Museum of Ontario Archaeology).

tural response to demographic increase throughout the fourteenth and early fifteenth century, not by economic competition between corporate groups (Hayden and Cannon 1982), social display (Varley and Cannon 1994), or defense (Finlayson 1985). In light of the Middleport growth rate of 1.1 percent per annum, a series of "baby boom" generations would have been created throughout the fourteenth and in the early fifteenth century. Upon reaching maturity and marriage, each "baby boom" generation would have required a large number of new compartments to be added to existing longhouses *within the 30-year lifespan* of each house. It is interesting to note that spacing between hearths in Huron longhouses of the mid-fifteenth century increases (Varley and Cannon 1994), suggesting an attempt to deal with overcrowding at this time. Longhouse length declined substantially in the early sixteenth century, with an average of only 30 m for Neutral houses by A.D. 1580 (Lennox and Fitzgerald 1990, 445). Reasons for the decline could be a switch in village government, from dominant matrilineages to clan segments, enabling more fluid longhouse membership (Engelbrecht 1985, 15–17; Warrick 1996, 20).

Precontact Huron-Petun and Neutral villages were surrounded by a variety of hamlets of two or three houses (e.g., Bradley Avenue [Lennox 1995]), agricultural field cabins (e.g., Ronto, Windermere, Smallman [Pearce 1996]), and special-purpose camps (e.g., Birch [MacDonald and Cooper 1992]). Cultural resource management archaeology over the last 20 years has uncovered several examples of each site type, particularly in the London, Waterloo, and Hamilton regions (Lennox 1995; Pearce 1996), suggesting that many fifteenth- and sixteenth-century Iroquoians lived their lives away from the large villages during the spring, summer, and fall.

Concomitant with the growth of longhouses, precontact Huron-Petun and Neutral sites expanded to cover areas of 4.0 ha or more (fig. 7.12). Unlike longhouse

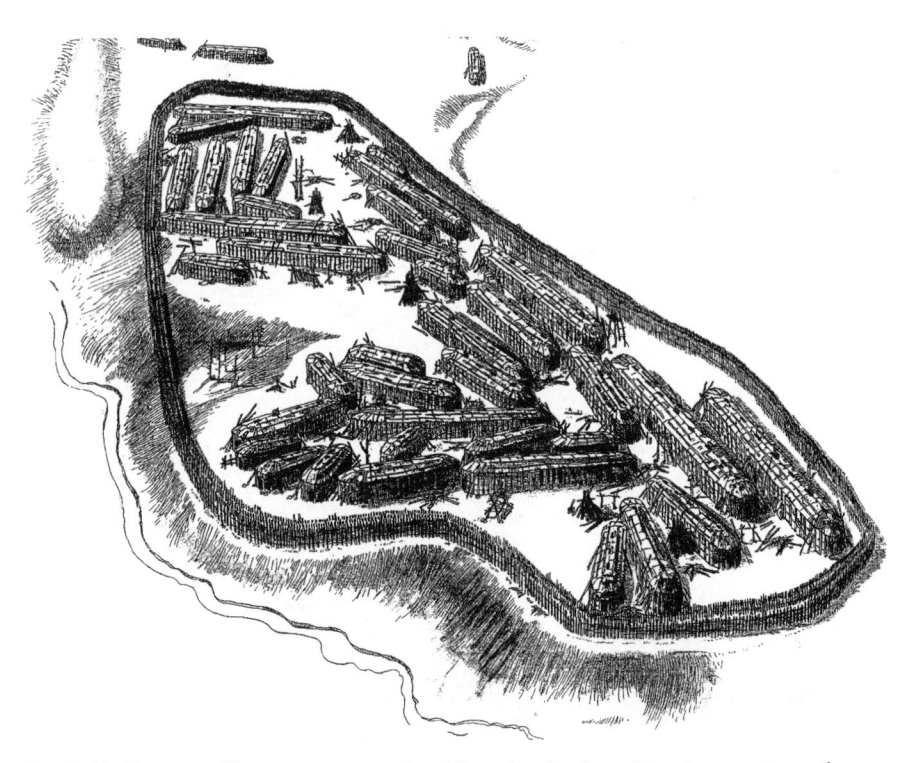

Fig. 7.12. Draper village reconstruction (drawing by Ivan Kocsis, courtesy of Museum of Ontario Archaeology).

growth, which was primarily driven by intrinsic population growth and correspondingly high rates of nuclear family formation, the sudden appearance of massive villages in mid-fifteenth-century Ontario probably resulted from the amalgamation of several smaller neighboring settlements. The Draper village, for instance, grew from an original core of 1.2 ha to a total size of 4.2 ha (including Draper South Field expansion) by the accretion of five separate settlements during its estimated 35-year lifespan (Finlayson 1985; Warrick 1990, 239–43) (fig. 7.13). A similar developmental history is inferred for the early fifteenth-century Cleary site (Warrick 1990, 240), the mid-fifteenth-century Parsons site (Williamson and Robertson 1998) and the mid-sixteenth-century Coulter site (Damkjar 1990). Based on the appearance ca. A.D. 1400–1450 of the defensive siting of settlements, on high ground by forks in streams as well as on multiple-row palisades, scattered human bone in village middens (Warrick et al. 1987), and osteological evidence for death by interpersonal violence (Williamson 1978) in Ontario Iroquoian and St. Lawrence Iroquoian sites, warfare was probably the motivating factor behind such unprecedented growth in settlement size (Finlayson 1985, 439; Pearce 1996; Trigger 1985, 99–103). Theft, murder, political intrigue, blood feud, or competition over hunting territories may have led to outright warfare between emergent, nonallied Huron-Petun, Neutral, and St.

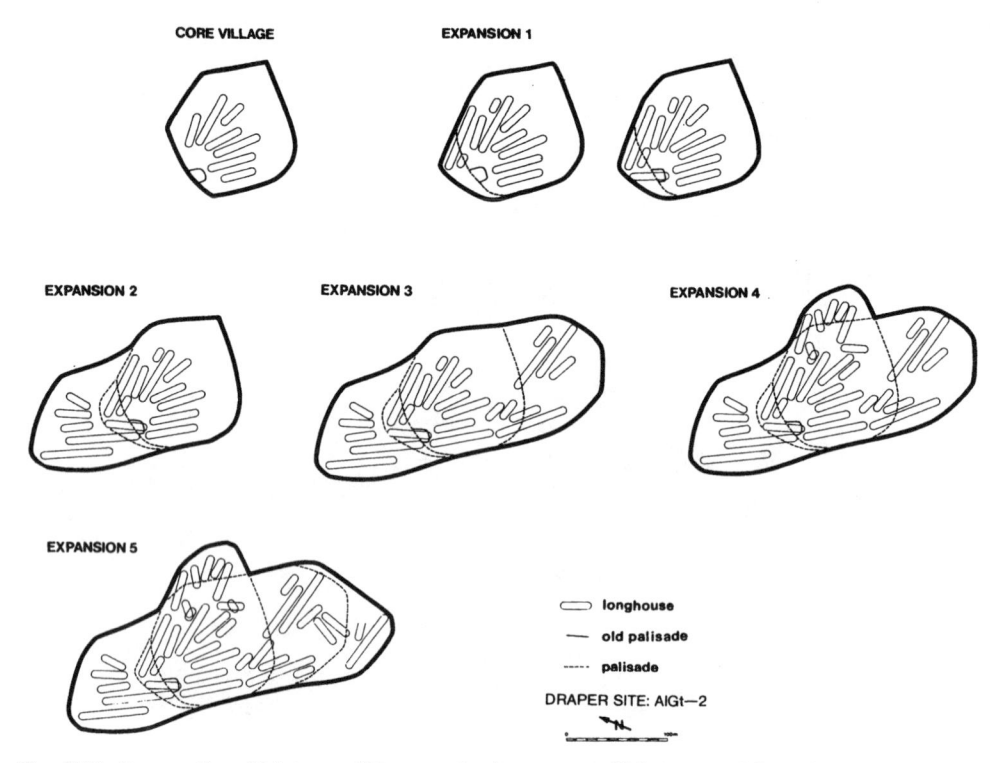

Fig. 7.13. Occupational history of Draper site (courtesy of Museum of Ontario Archaeology).

Lawrence Iroquoian tribes. However, the presence of St. Lawrence Iroquoian pottery and abundance of Onondaga chert tools in late fifteenth-century Huron-Petun sites in the Toronto region (Williamson and Robertson 1998, 147–49) suggest peaceful interaction with Neutral (trade) and St. Lawrence Iroquoians (marriage exchange).

In the fifteenth and sixteenth centuries, interaction between Iroquoians and Algonquians in Ontario was both belligerent and peaceful. On the belligerent side, the Neutral appear to have been engaged in a protracted war with Central Algonquians, known to archaeologists as the Western Basin Tradition (Murphy and Ferris 1990). In the late fifteenth century, Neutral villages were surrounded by multiple-row palisades and earthworks. Earthworks are evident at Clearville, Southwold, and Lawson (fig. 7.14), and there is evidence at all of these sites of shell-tempered Western Basin pottery, presumably the handiwork of women captives (Lennox and Fitzgerald 1990, 418, 419). Fifteenth-century Western Basin sites are also encircled by earthworks, such as the Parker and Weiser sites near Sarnia (Murphy and Ferris 1990, 257–59). Hostilities seem to have increased during the sixteenth century, indicated by the virtual withdrawal of Neutrals from the Chatham and London regions to lands east of the Grand River by A.D. 1550 (Lennox and Fitzgerald 1990, 438).

Fig. 7.14. Lawson site excavation and reconstruction, London (courtesy of Museum of Ontario Archaeology).

In contrast to the Neutral, the Huron-Petun experienced peaceful coexistence with their Algonquian neighbors to the north. Increased trade between the Huron-Petun and Shield Algonquians beginning ca. A.D. 1450 can be inferred from village site distributions. Before this date, Huron-Petun settlement was concentrated far south of the Frontenac Axis, with its relatively short growing season and extremely shallow, stony soils (Chapman and Putnam 1984). During the mid-fifteenth century a number of Iroquoian settlements were established along the southern margins of the Shield, such as the Jamieson and Quackenbush sites. Based on excavated finds of literally hundreds of stone axe fragments in various stages of manufacture from Quackenbush, it has been postulated that this village controlled a major portion of the stone axe trade amongst fifteenth-century Ontario Iroquoians (Peter Carruthers, personal communication, 1988). Neighboring Algonquian hunters probably supplied foodstuffs (dried fish and meat), furs, and deer hides to the Iroquoian inhabitants in exchange for dried maize, tobacco, nets, pottery, and axes (Trigger 1976, 166–74). The gradual northwesterly movement of Huron-Petun population throughout the fifteenth and sixteenth centuries is the result of intensification of these exchange networks between Algonquian hunters and Iroquoian farmers (Trigger 1976, 166–74; 1985, 160).

Stabilization of precontact Huron-Petun and Neutral population by A.D. 1500 was the result of a lower fertility rate, not increased infant mortality (Jackes 1986). Skeletal analyses of the Uxbridge population, dating ca. A.D. 1460–90, have revealed a rather unhealthy picture of fifteenth-century Huron life: chronic protein-calorie malnutrition, a very high incidence of tuberculosis (at least 4 percent skeletal involvement [Pfeiffer 1986]) (and presumably other density-dependent diseases and parasites), and a number of deaths and injuries caused by interpersonal violence (Pfeiffer 1986; Pfeiffer et al. 1986). In summary, chronic malnutrition, high disease loads, overcrowded house life, and stress caused by endemic tribal warfare would have effectively lowered the fertility of late fifteenth-century Ontario Iroquoian women.

By the early sixteenth century, Huron-Petun and Neutral site distributions show a definite contraction of earlier territories—the Huron-Petun had almost abandoned the north shore of Lake Ontario and the Neutral had essentially moved east of the Grand River by A.D. 1534 (Lennox and Fitzgerald 1990; Fitzgerald 1990a; Warrick 1990). The concentration of village sites is interpreted as the formation of tribes. Assigning late fifteenth- and early sixteenth-century sites and site clusters to either the Huron-Petun or Neutral has its difficulties (Ferris and Spence 1995; P. Ramsden 1996), particularly for the Crawford Lake region and the Credit and Humber River valleys. Pottery decoration is relatively simple and uniform across southwestern and south-central Ontario at this time (fig. 7.15). In general, Crawford Lake sites are considered ancestral Neutral (Finlayson 1998) and those in the Credit and Humber River valleys are probably ancestral Petun or Tahontaenrat (the last tribe to join the Huron confederacy ca. A.D. 1610) (Warrick 1990, 374).

Fig. 7.15. Pottery rim sherds, Draper site (courtesy of Museum of Ontario Archaeology).

Precontact St. Lawrence Iroquoians

St. Lawrence Iroquoians were the first Iroquoian people to make direct contact with Europeans in 1534, on the Gaspé coast (Biggar 1924). Archaeologically, they are represented by dozens of site locations along the St. Lawrence River (Chapdelaine 1989; 1995; J. Jamieson 1990a; Pendergast 1975; 1993b; Tremblay 1999), containing pottery decorated in a highly distinctive style (fig. 7.16). St. Lawrence

Fig. 7.16. St. Lawrence Iroquoian vessel (courtesy of William R. Fitzgerald).

Iroquoians settled Grenville County and Lake St. Francis regions in the late thirteenth or early fourteenth century, as a result of migration and colonization from either Ontario or New York State. Earlier St. Lawrence Iroquoian sites in the lower St. Lawrence River valley, near the Saguenay River in Quebec, demonstrate in situ development from the late tenth (Middle Woodland times) to the sixteenth century (Chapdelaine 1995; Tremblay 1999). In the latter region, pottery decoration in the late thirteenth century reveals a shift from a relationship with New York State Iroquoians to Ontario Iroquoians. It is also at this time that maize agriculture appears for the first time in the Quebec City area (ca. A.D. 1250–1300) (Tremblay 1999). It is conceivable that both maize and pottery styles were adopted by St. Lawrence Iroquoians as a result of a Uren colonization of eastern Ontario.

The St. Lawrence Iroquoians occupied five major areas in the early sixteenth century: Jefferson County in New York State (at least two and possibly four distinct communities with a total population of perhaps 2,500) (Pendergast 1985; 1993b; Engelbrecht 1995); Grenville County in eastern Ontario (Pendergast 1975; 1985; 1993b) (representing two distinct communities and a population of about 2,500); Lake St. Francis Basin west of Montreal (one community of 1,000 persons); Montreal Island (including Hochelaga, with an estimated population of 1,500 [Trigger 1972, 15]); and east of Montreal as far downstream as the Quebec City area (including villages east of Montreal, 500 persons [Chapdelaine 1989]) and Stadacona (500–600 persons [Heidenreich 1990, 475]) and related small villages or hamlets near Quebec City

(Chapdelaine 1995) for a combined population of 2,000–3,000 (Heidenreich 1990). Except where referenced, population figures are calculated from village site areas (using 50 hearths/ha) as provided by James Bruce Jamieson (1990a), and occupation dates from James F. Pendergast (1993a). The grand total of 8,000 St. Lawrence Iroquoians in A.D. 1500 generally agrees with two independent population estimates for the St. Lawrence Iroquoians ca. A.D. 1535: 5,000 (disregarding villages west of Montreal [Heidenreich 1990]) and 10,000 (Clermont 1980).

The St. Lawrence Iroquoian settlement of Ontario is concentrated in two areas: Grenville County (south of Ottawa) and Lake St. Francis (east of Cornwall) (fig. 7.10). As mentioned earlier, site chronologies are still problematic, but it would appear that each cluster was occupied from A.D. 1300 to A.D. 1550 and contained large inland village sites, situated several kilometers from the St. Lawrence River (J. Jamieson 1990a; Pendergast 1993b). In the fifteenth century, St. Lawrence Iroquoian villages, such as Roebuck, Beckstead, Cleary, and Maynard-McKeown (Chapdelaine 1989; J. Jamieson 1990a; Pendergast 1993b; 1997), covered 2.0–3.25 ha; were encircled by earthworks, ditches, and multiple-row palisades; and contained a number of tightly packed longhouses, ranging in length from 18 to 41 m (J. Jamieson 1990a). There is evidence that large St. Lawrence Iroquoian villages, like those of the Huron-Petun and Neutral, were formed by the amalgamation of several smaller villages and hamlets (Pendergast 1997). Defensive considerations appear to have been paramount in late fifteenth-century St. Lawrence Iroquoian village organization.

Sometime in the sixteenth century, the St. Lawrence Iroquoians disappeared from their homeland. Jefferson County and Grenville County appear to have been abandoned by the middle of the sixteenth century (Chapdelaine 1989; Engelbrecht 1995; Pendergast 1985) and the Hochelaga and Stadacona groups disappeared sometime before A.D. 1580 (Pendergast 1993b; Trigger 1985, 146). The dispersal of the St. Lawrence Iroquoians is best explained by the formation of the Iroquois Confederacy and escalating warfare between various Native groups in the sixteenth century. Intense debate surrounds the relationship between the Huron-Petun and St. Lawrence Iroquoians (Trigger 1985, 144–48), but there is a growing consensus that the western St. Lawrence Iroquoians sought refuge among the Huron-Petun to escape constant raiding and harassment by the New York Iroquois (J. Jamieson 1990a; P. Ramsden 1990a; Sioui 1992a, 83–86). The Iroquois or Five Nations Confederacy, according to a reanalysis of oral tradition and solar eclipse chronologies for the Northeast, seems to have originated ca. A.D. 1536 (Snow 1996b, 60). Early in the sixteenth century, it would appear that the St. Lawrence Iroquoians became embroiled in a serious war with the eastern members of the Five Nations Confederacy and were ultimately defeated and incorporated into Onondaga and Mohawk villages (Bradley 1987a; Engelbrecht 1995; Snow 1996b, 76). Some survivors sought refuge in Huron-Petun villages in Victoria County (Pendergast 1993b; P. Ramsden 1990a). St. Lawrence Iroquoian pottery is present in many Huron-Petun sites, dated

A.D. 1450–1600, in relative abundance, often in excess of 5 percent of all pots recovered and over 10 percent in certain sixteenth-century sites (Warrick 1990, 377).

European Contact and Depopulation

The ultimate fate of the St. Lawrence Iroquoians brings us to the possibility that they suffered massive depopulation as the result of European contact and the spread of contagious disease. Before the recorded disease outbreak in December 1535 amongst the St. Lawrence Iroquoians of Stadacona (Biggar 1924, 204), there is no archaeological (Snow 1995b; Warrick 1990) or palaeodemographic evidence (Sullivan 1997) of epidemic disease or depopulation of Iroquoians as a result of European exploration of the Atlantic Coast in the early sixteenth century. Henry F. Dobyns (1983) and others (Ramenofsky 1987; M. Smith 1987; Upham 1992) believe that certain portions of North America were depopulated by pandemics of European disease, speeding far inland, in advance of the first footprints of Europeans on Native lands. However, the most recent research on Native North American population at the time of contact suggests that Old World disease preceded European contact only in portions of Central America and Peru (N. Cook 1998) and perhaps the American Southeast and Midwest (Ramenofsky 1987; M. Smith 1987). In every other region of North America, Old World disease and Native depopulation followed direct European contact, often in the form of localized outbreaks of disease. Factors that prevented the pandemic spread of Old World disease across sixteenth- and early seventeenth-century North America include long trans-Atlantic voyages (normal voyages of a month or more acted as a quarantine period for most infectious diseases); lack of European children in the first colonies of the Northeast (the most contagious Old World diseases were primarily childhood illnesses in sixteenth- and seventeenth-century Europe); infrequent land-based contacts with Natives before colonization; lack of domestic animal reservoirs or vectors for disease among Natives; low population densities of Native societies (at least in northeastern North America); physical, social, and demographic buffer zones between Native groups (preventing localized disease outbreak from becoming epidemic or pandemic) (Milner 1992; Snow and Lanphear 1988; Thornton et al. 1992). It is significant to note that the earliest material evidence of indirect European contact (i.e., iron, copper, brass, glass artifacts) in Ontario has been found in Iroquoian sites occupied in the mid-sixteenth century (Fitzgerald 1990a). It is unlikely that Iroquoians experienced calamitous depopulation from European disease in the sixteenth century.

Conclusions

The last 35 years of archaeology in southern Ontario have revealed a complex and dynamic history of Iroquoian occupation before European contact. Settlement pattern, population, subsistence, and sociopolitical organization experienced significant transformation from A.D. 500 to A.D. 1534. The introduction of maize agriculture and concomitant sociocultural accommodation to a new form of subsistence and use of the land launched Ontario Iroquoians on a trajectory that involved dramatic population growth, colonization of new territory, development of matrilocal/matrilineal society, and clan and tribal political organization. This process culminated in stabilization of Iroquoian population throughout the Northeast and the emergence of the Five Nations Iroquois Confederacy at the time of the first encounters between Iroquoians and the white-skinned strangers from the east in 1534. Precontact Iroquoian archaeology in Ontario is an exciting field with a rich database rivaling any other in the world. Future research holds much promise.

Acknowledgments

This paper, like any synthesis of a vast body of archaeological data, benefited greatly from informal conversations over the last year with friends and colleagues, particularly Jeff Bursey, Neal Ferris, Laurie Jackson, Paul Lennox, Dave Smith, Ron Williamson, and Phil Woodley. Bill Finlayson, Bill Fitzgerald, Paul Lennox, Bob Pearce, Dave Smith, Ron Williamson, and Penny Young provided maps and artifact and site photos. Phil Woodley kindly drafted the site distribution maps. Wilfrid Laurie University, Brantford Campus, provided logistical support (photocopying, computer) and the Ontario Ministry of Transportation kindly permitted me to take a leave from government bureaucracy to return to the academic world. I wish to extend warm thanks to everyone and would like to emphasize that the opinions expressed in this paper and any errors or omissions are entirely my responsibility.

8 | Aboriginal Settlement Patterns in Late Woodland Upper New York State

ROBERT J. HASENSTAB

Village Movement as a Correlate of Behavior

WILLIAM A. RITCHIE AND ROBERT E. FUNK (1973, 1–2) differentiate between two types of settlement pattern: micro and macro. Microsettlement patterns include archaeological features within habitation sites that reflect the "general community plan"—for example, post molds of housing or defensive structures and pits used for storage or burial of the dead. Macrosettlement patterns involve the distribution of whole communities over a landscape, reflecting their adaptation to the environment—both natural and cultural.

This paper focuses on macrosettlement patterns of the Late Woodland period in upper New York State; viz., the locations of villages occupied by the Five Nations League of the Iroquois and their ancestors (fig. 8.1). With the advent of maize horticulture at the beginning of the period, sedentary, nucleated villages became the focus of economic and social life (Fenton 1940, 167). Throughout the Woodland period, villages became larger in size, more densely occupied, and more complex (Ritchie and Funk 1973; Tuck 1971).

Villages were constructed by communities, were occupied for a generation, more or less, and were relocated as the need arose—either because of physical factors, such as soil exhaustion, or because of social forces, such as warfare. Because the relocation of a village was a strategic decision (Heidenreich 1971, 109), the movement of villages over time should reflect collective human behavior; namely, it should reveal the changing concerns of communities vis-à-vis their physical and social environments. Before social correlates of macrosettlement can be identified,

Previously published in *A Northeastern Millennium: History and Archaeology for Robert E. Funk,* ed. C. Lindner and E. V. Curtin, *Journal of Middle Atlantic Archaeology* 12 (1996): 17–26. Printed with permission by the *Journal of Middle Atlantic Archaeology*.

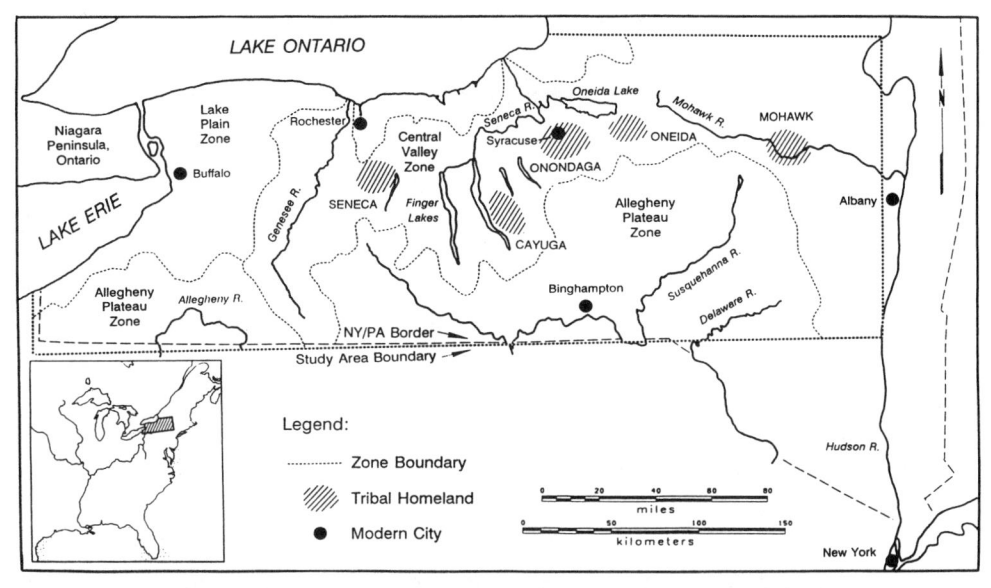

Fig. 8.1. The study area showing the homelands of the Five Nations and the three physiographic zones in upper New York State.

basic factors relating to the physical environment must be understood. William N. Fenton (1940, 165) argues of the Iroquois that "a final demonstration of their cultural origins requires basic studies of their adaptation to the environment."

This study analyzes the locations of known prehistoric Iroquois villages in upper New York State with respect to a variety of environmental variables. Factors of both the physical and social environments are considered. Macrosettlement change throughout the Late Woodland period is ultimately attributed to social factors.

Studies of Iroquoian Settlement Patterns

As part of the cultural ecology movement of 1960s anthropology, archaeologists focused on settlement patterns and prehistoric peoples' adaptation to the environment (cf. Ritchie and Funk 1973, 1). Because Iroquois village sites are obtrusive and were regularly relocated, they served as a ready database for settlement archaeologists throughout the region: in the Huron area of Ontario (Heidenreich 1971); in the Neutral and Wenro areas of western New York (White 1961); in the areas of the Seneca (Wray and Schoff 1953), the Onondaga (Tuck 1971), and the Oneida (Pratt 1976) in central New York; and in the Mohawk Valley of eastern New York (Lenig 1965). Most of these early studies attempted to establish local culture histories by tracing prehistoric communities through their village removal sequences.

These studies were synthesized in the landmark publication by Ritchie and Funk (1973). That study served as the inspiration for the present study, which began as a pilot study (Hasenstab 1978) and led to a Rochester Museum fellowship (Hasenstab 1981). That fellowship included field study under the late Charles F. Wray, focusing on village locations of the Seneca sequence, and ultimately culminated in my dissertation (Hasenstab 1990). Concurrent with my research and undoubtedly inspired by the same 1973 publication were a number of other studies focusing on Late Woodland settlement in upper New York State (Allen 1996; Bamann 1993; Bradley 1987a; Hunt 1990; Knoerl 1988; Niemczycki 1984; Prezzano 1992; Wykoff 1988).

Sorting Out Settlement: The Use of a Geographic Information System (GIS)

The database used in this study contained over 600 Late Woodland sites (including 350 villages) inventoried from the files of the State University of New York-Buffalo, the Rochester Museum, and the New York State Museum in Albany (Hasenstab 1990, 64–118; 1996). The study area chosen was the homeland of the Five Nations Iroquois between Albany and Buffalo. This area was divided into three physiographic zones for purposes of spatial comparison: the lake plain of the lower Great Lakes; the central valleys comprised of the Genesee, Seneca, and Mohawk river drainages; and the Allegheny plateau including the Allegheny and Susquehanna drainages of the southern tier of New York. The central valley zone contained the homelands of the Five Nations—the Seneca, Cayuga, Onondaga, Oneida, and Mohawk—and thus will be the focus of this paper.

Site occupations were divided into five major periods for chronological analysis: Owasco (A.D. 1000–1300), Transitional Iroquois (A.D. 1300–1400), Prehistoric Iroquois (A.D. 1400–1525), Protohistoric (A.D. 1535–1610), and Historic Contact (A.D. 1610–87). Two major analyses were performed: (1) spatial, being an identification of settlement patterns within each of the three zones during each period; and (2) chronological, being an analysis of trends in settlement over the five periods or shifts in settlement between periods.

A set of computer-encoded environmental maps, or a geographic information system (GIS), was compiled to analyze site locations. This analysis included variables affecting maize horticulture, hunting and gathering, and long-distance canoe transport: namely, various data on soils, climate, forests, wetlands, and waterways, totaling 50 data layers in all. Locations of sites were compared statistically against those of random control points in the GIS to determine which of the 50 environmental variables were critical in defining site location. Those were presumably the variables used by the village inhabitants in selecting site locations.

Results: Environmental Factors Affecting Late Woodland Settlement

Figure 8.2 presents major trends in the movement of central-valley-zone, or Five Nations Iroquois, villages from the beginning of the Late Woodland period through and including the Protohistoric period, after which the trends are reversed. The essential trend is a movement from valley-bottom locations into the uplands or zones of higher elevation. With respect to environmental features affecting subsistence resources, there is a decrease in emphasis on hunting-gathering and an increasing focus on features favorable to maize horticulture. In particular, villages move into zones of lower forest productivity and away from areas containing wetlands, while they move into zones of higher rainfall and—though not shown in figure 8.2—zones of richer soils (i.e., heavy limestone tills versus sandy outwash terraces). At the same time, villages move away from canoe-navigable waterways. Following is a description of each environmental variable as it would have affected settlement.

Movement into Hilly Terrain: The Local Village Setting

By the time of the Protohistoric period, villages of most Iroquois tribes were situated on hilltops (Fenton 1940, 172, 199, 201, 213, 220, 225, 226). At the time of con-

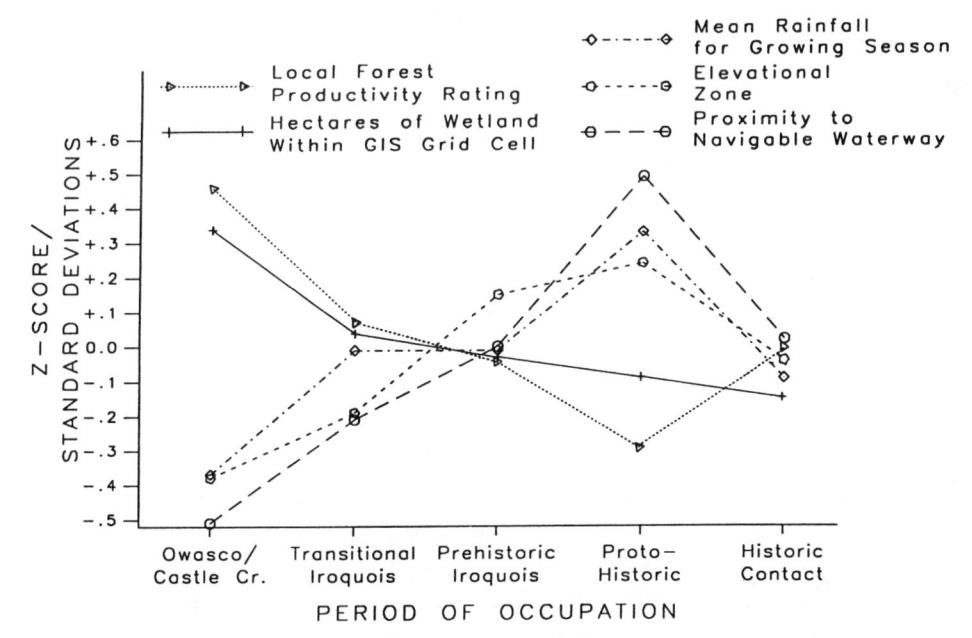

Fig. 8.2. Changes in village locations in the central valley zone with respect to five environmental variables. Plotted for each variable and time period is the average deviation in village location from the mean value of the variable for all time periods.

tact the Onondaga referred to themselves as "the great hill people" (Tuck 1971, 1), and the Seneca called themselves "people on the hills" (Morgan 1969 [1851], 51–52). Even the Petun of Ontario—commonly known as "the tobacco nation," were also referred to as the *Tionnontate,* or "mountain people" (Trigger 1976, 1:91). The pattern of hilltop occupation began in the Owasco period with a movement of villages from valley bottoms into upland terrain (Bradley 1987a; Ritchie and Funk 1973, 165–78; Tuck 1971).

There were many advantages of hilltop living including those of simple human comfort. Hills provided relief from the swarms of mosquitoes in lowland swamps that later plagued the early Euroamerican settlers (Charles Hayes, personal communication 1982). The movement away from wetlands cited above may relate to this factor.

During the winter months, hills broke the fierce winds blowing across the Lake Ontario plain. Wray (1982) noted that many of the Seneca villages, including Adams, Cameron, Culbertson, and Reed, were situated with high hills to the west to block the prevailing winds.

Villages outside the valley bottoms were located along aquifers, or zones where beds of porous bedrock come to the surface (Charles Wray, personal communication 1982; Pratt 1976, 6). Here springs issued from the hillsides and provided fresh running water year-round for the sedentary villagers; for example, at the Adams site (Squier 1851, 63). Interestingly, many village locations plotted on early twentieth-century, 15-minute quadrangles show permanent springs nearby, while the same locations on modern 7.5-minute quadrangles show no sign of surface water. These streams have apparently been filled with sediment from agricultural runoff, were often plowed over, and are no longer visible.

One other benefit of the hilly terrain to village setting is defensibility. In particular, hilltops surrounded by steep slopes were ideal for defensive fortifications. Such sites also provided strategic vantages over the surrounding terrain including trails, waterways, and other avenues of attack. These features would have become more important as hostilities heightened.

Microclimate and Growing Season

One property of hilly terrain, namely cold air drainage, affects not only human comfort but more important to horticulturalists it affects the incidence of frost and hence the effective growing season (Hasenstab 1982). Most Iroquois villages in the rolling hill country of New York were situated between elevations of 900 and 1,200 feet, whereas the adjoining valley bottoms range 500–800 feet and the ridgetops of the highest elevations range 1,500–2,500 feet, depending on the locale. In rugged terrain of the Appalachian highlands these intermediate elevations are referred to as "thermal belts" and tend to remain frost free during temperature inversions characteristic of autumn nights. Cold air from cooling ground drains downhill and accumulates in valleys, while radiating heat rises and is trapped under the inversion layer along the thermal belt. The association of Iroquois villages with this frost-free zone was first noted by Stanford J. Gibson (1971) in central New York. Meteorological monitoring has demonstrated that thermal belts can have growing seasons up to 30 days longer than adjoining areas upslope and down (Hasenstab 1982). This may have been a particularly significant factor during the Little Ice Age. Both William R. Fitzgerald (1992) and Susan E. Bamann (1993) argue that climatic deterioration during the Little Ice Age was a significant factor of settlement during the latter part of the Late Woodland period.

Another climatic factor that may have affected settlement was the ameliorating effects of the large lakes on land masses downwind to the east. Eleazer D. Hunt (1990) argues this lake effect was a significant factor among the Erie in southwestern New York, and James F. Pendergast (1993b) argues similarly for the St. Lawrence Iroquois at the east end of Lake Ontario. It may also have affected Five Nations groups to the east of Seneca, Cayuga, and Oneida lakes. The Lake Erie plain and Finger Lakes region today are prime vineyard areas owing to this phenomenon.

Lake Effect and Rainfall

Kathleen M. S. Allen (1996) notes that rainfall may have been a factor affecting settlement during the Prehistoric Iroquois period. Milton William Wykoff (1988, 16–82) argues for a period of drought in the Northeast beginning around A.D. 1280 and continuing through the 1300s—the Transitional Iroquois period here. To this drought he attributes the expansion of Ontario Iroquois groups across the Niagara Peninsula into New York State in search of moister soils. However, both Wykoff (1988, fig. 21) and I (Hasenstab 1990, maps 35, 36) show the lake plain in New York to be a relatively dry zone. In contrast, the higher elevations along Lake Erie and those southeast of the Finger Lakes receive greater summer rainfall owing to moisture from air masses being blown off the lakes, being forced upward, and thus cooling. Allen and Wykoff both argue this higher rainfall accounts for the Erie occupations in western New York—an argument supported by the GIS analysis (Hasenstab 1990, 150; 1996). My analysis also shows rainfall to be a significant factor in the patterning and changing of settlement in the Five Nations Iroquois area southeast and east of the Finger Lakes. Movement into the uplands here could relate to the drought cited by Wykoff.

Soils: Texture and pH

Associated with movement into the uplands was a change of village locations from glacial outwash sands of the valley bottoms to the heavier till soils of the uplands (Hasenstab 1990, fig. 34). Ethnohistoric accounts indicate the Iroquois cultivated the heavy, stony soils on their hill slopes and not on remote valley-bottom soils as is commonly misunderstood (Hasenstab 1986). Rudolphe D. Fecteau (1985, 98–99) documents a similar movement of Glen Meyer villages from sandy soils to heavier clay and till loams in Ontario. Wykoff (1988, 120–21) claims this movement was a response to drought.

My analysis (Hasenstab 1990, 149; 1996) shows that by the Prehistoric Iroquois period, i.e., A.D. 1400, the most significant variable accounting for Iroquois village location across space during each time period was rating-of-soil for corn cultivation. When soils were further analyzed by attribute, the key variable was revealed to be lime status. This status was presumably linked to the Iroquois' interplanting of beans with maize (Hasenstab 1986). Beans supply nitrogen, the chief nutrient required by corn, through the action of nitrogen-fixing bacteria. These bacteria, in turn, grow best in limestone soil. Furthermore, they thrive in moist soils, but in droughty soils they are inactive and the interplanting of beans with maize does more harm than good. This finding may in part account for the movement of villages onto moist soils and into aquifer zones.

Distance from Canoe-Navigable Waterways

Whereas soils account most for the patterning of villages across space *during* each of the later time periods, waterways account for most of the change or shifting in settlement *between* periods and throughout the Late Woodland period in general. These results, which in part are artifacts of the differing statistical procedures used (synchronic pattern recognition analysis versus diachronic regression and rank order analysis), imply in reality that while agriculture was holding constant as an important settlement concern throughout the later periods, waterways were becoming increasingly more important from one period to the next. In particular, the GIS analysis reveals that by far, the variable contributing most to the trend of upland village movement is distance from canoe-navigable waterways (Hasenstab 1996). Villages continue to move farther away from canoe-navigable waterways until the Protohistoric period, after which the trend is reversed.

The observed trend was coincident with an increase in hostility throughout the region. That this trend was a response to the hostility is supported by other patterns that imply avoidance of contact with outside groups. During all the time periods, distance from drainage divides was a significant locational factor (Hasenstab 1990, table 10C). Villages tended to be clustered within the interiors of drainages, avoiding what were probably territorial boundaries, or the so-called hinterlands, along drainage divides. At the same time, villages also avoided features such as portages between waterways and falls along streams (Hasenstab 1990, table 15; 1996). These features would have been active locations for long-distance canoe traffic. While some have argued that the Iroquois relied on overland trails, it should be realized that the historic fur trade, upon which the argument is based, was conducted primarily on horseback. Before the introduction of the horse, canoes would have been the major means of bulk transport (Hasenstab 1987).

Movement according to Cardinal Direction

The transition from the Prehistoric Iroquois period to the Protohistoric period (ca. A.D. 1500) represents the time of maximum hostility throughout the region (Jamieson 1990b). The GIS analysis shows that at this time, the second most significant variable accounting for settlement change, aside from waterways, is simply the universal transverse mercator (UTM) coordinates of sites (Hasenstab 1990, table 13C; 1996). Namely, village locations were shifting eastward throughout the central valley zone. Thus, movement into the uplands southeast of the Finger Lakes was not the primary trend, but rather movement away from canoe routes and toward the east.

Discussion: Social Factors Affecting Settlement

Lewis Henry Morgan (1969 [1851] 72, 41) commented that the Five Nations Iroquois "themselves declared that their country possessed many advantages superior to any other part of America." Indeed the upland areas they occupied included aquifers, thermal belts, lake-effect rains, and limestone soils. However, the settlement analysis reviewed here shows that the primary variables accounting for the shift into upland locations were not those of the physical environment, but rather those related to social factors. In particular, increasing hostilities throughout the region seem to have promoted a movement away from canoeable waterways and, between the prehistoric and protohistoric periods, a general shift eastward.

I have argued elsewhere (Hasenstab 1987; 1990; 1992) that it was conflict over territories that prompted warfare in the Five Nations Iroquois area and a retreat of groups toward the east. Beginning in the Transitional Iroquois period and continuing into the Prehistoric Iroquois period there was an influx of Ontario Iroquois groups into western New York (Niemczycki 1986; 1988, 85; White 1976, 135–36). This influx resulted in a dramatic increase in site density in the lake plain zone of western New York (Hasenstab 1990, table 9, fig. 29; 1996). Sites in this zone, in contrast to central valley sites, focused on canoeable waterways, falls along them, and portages between them (Hasenstab 1990, 151, 153, 155–56, table 15; 1996). This focus suggests that bulk transport may have been a key factor of settlement and is supported by the occurrence of massive fortifications at nearly all falls along canoeable waterways, for example Shelby Fort, Fort Hill LeRoy, and Akron Falls Fort (Hasenstab 1987).

Lake plain sites also favored areas of optimal forest and wetland areas (Hasenstab 1990, 155–56). This pattern, combined with evidence for game shortages in Ontario at this time (see Fitzgerald 1992), has led me to hypothesize that the influx of Ontario groups into New York represents an expansion of hunting territories (Hasenstab 1992). The fortified sites at portages are hypothesized to represent bulk breaking stations for the extraction of hides and cured meat from the area (Hasenstab 1987).

These intrusions were followed by increased evidence of hostility in the Five Nations area and a shift of tribal village clusters in an eastward direction. This shift is documented for the Cayuga area (Niemczycki 1984, fig. 12; 1991, table 1, fig. 1), the Onondaga area (Bradley 1987a; 1989), the Oneida area (the Oneida splitting east from the Onondaga; see Pratt 1976; 1991, 40), the Mohawk valley (MacNeish 1952, 83, 84, 87; Snow 1989), and the St. Lawrence valley (Pendergast 1993b, figs. 1–3). These eastward shifts are seen here as a response to territorial expansions and hostilities emanating from the west, namely, from Ontario (cf. Fitzgerald 1992).

Conclusion

The Late Woodland period experienced social change more rapid and dynamic than did any other period in the prehistory of the Northeast. Within a few centuries a group of populations in upper New York State was transformed from seminomadic hunter-gatherers to the highly organized League of the Iroquois. Change can be observed archaeologically in successive village occupations, where villages were occupied for roughly a generation at a time.

Macrosettlement, or the distribution of villages over the landscape, is viewed here as a form of human behavior operating at the scale of whole communities. The locating of a village is seen as an adaptation of a society and its economy to the surrounding environment—both natural and cultural. In Late Woodland upper New York State many changes were taking place: societies were developing lineage-based residence and descent systems; economies were changing to ones based on intensive maize horticulture; the natural environment was changing in terms of rainfall and growing season; and the social environment was becoming increasingly competitive and hostile. Changes in settlement reflected the interplay of all these trends.

The study reviewed here tracks settlement change by controlling for a variety of environmental variables with the use of a geographic information system (GIS) and multivariate statistical techniques. The study concluded that while settlement responded to a changing economy and physical environment, the most significant change is attributable to a changing social environment. In particular, defensive responses to increased hostilities have been shown to constitute the majority of change in Late Woodland macrosettlement. A hypothesis to explain this hostility in terms of competition over hunting territories has been put forth and remains to be tested by future research.

Acknowledgments

This study was made possible by a fellowship from the Rochester Museum and Science Center. I would like to thank the staffs of State University of New York-Buffalo, the Rochester Museum, and the New York State Museum for facilitating the compilation of site file data. I thank my graduate advisors, Dena Dincauze and H. Martin Wobst, for guiding me through the dissertation research. Finally, I thank Chris Lindner and Ed Curtin for giving me the opportunity to honor Robert Funk with this paper.

9 | The Iroquoian Longhouse
Architectural and Cultural Identity

MIMA KAPCHES

Introduction

IN NORTH AMERICA THE IROQUOIAN PEOPLES are unique. Well known and documented in the historic literature, their history extends several centuries into the archaeological past. One facet of the uniqueness of the Iroquoians is their specialized house form, the longhouse, and its important cultural symbolism for these peoples. The Iroquois of New York State called themselves the "People of the Longhouse" and much of their cultural and political imagery was an extension of the physical layout of the longhouses (Morgan 1969 [1851]). For the Iroquoian speakers north and south of the lower Great Lakes the longhouse was more than a dwelling style, it was a unique architectural feature with significant cultural identity. The working premise of this paper is that the Iroquoian longhouse, with its definable attributes, is an archaeologically recognizable indicator of cultural identity, i.e., *Iroquoian*. The corollary of this premise is that non-longhouse house forms, when found on sites adjacent to the Iroquoian area, or on Iroquoian sites, may *not* be Iroquoian. To discuss this premise it is necessary to identify the architectural features of an Iroquoian longhouse, and to define some aspects of architectural variability of that house form, and this is one of the goals of this paper.

Another theoretical approach to the study of archaeological architecture quantified the use of what was termed *spatial dynamics*, or the changes in actively used organized space within structures through time (Kapches 1990). The analytical approach of this paper, directed at architectural reality and cultural variability, is considered to be complementary. The challenge to archaeologists is to move beyond

Previously published in *Meaningful Architecture: Social Interpretations of Buildings*, ed. M. Locock, Worldwide Archaeology Series no. 9 (Hampshire, UK: Avebury, Aldershot, 1994), 253–70. Printed with permission by Martin Locock.

the limited structural data and attempt to make the structures understandable within the human framework. By examining structural variability related to domestic architecture, as it changes through time, one is also expanding the boundaries of analyzing the social/cultural dimensions of structures.

Parameters

To conduct this study it is necessary to establish chronological and cultural (geographic and tribal) parameters. The Iroquoian chronology is lengthy, and the tribal developments are diverse and complex. It is therefore essential to define the time periods and cultural areas to be addressed.

The first distinction is that between the terms *Iroquois* and *Iroquoian*. South of Lake Ontario in New York State there existed the well-known League of Five Nations, or the Iroquois Confederacy. These Iroquoian speakers consisted of the Mohawk, Oneida, Onondaga, Cayuga, and Seneca tribes. North of Lake Ontario there were also Iroquoian-speaking tribes, the Huron, the Neutral, and the Petun, who were not part of the Confederacy (fig. 9.1). These latter tribes are called *Ontario Iroquoians,* but are not called *Iroquois,* which is a name used to specify the Five Nations. In the discussion to follow, the archaeological focus will be on the Ontario Iroquoians, not the Iroquois south of the lake. This focus is because a survey of the

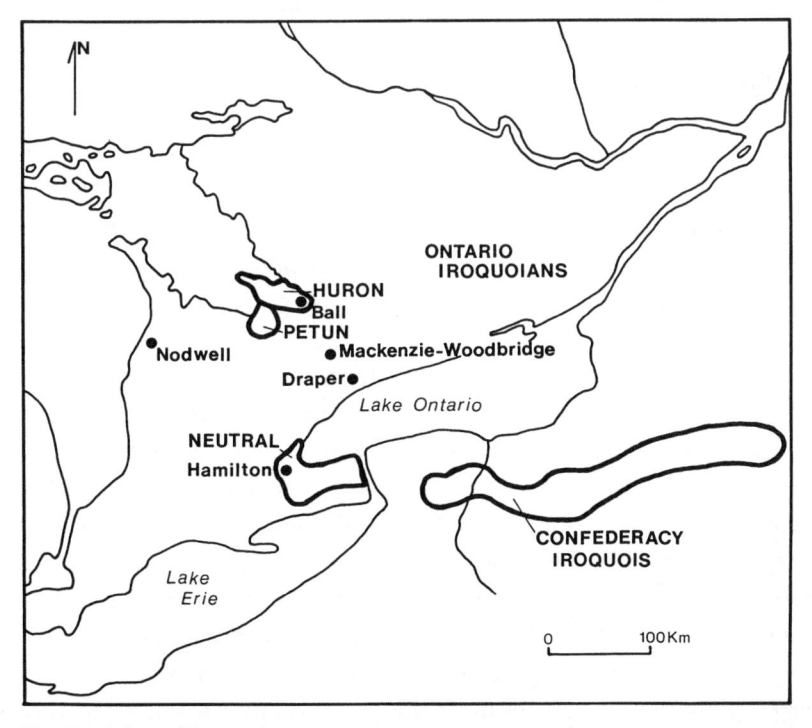

Fig. 9.1. Map of Iroquoia.

published literature from New York State reveals few well-documented, large-scale village excavations, in contrast to the wealth of data from Ontario. However, because observations and anthropological data about the Iroquois are pertinent they will be referred to in the course of the paper.

The chronological parameters of the paper are related to the Ontario data. In Southern Ontario archaeologists have assigned the date A.D. 1615 as the threshold of the historic period, in which literate Europeans first visited Ontario and began writing accounts of their experiences and described the peoples whom they encountered. The date of the arrival of Samuel de Champlain in Huronia is A.D. 1615, where he wintered at the Huron village of Cahiagué. Sites occupied before A.D. 1615 are categorized as prehistoric. In this presentation, both prehistoric and historic data will be included. Chronologically, the study will cover the late prehistoric to early historic Ontario Iroquoian periods, ca. A.D. 1350 to ca. A.D. 1640.

Culturally, the data will mostly be drawn from Ontario Iroquoian sites of the Huron continuum. Neutral data from the historic period will also be presented. Although architectural similarities will be presented for these different tribes, architectural variability will be highlighted.

By the conclusion of this paper several points will have been reviewed: the construction of houses, the layout of houses, the symbolism of houses, and the tribal variability of houses. Combined, these data will support the argument for the cultural and architectural definition of the Iroquoian longhouse.

The Iroquoian Longhouse

The Iroquoian speakers north and south of Lake Ontario lived in multiple-family dwellings called longhouses. The longhouse was the focus of the Iroquoian matriliny. Descent was matrilineal, reckoned through the female line, and residence was matrilocal: daughters brought their husbands into their mother's home to live. Although there were some exceptions, this was the general rule for both the Ontario and the League Iroquoians (Trigger 1976).

The longhouse was intensively occupied from the fall to the spring, with many social and symbolic activities taking place. In the warmer summer months, the longhouse was less intensively occupied, as women and children left the confines of the structure to attend the crops in the adjacent fields and to live in less formal structures, smaller cabins, or lean-tos. During this season the men were often trading or hunting away from the village.

For the Ontario Iroquoians we have little information on the symbolism of the longhouse within the cultural sphere. The reason for this lack of information, which affects much that is known (or not known) about them, is the early date of their dispersal by the League Iroquois. By the middle of the seventeenth century the Ontario Iroquoians no longer existed as a distinct cultural entity in southern

Ontario. They had been massacred, nearly completely annihilated, and driven out of the area by the League Iroquois (Trigger 1976). For this paper, the result of these wars is a lack of observation and recording of anthropological data on the Ontario Iroquois. In contrast, because of their continued existence, the data on the League Iroquois are more complete. It is not possible, however, to directly infer that all the data from the League can be applied to the Ontario Iroquoians.

The confederation of the League of Iroquois is thought to have occurred in the fifteenth century (Tuck 1978). The Iroquois "likened their confederacy to a longhouse, having partitions and separate fires, after their ancient method of building houses, within which the several nations were sheltered under a common roof" (Morgan 1969 [1851], 51). These "People of the Longhouse" were "one family... and these ties of family relationship were carried throughout their civil and social system... and bound them together in one common... brotherhood" (Morgan 1969 [1851], 60). There was no similar political/religious symbolism reported for the Ontario Iroquois. In Ontario it is apparent that the longhouse was the focus of cultural/symbolic activity, but it is not possible to assume the greater political/symbolic significance of the longhouse as seen by the League.

What activities were conducted in the longhouse? Sleeping, food storage, food preparation, storage of tools and raw materials, preparation of finished goods, childbirth, death, ceremonials, political meetings: in short, all activities. The longhouse had a nonspecific-function interior (Kapches 1990). This means that the range of activities could be carried out at any place inside the house, and there were no special rooms assigned for these functions. There were structural elements in the interior that demarcated space: the end-cubicle or end-storage area, and the platforms or benches along the sides of houses. In the central area of the house the fire pits, or hearths, were situated. The arrangement of families inside the house was not random. Each family occupied one side of one hearth; therefore each hearth had two families, on opposite sides of the longhouse. Each family had storage space for personal goods on their platform, and also space for hanging goods on the poles suspended from the rafters. In Ontario, in contrast to New York State, there is no clear archaeological evidence for interior partitions dividing the platforms and the central corridor space, as on the Iroquois sites. Although the storage of personal items seems to have been specific according to familial placement in the house, the storage of food and firewood was communal. Firewood was stored under sidewall platforms, and food was stored in huge elm-bark casks placed in the end cubicles.

Longhouse Construction and Raw Materials

The construction of most houses seems to have taken place during the spring and summer months, when the saplings and the bark were pliable. Descriptions of the details of longhouses observed by the French include: the lodges had a bower or arbor shape, hence a rounded roof; they were covered with tree bark (cedar, ash, elm, or fir) with splints to hold this bark in place; there were no windows, no cellars, only one storey; no chimney—only a smoke hole in the ceiling protected by a bark flap; a door at each end; a platform about four to five feet (1.2–1.5 meters [m]) high along each side, beneath which wood was stored; the porches or end cubicles were for storing food; there was a passage down the center; and food and goods were stored in bark- or grass-lined pits, which were subsequently covered with bark and soil for protection from fire (Biggar 1929; Sagard-Théodat 1939 [1632]; Morgan 1969 [1851]).

Archaeologically, it is observable that longhouses are predominantly 22 to 26 feet (6.6–7.9 m) wide. The French missionary Brébeuf described "the usual width (of the house) is about four brasses. Their height is about the same" (Thwaites 1896–1901, 8:105–7). This description is most often interpreted as the width of the longhouse equals the height of the longhouse. There is considerable debate amongst Iroquoianists about the height of longhouses as reflected in reconstructions (Kapches 1992). This debate will not be reviewed in depth here as it is the subject of ongoing research by the author on construction materials and architectural techniques.

Iroquoian Archaeological Terminology

The archaeological evidence for Iroquoian structural remains appears as features in the soil. These features are the result of human activity, and exist as remnants of the occupation. The main features are post molds, hearths, and pits. Building with stone is not known for Iroquoia, and all structures were constructed of wood, with posts placed directly in the ground. Post molds are the building blocks of Iroquoian archaeology. The term *post mold* is here used to describe the archaeological feature created by a post's being driven into the ground and then decaying, leaving a discoloration in the soil visible both from the surface as a circular stain, and in cross-section as the pointed straight-sided outline of the post. True post holes, with large holes dug to place smaller identifiable posts, are not recognized in Iroquoia. However, similar features, perhaps best termed *post pits*, with small-circumference pits dug for the placement of posts (which are not usually clearly identified) are present (Kapches 1990). *Hearths* are recognized by the occurrence of oxidized soil, reddish in color, and are irregularly oval in outline. Hearths are often shallow features, not extending below the plough zone, some 10 to 12 inches (0.25–0.30 m) below the surface. Being shallow, they are easily destroyed by agricultural activities, and their presence is often inferred by other features (a plethora of small post molds) associated with them. Finally, *pits* are holes dug into the ground of variable size and shape. Often pits have artifacts in them, and when they were abandoned they were filled with layers of garbage debris from the occupation of the house.

A Typical Archaeological Longhouse

Standard details of an Ontario Iroquoian longhouse are shown in figure 9.2. This figure shows House No. 7 from the prehistoric, mid-fourteenth-century Nodwell site (J. Wright 1974). "A" is the plan published in the report. It is included to

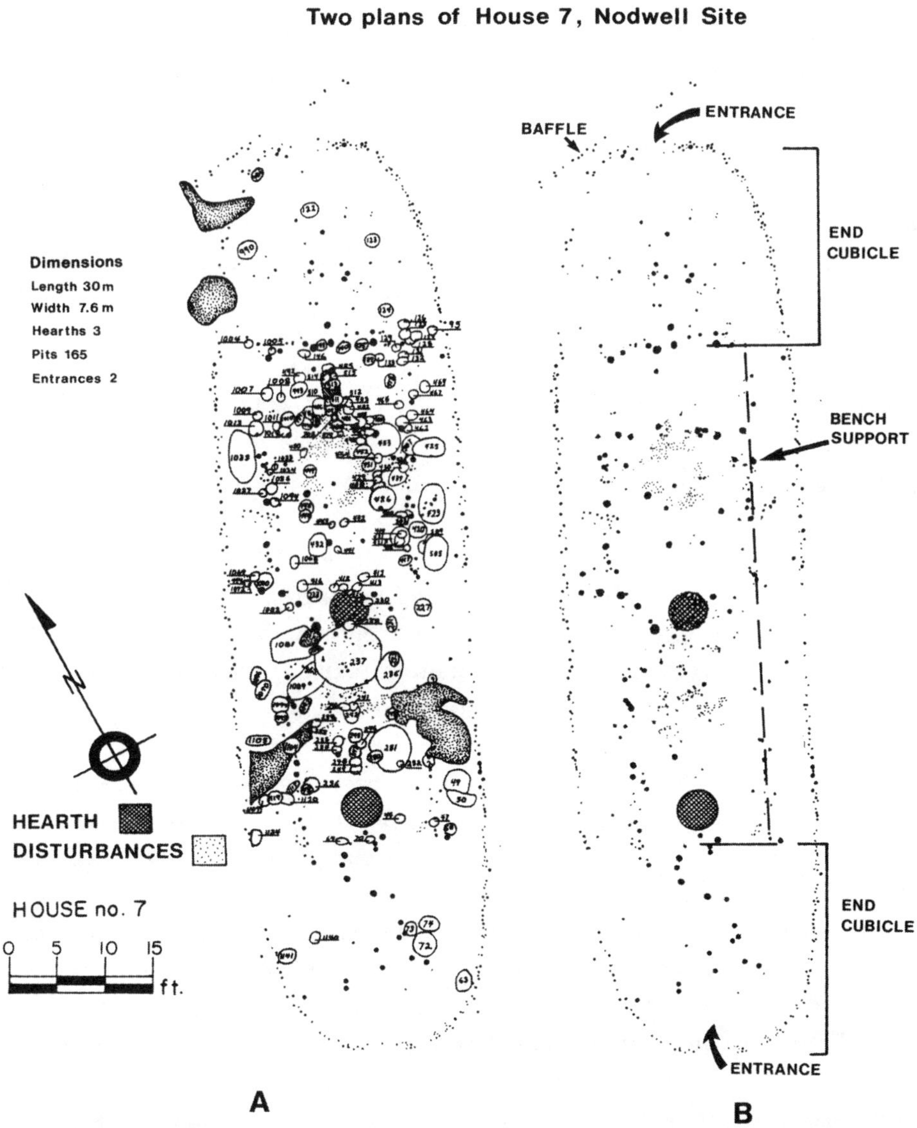

Fig. 9.2. Two plans of house 7, Nodwell site.

give an idea of the complexity of floor plans as they are published. This is a typical example of an Iroquoian longhouse. The house was 99 feet (30.0 m) long, 25 feet (7.6 m) wide, with end cubicles at each end of the house, sidewall benches at approximately five feet (1.5 m) out from the wall on each side of the house, one definite doorway at the end with an external protecting baffle (which is a rare feature), a possible door at the other end, one definite hearth, and two possible hearths located in the central corridor. The diameter of the wall posts was 2 to 3 inches (0.05–0.08 m), and the larger interior support posts were 5 to 8 inches (0.13–0.20 m) in diameter. There were 165 pits inside the house and these are situated, for the most part, in the central corridor area of the house.

Figure 9.2B shows House 7 with the storage pits excluded, because pits inside houses were covered with bark and earth, and so are not considered part of the construction of the house (see Kapches 1990 for a discussion of this). What remains are the details of the superstructure.

The side walls of the house are made of single and staggered rows of posts. It was thought that the bark walls were positioned firmly between these two rows, with additional exterior splint-work to fasten the bark. However, a brief reference to building mentions that the bark shingles were the last "to be put in place to finish" a house (Fraser and Jones 1909, 303). This reference suggests that the poles were staggered to allow for cross-members to support the exterior attachment of bark shingles. The bark, whichever variety of wood was selected, was prepared as large shingles, which were layered in an overlapping pattern. The grain of the shingle was vertical, allowing the rainwater to run off the house. The diameter of the posts indicates that saplings were selected for the walls.

Inside the house, there are larger support posts positioned at a distance of five feet (1.5 m) from the walls. These are bench-support posts and can be easily identified in the plan. They occur bilaterally down the center of the house. To support the sidewall benches, posts were placed horizontally between these supports: at Nodwell it was discovered that these cross-supports actually wedged very firmly, providing excellent support for the benches. Additional support for the bench was provided by attachment to the sidewall posts. These posts also provided support for the roof and allowed for the attachment of posts to provide space for hanging items in the rafters of the house. Note as well, by comparing with view A, that it is not usual for storage pits to occur underneath the benches.

At both ends of this house there are rows of posts that demarcate the end cubicle area from the rest of the house. The end cubicle area is often devoid of storage pits, as storage of food in these cubicles was in large bark casks.

The duration of the occupation at Ontario Iroquoian village sites was observed to be about 10 to 15 years. After that time the villages were abandoned, new locations chosen, and the village relocated. At some villages, archaeologists are now suggesting that the occupation may have been longer, perhaps as long as 30 years

(Warrick 1988). Evidence for longer occupation may be discerned in the rebuilding activities seen in the walls of the houses. Villages occupied for a shorter period of time would not have a lot of rebuilding activities observable in the floor plans.

Examples of Longhouse Structural Variability

Structural variability can be created by limitations of available raw materials and/or the effects of cultural factors, i.e., present only in houses of a particular tribe. For the Ontario Iroquoians there were no significant changes in the raw materials employed in the construction of houses for the time period under study. Therefore, it is argued that structural variability is the result of cultural factors. Those features that appear to be the result of architectural variability will be described employing examples of Ontario Iroquoian longhouses.

House 4 from the prehistoric, proto-Huron, Draper village site, ca. A.D. 1450–1550, is presented in figure 9.3B (Finlayson 1985). This house has been lengthened two times at each end, four times altogether during its occupation. The original house was 36.7 meters long; when the expansions were complete the house was 62.8 meters long. It is usually thought that houses were expanded rather than retracted. As families grew in size, or as in the case of the Draper site, as the community grew, the houses were lengthened to encompass more people. The expansion episodes are evidenced by the tapered rows of posts that appear inside the house. Also visible are the support posts for the sidewall benches, as well as the lack of pits underneath the benches, and the similar lack of pits in the end cubicles. Of note is the observation by the excavating archaeologist that as well as two doorways in the ends of the house, it is likely that there were doors at midpoints on either side of the house. Observe the overlapping and crowded rows of post molds constituting the walls; these suggest rebuilding of the walls, and further suggest a longer period of occupation of this village. See in House 6 at the top of the figure the complete rebuilding and moving of the wall of a house. In this figure the several rows of posts in lines below House 4 are palisade rows.

Figure 9.3A is House 12 from the prehistoric Draper, proto-Huron village site (Finlayson 1985). It is possible to determine several features of this house: limited storage pit presence on the sides and the end of the house, doorways at the ends, and complexity of central corridor feature concentration including many hearths and small pits. There are two aspects of this house that will be pointed out as examples of architectural variability. The first has to do with the lack, in some areas of the house, of obvious large posts along the sides, which would have provided support for the benches. There are at Draper, and at other sites, small circular or oval pits on the floors in the position where a support post would ideally have been situated. At some sites there are no bench wall support posts, just a distinct row of small pits. It is argued that these pits, termed *post pits,* were dug out for the placement of support

182 · *Precolumbian Dynamics*

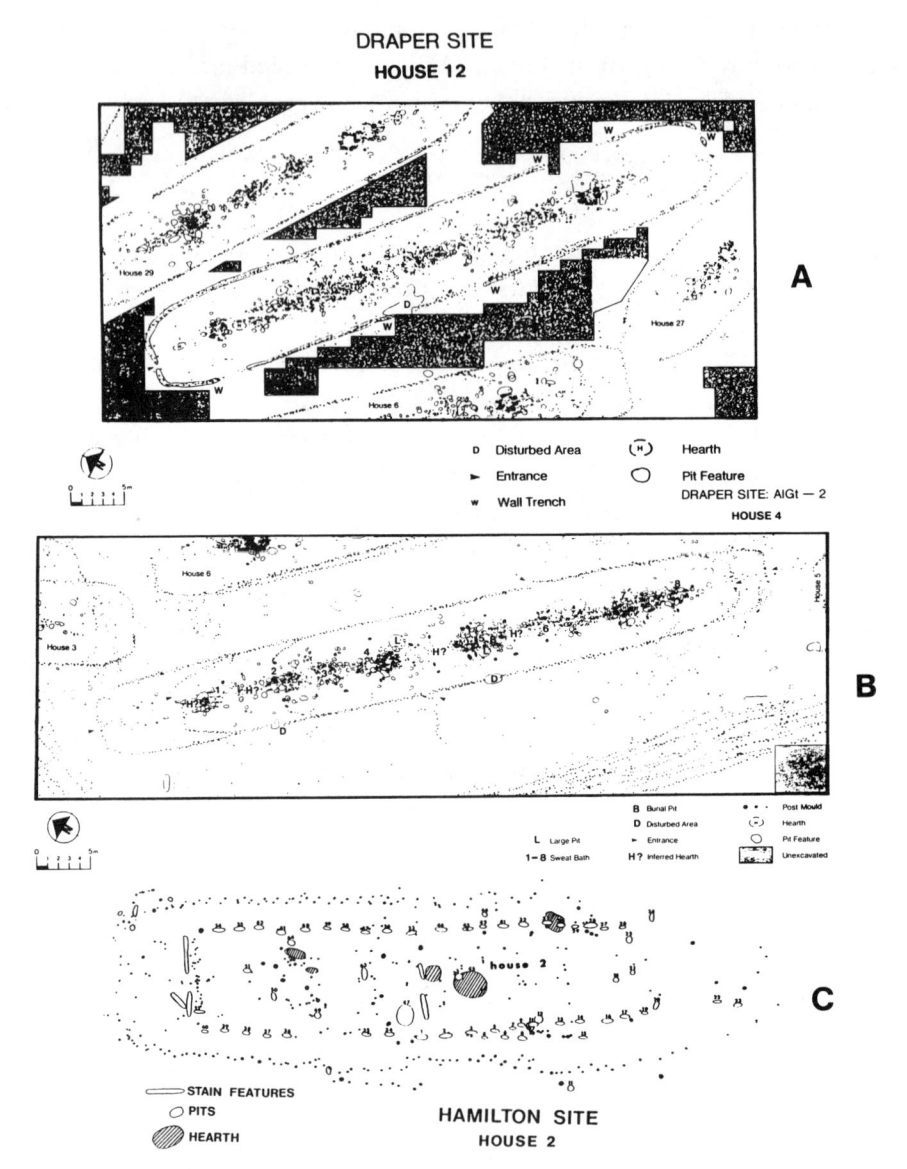

Fig. 9.3. Top: house 12 at Draper site. Middle: house 4 at Draper site. Bottom: house 2 at Hamilton site.

posts for the benches and the superstructure. The other major variation in the plan of House 12 is the presence of a trench dug along the wall of the house. Wall trenches have post molds at their bottom. They can be shallow or deep, and are quite variable. There are several ideas concerning the presence of these (see Kapches 1990); the accepted architectural rationale is that they were dug to aid the deeper positioning of the sidewall posts, and that they allowed the bark siding to be placed into the ground to assist in the prevention of drafts, and that the excavation of these features allowed for the planning of the layout of the structure during its construction. Culturally, it has been suggested that these features may indicate a Mississippian house-construction technique imported into Ontario Iroquoia (Kapches 1990).

House 2 in figure 9.3C is from the historic Neutral Hamilton site, ca. A.D. 1640 (Lennox 1981). The double staggered row of post molds forming the walls is obvious; however, the walls are poorly defined and even absent in some areas of this house. This absence is owing to difficulties during excavation. Following previous examples where there are support posts for the benches, at Hamilton there are linear and oval pits forming the border edge of the bench. As can be seen by comparing the distribution of these to those at the Draper site, these pits, called "slash pits," are more regular in plan view and in positioning. Another type of pit distinctive to Neutral sites is a "linear stain feature." These features can be seen at one end of the Hamilton house, to the exterior of the interior cubicle partition. As well, there are two stains in the central area of the house, interpreted as resulting from the disintegration of bark insulation flaps in the ground. The reason offered for the linear stain in the center of the Hamilton house is that it indicates an expansion event had occurred. These two stains, then, represent a partition of the end cubicle area of the original, pre-expansion house. The linear stains and slash pit features are tribally distinctive to the Neutral.

The Ball site, an historic Huron village, ca. A.D. 1615, provides another interesting structural variation seen in House 16 (fig. 9.4A) (Knight and Cameron 1983; Knight personal communication 1988). The posts of this house are paired and in single rows. At the north end, the house has been expanded. The absence of features at the two ends of the house suggests small storage cubicles. At Ball there is little definition of hearths in the central corridors of the houses, and thus the presence of hearth areas is inferred from clusters of small posts and associated pits. As at Draper House 12 there are no bench support posts. However, similar to the slash pits at the Hamilton, Neutral site, there are small pits positioned regularly in the house, at a standard distance from the walls, indicating the presence of sidewall benches. A unique feature of this house is the presence of definite interior partitions. Two interior partitions, along with the end cubicle partitions, divide this house into five compartments, three for living space and two for storage. The presence of partitions is more typical of houses of the League Iroquois (i.e., the Eaton site; Engelbrecht 1992). There is no indication that this house was occupied by any other than Huron peoples. This interior partition feature is not common at the Ball site.

There is a unique structure often found on Ontario Iroquoian villages: the cabin. The cabin is a small structure that is not a longhouse and is not a short longhouse (Kapches 1984). Before discussing cabins, the length of houses can be reviewed. The average length for longhouses was once estimated as 24 meters

184 · Precolumbian Dynamics

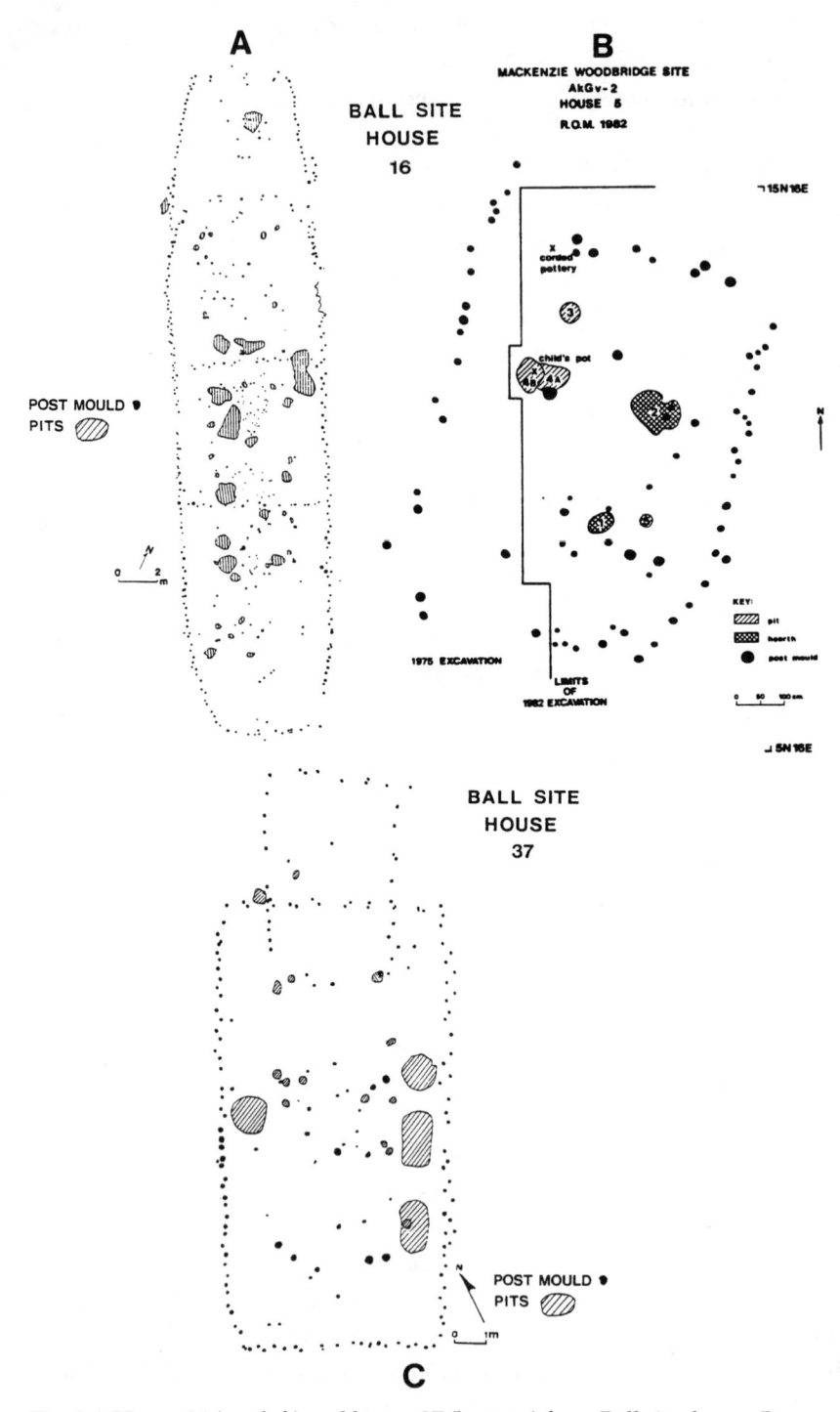

Fig. 9.4. House 16 (top left) and house 37 (bottom) from Ball site; house 5 from Mackenzie Woodbridge site (top right).

(Heidenreich 1971). Now, with a larger sample of excavated houses, it is apparent that there is considerable variability in house length even at one site. One longhouse excavated in Ontario, at the Moyer Site, is over 300 feet (91 m) (Wagner, Toombs, and Riegert 1973). Longhouses, by definition, are longer than they are wide. The average Iroquoian longhouse is 7 meters wide. Based on data estimating a width-to-length ratio (W:L) for longhouses (Kapches 1984), longhouses have a length that is two times greater than width (1:>2); short longhouses have a length less than twice the width (1:<2) but a length greater than the width and one-quarter (1:<1.25). Cabins are smaller structures and have a length that is less than the width and one quarter (1:<1.25). Cabins are considerably smaller than short longhouses. Short longhouses have the interior structural details of long longhouses, while cabins have considerable variability.

House 5 from the Mackenzie-Woodbridge site is a cabin (fig. 9.4B). It is 7 meters long by 5 meters wide. It has doorways in corners, a possible small platform on one wall, and a partition at one end. Cabins are found on late prehistoric and historic sites, both Huron and Neutral (Kapches 1984). They may have served as shelter for single families, or visitors, or were used by shamans for ceremonials. Despite the small size of cabins, they still exhibit some of the features of Iroquoian construction, such as hearths and pits in the interior area, away from the walls.

What is clear from these examples, and within the context of this paper, is that these are not longhouses. Small non-longhouse structures on Iroquoian sites must be considered individually because they are not Iroquoian on the basis of architectural attributes. That Iroquoians knew how to make cabins, and did so when needed as special-purpose structures, is not at question. What is at question is the ethnic identity of these structures. Cabins are known to have been constructed by Algonquians (Murphy and Ferris 1990; Reid and Rajanovich 1991), and Algonquians are known to have wintered on the outskirts of Iroquoian villages. The presence of cabins in the village is not usually assumed to indicate an in-village Algonquian presence. The difficulty of assigning an Algonquian identity to such structures on Iroquoian village sites leads instead to the conservative assessment that these houses are special-purpose structures built by Iroquoians.

The final structure that will be presented for review is House 37 at the Ball site (fig. 9.4C). This site is argued by Fitzgerald (1986) to be Cahiagué, the village where Champlain wintered in A.D. 1615–16. This assertion is based on the chronology of the glass trade beads at the site in comparison to other sites in the vicinity of the Ball site. There is some debate concerning Fitzgerald's analysis, as the excavator, Dean H. Knight, does not support this interpretation (Knight personal communication 1991). An examination of the architectural features of House 37 sheds some light on the impact of Europeans at that site. Although architecture may not assist in resolving the particular question of site identity, this structure has elements of European influence that provide another view of cultural attributes of architecture.

House 37 is described as 48 feet (14.6 m) long, by 30 feet (9.1 m) wide, with a possible door space along one wall, and with a small addition at one end (Knight and Cameron 1983). This structure, in comparison to those previously presented, shows distinct differences: right-angle corners, a rectangular shape; an addition with squared corners, also with a rectangular outline; the arrangement of pits, of which there are few, along the sides of the house under the sidewall bench area. House 37 is quite different from the Iroquoian longhouses and small Native-made cabins of Iroquoian and Algonquian origins in southern Ontario (Murphy and Ferris 1990; Reid and Rajanovich 1991). Because of the distinctive right-angle corners it has a European appearance, one that suggests that it had a true frame for the superstructure.

What is known about the structures built for Europeans at this early time period? From the eyewitness accounts it is known that Father Joseph LeCaron and other Frenchmen (soldiers) wintered with the Huron at the same period that Champlain did. Father LeCaron had a structure, a little cabin, built for him, where Champlain stayed when he visited him at Carhagouha, some distance from Cahiagué. In A.D. 1623–24 when Father LeCaron returned to Huronia with the lay brother Gabriel Sagard, Sagard detailed a structure built for them. He described it as a small lodge, or cabin, 20 feet (6.0 m) long by 10 to 12 feet (3–3.6 m) wide. It was a hut divided into two: on the door side there was the eating, sleeping, and meeting area. There was a partition to a small chapel, "an inner room" with an altar, and there was a small room between these two rooms for the storage of personal items. This description fits the layout of House 37. A large room with a door, a small added-on room for the altar, with a small vestibule or storage area separating the two rooms.

Although it is argued here that House 37 may have been for the occupation of the French during the existence of the site, there are other points to be considered before stating this without reservations. First, there are no unusual artifacts from House 37 that suggest it may have had other than nonnative occupants. This absence is not surprising, because the Europeans at this time, although some trading was involved, were not expressly in Huronia to trade. This was an exploration and a missionary trip, and intensive trading commenced much later, so at this early date little trade material is expected. Also, the Europeans were not self-sufficient. As guests of the Huron, they received their subsistence support and personal goods from the Natives, and therefore they existed with the use of Native-made items such as pottery vessels, furs, mats, and wooden bowls.

Another factor to be considered was that in the literature there are two cabins described as being built for Europeans, and both of these were built at some distance from the village, and therefore not in the village proper. This fact is of interest because House 37 is in the midst of the village, not on the periphery. However, the cabins built away from the village were for the French missionaries, who chose not to live in the village proper. Rather than accepting this situation of cabin construction as the only acceptable norm, it is suggested that intra-village construction was a variation. Indeed, it appears that Champlain and his soldiers wintered inside the village of Cahiagué, not in a cabin on the outskirts. Considering the political importance of Cahiagué as the major village of the area, it is unlikely that a guest of such importance as Champlain would have been allowed to reside outside the protective confines of the village palisade, especially considering this was a time when active warfare was being waged against the Huron by the League Iroquois.

A final point to be considered is that Atironta, one of the main headmen of the Arendarhonon tribe of the Huron, whose village was Cahiagué (and whose guest Champlain was), visited Quebec with Champlain in 1616. At Quebec Atironta stated that he wished to have Frenchman live among the Huron (Trigger 1976). House 37 may have been constructed at Atironta's request, based on the structural designs he saw at Quebec, in order to accommodate Frenchmen. In this interpretation House 37 would be a Native architectural view of a European structure. It is tentatively concluded that House 37 may be evidence of a structure built on an Iroquoian village in the European fashion.

Conclusions

Certain standard features of longhouses are repeated through time and in different tribal areas (Dodd 1984). These standardized features clearly culturally define the architecture of Iroquoian longhouses. As well, there exists considerable variability that can be associated with cultural expression, associated with tribal influences and introduced European architectural concepts.

It is critical to an understanding of archaeological architecture to be aware that vernacular structures are not immutable; they change according to various internal and external influences over time. That Europeans affected elements of Iroquoian architecture is expected and is apparent in an ongoing study on the longhouses of the contact-period Ontario Iroquoian sites. The Ball site, an early site in the European contact period, is a transitional site where the effects of European interaction in structural variability are limited. Further, just as the Native architecture changed, so did the European architecture, as seen in the earliest European buildings in Ontario (also part of a study currently being undertaken).

This paper has been an introduction to the architecture of the Ontario Iroquoians. Ongoing research will attempt to evaluate variability in the architecture of the Confederacy Iroquois and other Iroquoians of Northeastern North America not located in Iroquoia heartland. Also being evaluated is the architecture of adjacent peoples to determine the interaction of Iroquoian peoples through the presence or absence of the Iroquoian structures so essential to the definition of Iroquoian peoples.

Acknowledgments

I would like to thank the Architectural Conservancy of Ontario for allowing me to make a presentation of a version of this paper, "The Ontario Iroquoian Longhouse: A Study in Vernacular Architecture," at their conference on Vernacular Architecture, April 24–25, 1992, in Brantford, Ontario. Many thanks to Alec Reefer and Paul Dilse. I would also like to acknowledge the long years of careful work by Dr. Dean Knight of Wilfrid Laurier University at the Ball site. Dr. Knight has allowed me access to his unpublished data, which has provided an exceptional database for my research on Iroquoian longhouses.

PART THREE

| *Postcolumbian Dynamics*

| Overview

THE ARRIVAL OF EUROPEANS and colonialism in North America had a devastating effect on many Native groups, resulting in significant loss of life, land, and culture. As the readings in part 3 testify, the Iroquois experience during Postcolumbian times in the Northeast was mixed. Several populations were rapidly victimized by virulent new diseases and armed clashes, though others were able to delay the impact, owing partly to their remote locations away from initial Dutch, French, and English fronts. The earliest recorded encounter with Europeans occurred in A.D. 1534 when Jacques Cartier met Northern Iroquoians on his voyage along the St. Lawrence River. Other explorers and colonial settlements soon followed. Considerable documentary evidence exists on the Iroquois during the sixteenth-eighteenth centuries. This information, however, is partial, not only because it was produced solely by Europeans, as opposed to Natives, but also because authors often intentionally misled their readers for political and economic gain. Although archaeology has its own biases and cannot provide a complete view of the Iroquois past, the interpretation of thousands of material remains from hundreds of sites complements, and sometimes contradicts, colonial records.

The lead article in this section, by Martha L. Sempowski, elucidates the occurrence and timing of a major breach in interactions between the Seneca and Susquehannock, as indicated by historical sources at the beginning of the Contact Period. She hypothesizes that disruption in the exchange relationships took place shortly after the establishment of the Dutch in New York around A.D. 1609 and before A.D. 1615 when Samuel de Champlain reported animosity presumably between these two Iroquois communities. Analysis of such types of European and exotic trade goods as brass, glass beads, and marine shell from Seneca and Susquehannock sites suggests the involvement of both groups in separate spheres of interaction with Native and European populations for at least part of this time.

William E. Engelbrecht explores the question concerning what effect, if any, the colonists had on New York Iroquois political development during the Protohistoric Period (ca. A.D. 1500–1630). He maintains that although the Five Nations Iroquois and the League of the Iroquois originated during Precolumbian times and continued to develop after initial contact, European powers indirectly contributed to the consolidation of both organizations. Relying on archaeological remains, particularly from Onondaga and Seneca sites, as well as on oral history, the author argues that the isolation of the New York Iroquois from areas of colonial settlements until the eighteenth century provided extra time for their political development to proceed without direct European interference. In his words, "Though Europeans were the cause of increased warfare and mortality rates for the protohistoric Iroquois, their sociopolitical institutions evolved to meet these challenges" (Engelbrecht 1985, 180 [chap. 11).

Unlike Sempowski and Engelbrecht, Kurt A. Jordan focuses on structural remains excavated at a single postcolumbian site, Townley-Read, located near Geneva, New York, and occupied by the Seneca between about A.D. 1715 and 1754. Structure 1 measures 7.5 meters (m) long and 5.3 m wide, in sharp contrast to the older, much larger Iroquois longhouses, and is situated in a low-lying area of the site, as opposed to a nearby defensible ridgetop, which would have been preferred during the fifteenth-seventeenth centuries. Although Jordan admits that he is not entirely certain of the length, he uses Kapches's (1984) typology for Iroquoian house forms to define this feature as a "short longhouse," or less formally as a "shorthouse." Based on the remains of four main interior support posts, double layer of wall posts, domestic debris, and a central corridor with a previously destroyed central hearth, the author interprets the structure as a two-family dwelling that resembles closely a free-standing segment of a longhouse. Jordan compares the Townley-Read shorthouse to traditional Iroquois dwellings and discovers that it exhibits different post types and post placement, lower density of wall posts, increased nail use, and lesser proportion of space dedicated to permanent and semipermanent features. He reasons that log or plank siding, instead of bark, was used to build Structure 1, resulting in greater durability and fewer posts for bracing as bark. This log- or plank-sided shorthouse counters the predominant model of eighteenth-century Iroquois housing that claims European-style log cabins replaced bark longhouses. As Jordan emphasizes, the Townley-Read short longhouse and other Iroquois houses of the mid-eighteenth century remained recognizably Iroquoian in floorplan and construction, built fundamentally differently from European methods of log construction, thereby demonstrating much more continuity with indigenous architecture and culture.

In the next paper, William R. Fitzgerald directs our attention to changes experienced by the Neutral of southern Ontario during the sixteenth and seventeenth centuries. The explanation of cultural developments among the Neutral during this time, according to the author, has been influenced by the coincidence of such changes with the appearance and encroachment of the colonists. Fitzgerald adds that, despite the deleterious colonial impact on Ontario Iroquoian societies, by the time Europeans became a serious threat, many of these Native groups were already in the process of "devolution," initiated during the sixteenth century. His study reevaluates available archaeological, ecological, and climatic evidence of various human and natural factors that affected Neutral cultural change directly and indirectly. Among the trends identified in the archaeological record of this Iroquoian nation between the fifteenth and seventeenth centuries are decreasing and dispersing populations, shifting residential and subsistence patterns, increasing ritualism, and adoption of foreigners and exotic material goods. One explanation for the Neutral demise, which occurred in the A.D. 1650s, is that sustained climatic deterioration (known as the Little Ice Age), beginning by A.D. 1550, severely weakened this society that had become dependent on farming in a horticulturally marginal environment.

The subject of European diseases among the Huron and Petun is examined by Gary A. Warrick in chapter 14. Citing historical, epidemiological, archaeological, and bioarchaeological data, the timing and impact of depopulation among these Iroquoians are reconstructed. Epidemics, especially from smallpox and measles, spread rapidly among indigenous peoples, resulting in high mortality rates because they lacked sufficient immunity. Not only was disease contracted from highly contagious individuals, regardless of their ethnicity, but also from infected trade goods. Many historians assume that large numbers of Native Americans in the Northeast were decimated by European contagions, either immediately preceding or at the time of direct contact in the sixteenth century. The Huron-Petun indeed suffered tremendous loss of human life from the epidemics recorded in A.D. 1634–40 (Warrick estimates a 60 percent population decline), but no archaeological or bioarchaeological evidence exists for any substantial outbreak of European disease among this community in the sixteenth century. The author suspects the same for other Native groups in northeastern North America.

10 | Early Historic Exchange Between the Seneca and the Susquehannock

MARTHA L. SEMPOWSKI

Introduction

UNDERPINNING SEVENTEENTH-CENTURY fur trade in the New World was a preexisting web of Native interrelationships that are critical to understanding later patterns of interaction among Europeans and particular groups of Native peoples. Furthermore, knowledge of these earlier relationships must be sufficiently specific and fine-grained to elucidate the timing of the subtle shifts and realignments that took place, often quite abruptly, during the protohistoric period. Relations between the Five Nations Iroquois and the Susquehannock represent a potentially informative case in this regard in that historic sources indicate a major breach in interactions between them. This breach occurred sometime during the protohistoric or early historic period and endured into the late seventeenth century with apparently far-reaching political and economic consequences throughout the Northeast. However, significant questions remain regarding the timing of that disruption and thus its relationship to specific archaeological data sets in various regions. The goal here is to discern archaeological evidence indicative of disrupted interactions between the Susquehannock and the Seneca, one of the five tribes of the early historic League of the Iroquois, and to try to ascertain the approximate date of occurrence.

Background of the Question

The issue of relations between the Susquehannock and their New York neighbors is set within the broader context of questions surrounding the reinvigoration of Native exchange networks that occurred throughout the Northeast in the mid- to

Previously published in *Proceedings of the 1992 People to People Conference: Selected Papers,* ed. C. F. Hayes III, C. C. Bodner, and L. P. Saunders, Research Records no. 23 (Rochester, N.Y.: Rochester Museum and Science Center, 1994), 51–64. Printed with permission by Rochester Museum and Science Center.

late sixteenth century. Through these networks, highly prized materials such as marine shell and European manufactured goods, destined primarily for mortuary use, began to circulate in some quantities among Native groups. There appear to have been at least several distinct spheres of interaction operating in the region during this early period, but there is a growing consensus that most of the exotic material reaching Iroquoians in New York and Pennsylvania during the early part of the period originated along the mid-Atlantic coast and was transmitted inland and northward through Native intermediaries from the south (Bradley 1987a, 89–103; Bradley and Childs 1989; 1991, 8 [chap. 15]; Ceci 1985, 13–14; Pendergast 1989, 102–3; Vandrei 1984, 9–11; Wray et al. 1987, 250–51). Evidence is mounting that this early southeasterly network was to some extent distinct from and independent of that in which the Neutral and Huron of Ontario were involved during this period. Perhaps the strongest evidence in that regard is the widespread occurrence throughout Pennsylvania and New York of characteristic rolled brass spirals and "hoops," which are all but absent in contemporary Ontario Iroquois sites (Bradley and Childs 1991, 8 [chap. 15]). Distinctions are also apparent in the species of marine shell recognizable in sites in the two regions, leading to the suspicion that the marine shell within this New York/Pennsylvania network may have come from coastal groups located farther north than those supplying the shell to the Ontario groups (Wray et al. 1991, 394–95). There are also noteworthy differences in the types of brass and copper kettles typical in the two areas and in the size and shape of iron axes (cf. Fitzgerald 1988, 5–9, fig. 11; Kenyon and Kenyon 1987, 12–13; Wray et al. 1991, 324, 395).

Thus the general assumption has been that congenial relations prevailed between the Susquehannock and the Five Nations for some time during the latter half of the sixteenth century (Kent 1993 [1984], 18), and that the Susquehannock probably served as an important intermediary between the Five Nations and coastal Algonquian groups (Bradley 1987a, 89–103; Pendergast 1989, 102–3; Vandrei 1984, 9–11; Wray et al. 1987, 250–51). Subsequent studies, demonstrating a marked hiatus around the turn of the seventeenth century in the occurrence of marine shell on Seneca and Mohawk sites in New York, have pointed to a probable disruption in the southeasterly network by which marine shell had previously been reaching Iroquoia (Ceci 1985, 14; Kuhn and Funk 1994; Sempowski 1989, 90–92), and suggested that the source of the problem may have been some sort of rift with the Susquehannock. Other circumstantial evidence also seems to point toward broken relations between the Susquehannock and New York Iroquoians. Coinciding with the decline in shell in the Seneca area and elsewhere, and conceivably related to it, is the rather abrupt disappearance in New York of the brass spirals and "hoops" that had previously been so widespread in Iroquoia south of Ontario (Bradley and Childs 1991, 8 [chap. 15]). It may be worth noting that these spirals appear to continue longer in the Susquehannock area than elsewhere (Bradley and Childs 1991, figs. 5 and 6 [chap. 15]; Kent 1993 [1984]). Susquehannock pottery styles have also been noted on some New York Iroquois sites around this time (Bradley 1987a, 58–60; Kuhn and Funk 1994; Wray and Schoff 1953, 56), raising speculation about the presence of Susquehannock captives on New York Iroquois sites (Kuhn and Funk 1994). Unfortunately, differences in the current dating of the relevant Susquehannock, Seneca, and Mohawk sites present questions about the exact timing of these various phenomena (Kuhn and Funk 1994). Finally, Barry C. Kent has suggested the possibility that political problems with the Iroquois may have been one factor propelling the Susquehannock southward from the upper Susquehanna River Valley to the Schultz site in Lancaster County, although he has admitted that there is little direct archaeological evidence of conflict (Kent 1993 [1984], 18). Along with Hunter, Kent has posed as well the alternate possibility that the Susquehannock may have been motivated by a desire for greater proximity to sources of exotic goods from the coast (Hunter 1969 [1959], 13; Kent 1993 [1984], 19).

Also relevant to this issue is the more westerly sphere of alliances that tied Ontario Iroquoians to groups in the Ohio and Allegheny river valleys, and through them to influences from the southern mid-Atlantic coast (Dincauze and Hasenstaab 1989; S. Jamieson 1992, 78–81), a phenomenon also suggested with somewhat different emphases by William C. Johnson (1990, 11–12; 1992, 12–13). Along this network, exotic ideas and goods are said to have been transmitted from the "Mississippified" polities in the south to groups in Ohio, western Pennsylvania, and southern Ontario. James F. Pendergast (1992, 7–8) has argued that by 1608, the "Massawomeck," a group tentatively identified by Johnson (1992, 12) with the archaeological complex known as Monongahela, had become the crucial middlemen in the marine-shell trade between the mid-Atlantic coast and southern Ontario. Susan M. Jamieson (1992) has maintained that during the protohistoric period, the Ontario Iroquois actively restricted the Senecas' access to this network, its sources of marine shell, and its influences of "Mississippification." While Johnson (1990; 1992, 12–14) has proposed that the Susquehannock and the Seneca were cut off from this lucrative network, Fitzgerald (1990a, 589–90) has concluded from glass-bead evidence that connections continued between the Susquehannock and Ontario Iroquois throughout the early Contact Period.

If we assume that some realignments between coastal Algonquian suppliers of marine shell and inland middlemen groups (e.g., Monongahela versus Susquehannock) occurred early in the seventeenth century, this explanation may account for the sharp drop in marine shell in Seneca and Mohawk sites, but it fails to explain what might have disrupted relations between the Susquehannock and the New York groups. However, if it could be shown that the Susquehannock were not entirely excluded from the Allegheny Valley/Ohio Valley/Ontario sphere but enjoyed some sort of ongoing connections, possibly through real or fictive kinship ties, we might gain some important insights into the bases for the seventeenth-century hostilities that plagued the Susquehannock and their New York neighbors.

An historical account from as early as 1615 suggests the possibility that the Susquehannock and New York Iroquois were already seriously at odds. In that year, Samuel de Champlain reported sending Etienne Brûlé to take advantage of military support offered by a group commonly identified as the Susquehannock (Bradley 1987a, 223, fn. 2; Jennings 1978, 362; Tooker 1984, 3), in a French/Huron attack on an Iroquois village (Biggar 1922–36, 3:53–56; Bradley 1987a, 113, 223, fn. 2). If this account does indeed refer to the Susquehannock, it suggests that the animosity that was to characterize Susquehannock/Iroquois relations up until the dispersal of the Susquehannock by the Seneca in 1675 (Thwaites 1896–1901, 33:73; 59:251; 60:173) (as cited in Tooker 1984) was already in place at this early date. The question is when did the rupture, which was complete enough to produce the kind of enmity that the French and Huron were proposing to exploit in 1615, occur? And can archaeological evidence be found to confirm and elucidate it?

With no pretense of being able to explicate the entire scenario, the immediate goal of this study is merely to examine the limited question of whether the Seneca and the Susquehannock were involved in the same or different interaction spheres during the critical decades surrounding the turn of the seventeenth century. The assumption is made that if a disruption in mutual exchange between the Susquehannock and New York Iroquois had occurred during that time, it would likely be reflected in qualitative and quantitative differences in the material record of that exchange. With the Seneca as the focal New York group, the present study begins to explore this theoretical possibility. Common items of exchange, such as glass beads, brass ornaments, and marine-shell objects from Seneca and Susquehannock sites pertaining to the end of the sixteenth and the beginning of the seventeenth centuries were examined to see whether they would provide evidence that the two groups were participating in different spheres of interaction, and if so, how early a disjunction might have occurred.

Method of Investigation

With the assumption that groups involved in a common sphere of interaction would have been acquiring very similar kinds of European and exotic goods, and in roughly similar quantities, I conducted a preliminary comparison of the types and frequencies of several specific categories of "trade" items that occurred in the Susquehannock and Seneca regions.

Sources of Data

During the period in question, the two groups were situated about 250 miles apart with the Susquehanna and Chemung Rivers and the Finger Lakes providing potential access between the two regions (see fig. 10.1). The Cameron site (Hne 29–2) and the Dutch Hollow site (Hne 1–1) were selected for the Seneca side of the comparison, because they represent the two consecutive occupation periods in the Seneca sequence that are most likely to provide evidence relating to the period in question. According to our most recent revisions of the Seneca chronology (Wray et al. 1991, fig. intro-4, 400–411), they are thought to have spanned the period from the 1590s to 1620. Excavations at the Cameron site uncovered a total of 118 burials, and the data used here have been extracted from that compiled and published by the Seneca Archaeology Research Project (Wray et al. 1991). For the Dutch Hollow site, the study was restricted to the 70 burials excavated by William A. Ritchie and associates from one of three burial loci at the site (Ritchie 1954). Data from this cemetery, which are currently being prepared for publication by the Seneca Archaeology Research Project, are thought to be relatively consistent with that collected from the remainder of the site. All of the materials and records studied from these two Seneca sites are housed in the Rochester Museum and Science Center.

For the Susquehannock side of the comparison, the Schultz site (36La9) was selected. While it is a multicomponent site, it includes a large Susquehannock burial area. This study focused on 120 burials excavated by the Pennsylvania Historical Museum Commission (Smith and Graybill 1977) from a single cemetery area. Materials and records pertaining to the Schultz site are housed in the State Museum of Pennsylvania and were kindly made available to me for study by Senior Curator Steven Warfel. Despite the fact that Barry Kent dates the Susquehannock occupation of the Schultz site earlier (between 1575 and 1600) (1993 [1984], 332) than the dates currently being hypothesized for the two Seneca sites, it was chosen for the Susquehannock side of the comparison because of the presence of two particular glass-bead complexes that are considered to be unusually sensitive temporal markers. These are the "Indigo and White" tubular and oval bead, horizon, which predominates in Glass Bead Period 2 in the Northeast; and the "Polychrome" horizon that represents Dutch Period 1 in New York and Pennsylvania (also called New York Period 3), according to Ian T. Kenyon and William R. Fitzgerald (Fitzgerald 1990a; Fitzgerald et al. 1994; Kenyon and Fitzgerald 1986).[1] The occurrence of these

1. I was recently informed by James Herbstritt that striped polychrome beads have also been found at one of the Washington Boro sites (Ibaugh-36La54) thought to postdate the Schultz site occupation in the Susquehannock region (Herbstritt personal communication 1993). This finding raised the possibility that this site might have made a better candidate for comparison with Cameron and Dutch Hollow, although Kent's tally of beads from the Washington Boro village site (36La8) (Kent 1993 [1984], fig. 56) certainly did not suggest that, nor did Fitzgerald's assessment of that site's bead assemblage (1990a, 590). Nevertheless, I was subsequently provided by Herbstritt with data pertaining to a large sample of beads from the Ibaugh site, which had been classified according to Kent's system of glass-bead classification. After translation into the Kidd and Kidd classification system, it became apparent that while examples of the "Polychrome" complex did occur there, they were few in number and represented a very small proportion (less than 2 percent) of the total assemblage. One bead type from that complex that is quite

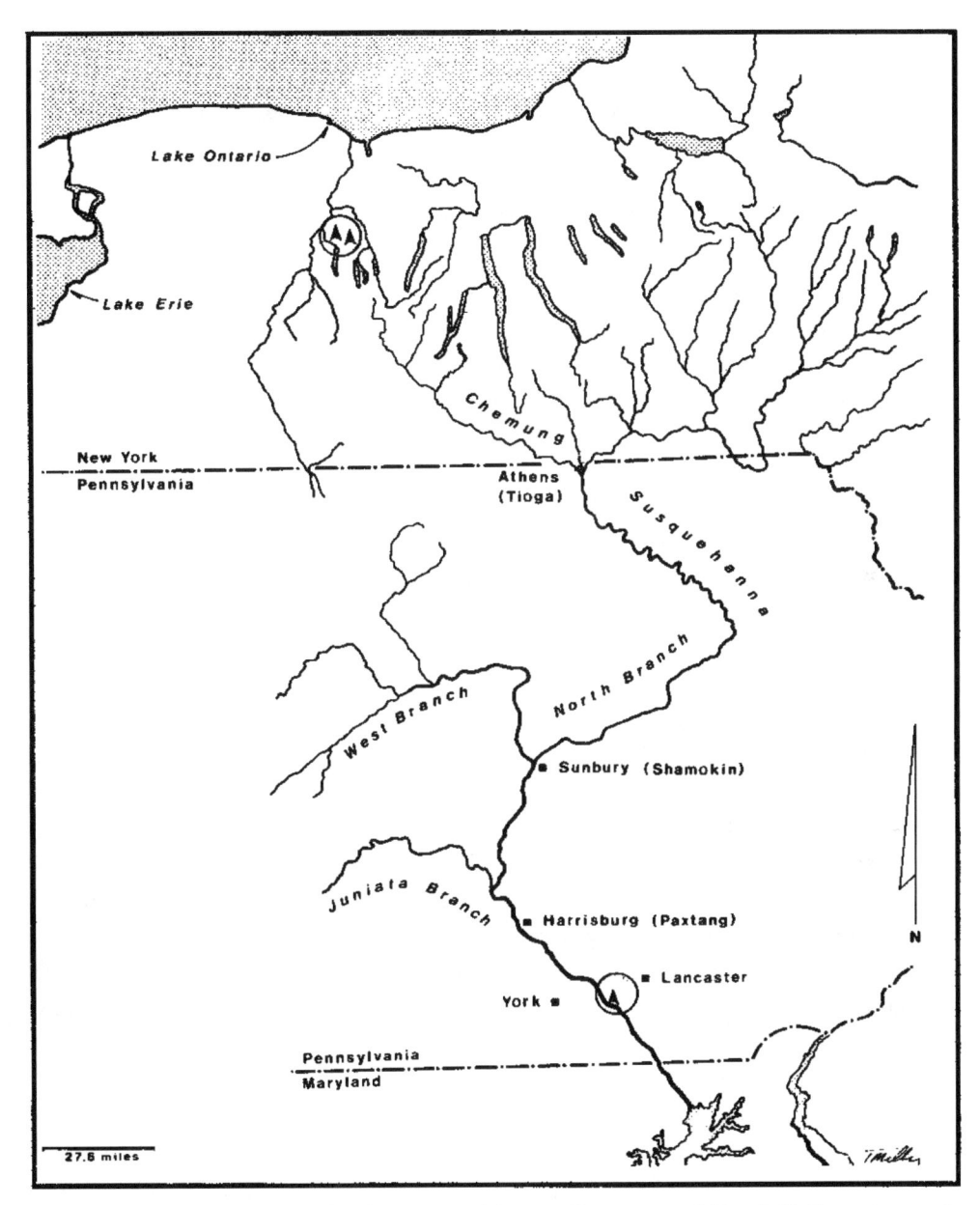

Fig. 10.1. Map of region showing locations of Seneca Cameron and Dutch Hollow sites and Susquehannock Schultz site. Drawn by Patricia L. Miller.

typical at both Schultz and Dutch Hollow, the tumbled "star" bead, is either missing or very rare in the Ibaugh glass-bead assemblage, and the "Indigo/White" complex found at both Cameron and Dutch Hollow is almost nonexistent (0.1 percent). Furthermore, the high frequency of cored White, cored Redwood, cored Brite Navy beads, cored striped, and uncored blue beads of other shades at Ibaugh seemed to point toward placement in the succeeding period, known as "Dutch Period 2," as Fitzgerald has suggested for the other Washington Boro sites (Fitzgerald 1990a, 590).

critical bead groups at Schultz and at the selected Seneca sites are considered to be an indicator of at least partial or overlapping contemporaneity. Furthermore, Kent has repeatedly affirmed that the basis for his proposed dates for the Susquehannock sites was Charles F. Wray and Harry Schoff's (1953) Seneca chronology (Kent 1993 [1984], 19, 330–32), and since that framework has undergone several subsequent revisions (Wray 1973; Wray et al. 1987; Wray et al. 1991, fig. intro-4, 400–411), the glass-bead parallels seem to represent a more secure basis than absolute dates for selecting sites for comparisons (for further discussion of this issue, see below). Thus, information and materials relating to a total of 188 Seneca burials and 120 Susquehannock burials constitute the comparative base utilized for examining the question of potential differences in the trade materials available to the two groups.

Data Analysis

Brass, glass, catlinite, and shell assemblages from both regions were examined in terms of the frequencies, dimensions, and morphological characteristics of the objects. Although all of the glass beads were personally examined and many of them measured, time constraints dictated that the beads from the State Museum of Pennsylvania collections be translated into the Kidd and Kidd classification system (1983 [1970]), which is currently being prepared for publication by the Seneca Archaeology Research Project from the detailed descriptions and counts provided by Ira F. Smith and Jeffrey R. Graybill (1977, fig. 5). Thus there may be some errors on my part in the identification of particular shades, especially the "light blues," from the descriptions. Nevertheless, because of the way in which the beads were grouped for comparison between the two samples (see table 10.1), such problems are not expected to have seriously affected the overall comparisons. Once classified according to the Kidd and Kidd bead typology, the varieties were grouped into nine general categories to facilitate the comparison of the respective bead profiles of each of the two areas. Table 10.1 contains a full tabulation of the varieties included under each grouping.

Group 1: Uncored "Indigo and White" Beads

These consist of tubular and oval shaped beads, either of opaque White or translucent Brite Navy Glass (see fig. 10.2). There is considerable variation in the intensity of the color of these blue beads classified as Brite Navy. Color appears to depend a great deal on the thickness of the glass. There is also a certain degree of size variation, which will be discussed below.

Group 2: Faceted "Star" Beads

Multilayer tubular "star" beads with five to seven layers of glass make up this grouping (see fig. 10.2). These beads vary enormously in size, from small (2–4 millimeters [mm]) to very large (over 10 mm), and in the range of occurrence—both in time and space. Although there are exceptions, most have been ground or faceted at the ends, exposing underlying layers.

Group 3: Tubular, "Flush-eye," and Frit-cored Beads

This group of beads includes many disparate varieties that did not occur in great quantity in any of the sites here and did not fit easily into any of the other categories (see fig. 10.2). For the most part, it consists of tubular beads, cored and uncored, that were not included in the Group 1 "Indigo and White" complex. It also encompasses cored and uncored "flush-eye" beads and the unusual frit-cored beads.

Group 4: Tumbled "Star" Beads

This grouping consists of multilayer "star" beads that have been heat tumbled to produce a rounded appearance and to expose somewhat the colors of the underlying layers (see fig. 10.2). Beads are generally medium to large, and include some with an outer layer of Dark Palm Green or White, as well as the more typical Brite Navy. Also included are a few that have had stripes inlaid into the final layer of glass.

Group 5: Large Striped Beads

This grouping consists of the large (over 6 mm) "broadly striped" beads that include uncored varieties of Redwood and Black beads, frequently involving either compound stripes or stripes of several different colors, as well as cored Brite Navy beads with varying numbers of White stripes (see fig. 10.2).

Group 6: Uncored Monochrome Beads

Encompassed in this grouping are the generally small- to medium-sized, uncored monochrome beads of round, circular, and oval shape. They include a wide range of bead varieties, including the ubiquitous semitranslucent Robin's Egg Blue round beads, as well as White, Black, Redwood, and various other shades of blue (see fig. 10.2).

Table 10.1

Comparison of Glass Beads from Early Historic Seneca and Susquehannock Sites

	SENECA			SUSQUEHANNOCK	
	Dutch Hollow	Cameron	Total	Schultz	
Burials:	70	118	188	120	
n:	4877	522	5399	3028	
Group 1: Uncored "Indigo and White" Beads (T,O)					
Ia5	3	200	203	167	
Ia19	—	9	9	219	
IIa15	31	114	145	835	
IIa57	23	12	35	306	
Totals			392	7.3%	1527	50.4%
Group 2: Faceted "Star" Beads (T)					
IIIk3/3*	6	—	6	70	
IIIm1/1*	1	1	2	—	
Totals			8	0.1%	70	2.3%
Group 3: Cored and Uncored Tubular, "Flush-eye," and Frit-cored Beads					
Ia1	3	—	3	—	
Ia16	—	—	—	1	
Ib'2	—	4	4	1	
If5	1	—	1	—	
IIg3*	—	—	—	1	
IIg4	2	4	6	4	
IIIa2	—	1	1	—	
IIIa9	—	—	—	1	
IIIa12	1	—	1	5	
IIIb9	1	—	1	6	
IIIbb7	1	—	1	—	
IIIc1	—	—	—	1	
IIIc'3	5	—	5	—	
IVg1	1	—	1	29	
Frit-cored	—	—	—	11	
New Varieties					
Ia_*(1)	1	—	1	—	
Totals			25	0.5%	60	2.0%
Group 4: Tumbled "Star" Beads (R)					
IVk3/4	184	—	184	209	
IVk6/7	2	—	2	5	
IVn1	—	—	—	37	
IVn2/3	1	—	1	21	

	SENECA			SUSQUEHANNOCK	
	Dutch Hollow	Cameron	Total	Schultz	
IVn4	3	—	3	—	
Totals			190	3.5%	272	9.0%
Group 5: Large Striped Beads (R, F)					
IIb7	—	—	—	1	
IIb13*	1	—	1	—	
IIb14*	—	—	—	1	
IIb15	5	—	5	5	
IIb62	—	—	—	5	
IIbb1/1*	17	—	17	11	
IIbb2	1	—	1	—	
IIbb5	—	—	—	43	
IIbb7	2	—	2	—	
IVb29–32	80	—	80	5	
IVb33–36	18	1	19	35	
New Varieties					
IIbb_*(3)	1	—	1	—	
Totals			126	2.3%	106	3.5%
Group 6: Uncored Monochrome Beads (R, C, O)					
IIa1/2	83	4	87	—	
IIa3	1	—	1	—	
IIa6/7	11	—	11	48	
IIa8	1	6	7	—	
IIa10	—	—	—	4	
IIa13/14	18	28	46	20	
IIa17	36	—	36	—	
IIa19	3	—	3	—	
IIa20*	14	—	14	—	
IIa33	70	—	70	—	
IIa40	122	81	203	—	
IIa40/41	32	—	32	127	
IIa42	1	—	1	—	
IIa43	—	19	19	152	
IIa44	18	—	18	—	
IIa45	31	—	31	—	
IIa46/47	194	37	231	229	
IIa48/49	222	—	222	—	
IIa50/51	61	—	61	—	

(continued on next page)

Table 10.1 (cont.)

Comparison of Glass Beads from Early Historic Seneca and Susquehannock Sites

	SENECA				SUSQUEHANNOCK	
	Dutch Hollow	Cameron	Total		Schultz	
IIa55/56	118	1	119		169	
IIa59	7	—	7		—	
IIa?	—	—	—		7	
Totals			1219	22.6%	756	25.0%
Group 7: Cored Monochrome Beads (R, C, O)						
IVa1/2/3/5/6	283	—	283		2	
IVa4	1	—	1		—	
IVa8	1	—	1		—	
IVa11/13/14	114	—	114		—	
IVa12*	1886	—	1886		39	
IVa18	—	—	—		50	
IVa19/19*	405	—	405		107	
New Varieties						
IVa_*(4)	120	—	120		—	
Totals			2810	52.0%	198	6.5%
Group 8: Small/Medium Cored Striped Beads (R, C)						
IVb2*	1	—	1		—	
IVb3/4/10/11	92	—	92		3	
IVb7*	5	—	5		—	
IVb13	14	—	14		—	
IVb14	1	—	1		—	
IVb15/16	293	—	293		—	
IVb23	105	—	105		17	
IVb24	8	—	8		—	
IVb?	—	—	—		4	
IVbb1	2	—	2		—	
IVbb4/7	12	—	12		—	
New Varieties						
IVb_*(10)	1	—	1		—	
Totals			534	9.9%	24	0.8%
Group 9: Uncored Striped Beads (R, C)						
IIb2	2	—	2		—	
IIb3	15	—	15		—	
IIb12	1	—	1		—	
IIb18	11	—	11		1	
IIb19	—	—	—		2	
IIb43	—	—	—		12	

	SENECA			SUSQUEHANNOCK	
	Dutch Hollow	Cameron	Total	Schultz	
IIb56	17	—	17	—	
IIb57	2	—	2	—	
IIb58/58*	4	—	4	—	
IIb59	2	—	2	—	
IIb64	4	—	4	—	
IIb65	1	—	1	—	
IIb67	1	—	1	—	
IIb68	11	—	11	—	
IIb70*	1	—	1	—	
IIb72/72*	3	—	3	—	
IIb74*	2	—	2	—	
IIb'13	14	—	14	—	
New Varieties					
IIb_*(10)	1	—	1	—	
IIb_*(11)	2	—	2	—	
IIb_*(12)	1	—	1	—	
Totals			95	1.8%	15	0.5%
Description of New Varieties					
Ia_*(1)	T	S	Tsl Brite Copen Blue		
IIbb_*(3)	R	L, VL	Tsp Brite Blue (appears Black)—7 or 8 Redwood on White stripes		
IIb_*(10)	R	M	Tsp Pale Blue—9 (3 groups of 3) White stripes		
IIb_*(11)	O	S, M	Tsp Pale Blue—2 Redwood stripes		
IIb_*(12)	R	M	Tsp Mint Green—4 Redwood and 4 White stripes		
IVa_*(4)	R, C	S, M	Tsl Robin's Egg Blue—Lt. Gray core		
IVb_*(10)	R	L	Op Redwood—Dk Rose Brown core—12 op White stripes		

Note: Classified according to Kidd and Kidd 1983 [1970].
* A slight variation of the bead variety identified by Kidd and Kidd (1983 [1970]).

Group 7: Cored Monochrome Beads

This grouping includes small- to medium-sized, cored monochrome beads of varying colors (see fig. 10.2). They range from round to circular, and in some cases, where very large numbers are available for study, appear to form a continuum from round to circular. Most common colors within this grouping are opaque Redwood,

Fig. 10.2. Most common glass-bead varieties in each of nine groupings used in this study. a. Group 1; b. Group 2; c. Group 3; d. Group 4; e. Group 5; f. Group 6; g. Group 7; h. Group 8; i. Group 9. Photograph courtesy of Rochester Museum and Science Center.

translucent Brite Navy, translucent Light Gray with a White layer that makes the bead appear white, and translucent Light Gray with an opaque Shadow Blue layer that makes the bead appear blue.

Group 8: Small/Medium Cored Striped Beads

This grouping includes generally small- to medium-sized, round and circular cored striped beads (see fig. 10.2). Most common are Redwood with either three or six White stripes and varying core colors; White with varying core colors and Redwood and Brite Navy stripes; and Shadow Blue with Light Aqua core and Redwood stripes.

Group 9: Uncored Striped Beads

This grouping includes a wide variety of small- to medium-sized, round and circular uncored striped beads, including the ubiquitous "gooseberry" beads (see fig. 10.2).

Results

Results indicate that glass beads occurred in a considerably higher percentage of graves at the Susquehannock site (30.0 percent) than at the combined Seneca sites (21.3 percent), but Susquehannock burials generally contained smaller quantities of beads. Therefore, overall, based upon the total number of excavated burials in each sample, roughly similar quantities of glass beads seem to have been available for mortuary use in the two areas (approximately 25–27 per burial).

However, a comparison of the glass-bead profiles for each area, based on the nine groupings outlined above, reveals some rather clear distinctions in the types of glass beads available (see fig. 10.3 and table 10.1). First, more than one-half of the glass beads at the Schultz site belong to Group 1—uncored Brite Navy (or Indigo), and White tubular and oval beads. This amount compares with a mere 7.3 percent of the total beads from the Seneca sample. A substantial relative difference is also noted for Group 2, the tubular faceted "star" beads, which are almost nonexistent in the Seneca sample, but represent a conspicuous 2.3 percent of the Susquehannock sample. The beads represented in both of these groupings have been identified with Glass Bead Period 2 (approximated at 1600 to 1609–14 in New York and Pennsylvania and 1600 to 1624–30 in Ontario) by Kenyon and Fitzgerald (Fitzgerald 1990a; Fitzgerald et al. 1994; Kenyon and Kenyon 1983; Kenyon and Fitzgerald 1986). The mixed Group 3, comprised of tubulars (other than those in Group 1), "flush-eye," and frit-cored beads showed a similar pattern of higher relative incidence in the Susquehannock sample (2.0 percent versus 0.5 percent). Interestingly,

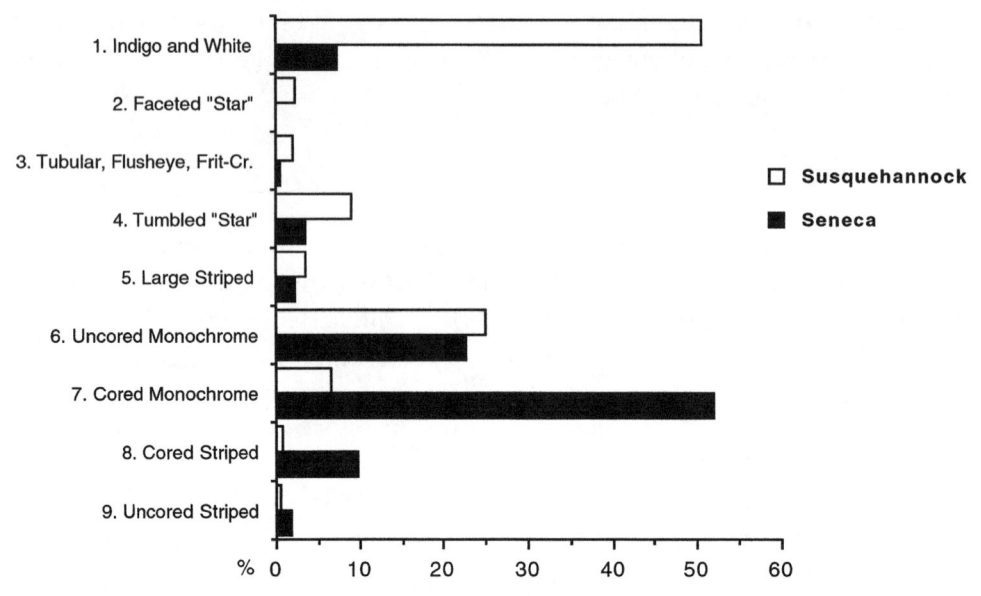

Fig. 10.3. Frequencies of glass-bead groups in Seneca and Susquehannock sites under study.

some of these beads (e.g., Kidd varieties IIg4, and Ib'2) are also identified as belonging to Glass Bead Period 2 in Ontario (Fitzgerald 1990a; Fitzgerald et al. 1994; Kenyon and Kenyon 1983; Kenyon and Fitzgerald 1986).

Better represented in both areas are the tumbled "star" or chevron beads of Group 4 and the large striped beads in Group 5. While the first are significantly more frequent in the Susquehannock sample (9 percent versus 3.5 percent), those comprising Group 5 occur in relatively close, albeit low, frequencies in the two samples (3.5 percent versus 2.3 percent). These two bead groups are considered diagnostic of the complex identified as the Dutch "Polychrome" horizon or Dutch Period 1 (approximated at 1609 to 1624) in New York and Pennsylvania by Kenyon and Fitzgerald (Fitzgerald 1990a; Fitzgerald et al. 1994; Kenyon and Fitzgerald 1986). These authors have pointed to the presence of this complex of beads at both the Schultz and Dutch Hollow sites and elsewhere in New York as a probable indicator of site occupations in the second decade of the seventeenth century (Kenyon and Fitzgerald 1986, 25–29).

Another grouping in which Susquehannock and Seneca samples show an even higher degree of similarity is Group 6, uncored round and circular monochrome beads other than those in Group 1. Most of these beads are not considered reliable temporal indicators, although the black varieties (Kidd varieties 11a6/7) found in both areas have been associated with Dutch Period 2 (Fitzgerald et al. 1994, 13). Close examination of table 10.1 also indicates some interesting patterns of differences between the two samples. In general, the Seneca sample shows much greater diversity, while the Susquehannock sample of uncored monochromes seems to consist primarily of uncored beads of varying shades of blue.

Dominating the Seneca assemblage, to about the same degree as the Group I complex does the Susquehannock, is Group 7 (52.0 percent versus 6.5 percent), consisting of a complex of small cored monochrome beads. Of particularly noteworthy frequency is a bead that is not included in the Kidd and Kidd typology, although it appears to represent a variant of one of those that he identifies. A small- or medium-sized circular bead with a transparent Light Gray outer layer, a Shadow Blue middle layer rather than the Brite Navy indicated by the Kidds, and a Light Gray core is classified here as IVal2*.[2] As is the case with the variant originally described by the Kidds, these beads actually appear "blue" to the naked eye, and thus have probably been quite frequently misidentified. Fitzgerald has recently included some of these Group 7 bead varieties with the "Dutch Cored" horizon (Dutch Period 2) that he proposes postdates 1624 (Fitzgerald et al. 1994, 13), although this particular bead variety (IVal2*), which is so frequent at Dutch Hollow, is not mentioned. Also significantly more frequent in the Seneca sample are the small cored striped beads, Group 8 (9.9 percent of the Seneca sample, versus only 0.8 percent of the Susquehannock).[3] Finally, uncored striped beads, Group 9, although relatively rare, show a slightly higher incidence in the Seneca area (1.7 percent versus 0.7 percent).

In addition to the distinctive patterns of bead frequencies exhibited by the two glass-bead profiles, there are also some rather significant differences in the size and shape of beads from the two regions. Most importantly, tubular white beads (Ia5) from each area show a very consistent difference in their diameters. With few exceptions, all of those in the Schultz sample are very thin, falling into the 2- to 3.5-mm range. The vast majority in the Seneca sample are at least 1 to 2 mm larger in diameter, with only 3 of the nearly 200 beads measured falling into the Susquehannock range. The Susquehannock bead sample also contains a significant number of unusually large indigo ovals that do not occur at all in the Seneca sample studied here (between 5 and 7 mm in diameter versus the 4- to 5-mm range typical of blue ovals in the Seneca sites).

Brass assemblages show both similarities and differences. Brass beads in both areas tended to be scarce in number and mostly of the rounded variety, rather than the typical long rolled tubulars that are so abundant in earlier sites (fig. 10.4). There were also a number of brass "seed" beads in the Susquehannock sample that do not appear in the Seneca sample. Brass spirals (fig. 10.5), which occurred in late sixteenth-century sites in both regions, as James W. Bradley and S. Terry Childs's distributional study has shown (Bradley and Childs 1991 [chap. 15]), were actually far more common in these Susquehannock burials at Schultz (13.3 percent) than in

---

2. Thanks are due to Donald Rumrill for bringing the somewhat obscure makeup of this cored "blue" bead to my attention.

3. Several varieties of cored striped beads also showed a fairly high incidence in the Ibaugh assemblage (see note 1).

Fig. 10.4. Rounded brass beads from the Cameron site (RMSC cat. no. 5041/41). Average diameter of beads = 0.66 cm.

Fig. 10.5. Rolled brass spiral from the Cameron site (RMSC cat. no. 5470/41). Diameter = 4.0 cm.

Seneca burials of any period, but particularly during the period under comparison here. Only three burials from Cameron and none from the Dutch Hollow site include them for an overall frequency of 1.5 percent. Lastly, common in the Susquehannock brass assemblage are bracelets produced in varying widths from pieces of what appear to be machine-pressed, corrugated sheet brass (fig. 10.6). No bracelets of this kind were found in either of the Seneca assemblages, and in fact, only one tiny specimen of corrugated brass (rolled into a tubular bead) was found in any context at either of the two Seneca sites.

Marine shell actually occurred in a smaller percentage of the Susquehannock (7.5 percent) than the Seneca (16.6 percent) burials studied, but again the amount of shell (in terms of bead quantities) available for use in mortuary contexts appears to be very similar in the two regions. More important, the assemblages of marine shell found in both areas also look very similar—small discoidal and tubular beads and a few pendants, but no large intact shells, and wherever ascertainable, no large sinistrally whorled *Busycon*.

In terms of other exotic materials, twelve catlinite discoidal beads and two catlinite effigies occur among these burials at the Schultz site (Smith and Graybill 1977, fig. 4), versus no catlinite whatsoever in the sample of burials studied from

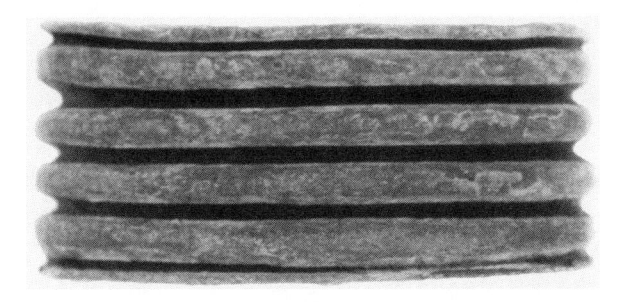

Fig. 10.6. Corrugated brass bracelet from the Schultz site (State Museum of Pennsylvania cat. no. La9/174). Diameter = 3.5 cm.

the Cameron and Dutch Hollow sites.[4] Twenty-six cannel coal beads and eleven cannel coal fragments, a material nonexistent in the Seneca comparison, were also found in the Schultz assemblages.

Discussion

Results of the artifact comparisons for these two regional samples at first appear somewhat ambiguous. On the one hand, the marine-shell assemblages seem to be very similar—both in kind and in quantity—in the two regions. There is also some overlap in the brass assemblages and in some of the types of glass beads that were available to both groups, particularly the relatively distinctive and short-lived large "Polychrome" beads attributed to very early Dutch trade. However, even more apparent are the rather striking dissimilarities in the exotic goods acquired by each group.

Brass spirals not only differ in overall frequency but are almost completely absent at the later of the two Seneca sites. Because these distinctive items occurred earlier in both areas, their continuity in the Susquehannock area and disappearance in Seneca territory appears to support the idea of disrupted exchange. Further, the unusual corrugated brass bracelets and the brass seed beads at Schultz have no equivalents in the Seneca sites. Finally, catlinite is not found at all in the Seneca comparative sample, and is, at most, exceedingly rare in the Seneca region during this period (see note 4); and cannel coal does not occur at all in the Seneca sample. However, it is the distinctions in glass-bead assemblages that seem most significant:

4. It should be noted that one maskette of either catlinite or red slate has been reported from another cemetery at the Dutch Hollow site; unfortunately it is not presently available for study. Also, several catlinite objects (a small bird effigy and four tubular beads) are attributed to the Factory Hollow site, thought to be contemporary with Dutch Hollow. While these objects have been identified as catlinite, their provenience is considered somewhat insecure because they originally formed part of the largely uncontextualized Dewey collection that was dispersed in a number of museums, including the New York State Museum where they now reside.

- the overwhelming proportion of the Indigo and White tubular and oval beads in the Susquehannock area;
- the markedly different size of those tubular white beads (Ia5) and oval dark blue beads (IIa57) that do occur in the Seneca sample;
- the incidence in the Susquehannock assemblage of tubular faceted star beads that are all but nonexistent in the Seneca sample;
- the corresponding domination of the Seneca sample by small cored monochrome and striped beads;
- the prevalence in the Seneca assemblage of many varieties of uncored monochrome beads that are unmatched in the Susquehannock sample.

One possible explanation that must be considered for these differences is simply that these sites do not represent contemporary occupations and that therefore such distinctions are to be expected. Several factors argue against such an interpretation. First, regardless of the exact occupation dates of the sites, which surely do not coincide exactly, there is no site in the Seneca sequence (neither earlier nor later) that has an Indigo/White glass-bead assemblage (Group 1) that does match this one at Schultz—either in terms of its overwhelming numbers or its frequency in the total assemblage, or in the occurrence of the very thin white tubular beads and the large-diameter dark blue beads. Even comparing the Cameron site where these beads do represent a high proportion of the total bead assemblage, we cannot ignore the fact that nearly five times as many of these beads resulted from a nearly equivalent number of excavated burials at Schultz. Second, there is no other site in the Seneca sequence that shows anything close to the frequency of faceted "star" beads (Group 2) exhibited at Schultz. Third, no earlier or later Susquehannock or Seneca site exhibits such similar proportions of the "Polychrome" beads (Groups 4 and 5), particularly the tumbled "star" beads (Group 5) (see note 1). Third, while the succeeding Washington Boro site in the Susquehannock area does show a higher frequency of the cored monochrome beads that predominate at Dutch Hollow, that assemblage apparently does not include the small cored "blue" beads (IVa12*) that constitute more than one-half of the beads at Dutch Hollow.[5] Overall, the Washington Boro glass-bead assemblage (as translated from Kent's classification system into that of Kidd and Kidd) seems to bear more similarities to those at succeeding sites in the Seneca area—Warren and Cornish. Thus it does not appear that a simple chronological explanation can account for the differences that have been identified here. Nevertheless, as in all complex answers, it may be partially applicable given that glass-bead evidence from the Washington Boro sites certainly suggests some temporal overlap with the later of the two Seneca sites—Dutch Hol-

---

5. Barry Kent has recently advised me that some of these beads may indeed have occurred at the Washington Boro (Ibaugh) site (personal communication, May 1994). If so, it appears that they must have been inadvertently misclassified as uncored beads. This possibility should be further explored.

low. Thus the Schultz site was probably abandoned sometime before Dutch Hollow was, at which time the Schultz inhabitants relocated to the nearby Washington Boro site (see below).

In terms of actual dates for these sites, Fitzgerald (1990a, 199–210) has proposed that the Indigo/White bead complex is of French origin and dates no earlier than about 1600. It lasted, along with French trade in Ontario, until approximately 1624–30. We have thus suggested initial dates for the Cameron site, where the first appreciable numbers of these beads occur in the Seneca area, at just before 1600 (ca. 1595) (Wray et al. 1991, 411). Based on that line of reasoning, I suspect that the Susquehannock probably also first occupied the Schultz site sometime around the same period.[6]

Kenyon and Fitzgerald have also presented very cogent arguments concerning the appearance of the large striped "Polychrome" horizon (Dutch Period 1) in New York and Pennsylvania sites (Fitzgerald 1990a; Fitzgerald et al. 1994, 10; Kenyon and Kenyon 1983; Kenyon and Fitzgerald 1986). They have suggested that these beads represent the earliest indication of Dutch trade in those regions sometime around 1609–14 and mark the cessation of the French-made Indigo/White bead complex in those regions.[7] They have proposed that this colorful complex of beads was in turn replaced by what Fitzgerald has called the "Dutch Cored" horizon (Dutch Period 2) sometime around 1624 (Fitzgerald et al. 1994, 13). I would argue on the basis of their comparative prevalence and occurrence in direct association with the "Polychromes" at Dutch Hollow that some varieties of small cored beads probably first appeared considerably earlier than 1624. Nevertheless, if we accept the dating of these complexes of glass beads, it seems clear that we can point to some partial or overlapping contemporaneity for the sites under study here, and that period of contemporaneity appears to fall primarily in the first and part of the second decades of the seventeenth century.

Having eliminated the probability of an explanation based solely on a lack of

---

6. William Fitzgerald has suggested the possibility of a very long occupation for the Schultz site, extending from Glass Bead Period 1 through Glass Bead Period 2 and into Dutch Periods 1 and 2 (i.e., from 1580 to beyond 1624). The evidence for occupation during the earlier period (Glass Bead Period 1) does not seem convincing to me, in that it seems to be based solely on the occurrence of the nondiagnostic Turquoise or Robin's Egg Blue medium round beads (IIa39 or IIa40) that occur even more commonly later on, and on 11 frit-cored beads, all apparently from a single burial context. Although admittedly rare, the latter are also known from later Seneca glass-bead assemblages.

7. Although Ian Kenyon and William Fitzgerald do not explain this divergence between the trade assemblages in the two regions as resulting from calculated exclusion by the Ontario Iroquois, as well as from the onset of Dutch trade, recent syntheses by Susan Jamieson (1992) and William Johnson (1990, 1992) would seem to imply this additional explanation. Far from being incompatible, the double thrust of these two factors seems to me to represent a very powerful explanation to account for the dramatic differences that Kenyon and Fitzgerald have identified.

contemporaneity between sites sampled from each area, we must resort to a more complex explanation for the distinctions that have been noted in the assemblages of trade materials from the two areas. I propose, as hypothesized, that to some degree the observed distinctions may be owing to differences in the political and kinship arenas within which each group interacted. In making the case, I will also outline the temporal parameters for the proposed disruption in interactions between the Susquehannock and the New York Iroquois, including the Seneca. The argument is a complicated one because, as is so often true, the social and temporal factors are intricately interwoven, making it difficult to extricate one from the other. Alternative explanations are of course always conceivable. However, the scenario proposed here seems to me to be the most plausible explanation for a wide range of discrete data relating to the Susquehannock and Seneca of this period.

We look first at the clear similarities that characterize the assemblages of the Seneca and Susquehannock. These are the presence in both areas (most frequently at the Cameron site on the Seneca side) of the "Indigo and White" (Group 1) beads; the common occurrence (almost exclusively at the Dutch Hollow site on the Seneca side), in roughly comparable frequencies, of the large striped "Polychrome" horizon (Groups 4 and 5); the occurrence in both areas of rolled brass spirals, again a similarity with the Cameron site, but in far lower frequency; and the similar marine-shell assemblages, also a similarity most apparent between Cameron and Schultz. This evidence would seem to support the long-standing thesis that there was a period, probably during the very late sixteenth century and into the first decade of the seventeenth, when both groups appear to be interacting within the same sphere. This interaction facilitated access to relatively small numbers of French-made "Indigo and White" beads and to small numbers of the very earliest Dutch trade beads to become available shortly after 1609—the tumbled "star" beads (Group 4) and the large striped beads (Group 5). However, I propose that only a small portion of the "Indigo and White" beads at Schultz were acquired during this period. The remainder, the overwhelming numbers, I suggest, resulted from subsequent interactions that followed a disruption in relations with the New York Iroquois sometime shortly after the Dutch trade got underway.

I propose that the vast majority of these Group 1 beads were acquired after that time, via the Allegheny Valley/Ohio Valley/Ontario exchange network to which the Susquehannock apparently enjoyed some (probably quite limited) access that the Seneca did not. In view of the fact that these beads continued to circulate in Ontario until at least 1624–30 (Fitzgerald 1990a; Fitzgerald et al. 1994), their relative volume at Schultz, compared to the Seneca sites, plus the size differences that have been noted, argue for this additional later source. The relatively higher incidence of faceted star beads in the Susquehannock sample, in comparison to the Seneca sample, a feature that has also been linked to the Ontario network (Kenyon and Kenyon 1983, fig. 2), lends additional support to this interpretation. Several other disparate pieces of artifactual evidence appear to link the Susquehannock, but not the Seneca, to this network: corrugated brass like that at the Schultz site has been found in several contemporary Neutral sites (Fitzgerald personal communication 1993); cannel coal ornaments are found in both the Schultz site and Monongahela assemblages; and catlinite, which is relatively abundant on the Schultz site as compared with the Seneca sites, is prevalent on Ontario sites of this period (Fitzgerald 1990a).

While the differentially large number of the "Dutch Cored Horizon" (Groups 7 and 8) beads on the Seneca Dutch Hollow site probably, to some extent, indicates the later duration of its occupation relative to that of the Schultz site (see above), I propose that it also reflects Seneca trade during this period when relations with the Susquehannock were disrupted. Particularly suggestive of this period of disparity are the cored light "blue" beads (IVaI2*), so common at the Dutch Hollow site but rare at the Schultz site, and apparently also at the subsequent Washington Boro site (see notes 1 and 5). Other varieties in this horizon that occur at Dutch Hollow but not at Schultz, such as the small cored White beads (IVaI1/13/14) and the small cored striped beads (IVb*), may be less time sensitive or may relate to a slightly later period after the Schultz abandonment, given that they do appear in considerable numbers at the Washington Boro site (see note 1).

Two other aspects of the archaeological evidence from the Dutch Hollow site may also become explicable within this scenario of disrupted relations—the disappearance of the rolled brass spirals that had been so abundant on sixteenth-century Seneca sites (cf. Wray et al. 1987; 1991) and the sharp decline in marine shell (Sempowski 1989). Furthermore, if both phenomena were in fact owing to a disruption in exchange with the Susquehannock, several implications would seem to follow. In the first case, that of the brass spirals, it may imply that the Susquehannock had been the source of these items—presumably as finished products—and that the Seneca did not fashion them themselves from scrap brass. The marine shell presents a more puzzling phenomenon. If disrupted relations with the Susquehannock were the cause of the decline in marine shell to the Seneca during the Dutch Hollow site occupation, it would appear to confirm the role of the Susquehannock as intermediaries in the exchange of marine shell from the Chesapeake Bay area that has been so widely accepted (Bradley 1987a, 89–103; Vandrei 1984, 9–11; Wray et al. 1987, 250–51). The difficulty is that at present, there is no evidence that marine shell continued in any greater abundance at the Schultz site than it does at Dutch Hollow. This finding may suggest that the coastal groups supplying marine shell had realigned themselves with other polities operating within the Allegheny Valley/Ohio Valley/Ontario sphere, as Johnson and Pendergast have proposed (Johnson 1990, 1992; Pendergast 1991a; 1992).

Finally, this archaeologically derived scenario would seem to be substantively and temporally consistent with Champlain's highly debated account of 1615, indicating not only hostile relations between the Susquehannock and the New York

Iroquois, but also an incipient alliance between the Huron of Ontario and a related group identified on a later map by Champlain as the Carantouanais. The latter group has been identified by many scholars as the Andaste or Susquehannock (Bradley 1987a, 223, fn. 2; Jennings 1978, 362; Tooker 1984, 3). Champlain stated that the Huron "received intelligence that a certain nation, allied to them, who dwell three long days' journey beyond the Onondagas, with which nation also the Iroquois are at war, wished to help them in this expedition with five hundred good men, and to make an alliance and swear friendship with us, having a great desire to see us, and that we should all carry on war together" (Biggar 1922–36, 3:53–54). More specifically regarding the Carantouanais or Susquehannocks' hostile relations with the Seneca (Iroquois), he added, "There are only three villages of them in the midst of more than twenty others with whom they are at war, unable to get help from their friends because these must need pass through the Senecas' country, which is thickly populated, or else make a wide detour" (Biggar 1922–36, 3:55).

Conclusions

In summary, this study has identified a pattern of similarities and distinctions in Susquehannock and Seneca archaeological assemblages. While these distinctions may be partially owing to a slight variance in the occupation periods of the sites studied, the temporal factor cannot adequately explain all of the distinctions. Thus it is proposed that, for a portion of this period, the Seneca and the Susquehannock participated in somewhat distinct spheres of interaction. Following a period of apparent mutual interaction, which may have been in place for some time before 1600, there appears to have been at least a partial disruption in relations and exchange between the Susquehannock and the Seneca. Whether this disruption includes the other New York Iroquois groups bears further investigation. This seems likely to have occurred sometime shortly after the onset of Dutch activities in New York around 1609, and if Champlain's account of animosity between the two groups in 1615 is valid, presumably before 1615. It is, of course, possible that problems had been brewing for some time between the New York Iroquois and their southern neighbors and had precipitated the Susquehannock's move south to the lower Susquehanna River Valley, as Kent has suggested (Kent 1993 [1984], 18).

In any event, following the proposed disruption in the earlier pattern of mutual exchange with the League Iroquois, the Susquehannock appear to have been involved, although probably in a relatively peripheral way, with the hypothesized Allegheny Valley/Ohio Valley/Ontario interaction sphere. It appears that the Seneca on the western edge of the New York Iroquois, and therefore geographically closest to the principal players in this sphere, were not involved, even to the extent that the Susquehannock were. The evidence brought forward here does not bear directly on whether they were deliberately shut out of that network, as Johnson (1990;

1992) and Jamieson (1992) have independently suggested, although the animosity between the Seneca and the Ontario Iroquois is historically well documented. Further, as Johnson (1992, 13–14) has hypothesized, the apparent subsequent elimination of the Monongahela, presumably by the Seneca, followed by an enormous influx of marine shell into Seneca territory, suggests that the Seneca's lack of access to that network and to southern sources of marine shell was a prickly issue that may have had grave consequences for at least some of their neighbors.

It is also unclear how aggressively the Susquehannock were being excluded from the Dutch trade during this period, but the fact that the Susquehannock initiated a formal request for trade with the Dutch in 1626 (Jennings 1968, 17; Myers 1912, 24, 38) suggests that they had been experiencing problems with access to the Dutch in the preceding years. By that time, of course, it appears that the Susquehannock had long since relocated from the Schultz site to the neighboring site of the Washington Boro village.

In addition to the preceding conclusions relating directly to the issue addressed in this study, several other unintended results have emerged. For example, if the conclusions outlined above are valid, the distinctions between the Susquehannock and the Seneca glass-bead assemblages may allow further refinement and partitioning of glass-bead assemblages in those areas. First, they suggest a reassessment of Group 1 beads for possible pre- and post-Dutch-period components, based on distinctions in relative quantities, frequencies, and bead sizes. They also reaffirm the simultaneous appearance of Groups 4 and 5 as part of the earliest Dutch beads to reach Native groups here, but may point to particular varieties, such as 3- to 7-stripe blue and white beads (Kidd varieties IVa29–32) that can be distinguished from those that occurred over a longer period of time, such as the 8- to 16-stripe blue and white beads (Kidd varieties IVa33–36). Lastly, they also appear to point to the temporal priority of uncored Shadow Blue beads (IIa46–48) and small cored "blue" beads (IVal2*), relative to small cored Whites and Redwoods in the later Dutch assemblages. Another unintended result is the possible implication that rolled brass spirals may have been transmitted to the Seneca and other New York Iroquois from (or through) the Susquehannock as finished objects, rather than being produced by all of these groups from scrap brass.

Finally, and most important, although it was completely unanticipated when the study was undertaken, it has raised a question about the traditionally accepted dates for the Susquehannock Schultz site (1575–1600) (Kent 1993 [1984], 332). I have suggested that Schultz seems more likely to have been occupied almost a quarter of a century later—from sometime in the 1590s until sometime between 1615 and 1620 when the occupants relocated to the Washington Boro site. It is with great caution and respect that I make this proposal for consideration by those far better versed than I am in Susquehannock archaeology and site chronology. Yet, the glass-bead data from the Schultz site, as discussed above, seem to favor inescapably a primarily early seventeenth-century occupation for the site. Even if my reasoning on this point proves faulted in the long run, I think this study emphasizes again that if we are ever to resolve interregional issues such as these, we must undertake collaborative studies aimed at achieving some reasonably valid level of cross-regional chronological alignment.

Acknowledgments

This paper has had a long incubation and owes much to the assistance, critiques, and suggestions of a great many individuals, including scholars on both sides of this Susquehannock/Seneca comparison. The final result, including any possible errors in fact or interpretation on what has proven to be a controversial subject, is, of course, my full responsibility.

I am indebted, first, to Research Director Charles Hayes and Curator Betty Prisch of the Rochester Museum and Science Center and to Senior and Assistant Curators Steven Warfel and Mark McConahay of the State Museum of Pennsylvania, whose well-organized archaeological collections of Seneca and Susquehannock materials provided the data source for the study. I am also most grateful for James Herbstritt's invaluable orientation to the Susquehannock collections in the latter institution, as well as for the additional data and careful commentary that he provided on the paper. William Engelbrecht, William Fitzgerald, Susan Jamieson, William Johnson, Robert Kuhn, and James Pendergast also responded most generously with their time and their thoughts when I sought their comments on an earlier version of the paper. However, I owe a special debt to Barry Kent, who gave most graciously of his time and expertise in a stimulating afternoon of exchange and interpretation of data from our respective areas. While our interpretations may differ in some respects, I look forward to an ongoing discussion with him of the many comparative issues of mutual interest.

In very early stages of the research, I was ably assisted by Annette Nohe and Kathryn Stark in the often tedious task of glass-bead classification, and Ralph Brown, Donald Rumrill, and Brian Fox provided technical advice and assistance at the other end with production of the "touchy" glass-bead illustration. Finally, I would like to thank Connie Bodner, Charles Hayes, and Lorraine Saunders for their editorial comments and suggestions, and for their patience with my lengthy deliberations on this paper.

11 | New York Iroquois Political Development
WILLIAM E. ENGELBRECHT

Introduction

NEARLY 150 YEARS elapsed between the European discovery of North America and the beginning of firsthand documentation of the New York Iroquois. What effect, if any, did Europeans have on Iroquois political development during this period? This paper argues that both New York Iroquois tribes and the League of the Iroquois developed gradually, the process beginning in prehistoric times and continuing into the historic period. During the Protohistoric period in New York (the sixteenth and early seventeenth centuries), Europeans indirectly contributed to the consolidation of Iroquois tribes and the League.

During the sixteenth and early seventeenth centuries, European trade goods were reaching New York Iroquois villages with increasing frequency, although there is little evidence of direct European contact with these groups. It is therefore difficult to identify changes that may have occurred in Iroquois society as a result of the European presence in North America. In order to assess Iroquois political development during this period, two separate lines of evidence will be used: archaeology and oral tradition.

To paraphrase William H. Sears (1961), archaeologists cannot dig up political systems. The data that archaeologists deal with generally constitute only an imperfect reflection of the actual past behavior the archaeologist is seeking to infer. If patterns of past behavior can be successfully inferred, the problem of relating this behavior to social or political institutions remains. An additional problem is that the archaeological database for the New York Iroquois is generally inadequate for inferring most aspects of sociopolitical organization. Despite over a century of archaeological investigation in New York State, there are numerous gaps in our

Previously published in *Cultures in Contact: The European Impact on Native Cultural Institutions in Eastern North America, A.D. 1000–1800,* ed. W. W. Fitzhugh (Washington, D.C.: Smithsonian Institution Press, 1985), 163–83. Printed with permission by the Anthropological Society of Washington.

knowledge of the Iroquoian occupation of the state. Many Iroquoian sites are poorly known, and some have been largely destroyed. There are few Iroquoian villages that approach total excavation, so we know little about the internal structure or population of most villages. My hope is that one benefit of this paper will be to focus attention on the need for new data as well as on the need to look at old data in new ways.

Using oral tradition to trace Iroquois political development also has limitations. Sometimes different or conflicting versions describing a particular event exist. Also, oral traditions are often rich in allegory and therefore cannot be interpreted in the same way as an historical narrative. Despite these problems, oral tradition, like archaeological data, does contain information about the past. The strategy employed in this paper is to seek possible areas of congruence between archaeology and oral tradition as they apply to Protohistoric Iroquois political development.

Tribal Development

The early seventeenth-century Seneca, Cayuga, Onondaga, Oneida, and Mohawk are commonly referred to as *tribes,* though modern Iroquois prefer the term *nations.* While the Oneida may have had a single village at this time, the other Iroquois groups consisted of two or more. It is assumed that these villages were not functionally differentiated. Because communities shifted their location a few miles every 10 to 20 years because of the depletion of soil and firewood in their immediate vicinity, over time a single community is represented by a number of sites in an area. Sequences of village movement have been worked out for a number of areas, including the Niagara Frontier, where a tribe of the Erie may have lived. With the exception of the Onondaga and Oneida, who were geographically close to one another, the tribes were separated by an average distance of approximately 55 miles. Figure 11.1 illustrates the areas in which sixteenth- and early seventeenth-century village sites are clustered.

The development of these population clusters remains to be worked out for all areas. Though the data are incomplete, there appears to be a trend toward increasing site size from the Owasco to the Iroquois period (Ritchie and Funk 1973, 364), implying the development of larger communities. In most cases, it is not clear whether these larger communities are the result of population increase or the merger of two or more smaller communities. In either case, defense was probably a major factor in encouraging the maintenance of larger communities. Many prehistoric sites are both palisaded and situated with reference to defensible terrain, suggesting that hostile external relationships were a fact of life during the Late Prehistoric and Protohistoric periods in New York.

These larger communities may have had organizational features characteristic of historic Iroquois tribes, but determining this from the archaeological record is

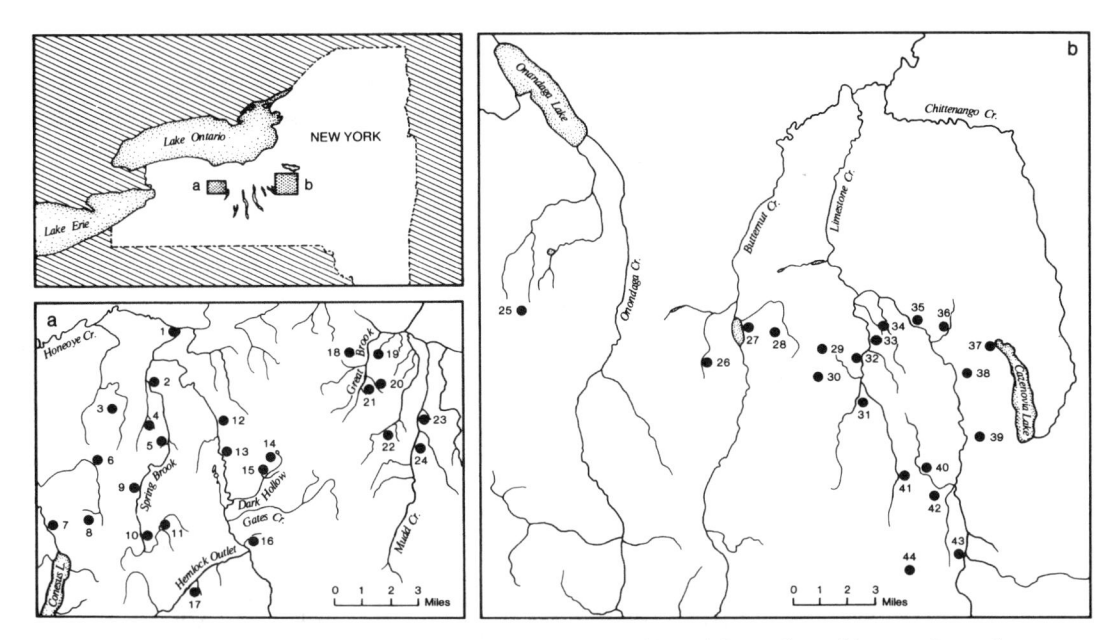

Fig. 11.1. Sixteenth- and seventeenth-century Seneca (a) and Onondaga (b) sites. Onondaga villages: 1. Rochester Junction; 2. Dann; 3. Kirkwood; 4. Powerhouse; 5. Lima; 6. Dutch Hollow; 7. Bosely Mills; 8. Feugle; 9. Cameron; 10. Adams; 11. Tram; 12. Warren; 13. Factory Hollow; 14. Conn; 15. Taft; 16. Belcher; 17. Richmond Hills; 18. Fort Hill; 19. Boughton Hill; 20. Bunce; 21. Beale; 22. Steele; 23. March; 24. Wheeler Station. Seneca villages: 25. Schoff; 26. Coye (Toyadasso) and Coye II; 27. Keough; 28. Bloody Hill; 29. Christopher; 30. Burke; 31. Carley; 32. Indian Castle; 33. Indian Hill; 34. Cemetery; 35. Nursery; 36. Barnes; 37. McNab; 38. Temperance House; 39. Atwell; 40. Quirk; 41. Pompey Center; 42. Sheldon; 43. Chase; 44. Dwyer.

difficult. Typically, historic Iroquois tribes were composed of two or more villages located not more than about 10 miles apart. Bruce G. Trigger suggests that "the need for defense produced larger settlements, until these reached the limits at which Iroquois slash and burn horticulture could operate efficiently. Once these limits had been reached, these same forces led to the development of defensive alliances in which friendly villages settled in close proximity" (1976, 158–59). Such alliances between villages would have formed the basis for the development of tribal identity encompassing two or more communities.

Two alternative processes of tribal development that might be reflected archaeologically are (1) the fusion of smaller communities to form larger communities, and (2) alliances between communities. Ideally the fusion of smaller communities into larger ones might be revealed through ceramic analysis, while alliances could be reflected archaeologically by the existence of contemporaneous village sites not more than about 10 miles apart. While a tribe may consist of a single village, closely spaced contemporaneous Iroquois village sites are taken to indicate the existence of a tribe for the purposes of this paper. Used in this manner, the term *tribe* could refer either to a loose alliance between communities or to a more integrated political organization.

The identification of tribes by the distribution of communities enables one to infer the minimum time depth of specific tribes. Similar site distributions in earlier times imply the existence of the same political unit. The initial appearance of the known tribal pattern (fig. 11.2) suggests that the particular tribe is at least that old. This information gives only a minimum estimate, however, because some variant form of tribal organization may have been in existence in the area earlier.

Onondaga and Seneca Archaeology

Rather than reviewing information for all historically known tribal areas, this paper focuses on two of the best known: the Onondaga and the Seneca. James A. Tuck (1971) noted changes in the Onondaga area in the fifteenth century that suggested to him the formation of the Onondaga tribe. These changes included the shift from small dispersed communities to two closely spaced communities, the large one probably being formed by the merger of two smaller communities. The close geographical proximity of the two communities suggests an alliance or nonaggression pact. It is this pattern of a large and a small community that persists into Protohistoric times in the Onondaga area. James W. Bradley (1979, 346) argues that there is further consolidation during the historic period, when the Onondaga lived in a single large village. The Onondaga data therefore suggest a continuing process of population nucleation or fusion, with a distribution resembling that of the early seventeenth-century Onondaga tribe appearing in prehistoric times.

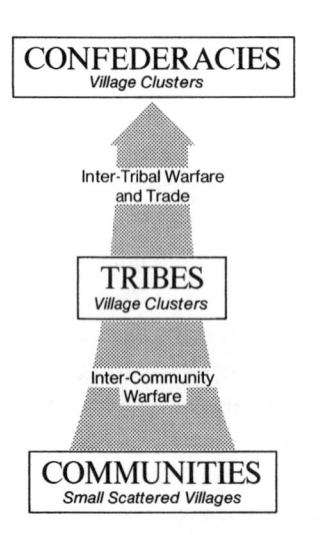

Fig. 11.2. Model of Iroquois political development and population distribution.

Data from the Seneca area present a different picture. Charles F. Wray (1973) has traced the historically observed pattern of two larger communities, each with an associated smaller community, back in time to about the mid-sixteenth century. While there are earlier Iroquoian sites in the area, their relationship to these later sites is not clear. I recently examined ceramics from two of these earlier sites, Footer and Farrell. Neither collection exhibited much ceramic similarity with collections from later Seneca sites (see table 11.1).

While the locations of Footer and Farrell suggest that the populations of these

Table 11.1

Coefficents of Agreement as Measured by Ceramic Similarity among Seneca Sites

SITE/DATE (A.D.)	Farrell	Footer	Belcher	Richmond Mills	Adams	Cameron	Factory Hollow	Dutch Hollow	Cornish	Warren	Powerhouse
Farrell 1300–1350		161	158	150	146	138	137	138	135	139	131
Footer 1350–1400			148	145	142	133	129	135	128	134	128
Belcher 1450–1550				173	151	145	137	143	133	142	134
Richmond Mills 1450–1550					159	165	155	160	147	159	152
Adams 1550–1575						148	141	149	137	155	140
Cameron 1575–1590							175	181	167	172	168
Factory Hollow 1580–1610								178	185	175	176
Dutch Hollow 1590–1616									173	177	177
Cornish 1600–1620										173	179
Warren 1615–1630											177
Powerhouse 1630–1650											

sites were ancestral to the sixteenth-century Seneca, ceramic analysis does not demonstrate a strong continuity. Other communities with different ceramic traditions probably merged with the descendants of the Footer and Farrell populations to form the large sixteenth-century Seneca communities.

To see if the fusion model developed from Tuck's Onondaga data could be applied to the Seneca, ceramics from the Adams site were examined. Adams is the earliest large western village in the Seneca sequence. If this village were the product of fusion of two or more separate communities, then ceramics from this site should be relatively heterogeneous, reflecting different ceramic traditions developed in different communities. Coefficients of homogeneity were calculated for Adams and six later Seneca sites, as well as for Farrell and Footer (see table 11.2). The ceramics from Adams proved to be the most heterogeneous (figs. 11.3 and 11.4), lending support to a fusion model for Seneca development. More information on early sites in the Seneca area and environs is needed to test this model further.

According to Tuck, in the Onondaga area the Christopher site represents the fusion of two earlier communities, one at Bloody Hill and one occupying the Keough site. Tuck was not able to examine a large sample from Christopher. Given that material is available, it should be studied to see if it is also more heterogeneous than that of later sites. Peter G. Ramsden (1978, 108) notes evidence of artifact heterogeneity on the Parsons and Draper sites, two large Huron sites probably dating to the early sixteenth century that, he believes, reflect the fusion of separate communities. Similar analyses of the first large fifteenth- and sixteenth-century sites in other areas should be undertaken to see if the ceramics are heterogeneous. If so, this heterogeneity would lend further support to the fusion model of Iroquois tribal development.

Oral tradition commonly states that there were two separate groups of Senecas at the time of the formation of the League (Parker 1916b, 87). This tradition agrees

Table 11.2

Coefficients of Homogeneity for Seneca Sites

Site	Date (A.D.)	Coefficient[a]
Farrell	1300–1350	.71
Footer	1350–1400	.74
Adams	1550–1575	.65
Cameron	1575–1590	.70
Factory Hollow	1580–1610	.74
Dutch Hollow	1590–1616	.72
Cornish	1600–1620	.76
Warren	1615–1630	.71
Powerhouse	1630–1650	.75

[a]The higher the coefficient, the more homogeneous the ceramic assemblage. Adams is the most heterogeneous.

Fig. 11.3. Ceramic vessels from the Adams site (Seneca, ca. A.D. 1565–75). These objects' diverse decoration illustrates the heterogeneity of this site assemblage. (RMSC cat. nos., clockwise from upper left: 614/94, 383/94, 269/94, 264/94; photographs courtesy of Rochester Museum and Science Center.)

with the Protohistoric and early Historic Seneca settlement pattern of two major villages, each with smaller settlements nearby. Different versions of the Seneca origin myth have been recorded by Morgan, Schoolcraft, Cusick, and others. As Mary Ann Palmer Niemczycki (1983, 25–26) has noted, these different versions may reflect different populations that merged to form the Seneca. In James E. Seaver's (1990 [1824]) account, a giant snake threatens the people but is eventually slain. William M. Beauchamp (1892) believed that this allegory preserved the memory of an early conflict that helped to unify the Seneca. This interpretation is compatible with George Hamell's equation of the serpent or fire dragon of Iroquois myth with forces of disharmony or disorganization (Hamell personal communication).

Conflict and population merger or fusion can therefore be inferred from both oral tradition and archaeology. During the Late Prehistoric period, blood feuds, religious motivation, and the desire to acquire prestige on the warpath led to escalat-

Fig. 11.4. Ceramic vessels from the Adams site (Seneca, ca. A.D. 1565–75). These objects' diversity illustrates the heterogeneity of this site assemblage. (RMSC cat. nos., clockwise from upper left: 609/94, 610/94, 268/94, 409/94; photographs courtesy of Rochester Museum and Science Center.)

ing conflict between Iroquoian communities (Trigger 1990a [1969], 52). With the advent of Europeans, competition for access to furs or to European trade goods further intensified Iroquois warfare. This warfare created widely spaced population clusters that provided the basis for tribal development. Marshall D. Sahlins (1961, 326) has noted that the degree of political consolidation within a tribe is dependent on external circumstances. Continued warfare would have operated to transform closely spaced allied villages into a single cohesive political unit.

Clans

The emergence of larger population units or tribes encouraged new forms of social integration. Elman A. Service (1962, 141) and others have stressed the role of pan-tribal sodalities in tribal organization, and Tuck (1971) postulated growth in organizations like the False Face Society during the process of Iroquois tribal formation. Clan affiliation became an important integrative mechanism as well. Clans were an important component of Iroquois political organization in historic times and clan affiliation remains important to New York Iroquois today. In historic times, members of the same clan were found in different communities or even in different tribes. Early European visitors to Iroquois villages noted clan symbols above longhouse doors that could be identified by traveling Iroquois seeking shelter among fellow clan members.

If we assume that Iroquois longhouses were generally occupied by members of a matrilineage and their spouses, then a study of the number and size of houses on different sites over time would reflect the number and size of lineages on these sites. While these data are incomplete, the general temporal trend seems to be that of: (1) increasing number of structures, and (2) decreasing size of structures. At one extreme is a site like Bates, dating to around A.D. 1200 and consisting of a single longhouse that may have housed around 50 people (Ritchie and Funk 1973, 251). At the other extreme are historically observed Iroquois villages consisting of many small houses, most of which must have housed nuclear families.

In the Onondaga area, the longest houses were found during the fifteenth century, and Tuck (1978, 328) noted a trend of decreasing longhouse size from the Prehistoric to the Protohistoric periods, even though sites continued to increase in size and the number of longhouses per site also increased.

Tuck suggests that this trend is related to tribal formation, perhaps from a relaxation of matrilocal residence rules as a result of greater freedom of movement between villages of the same tribe. Gary A. Warrick (1982) cites a similar trend in Ontario and suggests that longhouses began to decrease in size once alliances between communities were established. Such alliances could have given individuals or families greater residential flexibility, especially if the same clans were found in both communities.

The European presence in North America may also have contributed to decreasing longhouse size by increasing mortality rates. European-introduced diseases took a heavy toll on North American Indian populations, and the discovery of multiple primary burials on the Seneca sites of Adams, Tram, Steel, and Powerhouse suggests that the Protohistoric and Early Historic Seneca were no exception. Clans, being relatively large units, would have provided more stability and continuity during this demographically unstable period.

While the decreasing size of longhouses suggests that lineages as residential units were increasingly composed of fewer individuals, the increasing number of houses suggests that more lineages were appearing on sites. The increase in the number of houses could be explained by the fission of single lineages or the incorporation of small groups or lineages from other populations. In historic times, the

Iroquois adopted both individuals and groups, thus helping to maintain their population. With many smaller lineages present, clan segments probably took over many of the earlier functions of lineages within a community. In addition, shared clan affiliations provided a mechanism for fostering intercommunity or intertribal cooperation.

It is possible that the orientation of structures on Iroquois sites could reflect clans. Trigger (1981a, 35) notes the possibility that the tripartite arrangement of longhouses on the Mohawk site of Garoga could be interpreted as reflecting the three Mohawk clans of Bear, Wolf, and Turtle. However Ritchie and Funk (1973, 331) find that this arrangement best fits the shape of the hilltop on which Garoga is situated. In addition, the historic Mohawk Caughnawaga site (1666–93) shows a dual rather than tripartite division, which might reflect moiety organization. If the internal structures of more sites were known, hypotheses relating these arrangements to features of social organization could be tested.

Cemetery data can also be used to infer the presence of clans. There are often multiple cemeteries associated with Protohistoric Seneca village sites. The existence of these multiple cemeteries suggests the presence of social divisions, and it has been suggested that these represent clan or moiety cemeteries (Wray and Schoff 1953, 55). If such social divisions were not as important earlier, then earlier sites should be characterized by single, rather than multiple, cemeteries. With the exception of the twelfth-century Sackett site, this appears to be the case, though more data are needed.

In *Iroquois Cosmology*, John N. B. Hewitt (1928) relates a tradition of the formation of Iroquois clans. An individual states that "the time has now come when we should form clans which should exist. The reason that we should thus do, is that now, verily we have become numerous." And again: "There exists an unadjusted matter, we are separating one from another, continually, here upon earth" (Hewitt 1928, 597).

The tradition further states that mortality rates were unusually high at this time. People camped in groups on either side of a stream and were assigned their clan affiliation. This account suggests that clans arose in response to social need resulting from larger communities, disorganization, and increased mortality. The reference to a high death rate suggests the Protohistoric period.

Clans in some form may actually have great antiquity in the Northeast, as their widespread distribution suggests (Tooker 1971). The argument presented here is that they became increasingly important during the fifteenth through seventeenth centuries as Iroquois tribal organization developed. Larger communities and alliances between communities would have fostered the growth of integrative institutions such as clans. Such integrative mechanisms were well developed by the mid-seventeenth century, for Iroquois tribes successfully absorbed people from diverse groups at this time.

While the longhouse remains an important symbol of Iroquois life, the trend of decreasing longhouse size and increasing number of longhouses argues for the decreased importance of lineages as integrative features of social organization. In place of lineages, clans and clan segments assumed an increased role, contributing to the cohesiveness of Iroquois tribes and later to the League of the Iroquois.

Confederacy

In early historic times the Iroquois Confederacy or League of the Iroquois was composed of the Seneca, Cayuga, Onondaga, Oneida, and Mohawk. Just as these Iroquois tribes were formed by alliances between villages, so the League may have started out as a series of alliances between tribes. Trigger (1976, 163) suggests that the formation of a confederacy was an extension of the same forces that had already created tribal structures. As in the case of tribes, defense against a common enemy and a desire for peace between communities would seem likely reasons leading to such alliances. During the Protohistoric period, the increasing quantity of European goods on Iroquois sites suggests an increasing concern with nonlocal relationships.

Oral Traditions

The foremost student of the League of the Iroquois was Lewis Henry Morgan. Even today, over a century after his death and 130 years after the publication of *The League,* his description of the structure and functioning of the League continues to influence our thinking. Morgan received much of his information on the League from Ely S. Parker, a knowledgeable Tonawanda Seneca. However, the League as Parker described it to Morgan did not necessarily function in the same way in the seventeenth century. Though seventeenth-century accounts tell us little about the League, they do indicate that each Iroquois tribe had considerable autonomy. In fact, a number of writers have suggested that in the early seventeenth century the League was basically a nonaggression pact between constituent members, allowing each tribe to undertake enemy raids without fear of attack from neighboring allies. During the eighteenth century, Iroquois tribes often pursued independent diplomatic policies. This diplomatic independence gave the Iroquois flexibility in maintaining the balance of power between the British and French (Tooker 1981). Thus the available information suggests that the picture of unified action described by Morgan cannot be projected far back in time.

The question of when this alliance or League was initially formed remains to be answered. At present, it is not clear if it is a prehistoric or a protohistoric phenomenon and hence whether the European presence in North America had anything to do with its inception.

There are many oral traditions surrounding the formation of the League and they do not agree as to the time of formation. In one version, the Seneca join the League after a total eclipse of the sun during a time when the corn was ripe. A check of astronomical tables points to A.D. 1451 as the likely date for this eclipse in central New York (Tooker 1978, 420). Other traditions place the formation of the League sometime during the Protohistoric period: the length of a man's life before white men came to the country. Because of these contradictions, oral tradition has generally been dismissed as being of little use in determining the date for the founding of the League.

Deganawidah, who is credited with founding the League, is said (in some versions) to have been a Huron. The Huron also formed a confederacy, and for the early seventeenth century, their confederacy is better documented. Unlike the New York Iroquois, the separate groups composing the Huron confederacy were found together when the French first visited Huronia.

Archaeological research as well as accounts recorded by the French suggests that the formation of the Huron confederacy was a gradual process, the confederacy first being made up of two groups, the Attignawantan and the Attigneenongnahac (Trigger 1976, 163). The Huron claimed that the alliance between these two groups went back to around A.D. 1440. On the other hand, the Tahontaenrat probably did not join the Huron confederacy until about 1610 (Trigger 1976, 157). While the distribution of population in Huronia was more clustered than that of the New York Iroquois (perhaps ultimately to the Hurons' disadvantage), it seems logical that the formation of the League of the Iroquois might also have been a gradual process, the final alliance being but the last of a series of earlier alliances between some but not necessarily all of the five groups.

If the formation of the League of the Iroquois is best described as a series of alliances, then the conflicting oral traditions relating to its origins could be seen as referring to the formation of different alliances. For example, there may have been a prehistoric alliance or agreement between some or all of the tribes shortly after the eclipse of 1451 and then another between all of the Five Nations during the Protohistoric period. Some traditions say that the Mohawks were the first to join the League, whereas the Senecas were the last. These traditions support the idea that the League took shape over a period of time. Also, some traditions suggest that the names of the last two Seneca chiefs on the roll call of chiefs were added some time after the original council of the League (Tooker 1981, 7). This timing, coupled with the fact that the Senecas have the fewest League chiefs, may reflect their status as late joiners of the alliance.

Ceramics and the League

In 1971, I attempted to infer the formation of the League of the Iroquois from an examination of Iroquois ceramics. It was assumed that with the formation of the

League, there would have been increased communication and movement of women between tribes of the League, and that this movement would be reflected ceramically. Pots from sixteenth- and early seventeenth-century Iroquois sites were examined, as were pots from the Niagara Frontier, an area originally to the west of the League. It was anticipated that with the formation of the League ceramic similarity between constituent members would increase, whereas pottery from the Niagara Frontier would not show this pattern. A primary assumption behind this hypothesis was that the formation of the League of the Iroquois was a relatively rapid and unique event. The results of that study did not support the original expectation. No clear difference in ceramic patterning between League sites and non-League sites was observed.

Though there was a general trend of increasing ceramic similarity between all areas through time, the amount of this increase varied. From this variation one could infer that intertribal female contact and movement between some tribal areas was greater than between others. I have gathered additional data since the 1971 study, so that now computer-coded ceramic information is available on some 8,000 Iroquois pots from 42 village sites across New York State. These data reinforce the original inference that rates of intertribal female movement for any period are variable. Though ceramic patterning does not demonstrate that the formation of the League was a gradual process, these data can be interpreted in this light.

For example, ceramic analysis suggests little intertribal movement or interaction on the part of women in the Niagara Frontier and Seneca areas (Engelbrecht 1974a; 1978). While later Niagara Frontier sites show some Seneca-style pottery, in general ceramics from the two areas are distinctive. Sites in the Niagara Frontier cluster with one another on the basis of ceramic style and are ceramically homogeneous. Seneca sites show a similar pattern, being only slightly less homogeneous and slightly less similar to one another than are Niagara Frontier sites.

Historically, the population in the Niagara Frontier did not have an alliance with other New York Iroquois populations and this lack may be reflected in the area's ceramic distinctiveness. Seneca ceramics suggest that Seneca women were only slightly less isolated, a factor that may relate to the oral tradition that the Seneca were the last to join the League.

The Onondaga, Oneida, and Mohawk areas show a different pattern. In general, Onondaga and Oneida sites cluster with one another on the basis of ceramic style and show increased similarity with Mohawk sites through time (Engelbrecht 1974a; 1978). This increased similarity suggests increasing female movement between the Onondaga, Oneida, and Mohawk areas during the Protohistoric period. Iroquois woman regularly carried provisions for men on journeys (Thwaites 1896–1901, 38:255) and women could have traveled between tribes on their own. The Mohawk had easiest access to Dutch goods, and in 1634 Van den Bogaert saw Oneida women who had come to a Mohawk village to trade. Tribal exogamy may also be reflected in these ceramic patterns. While matrilocality for the Iroquois is generally assumed, there may have been exceptions. As the smallest New York Iroquois tribe, tribal exogamy may have been more common for the Oneida, who in the sixteenth and early seventeenth centuries apparently consisted of a single medium-sized village. Sites in the Oneida area show a clear trend of increasing ceramic heterogeneity through time, possibly reflecting the movement of women into the Oneida tribe (see table 11.3).

Recently William Andrefsky (1980) has argued that sites of the League Iroquois tend to have more trade material than do contemporaneous non-League sites in New York. This suggests a link between trade-related activities and League functioning. Trading between allied tribes could have increased tribal interdependence while intertribal cooperation in raiding allowed the formation of larger war parties.

Summary

In this paper, the terms *tribe* and *confederacy* have been used to refer to a range of organizational forms, from loose alliances to more tightly organized polities. However, power was never so centralized in historic Iroquois tribes as to preclude a measure of individual or kin group independence. Likewise, tribes appear to have preserved a measure of autonomy within the League of the Iroquois. Within both tribes and the confederacy, the degree of political consolidation probably increased over time.

During the Prehistoric period, warfare led to larger communities and to alliances between communities (tribes). Tribal development was facilitated by the development of tribal sodalities and an increased role for clans. Continuing warfare encouraged alliances between tribes (confederacies). During the Protohistoric period, the European fur trade resulted in increased conflict, thereby accelerating trends already operating prehistorically.

Table 11.3
Coefficients of Homogeneity for Oneida Sites

Site	Date (A.D.)	Coefficient[a]
Nichols Pond	1450–1500	.71
Buyea	1500–1550	.64
Bach	1540–1555	.63
Diable	1550–1570	.65
Wayland Smith	1570–1595	.60
Thurston	1625–1637	.58

[a] The higher the coefficient, the more homogeneous the ceramic assemblage. There is a clear trend of increasing heterogeneity through time.

The Iroquois Confederacy eventually defeated surrounding tribes and confederacies, adopting many people in the process. These large-scale adoptions helped the Iroquois to counter the increased mortality resulting from European-introduced pathogens. Because the Iroquois were geographically separated from areas of European settlement until the eighteenth century, they had more time than did more easterly groups to develop politically without direct European disruption.

In the seventeenth century surrounding Native American groups were no longer a threat to the Iroquois, but the major European powers continued to pose an external threat and we may assume that the League of the Iroquois continued to evolve as a political institution in response to this threat. Witness, for example, the incorporation of the Tuscarora in the early eighteenth century, when the Five Nations became the Six Nations. This incorporation can be viewed as a continuation of the process of alliance building begun by the Iroquois in prehistoric times.

The European discovery, exploration, and eventual colonization of the New World resulted in major changes in the way of life of the Native peoples of North America. Many groups ceased to exist while others were fragmented and displaced. Occasionally, as in the case of the New York Iroquois, populations successfully maintained themselves in their traditional homeland during the colonial period. Though Europeans were the cause of increased warfare and mortality rates for the protohistoric Iroquois, their sociopolitical institutions evolved to meet these challenges.

Acknowledgments

I am pleased to thank William Fitzhugh of the Smithsonian Institution, who asked me to present a talk to the Anthropological Society of Washington on the effect of early European contact on Iroquois institutions, thereby providing the focus of this paper. This study was in part made possible by an Arthur C. Parker Research Fellowship from the Rochester Museum and Science Center. The staff of the Rochester Museum, including Charles Hayes III, Charles Wray, and George Hamell (now with the State Museum in Albany), and Tricia Miller, who provided the photographs, was most helpful. Charles Vandrei and Mary Ann Niemczycki, both of the State University of New York at Buffalo, made helpful comments on an early draft of this paper. Finally, I would like to thank Elaine Henzler, secretary of the Anthropology Department at Buffalo State College, for her assistance in typing this paper.

12 | An Eighteenth-Century Seneca Iroquois Short Longhouse from the Townley-Read Site, ca. A.D. 1715–1754

KURT A. JORDAN

Introduction

THIS PAPER REVIEWS the excavation of what is interpreted as the traces of an eighteenth-century Seneca Iroquois dwelling at the Townley-Read site (fig. 12.1; NYSM 2440; RMSC Plp-016) near Geneva, New York. Townley-Read Structure 1, classified as an intercultural/creolized short longhouse, was excavated by the Townley-Read/New Ganechstage Project in 1999. On present evidence, the Seneca occupation of the site took place from approximately A.D. 1715 to 1754 (K. Jordan 2002, 274–91).

The Townley-Read/New Ganechstage Project has conducted archaeological investigations at the Townley Read site from 1996 through 2000. Project fieldwork, codirected by Dr. Nan Rothschild of Columbia University and the author, included Columbia University Summer Archaeological Field Schools in 1998 and 1999 and a Hobart and William Smith Colleges Field Course in Iroquois Archaeology in Spring 2000. The project has been supported by grants from the National Science Foundation and the Early American Industries Association and advised by Peter Jemison of the Seneca Nation of Indians. The major findings of the project at Townley-Read to date include: (1) surface artifact densities indicating a dispersed eighteenth-century community with houses 60–80 meters (m) apart in a nondefensible location; (2) the post mold outline of the 7.5 m x 5.3 m Seneca short longhouse (Structure 1) detailed in this article; (3) the subplowzone remnant of a 3.5 m x 1.7 m

---

Previously published in *The Bulletin: Journal of the New York State Archaeological Association* 119 (2003): 49–63. Printed with permission by *The Bulletin: Journal of the New York State Archaeological Association.*

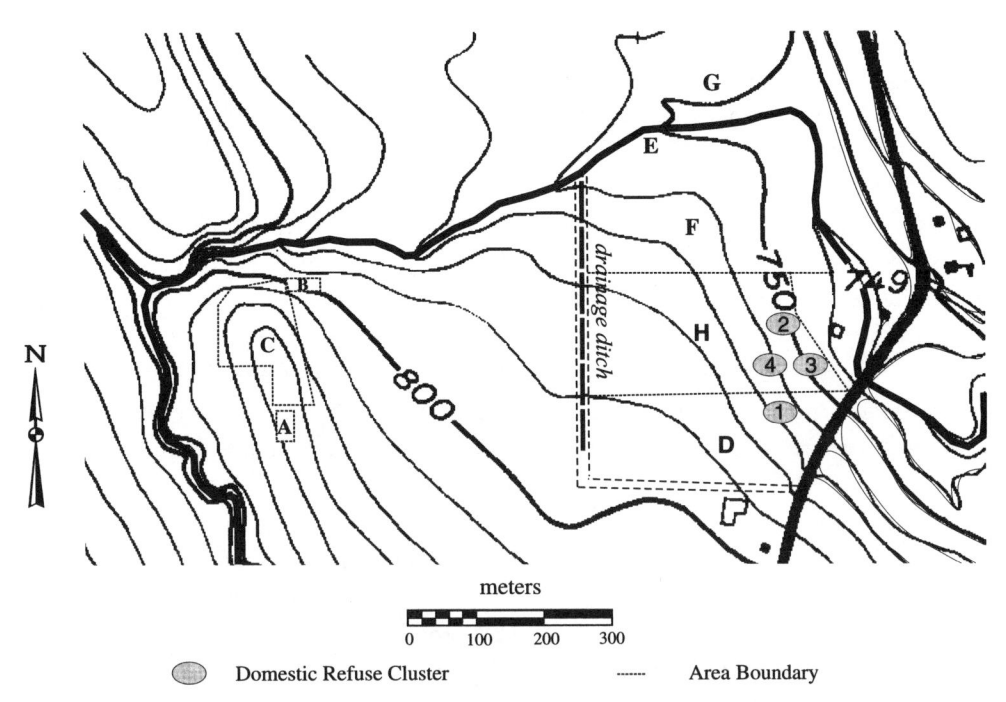

Fig. 12.1. Topographic map of the Townley-Read site (NYSM 2440; RMSC Plp-16), occupied ca. A.D. 1715–54. Letters mark areas that have been investigated or considered by the Townley-Read/New Ganechstage Project. A, B, and C are ridgetop areas with prehistoric deposits. D and H are low-lying areas with eighteenth-century domestic deposits. F is known to contain eighteenth-century materials but has not been investigated systematically. E and G were examined by the project but did not contain substantial cultural materials. Elevations are given in feet; contour interval 10 ft (3.0 m). Base map taken from USGS topographical map, 7.5' series, Stanley, New York quadrangle.

external firepit (Feature 5) that contained over 3,400 pieces of animal bone; (4) a buried plowed eighteenth-century trash deposit of at least 15 inches (in) x 10 in that contained animal bone, glass, brass, and smoking pipe remains; and (5) a previously unknown prehistoric component at the site. Our search for a rumored eighteenth-century European-run smithy at the site was unsuccessful. Additional information on the project can be found in my doctoral dissertation (K. Jordan 2002).

Archaeological Fieldwork

The main focus of the Townley-Read/New Ganechstage Project has been to isolate and excavate domestic-context archaeological deposits from the eighteenth-century Seneca village at Townley-Read. Unpublished records of previous research undertaken at the site (Conover ca. 1889; Wray 1979–82) offered conflicting opinions about the location of the eighteenth-century village. The project first investigated local historian George S. Conover's (ca. 1889) claim that the village was located on a western ridgetop overlooking an elbow in Burrell Creek. This ridgetop is one of the more defensible spots in the locality and has relatively easy access to water and good floodplain soil. Although these factors frequently were key to the placement of Iroquoian sites occupied between the fifteenth and seventeenth centuries, excavations on the ridgetop (fig. 12.1: Areas A, B, and C) produced no definite evidence for an eighteenth-century occupation, proving that Conover's claim was in error.

The ridgetop contained a light scatter of prehistoric and post-1788 Euroamerican artifacts. The most substantial concentration of prehistoric artifacts was found in Area A, interpreted as the by-products of one or more short-term uses of the ridgetop as a lithic core-reduction location, camp site, and/or hunting station by prehistoric (minimally Late Woodland) groups. The prehistoric artifacts recovered on the ridgetop may be the traces of resource-procurement forays by residents of the nearby Late Woodland Woodley village site (RMSC Plp-078; see MacNeish [1952] and Niemczycki [1984] for contrasting interpretations of the Woodley site's place in the Seneca and Cayuga sequences).

The lack of eighteenth-century residential deposits on the ridgetop had several interesting implications. First, it shifted the focus of the project to the low-lying eastern fields at Townley-Read (fig. 12.1: Areas D, F, and H), where avocational archaeologist Charles Wray and others had excavated at least 33 eighteenth-century burials between 1979 and 1982 (Wray 1979–82). Second, in terms of settlement pattern it meant that the Seneca residents at Townley-Read had ignored a defensible, traditional-looking site location on the ridgetop and settled only 700 m away in a low-lying area with essentially no defensive value. Third, it meant that Seneca houses and burials were located in fairly close proximity. Because it was a priority of the project to avoid disturbing Seneca graves, we needed a reliable method for determining where domestic deposits were likely to be found before we started digging.

Although the project experimented with a range of nonintrusive field techniques including geophysical surveys using ground-penetrating radar, magnetometry and conductivity instruments, and systematic metal detection, the most successful method proved to be simple surface examination of the plowed portions of the site. We employed a number of different variations, ranging from point-proveniencing each surface artifact in a given area using a total station, to counting artifacts within 20 m x 20 m squares. Use of 10 m x 10 m collection units with diagnostic artifacts point-provenienced within the site grid appears to offer the best compromise between maximizing the level of detail acquired about spatial relations and minimizing the amount of time and money spent.

To date a total of 6.5 hectares (ha) (16 acres) have been surface-mapped within

Areas D and H at the site. These surface investigations have allowed us to define four of what I have termed *Domestic Refuse Clusters,* or DRCs. DRCs primarily were defined by surface concentrations of small pieces of burned and unburned animal bone and tooth fragments. Any 20 m x 20 m square in which 20 or more animal bone/tooth fragments were found was defined as a DRC. These areas also contained most of the white ball clay smoking pipe and olive bottle glass fragments we found, items that are almost never found in early eighteenth-century Seneca grave assemblages. Project excavations to date have supported the idea that such surface artifact concentrations are reliable indicators of subsurface domestic remains. The manufacture of bone grease by Seneca women is likely to account for the highly fragmented character of the food bone refuse found at the site (K. Jordan 2002, 482–86; Watson 2000).

Excavations in DRC 1 in 1999 revealed it to be a definite houselot, containing the footprint of a short longhouse (Structure 1) and Feature 5, a large external firepit. During 2000, excavations in DRC 3 located a buried plowed midden horizon of at least 15 m x 10 m in size, so DRCs cannot automatically be assumed to be houses. Although they have not been adequately investigated to date, DRC 2 and DRC 4 likely represent houselots based on their similarity to DRC 1 in terms of their distance from Burrell Creek and placement half to three-quarters of the way down the slope toward the creek.

Within DRC 1, a 10 m x 40 m grid of shovel test-pits at 5 m intervals, sampling of a set of metal detector "hits" in a separate 10 m x 30 m area, and a series of 1 m x 1 m test units helped us to locate Post Molds 4 and 5, later determined to be the northwest and southeast main support posts for Structure 1. At this point a bulldozer was brought in to strip off the plowzone in an area of roughly 14 m x 43 m, which enabled us to recover much more information about the broader houselot area than would have been possible using hand excavation alone. Initially we left an island of plowzone soil around Post Molds 4 and 5 that turned out to enclose just about the entirety of Structure 1; we did not discover the size and alignment of the dwelling until mid-November when this soil was removed by a backhoe. The weather did not permit much more work during that field season; the project was able to fully clean and map the structure area, but the majority of wall posts were not excavated. Although we found several post molds and features likely to date to the eighteenth century outside Structure 1, their positioning was neither dense nor patterned enough to suggest that another structure was present within DRC 1 (K. Jordan 2002, 248–58).

Structure 1

The post mold pattern recovered at the western end of DRC 1 (fig. 12.2) is interpreted as the remains of a "short longhouse" dwelling used by the Senecas for part

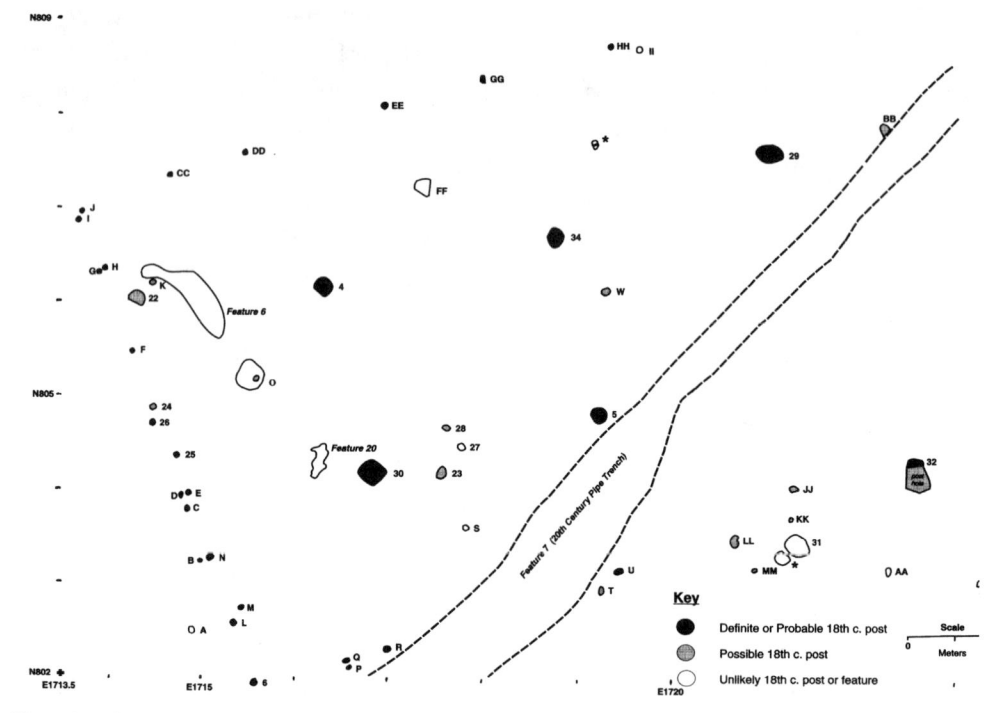

Fig. 12.2. Structure 1 post molds and features from the Townley-Read site, area D, domestic refuse cluster 1. Posts numbered or marked with an asterisk were excavated; posts marked with a letter were not excavated. Portions of features 6 and 7 were excavated; feature 20 was not excavated.

or all of the period between 1715 and 1754, termed Structure 1. To date the Townley-Read house is only the fourth full house plan recovered in the Seneca region from the period between A.D. 1550 and 1779, the others being located at the (1) Factory Hollow (Guthe 1958); (2) Cornish (Hayes 1967); and (3) Ganondagan (Dean 1984) sites, although I am skeptical that the Ganondagan remains represent a domestic structure (see K. Jordan 2002, 395–96).

A total of 53 dark, post mold-sized soil stains were present in the area of the structure. Of these 15 were excavated, 9 of which are interpreted as probable or definite, 4 as possible, and 2 as unlikely eighteenth-century post molds. Of the 38 unexcavated posts, 21 are interpreted as probable or definite, 9 as possible, and 8 as unlikely post molds based on their location, color, and/or the presence of small pieces of bone or charcoal within their fill. Two larger soil stains (Features 6 and 20) were located within the structure area; neither is thought to be cultural. Three smaller unnumbered features not thought to be cultural were also excavated. Additional details regarding the post molds and noncultural soil stains can be found in a draft site report (K. Jordan 2001a).

As I interpret it, Structure 1 at Townley-Read was 5.3 m wide and 7.5 m long

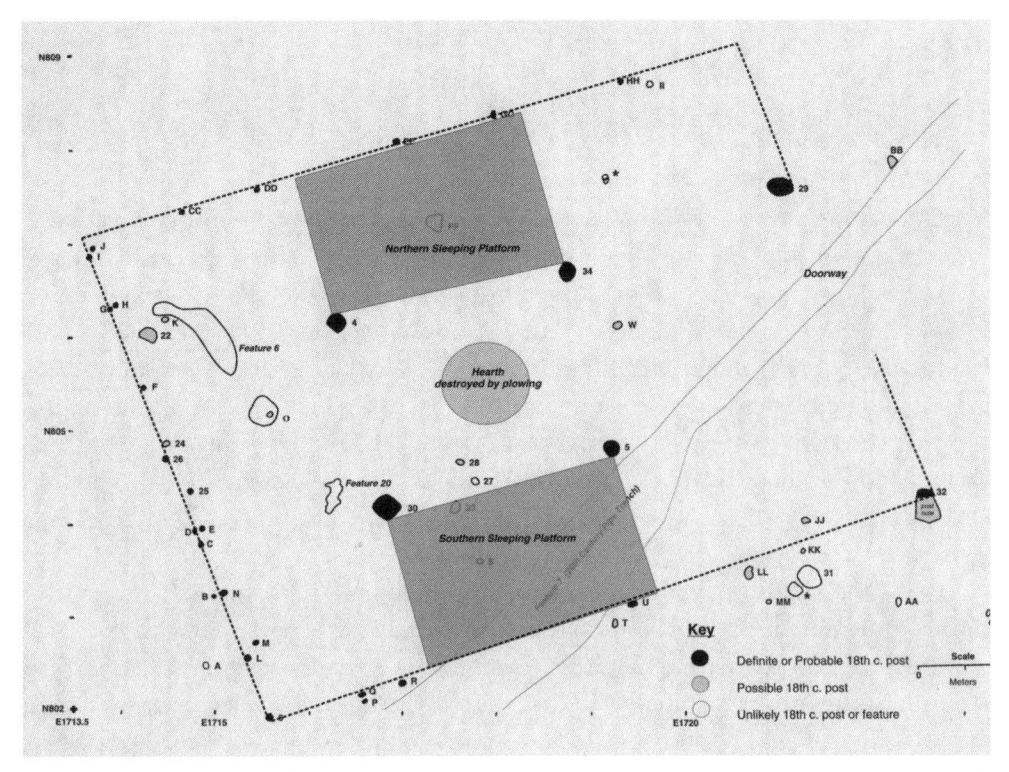

Fig. 12.3. Interpretation of size and internal features of structure 1 at the Townley-Read site, area D, domestic refuse cluster 1.

(17.3 ft x 24.6 ft)(fig. 12.3). The width measurement is fairly certain, because it is based on the western wall, which contains 14 definite and 2 possible posts, 5 of which were excavated. Post molds were found at close to right angles to the presumed corners of the west wall, making it unlikely that the structure extended beyond the 5.3 m dimension. The length figure has less evidence to support it. The north wall contains 6 probable posts, none of which was excavated. The south wall is even less substantiated, with only 4 definite and 5 possible posts. It also appears that part of the south wall was obliterated by a twentieth-century pipe trench (Feature 7). However, the large Post Mold 32 is on the line of the south wall and its position has been used to mark the eastern end of the structure. During November and December 1999 we made some attempt to chase out the north and south walls and the interior lines established by the two sets of main support posts. None of these attempts located any additional posts. Time constraints did not allow us to clean and map these areas as completely as I would have liked, but impressionistically I am 85 percent certain that we found the end of the house. Based on my interpretation of its size, Townley-Read Structure 1 is defined as a "short longhouse" using Mima Kapches's (1984) typology for Iroquoian houses, or, less formally, as a "shorthouse." I have interpreted Structure 1 as a two-family dwelling based on the presence of four main support posts and a central corridor, which suggest that the dwelling contained two sleeping platforms.

The architecture of the Townley-Read house is in many ways fairly traditional in form. The largest posts are located in the interior of the dwelling, where they provided the main structural support for the house and presumably framed a central corridor and anchored sleeping platforms. These four main support posts (PMs 4, 5, 30, and 34) ranged from 18 to 23.5 centimeters (cm) in diameter, averaging 19.9 cm, and extended from 12 to 36 cm below subsoil surface. All of these posts had rounded bottoms. Only three definite small external post molds (PMs 6, 25, and 26) were excavated. These posts extended from 11 to 18 cm below subsoil surface; the bottom of PM 6 (the southwest corner post) was fairly round in form, while the bottoms of PMs 25 and 26 from the west wall came to relatively sharp points. The surface diameter of all 31 definite, probable, or possible wall posts ranges from 4.0 to 13.0 cm, averaging 6.3 cm.

Post Molds 29 and 32, both of which are located at the eastern extreme of the structure, do not fit either the interior or wall post category particularly well. PM 29 is more or less on line with the northern set of main support posts; PM 32 is on line with the southern wall of the structure. Both posts are close to an equal distance from the western wall, prompting the interpretation that these posts formed part of the eastern wall of the house. PM 29 is 24.5 cm in diameter but extended only 10 cm below subsoil surface. To date, PM 32 is a unique find at the site: it was a rectangular post 18 cm x 7 cm in size that had been inserted into a dug post-hole. Its position in line with the south wall and the fact that we found no similar features make it almost definite that PM 32 was part of the structure rather than an intrusive feature such as a Euroamerican fence post. This use of large posts to support a wall represents a departure from the fairly traditional construction methods seen in the rest of the house.

Although we did not recover direct evidence for a central hearth, indirect evidence supports the claim that one was present. Flotation sample heavy fraction charcoal density was highest in PMs 32 and 34, intermediate in PMs 5, 6, and 29, and low in PMs 4 and 30, which suggests that the hearth may have been located somewhat to the east within the structure. In contrast, fire-cracked rock was concentrated to the west: large pieces of fire-cracked rock were present in the matrix of PMs 4 and 30 and smaller pieces were present in PMs 6, 29, and 34. Additionally, fire-cracked rock was recovered in the plowzone from three test units dug within the house area. Any noncentral firepit or hearthstone fireplace with a chimney probably would have been located along the doorless western wall, but the low charcoal density in PMs 4, 6, and 30 weighs against this idea.

Data from the post mold flotation samples provide a solid foundation to the claim that Structure 1 was a domestic dwelling. A total of nine soil samples were taken from possible or definite post molds within the house; two of these samples were taken from PM 32 (one from the dark post remains, and one from the post hole fill). The contents of post mold fill recovered from flotation and/or dry screening with 3 mm (0.125 in) mesh hardware cloth have a very "lived in" look, containing many small artifacts that represent the by-products of household activities and lost items. Seven of the thirteen excavated possible or probable post molds contained glass seed beads, including all four main support posts and Post Molds 6, 25, 29, and GG. A single tubular white wampum shell bead was found in the matrix of PM 4. Fish scales were recovered from PMs 4, 6, and 29 and from Feature 6; PM 6 contained a single muskrat tooth; four pieces of sheet brass kettle scrap were found in PM 4; and a single hand-wrought nail was recovered from PM 30.

There was some variety in the amount of cultural material found within individual post molds. The western main support posts (PMs 4 and 30) contained significantly more bone and other artifacts than the other post molds. Although these posts were larger and were driven deeper into the ground than the other posts within Structure 1, there were significant differences in artifact density as well as overall quantity. PM 4 contained 117 pieces of bone (including white-tailed deer and the only porcupine specimens found at the site to date) while PM 30 contained an astounding 394 pieces of bone (including deer bones, raccoon maxilla fragments, and fish ribs) and a raccoon tooth. Conrad E. Heidenreich (1971, 154) and Dean R. Snow (1995e, 100, 124) have interpreted post molds filled with large pieces of refuse as evidence that these posts were pulled when the structure was abandoned. Following this argument, the high concentrations of bone in PMs 4 and 30 make it likely that they were pulled while PMs 5, 29, 32, and 34 rotted in place. PMs 4 and 30 were clearly structural supports (in contrast to Snow's contention that only decorated, nonstructural posts were pulled at abandonment); their removal would imply that the structure was at least partially dismantled upon abandonment or at some point subsequent to abandonment.

Plowzone soil from the shovel test-pits and test units excavated within Structure 1 contained a variety of material types (see K. Jordan 2001a for a full inventory). Items indicative of consumption were animal bone and tooth remains (including specimens identified as white-tailed deer and black bear), two eighteenth-century olive bottle glass fragments, and native-made ceramic pipe and European white ball clay pipe fragments. Complete items of personal ornamentation consisted of two drawn round black glass beads and a rolled sheet brass cone bangle. There is evidence for possible manufacture of adornment items in the form of one burned blue and white glass pendant fragment that appears to have been discarded during production, a tabular fragment of possible red slate manufacturing debris, one shell fragment, and six pieces of scrap sheet brass (which also may reflect utilitarian usage). Other artifacts consisted of one sheet brass projectile point, possible eighteenth-century ceramic sherds (one aboriginal and eleven European-made), two pieces of clear flat glass that may be mirror fragments, iron nails and iron objects of indeterminate function, charcoal, ten pieces of lithic debitage, fire-cracked rock, and assorted intrusive nineteenth- and twentieth-century materials.

The Construction of the Townley-Read Short Longhouse

In terms of house plan, the Townley-Read shorthouse appears overall to have been built using a fairly traditional scheme. The main supports for the house were located in the middle of the structure with lighter posts around the outside. A central hearth and sleeping platforms were likely to have been present. Some of the indeterminacy of the eastern portion of the structure may be owing to the existence of a covered storage compartment (Snow 1997, 70), another traditional feature. Given the layout of the shorthouse, it probably housed two families, maintaining the multiple-family norm of earlier houses, although in abbreviated form. The Townley-Read structure looks very much like one freestanding segment of a longhouse.

Townley-Read Structure 1 can be compared to a completely traditional short longhouse plan recovered at the protohistoric Onondaga Atwell site (Ricklis 1967; this discussion relies on the summary and figure provided by James A. Tuck [1971, 165–70, fig. 7]). The Atwell structure was constructed entirely with traditional nonmetal tools before the onset of direct contact with Europeans: a small number of European brass items but no iron tools have been recovered from the site, which is dated to the last half or quarter of the sixteenth century by Tuck (1971, 165, 169–70) and to ca. A.D. 1525–50 by James W. Bradley (1987a, 50). The Townley-Read short longhouse manifests a surprising number of continuities with the Atwell structure despite at least 140 years between their construction dates. The dimensions of the Townley Read house (7.5 m x 5.3 m) are close to that of the Atwell structure (9.1 m x 5.5 m per Tuck [1971, 167]), especially in width. Both structures have more or less square corners and frequent large internal posts, and presumably both structures had central hearths. The dwellings each have the characteristic double layer of wall posts signifying that the posts were used to brace siding. According to Tuck (1971), an unusual circular pattern of posts at the west end of the Atwell house may have supported a corncrib or granary, so both short longhouses may have had only a single eastern door.

At the same time, the Townley-Read structure incorporated a number of innovations that were not present in the Atwell structure or most other earlier houses. The data from Townley-Read Structure 1 also can be compared to the detailed information available on structural features excavated at four other Iroquoian sites occupied during the A.D. 1670–1779 era, including: (1) Ganondagan, a Seneca site occupied from approximately 1670 to 1687 (and in which some of the residents of Townley-Read may have spent their early years) where one structure plan has been excavated (Dean 1984); (2) Conestoga, a multiethnic (in part Seneca) community near Lancaster, Pennsylvania, occupied from 1690 to 1740 where one incomplete and two complete house plans have been uncovered (D. A. Anderson 1995; Kent 1993 [1984]); (3) Primes Hill, an Oneida site dated to approximately 1696–1720 where a variety of post molds were found but no structural pattern could be discerned (Bennett 1988; personal communication 2001); and (4) Egli, a multiethnic community on the Susquehanna River occupied from 1753 to 1779 where again posts were excavated but no structural pattern was determined (Hesse 1975). Differences between the Townley-Read shorthouse and more traditional Iroquoian structures are most apparent in terms of post type and location, iron nail use, post frequency, and the allocation of organized and unorganized space within the structure.

With regard to post size (table 12.1), the posts used in Townley-Read Structure 1 fall within the range of sizes used at other Iroquoian sites from the 1670–1779 era, although there is a great deal of variation and no clear-cut trend emerges over time in these figures. The Townley-Read post size figures are quite comparable to those found at Primes Hill and what David A. Anderson (1995) has termed House 1 at Conestoga (located to the southwest in Kent [1993 (1984), fig. 107]), which appears to have used internal support posts and paired wall posts to brace semirigid siding. The Townley-Read posts are somewhat smaller than those excavated at Ganondagan, and much smaller than the posts employed in Conestoga House 2 (a non-Iroquoian or nontraditional structure in the center of Kent [1993 (1984), fig. 107]) and the massive rectangular posts used at Egli.

However, the *type* and *location* of some of the posts used in Townley-Read Structure 1 are quite atypical and unparalleled at any of the earlier sites. Novel post use at Townley-Read is illustrated by the shape of Post Mold 32, an unusual

Table 12.1
Post Mold Diameter Figures (cm) for Selected Iroquoian Sites

Site/Structure	Occupation Dates	Overall Average (all posts)	Smallest Wall Post	Largest Wall Post	Wall Post Average
Ganondagan/					
Trench 4 Structure	1670–1687	9.5	6.1	15.2	9.5
Primes Hill	1696–1720	7.8	5.1	12.7	7.3
Conestoga/House 1	1690–1740	7.0	n/a	n/a	n/a
Conestoga/House 2	1690–1740	12.7	n/a	n/a	n/a
Townley-Read/					
Structure 1	1715–1754	8.3	4.0	13.0	6.3
Egli	1753–1778	17.8 by 22.8	n/a	n/a	n/a

Sources: Anderson 1995; Monte Bennett, personal communication 2001; Dean 1984; Hesse 1975.

squared-off post with a dug post hole, and the use of large Posts 29 and 32 as part of the eastern wall. These features suggest some departure from traditional construction methods.

Iron nail use can be estimated through calculation of the ratio between nails recovered and the area excavated at a given site (table 12.2; for additional details regarding nail use see K. Jordan 2001b). Comparable nail density figures can be calculated for Townley-Read, Ganondagan, and Primes Hill because all three sites were plowed and likely had plowzones of roughly the same thickness; excavations at each site sampled portions of houselots; and each site contained sub-plowzone features. To make the data consistent with the other sites, the Townley-Read figures only include nails found in shovel-test pits or test units, excluding artifacts found by surface collection and from the bulldozer trench.

At Egli, 118 hand-wrought rosehead, L-head, T-head, and headless nails were recovered in an area greater than 455.2 m² (4,900 ft²). However, the raw nail density figure of 0.26 nails/m² is not comparable with the other sites because most of the topsoil in the examined area at Egli was cleared away by a bulldozer; nails were recovered only from topsoil left behind by the bulldozer and from features. I have arbitrarily increased the Egli density figure fourfold to fivefold to compensate for the lost topsoil.

Although the estimated figures of 1.04 to 1.30 nails/m² for Egli must be used with caution, current evidence indicates that the structures at Townley-Read and

Table 12.2
Iron Nail Density per Square Meter of Excavated Area at Selected Iroquois Sites

Site/Area	Occupation Dates	Excavated Area (m²)	Number of Eighteenth-Century Nails Recovered	Nails/m²
Ganondagan/ Trench 4	1670–87	157.9	22–28	0.14–0.18
Primes Hill	1696–1720	88.3	30	0.34
Townley-Read/ Structure 1 Area	1715–1754	11.8	10–16	0.85–1.36
Townley-Read/ Area D Total	1715–1754	37.4	25–42	0.67–1.12
Townley-Read/ East Fields Total	1715–1754	57.6	31–53	0.53–0.92
Egli (estimated)	1753–1778	455.2	118	1.04–1.30

Sources: Bennett 1988; Dean 1984; Hesse 1975. Iron "hardware" was recovered at Conestoga but not quantified (Kent 1993 [1984], 389).

Egli used a substantially greater number of nails than dwellings at the earlier Primes Hill and Ganondagan sites. All of these figures probably underestimate Iroquois nail use given that iron nails may have been collected for reuse when a site was abandoned and/or systematically removed from the archaeological record by modern collectors with metal detectors.

Gary A. Warrick (1988) has proposed a method for calculating the occupation duration of a given Iroquoian house based on the amount of wall post replacement that took place. However, the very low wall post density in the Townley-Read shorthouse suggests that the Warrick method cannot be used at Townley-Read. Even in the western wall of the shorthouse, where preservation and post recovery was quite good, original wall post density was only about 2.5 posts/m, well below almost all of the original, prerepair density figures for pre-1650 Huron and Neutral longhouses cited by Warrick (1988). Post density in the more or less straight line of posts in the north wall is even more sparse, with approximately 1 post/m. It would seem a logical conclusion that the Townley-Read structure used a different construction type and/or materials that needed substantially less reinforcement than the typical bark-sided longhouse. The Townley-Read dwelling also may have differed from more traditional bark-sided short longhouses used at contemporaneous Iroquois sites such as Onondaga (Bartram 1966 [1751], 41).

Kapches's (1990) conceptualization of the "spatial dynamics" of Ontario Iroquoian longhouses contrasts the degree of organized versus unorganized space within a structure's interior. Kapches classifies sleeping bench areas and the enclosed storage areas behind partitions (either in the house's interior or at the ends) as permanent allocations of space, hearth areas as semipermanent, and storage and refuse pits as temporary. Permanent and semipermanent areas together are considered to be "organized space." The analysis of the spatial dynamics of the 39.75 m^2 Townley-Read Structure 1 is restricted to the contrast between the "organized" sleeping bench and hearth areas and the "unorganized" rest of the house because there is no definite evidence for a cubicle area beyond the east wall. Sleeping benches—the only permanent features—took up about 7.85 m^2, or 19.7 percent of the total interior area. Because no intact hearth remains were recovered, I estimated the length of the proposed central hearth at one-half of the average length of the two sleeping benches (1.16 m) and its width at approximately 1.0 m, resulting in a semipermanent hearth area of 1.16 m^2, or 2.9 percent of total internal space. In total, the Townley-Read short longhouse contains 9.01 m^2 of organized area representing 22.7 percent of the total and 30.74 m^2 of unorganized area representing 77.3 percent of the total area of the structure.

The 22.7 percent organized area figure is substantially lower than Kapches's (1990) figures for most prehistoric to early historic true longhouses in Ontario. However, the Townley-Read shorthouse itself is smaller than almost all of the houses in Kapches's study. The closest parallel would be in Category I cabins (sized

110 m² or less) from the protohistoric or early historic Ball site (ca. A.D. 1600). The Ball site Category I averages of 16.5 percent sleeping benches and 1.9 percent hearths are quite close to the Townley-Read figures of 19.7 percent and 2.9 percent. Kapches defines the Ball Category I cabins as "special purpose structures with late Iroquoian organization [i.e., matrilineality]" (Kapches 1990, 64). The range of artifactual materials recovered from the Structure 1 area at Townley-Read argues against a special-purpose function for the shorthouse. As with Warrick's occupation span estimates, the conclusions reached by Kapches regarding the spatial dynamics of seventeenth-century houses may not apply to Iroquoian houses of the eighteenth century.

To summarize, in comparison to traditional Iroquoian houses the Townley-Read shorthouse exhibits different post types and post placement, a lower density of wall posts, increased nail use, and a lesser proportion of space dedicated to permanent and semipermanent features. The primary innovation at Townley-Read was probably that new siding materials had replaced bark. A number of first-person descriptions of eighteenth-century Iroquois housing describe the use of logs, hewn timbers, or split-log planks for siding (e.g., James Smith [1755] in Drake [1855, 193–94]; Richard Smith [1769] in Smith [1989 (1906), 131–32]). Many of the nontraditional construction elements exhibited by the Townley-Read shorthouse were probably a consequence of the new siding materials. Log or plank siding would have been more sturdy and durable and would not have required as many posts for bracing as bark. Nails of various sizes provided additional reinforcement for the structure. However, it is important to emphasize that although the Townley-Read short longhouse and other Iroquois houses of the mid-eighteenth century were in part made of logs, these houses remained recognizably Iroquoian in floor-plan and construction, and logs were used in ways fundamentally different from European methods of log construction.

The Classification of Eighteenth-Century Iroquois Houses

The archaeological and ethnohistorical literature on eighteenth-century Iroquois housing often claims that *"bark longhouses"* were abandoned in favor of *"log cabins"* (Grumet 1995, 346; Wallace 1969, 23; 1978, 442; Wray 1983, 41), and not infrequently eighteenth-century Iroquois houses are described as *"European-style log cabins"* (e.g., Aquila 1983, 32; Graymont 1972, 10; Richter 1992, 260–61; Snow 1995e, 472; 1997, 72; Weslager 1969, 59–62). This terminology should be amended, because these terms are at best misleading and at worst simply inaccurate. First, the word *cabin* can be used to refer to three different things:

1. a more or less temporary structure;
2. the size of a dwelling, regardless of its method of manufacture (obviously this is the sense of the word used by Kapches [1984], who defines an Iroquoian-style cabin as a residential structure with a length:width ratio of 1.25:1 or less); and

3. a dwelling made from notched logs laid parallel to the ground, or in other words a *European-style log cabin* (T. Jordan 1985; T. Jordan and Kaups 1989).

Archaeologists and historians must be careful not to conflate these three meanings, in particular guarding against taking the use of the word *cabin* (or the French *cabanne*) in historical sources to mean more than it should. Seventeenth- and eighteenth-century Europeans often used the term *cabin* only in the sense of a temporary structure, with no implications as to the size of a dwelling or the materials from which it was built. This point is clearly illustrated by the 1616 use of the word *cabanne* by Samuel de Champlain to describe bark-covered longhouses with up to 12 hearths (Snow 1997).

Cabin still has a productive place in ethnohistorical and archaeological parlance, but scholars need to exhibit considerable caution and precision in its use. Many Late Historic Period Iroquoian structures described as cabins in the literature are, in terms of size, true or short longhouses. For example, what John Bartram described as two-family "cabins" at Onondaga in 1743 were almost definitely short longhouses built using Iroquoian architectural principles (1966 [1751], 41). Similarly, the proportions of the structures recovered archaeologically at Townley-Read, Ganondagan (Dean 1984), and Conestoga (Kent 1993 [1984]), make them true longhouses or shorthouses rather than cabins in Kapches's terms. Because *cabin* can refer to structures constructed in either European or traditional Iroquois styles, the term should *always* be preceded by *Iroquoian-style* or *European-style* when used in the context of seventeenth- to nineteenth-century Iroquoian sites, and its use should be preceded by a careful consideration of the architectural principles used in the construction of the dwellings in question.

Were Iroquois houses of the mid- to late eighteenth century built in a European style? Assertions of this sort need to be made very carefully. We all readily can conjure up an image of a "European-style log cabin" in our minds, consisting of a dwelling made of logs set parallel to the ground and held together by notches at the corners, with a central eave-side door, windows on either side of the door, and a chimney at the gable end. This image has been a powerful symbol of Euroamerican pioneering since the nineteenth century (e.g., William Henry Harrison's [1840] "log cabin-hard cider" presidential campaign), and it is reinforced through many forms of popular culture. The issue is complicated by the fact that Iroquois people did in fact construct dwellings that looked just like this on reservations in the nineteenth century, for which there is substantial photographic (Snow 1994b, fig. 8.1; Tuck 1971, plate 44) and some archaeological (Lantz 1980) evidence. But did mid- to late eighteenth-century Iroquois houses look like the popular stereotype? I argue that they did not.

Many eighteenth-century Iroquois construction practices remained quite traditional and upon closer analysis almost all look decidedly non-European. Take for example the use of logs: the preponderance of documentary and archaeological evidence indicates that logs were used as a substitute for bark, not in corner-notched

European-derived forms. Logs, whether whole, hewn, or split into planks, were stacked one upon the other and braced by posts. Archaeological evidence from every reported eighteenth-century Iroquoian site includes a large number of post molds, suggesting that post supports were the predominant or even the exclusive construction type.

Perhaps the most telling construction detail is how the weight of a structure is distributed. As Kapches notes, European houses bear weight on corner posts or along walls, while traditional Iroquoian structures were supported by large posts in the interior of the structure (1993, 145–47). A modern log-builder estimates that properly done corner notches support 70 to 80 percent of the weight of a European-style log building (Langsner 1982, 121). Many documentary and archaeological sources demonstrate the continued use of decidedly non-European large interior supports in eighteenth-century Iroquois houses, further substantiating the idea that many Iroquois log dwellings were built using a core of Iroquoian architectural principles.

This is not to argue that there were no true European-style houses in eighteenth-century Iroquois villages. The post-1762 Dutch-style Brant House at Indian Castle (Guldenzopf 1986; Snow 1995e) is a case in point. But European-style houses were introduced much later than is implied by the secondary archaeological and ethnohistoric literature and there was no widespread independent adoption of European house forms across Iroquoia. In the parts of Iroquoia more remote from European settlement, European-style houses were rare and were introduced at a later date. This is illustrated by a survey of the documents from the 1779 Sullivan-Clinton expedition describing the destruction of Seneca settlements (contained in Conover 1887; Division of Archives and History 1929). The Sullivan-Clinton documents indicate that in 1779 most Seneca houses were sided with rounded or squared logs or hewn boards and contained an array of Native features, such as bark roofing, interior support posts, gable-end doors, end storage compartments, smoke holes, and berths on each side of a central fireplace. However, the soldiers also mention what they called "Tory Houses" or houses "built by white people" or describe definite European structural details (such as frame construction) at 7 of the 17 Seneca villages destroyed by the expedition. These houses were found either in the easternmost Seneca settlements located along the Chemung River or in settlements described as "new." No European-style houses were mentioned at the two largest settlements, Kanadesaga and Genesee Castle, which would have been natural locations for Tories to settle if they wanted to influence Seneca affairs. I conclude that Senecas themselves resided in at least some of the so-called "Tory houses," that proximity to Europeans was a factor in their construction, and that most European-style houses in the Seneca region were constructed after about 1765.

Instead of European construction styles inevitably diffusing to Iroquois populations after their introduction, their adoption by the Iroquois appears to have been based on specific material factors. The first was proximity to Europeans, with the "directed culture change" of houses built by missionaries (Fenton 1967) and colonial officials playing a significant role. Emerging Iroquois elites such as the Brant family used European framed house forms as an expression of growing social inequality. The widespread adoption of European-style dwellings by the majority of Iroquois populations appears to be linked to their taking up intensive agriculture and stock raising, something that took place most completely on post-Revolutionary reservations (Wallace 1969), but may have occurred earlier in the Mohawk Valley where substantial European territorial encroachment began in 1711 (see K. Jordan 1997; 2002, 444–67).

But does it suffice to say that most Iroquois houses before 1800 (especially outside the Mohawk Valley) were built using traditional architectural principles, and that by the late eighteenth century they coexisted with a small number of European-style houses within the same communities? At some level this opposition between traditional Iroquois and European-style houses seems misplaced. Eighteenth-century houses like the Townley-Read shorthouse clearly fit within the Iroquoian architectural tradition, but at the same time they differ: they were *much* smaller than traditional longhouses; they utilized a variety of European tools, construction techniques, and hardware in their construction; and some contained an occasional chimney or window. It would seem to be a more productive position to treat these houses as hybrid, intercultural, creolized, or "mutualist" (Orser 1996) artifacts, adding eighteenth-century houses to better-known examples such as shell bead wampum, wooden ladles, antler hair combs, brass ornaments and tools, and splint basketry that show a *convergence* of cultural values instead of the envelopment of one culture by another (see Engelbrecht 2003). In my dissertation (K. Jordan 2002, 431–40) I propose that the "intercultural/creolized" Iroquoian house be treated as a formal architectural type, distinguished both from more wholly traditional bark-sided Iroquois houses and fully European-style dwellings.

A more subtle typology of house forms that incorporates the intercultural/creolized house type results in a more detailed picture of Iroquois society and culture than the previous bifurcation between "traditional" and "European" forms allows. This shift in perspective, one that much better fits the available documentary and archaeological evidence than the predominant "European-style log cabin" model, has important implications. As an experiment, go back to some of the secondary sources that discuss eighteenth-century Iroquois culture and substitute the words *log- or plank-sided shorthouse* wherever you see the word *cabin* and observe how this change subtly modifies the overall picture of eighteenth-century culture change. The transformation in house forms can no longer be taken as automatic and seemingly devastating evidence for the disintegration of Iroquois culture. Instead it becomes something more complex that demonstrates much more continuity with traditional architecture and culture.

Acknowledgments

This paper differs substantially from my paper given at the 1997 Rochester Museum and Science Center Conference on the Iroquois Longhouse. In that paper (K. Jordan 1997), I argued that multiple-family longhouse dwellings were likely to have been common at eighteenth-century Iroquois sites outside the Mohawk Valley, based on the fact that the dynamics of household formation were likely to have differed in the Mohawk region as a result of European territorial encroachment. The 1997 paper was given before substantial fieldwork had taken place at the Townley-Read site. While I stand behind the conclusions stated in that paper, the excavation data recovered at Townley-Read have complicated the issue and I felt that this presentation of recent field data would be more useful to readers than my original, more theoretical argument. I would like to thank the organizers of the Longhouse Conference, and I am grateful to Charles F. Hayes III for allowing me to present this different approach. A version of this paper was given at the 2000 Northeast Archaeological Symposium held at the Cayuga Museum, Auburn, New York, and portions of it appear in my doctoral dissertation (K. Jordan 2002, chaps. 5 and 8). Special thanks to Adam Watson and Michael West, who analyzed the faunal materials from the site, and to Monte Bennett for providing unpublished excavation data from the Primes Hill site. Don Cameron, Bob DeOrio, Bill Engelbrecht, George Hamell, Peter Jemison, Julie Jordan, Bob Kuhn, Nan Rothschild, Nerissa Russell, Lorraine Saunders, Martha Sempowski, Dean Snow, and Nina Versaggi made comments and suggestions that greatly improved this paper. My use (and abuse) of their comments is of course strictly my own doing.

13 | Contact, Neutral Iroquoian Transformation, and the Little Ice Age

WILLIAM R. FITZGERALD

THE EXPLANATION OF CULTURAL DEVELOPMENTS among the Neutral Iroquoians of southern Ontario during the sixteenth and seventeenth centuries has been influenced largely by the fact that many of the changes occurred during the initial era of European presence in eastern North America. A reevaluation of the available archaeological, ecological, and climatic record, however, reveals other human and natural agents that contributed both directly and indirectly to those developments.

An underlying tenet of Iroquoian research as far back as the writings of Lewis Henry Morgan (1969 [1851], 144–46), and particularly following the work of Richard S. MacNeish (1952), William A. Ritchie (1969), and James V. Wright (1966), has been that Iroquoian culture was in a state of progressive development that reached its zenith during the seventeenth century. Exposure to Europeans, their material culture, and their diseases has traditionally been considered the dominant, if not the solitary, agent in the abrupt decline of Ontario Iroquoian societies (e.g., Warrick 1984, 131).

The profound effect of European contact on Ontario Iroquoian societies cannot be denied, but it has been proposed, upon a reappraisal of the archaeological evidence, that certain aspects of Iroquoian culture in Ontario had attained their cultural apogee by the fifteenth century. By the time European presence became an influential factor, Ontario Iroquoian society was already in the process of redefinition or, more precisely, devolution (Fitzgerald and Jamieson 1985), much like the contemporaneous chiefdoms of the southeastern United States (Peebles 1986; M. Smith 1987). The state of seventeenth-century Neutral Iroquoian society was the result of centuries of adaptations to a complex series of diverse circumstances and

---

Previously published in *Societies in Eclipse: Archaeology of the Eastern Woodlands Indians, A.D. 1400–1700*, ed. D. S. Brose, C. W. Cowan, and R. C. Mainfort Jr. (Washington, D.C.: Smithsonian Institution Press, 2001), 37–47. Printed with permission by the author, William R. Fitzgerald, and the editor, David S. Brose.

forces initially independent of, but later compounded by, the effects of European contact. Among trends observable in the archaeological record between the fifteenth and the seventeenth centuries are population contraction and dispersal, changing residential and subsistence patterns, a florescence of ritualism, and the adoption of foreigners and exotic material culture.

In 1615 Samuel de Champlain noted that the Iroquoian-speaking group concentrated around the western end of Lake Ontario was not involved in the hostilities between the Huron and the Iroquois (Biggar 1922–36, 3:99–100). That neutrality led Champlain and subsequent Europeans to refer to this group as the Neutral nation. To the Huron they were the Atiouandaronk (Thwaites 1896–1901, 8:116). Although the devastating attacks of the Iroquois between 1647 and 1651 effectively extinguished this distinctive culture, the cumulative influences that had earlier molded it and other northern Iroquoian cultures also bore responsibility for their redefinition and ultimate demise.

History of Archaeological Research

The Neutral Iroquoians have been of interest to archaeologists, historians, and relic hunters since their villages and cemeteries were first disturbed by forest-clearing activities in the early nineteenth century (see Lennox and Fitzgerald 1990, 405–8). In 1843 the American ethnologist Henry Schoolcraft was taken to the Dwyer cemetery west of Hamilton, Ontario, and he returned in 1844 and 1845 to collect additional artifacts. The first systematic archaeological investigations of Neutral sites were carried out in the late 1800s and early 1900s by David Boyle from the Royal Ontario Museum (Toronto). William Wintemberg from the Victoria Museum (Ottawa) conducted extensive surveys and excavations throughout Neutral territory during the first quarter of the twentieth century and was largely responsible for initiating chronological and classificatory studies for this group.

The 1950s and 1960s saw a florescence in Neutral research. Richard MacNeish, Norman Emerson, and James Wright incorporated Neutral data into broader Iroquoian developmental schemes, and Marian White undertook an intensive investigation of the Neutral in the Niagara region of New York and Ontario. During the 1970s and 1980s, substantial numbers of undergraduate and graduate theses from universities in Canada and the United States, as well as independent research projects and salvage excavations, added exponentially to our knowledge of the Neutral.

Neutral Distribution

Neutral Ontario Iroquoian occupations datable to the fifteenth century are dispersed in a broad band along the north shore of Lake Erie (fig. 13.1), at the present northern edge of the Carolinian biotic province. During the first half of the six-

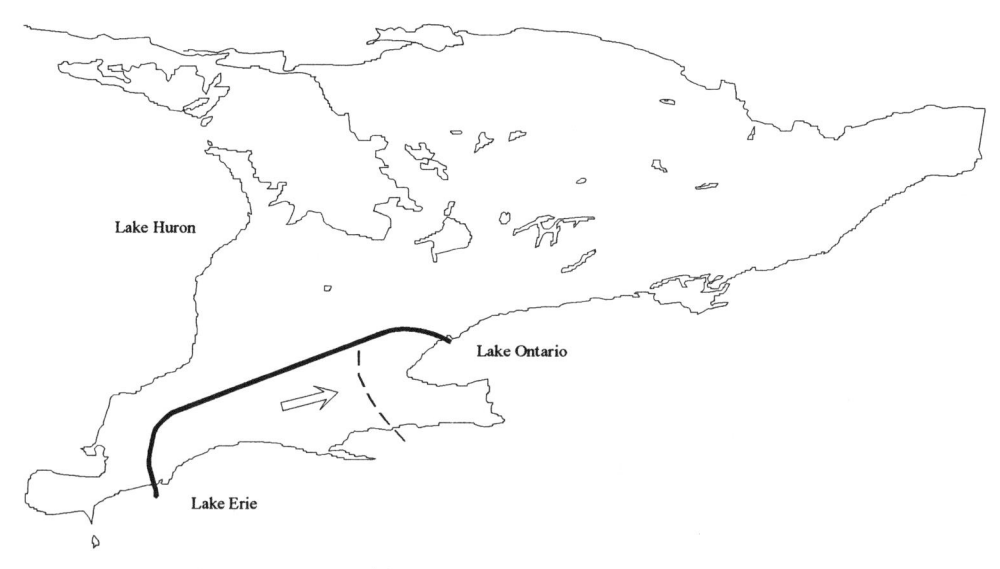

Fig. 13.1. Neutral territory in the fifteenth century (south of the heavy line) and by the mid-sixteenth century (east of the dashed line).

teenth century a large tract of Neutral territory west of the Grand River was abandoned (Lee 1959). The ensuing compaction of Neutral groups around the southwestern corner of Lake Ontario led to the formation of the well-defined tribal territories of the late sixteenth and early seventeenth centuries, and the Neutral allied themselves into a seemingly loose confederacy that persisted until their dispersal (Fitzgerald 1990a, 252–404). It was also during the second half of the sixteenth century that other Iroquoian groups undertook long-distance relocation. Huron groups in the Trent Valley and around the northwestern corner of Lake Ontario were withdrawing into the confederated territory described initially by Champlain (Ramsden 1990a). St. Lawrence Iroquoian groups were dispersed (J. Jamieson 1990a), and the Susquehannock migrated southward toward Chesapeake Bay (Witthoft 1969 [1959]).

Some believe that the migrations of the Huron, Neutral, and Susquehannock were motivated by the desire to relocate to areas where access to European goods was enhanced (Hunter 1969 [1959]; Ramsden 1978; Trigger 1985; 1991a). Even though Europeans had been in the Gulf of St. Lawrence since the end of the fifteenth century, they were there initially to fish, hunt whales, and explore, not to conduct commercial transactions with Natives (Turgeon and Fitzgerald 1992). Although ceremonial exchanges and ancillary bartering did take place along the coast and the St. Lawrence River, the majority of European goods obtained in these limited activities would have become dispersed long before they filtered inland. Only after Native groups could supply a commodity desired by Europeans might we expect an intensive commercial trade to have developed. Felt from beaver pelts became that commodity, but the French demand for non-Russian beaver did not become significant until the second half of the sixteenth century. It was not until the first years of the 1580s that the commercial fur trade commenced in northeastern North America, initially centered in the Gulf of St. Lawrence. Its onset is indicated by the dramatic increase of European goods of that era on Native sites in the Canadian Maritimes, along the Saguenay River, and around the lower Great Lakes.

It is inconceivable that the incredibly small quantities of goods that did filter indirectly into southern Ontario before 1580 might have triggered population movements of such magnitude. That the migrations clearly preceded the commercial fur trade is especially evident in the Neutral situation, where well-defined sequences of site relocations document successive stages in the introduction of datable European commodities (Fitzgerald 1990a). Supporting the notion that these migrations were not a consequence of competition for European goods is the virtual absence of such commodities in St. Lawrence Iroquoian settlements. Charles A. Martijn (1969) has suggested that the abandonment of the St. Lawrence lowlands was instead owing to the failure of horticulture caused by the onset of the Little Ice Age.

On the basis of the presence of heavily fortified Neutral frontier settlements and foreign Native ceramics on Neutral sites, it has been proposed that during the first half of the sixteenth century, Neutral groups in extreme southwestern Ontario were involved in hostilities with the neighboring Algonquian Fire nation (Fox 1980b). The Neutral abandonment might be interpreted as a means of increasing the buffer zone between the combatants. The initial cause of these hostilities is unclear, but like their seventeenth-century manifestations, which have been ascribed to competition over beaver hunting territories (Fitzgerald 1982a, 100), they might have been related to competition over resources, not so much in a capitalistic sense related to fur trade activities but more basically for survival.

At mid-sixteenth-century settlements within the area of contraction, the presence of substantial house and village expansions (fig. 13.2) and the continued practice of extensive settlement fortification indicate the incorporation of immigrants and the perception of an enduring threat (Fitzgerald 1991a). Similar expansions were occurring at contemporary Huron villages in the Trent Valley (Ramsden 1989).

The purported intensification of warfare in the lower Great Lakes throughout the precontact portion of the Late Woodland period has, since the 1950s, been linked to an increasing dependence on horticulture. Supposedly, warfare enabled the male members of society to continue to demonstrate their masculinity in some pursuit other than hunting (Engelbrecht 1987; Trigger 1981a; Witthoft 1969 [1959]). As faunal and carbon isotope evidence indicates (table 13.1; fig. 13.3), however, female-dominated farming activities never resulted in the abandonment of hunting.

The formulation in the 1950s and 1960s of the notion of males having to spend more time waging war in order not to feel emasculated is perhaps understandable

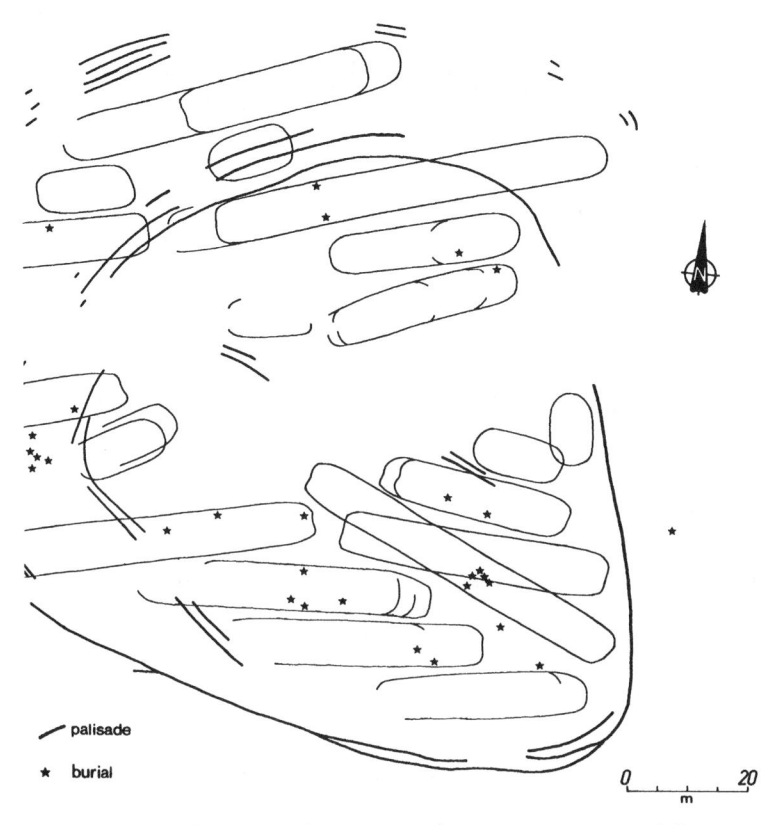

Fig. 13.2. Plan of the MacPherson site, showing expansion of the palisaded village. The core village was surrounded by an original palisade that was partially replaced at least twice by new rows of palisades to the northwest as the village grew.

in terms of a Cold War mentality. Yet the archaeological evidence implemented to propose an escalation of precontact warfare and cannibalism must be carefully scrutinized. "Brutalized" human remains—interpreted as such because they were shattered, charred, or modified to produce artifacts—have been recovered in archaeological contexts that can just as convincingly be related to burial practices or the by-products of burial rituals (e.g., Spence 1992; Woodley, Southern, and Fitzgerald 1992). Cremated remains and discarded skeletal items not included in secondary reburials probably have been inappropriately attributed to hostile actions, especially if recovered from plow-disturbed contexts, and most certainly if the skeletal elements belong to very young individuals. In addition, shallow primary interments are commonly scattered by recent agricultural activities (e.g., Saunders 1989). The fabrication of gorgets and other items from human bone should not necessarily be perceived as evidence of mistreatment or disrespect of enemies. Ornately decorated Roman Catholic ossuaries contain small skeletal fragments of

Table 13.1

Frequencies of Deer and Woodchuck Remains at Neutral Iroquoian Settlements

Period	Site	Mammal Sample Size	Deer %	Woodchuck %
1400–1500	Coleman	271	2.6	26.6
	Ivan Elliot	502	1.2	24.9
	Moyer	704	2.7	73.4
1500–1580	Buddy Boers	922	85.8	0.3
	Knight-Tucker	602	73.6	0.0
	MacPherson	291	78.4	0.3
	Raymond Reid	237	59.1	7.6
1580–1600	Cleveland	4,466	64.6	1.3
1600–1630	Brown	881	64.7	0.6
	Christianson	1,169	50.1	2.6
1630–1650	Hamilton	8,249	64.9	0.7
	Hood	2,250	75.2	0.4
	Walker	7,626	70.9	1.1

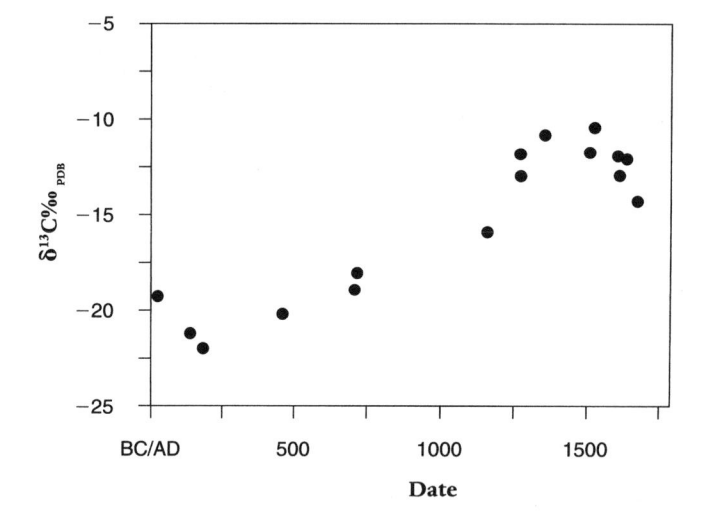

Fig. 13.3. Carbon isotope trends.

saints—hardly a situation to be construed as a display of interpersonal violence. Indeed, the Jesuits reported that the Neutral displayed the remains of family members within their longhouses, sometimes for prolonged periods, before final burial (Thwaites 1896–1901, 21:199).

Intercultural feuding cannot be denied as a fact of Iroquoian life (e.g., Abler 1980; J. Jamieson 1983). But its impact on the formation of precontact Ontario Iroquoian culture should not be exaggerated on the basis of the present extent of archaeological evidence and Eurocentric interpretations of the treatment of Iroquoian dead.

Cultural Trends

A brief overview of major cultural trends for the Neutral reveals that their society underwent significant transformation in the two centuries before its demise. These trends can be evaluated in terms of natural cultural evolution, foreign influences, and the limitations imposed on a society occupying a transitional biotic zone at the northern limit of productive horticulture during a period of worldwide climatic deterioration.

The Fifteenth Century

The widely distributed Neutral of the fifteenth century shared a number of traits that diverged from later expressions of Neutral culture. Longhouses attained their greatest lengths at this time—occasionally measuring more than 100 meters long (table 13.2)—from which can be inferred a relatively complex social organization. The significant enlargement of house length at this time has been attributed to the desire of families to attach themselves to despotic military warlords (Finlayson 1985, 438; R. MacDonald 1986, 178; Warrick 1984, 65–68) or successful traders (Hayden 1978, 112–14). Evidence from twentieth-century New Guinea has been used to argue both scenarios for fifteenth-century Ontario, but perhaps an alternative explanation can be suggested on the basis of a more comparable situation from the Great Basin of the western United States. For that area, Daniel O. Larson and Joel Michaelsen (1990) proposed that one result of an intensification of horticultural

Table 13.2
Trends in Neutral Iroquoian Longhouse Lengths

Period	No. Houses	Length (Meters) Range	Mean
1400–1500[a]	13	23–123	61.5
1500–1580[b]	33	12–78	29.5
1580–1630[c]	19	6–45	19.4
1630–1650[d]	18	6–28	15.3

[a]Sites: Coleman (R. MacDonald 1986); Ivan Elliot (Fitzgerald 1990b); Moyer (Wagner et al. 1973).
[b]Sites: MacPherson (Fitzgerald 1991a); Raymond Reid (Fitzgerald 1990b); Zap.
[c]Sites: Christianson (Fitzgerald 1982a); Cleveland (Noble 1972); Fonger (Warrick 1984); Thorold (Noble 1980).
[d]Sites: Bogle 1 and 2 (Lennox 1984a); Hamilton (Lennox 1981); Hood (Lennox 1984b); Walker (M. Wright 1981).

pursuits by the Virgin Branch Anasazi during the eleventh and twelfth centuries was the need to form larger social units in order to increase labor efficiency.

In southern Ontario, beans become increasingly visible in the archaeological record only after the beginning of the fifteenth century (Fecteau 1985, 171). This source of nonanimal protein might have encouraged an intensification of horticultural pursuits and perhaps ultimately population growth. The mammal component of faunal assemblages from sites of this century (that is, sites possessing the cultural attributes to be listed later) is notable for its low representation of white-tailed deer (Fitzgerald and Jamieson 1985; Lennox and Fitzgerald 1990), a dietary mainstay both before and after the fifteenth century. Although deer appear not to have been exploited extensively, smaller mammal species such as the woodchuck, an edible nuisance in agricultural fields, are frequently represented in the faunal sample (table 13.1).

Features associated with Ontario Iroquoian dwellings of this era are enclosed semisubterranean pits attached to longhouse exteriors. These have been interpreted as enclosed sweat lodges (R. MacDonald 1988) or storage structures (Fitzgerald 1991b). After the turn of the sixteenth century they are seen infrequently.

The pottery assemblage is characterized by a diversity of decorative motifs on the collar and neck areas of vessels and most notably by large, high-collared pots with elaborate decorations on the collars (fig. 13.4). Chronologically and stylistically, the assemblage forms a distinctive pan-Iroquoian horizon considered to represent the zenith of Iroquoian pottery manufacture (Ritchie 1969, 313). Regional expressions include the Huron Black Creek-Lalonde, the "classic" St. Lawrence Iroquoian, and the Iroquois Chance cultural phases (J. Jamieson 1990a; Ramsden 1990a; Tuck 1971). Ceramic smoking pipes with flared or elongated barrel-shaped bowls predominate.

Although foreign links are evident in the presence of marine shell and copper ornaments, the rare occurrence of such artifacts indicates that long-distance, interregional contacts were intermittent and perhaps indirect. This situation seems to negate Brian Hayden's (1978) model for increased house size. Species of marine shell recovered from Ontario have their origins along the Atlantic coast south of Chesapeake Bay and in the Gulf of Mexico (Pendergast 1989), and although New World copper from southern Ontario archaeological sites of this era has traditionally been assigned a Lake Superior origin, southern or eastern sources cannot be dismissed (cf. Rapp, Henrickson, and Allert 1990). Native copper outcrops have been noted in various places in the Appalachians from Georgia to New Brunswick since as far back as the 1560s, when Goulaine de Laudonniere, a Norman captain exploring the coasts of Georgia and Florida, referred to copper mines "in the mountains of Appalesse" (Sauer 1971, 206). Both Samuel de Champlain (Biggar 1922–36) and Marc Lescarbot (Grant and Biggar 1907–14) recounted explorations for copper in the Canadian Maritimes during the first decade of the seventeenth century.

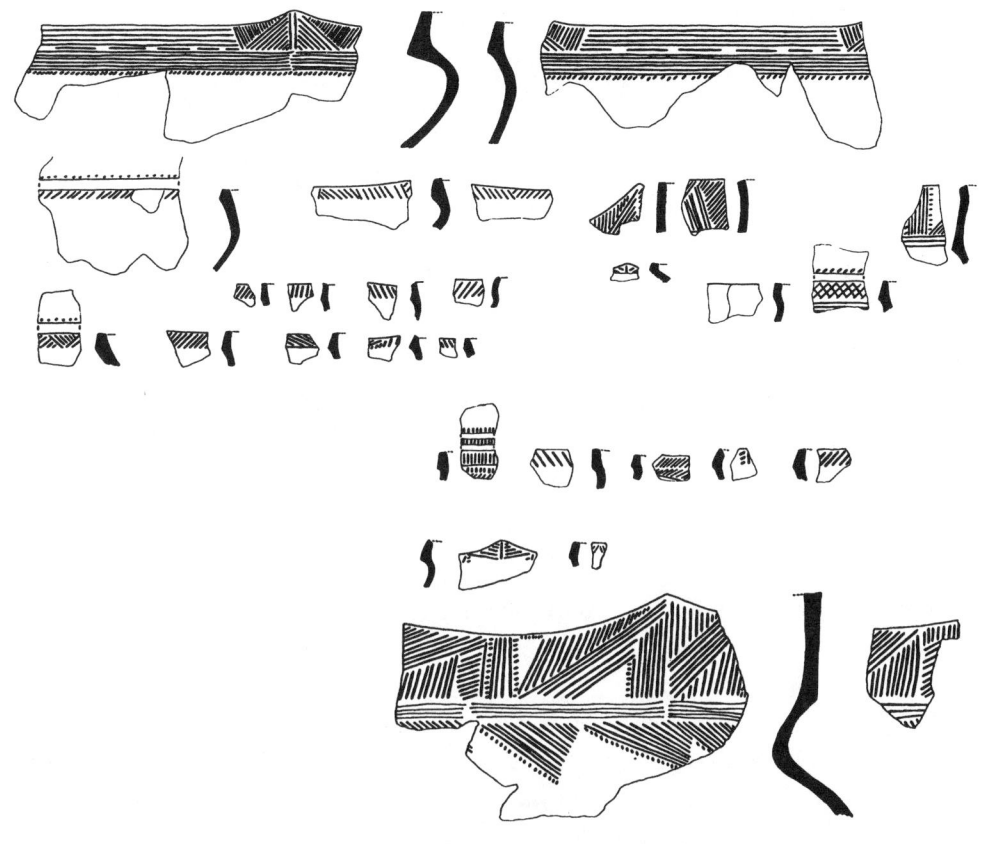

Fig. 13.4. Ceramic vessel rims from the fifteenth-century Ivan Elliot site.

The Sixteenth Century

The sixteenth century was a period of change and readjustment as the once widely dispersed Neutral consolidated into well-defined, confederated tribal areas around the southwestern corner of Lake Ontario. Changes in residential patterns are suggested by a trend toward reduction in longhouse size, a trend that becomes even more noticeable in the seventeenth century (table 13.2). When under stress, societies at the confederacy level tend to fracture into components (Tooker 1963, 122).

Structural features of Neutral longhouse interiors also underwent change. Regularly spaced, large-diameter posts situated approximately 1.5 meters from the side walls served as roof supports and compartmentalized lateral storage and sleeping sections. Similarly, house end cubicles were defined by posts set in rows parallel to the end walls. This pattern has been observed in all northern Iroquoian houses. A shift from post to plank partitions (lateral "slash" pits and linear end features) began around mid-century, a technological phenomenon that has, with few

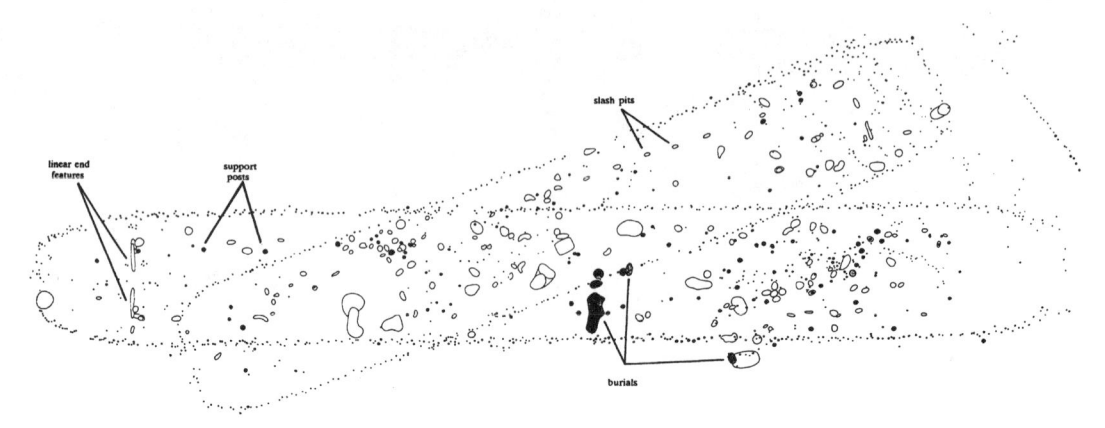

Fig. 13.5. Houses 5 and 6 from the sixteenth-century MacPherson site.

exceptions, been observed only in Neutral structures (fig. 13.5). If this shift was related to the appearance of European splitting implements, then adjacent groups might be expected to have adopted the practice too. This change was under way, however, before the post-1580 presence of substantial numbers of iron axes and chisels in the Northeast.

During the sixteenth and seventeenth centuries, the mammal assemblages recovered from Neutral settlements changed significantly, to domination by white-tailed deer (table 13.1). The large amounts of animal protein that were again being procured presumably necessitated a return to traditional large-game hunting practices.

During the sixteenth century and continuing into the seventeenth, the decorative motifs on ceramic vessel collars became progressively simplified and homogeneous (fig. 13.6). Pipe bowl shapes also shifted to short-barrel, collared, and coronet styles. In contrast to the apparent trend toward simplification of ceramic vessels and noneffigy pipes, during the sixteenth and especially the seventeenth century, zoomorphic and anthropomorphic effigies on ceramic and ground stone smoking pipes evolved rapidly (Mathews 1980; Noble 1979).

Exotic goods on southern Ontario habitation sites and in burials remained scarce until the last quarter of the sixteenth century, when quantities of Native marine shells and ornaments and European ornaments and utilitarian items suddenly exploded. Because the majority of these commodities were placed unaltered with the dead, the dramatic increase in the importation of such goods seems to indicate an intensification of ritualism and mortuary ceremonialism (cf. Trigger 1991a, 1204–5). The onset of the intensified European commercial fur trade at this time appears to have been a fortunate event that provided the Neutral with yet another abundant source of goods with metaphorical associations.

Also indicating an increasing concern with ritual, just before the flood of Euro-

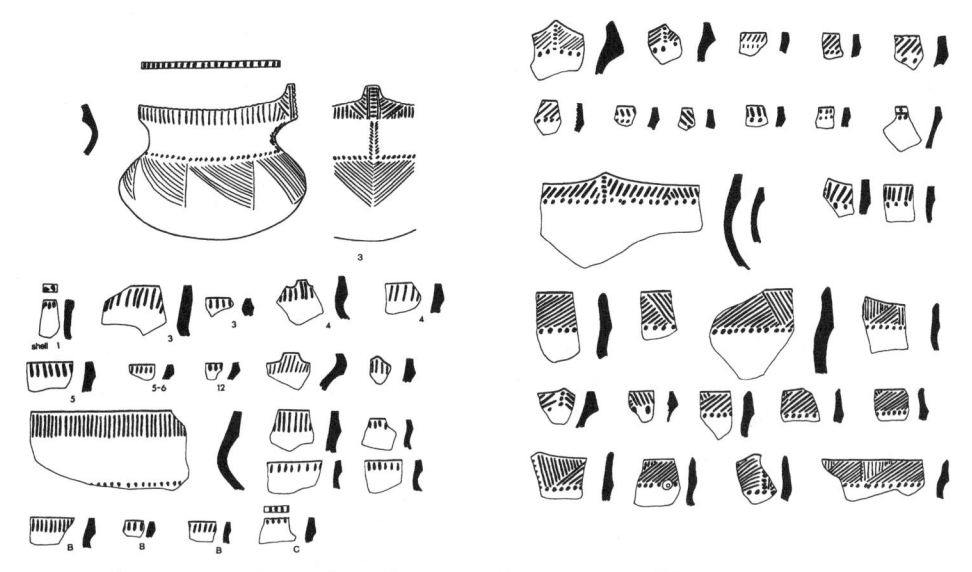

Fig. 13.6. Ceramic vessel rims from the sixteenth-century MacPherson site.

pean goods and marine shell, is the appearance on Neutral ceramic pipes and vessels of distinctively eastern Tennessee, Dallas phase, anthropomorphic falcon hunter-warrior icons (Fuller and Silvia 1984, 35–37; Lewis and Kneberg 1970, 96–97, pl. 54; Stowe 1989, 127).

The Seventeenth Century

Even though Neutral tribal areas remained intact into the seventeenth century, there are numerous indicators of cultural instability and turmoil, especially during the quarter-century before the Neutral's 1650 dispersal. Dwellings continued to decrease in length until, during the second quarter of the seventeenth century, they were shorter than any known from the previous two centuries (table 13.2).

On the seventeenth-century sites of the Spencer-Bronte Neutral tribal grouping, a shell-tempered ceramic tradition suddenly appears (Fitzgerald 1982a; Lennox 1981; 1984a; 1984b; Lennox and Fitzgerald 1990; Stothers 1981). It is especially well represented on sites dating to the 1630s and 1640s, a time when European epidemics ravaged the Ontario Iroquoians. The presence of these ceramics is a manifestation of the massive, historically documented, nontraditional Neutral invasions against the Fire nation (Biggar 1922–36; Thwaites 1896–1901), an Algonquian-speaking group situated around the western end of Lake Erie. In the early 1640s alone, more than 1,000 females—the pottery makers and their children—were brought back as captives to replenish a depleted Neutral population, something also practiced by the Iroquois during the 1650s (Engelbrecht 1987, 22–24).

During the 1630s and 1640s an assemblage of implements belonging to an extractive curing procedure appeared among the Neutral (Fitzgerald 1990a, 241–48). Among the items are long (generally greater than 100 millimeters) and frequently decorated animal bone "sucking" tubes, ceramic human effigy pipes that depict the practitioners of the procedure, and increasing frequencies of marine shell, copper, brass, and turtle shell rattles. Clearly the devastating epidemics, compounded by famines, were having serious physical and psychological effects on the population.

Foreign goods continued to be present in significant amounts, but these French- and Dutch-supplied items in most instances supplemented rather than replaced Native equivalents. The notable exception among the Neutral was the replacement of chipped stone cutting and ground stone chopping implements by iron knives and axes, respectively. The adoption of foreign material culture continued to be pragmatic and ritualistic. The deaths of large numbers of craftspeople during the epidemics did, however, accelerate the trend toward substitutions and dependence on European technology.

Additional Dallas-phase artifacts appear on Neutral sites dating to the seventeenth century: marine shell masks and antler combs with forked-eye or Thunderbird motifs, and marine shell gorgets with Citico rattlesnake motifs (Boyle 1900; Fitzgerald 1982b; I. Kenyon 1972). These depictions and articles have hunting and warring associations (J. Brown 1989; M. Smith and Smith 1989; Strong 1989).

Agents of Change

In the two centuries before their extinction as a cultural entity, the Neutral underwent a series of dramatic transformations. The widespread fifteenth-century expression of Neutral culture was characterized by elongated, multifamily residential structures, an elaborate ceramic tradition, and a subsistence base whose mammal component was dominated by small animals. In the sixteenth century, long-distance relocations probably precipitated by conflicts with adjacent Algonquian groups led to the formation of a confederacy of Neutral tribes compacted around the southwestern corner of Lake Ontario. The number of families living in a single structure declined dramatically, the effort expended on ceramic decoration waned, and subsistence shifted significantly toward increased dependence on deer. In the second half of the century, the numbers of artifacts associated with ritual and ceremony suddenly rose. During the seventeenth century, increasing contact with Europeans and their diseases, as well as conflicts with other Native groups, further stressed Neutral society. Longhouse fission accelerated, and the adoption of European technology, foreign captives, and curing cults characterized a rapid cultural breakdown.

Although the deleterious effects of contact with Europeans and their material culture are well documented, that vector of change in many instances only exacerbated developments that began before Europeans appeared in the Americas. The root cause of the Ontario Iroquoian demise remains perplexing. One explanation that requires greater scrutiny is that a sixteenth-century climatic deterioration severely weakened a society that had become increasingly involved in horticulture in a horticulturally marginal area.

For such a proposition to be supported, one must demonstrate, first, that significant climatic cooling took place and, second, that southern Ontario is a marginal horticultural zone. Climatic deterioration in a marginal agricultural area would have serious consequences, perhaps triggering the diverse yet interrelated chain of events in southern Ontario Neutral culture during the sixteenth and seventeenth centuries.

Climatic Deterioration

From across the northern hemisphere, weather records, glacier movement data, pollen cores, wine harvest dates, and even paintings convincingly attest to the onset of a sixteenth-century cooling, a period referred to as the Neo-Boreal or Little Ice Age (Grove 1988).

Between 1350 and 1500, Alpine glaciers retreated moderately, but the climate did not return to the mildness that characterized the turn of the millennium (Le Roy Ladurie 1971, 264). Although researchers assign varying duration to the Little Ice Age, they agree that it encompassed the later half of the sixteenth century and the seventeenth century. Reid A. Bryson and Wayne M. Wendland (1967, 296) suggested that the years between 1550 and 1850 saw cool summers and cold autumns, a climate that would have affected Native farmers in the Northeast severely.

C. U. Hammer, H. B. Clausen, and W. Dansgaard (1980, 235) suggested a longer duration, from 1350 to 1900, divided by minor interstadials from 1500 to 1550 and from 1700 to 1800. This pattern corresponds to the acidity profile from the Crete ice core in Greenland, where greater amounts of volcanic aerosol acids were deposited during periods of large-scale volcanism—an occurrence that has been suggested to contribute to climatic cooling (Porter 1981, 141).

Felix G. Sulman (1982, 1:131–32) also suggested a longer span, 1430 to 1850, for the main phase of the Little Ice Age for most parts of the world. During the 1430s the first severe winters were recorded after the balmy Viking age. Rivers in Germany froze, many French vines were killed by frost, and cold winters began to grow common.

By 1500, in the lowlands of northwestern Europe, summers were on the order of 0.7 degrees Celsius cooler than the summers of the medieval optimum. This trend led to a shortening of the growing season by as much as five weeks by the seventeenth century (Ford 1982, 77; Grove 1988, 413–14). Throughout sixteenth-century Europe there was a notable cooling between 1550 and 1600 (Grove 1988,

193; Le Roy Ladurie 1971, 281–87). For example, tree rings in Switzerland indicate that during the early stages of the Little Ice Age, summer temperatures were about 2 degrees Celsius lower than those of the late nineteenth and early twentieth centuries (Grove 1988, 193). During the early seventeenth century, the glaciers of Europe advanced decisively, and the years between 1643 and 1653 were marked by the severest winters in western Europe since the end of the Pleistocene (Sulman 1982, 1:131–32). Poor fishing and pestilence were among the consequences (Grove 1985, 149), and in marginal agricultural areas, where productivity depended on latitude and altitude, farmland became unproductive (Parry 1981; Pfister 1981).

This cooling period is also documented in the artwork of the period. The tradition of portraying winter landscapes, frozen rivers and harbors, abundant snowfall, and winter sports in Flemish paintings and prints was established by Pieter Bruegel the Elder (1528/30–69) in the later half of sixteenth century. Flemish immigrant painters were largely responsible for introducing the subject into the Dutch repertoire in the first quarter of the seventeenth century (Bugler 1979, 59; Gaskell 1990, 414).

For the lower Great Lakes area of North America, Rudolphe Fecteau (1985, 98–99) proposed a sequence of climatic fluctuations. During the Pacific I stage (1250–1450), the climate was characterized by decreased rainfall and cooler temperatures. It was then that southern Ontario communities located on sandy soils were abandoned. The Pacific II stage (1450–1550) was an era of climatic amelioration that permitted a northward movement of Carolinian biotic-zone fauna. During the Neo-Boreal (1550–1880), climatic deterioration included a cooling of temperatures by about 1 degree Celsius. The Recent stage (1880-present) has been marked by a general warming trend.

From Crawford Lake in southern Ontario, the fossil pollen record reveals that after 1360, pine and oak forests began to replace the previously dominant beech-maple forest (McAndrews 1988, 682). The presence of oak began to increase around 1370 and peaked around 1650, whereas white pine, a northern species near its southern limit at Crawford Lake, became more prevalent around 1390, peaking around 1860. John H. McAndrews (1988, 683) attributed the southward advance of northern species to the cooler climate of the Little Ice Age. The establishment of white pine stands in the vicinity of Huron Iroquoian sites datable to the early sixteenth century (Bowman 1979) further supports the onset of cooler climatic conditions.

Southern Ontario as a Marginal Horticultural Area

Biotic boundaries are not static. When climate changes, the boundaries shift, and when boundaries shift, the subsistence base may be affected, especially in sensitive areas in high latitudes where conditions for plant growth and horticulture are marginal (Grove 1988, 1; Harding 1982, 3; Parry 1981).

In late twentieth-century Ontario, corn could be grown effectively only as far north as what was seventeenth-century Huron territory. This pattern is determined by criteria such as the number of frost-free days, the number of growing-degree days, "corn heat unit" (CHU) values, the length of the growing season, and soil conditions (Fecteau 1985, 102–8). Corn heat units (based on days with temperatures of more than 10 degrees Celsius and nights with temperatures over 4.4 degrees Celsius) are especially useful in determining the viability of corn. The Ontario Corn Committee (1992) publishes geographical ranges for corn hybrids adapted to the climate of Ontario.

Because corn is one of the few annual crops that use the full frost-free period to complete its life cycle, varieties must be carefully selected to make optimum use of heat and to avoid frost damage. Tender crops such as corn and beans are damaged when air temperatures range between minus 1.5 degrees Celsius and the freezing point. In the late twentieth century, most shelled corn was grown in areas having CHU values of 2,900 or more, although some grain corn could be grown in areas that had as few as 2,500 CHUs (fig. 13.7) (D. Brown, McKay, and Chapman 1980, 33, 37–38). Bean production is most efficient in areas with greater than 3,000 CHUs (Fecteau 1985, 32).

Though it is a reasonable assumption that climate-dependent agricultural factors were reduced in southern Ontario during the sixteenth and seventeenth centuries, it is difficult to determine confidently how much farther south the limits of effective aboriginal horticulture might have shifted. Historical accounts from sev-

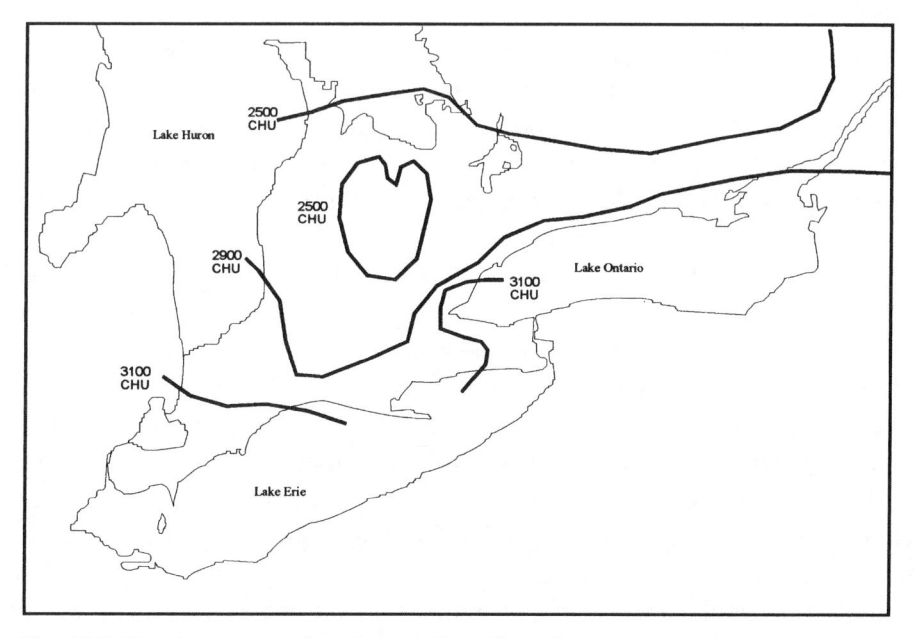

Fig. 13.7. Corn heat unit values for southern Ontario.

enteenth-century southern Ontario do, however, provide a notion of the extent of the climatic difference. On the basis of twentieth-century climatic conditions, Conrad E. Heidenreich (1971) suggested that one crop failure should be expected every 10 years. Between 1628 and 1650, however, when the Jesuits were among southern Ontario groups, severe winters, droughts, crop failures, and famines were documented almost annually (see Arès 1970; Thwaites 1896–1901). This undoubtedly reflected, in part, the climatic instability of the Little Ice Age: "Behold dying skeletons eking out a miserable life, feeding even on the excrements and refuse of nature" (Thwaites 1896–1901, 35:89).

The Cultural Unsuitability of Marginal Horticulture

If not supplemented with other foods or prepared with certain additives, corn has marginal nutritional value. A dietary mixture of corn and beans produces a combination of amino acids that is a good source of protein (Fecteau 1985, 30). Soaking, boiling, or cooking corn with lime (calcium oxide) or alkali (potassium oxide) also releases the essential lysine and tryptophan amino acids and niacin, a member of the vitamin B complex (Katz, Hediger, and Valleroy 1974). In societies that depend heavily on corn, supplementing the diet with protein, treating the corn with alkaline substances, or both are essential to avoiding malnutrition.

Iroquoians of southern Ontario occupied the area in and immediately adjacent to the Canadian-Carolinian Transitional (Mixed Forest) and Carolinian (Deciduous) biotic zones at the northern limit of productive horticulture. It is in such marginal areas, especially those along the boundaries of biotic zones, that climatic variations have the greatest potential for social and economic disruption. With the onset of climatic deterioration in the sixteenth century, the diminishing reliability and output of domesticated crops seems to have resulted in a return to a more traditional hunter-gatherer subsistence strategy (cf. Sioui 1992b) that favored an intensification of large-game exploitation.

The exponential increase in the proportion of deer remains on sixteenth- and seventeenth-century Neutral sites after a fifteenth-century lull suggests that hunting might have alleviated two climate-related stresses. In particular, if the reliability of the protein-rich but cold-sensitive bean was threatened by the colder climate of the Little Ice Age, an alternative source of dietary protein would have been required. Deer, being large, easy to capture, and especially abundant in areas of cedar swamps (Peterson 1966, 324), would have provided a ready supply. Another incentive for increasing deer procurement might have been a growing demand for warm winter clothing.

Analysis of stable carbon isotopes in human bone provides a ratio of carbohydrate to protein in the diets of past populations. Corn was the primary dietary source of carbohydrates for the Ontario Iroquoians, but bean protein cannot be distinguished from meat protein by this technique. Although it is clear that corn continued to be a significant contributor to the diet throughout this era, carbohydrate values were decreasing by the seventeenth century (see fig. 13.3) (Katzenberg, Saunders, and Fitzgerald 1993; Schwarcz et al. 1985). If corn consumption was decreasing, so, presumably, was the consumption of beans. The dramatic increase in deer exploitation may represent a replacement of plant protein by animal protein.

Pressures on a population that had become increasingly dependent on horticulture, especially at a climatically unstable time and in a horticulturally marginal area, might have led to increased competition for deer hunting territories and thus to intercultural conflicts (Gramly 1977). Such conflicts might have been avoided when horticultural products constituted a greater proportion of the diet. In southern Ontario, land suitable for horticulture is much more abundant and widespread than are tracts that would support high densities of deer.

Summary

Late Woodland Ontario Iroquoian culture developed amid the uncertainty of northern horticulture. The widespread introduction of beans by the fifteenth century might have brought about a trend toward the substitution of plant protein for animal protein in a diet that included a substantial quantity of otherwise nutritionally poor corn. With this development, more effort might have been directed toward other aspects of society if less time was spent on male-oriented subsistence pursuits. Cultural advancement and elaboration might have been related in part to the evolution of plant domestication.

Not only is northern horticulture an inherently unhealthy and hence maladaptive subsistence pursuit (see Patterson 1984; Pfeiffer and King 1983), but further stresses result when the stability of the horticultural base is undermined. Ontario Iroquoians attempted to adapt, a feat made easier by the flexibility of northern Iroquoian social organization. Like their hunter-gatherer ancestors and neighbors, during good times they were able to fuse into larger groups, whereas during lean and other stressful times they could split into smaller groups or move to areas of new resources. Although an increase in deer procurement might ultimately have become a successful subsistence adjustment to the restraints of a cooler and unstable climate, such an outcome was ultimately thwarted by the devastating effects of European epidemics. Native curing practices and the importation of captives to restock the population proved futile in the struggle to adapt to additional adversity. Attempting to combat famine, contagion, and Iroquois attacks while maintaining the basic necessities of life was too much to achieve, and by 1651 the decimated Iroquoian groups of southern Ontario succumbed.

Acknowledgments

Versions of this chapter were presented at a number of conferences in 1992: the Society for American Archaeology (Pittsburgh), Transferts Culturels en Amérique et Ailleurs (Québec), the Canadian Archaeological Association (London), and People to People (Rochester). Over the years, conversations with James Bradley, Shelley Saunders, Marvin Smith, and Bruce Trigger have provided valued insights. Bruce Jamieson in particular was instrumental in formulating a number of the notions that were developed. Paul Lennox, Rosemary Prevec, and Howard Savage generously provided access to unpublished faunal information. The chapter was largely written and revised while I was the recipient of a Social Sciences and Humanities Research Council of Canada Postdoctoral Fellowship.

14 | European Infectious Disease and Depopulation of the Wendat-Tionontate (Huron-Petun)

GARY A. WARRICK

Introduction

IN A.D. 1492, the population of North America (i.e., north of the urban civilizations of Central Mexico) was somewhere between 1.89 million (Ubelaker 1992) and 18 million (Dobyns 1983). By 1890, only 546,000 Native North Americans were alive (Ubelaker 1992). Most historians and archaeologists agree that the catastrophic depopulation of Native America was caused by epidemics of European disease, but there is disagreement about when this depopulation occurred. Some scholars believe that much of Native America experienced sixteenth-century pandemics of European disease far in advance of face-to-face contact with Europeans and support high pre-European population estimates (S. Cook 1973; Dobyns 1966; 1983; Crosby 1976; 1986; Ramenofsky 1987; Upham 1992). Others believe that Native American depopulation occurred as a result of local disease epidemics, after first direct contact with Europeans (Milner 1992; Reff 1991; Snow 1995d; 1996c; Snow and Lanphear 1988; Snow and Starna 1989; Ubelaker 1992). In the absence of sixteenth-century pandemics, historical first-contact population estimates for Native America are deemed to be an accurate reflection of precontact population, resulting in numbers that are one tenth of those cited by proponents of pandemics. Unfortunately, surprisingly few investigators (cf. Ramenofsky 1987; Snow 1995d; 1996c) have actually used archaeological data to trace the demographic history of a Native group to measure the timing of depopulation and precontact population numbers.

The debate over the population of the New World in 1492 is not confined to academia—Native Americans are keenly interested in knowing whether the first Eu-

Previously published in *World Archaeology* 35, no. 2 (2003): 258–75. Routledge. Printed with permission by Taylor and Francis Ltd., <http://www.tandf.co.uk/journals.>

ropeans to contact their ancestors found them in an unaltered precontact state or as the surviving, disease-scarred remnants of a formerly populous and complex society (Krech 1999, 83–84; Sioui 1992a). At present, population estimates for Native America in 1492 are unacceptably contentious. In order to achieve reliable estimates of Native population at the regional or hemispheric level, censuses of individual Native American groups or tribes must be compiled. The best method for estimating Native American population involves meshing data from historical accounts, epidemiology, archaeology, and bioarchaeology. The use of multiple data sets permits one to trace a particular Native population from precontact to late historic times and to assess the impact of European contact and disease. This paper examines the timing and demographic impact of the first European disease epidemics to affect the Wendat-Tionontate (Huron-Petun) who occupied southern Ontario, Canada, and demonstrates why archaeological data are crucial to the writing of Native American population history.

The Case of the Wendat-Tionontate

The Wendat-Tionontate, or Huron-Petun, are one of the best-known Native groups in all of North America and provide an ideal case study for examining the timing and impact of European disease epidemics for several reasons. First of all, seventeenth-century documents, written by French visitors to the Wendat-Tionontate country (Samuel de Champlain in the winter of 1615–16 [Biggar 1922–36], Gabriel Sagard in the winter of 1623–24 [Sagard-Théodat 1939 (1632)], and various Jesuit priests from 1634 to 1650 [Thwaites 1896–1901]), provide descriptions of daily life, census data, and eyewitness accounts of epidemic disease. Second, there is abundant archaeological data for the Wendat-Tionontate, including the partial and complete excavation of dozens of village sites occupied from 1000 to 1650, allowing one to make inferences about population change from settlement size and number (Warrick 1990). Lastly, several large burial populations have been exhumed and analyzed, permitting one to trace changes in pathology and vital rates from 1300 to 1650 (Pfeiffer and Fairgrieve 1994).

In the early seventeenth century, the Wendat-Tionontate were one of several confederacies of Iroquoian speakers in northeastern North America (fig. 14.1). Northern Iroquoians occupied the mixed deciduous forests of the St. Lawrence Valley-Lower Great Lakes region and numbered around 100,000, distributed in 30 distinct nations (Snow 1992b; 1996c; Warrick 2000 [chap. 7]). Before 1634, when the first recorded epidemics of European disease struck the Wendat, the combined Wendat-Tionontate population totaled 30,000–35,000, according to seventeenth-century accounts (Biggar 1922–36, 3:122; Thwaites 1896–1901, 6:59; 7:225; 8:115; 10:313; Sagard-Théodat 1939 [1632], 91). The Wendat consisted of four nations (Heidenreich 1971, 84–86; Trigger 1976, 30; 1990a [1969], 19–20) who occupied eighteen

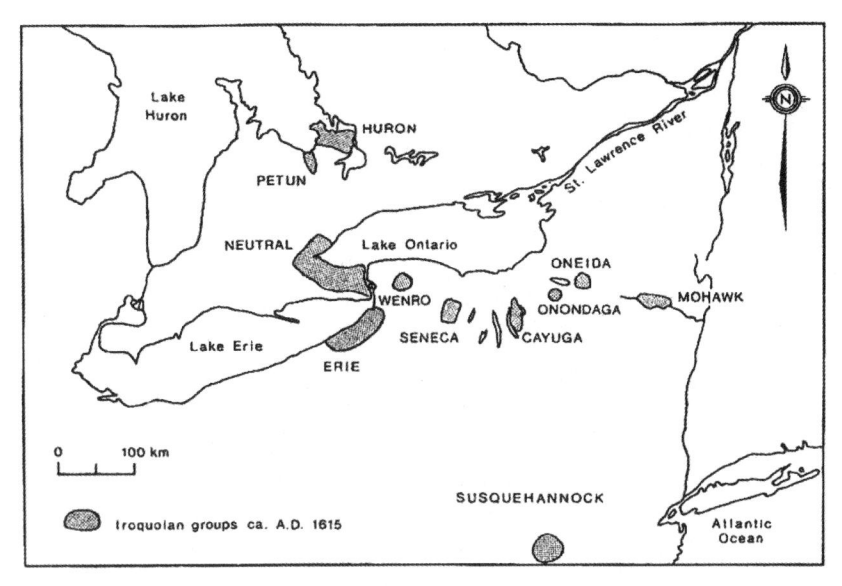

Fig. 14.1. Distribution of Iroquoian groups in northeastern North America ca. A.D. 1615

villages. The Tionontate, divided into two nations, occupied seven villages (Biggar 1922–36, 3:95–101, 122; 4:278–84, 302; Garrad and Heidenreich 1978; Sagard-Théodat 1939 [1632], 91). The typical village was 1.8 hectare (ha) in size and contained 30 to 40 longhouses surrounded by a double-row palisade (Warrick 1990, 391). Longhouses averaged 20 meters in length (Dodd 1984, 414), sheltering 30 to 40 people (Warrick 1990). Fireplaces for cooking and heating were arranged along the center of a longhouse, and each was shared by two nuclear families (Biggar 1922–36, 3:122–24; Thwaites 1896–1901, 8:105–7; Sagard-Théodat 1939 [1632], 93–95). The Wendat diet consisted of at least 50 percent maize, beans, and squash; 25 percent fish; and 25 percent wild game (primarily white-tailed deer) and fleshy fruit (Heidenreich 1971, 163–64; Katzenberg 1993). The French remarked on the robust health of the Wendat (Trigger 1990a [1969], 13).

Historical Population and Disease Epidemics among the Wendat-Tionontate

The first estimates of Wendat-Tionontate population are 32,000 by Champlain in 1615 (Biggar 1922–36, 3:122) and 30,000–40,000 by Gabriel Sagard in 1623–24 (Sagard-Théodat 1939 [1632], 91). Before the summer of 1634, the French Jesuits who had lived among the Wendat consistently estimated their population at 30,000 persons and the number of their villages at 20 (Thwaites 1896–1901, 6:59; 7:225; 8:115; 10:313). There are no recorded estimates of Tionontate population for the early 1630s, but in 1639 they are said to have occupied nine villages (Thwaites

1896–1901, 19:127). In the spring of 1639 and over the winter of 1639–40, the Jesuits took a house-by-house census of the Wendat-Tionontate:

> [W]e have had means to take the census not only of the villages, large and small, but also of the cabins, the fires, and even very nearly of the persons in all the country—there being no other way to preach the Gospel in these regions than at each family's hearth, whereof we tried to omit not one. In these five missions there are thirty-two hamlets and straggling villages, which comprise in all about seven hundred cabins, about two thousand fires, and about twelve thousand persons. (Thwaites 1896–1901, 19:127)

The total of 12,000 applied to both the Wendat and their neighbors the Tionontate. This census documents the impact of the 1639–40 smallpox epidemic—it counted hearths before the epidemic struck and survivors after the epidemic passed. Two thousand fires should translate into 20,000 people, assuming two families per hearth and five people per family. Instead, only 12,000 people are reported. This report implies the loss of 8,000 people over the winter of 1639–40, from smallpox, the last in a series of devastating diseases that visited the Wendat-Tionontate between 1634 and 1640.

The first recorded disease epidemic among the Wendat-Tionontate occurred in the late summer of 1634. A "sort of measles and an oppression of the stomach" (Thwaites 1896–1901, 7:221), accompanied by high fever, rash, vision impairment in some cases, and ending in diarrhea, spread throughout the western Wendat villages and lasted over the winter (Thwaites 1896–1901, 7:221; 8:87–89). Mortality rates were approximately 20 percent (Trigger 1976, 851). If the 1634 epidemic was measles *(Variola minor)* (Dobyns 1983, 17, 322; Trigger 1976, 500–501), mortality rates in a nonimmune population are characteristically 10–20 percent (Ramenofsky 1987, 148). Assuming that only the western half of the Wendat population and some Tionontate were infected (Thwaites 1896–1901, 10:77), the Wendat-Tionontate may have suffered a 10 percent depopulation—a loss of about 2,500 people. It is possible that this measles epidemic can be attributed to the arrival of 25 French children at Quebec in June 1634 (Trudel 1973, 184–85). It is generally agreed that Wendat traders were afflicted with measles upon contacting the sick and dying Algonquian and Innu at Trois Rivières, and possibly Quebec, in early July 1634 (Trigger 1976, 500–501).

A "pestilence, of unknown origin" (Thwaites 1896–1901, 11:13) hit the Wendat in early September 1636 and persisted until the spring of 1637 (Thwaites 1896–1901, 13:115, 163–65). This epidemic has been diagnosed as influenza, judging from its symptoms (i.e., bouts of very high fever and cramps) and that it affected both the French and Wendat (Thwaites 1896–1901, 13:95–101; Trigger 1976, 526–27). However, influenza is communicable for no more than three days (Benenson 1975), and probably would not have survived an Atlantic crossing on board a ship with fewer than 100 passengers. Furthermore, the sickness lasted at least two weeks among the few French residents of Wendat villages, and persisted throughout the winter and flared again in the early spring among the Wendat themselves (Trigger 1976, 526–27), uncharacteristic behavior for a flu. A more likely diagnosis is strep infection (e.g., tonsillitis) complicated by bacterial pneumonia, which often produces high fever and stomach cramps owing to swollen lymph glands and can result in 25 percent mortality in a population untreated with antibiotics (Ramenofsky 1987, 150–52). Strep infection can have a communicable period of weeks or months, depending on the strain (Benenson 1975), and is especially contagious in crowded dwellings where contact is intimate (e.g., sharing of drinking and eating utensils). It may have been transmitted by the Nipissing, who probably contracted the disease from new French immigrants at Trois Rivières (Trigger 1976, 521; Trudel 1973, 185). The western Wendat (Attignawantan Nation) lost 500 people, half of these in the large Ossossane village (Trigger 1976, 528). Mortality would have averaged 5–10 percent (Benenson 1975), reducing Wendat-Tionontate population by another 1,300–2,500 people. The Nipissing who wintered in the Wendat country lost 70 persons during this epidemic, approximately 10 percent of their population (Thwaites 1896–1901, 14:37).

Another epidemic of an unidentified childhood disease (no French contracted it) struck the Wendat in the summer of 1637 and lasted until the autumn of the same year (Trigger 1976, 528). The disease killed its victims quickly, sometimes within two days of onset (Thwaites 1896–1901, 15:69), but no symptoms are explicitly mentioned. Outbreak of the disease occurred before the Wendat trading season, and it probably entered Wendat-Tionontate villages via the Susquehannock, who had suffered an unspecified epidemic in February 1637 (Trigger 1976, 528). The ultimate origins of the infection were probably from the English colony in Virginia, a fast-growing colony with numerous children, whose population exceeded 4,800 in 1625 and 8,000 in 1640 (Delage 1993, 244). If the illness was scarlet fever (rash form of *Streptococcus pyogenes*), as suggested by Dobyns (1983, 322) and Snow (1992b) and supported by the lack of remarks about symptoms by the Jesuits, perhaps implying similar ones to the preceding epidemic of the 1636–37 winter (Trigger 1976, 528), the mortality rate is reportedly higher for this epidemic than the previous one (Trigger 1976, 528), suggesting at least 10 percent mortality overall, leaving only 23,000 Wendat-Tionontate alive in late 1637.

Smallpox ravaged the already decimated Wendat and Tionontate from the early fall of 1639 until the spring of 1640 (Dobyns 1983, 322; Trigger 1976, 588–89). In 1633, smallpox was transmitted to the Natives of coastal New England, reaching as far inland as the Mohawk by December 1634 (Snow 1992b; Snow and Starna 1989). In 1638, a British ship docked at Boston carrying smallpox (S. Cook 1973). This introduction was the one that inevitably found its way to the Wendat-Tionontate via a group of Kichesipirini returning from Abenaki country (Thwaites

1896–1901, 16:101; Trigger 1976, 588). Smallpox is directly communicable for two weeks but can live in a dried state in scabs and on clothing for longer periods (Benenson 1975; Ramenofsky 1987, 146). Victims typically die within five to seven days of first symptoms from severe fever and toxemia (Benenson 1975). The consequences for the Wendat-Tionontate were devastating: a 40–60 percent mortality rate for most villages has been conservatively estimated, based on documented outbreaks of smallpox in other "virgin-soil" situations (Heidenreich 1971, 97–98; Ramenofsky 1987, 146–49; Snow 1992b). Thus, based on disease mortality rates, the post-smallpox Wendat-Tionontate population would have been somewhere in the vicinity of 10,000–12,000 people, precisely the number documented by Jerome Lalemant in the 1639–40 census (Thwaites 1896–1901, 17:223; 19:127).

For the Wendat-Tionontate, the epidemics of European disease ended in the spring of 1640, leaving an estimated 12,000 scarred and battered survivors. In a period of six years, the Wendat-Tionontate were reduced from 30,000 to 12,000—a depopulation rate of 60 percent. Catastrophic depopulation of the Wendat-Tionontate evoked this reaction from Jerome Lalemant in 1642: "Where eight years ago one could see eighty or a hundred cabins, barely five or six can now be seen; a Captain, who then had eight hundred warriors under his command, now has not more than thirty or forty; instead of fleets of three or four hundred canoes, we see now but twenty or thirty" (Thwaites 1896–1901, 23:109).

European Disease in the Northeast before 1634

Before examining the archaeological record and burial populations of the Wendat-Tionontate for evidence of European disease and depopulation before the historically documented epidemics of 1634–40, it is important to investigate the potential for pre-1634 transmission of disease to the Wendat-Tionontate. It is possible that infectious disease reached Iroquoian peoples as early as 1524, as a result of the voyage of Giovanni da Verrazzano, who had direct contact with Native North Americans along the Atlantic coast from North Carolina to Maine (Morison 1971, 289–309). However, Dean Snow has argued (1980, 32–33; Snow and Lanphear 1988) that the average 42-day duration of trans-Atlantic crossings in the sixteenth and early seventeenth century and relatively small crew sizes acted to prevent the transmission of most European crowd contagions to North America. The communicable periods (i.e., incubation period plus period of illness [Burnet and White 1972, 124–25]) of most European diseases are less than 14 days (Benenson 1975; Ramenofsky 1987), except for smallpox (9–21 days and on clothing for months), plague (in fleas for months), whooping cough (14–28 days), strep infections (months), typhus (28 days including human body louse life cycle), and bacterial pneumonia (months) (Benenson 1975; Ramenofsky 1987). The trans-Atlantic sea voyage acted like a quarantine period for European sailors (Snow 1980, 32–33).

Nevertheless, there are several references in sixteenth- and seventeenth-century documents to disease outbreaks among Natives in northeastern North America.

The first recorded epidemic of European disease in the Northeast occurred in 1535. While overwintering near the village of Stadacona (near present-day Quebec City), Jacques Cartier (Biggar 1924, 204) observed in December 1535 that over 50 Stadaconans (about 10 percent of the village population [Trigger 1985, 237]) died from an unknown disease. The mortality rate, epidemic behavior, and timing of the disease outbreak suggest a European contagion (Trigger 1976, 193–94). Influenza and cold virus have been proposed (Snow and Lanphear 1988; Trigger 1981b), but the epidemic was probably bacterial pneumonia. People predisposed to pneumonia (staph or strep strains) as a primary infection are those who have chronic lung disease or previous respiratory infection and who live in cold, damp, and crowded dwellings (Benenson 1975; Ramenofsky 1987, 150). Skeletal pathology indicates that tuberculosis was endemic among fifteenth- and sixteenth-century Wendat-Tionontate (Hartney 1981; Pfeiffer 1984) and also present in fifteenth-century St. Lawrence Iroquoians (Hartney 1981). Furthermore, life in an Iroquoian longhouse during the winter was cold and crowded—at night occupants slept close to the central fires, huddled together for warmth (Thwaites 1896–1901, 17:13; Sagard-Théodat 1939 [1632], 93–94). Coughing, droplet spread, and inhalation are the main routes of infection. The communicable period for bacterial pneumonia varies, but the disease can survive in a person's upper respiratory tract for months (Benenson 1975). Primary infections of pneumonia, left untreated by antibiotics, result in 20–25 percent mortality through high fever and respiratory distress (Ramenofsky 1987, 152).

Archaeology and oral history both indicate that St. Lawrence Iroquoians abandoned the St. Lawrence Valley by 1580, as a result of warfare among themselves and with other Iroquoian nations (Bradley 1987a, 84–87; Engelbrecht 1995; Heidenreich 1990; J. Jamieson 1990a; Kuhn et al. 1993; Pendergast 1993b; Ramsden 1990b; Sioui 1992a, 83–86; Snow 1996c; Trigger 1985). The presence of distinctive St. Lawrence Iroquoian pottery in Wendat, Onondaga, and Mohawk sites between 1530 and 1580 indicates that at least 800 St. Lawrence Iroquoians resettled among the Wendat (Saunders et al. 1992, 120), 600 joined the Onondaga (Bradley 1987a), and perhaps a few hundred lived with the Oneida and Mohawk (Snow 1996c). The possibility that St. Lawrence Iroquoians were depopulated by European disease (Sioui 1992a, 41–42), causing regional destabilization, cannot be ruled out.

The Wendat's first contact with the French occurred at Quebec in 1609 (Biggar 1922–36, 2:67–71). Between 1610 and 1615, approximately 200 Wendat and Algonquians traded with the French on the St. Lawrence River. In the spring and early summer of 1611, some of the Ottawa Valley Algonquians were prevented from coming to trade because "many had died of fever" (Biggar 1922–36, 2:207). A fever causing relatively high mortality was probably of European origin, perhaps bacterial pneumonia, and perhaps was transmitted to Algonquians via their Innu allies who frequented the Quebec trading post each winter. There is no historical evidence for its spread to the Wendat-Tionontate.

In the winter of 1615–16, Champlain and 14 men overwintered in the Wendat country (Heidenreich 1971, 238). Although contact was intimate (Biggar 1922–36, 3:47), there was no apparent disease transmission. French traders occasionally overwintered in the Wendat-Tionontate country (5 or 6 traders in 1622–23; 14 in 1623–24; 10 in 1624–25; 8 to 10 in 1626–27; 21 in 1628–29) with apparently no ill effects on the indigenous population (Trigger 1976, 367–73).

From 1616 to 1622, an epidemic of viral hepatitis swept entire communities away (90 percent mortality) in southern New England, but did not spread more than 60 kilometers inland from the Atlantic coast (S. Cook 1973; Snow 1992b; Spiess and Spiess 1987), leaving Iroquoians unscathed. Gabriel Sagard recorded that the Weskarini (interior group of Algonquian, north of the Ottawa River) suffered relatively high mortality because of disease and hunger during the winter of 1623–24 (Sagard-Théodat 1939 [1632], 263). It is not known if the disease was a European one. Finally, in 1633, an outbreak of smallpox at an English trading post on the Connecticut River spread quickly to the Mohawk and other Five Nations villages (Snow 1992b), presumably through Mahican traders who had lucrative commercial relations with the Dutch and English in both the Connecticut and Hudson River valleys (Brasser 1978a). Smallpox did not reach the Wendat-Tionontate in 1633, probably because of hostile relations between the Wendat and Five Nations confederacies.

Archaeology and Wendat-Tionontate Depopulation

Ann F. Ramenofsky (1987) made the first serious attempt to use archaeological settlement data to estimate the sixteenth- and seventeenth-century population for an Iroquoian group, with the explicit goal of determining the timing of depopulation for the Five Nations Iroquois as a result of European disease. Relative estimates of population from roofed area of village sites produced ambiguous results because of biased site samples (only 26 sites representing three centuries) and imprecise time periods. In an attempt to improve upon Ramenofsky's (1987) research, two independent archaeological projects were launched in the 1980s to estimate fifteenth- to seventeenth-century population for the Mohawk (Snow 1992b; 1995d; 1996c; Snow and Lanphear 1988; Snow and Starna 1989) and the Wendat-Tionontate (Warrick 1990). Using estimates of 12–20 square meters (m²) of village area per person, Dean Snow (1995d) calculated absolute population figures and found that Mohawk population increased steadily from A.D. 1400 to 1635 (1,070–7,740 people) but experienced a 63 percent decrease between 1635 and 1640. When did depopulation occur for the Wendat-Tionontate?

The archaeological record for the Wendat-Tionontate offers several advantages for estimating past population from settlement remains. First, more than a century of archaeological investigation has located 460 village sites in south-central Ontario, approximately 61 percent of all village sites that ever existed and over 80 percent of all sixteenth- and seventeenth-century sites (Warrick 1990, 157–59; see table 14.1). Second, Wendat-Tionontate village sites were occupied for 10 to 50 years (Warrick 1988), with minimal reoccupation of the same site. Furthermore, excavation has uncovered partial or complete plans for 50 village sites (Warrick 2000 [chap. 7]), permitting one to calculate density of hearths (and people) per unit area of site. Lastly, many Wendat-Tionontate sites can be dated to 10- to 30-year periods (based on radiocarbon dates and pottery decoration and glass bead chronologies [e.g., Kenyon and Kenyon 1983; Fitzgerald 1990a]), corresponding to individual village occupations (Warrick 1988).

I (Warrick 1990) traced change in Wendat-Tionontate population in absolute numbers from A.D. 900 to 1650. The methodology used archaeological settlement data from 25 partially or completely excavated village sites, 460 known village sites, and seventeenth-century descriptions that two families shared each central hearth in a longhouse (Thwaites 1896–1901, 15:153; Sagard-Théodat 1939 [1632], 94). Central hearths are the most useful indicator of population in Iroquoian village sites. Based on excavated village plans, hearth densities in Wendat-Tionontate settlements were found to be relatively constant over several centuries, averaging 50 hearths per hectare of village area. Paleodemographic analyses of ossuary data

Table 14.1
Archaeological Estimates of Wendat-Tionontate Population

Time Period	No. of Confirmed Village Sites	No. of Historic Villages	No. of Missing Village Sites	Total No. of Coeval Village Sites	Total No. of Hearths	Population
A.D. 1647	21	n/a	0	21	1,920	11,520
A.D. 1633	35	29[a]	0	35	2,940	29,400
A.D. 1623	25	25[b]	0	25	3,150	31,500
A.D. 1615	19	25[c]	6	25	2,940	29,400
A.D. 1580–1609	25	n/a	6	31	3,370	33,700
A.D. 1550–1580	27	n/a	1	28	3,020	30,200
A.D. 1500–1550	76	n/a	0	37	3,330	33,300
A.D. 1450–1500	97	n/a	0	35	2,780	27,800
A.D. 1420–1450	45	n/a	0	32	2,590	27,200

Source: Data from Warrick (1990)
[a] Thwaites (1896–1901, 6:59; 7:225; 8:115; 10:313; 19:127).
[b] Sagard-Théodat (1939 [1632], 91).
[c] Biggar (1922–36, 3:95–101, 122; 4:278–84, 302).

from Fairty, Uxbridge, Kleinburg, and Ossossane provide average family sizes of 10 to 11 people per central hearth for the Wendat-Tionontate. Applied to archaeological hearth density, this size translates into 500—50 people per ha of village area. This estimate matches Snow's (1995; 1996) standard population density figure of 20 m² of village space per person for the Mohawk (except between 1550 and 1625 when hearth density rose to 70 hearths per ha among the Wendat-Tionontate [Warrick 1990, 232 35] and 12 m² of village space per person for the Mohawk [Snow 1995d; 1996c]). Hearth density was then multiplied by site area and number of people per hearth for 460 confirmed and dated Wendat-Tionontate village sites, representing 700 years of occupation. The time periods in table 14.1 are derived from radiocarbon dates, pottery seriation, and European trade item chronologies (Warrick 1990, 170–90). Adjustments were made to the village totals for each time period to accommodate site durations that were less than the length of the time periods, to avoid double-counting people. Coeval village numbers in table 14.1 represent the maximum number of villages that were simultaneously occupied in each time period. The cumulative size of these villages was used to calculate the total hearth number (using hearth density per hectare of village area), which in turn was multiplied by the period-specific family size.

Population estimates derived from hearth counts were plotted over time for the Wendat-Tionontate (fig. 14.2). The resulting graph displays a rapid population increase during the fourteenth century from 11,000 to 29,000 persons, representing a growth rate of 1.07 percent per annum (Warrick 1990, 353), a leveling off and then cessation in growth by 1475, and then a dramatic decrease in the 1630s (fig. 14.2). The important part of the curve, the sixteenth century, shows stability with no significant decrease (except for fluctuations around a mean of 30,000 Wendat-Tionontate from 1500 to 1623 [see table 14.1]). This result can be explained by a

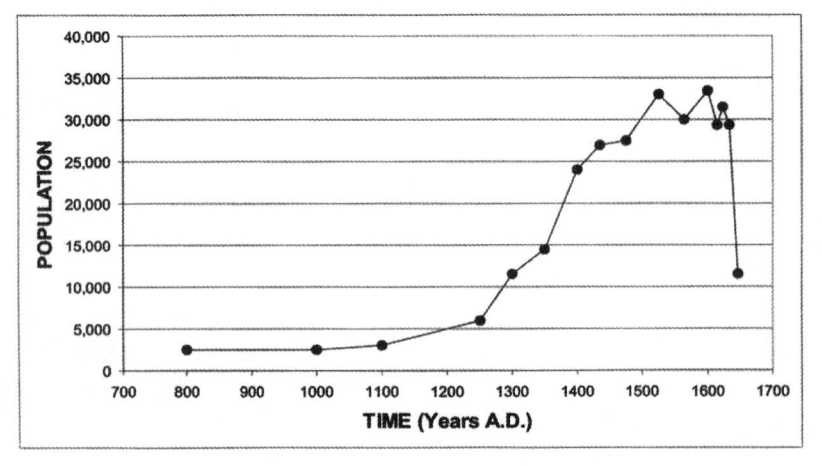

Fig. 14.2. Population growth curve for the Wendat-Tionontate A.D. 800–1650.

simple 10 percent error margin in archaeological census taking, not depopulation from a "1520s pandemic" (Dobyns 1983). A similar result has been obtained for the Mohawk. In fact, the Mohawk population was *increasing* throughout the sixteenth century (Snow 1995c; 1996c). Thus, for at least two relatively dense populations of the Northeast (particularly vulnerable to depopulation from contagious disease as a result of compact longhouse and village life), there is no evidence for early sixteenth-century pandemics and consequent depopulation.

Using archaeology to estimate the depopulation curve for the Wendat-Tionontate is a little more difficult. First of all, there was a high frequency of village abandonments, relocations, and amalgamations between 1635 and 1640. Many villages were abandoned after 1639 because they were no longer demographically or politically viable communities.

> The remnants of the Wendat found themselves living in villages that were too large for them. Many longhouses were empty or almost empty, since up to half of their inhabitants were dead. In the summer of 1640 this resulted in a decision to relocate the town of Ossossane, although the existing settlement was only five years old (21:159). The extra labour involved in founding a new, albeit smaller, town so soon after the last move must have been a very heavy burden to the people of Ossossane. It may be assumed that similar, premature moves were made in other parts of the Wendat country. (Trigger 1976, 602)

Second, the number of people per hearth was no longer 10 (i.e., two nuclear families): based on palaeodemographic data from Ossossane and the 1639–40 Jesuit census (i.e., documenting 2,000 hearths and 12,000 people), post-1640 hearth population was only 6 people (Warrick 1990, 306–9). Using the 1639–40 Jesuit lists of village names and number for the Wendat-Tionontate, matching archaeological sites to villages on the 1640s Jesuit map *Corographie du Pays des Wendats*, and multiplying hearth counts by 6 people per hearth yields a 1647 Wendat population of 8,600 persons and a Tionontate population of only 2,900 people, for a combined Wendat-Tionontate total of 11,500 (Warrick 1990, 404). One example of the difficulty in providing archaeological estimates of post-epidemic population from settlement remains involves the Tahontaenrat village of Scanonaenrat, occupied between 1635 and 1649. Identified in 1996 with the 5.6 ha Ellery site (Archaeological Services Inc. 1993), Scanonaenrat would have contained over 2,500 people estimated from site size. However, Scanonaenrat must have lost over half of its population during the epidemics of 1634–41. If the Tahontaenrat continued to live in their pre-epidemic village, which it appears that they did, then archaeologically the depopulation would be invisible, unless upon complete excavation the village site revealed an obvious contraction in size (i.e., abandonment of a section of the village, shortened longhouses, and a rearranged palisade configuration).

In summary, archaeological estimates of Wendat-Tionontate population indicate stability for 1475–1633 and a 60 percent depopulation between 1634 and 1640. There is no evidence of sixteenth-century disease epidemics or depopulation.

Bioarchaeology of the Wendat-Tionontate

Skeletal populations provide a unique data set for tracking temporal change in disease and mortality rates, which can identify the introduction of European disease. Beginning in the early fourteenth century, the Wendat-Tionontate began to bury their dead in communal ossuaries, often containing the disarticulated remains of hundreds of individuals, typically representing the dead that had accumulated over the 10- to 30-year lifespan of a village. In 1636, a French Jesuit, Jean de Brebeuf, witnessed and recorded one of these burial episodes near the Wendat village of Ossossane, which he called "Feast of the Dead" (Thwaites 1896–1901, 10:275–303). In 1947–48, this ossuary pit was identified and excavated (Kidd 1953; Fitzgerald 1990a, 222–26). (It should be noted that, in the summer of 1999, the Wendat people repatriated the bones and grave goods of the Ossossane ossuary and reburied them with appropriate ceremony in the original pit. Other ossuaries are being considered for repatriation.) Subsequent excavation of other Wendat-Tionontate ossuaries has amassed large skeletal populations, dating from 1300 to 1640. Three ossuaries characterize fifteenth- (pre-Columbian), sixteenth- (indirect European contact), and seventeenth-century (direct European contact) Wendat-Tionontate population: Uxbridge (1460–90), Kleinburg (1580–1600), and Ossossane (1624–36) (Pfeiffer and Fairgrieve 1994). Is there evidence in any of these populations for European disease and depopulation?

Skeletal analyses of the Uxbridge population (dating 1460–90 and containing 457 individuals [Pfeiffer and Fairgrieve 1994]) have revealed a rather unhealthy picture of late fifteenth-century Wendat life: chronic protein-calorie malnutrition, a very high incidence of tuberculosis (at least 4 percent skeletal involvement [Pfeiffer 1986]), 21 percent dental caries, and a number of deaths and injuries caused by interpersonal violence (i.e., tribal warfare) (Pfeiffer 1984; 1986; Pfeiffer and King 1983; Pfeiffer et al. 1986). Despite a high morbidity, however, the Uxbridge population had a lower juvenile mortality (70 percent survival to 15 years of age) and a slightly higher adult life expectancy (life expectancy at birth of 25 years) than the fourteenth-century Fairty population (Warrick 1990, 306). Palaeodemography indicates a stable population ($r = 0.0$) (Jackes 1986; Warrick 1990, 306), confirming archaeological estimates of population stability for the Wendat-Tionontate by 1475 (Warrick 1990).

Bioarchaeological analysis of the Kleinburg ossuary (dating 1580–1600 (Kenyon and Kenyon 1983) and containing 561 individuals [Pfeiffer and Fairgrieve 1994]) reveals a life expectancy at birth of 25 years, a low juvenile mortality rate (70 percent survival to 15 years), but a low fertility rate (Jackes 1986; Pfeiffer 1983). An extremely high rate of dental caries (41 percent [Patterson 1984]) is substantiated by paleodietary analyses suggesting a diet composed of at least 50 percent maize (Katzenberg and Schwarcz 1986). Paleopathology of Kleinburg indicates a lower incidence of tuberculosis, lower rate of bone infection, and higher rate of growth arrest lines than either the Fairty or Uxbridge populations, but otherwise the relative health of the Kleinburg people was comparable to that of earlier Wendat-Tionontate (Pfeiffer and Fairgrieve 1994; Pfeiffer and King 1983). There is absolutely no evidence for European epidemics in the Kleinburg mortality rates (Sullivan 1997). Palaeodemography indicates a stable population ($r = -0.002$) (Jackes 1986; Warrick 1990, 306), confirmed by archaeological population estimates (Warrick 1990).

The mortality profile of the Ossossane ossuary (dating to 1636 and containing 419 individuals [Pfeiffer and Fairgrieve 1994]), indicating elevated adolescent deaths (40 percent survival to 15 years), suggests impact from an epidemic disease (Jackes 1986; Saunders and Melbye 1990; Sullivan 1997). Infants (0–2 years) and the old (>40 years) are selectively killed by acute crowd infections, although adolescents and young adults (15–30 years) can experience high mortality rates from smallpox, measles, mumps, and chickenpox because of overreactive immune responses (Burnet and White 1972, 97–99). Ontario Iroquoian skeletal populations that were buried during the 1630s epidemics, at Ossossane and in the Neutral cemetery at Grimsby, reveal extremely high juvenile mortality rates for populations that we know were not growing, based on archaeological evidence (Jackes 1986). Paleopathological data suggest a population in comparable health to that of Fairty, Uxbridge, and Kleinburg (Pfeiffer and Fairgrieve 1994). Based on the historical identification of this ossuary, the dead would include victims of the 1634 measles epidemic. It is interesting that no signs of European disease were identified in the bones of the Ossossane people. Infectious diseases of European origin tend not to leave signatures in skeletal populations—victims die before bony lesions have a chance to form, and, for survivors, lesions produced by European diseases, such as smallpox and measles, if produced at all, tend to be nonspecific (Ortner 1992). One possible exception is the discovery of lesions attributed to smallpox in the bones of an adult male buried in a Neutral Iroquoian cemetery, in Grimsby, southern Ontario, dating 1640–50 (Jackes 1983). It is conceivable that this man was infected with smallpox as early as 1633–34 (Jackes 1983, 80). Glass bead chronology, in association with inferred season of death and distribution of multiple graves at the Grimsby cemetery, suggests that European epidemics did not affect the Neutral until the mid-1630s (Fitzgerald 1990a, 226–39).

In summary, palaeodemography and palaeopathology of Wendat-Tionontate skeletal populations between 1400 and 1650 document consistently moderate rates of caries, malnutrition, and endemic disease (e.g., tuberculosis), but no evidence of European disease before the first recorded epidemic of 1634.

Discussion: Iroquoians and European Disease in the Sixteenth and Seventeenth Centuries

Why were the Wendat-Tionontate and other Iroquoian groups living in the interior of the Northeast not infected with European disease before 1633? Factors that prevented the pandemic spread of European disease across sixteenth- and early seventeenth-century North America include long trans-Atlantic voyages, lack of European children in the first colonies of the Northeast, infrequent land-based contacts with Natives before colonization, low population densities of Native societies in northeastern North America, and physical and sociopolitical buffer zones between Native groups (preventing localized disease outbreak from becoming epidemic or pandemic) (Carlson et al. 1992; Milner 1992; Snow 1992b; Snow and Lanphear 1988; Thornton et al. 1992).

In the 1630s, shiploads of European colonists began arriving along the Atlantic seaboard. Infected children of these first colonies are believed to have been responsible for initiating a continuing series of disease epidemics among interior Native groups of the Northeast (Snow and Lanphear 1988). In seventeenth-century Europe, most acute crowd infections were childhood illnesses. Typically, most children would have been exposed to measles, smallpox, whooping cough, and other contagions by five years of age (Burnet and White 1972, 95). In 1629, there were only 117 residents of New France and about 500 in New England and 300 in New Netherland (Delage 1993, 243, 258; Trudel 1973, 165). Between 1630 and 1640, 700 colonists settled in New Netherland and 13,400 in New England (Delage 1993, 243). In contrast, New France added only 120 colonists in the 1630s (Delage 1993, 243). This suggests that most of the European diseases that inflicted such devastation on the Wendat-Tionontate probably originated from newly arrived Dutch or English children after 1630.

Early seventeenth-century France, England, and the Netherlands were unhealthy places to live, especially in the towns and cities. France's population was stagnant (Grigg 1980, 55–57), suffering famine in 1630 and disease epidemics in 1625, 1637, and 1638 (Delage 1993, 257–58). The rise of urbanization in Western Europe in the early 1600s (10 percent of France's population, 15 percent of England's, and 50 percent of Holland's were in towns of over 5,000–10,000 people [Grigg 1980, 95, 110, 156]) elevated the rates of epidemic disease and mortality (Wrigley 1969, 96–97), as reflected in a decline in both life expectancy at birth and total fertility rate from 1600 to 1650 (Livi-Bacci 1992, 84). Between 1612 and 1664, plague attacked the citizens of Amsterdam on nine separate occasions (Grigg 1980, 160) and attacked Paris on five occasions (Delage 1993, 258). Unfortunately for seventeenth-century Native America, the cities and towns of Western Europe produced the bulk of North American colonists. In fact, overseas emigrants from southeastern England in the early 1630s were predominantly (up to 80 percent) urban artisans and their families (Grigg 1980, 98). Similarly, 40–60 percent of French emigrants in the 1630s came from urban areas (Charbonneau and Robert 1987). The generally poor state of health of Europe's town and city dwellers in the early 1600s, the dramatic rise in colonization of North America between 1625 and 1640, and the predominantly urban origin of the first colonists of New France, New England, and New Netherland explain why the Wendat-Tionontate and their neighbors were decimated by European disease after and not before 1630.

The first encounters of Native Americans and European disease most often took the form of locally severe outbreaks. In northeastern North America, Native population densities were relatively low, and most Native nations lived in clusters of compact villages separated from other nations by hundreds of square kilometers of forest, i.e., deer hunting territories. Although all Wendat communities were within one or two days' walk of one another, the Wendat-Tionontate homeland was 21–28 days by canoe from Montreal and more than 40 days overland during the winter (i.e., 600 kilometers). A network of trails connected the Wendat-Tionontate to the Neutral (4- to 5-day walk or 120 kilometers) and beyond to their Susquehannock allies (at least 30 days overland or 800 kilometers). The Wendat-Tionontate were hostile with most of the Five Nations Iroquois. In turn, the Five Nations fought with the Algonquian groups to the north and east (Mahican) and with the Susquenhannock to the south (Heidenreich 1990; Trigger 1985). This fighting essentially isolated the Five Nations from European contact in the sixteenth century and interrupted the human chain of contact that could have carried European disease inland from the Atlantic Coast.

The demographic impact of European epidemics on the Wendat-Tionontate, causing close to 60 percent depopulation, is congruent with other "virgin-soil epidemics" (Crosby 1976). Aboriginal groups along the Northeast coast of North America were decimated in the early 1600s by European diseases (Carlson et al. 1992; S. Cook 1973; Snow 1980, 32–35; Snow and Lanphear 1988). Depopulation rates for New England Natives of the early seventeenth century range from 67 to 95 percent (Snow and Lanphear 1988, 24). Smallpox was the most virulent, with 50–90 percent mortality rates being recorded for virgin-soil epidemics of this disease (Johnston 1987, 20). The high residential density of Iroquoian villages and communal longhouse life would have hastened the spread of disease and death from secondary infections (e.g., pneumonia) (Burnet and White 1972, 16–17; Crosby 1976, 293–97). The deep spiritual concern for sick relatives, longhouse living conditions, and lack of quarantine are highlighted in an account of Wendat behavior during the 1639–40 smallpox epidemic by Jesuit Jerome Lalemant: "For the Wendats—no matter what plague or contagion they may have—live in the midst of their sick, in the same indifference, and community of all things, as if they were in perfect health. In fact, in a few days, almost all those in the cabin of the deceased found themselves infected; then the evil spread from house to house, from village to village, and finally became scattered throughout the country" (Thwaites 1896–1901, 19:89).

Conclusion

In conclusion, it is possible to identify the timing and demographic impact of the introduction of European disease on a Native American group, using historical, epidemiological, archaeological, and bioarchaeological data. Archaeological estimates of pre-Columbian Wendat-Tionontate population appear to match estimates provided in the early seventeenth-century documents—30,000 people. Furthermore, there is no archaeological evidence for depopulation of the Wendat-Tionontate before the recorded disease epidemics of the 1630s. It is interesting that Dean Snow (1995d) made a similar finding for the Mohawk. If the Wendat-Tionontate and Mohawk cases are representative of the Native population of northeastern North America, we must conclude that there was no sixteenth-century pandemic of European disease in the Northeast. In fact, contrary to the claims of Henry Dobyns (1983) and his supporters (Crosby 1986; Upham 1992), the only region in North America that contains any archaeological evidence for significant depopulation in the sixteenth century is the southeastern United States (Ramenofsky 1987; M. Smith 1987). Thus, for most regions of North America, the first European observations of Native American population numbers are probably an accurate reflection of precontact numbers. This conclusion implies that the Native North American population in 1492 was probably around two million, a figure derived from European first-contact population estimates (Ubelaker 1992).

PART FOUR

| *Material Culture Studies*

| Overview

A WIDE RANGE OF ARTIFACT TYPES comprised the assemblage of objects used by the Iroquois at different times in the past. During Precolumbian times, items were made from stone, bone, clay, shell, wood, and other natural sources. Although such raw materials continued to be exploited following initial contact, new ones were acquired from Europeans, most importantly brass, copper, iron, and glass. These so-called exotics were used "as is" (e.g., brass spoons, copper kettles, iron axes, and glass beads), or the metals were modified into such objects as projectile points, beads, and cone-shaped "tinklers" attached to clothing, among other forms. The authors of this set of five chapters analyze copper items, wampum (marine shell beads), glass beads, ceramic pots, and smoking pipes, just some of the many kinds of artifactual remains frequently recovered from Iroquoian archaeological sites.

In the first essay, James W. Bradley and S. Terry Childs examine puzzling small metal objects called spirals and hoops, made by Iroquois craftsmen using copper obtained from colonial settlers during the sixteenth and early seventeenth centuries. These sophisticated items are among the earliest that Native peoples made from European material. Spirals likely were worn as earrings, hair ornaments, and pendants, while hoops also may have been utilized as pendants. Both were manufactured by rolling sheet copper or copper alloy (from a piece of a kettle, for instance) into a tube, and then either coiling the object into a loose spiral or working it into a circle. The vast majority of the two artifact types have been recovered from sites associated with either the Susquehannock or Five Nations Iroquois, though in the early seventeenth century they also appear at Ontario Iroquoian sites. After about A.D. 1625, they essentially disappear from the archaeological record. Employing physical and chemical analyses, Bradley and Childs determine the composition, source, and fabrication of a sample of these metal items of adornment. They conclude by offering a new interpretation of spirals and hoops—though made from European materials, they were indigenous forms imbued with power drawn from traditional Iroquois cosmology and spiritual beliefs about the healing properties of copper.

No study of Iroquois material culture would be complete without discussion of wampum and European glass trade beads. The next article, by George R. Hamell, looks at how exchange of European objects (including beads) during the sixteenth and seventeenth centuries brought about profound changes in the ideational, sociopolitical, and economic subsystems of the Iroquois and other Native groups in the Northeast. Relying upon documentary sources, oral tradition, and archaeological evidence, Hamell proposes a semantics of color for wampum and glass beads and addresses the affective meanings various colors presumably conveyed to Northern Iroquoians during Precolumbian and Postcolumbian times. According to the author, both white and red are potent colors, symbolizing the sentient aspect of life (i.e., daylight and life itself) and the animate aspect of life (i.e., blood), respectively. Black is characterized by the absence of sentience and animacy, as in states of mourning. Hamell traces shifts in color preferences in glass trade beads among the Iroquois during the sixteenth and seventeenth centuries. The most popular glass trade beads (monochrome or polychrome) recovered from Iroquoian sites dating to this period were ones whose ground colors were either white, black, red, green (green-blue), or blue, and whose forms were primarily either tubular, oval, or spherical. Yellow was not a popular bead color as it was perceived as an unhealthy tone typically associated with disease.

Robert D. Kuhn, in the third piece, seeks to understand when and why warfare occurred among Iroquoian populations. In particular, he studies Native ceramic pots and smoking pipes (as well as settlement patterns) to reconstruct changing Mohawk interaction and conflict with Northern Iroquoian groups of southeast Ontario (i.e., Huron, Petun, and St. Lawrence Iroquoians) between A.D. 1400 and 1700. Stylistic and trace element analyses are applied to ceramics from these societies. Kuhn interprets Huron and St. Lawrence Iroquoian pottery that is made from Mohawk valley clays and recovered from several mid-sixteenth-seventeenth-century Mohawk sites, a period of increased hostilities among Iroquoian communities, as representing the work of Northern Iroquoian female war captives who were adopted into Mohawk groups. In contrast to the pottery, no Mohawk ceramic smoking pipes of Northern Iroquoian origin (based on clay sourcing) were recovered from Mohawk sites dating after about A.D. 1550, though four such examples were found in fifteenth-century Mohawk sites. Unlike pottery, pipes were made by men and were important gift or exchange items, believed to function within a reciprocal interaction network. Thus the author interprets the recovery of Northern Iroquoian pipes on Mohawk sites, before the sixteenth century, as a sign of peaceful trade relations before the onset of warfare. Charting the frequency of Northern Iroquoian ceramic traits in Mohawk pottery and smoking pipe assemblages provides an indication of when conflict originated between these two groups and how its intensity changed through time. The results of both ceramic analyses suggest that warfare between the Mohawk and Northern Iroquoians began and intensified during the early sixteenth century, unrelated to the European presence at first.

The following paper also examines pottery, but in a rather different approach from that of the previous article. Anthony Wonderley attempts to interpret the symbolism of humanoid effigies on Oneida ceramic vessels dating between approximately A.D. 1500 and 1650. He uses multiple clues to speculate that the meanings of the icons were related to corn, femininity, and the domestic environment. The effigies possibly depict cornhusk people, a mythological race of beings affiliated with maize and other crops, and hence may affirm the ways in which Oneida women performed their ritual duties with supernatural beings. Ultimately, Wonderley seeks to understand the ceramic effigies as they may have been perceived in the past by the Oneidas themselves, a distinct challenge.

We conclude with a work by Claude Chapdelaine, which is a detailed site-specific study of an astounding collection of 365 St. Lawrence Iroquoian smoking pipes that are some 500 years old. These ceramic artifacts were excavated from the Mandeville site, a relatively small village containing at least five longhouses on less than two acres, and situated about midway along, and just south of, the St. Lawrence River in Canada. The author addresses the variability, intra-site spatial relationship, function, and significance of the pipes in this unique collection, as he tries to understand why so many were recovered at this site. Like Wonderley in the previous reading, Chapdelaine is also interested in the symbolism of ceramic effigies, but on smoking pipes instead of on pots. As he and others have written, animal effigy pipes may represent guardian spirits, and human effigy pipes are possibly associated with ritualistic healing and curing activities performed by male specialists known as shamans. Whatever their meanings and uses, effigy pipes are considered sacred by contemporary Iroquois.

15 | Basque Earrings and Panther's Tails
The Form of Cross-Cultural Contact in Sixteenth-Century Iroquoia
JAMES W. BRADLEY AND S. TERRY CHILDS

Introduction

SPIRALS AND HOOPS are two related copper artifact forms that occur primarily on sixteenth-century sites in northeastern North America. Although initially viewed as European objects made for trade, analysis of the metals and the methods of fabrication indicate that these artifacts were produced by Native craftsmen. Indeed, they are among the earliest distinctive objects that Native Americans made from European material. Spirals and hoops also have a particular cultural distribution; they occur almost exclusively on Iroquoian sites within the Susquehanna, and adjacent, river drainages. As a result, these artifacts serve as a sensitive probe for examining a Native American response to European contact.

Description

Spirals have long been recognized as an early contact period artifact (Cadzow 1936). As early as 1953, both spirals and hoops were proposed as sixteenth-century forms based on their occurrence within the Seneca Iroquois sequence (Wray and Schoff 1953). Nonetheless, these artifacts were not described in the literature until more recently (Bradley 1987a; Wray et al. 1987). Based on a sample of nearly 200 specimens, these forms can now be defined and analyzed with some confidence.

Previously published in *Metals in Society: Theory Beyond Analysis*, ed. R. M. Ehrenreich, MASCA Research Papers in Science and Archaeology 8, no. 2 (Philadelphia: Univ. Museum of Archaeology and Anthropology, Univ. of Pennsylvania, 1991), 7–17. Printed with permission by Museum Applied Science Center for Archaeology (MASCA), The University Museum of Archaeology and Anthropology, University of Pennsylvania.

Both spirals and hoops are artifacts made from sheet copper or copper alloy. In spite of their overall differences, the two forms are of similar construction. Spirals were, most often, made from a thin, rectangular strip of metal that had been rolled into a tube, then coiled into a loose spiral. The ends were usually tapered and the overall piece carefully finished. Round in section, spirals average between 2 and 3 centimeters (cm) in diameter, although the range can be from 1 to 6 cm. In addition to size, there is also considerable variability in the tightness of the coiling. Occasionally spirals were also made from two pieces of sheet rolled together or even a single solid piece of metal. A typical spiral is illustrated in figure 15.1.

Hoops were also made from a thin, rectangular piece of metal that was first rolled into a tube, then worked into a circle, and finally flattened. The ends were usually finished to a spatulate shape, then lapped and tied. Hoops are generally larger than spirals. The average size is 5–6 cm in diameter although examples range from 1.5 to 17 cm. As with spirals, examples were occasionally made from multiple pieces of sheet worked together or a solid piece of metal. Figure 15.2 illustrates a typical hoop.

Even with minimal examination of the nearly 200 reported examples, two traits stand out. First, these are sophisticated artifacts. It required both technical knowledge and skill to produce them. Their occurrence on the sites of Iroquoian people

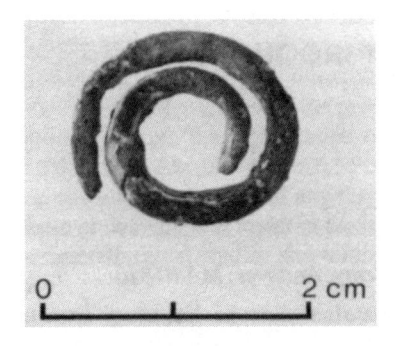

Fig. 15.1. Spiral #76/94 (Rochester Museum and Science Center), from the Seneca Adams site.

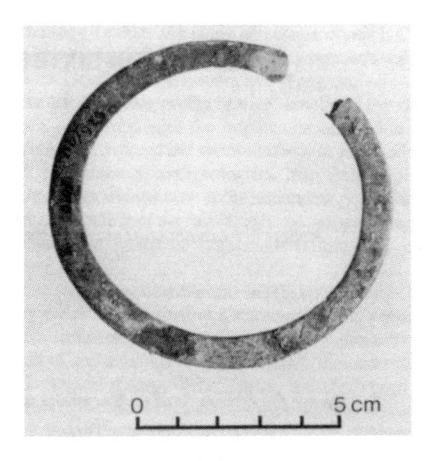

Fig. 15.2. Hoop #526/94 (Rochester Museum and Science Center), from the Seneca Adams site.

not known for a strong, indigenous metalworking tradition is quite notable. Second, while there is considerable variability in the sample, it is the degree of conformity in shape and style that is striking. These points are discussed in greater detail below.

Distribution

Spirals and hoops have a specific chronological and geographical distribution. Based on the existing sample, it is clear that these are primarily sixteenth-century artifacts; over 85 percent are from sites currently dated to the sixteenth century (table 15.1). While spirals are the more commonly occurring form, hoops appear to predominate on the earliest sites. While both forms persist on sites of the early seventeenth century, their occurrence drops off rapidly.

The chronological distribution of spirals and hoops is paralleled by a geographical specificity. As figure 15.3 indicates, these artifacts are concentrated on sites predating ca. 1575 within the Susquehanna and adjacent drainages. Culturally, the sites that produce these artifacts are associated with either the Susquehannock or Five Nations Iroquois. The distribution of spirals and hoops is as notable for where these forms do not occur as it is for where they do. For instance, no examples have been reported from either the St. Lawrence valley or the sites of the Ontario Iroquois. This provides strong support for the argument that much of the earliest European material to reach Native American people in the interior of northeastern North America originated from contacts along the mid-Atlantic coast rather than from the St. Lawrence (Bradley 1987a, 93–95).

During the last quarter of the sixteenth century, the distribution of spirals and hoops remains much the same. The greatest concentration of these artifacts continues to occur on Susquehannock and Five Nations Iroquois sites. The major change is the removal of the Susquehannocks from their upriver sites around Tioga Point to larger, more consolidated settlements in the Washingtonboro Basin (Kent 1993 [1984], 306). Also evident is the spread of these forms, especially spirals, onto the Monongahela sites of the upper Ohio valley and into the Niagara frontier (fig. 15.4). Wherever they occur, the evidence suggests that spirals and hoops were an Iro-

Table 15.1

Chronological Distribution of Spirals and Hoops

Sites Dating	No. of Spirals	No. of Hoops	Total
Pre-1575	44	51	95 (48.5%)
Post-1575	59	13	72 (36.7%)
17th century	21	8	29 (14.8%)
Total	124 (63.3%)	72 (36.7%)	196 (100.0%)

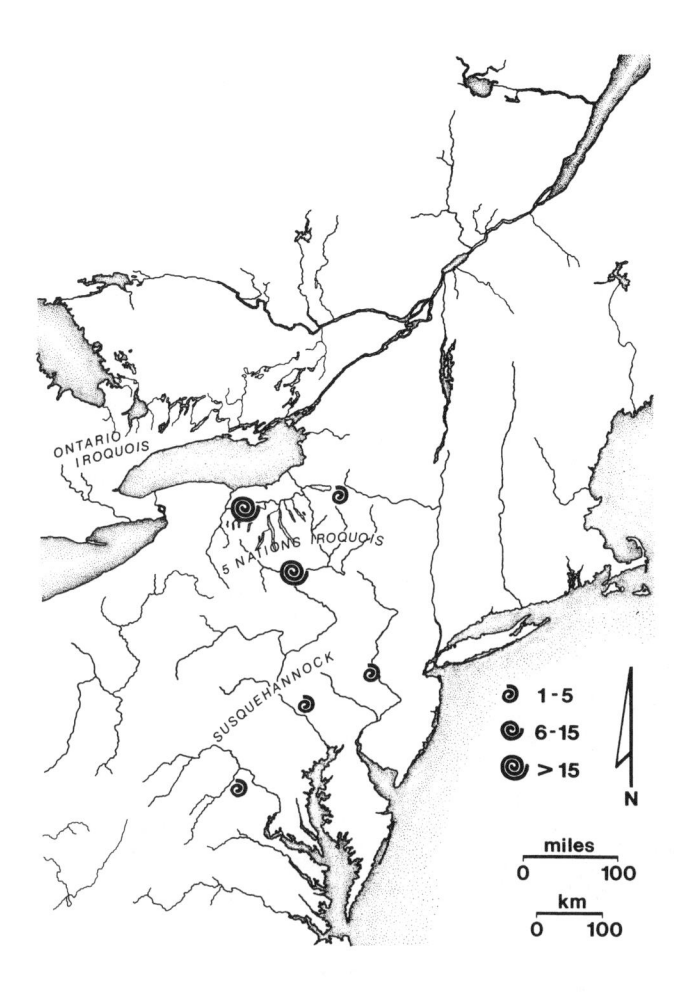

Fig. 15.3. Distribution of spirals and hoops on sixteenth-century sites before 1575.

quoian trait. As in the previous period, no examples have been reported from Algonquian sites, either around Chesapeake Bay or along the Atlantic coast.

By the seventeenth century, spirals and hoops are more thinly and broadly distributed. While still most prevalent on Susquehannock and Five Nations sites, these forms are much less common than they were on previous sixteenth-century sites. During the early seventeenth century, spirals are also found on sites further from the Susquehanna drainage, occurring in Huronia and possibly as far west as the Ft. Ancient sites along the Ohio River. After ca. 1625, spirals and hoops essentially disappear from the archaeological record. It should be noted that the decreasing occurrence of these forms takes place at the same time copper and brass artifacts, of both European and Native make, are becoming increasingly common.

Given the variability in this sample, closer examination of the two largest subsamples, Seneca (90 specimens) and Susquehannock (59 specimens), provides a clearer picture of how these forms were distributed. As figure 15.5 indicates, spirals and hoops quickly reach maximum expression on Seneca sites and then gradually

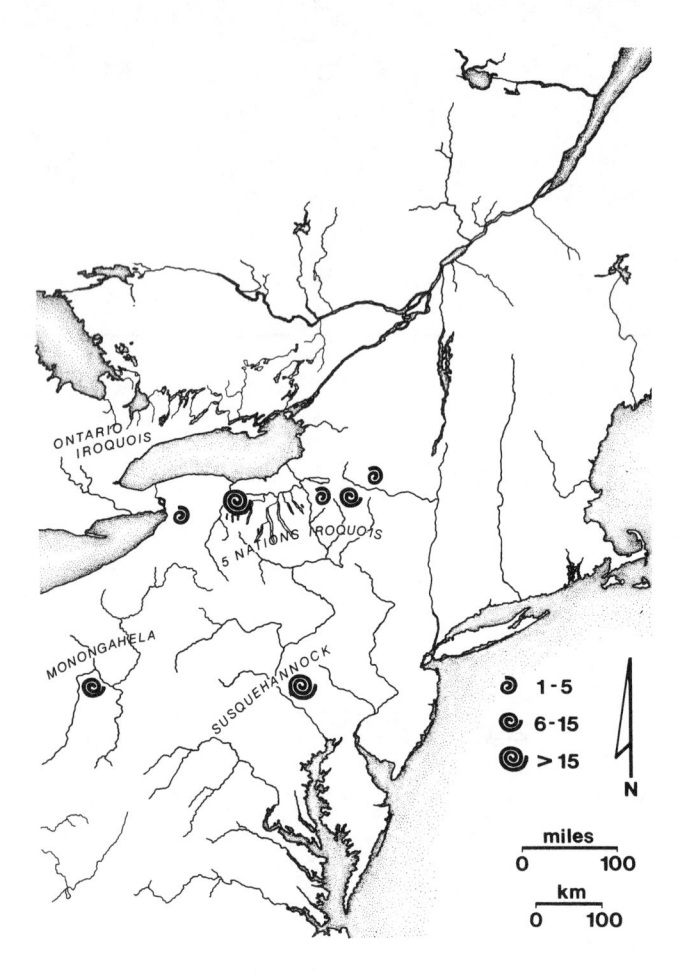

Fig. 15.4. Distribution of spirals and hoops on sixteenth-century sites after 1575.

tail off. The Seneca also appear to have preferred hoops over spirals. On Susquehannock sites, the pattern is quite similar (fig. 15.6). The curve looks different because Susquehannock sites before Schultz occur in a series of contemporary regional clusters rather than a series of seriated sites. Figure 15.6 also indicates that the Susquehannocks, in contrast to the Seneca, had a strong preference for spirals.

Mortuary Associations

While spirals and hoops have been recovered from middens and other occupation-related features, the majority have been found in burials. Spirals most commonly are located on or near the temporal bones, hence their traditional identification as "earrings." It is likely that they were used as either hair or ear ornaments although they were also worn as pendants. Hoops are most frequently found in the neck or chest area. While they often occur in sets, it is not clear how they were worn.

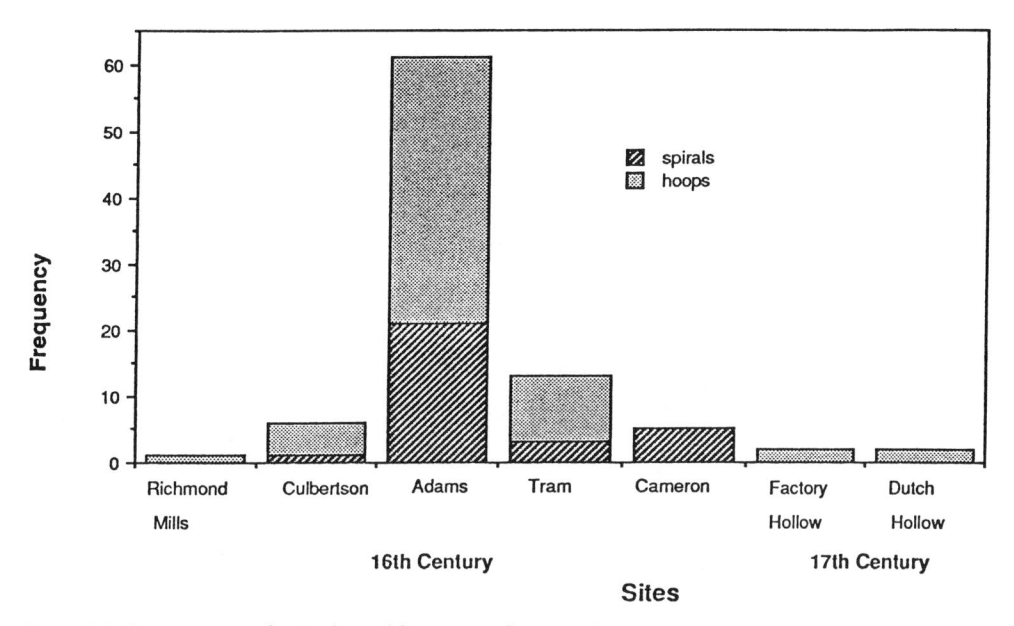

Fig. 15.5. Occurrence of spirals and hoops on Seneca sites.

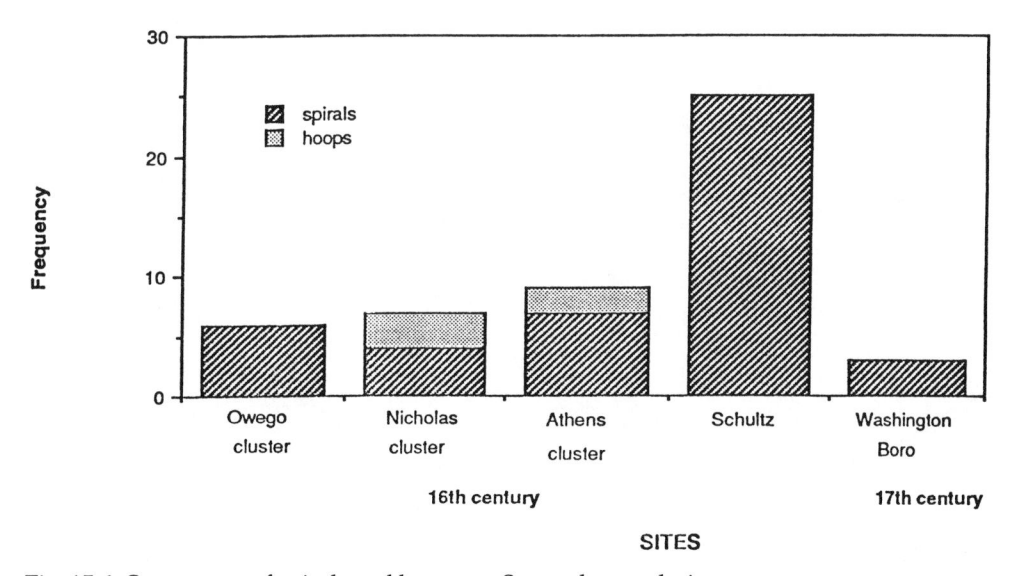

Fig. 15.6. Occurrence of spirals and hoops on Susquehannock sites.

Spirals and hoops are not a random occurrence in these burials. Table 15.2 summarizes their distribution in relation to total number of burials, burials with European materials, and age groups. Again, several patterns are evident. On pre-1575 sites, spirals and/or hoops appear in roughly 5 percent of the burials with no preference for the individual's age. On post-1575 sites, two changes take place. First, the occurrence of these forms in Seneca burials decreases, while in Susquehannock

Table 15.2
Mortuary Associations for Spirals and Hoops

Sites	Total Burials	Burials with European material	Burials with Spirals	Association by Age Group A	B	C	D	E	Burials with Hoops	Association by Age Group[a] A	B	C	D	E
SUSQUEHANNOCK														
Pre-1575	75	8 (10.7%)	4 (5.3%)	0	1	0	2	1	3 (4.0%)	0	0	1	2	0
Post-1575	120	86 (71.7%)	15 (12.5%)	7	5	0	0	3	0 (0%)	0	0	0	0	0
SENECA														
Pre-1575	266	47 (17.7%)	12 (4.5%)	2	4	2	4	0	19 (7.1%)	0	4	4	11	0
Post-1575	232	53 (22.8%)	6 (2.6%)	1	3	1	1	0	3 (1.3%)	0	2	0	1	0

[a] Age group associations: A—Infants (<1 yr); B—Children (1–12 yrs); C—Adolescents (12–18 yrs); D—Adults (>18 yrs); E—Unknown.

burials it more than doubles (at least in the case of spirals). This change may reflect the Susquehannocks' closer proximity to sources of European material after relocating to the Washingtonboro Basin. The second change is that these artifacts now occur almost exclusively with infants and children, both on Seneca and Susquehannock sites. Whatever these forms meant to Native people, it appears that they were not primarily markers of achieved status.

Materials and Technology

A variety of physical and chemical analyses were performed in order to address three questions: (1) Composition—from what materials were these artifacts made? (2) Source—where did the material(s) originate? (3) Fabrication—how were these objects made, and who made them? Among the methods used in the analysis were metallography, chemical analysis by electron microprobe and atomic absorption, and visual examination as well as other noninvasive techniques. This section reviews these analyses and applies the results to the three questions above.

Through a research grant from the Rochester Museum and Science Center, we were able to perform metallographic analysis on four objects: two spirals and a hoop from the Seneca Adams site, and a spiral from the Onondaga Dwyer site. The samples were prepared and analyzed by us (Childs) at the CMRAE (Center for Materials Research in Archaeology and Ethnology) laboratory, Massachusetts Institute of Technology. The results are summarized below.

Spiral #76/94

This small, delicate spiral (fig. 15.1), though now heavily corroded, was finely made and finished. Despite the corrosion, an irregular seam line was visible indicating that the piece had been hammered, trimmed, and rolled into a tube. Numerous small inclusions were distributed throughout the polished section. Chemical analysis by electron microprobe indicated that these were not cuprous oxides but contained appreciable amounts of lead. At least two kinks, or yield points, were also visible in the polished cross-section, indicating that the tube was not annealed fully enough to be worked into a smooth spiral. A final anneal was performed on this spiral after rounds of hammering and reheating (fig. 15.7). This is indicated by the presence of large, undeformed grains with well-developed parallel bands or twins.

Spiral #178/94

Spiral #178/94 (fig. 15.8) was similar to #76/94 in terms of general characteristics and construction. One major difference was the number and severity of yield

298 · *Material Culture Studies*

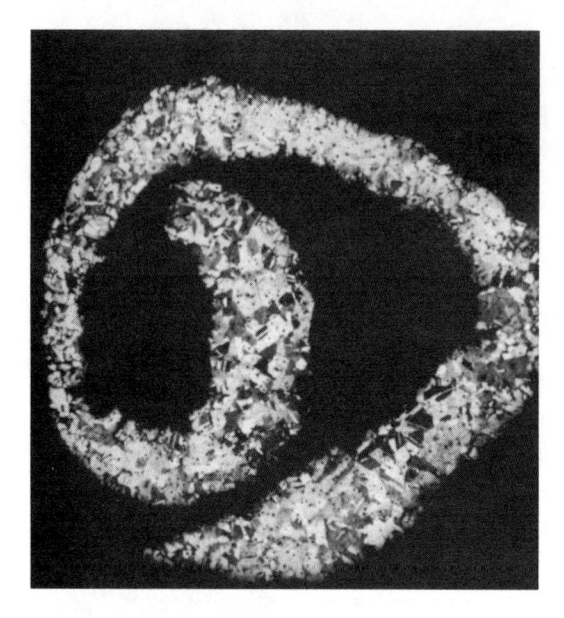

Fig. 15.7. Annealed structure in the cross-section of spiral #76/94 (see fig. 15.1). Potassium dichromate etch. Original magnification 32×.

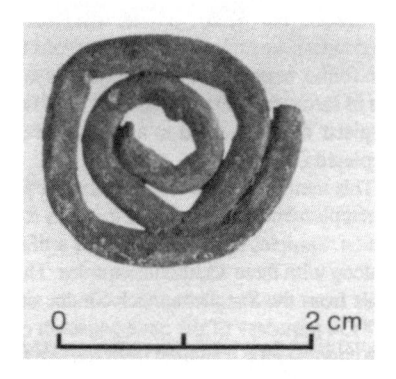

Fig. 15.8. Spiral #178/94 (Rochester Museum and Science Center), from the Seneca Adams site.

points, perhaps because of the length of the tube. While the tube was not sufficiently annealed during spiraling, the original sheet had been thoroughly annealed before being rolled into the tube. In cross section, the bends are smooth and each layer lies flush with the other. While the piece was subjected to a final anneal after spiraling, the last step was a light hammering to flatten the spiral. This step is reflected in the cross-section by the presence of smaller grains and slip bands at the inner corners of the bends.

Hoop #526/94

Large, finely made hoop #526/94 (fig. 15.2) was constructed in a manner similar to that of the preceding spirals. Instead of being fabricated from one piece of sheet, the original tube was made from two smaller pieces folded together. A section view shows that the tube was made with sufficient annealing to produce smooth and uniform bends without yield points. The final treatment of this piece was similar to that used on #178/94; while most of the metal was annealed, the grains along the inner surface of the bends were smaller and contained a considerable number of slip bands (fig. 15.9). These features appear to have resulted from the following sequence: flattening of the circled tube, annealing it one more time, then finishing the object with a few carefully executed blows at the edges to ensure uniformity and to smooth down the seam.

Spiral DW-1

Small spiral DW-1 (fig. 15.10) showed many of the same traits as the preceding pieces. While the seam from rolling the tube is more obvious, the spiraling was done with sufficient skill that each revolution was kept flush with its predecessor without yield points forming. The cross-section shows many inclusions, often elon-

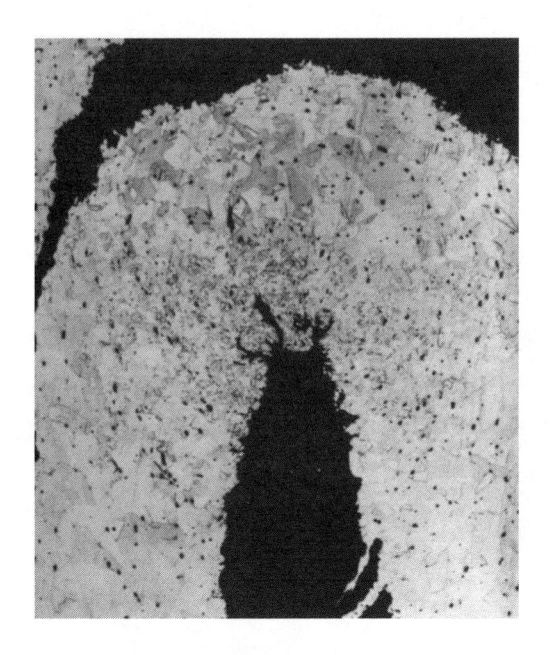

Fig. 15.9. Annealed structure at one bend in the cross-section of hoop #526/94 (see fig. 15.2). Note smaller grains on inside surface of bend. Potassium dichromate etch. Original magnification 100×.

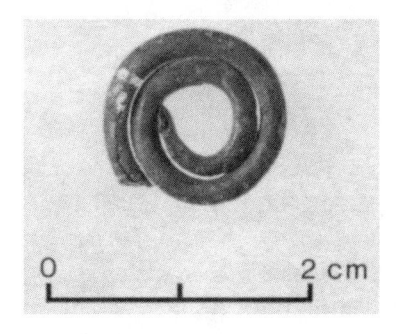

Fig. 15.10. Spiral (private collection) from the Onondaga Dwyer site.

gated from hammering. With the assistance of a polarizing attachment on the metallographic microscope, it was determined that these inclusions were cuprous oxides that are often found in smelted, relatively pure copper. The presence of large, uniform grains with twinning indicates that this piece was subjected to a final annealing after it was completed (fig. 15.11).

This metallographic examination for physical structure was supplemented by chemical analysis to determine composition. Samples from the same four artifacts were submitted along with three additional samples. These included two spirals from the Susquehannock Schultz site (36La9), #183 and #134 (courtesy of the State Museum of Pennsylvania), and a copper kettle fragment from the late sixteenth-century Onondaga Chase site, CZAS-3. The results of this analysis are summarized in table 15.3. Finally, an additional 28 spirals from Susquehannock sites were examined for metal color and presence of yield points. Several of these specimens were also tested with a Koslow Corporation Metal Identification Set (#1899). This set provided a quick, qualitative test for the presence of particular alloys.

Analysis revealed that all the tested specimens were smelted copper or copper alloy. The presence of oxide inclusions as well as compositions including zinc, tin, lead, and nickel support this conclusion. In terms of composition, the artifacts tested fell into two groups. The majority—all three Seneca and both Susquehan-

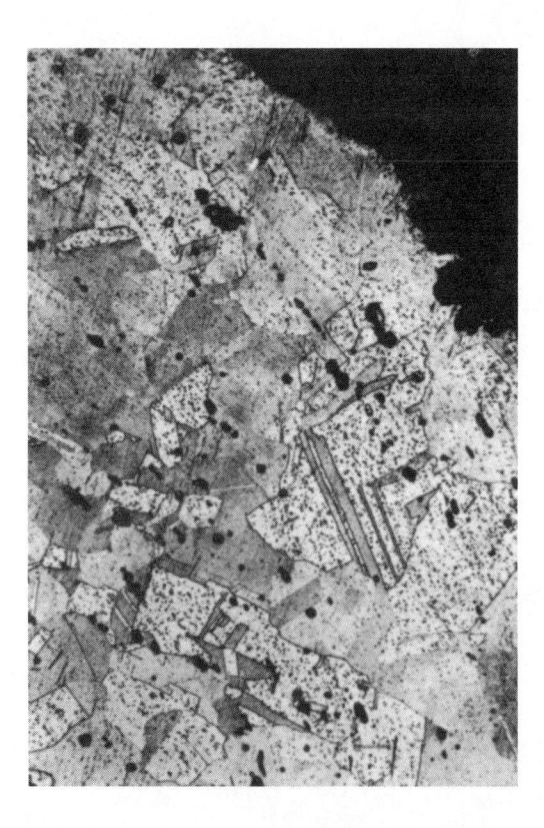

Fig. 15.11. Annealed structure in the cross-section of the Dwyer spiral (see fig. 15.10). Potassium dichromate etch. Original magnification 50×.

Table 15.3
Chemical Analysis by Atomic Absorption

Sample	Artifact Type	Cu[a]	Zn	Sn	Ag	Pb	Ni
SENECA							
76/94	spiral	73.59	25.14	IS[b]	0.027	0.85	0.24
178/94	spiral	81.47	16.73	1.31	0.069	0.25	0.02
526/94	hoop	67.86	30.69	0.03	0.027	0.98	0.26
SUSQUEHANNOCK							
36La9/134	spiral	81.90	13.59	3.26	0.12	0.68	0.09
36La9/183	spiral	88.44	10.98	IS	0.06	0.48	0.04
ONONDAGA							
DW-1	spiral	99.38	0.04	IS	0.08	0.30	0.05
CZA5–3	kettle frag.	99.74	0.003	0.003	0.06	0.16	0.03

[a] Calculated by subtraction.
[b] Insufficient sample.

nock examples—were the copper-zinc alloy, brass. While the two Onondaga examples were copper of a very high purity (+99 percent), it is important to note that both pieces were a smelted, not native, copper. Analysis of the additional 28 Susquehannock spirals suggested that approximately 50 percent were brass and 50 percent copper. Clearly, at least two different stocks of European metal were used in fabricating these artifacts.

Recent research on the sources of European metals available to Native Americans suggests that during the last half of the sixteenth century at least two different production and exchange networks were in operation. Best documented is the Basque network that brought copper kettles from Bordeaux and other Biscay ports to the Canadian Maritimes between 1580 and 1600. Archival sources describe these as "kettles of red copper" and provide important details on size, construction, and numbers taken for trade (Turgeon 1990, 85). Archaeological investigation has documented the occurrence of a distinctive copper kettle form, one that corresponds closely with those described in the documentary record. Unlike the traditional "trade kettle," this form is characterized by robust iron banding, patterned battery work (produced through mechanical hammering), and a distinct folded lip or shelf (Fitzgerald et al. 1993). Archaeologically, these kettles, and pieces of them, are found primarily in the Maritimes and the St. Lawrence river drainage. Analysis of a fragment from the Onondaga Chase site (see above) confirms that these kettles were indeed "red copper."

A second network appears to have brought brass to the mid-Atlantic coast during the third quarter of the sixteenth century. While the documentary record is less complete, Norman merchants from ports such as Honfleur and Havre were active along the Atlantic coast from at least 1559 on. In contrast to the Basque trade assemblage, the Normans appear to have preferred brass to copper (Turgeon 1990, 85). This preference is not surprising given the proximity of major brass production centers such as Aachen and Antwerp. Archaeologically, brass is the first European metal to occur on Susquehannock and Five Nations Iroquois sites. The distribution of brass artifacts on protohistoric Iroquoian sites suggests that the mid-Atlantic coast was the most likely source. In sum, both the documentary and archaeological records indicate that spirals and hoops were made from at least two different stocks of metal that arrived in the New World via different routes.

While metallographic analysis indicates how these artifacts were made, the question of who fabricated them remains. Three lines of evidence argue that these objects were made by Native people, not Europeans. First is the evidence that different metals were used to produce the same forms on the same site. If spirals were a European product, one would predict that their distribution would coincide with the sphere of influence of whoever traded them. Instead the distribution of spirals and hoops appears to be largely independent of European patterns of trade and more reflective of the indigenous exchange networks for marine shell and exotic lithics that drew on a wide range of sources. Indeed, the assemblages of brass and copper artifacts from sixteenth-century Iroquoian sites are notable for their heterogeneity of material.

A second argument for Native fabrication is that, while these artifacts bear none of the signatures of European craftsmanship, they are technically well within the documented abilities of Native Americans. Conspicuous by their absence are any indications that metal tools (such as files or vises) or common techniques for joining metals (brazing or soldering) were employed in the making of these objects. On the other hand, sophisticated sheet work that employed multiple anneals and all the manipulations needed to produce a spiral or hoop was practiced by Hopewellian craftsmen at least as early as 1800 B.P. (Greber and Ruhl 1989, 144–45). While this metalworking technology did not remain as visible in the archaeological record of the Northeast as it did among the Mississippian peoples of the Southeast (Leader 1988), these skills were apparently not lost. Native craftsmen appear to have taken the techniques developed for working native copper and applied them to the new materials brought by Europeans. The argument for Native fabrication is strengthened by the presence of trimmings and partially completed objects on Iroquoian habitation sites. After metallographic examination of several specimens from the mid-sixteenth-century Susquehannock component at the Engelbert site, Helene R. Dunbar and Katharine C. Ruhl (1974) reached the same conclusion: spirals and hoops were most probably made by Native craftsmen using European material but indigenous technology.

A final argument in favor of Native fabrication is that this provides the best explanation for the observed variability in spirals and hoops, both in terms of the objects themselves and in their distribution. As observed earlier, considerable variability exists in how spirals and hoops were made, yet it is the degree of conformity in shape and style that is striking. In this, spirals and hoops are most similar to Hopewellian earspools; different techniques were used to produce essentially the same form. To paraphrase Katharine Ruhl, the fabricators were evidently not constrained by one set of formulae in constructing these artifacts (Greber and Ruhl 1989, 145). The variability in distribution also argues for Native production as opposed to importation. The Seneca preferred hoops, while spirals were more popular among the Susquehannocks. Similar localized preferences are evident in other artifact classes that reused European metals (Bradley 1987a, 75).

To summarize, the three lines of evidence strongly support the hypothesis that these artifacts were the product of Native American craftsmen even though the materials used were of European origin.

Meaning

Traditional interpretations of spirals and hoops have assumed that these objects were European in concept as well as material. Whether made by Europeans as trade merchandise or copied by Native craftsmen, the value of these forms to Native Americans was presumed to lie in their European origin. In his article on archaeology and the fur trade, John Witthoft typified this view, seeing spirals and hoops as little more than European forms in a new context. Hoops were "metal rings from rigging" while "spiral brass earrings, worn in the left ears of Indian burials represent[ed] a direct transference of the ancient sailor's caste mark . . . against bad eyesight" (Witthoft 1966, 204–5). Based on no more evidence than this, the term *Basque earring* has crept into the literature along with its ethnocentric assumptions.

Given the strong evidence that these objects were made by Native Americans, we propose a different interpretation—that spirals and hoops, though made from European material, were Native forms that drew their meaning and power from traditional Native beliefs and cosmology. To argue for this interpretation we must revisit European contact and try to see it from an aboriginal point of view. To Native eyes, the first Europeans appeared as returning cultural heroes, otherworldly man-beings who rose up from beneath the World's rim on floating islands, bringing with them a wealth of Under(water) World substances. As George R. Hamell and others have pointed out, Europeans could not have chosen more appropriate materials to bring with them (Hamell 1987b; Simmons 1986). The brass trinkets and glass beads may not have had much value in European eyes, but to Native Americans, the objects offered by these strange man-beings were the traditional substances of life-enhancing and life-restoring power. Although the equating of ritual substances, native copper in this case, with European materials would certainly change, it helps to explain the initial Native response. In the beginning, Native Americans saw Europeans and their exotic material wealth as a part of their own world, not somebody else's.

What we propose is that spirals and hoops were a material residue of this initial Native response, one that revived the use of copper for ritual healing and invoked its traditional guardian, the Underwater Panther. The clearest expression of this linkage occurs among the Algonquian tribes of the Upper Great Lakes during the late eighteenth and nineteenth centuries. Here the Underwater Panther, the dominant power of the Underworld (and complement of the Thunderbird in the Upperworld) was portrayed as a powerful cat-like creature with horns and a long, spirally tail often described as made of or covered by copper scales. Those fortunate enough to find or possess a piece of copper from the Panther's tail had a charm of great healing power (Phillips 1986, 29–30).

While this is, admittedly, a nineteenth-century view, there are good reasons for arguing that this linkage is of much greater antiquity. Panthers are often represented in the archaeological record on seventeenth-century Iroquoian sites and usually occur on artifacts with strong ritual associations such as pipes and warclubs. The earliest version of the origins of the Iroquoian Little Water Medicine, in which the panther plays the key role in healing a slain warrior, was recorded by the Jesuits in 1636 (Thwaites 1896–1901, 10:177). Representations of panther manbeings (shamans wearing panther-skin robes) occur on precontact Iroquoian sites and have precedents extending back to the Middle Woodland (Brose et al. 1985, 185).

What we propose is that the explicit linkage between the healing power of copper and the Panther's spiral tail recorded in the nineteenth century was an echo of another, earlier linkage, one that grew out of the initial contacts between Europeans and Iroquoians. In addition to material wealth, Europeans also brought a wide range of new diseases. While Henry F. Dobyns's estimates on postcontact mortality rates among Iroquoians are excessive (Dobyns 1983, 313–25), there is no question that new diseases had an impact. It is our hypothesis that spirals and hoops represented an appeal to the healing power of the Panther, a means for invoking protection for those least able to protect themselves.

Conclusion

In sixteenth-century North America, copper was the preferred cross-cultural medium of exchange, just as shell (in the form of wampum) would be in the seventeenth century. Though valued by both Europeans and Native Americans, copper's worth was defined for each by very different cultural standards.

The quincentennial anniversary of Columbus's landing in the New World is a particularly appropriate time to examine these cultural differences and to try to see

Native Americans and their response to Europeans in an appropriate context. While our "Panther's tail" hypothesis may not be correct, we believe it is, at least, in the right direction. Rather than perpetuate the view of Native Americans implicit in the "Basque earrings" interpretation—a simple, passive people just waiting to be discovered—we prefer to see their behavior as analogous to our own, struggling to make sense out of the unexpected in life by trying to reconcile it with what we already know and believe.

Acknowledgments

We are pleased to acknowledge the assistance of several colleagues on this project. Among those who generously shared information with us are: Dolores Elliot, George Hamell, James Herbstritt, Barry Kent, Charles Lucy, Lorraine Saunders, and Martha Sempowski. We would also like to thank Stephen Warfel, curator for archaeology at the State Museum of Pennsylvania, for permission to test specimens from Susquehannock sites. Finally, the metallographic and chemical testing of the Seneca specimens was made possible through a grant from the Arthur C. Parker Fund, administered through the Rochester Museum and Science Center.

16 | The Iroquois and the World's Rim
Speculations on Color, Culture, and Contact

GEORGE R. HAMELL

CONTACT BETWEEN THE PEOPLES of the New World and of the Old World had ideational consequences for both. The event of contact, and more importantly the process of contact, initiated the reciprocal redefinition of the mythical realities that for centuries, if not millennia, had structured New World and Old World thoughts and behaviors about the other world. Neither the event nor the process of contact is over. For the Iroquois, dwelling beneath the Great Tree at the center of Earth-Island, indirect knowledge of contact at the eastern World's Rim and the indirect receipt of exotic trade goods emanating there, appear to have reified and reinvigorated the traditional ritual meanings and functions of light, bright (reflective), and white things. Not least among these were white marine shell and red, upper Great Lakes native copper, into whose meanings and functions were incorporated and assimilated analogous European trade goods of glazed ceramic, glass, and metal. This seemingly innocuous exchange of European baubles, bangles, and beads along the mid-Atlantic Coast of northeastern North America during the sixteenth century catalyzed profound changes in the ideational, sociopolitical, and economic subsystems of coastal and interior Native populations.

At the turn of the sixteenth century the indigenous populations of northeastern North America were either Algonquian, Northern Iroquoian, or Siouan speakers (Trigger 1978d). The latter were by far in the minority and were found nearer the mid-Atlantic coast, while the majority were speakers of diverse Algonquian languages. With the exception of the Meherrin, Nottaway, and Tuscarora of the coastal Virginia and Carolina regions to the southeast and the so-called St. Lawrence Iroquoians to the northeast, the remaining Northern Iroquoian speakers dwelt in the

Previously published in *The American Indian Quarterly* 16 (1992): 451–69. Reprinted with permission by the University of Nebraska Press, copyright © 1992.

interior in what is now north-central Pennsylvania, western and central New York, and southwestern Ontario, bordering the Great Lakes of Erie and Ontario.

These northern Iroquoian speakers have since been linguistically differentiated into 11 regional populations, which with caution can be identified with as many historically attested geosociopolitical entities, or tribes (nations), bearing the same linguistic identifiers (Lounsbury 1978; Trigger 1978d, 282–89, 357–417, 466–524). Caution is required because the event and process of contact seem to have been factors in the tribalization of at least some of these regional populations. Furthermore, many of the so-called historic Northern Iroquoian tribes were initially regional confederations of more or less biologically, linguistically, and ethnically distinct communities.

The seventeenth-century Seneca, or "the people of the great hill," are one such geosociopolitical entity (Hamell 1980; Hamell and John 1987; cf. Abler and Tooker 1978; Abrams 1976). Despite the implication of homogeneity, a Northern Iroquoian "tribal" designation frequently masked considerable linguistic, biological, and even ethnic-cultural diversity among its constituent populations. Countering the centrifugal tendency of this diversity was the stronger centripetal force of community-focused kinship and the reciprocal responsibilities of consequent social relations. Kinship was the paradigm that integrated Northern Iroquoian populations into successively larger geosociopolitical entities: beginning with the longhouse matrilineage, to the clan (and moiety), to the village, to the confederated villages comprising the tribe, and to the tribes comprising interregional confederacies, the Iroquois Confederacy—originally comprised of the Seneca, Cayuga, Onondaga, Oneida, and Mohawk—being the best-known example.

Glottochronology and comparative linguistic research among the Northern Iroquoians suggest that their historic distribution overlaps that of their probable "homeland": the northern Appalachian Plateau region of north-central Pennsylvania and south-central New York, and astraddle divides between major riverine systems draining toward the southwest, southeast, and northeast (Lounsbury 1978). From their ethnocentric perspective, the Real Men, or the Iroquois proper, indeed occupied the highest land upon Earth-Island.

The Northern Iroquoians, like many of their Algonquian and Siouan neighbors, were relatively recent swidden horticulturalists (Chafe 1964; Fenton 1978; Tooker 1970). The Three Sisters or Our Life Supporters—that is, maize, beans, and squash, as we so unhumanly refer to them—had been introduced to Northeastern Woodland populations about 1,000 years ago (Tuck 1978; J. Wright 1984). For thousands of years earlier, however, Northern Iroquoian speakers, like their Algonquian and Siouan neighbors, had been hunters, fishermen, and gatherers nearly exclusively (Ritchie 1980; Ritchie and Funk 1973). Swidden horticulture did not displace these earlier subsistence bases, but was incorporated within them. Its recent incorporation is tellingly revealed linguistically, ritually, and archaeologically.

The religion, or, as I prefer, the mythical reality of the Northern Iroquoians generally, and of the Iroquois proper, differed little from that of their swidden-horticulturalist and hunting, fishing, and gathering Algonquian and Siouan neighbors (Hamell 1987a). This mythical reality was in structure and process the ancient, shamanistically based worldview of the hunter, the fisherman, and the gatherer. It was a mythical reality also integrated by the reciprocal responsibilities of kinship. Northern Iroquoians, Algonquians, and Siouans did not live in a *natural* world, but in a *social* world inhabited by human kinds of people—real men (man-beings)—and by other-than-human kinds of people. The latter comprise the mind-less, will-less, and soul-less biological, geological, meteorological, and astronomical phenomena, which we call *nature* in distinction to *culture*.

Within Northern Iroquoian mythical reality, ritual was a social contract invested among human man-beings to maintain the social order that had been chartered by the Master of Life to obtain among all man-beings. Quite naturally, or I should say, quite culturally, social order was the ideal state-of-being, a state of individual and collective well-being: physically and spiritually, as well as socially. Failure to maintain this ritual or social contract precipitated entropy in relations, and in its asocial and antisocial consequences. For the Northern Iroquoian, such literal and figurative dark times, characterized by war, famine, and pestilence, were heralded by the return of the primal, white fire dragon (serpent≈panther) man-being of discord, the alter ego of the meteor (comet) man-being (Hamell 1991, 49–60).

Northern Iroquoian mythical reality was a generally equalitarian social order, although the reciprocal responsibilities that obtained among and between grandmothers, grandfathers, mothers, fathers, aunts, uncles, nieces, nephews, sisters, brothers, and cousins were not always symmetrical. Social distance—generational distance in particular—was a primary variable in structuring the context and content of social relations.

The World's Rim

At the turn of the sixteenth century the mythical reality of the Northern Iroquoians, like the mythical reality of their Old World contemporaries, was ethnocentric, anthropocentric, and geocentric. According to the traditional mythical reality of the Iroquois proper, they as Real Men dwell at the center, sheltered beneath a great white pine tree (man-being), located at the middle of the back of a great turtle (man-being) afloat in the middle of a great lake, beyond which lies the World's Rim (Fenton 1962). Daylight is provided by Elder Brother Sun (man-being) as he glides westward overhead along the interior surface of the sky dome from his place of emergence in the east, pausing overhead at noon to look down upon the affairs of men. At the World's Rim to the west, Elder Brother Sun begins his nocturnal passage east through the below world, and the traditional home of the souls of the deceased, to emerge once again in the east to the thanksgivings of human man-beings.

Surrounded by its cornfields, slashed and burned from the surrounding forest, the typical late prehistoric Iroquois village was the world in microcosm. The Woods'-edge surrounding the village was analogous to the World's Rim. Both were ritual thresholds, where mythical time and space converged: the setting and context for rites of passage, and for social exchanges between real human man-beings and other-than-human man-beings.[1] Among the latter are the grandfathers, keepers of precious substances or medicines of well-being and of the rituals associated with them, who habitually dwell at liminal places: in deep springs, rivers, and lakes, in caves and rocky places, and at the World's Rim, beyond the great waters surrounding Earth-Island.[2]

Such substances and rituals were the gifts with which those on vision quest, or the long-lost warrior or hunter, returned, having accidentally wandered to such extremes. While all knew of the World's Rim and of what one could expect to find there, few real human man-beings had ever actually journeyed there, and fewer still had ever returned. Nevertheless, the World's Rim was a reality, a mythical reality that underlay the cultural efficacy of substances and goods originating there, and most frequently received through exchange from other real human man-beings, who likewise knew of the ultimate source of such things, but again only indirectly through others.

At the turn of the sixteenth century, the eastern World's Rim of Iroquois mythical reality and the western World's Rim or edge of the world of European mythical reality were brought into physical and metaphysical, tangential relation, at first sporadically and then permanently. Here within a shared geographical and metaphysical frontier, the mythical reality of one world began its redefinition in relation to the mythical reality of the other world, a process that continues through the present.[3]

1. Both the World's Rim and the Woods-edge were places of requisite transformation, before entry. One must be made fit to enter either the Village of the Souls, or the villages of real human man-beings. This was a rite of passage requiring the individual's remaking: an act of physical, social, and spiritual purification, and concomitant kinship affirmation or confirmation. Historically, these rites of passage for departing or arriving kinsmen at the Woods'-edge included wampum and/or calumet ceremonies and the departure of war parties, and their return with scalps and captives, to take the place of deceased community members. For further discussion with citations, and appended narratives of such transformations, see Hamell (1981).

2. Principal among these grandfathers are the antlered or horned, great serpent, dragon, and panther man-beings of Northern Iroquoian (and Central Algonquian) mythical realities. The scales of these man-beings are most frequently identified with metallic substances (i.e., brass, copper, and silver), and, with decreasing frequency, muscovite mica plates, quartz crystals, archaeological silicious bifaces, and shell (Hamell 1983, 13–17; 1991, 68–74, 98–99).

3. For a very recent discussion of this process, see Trigger (1991a; 1991b). What Trigger seems to contrast in the title of his first paper is an *emic* versus an *etic* interpretation of the archaeological residue

Along this shared cultural frontier, exotic substances and objects of the mythical reality of the one culture acquired an elevated cultural efficacy within the other's mythical reality.[4] We tend to think that this process was one-sided. The seeming naïveté of the Indian response to European baubles, bangles, and beads is the stereotypical example. However, this process of the mundane of one mythical reality becoming the exotic of another mythical reality, assuming a disproportionate ideational efficacy within its recipient culture, was a reciprocal cultural phenomenon. How else do we explain the *Old* World ideational (religious or scientific) interest in *New* World artificialia? Twined fiber bags, quill-decorated moccasins, steatite smoking pipes, wooden ball-headed warclubs, and more, acquired and collected by European traders, travelers, scholars, and kings from the northeastern New World, were placed in proud display in so-called cabinets of curiosities, the ancestors of today's great Old World ethnographical collections and museums (Burch 1990; Hamell 1987c).

Light, Bright, and White Things Are Good to Think

The lure of exotic and of literally and figuratively precious substances brought the mythical reality of the *Old* World into tangential relations with the *New* World. What were among these substances, so precious in the Old World, that lured men in small boats to the ends of the world, as known? Gold, silver, diamonds, and pearls, which had long been, and still are, traditional Western European material metaphors of value, not only of *economic* value but of *ideational* value as well (Gombrich 1963, 12–29). Before bank books, stocks and bonds, and paper currencies—that is, paper symbols of wealth—these substances comprised tangible and conspicuous metaphors of cultural value, encoded and manifested linguistically and synesthetically within figures of speech, in clothing and adornment, and in works of art and architecture. Invested within these substances and the artifacts

---

of contact behavior. Although the former interpretation is equally rational, as Trigger acknowledges, he unfortunately terms it a "romantic" interpretation. Nor, as the paper's title suggests, is it an "either-or" choice of interpretation. Rather, Trigger argues in his two papers that both interpretations of the archaeological data are necessary for a closer approximation of the "truth." While Trigger correctly characterizes my approach to the interpretation of the archaeological data of contact as of the "romantic" school, I too had proposed that the indigenous mythical reality that initially mediated contact immediately began an ongoing process of redefinition, so that it would rationally reflect the reality of the here and now, as culturally constituted (Hamell 1987a, 79–88).

4. See Alfred Goldsworthy Bailey: "no treatment of primitive economics could be complete without some consideration of the religious factors, however brief it may be. . . . It will serve our purpose here if we bear in mind the fact that the efficacy of an implement, for example, was determined by factors which operated from beyond the material world" (1937, 47).

made from them was a millennia-old fusion of aesthetic and ideational interest and value.

Like most biological organisms, humans are phototropic: they grow toward the light. As sentient biological organisms, humans tend toward the light, whether it be the Sun or *the Son.* As sentient biological organisms, humans understand that light is life, and that light is the prerequisite to animacy and sentience. This is a fundamental and, I daresay, universal cultural axiom that has generated parallel dependent corollaries manifested cross-culturally in human thought and behavior, linguistic and physical.

Light (sources), bright (reflective), and white things are tangible metaphors for abstractions of greatest cultural value: for life itself, and for positive states of physical, social, and spiritual well-being. We should remind ourselves that the great value that Western culture places upon the Golden Rule, or upon a gem or pearl of wisdom, lies not with their economic worth, but with their reflective virtues.

For millennia in the Old World, such substances and artifacts fashioned from them have represented wealth as weal, or well-being. The Iroquois and other Northeastern Woodland Indian peoples would agree with this characterization of wealth as well-being. Among them, however, wealth as well-being is more generally appreciated as medicine: the insurance and assurance of physical, social, and spiritual well-being, individually or collectively invoked in ritual. Within ritual contexts, these concepts of well-being have traditionally constellated about white shell, and more recently about another, bright, light-reflective, white substance: a "white metal," silver.

In the interior mid-Atlantic region at contact, the "diamonds of the country" were the relatively scarce and small cylindrical or barrel-shaped beads of white marine shell, which were to become recorded in contemporary documents as *sewant* (Dutch), *porcelaine* (French), and *wampumpeague,* shortened to *wampum* (English).[5] It was Jacques Cartier in 1535, speaking of the St. Lawrence Iroquoians, who established the convention of making the comparison between the Northeastern Woodland Indians' interest and desire for these seemingly inconsequential small white

---

5. The term *wampum* is a shortened form of a southern New England Algonquian term, *wampumpeage,* which translates as "a string of white [shell beads]" (Hewitt 1907–10, 904; cf. Aubin 1975, 108). Although the term specifically refers to white (marine) shell beads, the abbreviated form, *wampum,* became a gloss for both the white marine shell beads and the purple ("black") marine shell beads of the same shape and size. The French term, *porcelaine,* referred specifically to the white beads only of this shape and size, originally. The term's primary contemporaneous referents were the exotic and precious, white translucent-bodied ceramics (china) originating in the Far East. The French term itself derived from the Italian term for the cowry shell, *porcellana,* whose substance these ceramics resembled. *Porcellana* translates "of a sow," and encodes the resemblance between the ventral opening of the cowry shell and the vulva of a sow (cf. Morris 1980, 1020).

(marine) shell beads, and that of Western Europeans for gold, silver, diamonds, and pearls.[6]

A Semantics of Color, Ritual, and Material Culture

Among the Northern Iroquoians, and the Northeastern Woodland Indians generally, color is a semantically organizing principle of ritual states-of-being and of ritual material culture. Three colors predominate: white, black, and red.[7] These col-

---

6. "The most precious article they possess in this world is *esnoguy*, which is as white as snow. They procure it from shells. . . . of which they make a sort of bead, which has the same use among them as gold and silver with us" (Biggar 1924, 158–60). Compare Paul le Jeune, speaking of the "great riches" of the Montagnais Algonquians in 1632: "Their gold and silver, their diamonds and pearls, are little white grains of porcelain" (Thwaites 1896–1901, 5:61).

7. It is noted that neither "white" nor "black" are true colors. Among some northeastern Woodland Indians, (light) green-blue-ness is semantically equivalent to that of white-ness. I can only briefly survey here some of the pertinent literature on color and color theory that informed the synthesis in this section of the text. For the neurophysiology or psychophysiology underlying cultural universals of light-ness (white-ness) and darkness (black-ness), and color (red, yellow, green, and blue) perception, see B. Berlin and Kay (1969); Borstein (1975); Ratcliff (1976); Wattenwyl and Zollinger (1979); and Witkowski and Brown (1977). For early criticism of Brent Berlin and Paul Kay's methodology, but nevertheless corroboratory ethnographic data, see Durbin (1972); Ember (1978); Hays et al. (1972); and Naroll (1970, 1232, table 1, 1278).

For an argument for the cultural appropriation of and cultural *imposition* of cultural (social) meaning upon these inherent, structural categories of mind, see Sahlins (1976). For a discussion that suggests that the cultural (social) meanings associated with the colors white, black, and red are not as arbitrary as Sahlins suggests, but are based within the affective associations of these colors, see Turner (1967, 59–92; 1973). Simplified, the human eye is neurophysiologically structured and programmed to differentiate the dark-ness to light-ness continuum, as well as the focal wavelengths of the four primary and true colors: red, yellow, green, and blue. The dark-ness (≈black-ness) to light-ness (≈white-ness) continuum provides the literal and figurative background of perception, against which these four colors are perceived and distinguished. These neurophysiological structures and the opponent-process (theory) of color perception undoubtedly underlie the culturally appropriated and informed, contrastive dyads of darkness-lightness, or blackness-whiteness, which also appear to be the only (near-) universal semantically antonymic dyad, and also undoubtedly underlie the culturally appropriated and informed, and (near-) universal, contrastive and complementary triad of white(ness), black(ness), and red(ness). Among dark-pigmented-eyed populations, such as the northeastern Woodland Indians, there is also a universal tendency not to neurophysiologically distinguish and, consequently, not to lexically distinguish between the colors green and blue. Either and both colors are often referred to by the same color term, which accounts for the "confusion" of these colors among these peoples as recorded in the historical and ethnographical records.

Published synthetic discussions of Northern Iroquoian color terms have not been found, and similar materials for the northeastern Woodland Indians, generally or specifically, are practically nonexistent. However, for a list of Seneca Iroquois terms for light-colored (white) and dark-colored (black), and for the colors black, gray, red, yellow, green, blue, purple, and brown, see Chafe (1963). For a discussion of Narragansett Algonquian color terms, see Aubin (1975).

Finally, any color may mean everything, or nothing, as some of the literature on color symbolism

ors organize ritual states-of-being into three contrastive and complementary sets: social states-of-being, asocial states-of-being, and antisocial states-of-being, respectively.[8] Ritual is the means to maintain a desired state-of-being, or to transform one state-of-being into an at least temporarily more desirable state-of-being. Within ritual contexts material culture functions to synesthetically manifest through its attribute of color the present state-of-being of its participants, and to synesthetically manifest through color, the desired state-of-being to be ritually effected. This may be the status quo, or one of the other two contrastive states-of-being.

The colors white, black, and red potentially organize ritual states-of-being and ritual material culture into either triadic or dyadic contrastive-complementary sets. White social states-of-being, black asocial states-of-being, and red antisocial states-of-being form the one contrastive-complementary triadic set; white *and* red social states-of-being in contrast to black asocial states-of-being form one dyadic opposition; and white social states-of-being in contrast to black and red antisocial states-of-being form the other.

Within these ritual states-of-being, the colors white, black, and red also individually manifest varying valences (+, 0, or -) of potency, evaluation, and activity (F. Adams 1973; Osgood, May, and Miron 1975), depending upon the state-of-being being ritually foregrounded and the state-of-being with which it is being contrasted. For example, white(-ness), the color of (day)light and thus of life itself, is the most potent color, and the most highly evaluated color if that potency is consecrated to socially constructive purposes.[9] However, white *and* red are both *potent*

---

demonstrates. Patterning in color symbolism only emerges when cultural (social) context and intended contrast of *significata* are controlled. In this paper I am interested only in the patterning in meaning that emerges from the ritual consecration of white, black, and red within social, asocial, and antisocial states-of-being. These may be considered *marked* states of biosocial being, which stand in contrast to an *unmarked* state of biosocial being, in which any and all colors are culturally, socially, and individually appropriate and acceptable. For example, within economic contexts black wampum beads have a greater economic value (twice that) than white wampum beads. In regard to trade textiles and dress, both black (or dark navy blue) and red broadcloth appear to have been preferable to white.

8. The semantics of color, ritual, and material culture proposed here has emerged from my ongoing research of the functions and meanings of wampum among the Northern Iroquoians and other northeastern Woodland Indians. For a fuller discussion of this proposal and for some of the data upon which it is based, see Hamell (1986; cf. Miller and Hamell 1986).

9. White-ness, like red-ness, was a ritually bivalent color. Within the context of ritual, whiteness connotes and denotes greatest potency, which may be ritually consecrated either to socially *constructive* or to socially *destructive* purposes. Depending upon one's perspective upon the operation of this great potency, it may be either positively evaluated or negatively evaluated, respectively, i.e., "white magic" or "black magic." Normatively, in its ritual context and consecration, "white magic" prescribes white things and proscribes black things; while normatively, in its ritual context and consecration, "black magic" prescribes black things and proscribes white things. It is whiteness's connotation and denotation of greatest potency that underlie the cultural efficacy of white entities. And so long as whiteness's great potency is ritually consecrated to socially constructive purposes, it is also positively evaluated. It

colors, because they are generally identified with the sentient aspect and the animate aspect (i.e., blood) of life, respectively.[10]

White and red are also positively evaluated colors to the extent that their (life) potency is ritually consecrated to socially constructive functions. However, because red is the most *active* or animate of the three colors, it is also bivalent: if its animacy is consecrated to socially destructive functions, it manifests antisocial states-of-being in contrast to white social states-of-(physical-, social-, and spiritual-) being; if its animacy is consecrated to socially constructive functions, it manifests social states-of- (physical well-) being. When conjoined, white and red manifest the sentient and animate aspects of social states-of-being, respectively, and are most frequently contrasted to black states-of-being, characterized by the absence of sentience and animacy, as in states of mourning.[11]

Life's Immortal Shell

Concepts of greatest (life) potency, and consequently of greatest positive cultural evaluation—which are semantically identified with whiteness—are the common ideational denominators underlying the ritual functions of white shell throughout the Northeastern Woodlands. Within social states-of-being, white

---

is the potential bivalency in the operation of whiteness's great potency that underlies the sometimes ambiguous and often paradoxical relations between human man-beings and white entities. This is the paradox of *Moby Dick,* which Herman Melville discusses at length but could not resolve in his chapter "On the whiteness of the whale" (Melville 1851).

10. Seneca (Iroquois) color terms are comprised of the verb root, meaning "to be the color of," and a noun root referencing some physical entity of which that specific color is a salient physical attribute. Consequently, Seneca color terms are not "basic" color terms, as defined by B. Berlin and Kay (1969). The Seneca term for *red* is comprised of the verb root meaning "to be the color of" and a noun root, of which the origin is reportedly uncertain, but which has the meaning "red" (Chafe 1963, 40). However, this noun root for red is undoubtedly cognate with and etymologically derived from the Seneca noun root for "blood" (cf. Chafe 1967, 83 lexical items 1736 and 1737).

Red ochre and vermillion were frequent offerings in Seneca burials of the seventeenth and eighteenth centuries. The presence of red ochre in similar contexts extends thousands of years back into prehistory within the same region. Red pigments are, alternatively, closely identified with antisocial states of being, such as warfare: the face and body paint of warriors, the red-painted warclubs and belt axes left upon the bodies of victims as declarations of war, and the red-painted wampum belts, so-called "hatchet belts" presented as war invitation belts.

11. The specific Seneca Iroquois term for *black* is comprised of the noun root for "charcoal," incorporated within the verb root meaning "to be the color of" (cf. Chafe 1963, 40; Chafe 1967, 62 lexical item 844). Traditionally, Seneca mourners extinguished their fires, blackened their faces, and remained in the "darkness" of grief until condoled. Seneca wampum strings and wampum belts denoting and connoting condolence were and are black. The same noun root is found in the Seneca term for *minister* or *priest,* as glossed in appellation, "Black Robe."

shell, whether freshwater or marine in origin and regardless of its natural or manufactured form, functions as a metaphor for light, and thus for life itself, particularly in its sentient aspect. White shell is a material metaphor for the biological continuity of life in general, and for the biological and social continuity of human life in particular (Hamell 1986).

This function and meaning of white shell underwrote the intense interest in white marine shell "ornaments," particularly in those small cylindrical beads, called *sewant, porcelaine,* and *wampum,* that became after contact the medium and the message of social exchanges between Native and Native, and between Native and newcomer. Red(-painted) and/or purple ("black") wampum beads, bead strings, and bead belts were the media of socially contrastive messages.

Light, bright, and white were and still are good to think with among the Iroquois and other Northeastern Woodland Indians. This ritual function and meaning of light, bright, and white material culture, shellwork in particular, may with confidence be projected far back into prehistory, as can the contrastive-complementary functions and meanings of black and red material culture. This proposed semantics of color, ritual, and material culture most probably accounts for the differential and deferential disposal in mortuary contexts during the Terminal Archaic and during the Early and Middle Woodland periods of white (marine) shell, white freshwater pearls, white ($\approx$ transparent) rock crystal, white chalcedony, white (muscovite) mica, white free-state metals (silver, galena); red cedar, red ocher (hematite), red chalcedony, red jasper, red pipestone (catilinite), red native copper; and black charcoal, black obsidian, black chalcedony (and chert), black (biotite) mica, and black meteoric iron. I suggest that in the reporting of archaeologically recovered ritual material culture, a presentation organized by color may be as meaningful, and perhaps more so, than its reportage by the traditional analytical categories of raw material and function.

Cultural and Contact Continuities

During prehistory, white, black, and red exotic substances moved hundreds of miles across exchange networks from their ascribed places of origin in distant regions where mythic time and space converged, at least from the ideational perspective of the recipient local community. To some extent the cultural efficacy of such luxury and status goods, as they are called by archaeologists, was positively correlated with the social distance of their ascribed place of origin. While the exchange of such substances across and within the interior mid-Atlantic region did not stop entirely about 1,000 years ago, it did diminish greatly during the Late Woodland period, that is, during late prehistory.

However, during this period there was a resurgence in the exchange of native copper originating in the Lake Superior region, and of marine shell emanating from the mid-Atlantic coast and most probably from the Chesapeake Bay region (Bradley 1987b). In a probable series of indirect exchanges between local communities, marine shell and marine shell "ornaments" passed from the coast, northwest up the Susquehanna River and its tributary drainages into what is now eastern and central New York State. This was one of the primary indigenous trade networks across which were to move the earliest European trade goods during early protohistory.

Within the region of the historic Seneca Iroquois, this resurgence of interest in native copper and marine shell is archaeologically evidenced by their increasingly frequent differential and deferential disposal in mortuary contexts. Their inclusion is coincident with the increasing frequency with which the deceased are accompanied by other so-called "grave goods," local or exotic in origin. This appears to have been a general cultural phenomenon throughout the Northeast during the sixteenth century.

A tenuous thread of archaeological data can be woven to link the resurgence of this mortuary behavior to that of the Middle Woodland period and earlier. It has been asserted that this resurgence of interest in native copper and marine shell, and in their differential mortuary disposal, was a late prehistoric, cultural phenomenon, as was the increasing practice of dedicating other goods to the deceased, and that neither behavior is directly correlated with contact (Wray et al. 1987, 251). However, given that the criterion dividing regional prehistory from regional protohistory is the presence or absence of European trade goods, such assertions have the potential for tautology. Rather, I would counter-assert that these archaeologically manifested behavioral changes within the historic homeland of the Seneca are contact-correlated phenomena. I assert, or more properly speculate, that these are behavioral responses to the Seneca's indirect knowledge of something (contact) happening at the eastern World's Rim.

I speculate that the earliest European trade goods remained among coastal Native groups who, in turn, and early in the sixteenth century, revived the interior-directed exchange of traditionally valued marine shell in order to obtain supplies of furs to trade to coasting Europeans. Marine shell was soon followed along these interior exchange networks by a limited repertoire of European trade goods, which by the middle of the sixteenth century were more readily and reliably available among coastal groups. As these European trade goods become increasingly available among the Seneca and other interior groups, these goods too began to be consecrated to burial. Of further interest and related significance, I suggest that a shift in preferred burial orientation begins at the same time, with the majority of the deceased heading west, literally, and perhaps metaphysically, early in the following century (Wray and Schoff 1953, 56).

What is significant is that most of these earliest European trade goods are monochrome and polychrome glass beads, and copper (and brass) pendants, beads, bracelets, and necklaces, non-"utilitarian" in form and function (Ritchie 1954; Wray 1985; Wray and Schoff 1953; Wray et al. 1987). The cultural interest in and the cultural efficacy of the earliest of these European trade goods were consequent correlates of their perceived exotic source, and of their colors and substance, which were perceived and received as analogous to traditional, indigenous substantial metaphors of cultural value. Although the earliest tools and weapons of iron (steel) had some indigenous precedent, if not in substance, then at least in function and/or form, we may also imagine that they too had a cultural or ideational efficacy, vastly disproportionate to whatever utilitarian function they were initially put.

Color as Cultural Sieve

The function of color and correlated affective meaning in articulating culture contact in northeastern North America is no better evidenced than in the exchange of indigenous shell beads and European glass trade beads. The exchange of glass trade beads was consumer driven by Indian interest in and desire for beads of particular colors, forms, and sizes. Consequently, we can infer that the archaeological frequency of glass trade bead types and the archaeological-numerical frequency of beads of each of these types directly reflect their relative popularity among their Eastern Algonquian and Northern Iroquoian consumers. It should not be surprising that the most popular glass trade bead types and glass beads generally were beads (monochrome or polychrome) whose ground colors were either white, black, red, green (green-blue), or blue, and whose forms were primarily either tubular, oval, or spherical (Kidd and Kidd 1983 [1970]).

The "blue" glossed here includes numerous lighter shades of blue, typologically and descriptively distinguished in the glass trade bead literature, and less numerous, darker shades of blue. I will suggest that these finer distinctions in hue, relative to the color "blue" or to any of the other "colors" distinctions that are critical to the contemporary analysis, description, and communication of glass trade bead types, were nevertheless largely irrelevant to their original consumers.

Distinctions in hue were apparently only of significance in their extreme; distinctions between lighter or darker shades of "colors" were significant in glossing some lighter-colored beads as "white," or in their allowance as "white" substitutes, or in glossing some darker-colored beads as "black," or in their allowance as "black" substitutes. Among Northeastern Woodland Indian consumers the colors distinguished among glass trade beads were more or less congruent with the focal colors of indigenous and "natural" entities of which these same colors were salient physical attributes: "white" things, "black" things, "red" things, "yellow" things, "green" things, and so on.

Small white tubular glass beads and small dark blue tubular glass beads were among the most popular glass bead types and among the most popular glass beads numerically by the turn of the seventeenth century in northeastern North America (Bradley 1983, 31; Kenyon and Kenyon 1983, 60–62, 68; Wray 1983, 42). While we may infer that the popularity of the white tubular glass beads was at least in part owing to their analogy to contemporary and indigenous small white marine tubular shell beads (i.e., "early wampum"), we cannot claim an indigenous marine shell analogy for the dark blue tubular glass beads.

To my knowledge, purple, glossed "black" marine shell beads were not manufactured until after contact (Ceci 1986; 1989, 71, table 4). No examples, regardless of marine shell source and bead form and/or size, have been reported from prehistoric archaeological contexts in the Northeast. The earliest purple marine shell beads of which I have knowledge are discoidal shell beads, manufactured from the purple ("black") spot of the quahog or hardshell clam *(Mercenaria mercenaria)*, that postdate ca. A.D. 1565 (Ceci 1986, 22; 1989, 72). The earliest purple ("black") tubular beads, made from this same shell and of wampum form, date to the turn of the seventeenth century (Ceci 1986, 30; 1989, 72). Consequently, on the basis of archaeological evidence in northeastern North America, one might posit the iconoclastic conclusion that the indigenous coastal manufacture of purple ("black") wampum beads was catalyzed by the contemporary popularity of the earlier occurring, dark blue tubular glass trade beads.

From the perspective of Iroquoia, the small white tubular glass beads that were popular in northeastern North America at the end of the late sixteenth century declined in popularity through the early decades of the seventeenth century, while the popularity of dark blue tubular glass beads increased. These trends in white tubular glass and dark blue tubular glass bead color popularity were concurrent with the increasing popularity of small red ("Redwood") tubular glass trade beads. By the 1650s and 1660s, dark blue tubular glass and red tubular glass beads peaked in popularity, as did tubular glass beads generally (Huey 1983, 99, fig. 4). During the last half of the seventeenth century, tubular glass beads of all colors rapidly declined in popularity, replaced by the increasing popularity of spherically shaped glass beads, primarily red or black in color.

This "red shift" in glass trade bead color preference during the first half of the seventeenth century is archaeologically evidenced among the Northern Iroquoians (Kenyon and Kenyon 1983, 69–70; I. Kenyon 1986, 58–59, fig. 2).[12] In 1654, among the Iroquois proper, these "little tubes or pipes of red glass . . . constitute[d] the diamonds of the country" (Thwaites 1896–1901, 41:109–11). In turn, these red tubular glass trade beads had late prehistoric—early protohistoric indigenous analogues in

---

12. Northern Iroquoian interest in "red" glass beads during this period is further archaeologically evidenced by beads whose exterior non-red stripes or non-red layers had been ground off to produce a monochrome brick-red surface (cf. Kenyon and Kenyon 1983, 69–70; I. Kenyon 1986, 58–59, fig. 2).

beads of similar size and shape manufactured from catlinite (red pipestone) found in the upper Great Lakes and in contemporary, locally manufactured, red slate imitations.

From this evidence, one should not conclude that either white beads or "black" (as used here, a gloss for dark blue or purple) beads declined in popularity among the Northern Iroquoians by the middle of the seventeenth century. White tubular *glass* beads did drastically decline during the early seventeenth century, and dark blue tubular *glass* beads were competing in popularity with red tubular *glass* beads by the middle of the seventeenth century. However, it would not be valid to conclude that white tubular beads and "black" tubular beads in general declined in popularity.

Quite the contrary, for these shifts in color preferences in glass tubular beads were contemporaneous with the increasing coastal manufacture and interior-oriented exchange of white wampum and "black" wampum (marine shell) beads (Ceci 1986; 1989; Sempowski 1989). Interior Northern Iroquoians still preferred small white tubular beads and small dark "blue" tubular beads, but preferred that beads of these colors, forms, and sizes be made of marine shell. Discussions of the dynamics of bead color, form, and size preferences in the Northeast during the sixteenth and seventeenth centuries must include beads of all materials: shell, stone, metal, and glass.

If we can infer that the archaeological frequency of glass trade bead types and the archaeological-numerical frequency of beads of each of these types directly reflect their relative popularity among their Eastern Algonquian and Northern Iroquoian consumers in the sixteenth, seventeenth, and eighteenth centuries, we can then infer that yellow glass trade bead types and yellow glass trade beads generally were unpopular (Kidd and Kidd 1983 [1970]). Just as the popularity and correlated ritual functions of beads of the colors white, black, red, green, green-blue, and blue were delimited by the affective associations of these colors, it is very probable that the unpopularity of yellow beads during this period was also attributable to the affective associations of this color, especially within ritual contexts. The direct and indirect evidence suggests that "yellow" was not a "healthy" color.

The Seneca (Iroquois) term for *yellow* translates literally as "to be the color of bile" (Chafe 1963, 40; 1967, 62 lexical item 873), as probably evidenced in the skin color of victims of jaundice or viral hepatitis. Among the Southern Iroquoian Cherokee, white, black, red, and yellow glass "seed" beads are used in the divinitory treatment of disease. Within this ritual context, white is emblematic of the happiness that comes with recovery from the disease, red represents the powerful spirit that conquers the disease, black represents the great lake in the Night Land into which the disease is cast, and yellow typifies the disease itself (Mooney and Olbrecht 1932, 218; cf. 118–19, 132, 152, 304; cf. Hamell 1983, 23).

Documentary evidence also suggests that yellow was not a popular color generally in northeastern North America during the sixteenth, seventeenth, and eighteenth centuries. At Narragansett Bay in A.D. 1524, Giovanni da Verrazano reported of the Algonquian Indians encountered there, that they did not value gold, because of its color, yellow; of which he further stated that this color was "especially disliked by them; azure and red are those (colors) in highest estimation with them" (Winship 1905, 15–16). Verrazano continues by noting that among the things most highly prized by the Indians were the "azure crystals" (glass trade beads) given them.

Indirect corroboration of the Mohawk (Iroquois) dislike of the color yellow, or at least their unappreciation of gold as a useful metal, was reported by Johannes Megapolensis Jr. in A.D. 1644 (Megapolensis 1909, 176). Further corroboration is found by the end of the seventeenth century in the Iroquois' selection of silver, or "white metal," and not gold, as the substance of which the symbolic, brightly polished "Covenant Chain" was forged and that linked them and their Indian and white neighbors in peace and trade. In council, the silver Covenant Chain manifested itself in the form of a white-grounded wampum belt, within which were frequently represented, in purple wampum, human figures linked in social relations.

Conclusion

Contact with Native peoples along the mid-Atlantic coast and in the interior was not an event, but a series of contact events, which took place at differing times in differing places. More important than the event or events of contact was the process of contact: a process mediated within the overlapping cultural frontiers of New World and Old World mythical realities, and wherein one culture's "truck" became, for a time, another culture's "treasure." In this cross-cultural exchange, colors and their affective meanings played significant roles, underappreciated then, and now.

Acknowledgments

I would like to thank James W. Bradley, Director, Robert S. Peabody Museum of Archaeology, Phillips Academy, Andover, Massachusetts; and Paul R. Huey, Senior Scientist (Archaeology), Bureau of Historic Sites, New York State Office of Parks, Recreation and Historic Preservation, Peebles Island, Waterford, New York, for their helpful comments on an earlier draft of this paper.

17 | Reconstructing Patterns of Interaction and Warfare Between the Mohawk and Northern Iroquoians During the A.D. 1400–1700 Period

ROBERT D. KUHN

Introduction

THE SEVENTEENTH-CENTURY CONFLICT between the Five Nations Iroquois of New York and the surrounding Iroquoian tribes in southeast Ontario, New York, and Pennsylvania (the Huron, Petun, Neutral, Wenro, Erie, and Susquehannock) is well known from numerous primary accounts (Biggar 1922–36; Thwaites 1896–1901; Sagard-Théodat 1939 [1632]) and secondary accounts (Grassman 1969; Trigger 1976; 1978c). It is clear from these sources that by the time of the great dispersals at the hands of the Five Nations Iroquois in 1649 and the 1650s this warfare was intensive and primarily rooted in competition over control of the European fur trade (Trigger 1976). But the beginning of this conflict is not as well understood as the finale. When did conflict between the New York Iroquois and the Northern Iroquoians of southeast Ontario begin? Were the origins of this conflict related to the European fur trade? How did the St. Lawrence Iroquoians fit into the picture? Because written records for earlier periods are lacking, the answers may only be found in the archaeological record (Bradley 1987b, 42; Trigger 1985, 118).

Reconstructing warfare patterns is problematic because of the limitations of the archaeological record (G. Wright 1974). Palisaded villages and the remains of human bones in refuse middens indicate that warfare was occurring prehistorically (Milner 1999). Among the eastern Iroquois (Mohawk, Oneida, Onondaga) conflict was occurring by circa 1200 if not earlier (Tuck 1978, 326). Most agree that

Previously published in *A Passion for the Past: Papers in Honour of James F. Pendergast,* ed. J. V. Wright and J.-L. Pilon, Mercury Series, Archaeology Paper no. 164 (Gatineau, QC: Canadian Museum of Civilization, 2004), 145–66. Printed with permission by Robert D. Kuhn.

initially warfare took the form of blood feud motivated by revenge or prestige acquisition (Snyderman 1948; Trigger 1985, 97–98; Tuck 1978, 326); however, to what extent the nature and intensity of warfare changed through time continues to be debated (Niemczycki 1988, 79, 82). Numerous studies have attempted to examine warfare, interaction patterns, or related issues in Iroquoia (e.g., Bradley 1987a; Engelbrecht 1971; Milner 1999; Whallon 1968).

This study attempts to examine changing Iroquoian warfare and interaction patterns over the 1400 to 1700 period by analyzing the archaeological evidence from one Iroquois tribe, the Mohawk. Located in the middle Mohawk valley of New York, the Mohawk are the easternmost tribe of the Five Nations Confederacy. Thanks to archaeological investigations conducted by Donald Lenig (1965), William A. Ritchie and Robert E. Funk (1973), and Dean R. Snow (1995e), there is a remarkably complete record available from fifteenth-, sixteenth-, and seventeenth-century Mohawk sites. Historical documentation on the Mohawk from the seventeenth and eighteenth centuries is equally rich (Fenton and Moore 1977; Grassman 1969; Snow et al. 1996).

Stylistic Analysis of Mohawk Pottery

Assigning ethnicity based on pottery assemblages must be done with great caution because a direct correlation between archaeological cultures and actual ethnic groups does not exist (Engelbrecht 1999, 51; Fox 1990b, 462; Ramsden 1996, 107; Sutton 1995, 72; Williamson and Robertson 1994, 39). Nevertheless, most archaeologists "regard ceramics as the most sensitive indicators of time-space differences and ethnic divisions" (Starna and Funk 1994, 48). During the fifteenth, sixteenth, and seventeenth centuries, some Iroquoian groups did decorate their pottery with motifs that were generally indicative of their tribal affiliations (Lenig 1965; MacNeish 1952; James Wright 1966, 15). Interestingly, the discovery of sherds decorated with the styles of other tribal groups, often referred to as exotic pottery, is a common occurrence on Iroquoian archaeological sites (MacNeish 1952; Pendergast 1993b, 29–31; Trigger 1985, 105). William E. Engelbrecht (1984) has evaluated this phenomenon and he isolates a number of possible explanations for the occurrence of foreign or exotic pottery on Iroquoian sites including intermarriage, trade, capture, and migration (see also J. Jamieson 1990b, 82; Latta 1991; Ramsden 1990b).

A complete review of explanations for exotic pottery is beyond the scope of this paper. In different cases each may hold true. For example, in southeast Ontario, where sedentary horticultural Iroquoian communities were interacting with nearby hunter-gatherer bands of Algonquians, it seems likely that ceramic traditions were shared (Dawson 1979, 27); that pottery may have moved freely between groups as subsistence resources were traded or exchanged (Fox 1990b, 463; Sutton 1995, 77; Warrick 2000, 418, 452 [chap. 7]); or that pottery moved between groups through other forms of nonviolent contact (Trigger et al. 1984, 10). In eastern New York, however, where Iroquois tribes were historically at war with Northern Iroquoian populations located great distances away, the interpretation that rare examples of exotic pottery were the work of female war captives seems a more likely scenario (Kuhn et al. 1993, 84; Trigger 1985, 106). In addition, high percentages of exotic pottery within archaeological site assemblages are probably evidence of the migration of a large group of people, either forced or voluntary (Engelbrecht 1991, 8; J. Jamieson 1990b, 82; Kuhn and Snow 1986, 30–31; Lennox and Fitzgerald 1990, 418–19).

How should archaeologists develop appropriate interpretations of exotic pottery on archaeological sites? For the Mohawk, the rich documentary record encourages use of the direct historical approach (Ritchie and Funk 1973, 359; Steward 1942). For example, a well-known event during the Beaver Wars that was chronicled in the *Jesuit Relations* is the dispersal of the Huron by the Five Nations Iroquois in 1649. Many were either captured or coerced to join the Mohawk during and after this event, including, in 1657, the entire Attignawantan tribe of Huron. One hundred Mohawk warriors accompanied these Huron during their migration from settlements on the Isle of Orleans near Quebec to their new homeland in eastern New York (Grassman 1969; Thwaites 1896–1901, 43:187; Trigger 1976). This migration suggests that the influx of Huron people into Mohawk communities at this time was sizable.

The evidence of an event like this is readily apparent in the archaeological record. At the Mohawk Jackson-Everson site, which dates to the third quarter of the seventeenth century, a majority of the ceramic assemblage is composed of Huron pottery types. Sherds of Huron Incised and Warminster Crossed pottery from this site are illustrated in Kuhn (1986a, 87–89). The ceramic assemblage is composed of approximately 80 percent Huron pottery. This composition appears to be consistent with Jesuit assessments of Mohawk village composition. The Jesuit Lalemant, visiting the Mohawk in 1659–60, recorded that foreigners living among the Mohawk outnumbered the Mohawk themselves (Thwaites 1896–1901, 45:205–9).

Trace element analysis of Huron pottery from Jackson-Everson and other Mohawk sites has shown that these ceramic specimens were manufactured from Mohawk valley clays (Kuhn 1986a). Therefore, these pots do not represent trade items or possessions that were brought to the Mohawk valley by captives or immigrants. Given the documentary record, there seems little doubt that Huron pottery on Mohawk sites of this period represents the work of Huron women who were captured or coerced into joining Mohawk communities. During their tenure in Mohawk villages they were producing pottery that they decorated in traditional Huron styles.

There are no historical accounts of large Northern Iroquoian migrations into Mohawk territory before the dispersal of the Huron in 1649. Nevertheless, the capture of Northern Iroquoians, Algonquians, and Frenchmen by the Mohawk throughout the first half of the seventeenth century is well documented (Grassman 1969; Snow et al. 1996). This includes the practice of taking foreign women as captive brides. For example, the account of Pierre Esprit Radisson, who was captured and adopted by a Mohawk family from 1651 to 1654, clearly documents that the Mohawk practice of taking captive brides had been going on for decades. Radisson states that his 60-year-old Mohawk father was a great warrior who had captured his wife in Huronia (Snow et al. 1996, 81). Given that Radisson notes that they had lived together more than 40 years, this event probably took place as early as circa 1615. It seems likely that female captives like Radisson's adoptive mother were pottery producers during their long tenure with the Mohawk. They may have produced Northern Iroquoian or Huron-style wares and even taught these traditions to others. After all, Radisson's mother had five daughters during her lifetime among the Mohawk.

The evidence of this practice occurs on early to mid-seventeenth-century Mohawk sites in the form of low frequencies of exotic pottery. Examples of Huron styles including Huron Incised, Warminster Crossed, Warminster Horizontal, Sidey Notched, and Seed Incised pottery all occur on Mohawk sites of this period but typically in very small quantities. While some of these wares are unadulterated Huron types like those encountered at the later Jackson-Everson site, others incorporate Mohawk design elements and are perhaps better described as Huron-like. These specimens probably represent the work of individual captives, undoubtedly women, producing pottery in Mohawk villages. Although the "captive bride" explanation for exotic pottery has been heavily criticized (Latta 1991, Ramsden 1990b, 92–93) there is strong documentary evidence that supports the idea and it appears to be the most appropriate interpretation for Huron and Huron-like pottery on Mohawk sites.

As Michael W. Spence (1999, 277) has noted, outsiders entering a community through marriage were "cultural seeds" who would "play a role in the enculturation of the next generation" and have "a profound and enduring effect on the local culture." Among the Mohawk the influence of foreign female potters working in their villages appears to have led to significant changes in the Mohawk design tradition during the early to mid-seventeenth century. The frequency of certain traditional Mohawk pottery attributes declines and new attributes are introduced to the design vocabulary during this period. It seems that many of these changes are the result of external influences because early to mid-seventeenth-century Mohawk ceramic assemblages are more similar to those of Northern Iroquoian groups than to Mohawk ceramic assemblages from earlier periods. The 1620–40 Mohawk Cromwell site pottery assemblage represents a good example of these changes. Trends in individual design attributes are presented along with illustrations of Huron-like pottery in Kuhn (1994a, 32, 34). The interpretation that captive women from Northern Iroquoian groups like the Huron were being assimilated into Mohawk life and having an influence on Mohawk cultural traditions appears to be the most parsimonious interpretation of these trends.

The archaeological signatures on earlier and later seventeenth-century Mohawk sites are quite distinct, reflecting different historically documented demographic patterns and events. During and after the great diaspora of the 1650s, large groups of captives or coerced immigrants were coming into Mohawk communities that were in a state of upheaval from war, disease, and missionary activities. On Mohawk sites of this period large numbers of pure Huron-style pottery occur, uninfluenced by Mohawk ceramic traditions. On earlier seventeenth-century sites that date before the diaspora, individuals were being incorporated into Mohawk communities as a result of the warfare-capture-adoption complex that was such a well-documented component of Iroquoian warfare (Richter 1992, 65–74). On these sites pure Huron-style pottery is less frequent but Mohawk ceramic assemblages are more heterogeneous and incorporate attributes of Northern Iroquoian origin. Nevertheless, at a more general level the historical and archaeological evidence reflects a single process of culture change occurring because a tradition of captive assimilation created a unique form of increased interaction between societies at war. It is this historically documented pattern that best accounts for the occurrence of exotic pottery on Mohawk archaeological sites as well as for broader trends in the Mohawk pottery design tradition of the seventeenth century.

The correlation between the historical record and the archaeological record for the seventeenth century provides a reasonable basis for projecting similar archaeological interpretations back in time, despite the absence of corresponding written records for earlier periods. Small frequencies of exotic ceramics can be identified in most sixteenth-century Mohawk artifact assemblages. Although other explanations are possible, interpreting these items as early evidence of the warfare-capture-adoption complex of the Iroquois continues to be the most appropriate approach.

In contrast to the Huron exotics on Mohawk sites from the seventeenth century, most of the foreign pottery on sixteenth-century Mohawk sites has characteristics of St. Lawrence Iroquoian design motifs and attributes. Statements that St. Lawrence Iroquoian pottery does not occur on Mohawk sites (e.g., Heidenreich 1990, 482; J. Wright 1990, 501, 502) are incorrect. Examples of these wares have been illustrated in Kuhn et al. (1993) for the mid-sixteenth century Mohawk Garoga, Klock, and Smith-Pagerie sites. The presence of these wares on Mohawk sites corresponds closely with the period during which Iroquoian populations abandoned the St. Lawrence valley. They have been interpreted as evidence of conflict between the Mohawk and St. Lawrence Iroquoian groups leading to the capture and assimilation of St. Lawrence Iroquoian people into Mohawk communities (Kuhn et al. 1993).

All of this evidence suggests that a broader analysis of exotic pottery on Mohawk sites could provide a strong basis for interpreting interaction patterns with Northern Iroquoian groups during the late prehistoric to historic period continuum. If styles and attributes of Northern Iroquoian ceramics in Mohawk pottery assemblages indicate the presence of female war captives, then charting the frequency of these traits could provide an indication of when conflict originated and how the intensity of that conflict changed through time.

To conduct this study pottery assemblages of typed rim sherds from Mohawk sites dating between 1400 and 1700 were analyzed using a type and attribute analysis for Iroquois pottery developed by Engelbrecht (1971). For a majority of the sites the study utilized existing collections at the State University of New York at Albany, the New York State Museum, the Mohawk-Caughnawaga Museum, the Frey and Richmond collections, and the private collections of the late John Jackowski and the late Donald Rumrill. In addition, rim sherd data previously collected for the Mohawk Barker, Wagner's Hollow, and Martin sites were also graciously shared by William Engelbrecht for use in the study. Finally, the published work of Richard S. MacNeish (1952, 70–80) was evaluated and deemed consistent with the approach employed here and worthy of inclusion.

The sites and samples included in the analysis are listed in table 17.1. All 16 sites represent major, single-component, year-round Mohawk village sites that were probably occupied for a period of 10 to 50 years. The site names and chronology follow Snow (1995e) with minor chronological revisions where appropriate, based upon more recent research.

Table 17.1
Mohawk Site Chronology and Ceramic Assemblage Sizes

Site	Date	Rim Sherds
Second Woods	1400–1450	24
Getman #1	1450–1500	185
Elwood	1450–1500	280
Otstungo	1500–1525	539
Cayadutta	1525–1545	722
Garoga	1525–1545	1348
Klock	1540–1565	422
Smith-Pagerie	1560–1580	386
Barker	1580–1614	156
England's Woods #1	1580–1614	24
Rice's Woods	1600–1620	144
Wagner's Hollow	1614–1626	174
Martin	1614–1626	161
Cromwell	1626–1635	91
Rumrill-Naylor	1635–1646	14
Jackson-Everson	1666–1680	15

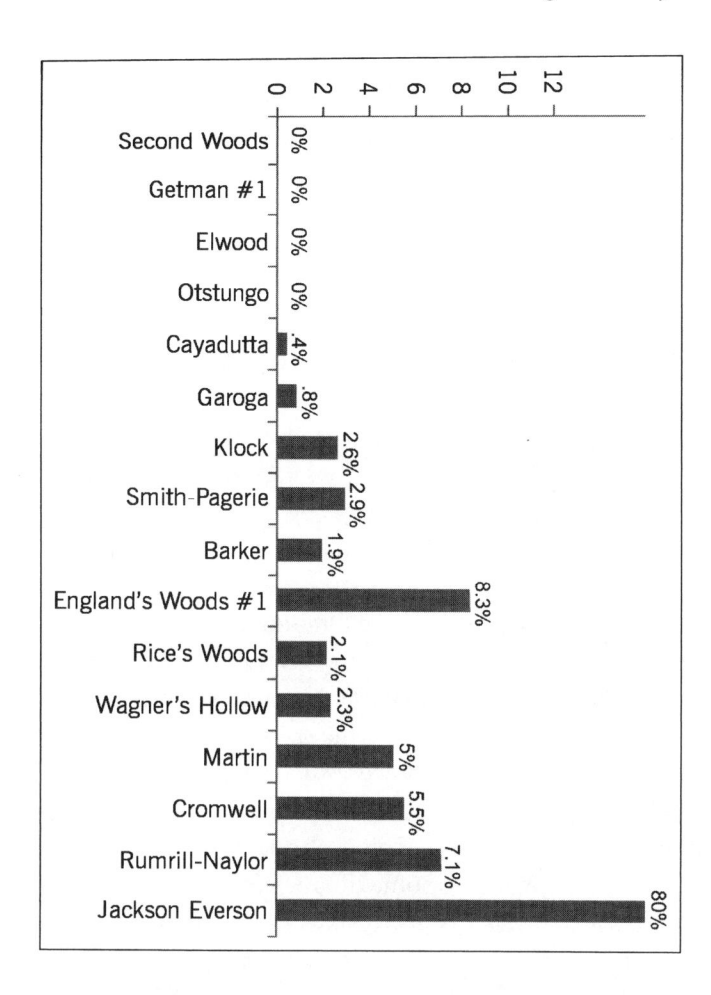

Fig. 17.1. Frequency of Northern Iroquoian pottery in Mohawk ceramic assemblages.

The frequency of Northern Iroquoian motifs in the typed rim sherd assemblage from each Mohawk site was calculated. The results are presented in figure 17.1. There are key types and attributes that can be used to differentiate Huron pottery from St. Lawrence Iroquoian pottery; however, there is also overlap of some attributes in the ceramics of these two groups (Bradley 1987a, 215). In fact, as Timothy J. Abel (2001) has recently demonstrated, pottery assemblages from some of the St. Lawrence Iroquoian sites located in Jefferson County, New York, produce high quantities of Huron-style ceramics. Therefore, motifs and attributes of all Northern Iroquoian groups were included together in figure 17.1 to improve the objectivity of the analysis. The relative degree of Huron or St. Lawrence Iroquoian influence on the Mohawk will be evaluated in the discussion and interpretation based upon the author's intuitive pottery sense developed from working with these collections.

The results demonstrate that Northern Iroquoian ceramic traits are absent on fifteenth-century Mohawk sites. The earliest conclusive evidence of Northern Iroquoian-style pottery is at the Cayadutta and Garoga sites (1525–45). Therefore, it may be concluded from the results of this analysis that the conflict between the Mohawk and Northern Iroquoian groups originated during the early sixteenth century. Corroborative evidence for this conclusion is available from both Onondaga and Oneida archaeology. James W. Bradley (1987a, 56–58, 85) and Peter P. Pratt (1976, 98) indicate that the earliest occurrence of similar exotics among these eastern Iroquois and tribes is during the 1500 to 1550 period. Both attribute the occurrence of these wares to hostilities (also see Pendergast 1993b, 17–20, 26–27 for a summary).

There remains some question regarding the presence or absence of exotic ceramics at the Otstungo site because of the lack of clarity in MacNeish's (1952) publication. It is not possible to determine if his reported exotic Onondaga ceramics on Mohawk sites include pottery with St. Lawrence Iroquoian traits because MacNeish equated the two groups with one another. Interpretation of MacNeish's (1952, 80) results is further compounded by an apparent typographical error (Roebuck Underlined?) in his list of exotic types. No Northern Iroquoian exotics appear in MacNeish's sample from the Otstungo site if the attribution of pottery to the Onondaga is accurate. Other collections of pottery from Otstungo examined by the author (n = 212) contain no ceramics with Northern Iroquoian traits.

The frequency of Northern Iroquoian motifs in Mohawk assemblages gradually increases over the course of the sixteenth century. The majority of the wares from this period are suggestive of St. Lawrence Iroquoian ceramic styles and attributes. Traits including annular punctates, corn ear motifs, criss-crossed lines, and pottery types including Durfee Underlined, Roebuck Low Collar, and Lanorie Crossed can be attributed to the St. Lawrence Iroquoians with some degree of confidence.

The occurrence of St. Lawrence Iroquoian traits in sixteenth-century Mohawk assemblages coincides closely with the documented dispersal of Iroquoian populations from the St. Lawrence valley sometime between 1543 and 1603. Abandonment of the region likely occurred early in this period (by 1580) given the general lack of European trade goods on St. Lawrence Iroquoian sites (Pendergast 1985, 34–35; Snow 1995e, 143). The ceramic evidence strongly suggests that some of these St. Lawrence Iroquoian peoples were incorporated into Mohawk communities.

There is a general consensus that the majority of the St. Lawrence Iroquoians were adopted into Huron communities based upon the high frequency of St. Lawrence Iroquoian pottery on numerous Huron sites (J. Jamieson 1990a, 403; Pendergast 1993b, 27–28; Ramsden 1990a, 383; 1990b, 91; Snow 1995e, 216; Warrick 1990, 377–78). Similar ceramic evidence can be used to argue that a smaller number found their way into eastern Iroquois communities. There is considerable debate regarding the size of this population influx. I and my colleagues (Kuhn et al. 1993) argued that it was probably a small number of people based upon the low frequency of exotic ceramics in sixteenth-century Mohawk assemblages. However, Snow (1995e, 198, 216) argued for a fairly large migration of St. Lawrence Iroquoians into Mohawk territory based upon demographic evidence, and Bradley

(1987a, 85) proposed that a "sizable group" was incorporated into Onondaga villages based on frequencies of exotic pottery similar to those presented here for the Mohawk. Engelbrecht (1995) originally favored the latter hypothesis but now appears to support the former (Engelbrecht 2004), based on different approaches to interpreting the pottery data.

It is probably not possible to resolve this issue at the present time because of the limitations of the Mohawk ceramic evidence. The key 1580–1614 period, when the impact of new St. Lawrence Iroquoians living among the Mohawk would likely be best reflected in Mohawk material culture, is poorly represented in the sample. The frequencies from the Barker and England's Woods sites are substantially different. There are only two exotic sherds (one Durfee Underlined, one Warminster Crossed) in the England's Woods site assemblage but the frequency is high because the sample is small. It may not be representative. On the other hand, the frequency presented for the Barker site, which is based on Engelbrecht's data, may be too low. Recently, Ralph C. Rataul (2001) reexamined the pottery from the Barker site under my guidance and the guidance of noted Mohawk archaeology expert Wayne Lenig. He recognized a number of Lanorie Crossed sherds that Engelbrecht had not identified (or misidentified as Middleport Criss-Cross) and estimated that pottery of St. Lawrence Iroquoian derivation composed almost 4 percent of the assemblage. Furthermore, this estimate does not include the uniquely high percentage of low collar sherds in the Barker site assemblage, which may also indicate St. Lawrence Iroquoian influence but is not reflected in an analysis of pottery motifs. The data necessary to resolve this issue will require extensive and controlled excavations of late sixteenth-century Mohawk sites in order to gather large and representative artifact assemblages as well as settlement pattern evidence of village expansions characteristic of the incorporation of refugee populations (see J. Jamieson 1990b, 82). This work remains to be done.

It is well worth noting that the timing and frequency of St. Lawrence Iroquoian pottery on Mohawk and eastern Iroquois sites differ significantly from the pattern on Huron sites. St. Lawrence Iroquoian pottery on Huron sites occurs earlier in time and in much higher frequencies (Warrick 1990, 377). This pattern suggests that the relationship between the eastern Iroquois and the St. Lawrence Iroquoians may have been different from the Huron's relationship with that group.

The first appearance of Huron-style pottery in the Mohawk sequence is at the Garoga site (1525–45). MacNeish (1952, 80) identified two sherds of Huron Incised pottery in the Peabody Museum collection from Garoga and there are also two examples of Huron Incised-like sherds in the New York State Museum collections from the site. In addition, figure 17.2 illustrates two other exotic rim sherds that are suggestive of Huron influences. Low collars, square castellations, deeply incised lips, poorly defined collar-neck juncture, and stamping are all attributes that are rare on sixteenth-century Mohawk pottery but common on ceramics from south-

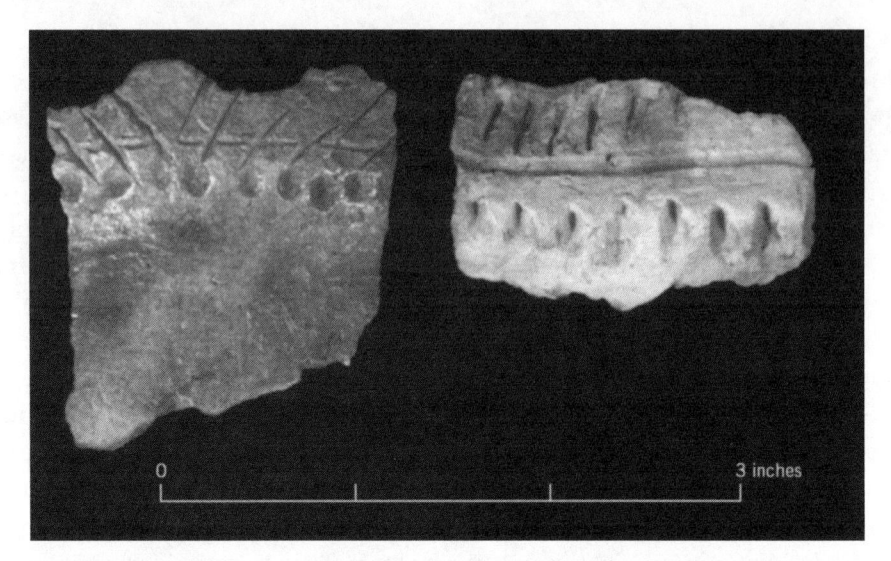

Fig. 17.2. Exotic pottery from the Garoga site: *l.* Sidey Crossed variant(?), *r.* Seed Incised variant(?).

east Ontario. Given the high frequency of Huron types on Jefferson County sites (Abel 2001), the possibility that this pottery may reflect St. Lawrence Iroquoians cannot be dismissed, but the likelihood that it reflects Mohawk interaction with the Huron should also be considered. Pendergast's (1993b, 26) conclusion that there is "no compelling archaeological evidence" for sixteenth-century hostilities between the Huron and the Iroquois seems overstated, given the evidence.

Huron pottery types are rare on sixteenth-century Mohawk sites and usually outnumbered by St. Lawrence Iroquoian pottery. During the early seventeenth century this relationship starts to reverse and Huron exotics begin to outnumber St. Lawrence Iroquoian wares although the latter still occur (fig. 17.3). Because the St. Lawrence Iroquoians were dispersed during the sixteenth century this reversal probably reflects the fact that no new St. Lawrence Iroquoians were coming into these communities and the older populations were assimilating. In contrast, the Huron were still an independent group of tribes in southeast Ontario and Huron captives were probably beginning to be brought into Mohawk communities more frequently during this period than previously.

During the seventeenth century the frequency of Huron wares on Mohawk sites increases steadily (figs. 17.4 and 17.5), mirroring the increasing intensity of the Huron-Mohawk conflict and ending with the great diaspora at mid-century. Ceramic assemblages from Mohawk sites dating to the second half of the seventeenth century are composed of as much as 80 percent Huron pottery (Kuhn 1986a). This fact is in keeping with Jesuit statements. The Jesuit Fremin, among the Mohawk in 1667, found the easternmost village of the Mohawk composed of two-thirds Huron and Algonquian captives (Thwaites 1896–1901, 51:121–27).

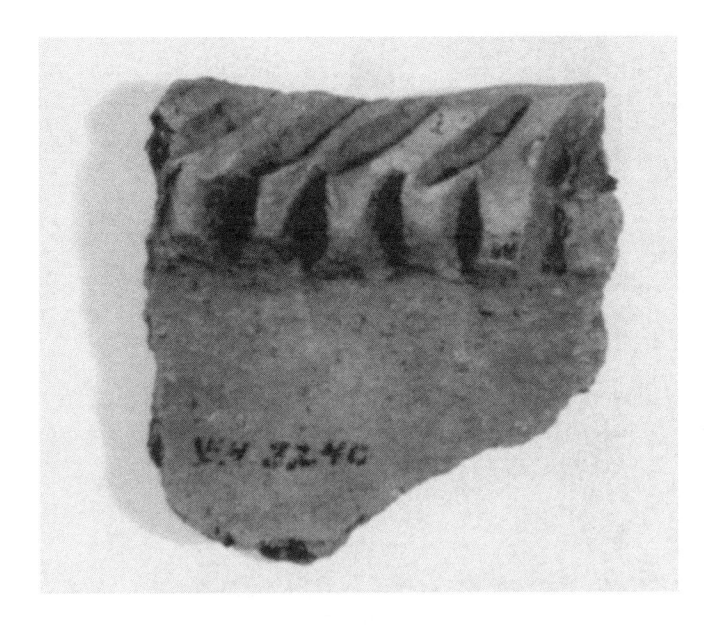

Fig. 17.3. St. Lawrence Iroquoian-like low collar stamped rim sherd from the Martin site.

Fig. 17.4. Huron-like Seed Incised variant rim from the Martin site.

Trace Element Analysis of Mohawk Ceramic Pipes

Some researchers have attempted to assess interaction between tribal groups based on the occurrence of exotically-styled ceramic smoking pipes in site assemblages (Bradley 1987a, 61–62; Pendergast 1981, 33–34; 1985, 34–35), an approach similar to that applied to pottery assemblages. This approach is fraught with difficulty because, unlike pottery, most pipe styles were pan-Iroquoian in distribution.

The documentary record suggests that women made the pots (Sagard-Théodat 1939 [1632], 109) and men made the pipes (Boucher 1664, 55) among the Iroquoians

Fig. 17.5. Huron Incised rim sherds with basal notching from the Martin site.

of the northeast. Also, village domestic activities were the domain of the women while trading and political activities were the domain of the men (Fenton 1978, 297–99; Tooker 1964, 58–59; Trigger 1990b, 130–31). This sexual division of labor led to homogeneous pottery styles and heterogeneous pipe styles, reflective of the different spheres of interaction characteristic of the manufacturing cohorts. Therefore, while some pottery styles are generally diagnostic of some tribal affiliations (Lenig 1965; MacNeish 1952; James Wright 1966, 15) pipe styles are frequently pan-Iroquoian (Mathews 1976; Tuck 1971, 224). Stylistic information appears to have been freely disseminated throughout Iroquoia by males interacting for economic, social, or political reasons. As a result, similar pipe styles were produced by many individuals throughout a large region.

Unfortunately, the pan-Iroquoian distribution of most pipe styles makes it difficult to objectively identify exotic pipes based solely on design motif. The type of analysis conducted with pottery styles cannot be applied to pipes with the same degree of reliability.

An alternative methodology that can be successfully applied to ceramic smoking pipes is trace element analysis. A program of elemental clay source analysis of Iroquoian ceramics using X-ray fluorescence (XRF) and particle-induced X-ray emission (PIXE) spectrometry has been underway for a number of years at the State University of New York at Albany. This approach has been used successfully to identify the presence or absence of pipes of exotic origin in archaeological site assemblages (Kuhn 1986b; Kuhn and Sempowski 2001). Related studies have shown that pipes of so-called exotic styles sometimes do come from foreign clay sources (Kuhn 1985) but often they do not (Kuhn 1986a; 1994b; Kuhn and Sempowski 2001). These results support the conclusion that attempting to interpret pipe styles alone, without information on the source of clay manufacture, is a questionable approach.

Like exotic pottery, the occurrence of exotic pipes in Iroquoian assemblages may have many explanations. Some have argued they indicate the presence of captive males (Pendergast 1985, 34–35) but this interpretation has been challenged (Heidenreich 1990, 482; J. Jamieson 1990b, 82). Others have suggested that smoking pipes were trade items (Brasser 1978b, 83; J. Jamieson 1990b, 82; West 1934, 292). The historical record would seem to favor the latter idea, with trade viewed in the context of Native gift giving, exchange, and reciprocity. It is documented that tobacco pipes were given to Europeans as gifts (John Smith 1910 [1608], 118) and that the Iroquois presented pipes as gifts to other tribes as a symbol of alliance and friendship (Jacobs 1966, 24). Unlike pots, pipes were small, portable, and imbued with power. Trade and exchange between tribes may have included pipes because the symbolism of pipes and tobacco made smoking an important part of Iroquoian social and political relations (Heidenreich 1978, 371; Tooker 1964, 50).

If pipes were important gift or exchange items, then the identification of pipes from other tribes or regions in Mohawk assemblages likely indicates that the Mohawk were participating in a reciprocal interaction network. This interaction would appear to represent a pacific relationship between the tribes in keeping with the Iroquois maxim "Trade and Peace we take to be one thing" (Wraxall 1915, 195).

To conduct such an analysis, trace element data on pottery and pipes from 11 Mohawk, 2 Huron, and 3 St. Lawrence Iroquoian sites were collected using XRF (table 17.2). Samples for this analysis derived from the collections of the State University of New York at Albany, New York State Museum, Royal Ontario Museum, University of Toronto, National Museum of Man in Ottawa, and the private collections of the late Donald Rumrill and the late John Jackowski.

Trace element data on pottery from southeast Ontario, the Mohawk valley, and the St. Lawrence valley were used to determine if clay resources from the regions could be successfully differentiated. This approach was based on the assumption that the vast majority of pottery found on a site was manufactured from locally available clays (Crépeau and Kennedy 1990, 72; Kuhn 1989, 29). If pottery samples could be successfully differentiated, then trace element data on Mohawk pipes of known provenience could be used to determine their probable region of origin.

An in-depth discussion of the methodological approach, XRF analysis, and statistical analyses employed in this research is presented in Kuhn (1985) and will only be briefly summarized here (see also Kuhn and Sempowski 2001 for a more accessible source). In the nondestructive XRF technique each sample to be analyzed was bombarded with X-rays from a radioisotope. The absorption of these primary X-rays cause the sample to emit fluorescent X-rays whose energies are characteris-

Table 17.2

Ceramic Samples Used in the Trace Element Analysis

Region	Site	Pottery	Pipes
Mohawk	Getman #1	10	54
	Elwood	50	22
	Otstungo	7	5
	Garoga	10	68
	Klock	10	8
	Smith-Pagerie	10	10
	Rumrill-Naylor	32	17
	Bauder	5	0
	Oak Hill #1	36	29
	Allen	30	0
	Jackson-Everson	5	10
Huron	Thomson	50	0
	Warminster	55	0
St. Lawrence	Roebuck	4	0
	Lanorie	6	0
	Salem	6	0
Total		326	223

tic of the elements present in the sample. A lithium doped silicon diode and high energy resolution solid state detector were employed for collecting data.

Six trace elements were considered including iron (Fe), rubidium (Rb), strontium (Sr), yttrium (Yt), zirconium (Zr), and barium (Ba) because these elements have been shown to be useful in other trace element research (Trigger et al. 1980; 1984) and because preliminary observations suggested that they would be useful for differentiating the samples in this study. The radioisotopes cadmium 109 and americium 241 were used to excite the sample for collecting data on these elements.

The trace element data were analyzed statistically using discriminant function analysis. Discriminant analysis produces classification functions using that set of trace elements which best discriminates among the pottery groups. These functions may then be used to classify pipe specimens based on their trace element composition. Discriminant analysis also produces jacknifed classification results that may be used to evaluate the accuracy of the classification functions. In the jacknife technique each case is classified into a group according to the classification functions computed from all the data except the case being classified. In this way, the data were used to evaluate the discriminant functions' ability to correctly identify individual ceramic specimens. Likewise, posterior probabilities were computed from the Mahalanobis D statistic as a means of evaluating the classification of individual pipe specimens. A conservative 95 percent posterior probability was assigned for classifying individual specimens into the exotic group.

The results of the discriminant function analysis indicated that trace elements could be used to differentiate between the pottery samples. Using the classification functions generated by the discriminant analysis, Mohawk-Huron pottery samples were classified correctly 87.4 percent of the time, Mohawk-St. Lawrence pottery samples were classified correctly 82.0 percent of the time, and Huron-St. Lawrence pottery samples were classified correctly 72.7 percent of the time. The relatively high level of discrimination between the Mohawk and the two Northern Iroquoian groups (both over 80 percent) suggests that exotic pipes from these groups in Mohawk assemblages should be identifiable using this classification technique.

The discrimination between Huron-St. Lawrence pottery is less than the discrimination between either group and the Mohawk sample but is consistent with the results of a similar study conducted by Bruce G. Trigger et al. (1980). The lower level of discrimination between these groups as compared to the Mohawk is probably related to geographic distance. The clays of southeast Ontario and the St. Lawrence valley are likely more similar to each other because of the close geographic proximity of these regions compared with the distance between either and the Mohawk valley. Others have suggested that pottery was moving between the Huron and the St. Lawrence Iroquoians (Trigger et al. 1980) and the possibility that this factor is confounding the results cannot be entirely dismissed. In any case, the results would seem to indicate that while the classification system should be useful for identifying Northern Iroquoian pipes in Mohawk assemblages, the ability to specifically attribute them to either southeast Ontario or the St. Lawrence valley will not be possible with the same level of confidence.

Table 17.3 presents the classification results for the Mohawk pipe sample using the classification functions established by the discriminant analysis. Of 223 Mohawk ceramic pipes, 4 were identified as Northern Iroquoian in origin with a posterior probability of 95 percent or higher, indicating that this attribution can be made with a high degree of confidence. This conclusion is further supported by the fact that, excluding two isolated outliers, the elemental composition of these four pipes fell outside the entire range of the Mohawk pottery control group.

A significant trend is apparent when the temporal distribution of these four

Table 17.3
List of Northern Iroquoian Pipes in Mohawk Assemblages by Time Period

Case	Posterior Probability	Exotic Pipes	Percent	Period
325	97.3%			
409	95.9%	3/76	4.0%	1400–1500
440	95.6%			
237	96.6%	1/73	1.4%	1500–1550
		0/18	0.0%	1550–1600
		0/56	0.0%	1600–1700

pipe specimens is considered (table 17.3). Northern Iroquoian pipes occur on fifteenth-century Mohawk sites but decline in frequency of occurrence thereafter. Only a single exotic pipe occurs on early sixteenth-century Mohawk sites and no such examples are to be found on Mohawk sites dating after approximately 1550.

In general, little can be said regarding the relationship between exotic pipes and decorative pipe styles because the majority of the specimens included in this study were small pipe fragments or undecorated stems. However, a single informative example of a correlation between pipe styles and foreign manufacture is worthy of special note. One of the pipes made from exotic materials that was identified in the assemblage of the Getman #1 site is a crude pipe stem decorated with rows of punctations. This specimen is illustrated in Ritchie and Funk's (1973, 308, plate 178 #13) report on the site. The poor quality of the specimen and the punctate decoration are both unique attributes within the pipe assemblage from the site but they are both typical of pipes found on Early and, to a lesser extent, Middle Ontario Iroquois sites in southeastern Ontario and the Niagara Frontier. This pipe type also occurs on St. Lawrence Iroquoian sites to a lesser degree (Abel 2001, 265, 271). In this instance, the exotic origin of the pipe suggested by the unique technique of decoration is confirmed by the compositional analysis of the pipe clay.

The identification of exotic Northern Iroquoian pipes on fifteenth-century Mohawk sites suggests that interaction and exchange of material items were taking place between these two regions at this time. It is argued here that these exotic pipes relate to a broad-based interaction sphere that existed across New York and southeast Ontario beginning during the preceding fourteenth century. There is convincing evidence that the fourteenth century was a period of extensive interaction including what Mima Kapches (1995, 91–92) refers to as "across lake sharing" between the Iroquoians of Ontario and New York, that was perhaps the result of "an expanding network of trading partnerships" (Williamson and Robertson 1994, 38). Also, James Wright (1966, 62–63) and Cynthia J. Weber (1971, 58–59) have noted a possible pipe complex diffusion from eastern New York to southeastern Ontario during this period. The fact that New York pipe styles show an expanded stylistic range including new varieties (Ritchie 1980, 303) may also indicate increasing interaction.

Trigger (1990b, 123) describes the fourteenth century as a time of "revolutionary change" and Kapches (1995) argues that a transformative social movement occurred during this period that gave rise to the classic Iroquoian cultural pattern. This pattern included the movement of people into western New York (Niemczycki 1988, 82) and eastern Ontario (Warrick 2000, 445 [chap. 7]). For the eastern Iroquois it did not involve the movement of people but rather an exchange of ideas and cultural patterns with Northern Iroquoians (Kapches 1995, 93), possibly related to the "massive social and political changes that accompanied village fusion" (Trigger 1990b, 124) and/or the rapid population increase that characterized this period in Ontario (Warrick 1996, 16; 2000, 444 [chap. 7]).

The connection between the interaction patterns of the 1300s and the movement of pipes recorded here for the 1400s perhaps receives some small measure of support from the characteristic attributes of the Getman #1 pipe previously discussed, because this style of crude, punctated pipe occurs predominantly on fourteenth-century sites in Canada, although a small number of this type do persist into later times (J. Wright 1966, 71).

The hypothesis that the interaction patterns of the fourteenth century continued through the fifteenth century deserves thoughtful consideration because traditionally the fifteenth century has been described as a period of declining interaction resulting from an increase in warfare. The differentiation of pottery styles that occurred during this period is frequently referenced as evidence of declining interaction. However, changes in pottery may not be a good measure of overall interaction patterns. Kapches (1995, 90–91) has argued that the transition to a matrilineal/matrilocal system occurred among the Iroquoians during the fourteenth century. This is in contrast to alternative interpretations that have dated this important sociocultural change to before 1300 (Warrick 1996, 16; Williamson 1990, 317–19) and perhaps even a number of centuries earlier (Trigger 1990b, 123, 128; Whallon 1968). However, if Kapches is correct, the increasing differentiation of pottery styles between some tribes during the 1400s might simply be the result of changes in female residency and marriage practices that occurred during the previous century of transition. Because women made the pots, the change to a matrilineal/matrilocal system that allowed females to remain in their family longhouses and villages for their entire lives may have led to increased regional and tribal differentiation in pottery styles. There may be other possible explanations for the ceramic patterns of this period (Williamson 1990, 318) that are not based upon an assumption of declining regional interaction or trade patterns.

In contrast to the village-based pottery traditions of Iroquoian females, it was the men in Iroquoian society that were most involved in trade, sociopolitical activities, and other forms of external interaction (Trigger 1990b, 130–31). Therefore, the distribution of pipes, as a male-related item, may provide a superior measure of interaction patterns related to sociopolitical relationships between tribal groups. Given that the results of this study demonstrate that the movement of exotic pipes continued through the fifteenth century, it is argued that, at least on one level, the interaction characteristic of earlier times appears to have continued during this period.

Ronald F. Williamson and David A. Robertson (1998, 147–49) have suggested that peaceful interaction and/or trade was occurring between the Huron-Neutral and Huron-St. Lawrence Iroquoians during the fifteenth century. The Neutral appear to have been in intense conflict with the Central Algonquians of the Western Basin Tradition (Lennox and Fitzgerald 1990, 418, 419) at this time, but the Huron coexisted peacefully with their northern Algonquian neighbors (Warrick 2000, 451 [chap. 7]). Perhaps it is time to dismiss the notion of pan-Iroquoian warfare and recognize that intertribal relations were likely far more complex.

The frequency of long-distance interaction apparently began to decline during the beginning of the sixteenth century and ceased entirely before 1550. The Garoga site was the only sixteenth-century site to contain an exotic pipe and this was a singular example. This decline and cessation of interaction between the Mohawk and Northern Iroquoian groups as reflected by the decline in the trade and exchange of symbolically, socially, and politically important ceramic smoking pipes may reflect the end of peaceful relations between these groups and the onset of the conflict that was to continue into the seventeenth century.

Mohawk Settlement Pattern Data

Two independent lines of evidence—stylistic analysis of pottery and trace element analysis of pipes—appear to correlate. They suggest that the first half of the sixteenth century was a time of changing interaction patterns in which long-standing peaceful relations between the Mohawk and Northern Iroquoian groups were deteriorating and open conflict was developing. A third source of archaeological evidence also reflects this change and further corroborates the results. Mohawk settlement pattern data reveal a significant change in the selected type of site locations occurring around the beginning of the sixteenth century. It seems clear that this change reflects a response to increased warfare at this time.

Mohawk sites that date between 1300 and 1500 are usually located on open level lands, near a water source and arable fields. While the few extensively excavated Mohawk sites from this period have palisades, it would appear that defensive concerns were only one of many considerations in the selection of site locations. Beginning circa 1500, Mohawk sites became far more defensively oriented. They are situated at locations that take advantage of natural defenses and are heavily fortified. This practice continued through the sixteenth century.

Topographic maps of fifteenth- and sixteenth-century Mohawk sites illustrate this shift in settlement patterns (fig. 17.6). The Getman and Elwood sites are representative fifteenth-century examples. Both sites are located on open level lands with no natural defenses. Other fifteenth-century Mohawk sites such as the Second Woods site also fit this pattern. In comparison, the sixteenth-century Otstungo and Garoga sites are situated in highly defensible positions protected by steep, elevated terrain and water. Indeed, the maps hardly do justice to the remarkable locations of these sites. Both are perched high on ridges protected on three sides by precipitous ravines. In the case of Otstungo the sheer 80- to 100-foot-high rock escarpment that defines the western boundary of the site is insurmountable. At both sites the neck of the ridge, which constituted the only easy access to the site, was protected either by a double palisade or a palisade and earthwork ditch and embankment. The palisade found at the Garoga site was substantially heavier than those on earlier sites (Ritchie and Funk 1973, 367). This distinct settlement pattern is typical of other six-

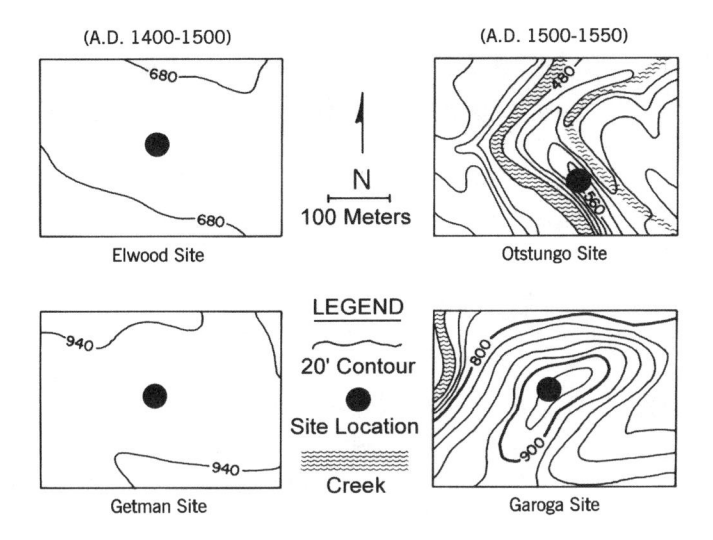

Fig. 17.6. Topographic maps showing location of the Mohawk Getman, Elwood, Otstungo, and Garoga sites. The figure illustrates the shift in settlement patterns that occurred around 1500.

teenth-century occupations in the Mohawk valley such as the Cayadutta, Klock, and Smith-Pagerie sites.

It would appear that a change in the importance of defense, probably representing a significant increase in warfare, occurred among the Mohawk during the early sixteenth century. The Elwood-Otstungo example is particularly important and interesting because it is generally agreed that the two close sites (they are less than 3.5 kilometers apart) represent a single community relocating over time (Bond 1985, 28). At the time this community established the Elwood site the defense of the settlement was apparently far less important than when they established their site at Otstungo a generation later. In contrast to earlier settlements the locations of Mohawk sites during the sixteenth century were selected specifically and primarily with defense in mind even when these sites were less than optimal in terms of living space (Ritchie and Funk 1973, 314) or subsistence needs (Bond 1985).

The Mohawk settlement pattern data may be reflecting a distinct and significant shift in the nature and intensity of warfare beginning around 1500. The settlement pattern data do not provide information concerning the participants in this conflict with the Mohawk. Warfare may have been developing between the Mohawk and many of their neighbors at this time. Nevertheless, the correlation between the timing of this change in settlement pattern and changes in Mohawk relations with the Northern Iroquoians certainly suggest that this was one source of the animosities.

Discussion

Three independent lines of archaeological evidence have been presented that aid in reconstructing the patterns of Iroquoian culture history during the late prehistoric to historic period continuum. Each suggests that the origins of conflict between the Mohawk and the Northern Iroquoians date to the 1500 to 1550 period. The results of the analysis shed light on a number of issues related to Iroquois culture change.

It has long been maintained that interaction patterns were generally restricted and localized during Iroquois prehistory (Bradley 1987a, 25, 34; Ritchie 1980, 293; Trigger 1981a, 33; Tuck 1978, 328). The primary archaeological evidence for this position has included (1) the lack of exotic goods found on sites dating between 1300 and 1500, and (2) the evidence for warfare in the form of village palisades and human remains in refuse middens, which presumably acted as a deterrent to interaction (Tuck 1978, 326, 328). This traditional view of the Iroquois as individual, localized communities increasingly drawn into conflict and competition has promoted the interpretation that Iroquois tribalism originated as a response to increasing warfare (Tuck 1971, 213; Bradley 1987a, 25).

While the lack of trade items on prehistoric Iroquois sites is suggestive of restricted interaction, caution should be used when interpreting this type of negative evidence. Trade items are difficult to identify archaeologically unless they embody diagnostic features such as visually recognizable exotic styles or materials (G. Wright 1974). The current study serves as a case in point because it demonstrates that previously unrecognized exotic pipes can be identified by typing their clay composition. The results of the trace element analysis suggest that exotic pipes were moving between Iroquoian communities during the fifteenth century. Although most of the archaeological evidence indicates that Iroquois villages during this period were relatively isolated, inward-oriented communities, at least at one level it appears that long-distance interaction was occurring. This interaction, represented by exotic pipes in Mohawk assemblages, may have been sociopolitical in nature given the symbolic associations of this male-related artifact type.

Although conflict may have acted as a deterrent to interaction, the relative intensity of prehistoric warfare during this period is difficult to measure and varied over time (Milner 1999). Unlike the seventeenth-century pattern, earlier (pre-1400) Iroquoian warfare was probably "a delicate balance of suspended blood feud" (Fenton 1978, 315) in which conflict took the form of raiding and small ambushes (Milner 1999, 126–27). James Bruce Jamieson (1990b, 83) describes this pattern as traditional tribal warfare and indicates that it did not include large-scale conflicts. This condition may not have posed a serious deterrent to interaction and intercommunity or intertribal contacts.

Jamieson (1990b, 83–84) argues that traditional tribal warfare gave way to more intense territorial warfare beginning around 1400. Similarly, George R. Milner (1999, 125) argues that "heightened hostilities" from competition over "prime patches of land" occurred around 1400 with the onset of the Little Ice Age. In addition, Gary A. Warrick (1996, 18, 19) states that "Iroquoian warfare appears to have escalated at the beginning of the fifteenth century" and that during the sixteenth century "warfare persisted at the same intensity as during the preceding fifteenth century." Serious questions must be raised regarding the timing that has been proposed for the escalation of warfare and whether it can be applied to the Mohawk and the eastern Iroquois.

While these estimates may be valid for southeast Ontario or other parts of the northeastern woodlands, it is impossible to reach similar conclusions based upon the archaeological record for the eastern Iroquois. Fourteenth- and fifteenth-century villages are not sited in locations especially conducive to defense and have similar palisading (e.g., Ritchie and Funk 1973, 255, 292; Snow 1995e, 101; Tuck 1971, 49). There is no evidence of increasing warfare over the 1300 to 1500 period. In contrast, a very substantial change to defensive site locations and heavy palisades occurs at the beginning of the sixteenth century, undoubtedly indicating a major escalation of warfare at this time. The pottery and pipe data corroborate this interpretation.

The results of this study also are relevant to interpreting the role of European contact and the fur trade on patterns of Iroquoian warfare. The changes in settlement pattern evident at the Mohawk Otstungo site indicate a significant change in the nature and intensity of warfare at the turn of the sixteenth century. Despite extensive professional excavations at this site (Snow 1995e, 115–38) no European trade goods have been found. The faunal assemblage from the site also has a low frequency of beaver and other fur-bearing species (Kuhn and Funk 2000, 41). From this evidence it appears that the initial escalation of warfare around 1500 clearly predates Mohawk involvement in the European fur trade. The intensification of warfare at this time is probably rooted in the gradual process of tribal development rather than in European contact.

Nevertheless, it is also clear that the fur trade began to influence patterns of Iroquoian conflict during the sixteenth century. The pottery and pipe evidence presented in this study indicate that by the second quarter of the sixteenth century the Mohawk were directly involved in conflict with Northern Iroquoian groups. It is during this same time period that the first European trade goods appear among the Mohawk at the Garoga site (Ritchie and Funk 1973, 327). It is also during this period that a significant increase in beaver occurs in the faunal assemblages of Mohawk sites (Kuhn and Funk 2000, 41). All of this evidence would seem to suggest that during the second quarter of the sixteenth century the conflict between the Mohawk and Northern Iroquoian groups was stimulated by the fur trade.

Conclusion

Three independent lines of archaeological evidence were brought to bear on questions concerning trade, interaction, and warfare patterns between the Mohawk and Northern Iroquoians. To a large degree the three lines of evidence produced consistent results that suggest that conflict and warfare between these groups originated during the early sixteenth century. The preceding centuries appear to be characterized by interaction, long-distance trade or exchange between these groups, and lower levels of conflict. A dramatic increase in warfare around the beginning of the sixteenth century clearly predates European contact but control of the fur trade soon became an important aspect of the warfare between these groups.

Acknowledgments

Much of the data for this study was gathered many years ago as part of my dissertation research (Kuhn 1985). I would like to thank the following individuals and institutions for providing samples of ceramic artifacts used in the trace element analysis aspect of this study: James V. Wright and Karen Murchison—Canadian Museum of Civilization, Mima Kapches—Royal Ontario Museum, John Reid—University of Toronto, Robert E. Funk and Beth Wellman—New York State Museum, Dean R. Snow—State University of New York at Albany. I would like to thank William Engelbrecht—Buffalo State College, for providing stylistic data on Mohawk ceramics collected during his dissertation research; Robert E. Funk and Beth Wellman—New York State Museum, for providing access to that institution's ceramic collections; the late Mr. Donald Rumrill of Gloversville, New York, and the late Mr. John Jackowski of Amsterdam, New York, for allowing me to analyze their collections of Mohawk pottery. I would also like to thank Bill Engelbrecht, Jim Bradley, and Jim Wright for their comments on an earlier version of this paper. Finally, this paper is dedicated to Jim Pendergast, who enthusiastically encouraged my interest in Iroquoian archaeology and ceramic analysis.

18 | Oneida Ceramic Effigies
A Question of Meaning
ANTHONY WONDERLEY

Introduction

"THE MOST INTRIGUING ITEM in an Oneida pottery collection is the effigy face or figure," observed Ted Whitney (1971, 12) of human-like depictions found on ceramics from the late 1400s to the mid-1600s A.D. I agree. Representations of undeniable conceptual importance, these consciously fashioned icons or symbols constitute the largest database available to us of material symbols significant to Oneidas long ago.

This article outlines a four-step approach to investigating the meaning(s) these images may have conveyed to their users. First, I evaluate the effigies as an artistic tradition, emphasizing how Oneida imagery focused thematically on one humanoid figure or on a limited set of anthropomorphic representations. Over time, the figure became more clearly defined in a naturalistic sense through the addition of standardized anatomical detail. The potters' design grammar evidently required that effigies could occur at only one location—on the exterior of a pot at or below a castellation (an upward flaring point at the top of a vessel's collar). Analyzing the imagery present at the castellated position, I suggest the humanoid effigy was linked iconographically to corn.

One must assume, I think, that the cultural meaning of effigies was consistent with the social setting in which effigy-bearing pots were employed. Consequently, the second kind of research is reviewing historical and archaeological evidence bearing on how these objects were made and used. Effigy pots were part of the domestic, utilitarian ceramic assemblage—a culinary complex centered on boiling corn. Knowledge of food preparation and of pottery-making was in the heads and hands of women. Within this sociocultural setting, one in which corn and kettles

Previously published in *Northeast Anthropology* 63 (2002): 23–48. Printed with permission by *Northeast Anthropology*.

resonated with cultural meaning, the most likely connotations of effigies included domesticity, femaleness, and corn.

On the basis of those criteria, the third operation is the attempted identification of the being(s) depicted. The most likely candidate among the corpus of ethnographically attested Iroquois beliefs is a mythological race of cornhusk people.

Perhaps the closest we can approach to a past mindset is to project back in time a characteristically Iroquois outlook on humans' place and duty in the cosmos. The fourth step, then, is the proposal that effigies make sense as evidence of a covenant between human women and non-human beings, presumably cornhusk people.

The last of these points is introduced first in a review of what archaeologists have made of effigies. I then present the basic data pertaining to effigy distribution and sequence.

Iroquois Effigy Traditions and Oneida Archaeology

Archaeological Approaches to Effigies

Ceramic effigies have attracted little scholarly notice in the Northeast. Most Iroquois ceramicists have ignored them altogether in sociologically oriented research emphasizing data quantification. Typically, such researchers apply statistical gauges of sameness or difference to samples of measurements taken from vessel forms and collar designs. Resulting measures of heterogeneity or homogeneity are interpreted behaviorally as reflecting, for example, the intensity of inter-regional hostility (Whallon 1968), forms of economic exchange (Engelbrecht 1974b), or degrees of craft specialization (Allen 1992).

An alternative approach stresses how Iroquois pots may have functioned as beacons broadcasting information pertaining to ethnicity and group membership/values.

> Pots were used for cooking on the hearth in the center of each longhouse compartment and were visible to everyone on a daily basis. Because maize stews were cooked for long periods of time, pots would often sit on the hearth for many hours. With the base of the pots either sitting in or dangling over the fire, the pronounced, geometrically incised collars on the vessels were a prominent, central icon for anyone entering the longhouse compartment.... [S]tylistic information was exchanged not only when pots were sitting in the hearth but when groups of women gathered to make pots. The slab-building of pots of consistent size and shape and the repetitive incising of decorations on collars provide the potential for pots to embody messages about group membership, the role of women, social integration, and the egalitarian ideal of Iroquois society. Thus, pots, as a central and visible output of the joint effort of women within the matrilineage, had the potential for carrying social messages in both manufacture and use. (Chilton 1999, 59)

Though obviously closer to the concerns of this study, that perspective (also) does not address the subject of effigy meaning. Indeed, effigies on pots have been considered in the Iroquois archaeological literature only when lumped together with other forms of representational imagery (on figurines, and effigy combs and pipes, for example) in very general culture-historical interpretive schemes. One suggestion is that faces appearing in the archaeological record about a millennium ago signaled the appearance of the False Face medicine society with masks (Ritchie and Funk 1973, 367; Tuck 1971, 213). Another interpretation relates a florescence of Iroquois material culture (including an increase in imagery) during the sixteenth and seventeenth centuries to an upsurge in ritual activity linked, in turn, to the European encounter (Hamell 1987a; 1998). The latter circumstances may also be connected, according to James W. Bradley (1987a), to the formation and revitalization of the Iroquois League.

My approach to effigies is inspired by the hope of understanding something of the world as it may have been perceived by the makers and users of the artifacts (Hall 1977). An obvious impression conveyed by Iroquois representational images, as Daniel K. Richter (1992, 28) observes, is that these people "devoted their highest artistic and technical talents to materials that connected them to the spirit world." When one looks, for example, at their effigy pipes,

> [i]t is likely . . . that this increased use of effigy pipes is a material reflection of a deep and fundamental aspect of Onondaga culture. [They] were preoccupied with maintaining good and correct relations with the spirit world and all its (super)natural forces. . . . This meant avoiding offensive behavior and rigorously heeding whatever demands were made, usually through the medium of dreams. From an Onondaga perspective, compliance with such requests through prescribed ceremonies and rituals was prerequisite to health, abundance, and success in hunting and war. (Bradley 1987a, 123)

Iroquois imagery resulted from their perception of the world and any attempt to approach such meaning requires close attention to (specifically) Iroquois outlook and culture. Although ceramic effigies have not been examined in this fashion, a different kind of Iroquois representational material has been so studied.

Several archaeological researchers have focused on culturally appropriate information in efforts to interpret Iroquoian effigy pipes (e.g., Mathews 1976; 1980). A pipe effigy typically depicted an animal or human facing the smoker. Such "self-directed" representations "related to the spiritual communications between men and their guardian spirits, cultivated by means of meditation while contemplating the representations of these spirits" (Brasser 1980, 100). Hence, the act of smoking was a private ritual of communication between the pipe owner and the effigy being.

Because smoking among the Iroquois was a male activity, most pipes belonged to men. A man presumably contracted a ritual relationship with a guardian who could bestow success in male activities. An appropriate and particularly potent supernatural guardian would be panther, an archetypal warrior and sorcerer in Iroquoian thinking according to George R. Hamell (1998, 272–73, 287). Such an interpretation implicitly carries predictive power. We should see panther-related imagery on men's pipes and war clubs (as apparently we do), and we should find different imagery expressed when the social contexts and purposes do not focus on exclusively personal and male concerns. Thus the cultural meaning of effigy pipes is clarified, and the imagery of the object is related to the object's use and user.

As our Iroquois pipe-smoker probably understood it, humans and other-than-human beings were linked by reciprocal social responsibilities to maintain their common world. The social order was (and is) underwritten by ritual contract in which the human obligation is to acknowledge and give thanks for the cosmos (Hamell 1987a, 77). The essence of this ancient worldview is preserved today in the Iroquois Thanksgiving Address, a kind of all-purpose ritual speech in which humans gratefully affirm they still are performing their proper duties (Chafe 1961). By renewing their covenant in this fashion, human beings contribute their crucial and ordained part to continuance of the universe. Simultaneously, respectful acknowledgment encourages other spiritual beings to render their assistance to humans (Shimony 1994, 140).

These are valuable clues for visualizing Iroquois symbolic material through Iroquois eyes. Applying them to the results of iconographic, contextual, and ethnographic research (discussed below), I propose Oneida effigies may be the surviving material correlates of a specifically human female obligation. The effigies bespeak silent invocation, a form of thanksgiving offered in fulfillment of ritual contract by Oneida food-providers to non-human beings responsible for making possible agricultural harvests.

Areal Distribution

Though best known among the Oneidas and other Iroquois of present upstate New York, anthropomorphic effigies occurred rather widely throughout the Northeast. Before outlining the archaeological evidence for the development of effigies in Oneida country, I summarize the distribution of effigies in the Northeast with remarks on other Iroquois effigies.

Pottery effigies similar to Oneida examples are reported from protohistoric to seventeenth-century contexts across much of the Northeast (fig. 18.1). Effigies depicting faces occurred among people who spoke Algonquian languages in a region embracing the Upper Delaware region of Pennsylvania and New Jersey (Kraft 1975); eastern New York (Lopez and Wisniewski 1989, 238); and southern New England (Grumet 1995, 143; Snow 1978, 66; Willoughby 1935, 197).

People who spoke Iroquoian languages fashioned face and figure effigies on

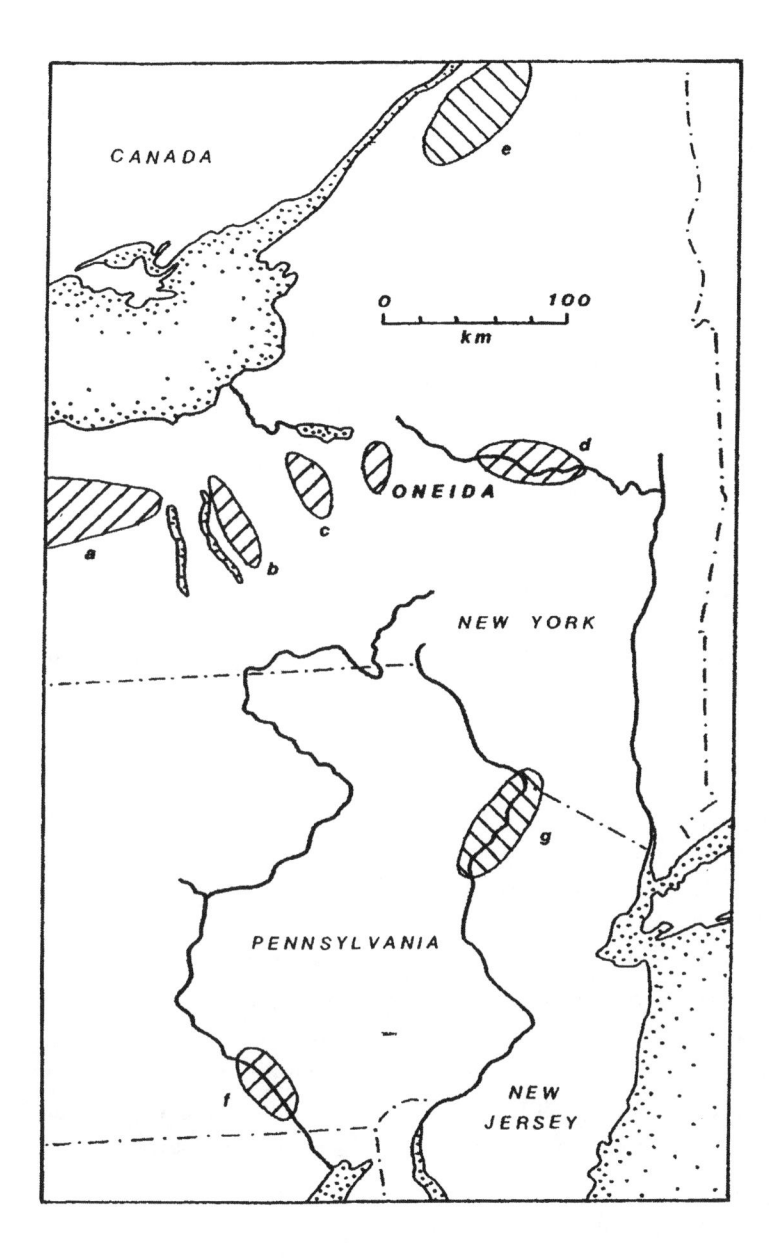

Fig. 18.1. Locations of Oneida and other ceramic effigy traditions mentioned in text. (a) Seneca; (b) Cayuga; (c) Onondaga; (d) Mohawk; (e) Jefferson County St. Lawrence Iroquoian; (f) Susquehannock; (g) Minisink.

ceramics distributed from at least the Susquehanna River drainage of Pennsylvania to the Canadian shores of the St. Lawrence. In the south, human-like figures are characteristic of Susquehannock pottery (Kent 1980, fig. 3; Skinner in Moorehead 1938, 60, plates xx and xxi). In the north, abstract effigy faces are typical of St. Lawrence Iroquoian pottery, including that of Jefferson County, New York (Parker 1920, plate 47; Pendergast 1968, plates IV-2, 5, 6; Pendergast 1991b, 61; Skinner 1921, plates xxvii-xxix; Wintemberg 1936, plates v and viii-ix).

Possible antecedents in the form of apparent faces applied or incised somewhere on ceramic vessels are sporadically reported around the horizon of A.D. 1000 throughout much the same area: from coastal New York (Lopez and Latham 1960), to the Susquehanna River, to southern Ontario (J. Wright 1972, plates 16a and 17a).

William M. Beauchamp regarded effigy faces and figures as "the highest achievement" in Iroquois ceramic art (1898, 92). Although rare in Cayuga pottery, effigies probably are present among ceramics of all of five original nations of the Iroquois League (Mohawk, Oneida, Onondaga, Cayuga, Seneca) in New York (figs. 18.2 and 18.3). If explicit discussion of effigies is any guide to their frequency, one would have to guess they occur commonly among Onondaga and Seneca assemblages. The highest frequencies of all may derive from Oneida country.[1]

The Onondaga effigy phenomenon is intimately related to and possibly identical with that of the Oneidas (described below). Researchers have said Onondaga and Oneida effigies look the same (Gibson 1968; MacNeish 1952, 68–69). More important, Onondaga effigies resemble Oneida examples in origin and development. Described as large and sometimes grotesque faces placed beneath castellations, effigies appeared suddenly in the Onondaga archaeological record sometime before 1500. During the sixteenth century, bodies were added to the faces to become full-figure images (Bradley 1987a, 38, 55). Between 1600 and 1655, "Small effigies, both applied and incised, continue to be placed beneath castellations" (Bradley 1987a, 122) (figs. 18.2b-c, 18.3b, and 18.3d).

Seneca effigies, in contrast, may have appeared slightly later in time and are said to have been uncommon during the first half of the sixteenth century (Hayes 1980; Wray 1973, 12). After about 1550, "[e]ffigy pottery increased in occurrence, with mask like human faces or stylized human figures beneath castellations" (Wray 1973, 12; cf. Ritchie 1954, plates 29.2 and 30.2).

Yet Seneca effigy practice of the late 1500s focused neither on face nor figure. The decorative feature most frequently placed beneath a Seneca castellation was an applied strip of clay indented with a series of horizontally parallel hash marks (Cervone 1991; Wray et al. 1987). Seneca archaeologists define this effigy as the "ladder motif" (fig. 18.2a). While the ladder motif is occasionally present among eastern Iroquois assemblages, it is rare in proportion to anthropomorphic effigies.

The Oneida Effigy Sequence

When Richard S. MacNeish published the first description of Iroquois pottery types in 1952, virtually all that he said about effigies anywhere related to Oneida

---

1. MacNeish thought effigies were rare everywhere (1952, 8), but one must still rely on impressionistic judgments in any comparison because we lack a standard measure of effigy frequency. For example, in Seneca country during the period of about 1560–95, the ratio of effigy occurrence to vessels (whole pots or rims thought to be from distinct vessels) is about 1:31. No comparable Oneida figure can be offered based on entire or reconstructable pots.

Oneida Ceramic Effigies • 349

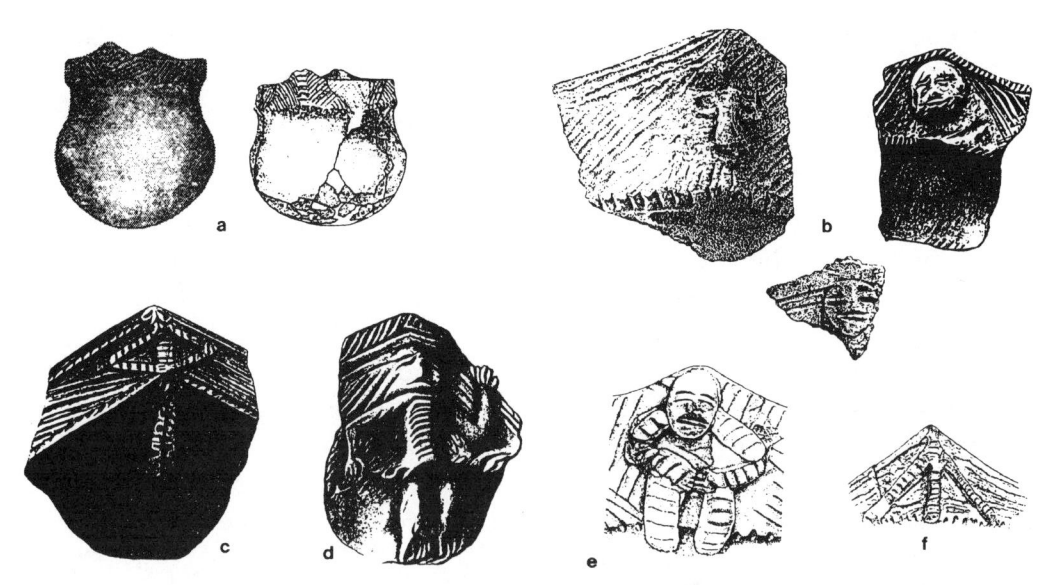

Fig. 18.2. Iroquois effigies (not to scale). (a) Seneca vessels with ladder motif at castellation (Wray et al. 1987, figs. 3–40h, 3–41g); (b) Onondaga faces (Bradley 1987a, fig. 4a-b; Beauchamp 1898, fig. 52); (c) Onondaga figure (Beauchamp 1898, fig. 54); (d) Mohawk figure (Beauchamp 1898, fig. 41); (e) Seneca figure (Wray et al. 1987, fig. 3–36a); (f) Seneca effigy (Cervone 1991, fig. 7–54e).

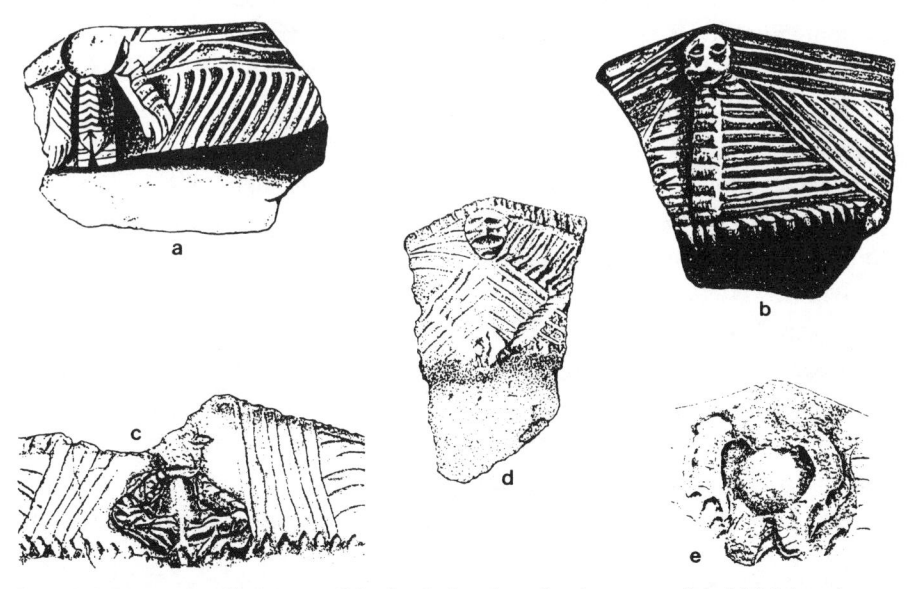

Fig. 18.3. Iroquois effigies possibly depicting females (not to scale). (a) Mohawk (Beauchamp 1898, fig. 108); (b) Onondaga (Beauchamp 1898, fig. 51); (c) Seneca (Wray et al. 1987, fig. 3–36b); (d) Onondaga (Bradley 1987a, fig. 4d); (e) Seneca (Cervone 1991, fig. 7–54d).

materials. He defined a sequence of Oneida effigies beginning with faces, then adding bodies fitted to the faces. That remains an accurate description after a half-century (1952, 68–69).

Faces first appeared within the Oneida archaeological record probably in the second half of the fifteenth century[2] at the Buyea and Goff sites (Pratt 1976, 100) (fig. 18.4). Placed beneath a castellation and 2.5 to 5 centimeters (cm) in length, most were anthropomorphic with two eyes, an obvious nose, and a mouth. Highly variable in style, some depictions look so simple or conventionalized as to seem abstract. Other more naturalistic renderings range between what could pass as grotesque caricature or realistic portrait. They also are diverse technically. Some apparently were modeled into the vessel fabric; the majority seem to have been sculpted on a disk or lump of clay that was then applied to the vessel wall. Individual facial features were incised, modeled, and punctated, and often more than one technique was employed on the same face. Most commonly, eyes were indicated by means of two horizontally parallel incisions.

At approximately A.D. 1500, distinct limbs were also applied to Oneida vessels recovered from the Olcott site (fig. 18.5 j-k). They may have been connected to the faces but, on the extant ceramic fragments, they seem disembodied and disarticulated. The apparent arms and legs usually are incised with hash marks.

The beginning of full-figure depiction in Oneida effigy art dates to the early 1500s at the Vaillancourt site. One sherd bears an upper torso and arms, all hash-marked, attached to a face (fig. 18.6g). However, faces without bodies or body parts predominate at this site (figs. 18.6 and 18.7). By about the middle of the sixteenth century at the Bach and Diable sites, a fair number of arms and legs were linked unequivocally to faces. In some cases, limbs and faces were attached, in proper anatomical fashion, to torsos (fig. 18.8). Clearly, these body parts were intended to be understood as part of an anthropomorphic figure.

Faces without bodies continued to be depicted throughout the sequence. Such isolated faces or heads (size highly variable) do not obviously differ from those attached to bodies.

During approximately the fourth quarter of the sixteenth century, the techniques used to represent the effigy image included diverse mixtures of appliqué and incision (Cameron site, see fig. 18.9). There was, however, greater consistency in depicting the figure's posture from this time through the early seventeenth century (Beecher, Thurston, and Marshall sites). The orientation of the arms typically was downward, often with elbows out and hands at hip (figs. 18.10 and 18.11).

2. The basic Oneida sequence of sites was defined by Pratt (1976) and Whitney (1970). All dates are approximate. Those early in the sequence are my estimates based on dates suggested for neighboring Mohawk (Snow 1995e) and Onondaga (Bradley 1987a) areas. Beginning with the A.D. 1570 date (Cameron site), I use dates proposed by Bennett (1983).

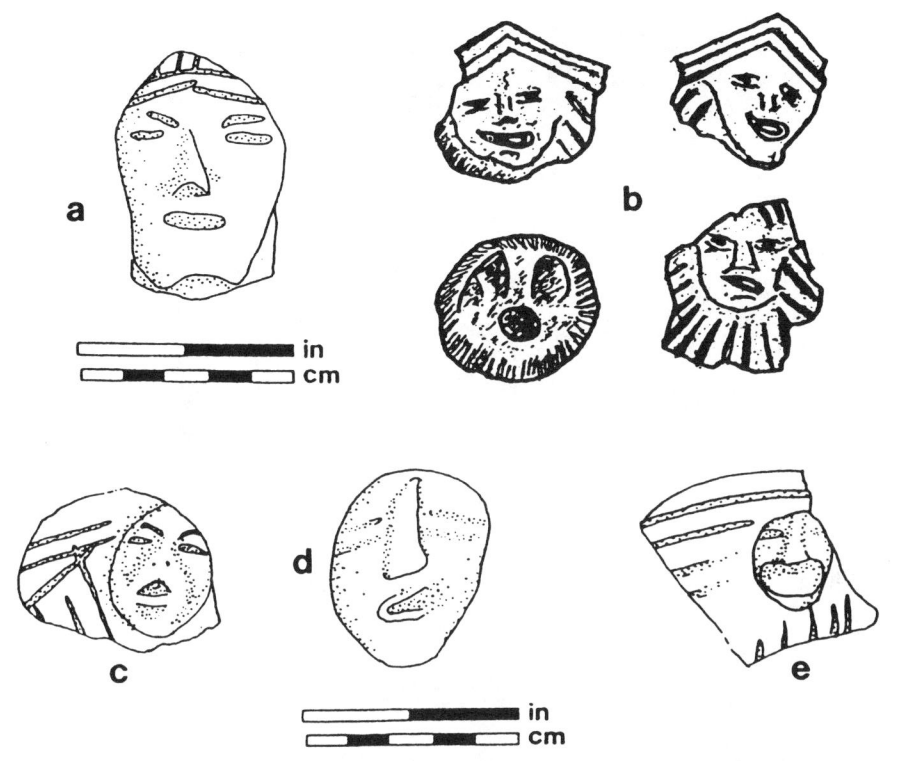

Fig. 18.4. Oneida effigies (ca. 1450–1500) from the Buyea (a-b) and Goff (c-e) sites (Whitney 1970, plate 4 [b: scale unknown]; and courtesy of Richard Hosbach [a], New York State Museum [c-d], and Longyear Museum, Colgate Univ. [e]).

Limbs and torsos continued to be hash-marked. Both MacNeish (1952, 68) and Peter P. Pratt (1976, 122) remark on the increasingly conventionalized appearance of the effigy image at this point late in the sequence.

A new trait at the Beecher site (ca. 1595–1620), according to Pratt, was "Thurston Horizontal pottery with the highly conventionalized medallion-like full human effigy beneath the castellation" (1976, 126). This kind of pottery remained the characteristic vehicle for effigy imagery at the succeeding Thurston (ca. 1625–37) and Marshall sites (ca. 1637–40) (fig. 18.12). Describing effigies on Thurston Horizontal from Marshall, MacNeish states:

> Often on pots of this type from historic sites there are human effigies under the castellations. The head is round with the facial features fairly distinct; the body is short and rectangular, usually with closely spaced horizontal lines crossing it. The arms extend out and downward from the body and are indistinct; they also are crossed by horizontal incisions. . . . The legs extend straight down from the body. Often the lower legs extend below the collar, while the thigh is on the collar. This gives the legs a slightly flexed appearance. The feet may come together or be slightly apart. The legs are also crossed by horizontal incisions. (1952, 66, 68)

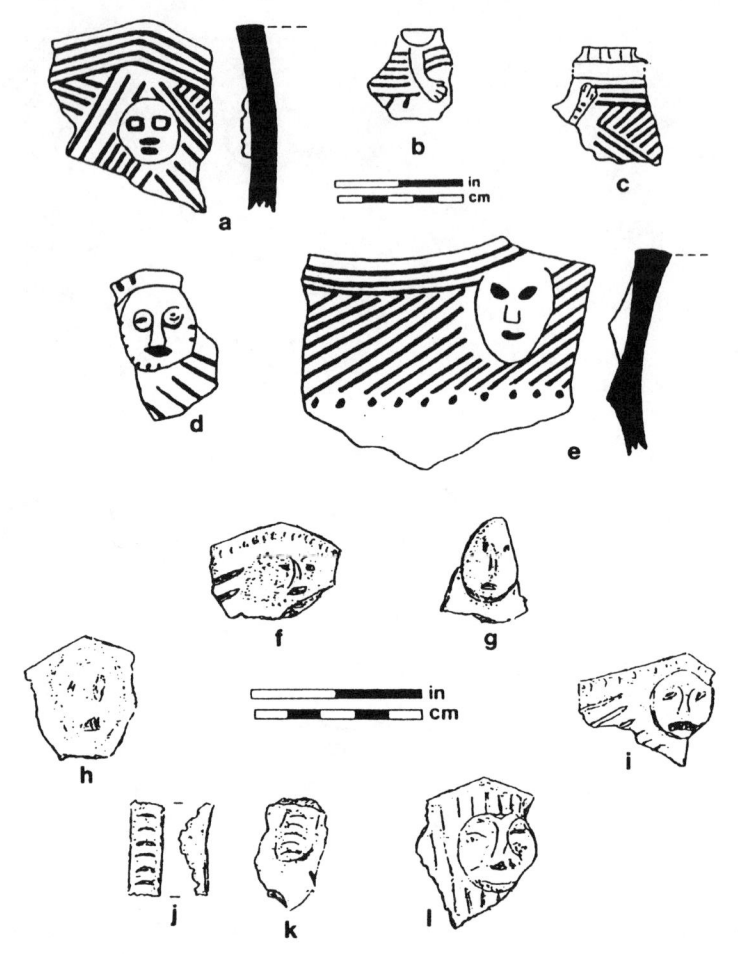

Fig. 18.5. Oneida effigies (ca. 1500–1525) from the Olcott site (Pratt 1963, plates 3–5 and 7–8; Whitney 1971, plate 7, nos. 1–7).

On most effigy figures from the Thurston and Marshall sites, the torso is indicated by means of two vertically parallel bands or ribbons. They are hash-marked; often there is an apparent open space left between them. Below the torso area, the ribbons resolve into the figure's legs. In addition, many figures have what look like wavy or possibly spike-like protuberances projecting outward from the exterior borders of the image (figs. 18.10j and 18.12).

Native-made ceramics declined rapidly after 1640, the effigy tradition apparently ending with the abandonment of fired clay vessels (Bennett 1984b, 19, 31). The latest effigies I have seen derive from the Sullivan site (ca. 1660–77; Longyear Museum, Colgate University).

How many Oneida pots actually carried effigies? The only statistic available is a relative and extremely crude one: the ratio of rims with effigies to total number of rim sherds. At the first appearance of effigies late in the fifteenth century (Buyea

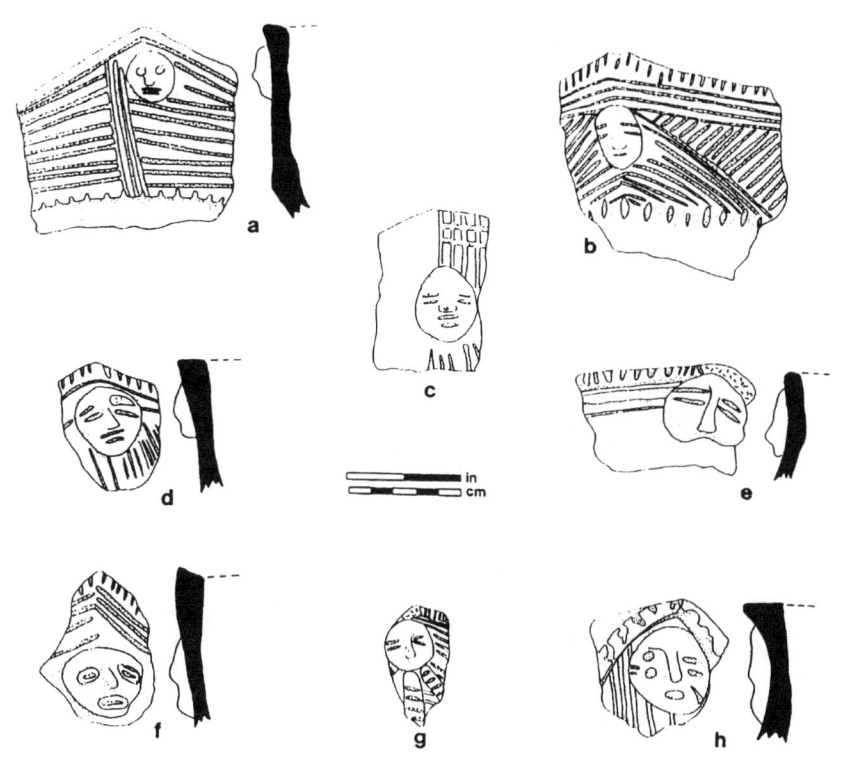

Fig. 18.6. Oneida effigies (ca. 1500–1525) from the Vaillancourt site (rim sherd silhouettes after Pratt 1961, plate 2a; courtesy of Richard Hosbach [b], Alexander Neill [c], and Longyear Museum, Colgate Univ.).

site), that ratio is 1:60. At a late sixteenth-century site (Cameron) it is 1:20; at an early seventeenth-century site (Beecher) it is 1:7 (Bennett 1979, 17; Bennett and Clark 1978, 25; Whitney 1970, 7). If these figures are representative, they indicate effigies became more popular over time.

The Oneida ceramic imagery of effigies may be medium-specific. My impression is that the same images occur rarely or not at all on other contemporaneous classes of representational material including effigy pipes and carved combs and figurines. Other classes of material representation seem far more variable in content and far less obviously patterned.

Oneida Effigy Art: Formal and Iconographic Observations

There is substantial variation in the construction or technical realization of the effigy throughout the Oneida effigy sequence. From the beginning, applied and incised techniques coexisted for constructing a face. When the sample from one site is relatively large as it is from Cameron, what is striking is the number of combinations and technical variations employed to realize the figure (fig. 18.9). Yet, however the effigy was created, the figure itself was standardized.

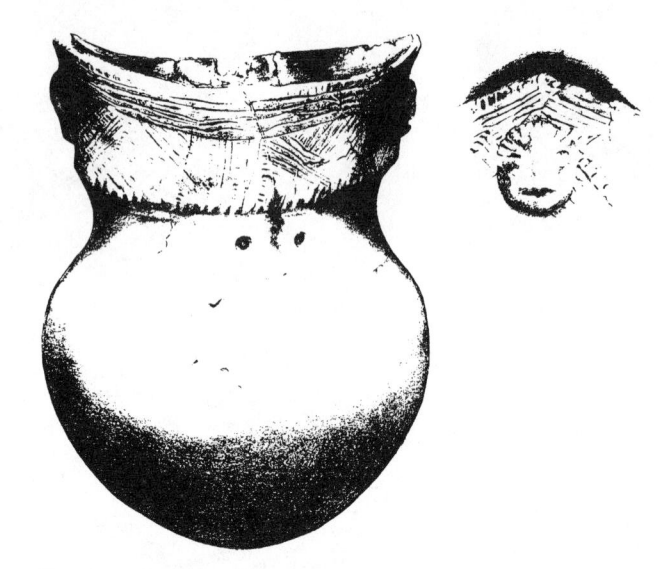

Fig. 18.7. Oneida effigy vessel (ca. 1500–1525), ca. 28 cm high, from the Vaillancourt site (courtesy of Longyear Museum, Colgate Univ., #2087; drawing by Julia Meyerson). The detail drawing depicts the only intact effigy face (one of two originally).

Figural effigies made by other New York Iroquois generally lack sexual indications. However, when sexually specific features are depicted, invariably they seem to be female as indicated by apparent genitalia or protuberant bellies (fig. 18.3). Judging by several examples created with what look like cleft crotches, the same probably is true of Oneida effigies (figs. 18.9i and 18.9o).

Variation in figural imagery was very limited. Effigies on the same complete pot look about the same. In a dozen examples I have examined, I cannot identify obvious distinctions between or among the figures placed on one vessel (fig. 18.12). The implication is that one vessel's effigies were intended to denote the same image of a humanoid figure (cf. Wray et al. 1987, 76).

Hardly any imagery departs from the human-like figure. Pratt identified, at the beginning of the effigy sequence (Goff site), two depictions of animals (1976, plate 17, nos. 14 and 18).[3]

Theodore Whitney reported an effigy ear of corn from the Olcott site (fig. 18.13d) and mentioned a second, said to be stylistically different, from the Bach site (1971, 12). Another aberrant effigy (Cameron site) is composed of three hash-marked fillets joined at one point (fig. 18.13b). One other example (Vaillancourt site) is the ladder motif so popular in Seneca country (fig. 18.13c). With these few

---

3. One of the effigies from the Goff site illustrated by Pratt is in the Longyear Museum, Colgate University holdings. It looks like a fat (pregnant?) frog.

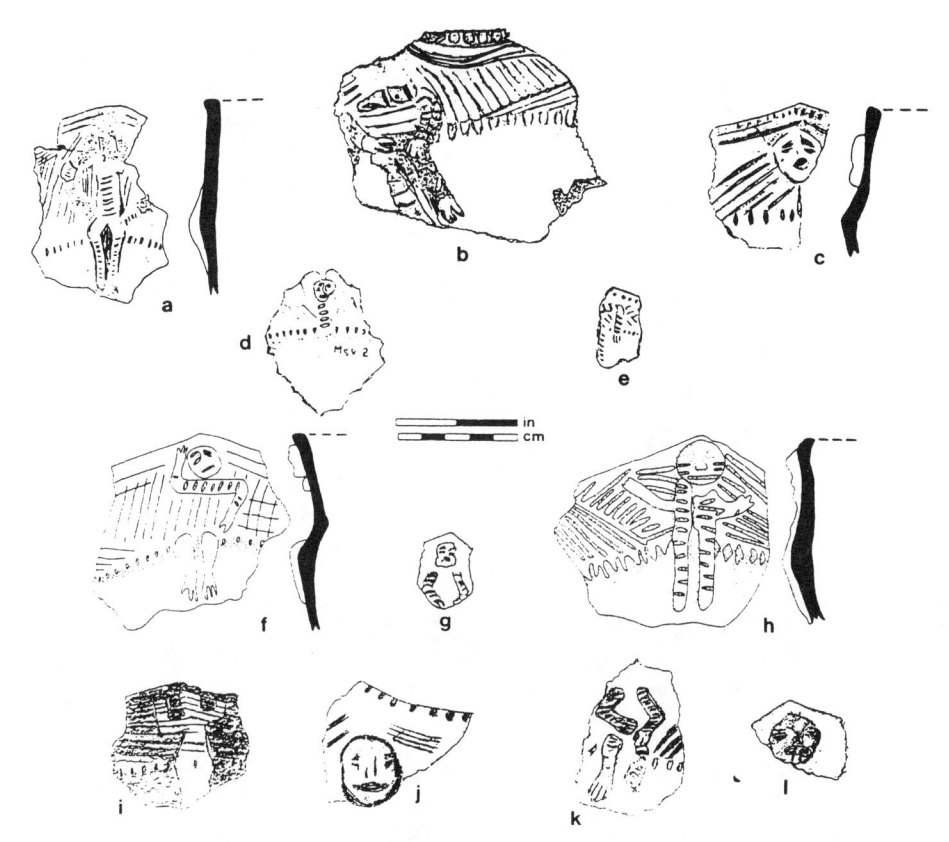

Fig. 18.8. Oneida effigies (ca. 1525–70) from the Diable (a-e) and Bach (f-l) sites (Gibson 1963, plates 3 and 4; Gibson 1991, fig. 7; Whitney 1967, plate 5; Whitney 1974, plate 4; Whitney in Young 1995, plate 1; after Pratt 1976, plate 20, no. 6 [h]).

exceptions, all other effigies reported from about a century and a half fit neatly within a corpus of anthropomorphic representation.

Just as all effigies on one vessel look as though they depict one humanoid figure, all anthropomorphic effigies on Oneida pots may have depicted the same subject. This is a logical supposition suggested by the manner in which the image evolved over time. It followed a coherent trajectory informed by a consistent representational logic dedicated to depicting the anthropomorphic theme naturalistically.

Change occurred in the direction of greater representational detail. An initial impulse to depict facial features was followed by the addition of more naturalistic features: first limbs; then limbs and torso areas recognizable as such in realist terms and clearly shown to be of an anatomical piece with the faces. Over time, additional specificity of detail included the distinctive bifurcated torso ribbons. While some effigies are more realistically depicted than others, verisimilitude (in the sense of photo-realism) is not the key feature of this representational development. As MacNeish observed, "No attempt seems to have been made to reproduce actual body contours or dimensions" (1952, 68). Rather, it is as though details were cumula-

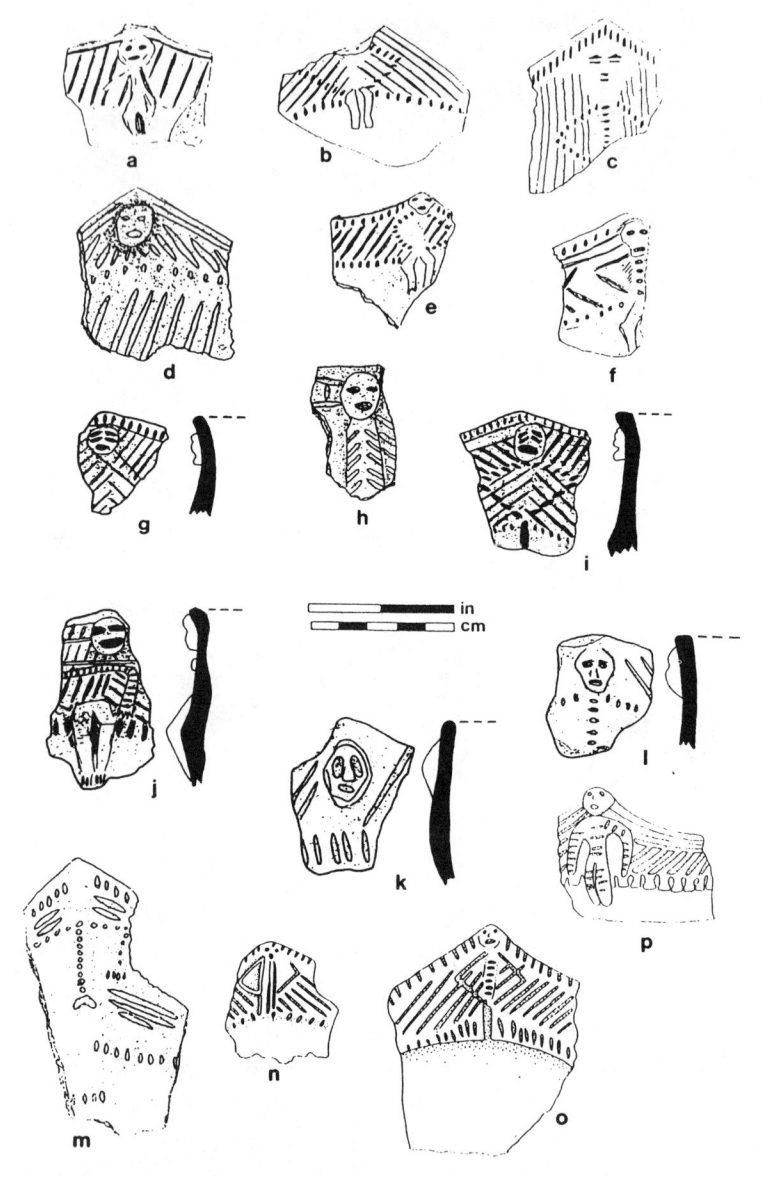

Fig. 18.9. Oneida effigies (ca. 1570–95) from the Cameron site (Bennett 1981, plates 13 and 14; Bennett and Bigford 1968, plate 9; Bennett and Clark 1978, plates 31 and 32; Bennett and Hatton 1988, plate D; and courtesy of Alan Sterling [n], Longyear Museum, Colgate Univ. [o], and Rochester Museum and Science Center [p]).

tively provided that would increasingly sharpen the definition or recognition of what was being depicted.

Oneida potters must have agreed on what they were representing and they had rules about how the theme was properly presented. First, effigies had to be placed on the outer surface of a vessel's collar in the presence of incised decoration. I can't

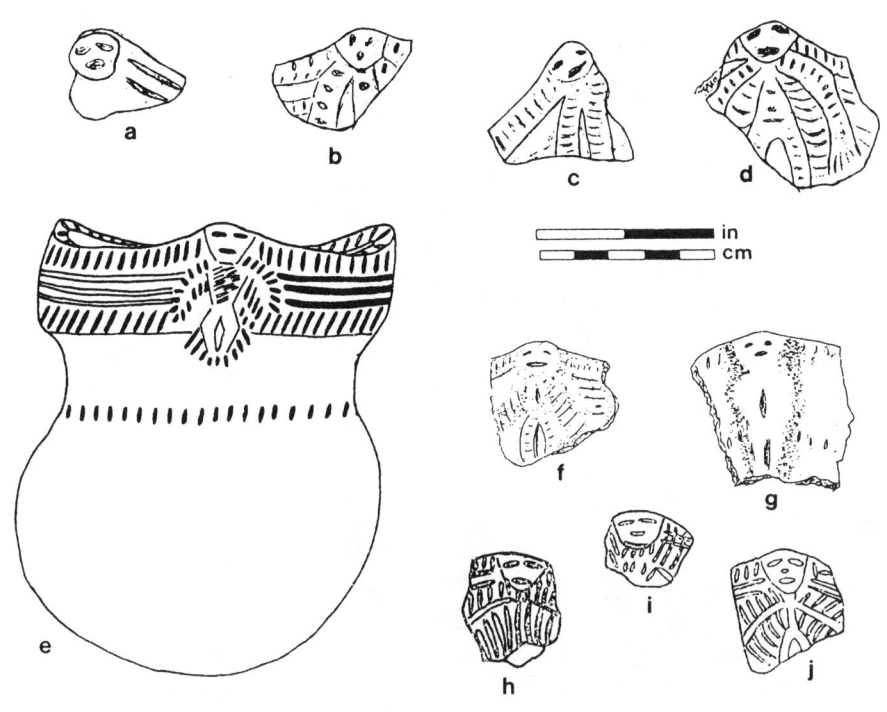

Fig. 18.10. Oneida effigies from the Beecher/Blowers (a-d, ca. 1595–1625) and Thurston (e-j, ca. 1625–37) sites (Bennett 1979, plates 16–18; Bennett 1991, fig. 3; Whitney 1974, plate 5). The illustrated vessel [e] is about 13 cm high (Bennett 1984a, plate 6).

tell whether there is any correlation between the presence of an effigy and a specific pattern of incised decoration. Certainly effigies occur on a wide range of pottery "types" that (originally) were descriptions of collar characteristics and decorative patterns thought to co-occur as a congeries indicative of an ethnic group or tribe (Ritchie and MacNeish 1949). Over time, effigies occur on types that MacNeish characterized as Mohawk, Onondaga, Cayuga, and, of course, Oneida (MacNeish 1952). For most of the Oneida effigy sequence, it looks as though sets of parallel lines, usually obliquely or horizontally oriented, were employed as backdrop to the effigies, a framing device setting off the image. Later incised design, especially the horizontal lines of what is often called Thurston Horizontal, tends to be more fully integrated into the presentation of effigy image. Possibly this combination is more frequent than any other.

Second, effigies had to be located at or just below castellations. Not all castellated vessels had effigies, but virtually every effigy occurred with a castellation. One effigy per castellation was standard. Complete vessels known to me (n = 26) have one to six castellations, most commonly two (14 examples) or four (8 examples). Sixteen of those vessels bear effigies: usually two in number (n = 12) but with one, three, and four effigies also present. If the number of effigies was meaningful

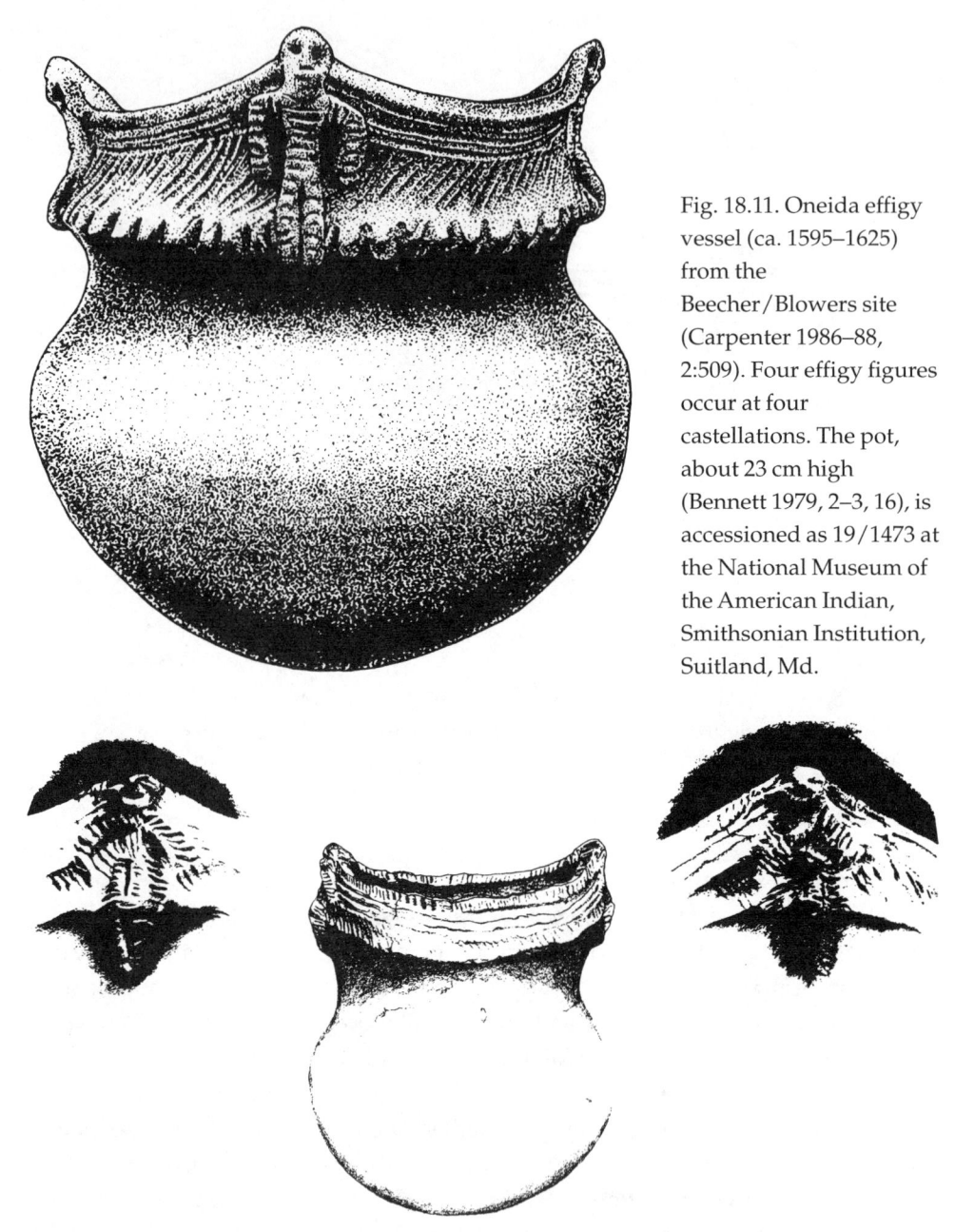

Fig. 18.11. Oneida effigy vessel (ca. 1595–1625) from the Beecher/Blowers site (Carpenter 1986–88, 2:509). Four effigy figures occur at four castellations. The pot, about 23 cm high (Bennett 1979, 2–3, 16), is accessioned as 19/1473 at the National Museum of the American Indian, Smithsonian Institution, Suitland, Md.

Fig. 18.12. Oneida effigy vessel (ca. 1625–37), ca. 16 cm high, from the Thurston site (courtesy of Longyear Museum, Colgate Univ., #2436; drawing by Julia Meyerson).

to their depiction, two was the most important frequency. But because other frequencies were acceptable, one specific number seems unlikely to have been symbolically crucial.

The principle of physical placement is essential to internal design analysis. If only a single location is appropriate to the humanoid effigy, any other image at that

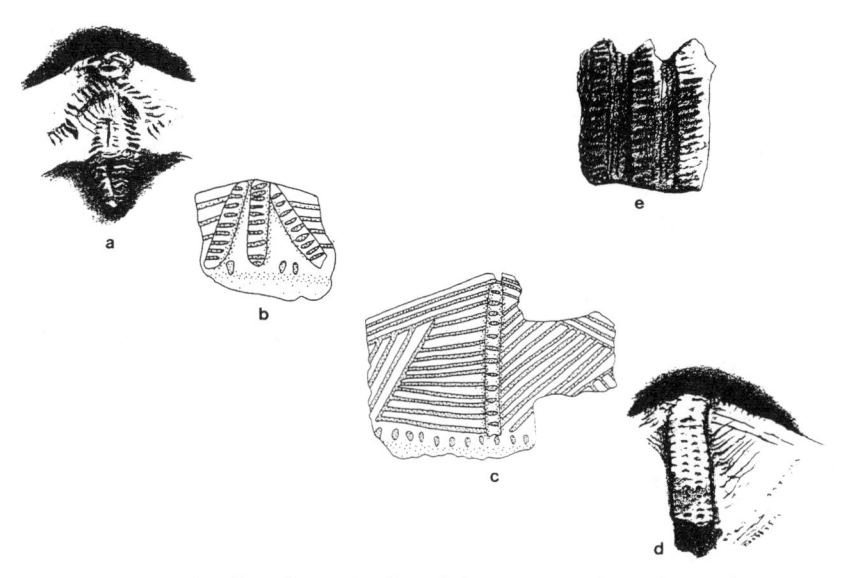

Fig. 18.13. Oneida effigy forms (a-d) and the "corn ear" rim design (not to scale). (a) full-figure effigy (Thurston site, see fig. 18.12); (b) design composed of three fillet bands (Cameron site); (c) ladder motif (Vaillancourt site); (d) apparent ear of corn (Olcott site); (e) rim sherd with corn ear design (Bach site)(drawings a, d, and e by Julia Meyerson; and courtesy of Monte R. Bennett [b], Richard Hosbach [e], Alexander Neill [c], and Longyear Museum, Colgate Univ.).

position might reasonably bear some conceptual link to the human-like figure or figural theme. Although there is little departure from the central image after the initial appearance of effigies in the archaeological record, the anomalies become particularly interesting in this iconographic sense.

The aberrant effigies are illustrated in figure 18.13. Here are shown all non-humanoid images in Oneida ceramic art (known to me) that (a) coincide with the development of the human-like figure after about 1500, and (b) occupy the position of the effigy figure at a castellation.

The ladder motif (fig. 18.13c) relates to the fully developed effigy figure (fig. 18.13a) in an obvious fashion. In effect, the body and legs of the figure are composed of two ladder motifs. In Seneca country, Charles F. Wray et al. (1987, 79) noted the resemblance of the ladder motif to an ear of corn removed from the "corn ear" design, the most obviously representational feature of St. Lawrence Iroquoian pottery. The corn ear was not a castellated effigy but a series of raised, vertically oriented ridges placed continuously around the vessel rim (fig. 18.13e).

The effigy composed of three applied fillets (Fig. 18.13b) also relates in obvious fashion to the ladder motif: it resembles three ladder motifs joined together. Gian C. Cervone (1991, 274) remarked that a nearly identical Seneca example (fig. 18.2f) looks like an abstracted figure. At the same time, its hash-marked strips relate it conceptually to both kinds of Seneca effigy: the ladder motif and the humanoid figure.

Barry C. Kent (1993 [1984], 144) offered a similar analysis of Susquehannock effigies: perhaps the ladder motif is a stylized full-figure effigy because both share the same horizontal gashes. And as Hamell (1979, fig. 7 caption) observed, the hash marks on effigies (presumably including the humanoid figure and the ladder motif) resemble corn husk or corn stalk materials. I see the same thing.

A technical illustration, figure 18.13 can also be read as an iconographic chart. As such, it illustrates two representational poles: a humanoid effigy on the upper left, an apparent corn cob on the lower right. Between these naturalistic extremes is a representational gradient or continuum. By the criteria of physical resemblance and shared structural elements, the human figure and the corn cob can be demonstrated to shade into each other smoothly and continuously. A plausible interpretation is that the humanoid effigy has something to do with corn.

In sum, Oneida effigy art was a coherent, highly patterned tradition. Its figural imagery, consistent and limited, suggests we may be looking at one humanoid or a limited set of anthropomorphic representations. The development of the effigy representation over time seems to follow an internal logic of increasing detail or clarification. Principles of design grammar and application included rules about effigy placement at a castellation and in conjunction with incised decoration. The aberrant but apparently related imagery occasionally found on castellations iconographically implies corn-related meaning.

Archaeologically, the question of how meaning may have been constituted requires looking first at how the material symbols were situated in social practice (Hodder 1986; 1987). Of necessity, one must pay close attention to associations and contexts. Who made the effigy pots? How were the vessels used? In what settings were they employed?

Manufacture, Use, and Social Contexts of Oneida Effigy Vessels

Visiting the Hurons in 1623, the Recollect missionary Gabriel Sagard observed that it was the women who made the pottery (Sagard-Théodat 1939 [1632], 109). Sagard's description apparently is the only firsthand testimony that pottery-making was women's work. Yet it is a sound assumption that women were the potters among the Iroquois also. Both Hurons and Iroquois rigorously maintained a division of labor along sexual or gendered lines and both assigned the same complex of related tasks to the domain of women. For Hurons and Iroquois, making pots was a logical and integral part of female tasks including food preparation and cooking (Allen 1992, 135, 141).

Sagard implied that pots were made by women in the normal course of women's work. If all women made pots, pottery-making was not a specialized craft occupation—a conclusion congruent with Whitney's (1974, 10) observation that a wide range of workmanship is evident among Oneida ceramics, and with Kathleen M. S. Allen's (1992) archaeological inquiry into Cayuga pottery. Pottery-making was a localized activity. Pots were of the women's domain in the clearing, the village, and the hearth. Made at home of local materials, few were carried far from where they were made (Engelbrecht 1978, 141; Kuhn 1985, 30–33; Latta 1991).

Sagard also explained how the vessels were used. Huron pots were set directly over the fire (Tooker 1991, 112). The same probably was true of Iroquois vessels (Parker 1910, 46, 60; Waugh 1916, 56). That is what Lafitau was told when, in the early 1700s, ceramic vessels were a more recent memory (Fenton and Moore 1977, 60). Of course, pots also may have been suspended above the fire as attested later in time among the Oneidas (R. Smith 1989 [1906], 132) and observed at an early day in New England (Willoughby 1935, 198). It is a logical possibility suggested by the structure of the collars (under which fiber could be strung for suspension) and the expression "hanging the kettle," meaning to prepare food and behave as hospitable host.

However they were supported, the vessels were placed over the fire primarily to boil water used in the preparation or cooking of corn (Allen 1992, 137; Biggar 1929, 126; Harrington 1908, 581–82; cf. Willoughby 1935, 198). The most common dish was a corn soup—a mush or gruel the Jesuits called *sagamité*—brought to a boil in the pot (Waugh 1916, 90–93, 95, 116). "The ordinary sagamité," said Sagard in a passage describing the Huron but equally applicable to the Iroquois, "is raw maize ground into meal, without separating the flour from the hull, boiled very clear, with a little meat or fish if they have any . . . it is the soup, meat, and dessert of every day, and there is nothing more to expect at the meal, for even when they have some trifle of meat or fish to share among them (which rarely happens except at the hunting or fishing season) it is divided and eaten first, before the soup or sagamité" (Sagard-Théodat 1939 [1632], 107). "Every morning," according to Lafitau, "the women prepare this sagamité and bring it to a boil for the nourishment of the family" (Fenton and Moore 1977, 60). This may have been the only regular meal of the day although the pot was left near the fire so that anyone could eat anytime (Allen 1992, 137–39; Waugh 1916, 46–47).

Europeans in early New England observed that Indians had two or three pots "to boil vittles in," ranging in size from a quart to a gallon (Willoughby 1935, 197). Similarly, Gary A. Warrick (1988, 30) suggests that "Iroquoian potters fashioned only one form of vessel for everyday use in basically two to three modal sizes." Allen (1992, 139) concurs that there was little functional variation. In Iroquois ceramic assemblages, there are little vessels and big vessels but they are the same kind of vessel used in the same way. Oneida pots with effigies differ in no formal respect from castellated vessels lacking effigies; presumably they did the same job.

Among Oneida archaeological ceramics, there is evidence for a very large pot (estimated diameter 46–51 cm) and an intermediate vessel size (ca. 23 cm in diameter and height) capable of holding perhaps four liters (Bennett 1979, 16; Whitney 1971, 9). Most surviving pots, however, are much smaller. Castellated vessels (n = 22) average about 12 cm in diameter and 16 cm in height. Such containers probably held something like one to two liters (Pratt 1976, 142).

Evidently, these latter indicate the size of the basic cooking pot. Mary Jemison (Seaver 1990 [1824], 31) pointed out how, during the late 1700s, the essential cooking utensil was "a small kettle"—in her day, of course, a metal container. The vast majority of brass kettles known from seventeenth- and eighteenth-century Iroquoia are quite small. They testify to continuity in cooking habits going back to the small ceramic vessels that Jacques Bruyas, a French missionary among the Mohawks, documented linguistically. By about 1675 when kettles were of European make, the word for earthen pot was *ontakonwe,* rendered as real or original kettle (Beauchamp 1895, 220).

Most complete or measurable Oneida pots (including vessels with effigies) derive from graves. This raises the possibility that these objects were especially made for mortuary as opposed to domestic use.

Cemeteries close to living areas apparently first occur at the Beecher site late in the sixteenth century. Pots frequently were found with those burials (in 8 of 19 graves) (Pratt 1976, 126–28). One effigy vessel from a grave at that site was observed to contain food residue (Bennett 1979, 16).

At the succeeding Thurston and Marshall sites, ceramic vessels continued to be interred with the burials (18 of 68 reported graves, some of them multiple burials) and buried with all segments of the population (ten males—juvenile and adult, nine females—juvenile and adult, and three children). Most pots with burials were effigy vessels (Pratt 1976, 129–32, 137–38). Among them are miniature pots and several sets of similar-looking vessels (Bennett and Cole 1976, 9; Pratt 1976, 130, plate 33). In general, I cannot tell whether these burial pots were used for cooking. Possibly some were made especially for interment.

On the other hand, the Oneida effigies on potsherds are indistinguishable from those occurring on vessels placed in graves. From the Buyea and Goff sites at the beginning of the effigy sequence through at least Thurston near the end, and including every intervening station, the fragmentary effigy material derives from the debris of living village life (habitation areas and middens). Therefore, it seems likely the same effigy pottery was used by the living and the dead.

Documentation about Native burial practice spanning two centuries is clear on this subject. Pots were used in death as they were in life: to provide food (Kuhn 1985, 64–67; Morgan 1962, 174). For example, a man's grave among the Iroquois in the 1650s was "filled with provisions for the sustenance of his soul" (Thwaites 1896–1901, 43:269). Among the Hurons in the 1620s, the souls of the deceased,

> though immortal, have still in the next life the same need of drinking and eating, of clothing themselves and tilling the ground, which they had while still clothed with

their mortal bodies. This is why with the bodies of the dead they bury or enclose bread, oil, skins, tomahawks, kettles, and other utensils, in order that the souls of their relatives, may not remain poor and needy in the other life for lack of such implements. For they imagine and believe that the souls of these kettles, tomahawks, knives, and everything they dedicate to them, especially at the great festival of the dead, depart to the next life to serve the souls of their dead, although the bodies of these skins, tomahawks, kettles, and everything else dedicated and offered remain behind and stay in the graves and coffins along with the bones of the deceased. (Sagard-Théodat 1939 [1632], 172)

Oneida ceramic vessels (including those bearing effigies) seem most likely to be the material correlates of women's activities in the home and, especially, of cooking corn. This inferred social setting provides no encouragement to a reading of effigies concerned with male politics (League) or male medicine societies (False Faces) as others have suggested (Bradley 1987a; Ritchie and Funk 1973, 367; Tuck 1971, 213). If the symbolic meaning of an object is in any way appropriate to its context and use, then an Oneida effigy probably is linked to corn and food preparation in a realm of domesticity and femaleness. Obviously, vessels with effigies could have been used in many other ways as well. But whatever the range of applications may have been, effigy pottery belonged to an Oneida village's domestic and utilitarian ceramic complex.

This archaeological characterization (utilitarian, domestic) carries the connotative freight of being ordinary, quotidian. That does not mean the pottery could not also have been symbolically meaningful or even sacred. On the contrary, these objects were imbued with associations that, although familiar, were highly valued in Iroquois culture.

Corn, of course, was esteemed as one of the Three Sisters, the life-providing triad of food crops that included beans and squash. In Iroquois folklore of the late nineteenth and early twentieth centuries, corn was visualized as a woman, usually one who withdrew her gift of food if neglected or slighted (Beauchamp 1922, 22; Hewitt 1918, 636–53; Parker 1989, 205–7; Randle 1953, 630). It was good manners, according to Parker (1910, 62–63), to thank the Creator for the gift of food. Failure to do so meant that the goddess of harvest was not properly appreciated (cf. Morgan 1962, 205).

Vessels containing corn resonated with additional meaning. While providing the stage on which effigies performed their symbolic roles, kettles also inspired metaphors expressing key cultural values. Hanging the kettle evoked hospitality, sharing, friendship, and peace. What William N. Fenton (1998, 49) calls the law of the kettle means that all Iroquois people understood hospitality to be "a right and a duty to share." "The kettle is repeatedly brought up in travel writings not as a mere object but as the attracting pole of an act of socialization. . . . 'Bringing out the kettle' signified a convocation at which food—the source of life, it need hardly be said—was to be shared" (Turgeon 1997, 10). The kettle was also "the object of mediation par excellence between this life and the 'other life' " (Turgeon 1997, 11). The Huron "Feast of the Dead," a reburial of all the community's deceased every 12–15 years, was actually called "the kettle" in Huron.

Oneida effigies, then, were found on vessels made by women and repeatedly used by women in the most basic nurturing roles of providing sustenance—cooked food, usually some form of corn boiled within the vessel—to their immediate families in the course of normal, day-to-day living in the home. The audience—those who read the symbolic text of effigies—included everyone. Yet the creators of the effigies were women and it was to women that the effigies would have been most resonant. The effigies must have something to do with food, Whitney (1974, 9) suggested, and they may have invoked "the good will and protection of the spirits entrusted with the feeding of a people."

Identifying Effigies: Cornhusk People

Because no description of ceramic effigies has survived, we cannot consult the historical record to confirm or deny a connection between pottery imagery and corn. However, we can try to establish the image's identity by searching the literature of Iroquois ethnography, folklore, and mythology for some belief meeting the criteria suggested by iconographic and contextual inquiry. The successful candidate must emphasize or encompass full-figure imagery reasonably related to corn, and should be conformable with domesticity and femaleness. I think the subject most clearly satisfying these criteria is a race of beings responsible for the present-day Husk Face medicine society among the Iroquois, mythological cornhusk people for whom great antiquity is suspected (Fenton 1987, 383, 400, 444; Tooker 1970, 152).

Diminutive beings personifying plant fertility, cornhusk people are an industrious agricultural people "associated with planting and cultivating of prodigious food crops" (Fenton 1987, 490). They are especially concerned with growing corn and it is cooked corn food that they crave (generally cornbread and unroasted corn mush). Cornhusk people are regarded as messengers of the Three Sisters who prophecy—quickly, because they must return home to tend crying babies—bountiful crops and many children (Fenton 1987, 383–404; Shimony 1994, 142–56; Speck 1995, 88–96; Tooker 1970, 72). Their leadership is dominated by women, and the cornhusk folk are strongly linked to women (Fenton 1987, 105, 408; Kurath 1968, 49, 182).

Legends of the cornhusk people specify an appearance completely covered over by corn tassels or cornhusks: these beings "dress in cornhusks" (Fenton 1987, 399). This characteristic still came through in the Husk Face Society origin stories collected early in the twentieth century. In these tales, Husk Face knowledge came from a hunter's encounter with a cornhusk person "dressed up in corn tassels"

(Speck 1995, 96). The hunter was informed, "you must tell your people that you and they must prepare something with cornhusks which shall resemble the form of my body" (Fenton 1987, 387). Thereafter, people were to pattern masks in imitating the appearance of cornhusk folk (Fenton 1987, 389).

Insistence on this specific feature of bodily appearance seems consistent with what the Oneida effigies looked like and with the logic of their development. Oneida effigies increasingly defined the anatomical details of a complete figure, a figure typically decorated with hash marks possibly related to corn. Interestingly, an anthropomorphic being with corn-like appearance may be associated with ceramic effigies elsewhere.

The archaeology of ceramic effigies outside upstate New York is most completely documented for the Minisink culture of the upper Delaware River, primarily in Pennsylvania and New Jersey. From perhaps the fifteenth century to (presumably) the abandonment of Native-made ceramics sometime in the seventeenth century, stylized effigy faces were created on Munsee Incised pottery (fig. 18.14). As with the Oneida and other Iroquois, effigies were situated on collar exteriors beneath castellations, on surfaces bearing linearly incised decoration (Kraft 1975, 126–31).

Kraft (1975) identified the Minisink potters as probable [proto] Lenape or Delaware, that is, as Algonquian speakers. He believed faces depicted in all representational mediums (notably pendants and pipes) represented masks, ethnographically attested among the Delaware as well as the Iroquois. The same interpretation, of course, was proposed at about the same time by several Iroquois archaeologists. Unlike his Iroquois counterparts, however, Kraft (1972, 5–6) was at-

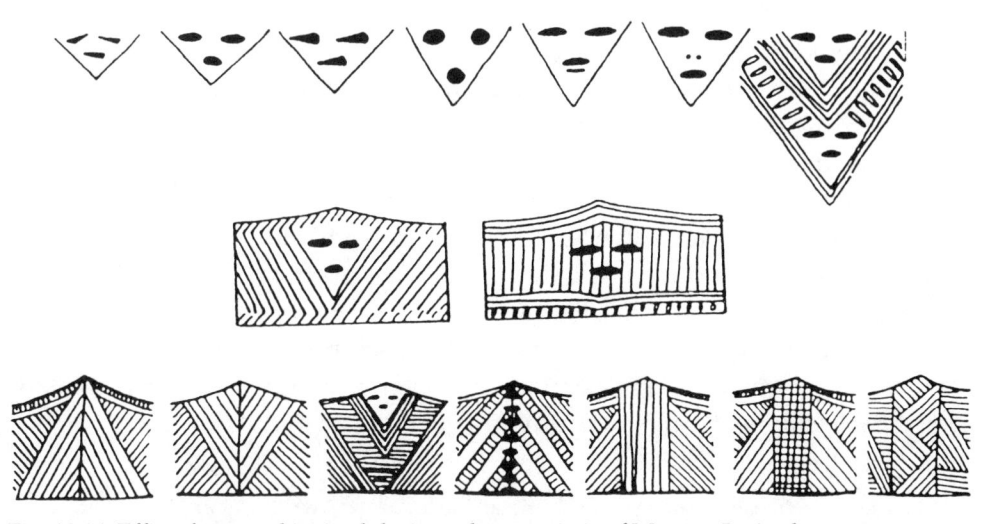

Fig. 18.14. Effigy faces and incised designs characteristic of Munsee Incised pottery, Minisink Culture of the upper Delaware River (Kraft 1975, fig. 15).

tracted not to wooden False Face masks but to cornhusk masks. He emphasized that Delaware culture once featured a corn harvest ceremony in which "two messengers dressed in suits of corn-husk clothing and wearing masks with corn husk 'hair' ride through the Delaware settlements as a signal that the ceremony will soon occur" (Speck 1937, 79). The subsequent dance was led by these two costumed figures.

Here, then, in possible association with archaeological effigies, is a surviving tradition insisting on full-figure cornhusk appearance. Perhaps equally significant, the corn harvest ceremony "was a festival of thanksgiving in which acknowledgment was made to mother Corn for the blessings of abundance, and an appeal made for the continuation of health, a form of blessing never forgotten for a moment by Delaware supplicants" (Speck 1937, 79). Here also full-figure cornhusk appearance specifically was linked to a human obligation to acknowledge corn.

A theme in Delaware folklore to this day stresses that the corn spirit is a woman believed to be extremely jealous (J. Miller 1997, 118). Corn Mother withdraws when offended, and she is easily offended by irreverence or even by the improper treatment of corn. People induce her return and attempt to ensure her presence by ceremonially acknowledging her nature, by paying her proper respect (Bierhorst 1995, 11, 34, 44, 56, 84, 91–92).

Effigy Meaning: Covenants with Cornhusk People

Let us suppose several lines of mutually supporting evidence suggest effigies were linked in meaning to corn, and that effigies may well have evoked cornhusk people. How should we imagine Oneida people regarding or reacting to these images?

One possibility is that effigies were actively and, perhaps, publicly invoked as gods as attested by an incident in 1637. Attempting to ward off disease destroying their village, Hurons created a number of "straw men"—life-size figures evidently constructed from the material of corn plants (Thwaites 1896–1901, 13:261–67).[4]

These effigies, full-figure representations larger than Oneida ceramic images but probably similar in appearance, were "their idols and their tutelary gods; it was in these grotesque figures that they put all their trust" (Thwaites 1896–1901, 13:231). Attempts to ward off what must have been European-derived sickness, these straw men were anguished cries for deliverance in a time of crisis. In contrast, Oneida ceramic effigies, staples of households for a century and a half, speak of something less dramatic and more private.

4. "L'homme de paille" is given in the printed French text for what is glossed as "straw man" (Thwaites 1896–1901, 13:262, 266). The identification of this straw as being from maize seems, to me, linguistically plausible. It is historically likely given the presence of maize and the absence of European straw materials at this time and place.

When Kraft developed his argument relating faces on Delaware archaeological material to cornhusk masks, he could draw on a striking feature of material culture. The Delaware ceremonial pattern was "inclined to the use of carved images of the human face and form, either as masks, effigy figures or face sculpturings" (Speck 1937, 11). He emphasized a specific kind of artifact: wooden drumsticks with effigy faces used in the Big House ceremony (fig. 18.15). In the course of this important ritual, effigy drumsticks replace plain drumsticks. "This substitution," Kraft noted, quoting ethnologist Frank Speck, "is an allegory of the increasing sanctity of the rites" (Kraft 1975, 130; original in Speck 1937, 67). A Delaware view of the matter was different. The carved heads on the effigy drumsticks, said a Native informant, "meant that human beings were giving thanks" (Harrington 1921, 140). I think the same could be said of Oneida ceramic effigies.

Concerned with maintaining correct relations with the spirit world, Oneidas probably regarded these images within the terms of a distinctively Iroquois perspective likely to be of considerable antiquity: ongoing social contracts operative between humans and non-human partners maintain the universe. The human duty is to acknowledge and thank the other beings for fulfilling their responsibilities and, by so doing, to encourage the other beings to continue to perform their functions. Given this conceptual framework, I suggest effigies attest to Oneidas' holding up their end of the cosmos-maintaining pact. Given the probable content and context of the imagery, I think the effigies imply prayers of gratitude offered by women food-providers to non-human beings (very possibly cornhusk people) in fulfillment of such mythic contract.

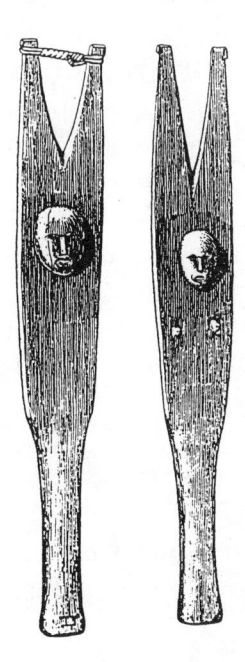

Fig. 18.15. Sacred drumsticks used in the Delaware Big House Ceremony (Harrington 1921, fig. 11). Example on left is 18.6 in. high.

Whether effigies were bound up with public ritual or paraphernalia for ceremonies is unknown but seems to me unlikely. A number of researchers have remarked on the gendered dichotomy of behavior in Delaware culture, particularly as it pervades ceremonial pose and responsibility (J. Miller 1997, 123). Speck pointed out how Delaware men are the ones who direct and seem to actively participate in the ceremonies (including Corn Harvest). In contrast, women's functions comprise little more than preparing ceremonial foods ("symbol of plant economy as female sphere") and "silent supplication" (Speck 1937, 26).

Because Iroquois culture was similar in this respect, effigies probably were not linked to male public-speaking, or to male communion with the other world via the burning or smoking of tobacco. Far more plausibly, they are reifications of saying grace, material correlates of Oneida women privately giving thanks for the gift of food.

French missionaries arrived too late in Iroquois country to document ceramic effigies but they did describe similar behavior. Jesuits, who customarily employed visual imagery in their missionizing efforts (Axtell 1985, 113–16; Richter 1992, 115–16, 125), reported that Iroquoian people responded to three-dimensional icons by dramatically intensifying private and individual forms of worship (e.g., Thwaites 1896–1901, 60:101). They witnessed (mostly) the praying and chanting of women because women comprised the majority of converts and it was the women, Jesuits thought, who learned the prayers sooner than the men (Thwaites 1896–1901, 63:175). Nevertheless, the entire community appreciated Christian statuary (Thwaites 1896–1901, 59:241) said to be "pleasing to their eyes" (Thwaites 1896–1901, 61:211).

Native people enjoyed looking at such images because they represented supernaturals. That does not necessarily mean the objects were worshipped as idols. As Frank Speck observed (1931, 36) of carved Delaware faces, "[t]hey stand as concrete representations of the spirit-forces as something to look at, to focus attention upon while the mind is centered upon the abstraction." To see such a being was one proof of the being's reality. The best way to convert the Iroquois, argued a priest in 1682, "is to make them see with their own eyes what we tell them with our voices" (Thwaites 1896–1901, 62:95). Another Jesuit in 1634 reported a religious debate in which the Native person scoffed at the idea of an invisible god. "Thy God," the Montaignais concluded, "has not come to our country, and that is why we do not believe in him; make me see him and I will believe in him" (Thwaites 1896–1901, 7:101).

Acknowledgments

Versions of this work were presented at the Annual Conference on Iroquois Research held in Rensselaerville, New York, in October 1998; the Northeast Archaeological Symposium in Auburn, New York, in October 1999; the Annual Conference of the New York Archaeological Association in Sparrowbush, New York, in April 2001; and the Annual Meeting of the Eastern States Archaeological Federation in Watertown, New York, in November 2001.

The opinions expressed here are solely the author's, but I am profoundly grateful to my employers, the Oneida Indian Nation, for encouraging this research. I appreciate suggestions offered by William Engelbrecht and George Hamell. I thank Charles R. Cobb, R. David Drucker, Richard Hosbach, Timothy A. Kohler, Steven Paul McSloy, Michael S. Nassaney, and an anonymous reviewer for editorial help. My thanks go also to those who allowed access to Oneida effigies in their care: Gary Urton (Longyear Museum, Colgate University, Hamilton, N.Y.), Betty Prisch (Rochester Museum and Science Center), George Hamell, Lisa Anderson, and Penelope Drooker (New York State Museum), Monte Bennett (Earlville, N.Y.), Alan Sterling (Canastota, N.Y.), Richard Hosbach and Alexander Neill (Norwich, N.Y.).

Two kinds of credit are given in the pottery illustrations. First, drawings from published sources are cited in the format used for in-text attribution elsewhere in this paper. Second, the collection in which the illustrated sherd resides is identified with the phrase "courtesy of." Pottery drawings not attributed to an artist or published source are by the author.

19 | The Mandeville Site
A Small Iroquoian Village and a Large Smoking-Pipe Collection—An Interpretation

CLAUDE CHAPDELAINE

The Site

THE MANDEVILLE SITE was found in 1961, but initial archaeological work only started in 1969. During five seasons of field activities, archaeologists excavated 1,283 square meters (m²), corresponding to about 18 percent of the entire site.

The site is located on the first terrace on the west side of the Richelieu River, 8 km upriver from its confluence with the St. Lawrence. However, it is important to remember that the site is only 2 kilometers (km) distant from the south shore of the St. Lawrence, and there may have been a trail leading to the latter. In 1643, to avoid a French post located at the mouth of the Richelieu River, the Mohawks are said to have taken a trail, some two leagues before arriving at Fort Richelieu, along which they portaged their canoes to the St. Lawrence (Thwaites 1896–1901, 24:65).

The site is located on a sandy terrace about 10 meters (m) above the river and is protected from western winds by a second terrace, 8 m above the first one and about 125 m further inland. It might be considered surprising that the village was not established on that second terrace, but its protected nature was obviously more important than being away from the river.

The excavation has produced evidence suggesting the presence of a small village comprising at least five longhouses. A large area for outdoor activities has been found along the edge of the terrace and a small midden has been located on a gentle slope at the south end of the village. A cemetery of ten individuals was also ex-

---

Previously published in *Proceedings of the 1989 Smoking Pipe Conference: Selected Papers,* ed. C. F. Hayes III, C. C. Bodner, and M. L. Sempowski, Research Records no. 22 (Rochester, N.Y.: Rochester Museum and Science Center, 1992), 31–40. Printed with permission by Rochester Museum and Science Center.

cavated. No evidence of a palisade has ever been identified, and we must conclude that this small village covering less than two acres was probably not palisaded.

Seven radiocarbon dates exhibit a large variability ranging from A.D. 750 to 1550 (uncorrected). Among these, two very close dates of 1540 and 1550 may well represent the occupation time of the village, and we suggest that Iroquoians were living on the Mandeville site during the early sixteenth century.

The Collection

The Mandeville site has produced a large collection of 537 domestic pottery vessels, more than 350 small pots, and 365 smoking pipes (Chapdelaine 1989). The smoking pipes were of great help in suggesting the approximate date and the function of the site, and we will discuss in this paper their morphology, size, style, spatial context, formation process, and cultural variation. They make up the largest smoking-pipe collection actually known from the St. Lawrence valley. The technological level was not studied in detail, but we can summarize some attributes. The clay is not as heavily tempered as that used to make the pots. The firing seems very good and more than 60 percent of the pipes show a gloss or luster resulting from a polishing of the surface before the firing process. Many smoking pipes exhibit an indisputable highly technical skill on the part of the makers.

Morphology and Style of the Smoking Pipes

In describing the smoking pipes, a general morphological approach was used to determine the minimum number of pipes. The most complete bowl fragments were compared to identify the bowls that might be used as units of analysis. This is the most popular procedure also utilized for establishing the rimsherds representing a vessel. The 365 units of analysis or bowl fragments outnumbered significantly the isolated stem fragments having a mouthpiece (table 19.1). This minimum number is approached only by the Roebuck site with 282 specimens (Wintemberg 1936). However, the Roebuck site is quite different (James Wright 1987). It is much larger than the Mandeville site, 8 acres vs. 2 acres; 40 longhouses vs. 5 longhouses; and 1,500 inhabitants vs. 200 occupants. The ratio of number of pipes seems to be much higher in Mandeville than anywhere else in Iroquoian country when estimated on the basis of acreage, number of longhouses, and population.

Morphology

Looking at the different categories of fragments, it becomes obvious that the skill of the makers was highly variable, and we get the impression of different

Table 19.1
The Mandeville Site Smoking-Pipes Collection

	Decorated	No Decoration	Total
Analyzable Pipes			
Effigy	43	30	73
No Effigy	133	159	292
Total			365
Lip Fragments	39	234	273
Elbow Fragments	1	142	143
Stem Fragments			
Without Mouthpiece	7	446	453
With Mouthpiece	3	223	226
Total			679
Bowl Fragments	47	325	372
Undetermined Pipe Fragments	4	145	149
Total Earthenware Pipe Fragments			1981

trends in the manufacturing process. Both the bowl forms and the large numbers of effigies show a high degree of variability (table 19.2, figs. 19.1–19.3).

The most popular type of bowl is the trumpet form, and this is confirmed by a brief analysis of the isolated lips from fragmentary bowls where 58 percent of these fragments are typical of the trumpet type. Conical bowls are second, but decoration around the bowl characteristic of the "ring" type is very rare. The third type is the vasiform pipe, but this category is not homogeneous.

The opening of the bowl is independent of the form, being consistently circular or slightly oval on 269 pipes out of 273 analyzable bowl openings (98.5 percent). The elbow angle varies between 90° and 120°, and the shape of the stem is circular or slightly ovoid (± 80 percent) while the mouthpiece is in half of the cases slightly modified or used (52 percent). We have four calumet pipes, all with a flat base, and four other fragmentary specimens with a flat base might be other examples of this kind of pipe without a stem.

Values have been provided in an earlier publication (Chapdelaine 1989) for other attributes of the samples such as the surface treatment, the interior profile of the bowl, the diameter of the hole, the position of the hole (more than 50 percent are not at the center of the stem and approximately 20 stems have two holes), and the position of the decoration or of the effigy.

Size

As is very often the case elsewhere, complete pipes are extremely rare, being limited to only a dozen specimens. Fortunately, there are 67 complete bowls, and it

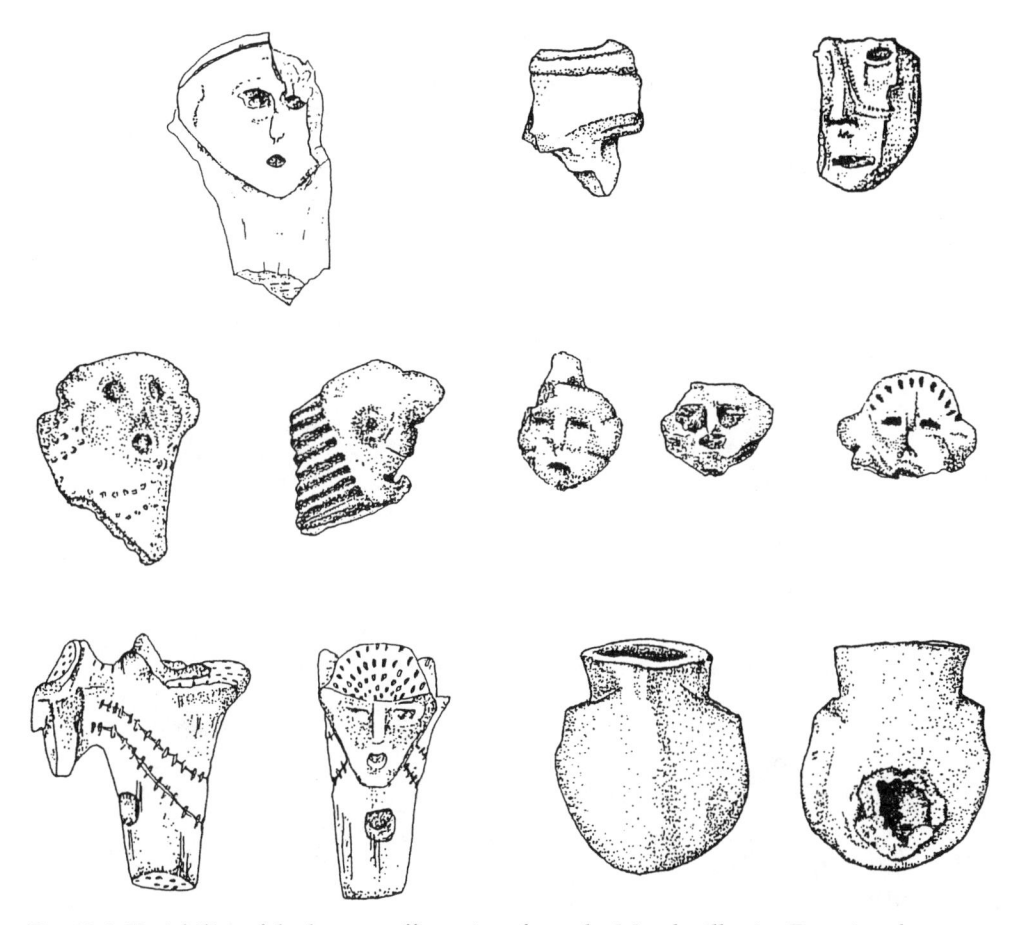

Fig. 19.1. Variability of the human effigy pipes from the Mandeville site. Drawings by Diane Bisson.

was possible to estimate their capacity. As a second step, the capacities of 247 fragmentary bowls were evaluated and extrapolated. For the 67 most complete pipes, the correlation coefficient between internal diameter and height of the bowls is r=0.759, between internal diameter and capacity r=0.824, and between height and capacity r=0.886. These correlations suggest three general sizes: small (= 1.9 cubic centimeters [cc]), medium (> 1.9 = 5.9 cc) and large (> 6 cc). The small size is overrepresented in this sample of 67 pipes. Within this small category, a miniature type can be defined by a capacity of less than 0.8 cc (the bowl is less than 12.6 millimeters [mm] in diameter and 31.0 mm in height). The distribution of the size for the 314 pipes proved interesting (table 19.3). Miniature pipes and large pipes are less common, and within the medium size category, the smaller subtype (2–3.9 cc), with 114 out of 144 pipes (79 percent), is the most popular. The fact that 65 percent of the pipes have a capacity of less than 4 cc should be noticed. This 4-cc capacity is the equivalent of today's king size cigarette. The larger pipes are always of the trumpet

Table 19.2

Mandeville Pipe-Type Frequencies

	Frequency	%
Trumpet	135	37.0
Trumpet + Vasiform	6	1.6
Conical	61	16.7
Conical with a Beak[a]	10	2.7
Vasiform	41	11.2
Barrel	1	0.3
Coronet	20	5.5
Bulbous	10	2.7
Cylindrical	1	0.3
Idiosyncrasy	6	1.6
Undetermined	1	0.3
Human Effigies	32	8.8
a) Heads Only (30)		
i) Single		
Roebuck face	3	
Maskette	2	
Calumet	2	
Ghost Face	4	
Ear Pierced	1	
Head with a Horn	1	
Crude Face	8	
Human (?)	3	
ii) Multiple		
Double Human Effigy	3	
Triple Human Effigy	3	
b) Body (2)		
Phallus	1	
Body	1	

form, and the effigy pipes are common in the lower medium size. Aside from these general differences, the size variations between effigy and non-effigy pipes cannot support the hypothesis that the making of an effigy on a pipe was a determinant of size. The chi square, with a degree of liberty equal to 5, is not significant ($X^2=7.168$), and we cannot rule out chance, with a probability of almost 21 percent (X^2 at $0.10=9.24$; X^2 at $0.05=11.07$). Regardless of form, the Iroquoians were putting in their pipes the amount of tobacco equivalent to that in a twentieth-century cigarette. This result is not in great contrast with early European pipes (based on the measures of only two pipes), which had a capacity of about 6 cc.

Style

	Frequency	%
Human/Animal Effigy	2	0.5
Human or Animal (?)	2	0.5
Moon Effigy	1	0.3
Animal Effigy (29)		8.0
Canis	8	
Bird	6	
Bird with Open-mouth Bowl	2	
Reptile	5	
Coiled Snake	2	
Turtle	1	
Animal (?)	5	
Undetermined Effigy	4	1.1
Missing Effigy	3	0.8
Total	365	99.9

[a] Placed in this category are five pipes that are considered a variant of the boat type with pointed ends and separators inside but with no figure in the boat.

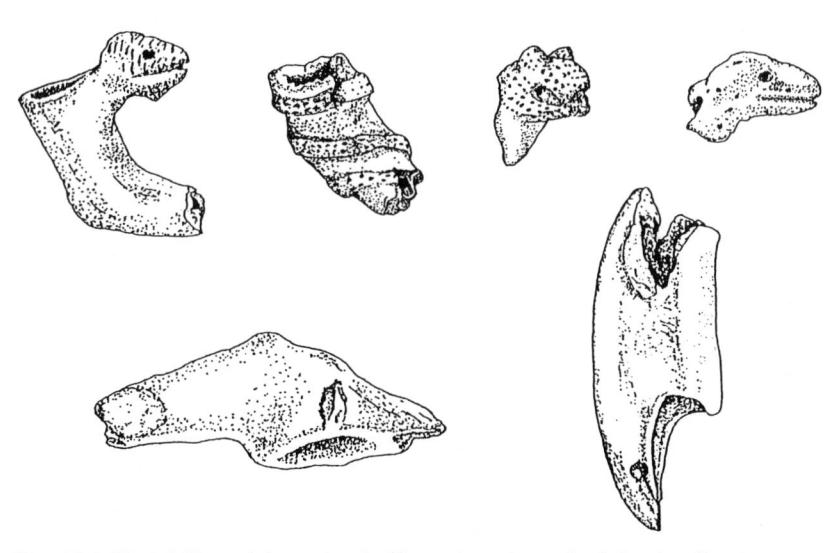

Fig. 19.2. Variability of the animal effigy pipes from the Mandeville site. Drawings by Diane Bisson.

Stylistically, it is important to note that 53.2 percent of the pipes were not decorated (194/365) and that the decision of adding an effigy does not make a significant difference in the frequency of decorated smoking pipes (table 19.1). The stem is seldom decorated. The low frequency of decoration on the bowls is similar to that

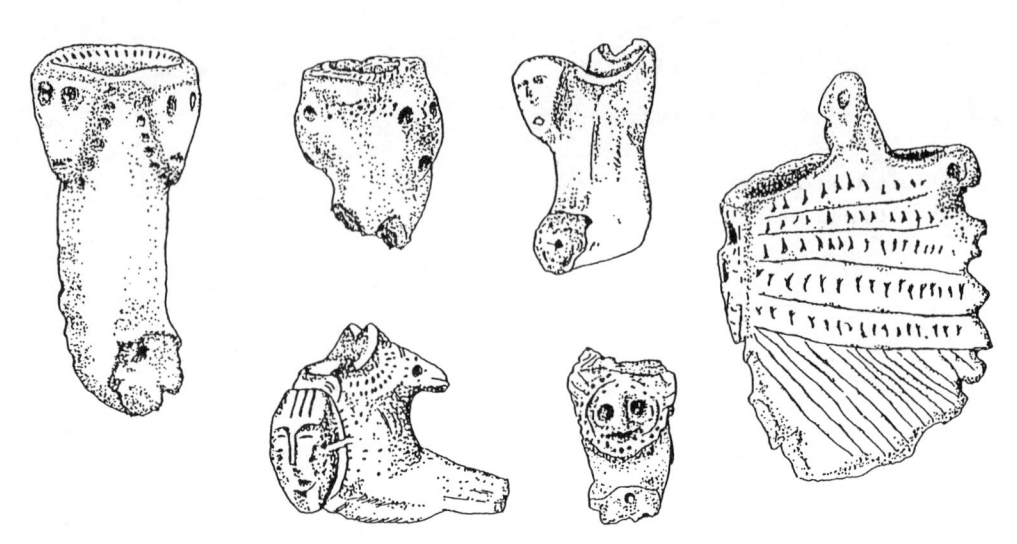

Fig. 19.3. Human or human/animal effigy pipes from the Mandeville site. Drawings by Diane Bisson.

Table 19.3
Mandeville Pipe-Bowl Capacity

	Effigy		No Effigy	
CATEGORIES/TYPES	F	%	F	%
Large (≥ 6.0 cc)	0		16	5.8
Medium ($>1.9 \leq 5.9$ cc)	4	10.5	43	15.6
Small ($>0.8 \leq 1.9$ cc)	17	44.8	74	26.8
Miniature (≤ 0.8 cc)	1	2.6	15	5.4
Lower Medium ($>1.9 \leq 3.9$ cc)	13	34.2	101	36.6
Upper Medium ($>3.9 \leq 5.9$ cc)	3	7.9	27	9.8
Total	38	100.0	276	100.0

of the pottery on the site. Neither the interior (7 cases) nor the lip (30 cases) is often embellished. On the 43 decorated effigy pipes, 22 were decorated on the effigy only.

Punctate and incised lines are the dominant techniques of decoration, but the cord-wrapped stick was used in 9 cases. On the bowls the motif design can be either complex, as in the case of chevrons (83/171=48.5 percent), or simple, as in the case of obliques, (65/171=38.0 percent), with 23 motifs being undetermined (13.5 percent). Only 31 percent of the trumpet form specimens are decorated, but they include 13 examples of the distinctive motif of the St. Lawrence Iroquoians composed of large incised horizontal lines with dots at the end of each line.

The Mandeville pipes constitute one of the most important collections of its kind in Iroquoia and indicate that the "Pipe-Tobacco-Smoking Complex" occupied a very central place in the daily life of this particular community. The trumpet form was the most popular, but the diversity of bowl forms with the addition of effigies presents a rare opportunity to glimpse the vivacity and creativity of a group that placed a high value on this practice.

Context

The Mandeville pipes are not only important because of their impressive number, but also because they were found in a well-detailed archaeological context. First, an attempt will be made to elucidate their spatial relations before cautiously going on to determine their specific function.

When looking at the distribution of pipes over the site, can it be postulated that the style and the form will be different among the longhouses because the men were responsible for making the pipes and that they were not kin-related like the women who made the pottery? To answer this question, the presence of trumpet and effigy pipes over the different sectors of the site was contrasted, and no significant difference was found ($X^2=4.56$). The chi square of the human and animal effigy pipes in the sectors of the site was also not significant ($X^2=2.43$). In each case, the probability that the spatial distribution of the two types occurred by chance is respectively 21 percent and 49 percent. There is no evidence suggesting that the precise location of an effigy pipe is related to a specific longhouse. However, the presence of trumpet and effigy pipes in the different sectors of the site shows similar frequencies.

A similar phenomenon was observed at Draper where pipe attributes "have a largely homogeneous spatial distribution; that is, the different mental templates which influence the manufacture of each artifact do not seem to be restricted to certain areas of the town" (von Gernet 1982, 50).

This spatial homogeneity of the pipes across the site was also noted for the pottery collection (Chapdelaine 1989). Can it be possible that women were responsible for making the pipes? This possibility may be supported first by the fact that similar skills are required for both pottery and pipe production, and second by the resemblance between decorative technique and motif between both ceramic forms. This view challenges the historic account made by Boucher, stating that the men made their own pipes (Boucher 1664, 101).

The pottery styles and also the different kinds of pipes of the different longhouses are quite similar, contrasting with the findings of James V. Wright for Nodwell concerning the conservative vs. progressive nature of the material culture of the different longhouses (Wright 1974). There is the impression of homogeneity between the longhouses of the Mandeville site, and it may be concluded that they are contemporaneous in spite of overlapping structures. Curiously, the artifactual sample from the midden seems representative of the whole collection, even if its composition comes from two longhouses and an area used for different outdoor activities.

The pipe distribution in the longhouses is puzzling. The pipes are more often found within what might be considered a familial area than the pottery, but fragments of the same specimen are spread throughout several familial sectors, covering sometimes a distance of 5 to 10 m. Could this be evidence for close links between men of the same longhouse? Could it also be that the women smoked inside the house given that the observed pattern is similar to the distribution of the pottery? Within the two best preserved longhouses (nos. 1 and 2), it can be observed that the central fireplaces have the highest density of pipes, and that the extremities of the longhouses are not very rich. It may support the hypothesis that the families occupying the extremities of these houses did not live there for a long period of time; or that storytelling and other activities during wintertime was done primarily around the central hearths of the longhouse.

Function

The function of the smoking pipes is problematic. We will try to relate this question to what might have been the systemic context of the smoking pipes. Not all the alternatives found in the literature will be reviewed (Mathews 1976; 1980; 1981a; 1981b; 1982; Noble 1979; von Gernet 1988), but the contextual data relevant to the subject will be presented.

Effigy pipes can be considered as sacred objects representing "guardian spirits" in the case of animal effigy pipes, and the human effigy pipes may be associated with "shamanistic activities" (Mathews 1980, 303–4). Some supportive evidence brought up by Mathews is the fact that some effigies were "purposefully broken and some have the face mutilated" (Mathews 1980, 303). In the Mandeville site collection, the effigy pipes consist primarily of the heads broken off the bowl, and the two parts could not be mended. The discard pattern of the bowls is different from the heads for most of the effigy pipes. It might be added that because the effigy heads are not molded to the bowl in most cases but represent an addition of clay, this part may be considered fragile and a high rate of breakage is to be expected. However, if we consider the effigy pipes to be sacred objects or contributing to socioideological activities of particular segments of the community, we can expect a different mechanism for the discard behavior. A discard pattern can be imagined in which effigy pipes would be stored safely away from dogs and children. A high density of pipes may be expected in the pits inside the longhouses, or as grave goods. A high ratio of effigy pipes in the midden or lying on the floor of the houses might be regarded as evidence for the common rather than sacred use of effigy pipes.

At Mandeville the data suggest very clearly that the discard location of the effigy pipes is not at all different from the non-effigy pipes. A chi square of 0.171 with a degree of liberty of 1—with a probability of 67 percent for no relation between the type of pipes and their presence in pits or others features like post molds or hearths—provides strong support for postulating the absence of any social rule guiding the disposal of these effigy pipes. The actual distribution of the two basic categories of pipes in the pits context as opposed to the floor of occupation, the outdoor area, and the midden is the same as for the pottery and small pots samples.

It is also important to note that the number of human effigy pipes is twice that of the animal effigies in the midden (12 against 6). Thus the sacred character of the pipes is not supported by the discard behavior and also by the fact that there is no difference between the ratio of effigy and non-effigy pipes stored away in pits and other features. They are mostly left broken in refuse along with other materials. One may argue that the sacred nature of the effigy pipes ends when they are broken. No effigy pipes were found in the graves of the small cemetery, and it is not a common practice elsewhere to give this kind of pipe as an offering to the dead. One broken specimen, a human face of the Roebuck human type, cannot really be considered an argument against the sacred perception of the smoking effigy pipes because it was used as a pendant or a charm with the head upside down. It was found on the occupation floor of a longhouse.

The archaeological context of the pipe sample is similar to that of the pottery and all the other items of material culture. Using general guidelines for the systemic context, our data do not support the sacred character of the effigy pipes. The impression is that the animal or human effigy pipes are discarded anywhere. No special distribution patterns for these guardian spirits or shamanistic pipes can be recognized.

It is tempting with the Mandeville collection to contest the postulate that only men were making the pipes. Is it possible that the women were responsible for the firing (Noble 1979, 82)? Can it be that the decoration on the non-effigy pipes was done by women? A comparative study of pottery and pipes might indicate some relationships, but for the Mandeville assemblage, it seems that a distinct set of motifs and techniques are involved. Some patterns found on the pottery can be recognized, and most often on the vasiform type. Also, was it only the men who used the pipes? Jacques Cartier stated that only men used them (Biggar 1924, 184). The number of pipes found in the longhouses can be used to either support the length of occupation of the structure or the longevity of the pipes. There are no data on the use-life of the pipes nor on the number of pipes owned by a smoker. In longhouse

No. 1, 79 pipes were found. Using the hypothesis that a man needs two pipes and that they last one year with the chance to find one of the two inside the house, the 79 pipes represent an occupation of eight years if there are ten smokers living in this particular house with a central axis occupied by five distinct fireplaces. These numbers can be manipulated to support the possibility that the women were also smoking inside the house. There is no argument except that it might explain this unusual high density of pipes.

The smoking pipes from the Mandeville site allow us to imagine the role played by the men in bringing into the community new ideas about the style of pipe making because they were outside of the village for part of the year. It is then possible to think of the pipes as good chronological markers and as representative of the cultural relations between regions.

Unfortunately, it is still impossible to produce a quantitative analysis on pipes within the St. Lawrence valley (table 19.4). A brief review of the available data on pipes from the Roebuck site confirms the early sixteenth-century occupation of the Mandeville site. In fact, if the effigy represents a good chronological indicator, the 20 percent effigy pipes at the Mandeville site is the highest in the St. Lawrence valley. It is also confirmed by the chronology proposed by William C. Noble for the Ontario Iroquois pipes (Noble 1979). He suggests that effigy pipes started to become popular after A.D. 1450 and that the anthropomorphological pipes were more frequent on sites dating A.D. 1500–1550 (Noble 1979, 81). The frequency of effigy

Table 19.4
Effigy Pipes on St. Lawrence Iroquoian Sites

Sites	Number of Pipes	Number of Effigy Pipes	% Effigy Pipes
CENTRAL REGION			
Dawson	39	4	10.3
Mandeville	365	73	20.0
Lanoraie	43	5	11.6
Bourassa	8	1	12.5
WESTERN REGION			
McIvor	41	3	7.3
Glenbrook	54	6	11.1
Roebuck	282	26	9.2
Summerstown Station	48	4	8.3
Beckstead[a]	58	1	1.7
Grays Creek	14	(1)	(7.1)
Salem	135	5	3.7
Berry	4	0	0.0

[a] Data were compiled from the two publications for this site (Pendergast 1966; 1984).

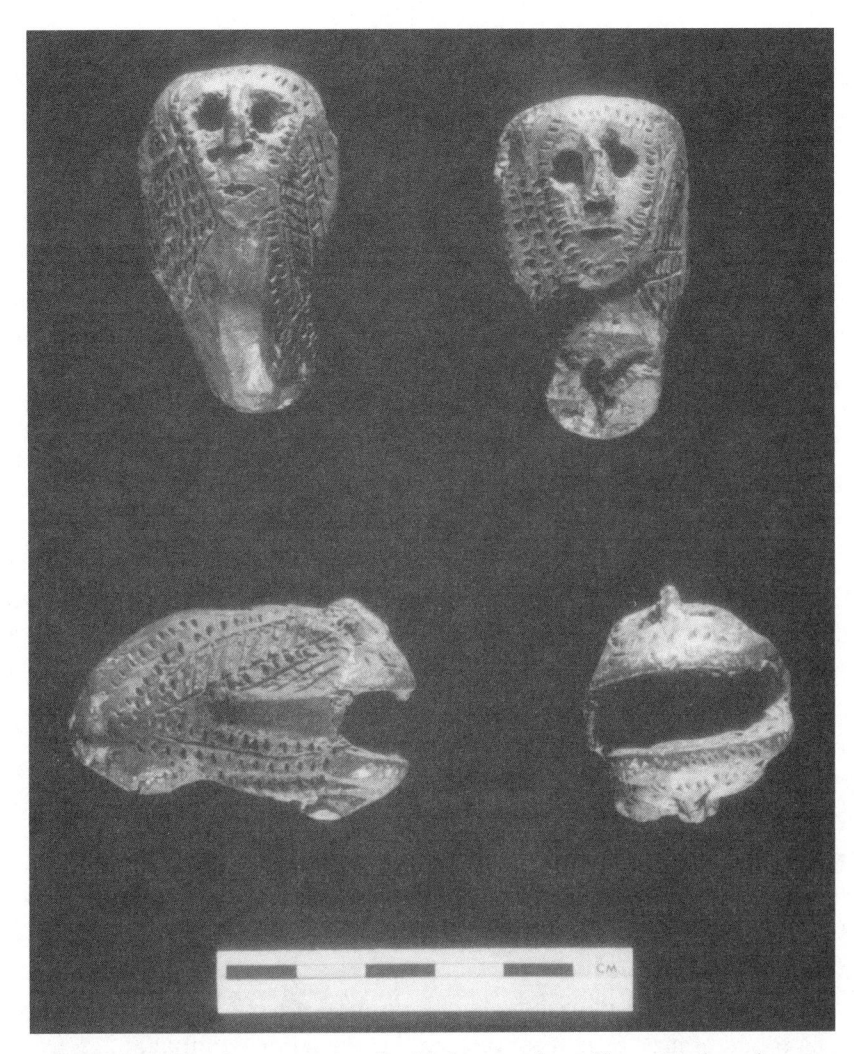

Fig. 19.4. This smoking pipe is a double human face effigy pipe found on the occupation floor of a longhouse at the Mandeville site, Tracy, Quebec. It is decorated with small linear impressions and incised lines making a complex motif. The stem is missing. Photograph: Marc Laberge, Vidéanthrop Inc.

pipes, the number of human effigies, the number of double and triple faces, and the two "dual effigy pipes" indicate a sixteenth-century site (figs. 19.1–19.4). Four bowls resemble the boat type of which there are two specimens from Onondaga sites dated to the first half of the sixteenth century (Bradley 1987a, 62). Therefore, the pipes tend to confirm the two radiocarbon dates of approximately A.D. 1550.

When the Mandeville and Roebuck collections are briefly compared, the same popularity of the trumpet form is found, but the absence of certain types in the Roebuck sample place it earlier than Mandeville in the sequence. For example, the

Janus type, the open-mouth bowl, the double bowl, the pipe type with no stem, and the human/animal dual effigy type are all absent at Roebuck. In the Mandeville sample, these types are represented by a total of 17 smoking pipes. It is also curious that the bowl with no stem is not described in Noble's list (1979, 71). It may well be considered a distinct type, and its development might be the middle St. Lawrence valley with the oldest specimen coming from the Lanoraie site, a mid-fourteenth-century village 8 km distant from the Mandeville site (Clermont et al. 1983).

The pipes are not suitable at the moment for establishing a precise seriation for the St. Lawrence Iroquoian sites. James F. Pendergast has suggested some trends that are useful (Pendergast 1972, 296, table 6), but they are too general to distinguish sites dating to the fifteenth or sixteenth century.

Conclusion: A Small Site and a Big Collection—An Interpretation

This last question is linked to a delicate problem of formation process in order to explain the presence of this large sample of 365 smoking pipes in a small village. It is common to find a great disparity in the total number of specimens of the different categories that usually form the archaeological record of an Iroquoian site, and this poor representation must be examined carefully. For example, it is often noted that the scarcity or abundance of effigy pipes varies within sites of the St. Lawrence valley (table 19.4), as do pottery, lithics, and bone tools. Small pots have also a variable density over Iroquoia as do clay waste and clay beads. A complete study of the formation process of the Mandeville collection is not the intention here, but rather to discuss those factors that might be involved in the disposition of smoking pipes in particular.

There are some factors that will not be discussed such as the different methods of excavation or the destructive effect of plowing on specific sites. They will be considered as constant factors, just as we accept the assumption that all the Iroquoian groups were participating with the same intensity in the pipe-tobacco-smoking complex.

The Iroquoians from Mandeville were living like the other Iroquoians in longhouses occupied on a year-round basis. They were producing garbage to be disposed of in two ways: interior pits and outside middens, usually on the sloping area of the site. They may also have accumulated debris inside the longhouses as was described by Cartier in the sixteenth century (Biggar 1924, 177). During their occupation of the village, they must have on occasion cleared away from their houses the detritus accumulated during wintertime. If they had left their village before doing this cleanup, the houses would show a high artifact density, as is the case for the Mandeville houses, but not for most of the longhouses of other sites (Ritchie and Funk 1973; Stopp 1984; J. Wright 1974). In fact, the only other longhouse with a high artifact density is from Lanoraie. It could also be possible that the high density might reflect a hasty abandonment of the site because of war or fire. The latter is not supported by the Mandeville site, but because the village was not protected by a palisade, it is possible that the villagers left the site because of the war and that they never returned to live there.

The third scenario involves the way people deal with their garbage. In an ethnographic study of sedentary groups, Priscilla Murray (1980) found that only two groups allowed debris to accumulate inside living areas, and both were the only two groups inhabiting longhouses. No Iroquoian groups were selected for this study, but the parallel is there with a suggestion that the differential rates of accumulation within prehistoric Iroquoian longhouses are simply a matter of the extent to which living floors were cleaned.

As for the Mandeville site, it is obvious that the pipe-tobacco-smoking complex was a prominent part of the daily life of the community. The site might have had a special status. In a marginal area between Hochelaga and Stadacona, this community may have corresponded in the St. Lawrence valley of the sixteenth century to the Petuns of the seventeenth century in the Great Lakes: the primary producers of tobacco. The region of Lanoraie is still today an important area for tobacco cultivation. It may also be that the Mandeville village was the home of some powerful shamans or a central place for holding various ceremonies. It may simply be a village participating in the smoking complex where women and men were smoking daily for the sake of feeling good, aside from all the other symbolic aspects of rituals involving the use of tobacco. This large sample would then be the result of the combined effects of the extent of housecleaning, the time of departure for another village, and the way they were forced to leave the area. Despite all these speculations, the Mandeville site will remain a truly puzzling village where the men, and possibly the women, smoked their *Quyecta* during the intense social activities that were held inside the houses during the wintertime.

Acknowledgments

I would like to thank Dr. Norman Clermont for helping me to clarify the structure of this paper and Charles A. Martijn for providing me with many helpful comments and editing advice. I remain solely responsible for the ideas expressed in this text.

PART FIVE

Contemporary Iroquois Perspectives, Repatriation, and Collaborative Archaeology

| Overview

MOST ARCHAEOLOGICAL TREATMENTS of the Iroquois contain very little, if any, input from contemporary Iroquoian peoples themselves. This absence may come as no surprise, especially because exceedingly few Iroquois are archaeologists, and because generally archaeologists and American Indians-First Nations of Canada have been in conflict over the excavation of indigenous skeletal remains and burial objects, as well as over the larger issue of who should control representations of the past. Simply put, Native mistrust and scorn of archaeologists and archaeology have been both deep and rampant for many years. Although several publications, including a few of the readings in parts 1–4, incorporate Iroquois oral tradition into archaeological interpretations, the extent of Iroquois involvement in the discipline has been minimal. In recent years, however, this situation, at least in the United States, has begun to change in critical ways, largely as a result of two seminal pieces of federal legislation: the Native American Graves Protection and Repatriation Act (NAGPRA) of 1990 and the 1992 amendments to the National Historic Preservation Act (NHPA) of 1966.

Both NAGPRA (Public Law 101–601) and the 1992 amendments to the NHPA (Public Law 102–575) put into place formal consultation procedures between Native Americans and archaeologists. Briefly, NAGPRA pertains to the protection of American Indian burials on land belonging to federally recognized tribes (including the Six Nations Iroquois) and to the federal government. This statute also established a framework for the returning of Native skeletal remains, funerary objects, sacred objects, and objects of cultural patrimony kept in federally funded museums. American Indian individuals and federally recognized tribes may receive these materials, upon request, if they can demonstrate cultural affiliation to such items. The 1992 amendments to the NHPA authorized federally recognized tribes to take on more responsibility for the preservation of significant historic properties on their land and to create Tribal Historic Preservation Offices/Officers. Further, for development projects on land owned by such tribes or by the federal government, or for projects involving federal funding or permitting, archaeologists may be required to consult with Tribal Historic Preservation Officers and other indigenous people in advance of such undertakings.

Thus, for some 15 years, not only have NAGPRA and the NHPA begun to improve the often contentious relationship between archaeologists and many Native communities, but they also have broadened the role of American Indians, including the Iroquois, in archaeology (see Dongoske et al. 2000; Ferguson 1996; Kerber 2006; Klesert and Downer 1990; Silliman 2007; Swidler et al. 1997; Watkins 2000). Archaeological collaboration with the Iroquois and other aboriginal groups has also occurred voluntarily, particularly in the past decade, beyond the narrow scope of regulatory compliance mandated by the two statutes. Actually, collaborative ethnography in the United States began in the early 1840s when Lewis Henry Morgan met Ely Parker, a Seneca, which led to the two working together on writing *League of the Ho-de-no-sau-nee*, or Iroquois (published in 1851).

Today archaeology is not just performed on Iroquoian sites, but it is increasingly done by, with, for, and among the Iroquois, especially in New York. Archaeologists, as a whole, are much more sensitive in their treatment and reporting of Native skeletal remains (as are museum curators who no longer exhibit such materials). In addition, fewer human burials are being excavated by archaeologists and avocationals alike, even though in states like New York the law permits disturbance of unmarked graves on private property.

The five readings in this section, including four prepared by Haudenosaunee writers who are not archaeologists, present a range of insights into such timely topics as contemporary Iroquois perspectives, repatriation, and collaborative archaeology. Although the research sources section for part 5 is considerably smaller than that of the others, the number of publications is growing as are examples of Iroquoian involvement in archaeology.

Doug George-Kanentiio, a Mohawk, opens with discussion of pertinent issues addressed previously in several reprints, including origins of the Iroquois and the Five Nations Confederacy, but from a very different perspective. Based on stories told by the elders, the Iroquois originated in the American Southwest desert and gradually moved east where numerous small bands split off to become the nations later encountered during European contact. Similarly, he recounts oral history of the founding of the League. A solar eclipse marked the first convening of the Haudenosaunee Grand Council late one day at the time of year when the corn was ripe and the grass was knee high. Relying on astronomical evidence discussed by Barbara A. Mann and Jerry L. Fields (1997), in combination with oral tradition, George-Kanentiio reasons that the birth of the Iroquois Confederacy occurred precisely on the afternoon of August 31, 1142. David Henige (1999), however, seriously questions the logic and methodology used by Mann and Fields (1997). It is safe to say that dating the League's origins remains a debatable issue among many researchers.

George-Kanentiio (2000, 26) also comments on a double standard in the way scholars have treated Iroquois accounts of the past: "Like all Native people in the Americas, the Iroquois have endured academic paternalism, which discounts as quasi-fantasy our history as passed across the generations by word of mouth. Yet it is these same social scientists who aggressively seek out Native 'informants' to enlighten them as to the spiritual and social practices that define Iroquois life."

In the following essay, Peter Jemison, a Seneca, explores the broad question of who owns the past. He summarizes dialogue from a symposium held on this controversial subject in 1989, just before NAGPRA became law. The participants included Iroquois individuals, and archaeologists and a physical anthropologist from the Rochester Museum and Science Center, which has a long record of organizing archaeological research and displays on the New York Iroquois. It is striking to compare the different voices and positions articulated in these brief, but revealing, excerpts. At the end of the piece, Jemison answers his rhetorical question posed at the outset: the federal government now "owns the past" because NAGPRA requires that museums study Native remains in their collections to determine cultural affiliation before repatriation.

Richard W. Hill Sr., a Tuscarora, also focuses on the politics of repatriation, specifically of sacred wampum belts held in several museum collections. He retells some of the arduous legal and political battles fought by the Iroquois for more than 30 years, before and after NAGPRA was enacted, to recover these objects of cultural patrimony. According to Hill, the long-awaited return of the wampum belts contributes to Haudenosaunee empowerment, revitalization, and survival. The author concludes by arguing that museums can play a critical role in the Native American future by considering new kinds of partnerships that go beyond the object: "Repatriation is not an end, it is, in many ways, a new beginning. Through the process and relations it engenders, museums will come to understand that cultural preservation is not only about keeping objects from decaying but also about keeping ideas, values, and beliefs viable for the many generations to come" (Hill 2001, 137).

Like the preceding Native authors, Salli M. Kawennotakie Benedict, a Mohawk, offers a distinctive Iroquois perspective on a number of current archaeological topics, including the relationship between archaeologists and aboriginal groups. She claims that among the Mohawks of Akwesasne in Canada not only has this interaction traditionally lacked respect and trust, but that the way archaeology has been performed there (and elsewhere in Native America) is akin to other acts of oppression and cultural genocide perpetrated on indigenous peoples by Western civilization. Benedict stresses the principle of "capacity building" at Akwesasne and the need to enlist the involvement and permission of all interested parties in the archaeological process to achieve a more positive outcome, grounded in mutual trust and respect.

In the final chapter of the volume, I underscore the importance, and assorted challenges and benefits, of archaeologists and Native Americans working together on varied educational, research, and museum-related projects. Two case studies in collaborative archaeology are presented involving the Oneida Indian Nation of New York and nearby Colgate University. The first centers on an archaeological workshop, at nonsacred sites, offered by the university to more than 100 Iroquois teenagers for nine consecutive years. During the past few summers, the project has been located on Oneida territory and has been funded almost entirely by the nation. The other example is of ongoing collaboration between the Oneidas and the university over the repatriation, exhibition, and curation of certain Oneida archaeological remains in Colgate's Longyear Museum of Anthropology. This cooperation stems from experiences in which both groups have continued to work together in compliance with NAGPRA and in voluntarily reaching agreements on other issues. As my paper demonstrates, collaboration is valuable to archaeologists and the Iroquois alike, especially when power and control are shared equally.

20 | Iroquois Roots
DOUG GEORGE-KANENTIIO

The Bering Strait Theory

IMAGINE YOU ARE PART of a small group of nomadic hunters, compelled for some unknown reason to leave your territory and drift to the northeast. Your group's journey may take decades to complete and might even continue long after your death. It began in the middle of a vast continent and involves moving toward a barren land of high mountain ranges marked by long, brutally cold winters.

While hunting was a challenge in your former region, it proves much more difficult as your band heads deeper into the frigid north. Finally, after seasons of deprivation and starvation, the scouts ahead of your group come to the shore of a great salt sea, the other side of which is lost in heavy fog. Ahead of you unfolds a vast plain of treacherous bog across which no large mammal can pass. Because this marshy land lies stretched between two polar oceans, it is swept by hurricane-force storms that drive the temperatures so low skin turns to ice wherever it is in contact with the air.

Superhuman effort is needed to endure the horrors of your journey, but the ever-dwindling band presses on, driven to the east by a strange compulsion that defies understanding.

Most of your group dies of hunger on the bogs, but a few manage to stumble forward until they reach a new land, void of human habitation. Once again there are unceasing mountain ranges to climb without any expectation the arctic atmosphere will end.

Finally, there is a glimmer of hope. Far ahead you spot a bright band of blue and white shimmering in the distance. Perhaps these are low-lying clouds covering a sheltering valley where you might once again shed your heavy animal pelt cloaks and bask in the warm sun.

Previously published in *Iroquois Culture and Commentary* (Santa Fe: Clear Light Publishers, 2000), 17–34. Printed with permission by Clear Light Publishers, Santa Fe, New Mexico, <www.clearlightbooks.com>.

As you get closer to the area your spirits are crushed, for directly before the company is a tremendous glacier two miles high and stretching beyond sight from the north to the south. Some of your band want to return across the bogs but others insist there is a way through the ice. As if by magic they find a chasm in the glacier. They eagerly enter and walk its entire 1,500-mile length without food of any kind while contorting their frail bodies through a narrow wind tunnel marked by 200-mile-per-hour tempests.

They emerge from the glacier to discover a fertile land of woolly mammoths, giant bison, and vast herds of horses. Your group is overjoyed by what they find and quickly populate the continent. Mysteriously, they ignore the smaller game creatures and risk their lives to exterminate the largest animals.

In time, your descendents will drift apart and within an astonishingly short period develop over 500 languages and dialects to communicate across hundreds of nations spread over two continents.

As strange as the above sounds, it is the basis upon which many otherwise intelligent scientists have determined the Western Hemisphere was first populated by human beings. Anyone with a shred of common sense will come to the conclusion that the Bering Strait migration theory is irrational. It is a theory only, for no true physical evidence exists that supports this concept. It is also illogical, for the only time a land bridge connected Asia and the Americas was during the ice age of 10,000 years ago, when human life in that region was impossible.

Then there is the other serious problem with the Bering Strait theory: it collapses when archaeologists find evidence that humans were here long before the end of the last ice age. Such evidence has been uncovered in South America, New Mexico, and California.

But if Indians did not come from Asia, where did they originate? The answer lies within Native oral histories for those willing to listen, learn, and believe.

Origins of the Iroquois

Central to the beliefs of every culture is the story of where they came from and how they arrived at their current time and place. While many origin stories are almost mythical in nature, others are surprisingly consistent with hard physical or linguistic data. Oral traditions inevitably contain valuable insights into the culture and mannerisms of any people, and none more so than those people who, because they lack a method of writing, rely exclusively on collective memories passed down through the ages by the sacred act of storytelling.

Such is the case with the Iroquois, a people who until recently passed on all their history by the spoken word. How accurate are these legends? I contacted my friend Dr. Dean Snow, an archaeologist at the State University of New York at Albany who has spent many years collecting material from various Mohawk settlements in central New York.

I asked Dr. Snow specific questions as to where he thought we came from, based solely on the evidence he had collected. His conclusions largely substantiate what I had been told by the elders of the Mohawk Nation, namely that we were originally a people from the desert area of the American Southwest who had gradually moved into this region over a period of many generations.

When our people tell a story they do not refer to specific years but recall special events, exceptional people, a specific land form, or an unusual celestial phenomenon. Eclipses of the sun are remembered and passed on, as are political and social upheavals. All of this is brought together in the form of a story to be told by our oral historians—men and women who traveled from one Iroquois village to the next during the winter cold, carrying with them the legends of our nations.

We are told our story began with the coming to earth of the Sky Woman, a person from a world beyond the stars who was drawn to this planet by curiosity. Instead of firm land, she found endless water because a great flood had covered the earth. Only through the intervention of certain animals was she able to avoid drowning in this endless sea.

By a series of miracles, she was able to have mud dredged from the ocean floor and placed upon the back of a giant turtle. By dancing upon it, she caused this muck to grow until it became the continent of North America, which the Iroquois call Turtle Island. Heavy with child, the Sky Woman gave birth to a daughter. When this daughter grew up, she was impregnated by the western wind with male twins.

Through another series of adventures, which take many hours to tell, this new land was given form and populated with plants and animals by the grandsons of the Sky Woman, one of whom was good and the other very bad. The good twin made humans in his image but his jealous brother corrupted these early people, giving them characteristics such as greed, hatred, and anger.

In time, after a great struggle, which took place on the southern shores of Onondaga Lake, the evil twin was defeated by his brother, but his deeds could not be undone. From that day to this, life on earth has been a constant struggle between the forces of light and darkness.

Our elders tell us we first grew to become a distinct people in the Southwest, in the land where the Hopi live. Indeed, to this day the Iroquois refer to the Hopi as our cousins, relatives whom we remember even after the passing of thousands of years.

For some reason, the Iroquois began to wander away from the Southwest and eventually settled at the eastern edge of the Great Plains where the Missouri and Mississippi River meet, near current-day St. Louis. It is said we were close allies with the Wolf Nation, now called the Pawnee. (In the movie *Dances With Wolves*, they are shown as the Indians with the Mohawk haircut attacking Lt. Dunbar's Lakota friends. It is entirely possible they borrowed their hairstyles from us, given that the Iroquois were a very important political and economic force in the Midwest throughout the seventeenth and eighteenth centuries.)

After many generations, the Iroquois again moved, this time toward the northeast following the Ohio River. During the course of this journey several small bands split off to venture north, where, over time, they grew into the Tobacco, Neutral, Huron, Petun, Wenro, and Erie nations. Another group went to the southeast and became the Cherokees, while a large number settled in central Pennsylvania and were known as the Susquehannas or Conestoga Nation.

Undeterred by these divisions, the main Iroquois party continued on, paddling their canoes along the shores of the Great Lakes and down the St. Lawrence River until they were stopped at a place near Three Rivers, Quebec, by the Algonquins. It is said the Iroquois were enslaved by the Algonquins and spent many years laboring for a people we called the Adirondacks, or "bark eaters," because they had the habit of flavoring their food with shredded bark.

After many years had passed, the Iroquois managed to escape. They retraced their steps along the St. Lawrence and into Lake Ontario. As they were about to land near the mouth of the Oswego River, they spotted the Adirondacks coming fast in an effort to recapture them. In a scene reminiscent of the "Divine Wind," or kamikaze, said to have protected the Japanese against invasion, a great storm came from the west and upset the canoes of the Adirondacks, drowning many of their men and driving the rest far into the lake.

Having landed safely, the Iroquois liked what they saw. Within a few years their population had grown so quickly that it was necessary to expand further into that territory. One group decided to set up their villages along the Mohawk River and became known as the People of the Flint because of the flint quarries in this eastern area. In the Iroquois language, they are the Kaiienkehaka, but are also called the Mohawks.

To the west of the Mohawks were the Oneidas, followed by the Onondagas, the swamp-dwelling Cayugas, and along the Genessee River, the People of the Great Hill or Senecas. Another group went far to the south to what is now North Carolina, but eventually retraced their steps to this region in the early 1700s. They are called the "shirt-wearers" or Tuscaroras.

This is a very abbreviated summary of the Iroquois story of our beginnings, of how we came to be in New York State. Nothing has ever been found that contradicts this story. In fact the physical and linguistic evidence supports what our elders have been telling us all along, namely that we are a people with roots in distant lands far to the west, but as a nation and a people we are of this land and no other.

The Great Law of Peace

The Iroquois people have lived in the North American Northeast from time immemorial, our language, culture, and lifestyles interwoven with the powerful rivers, great forests, and fertile valley bottomlands that compose our ancestral homelands.

Long ago, when the Iroquois lived as one family on the southern shore of Lake Ontario, we were given a series of moral teachings by a messenger sent to us from the spirit world. These instructions formed the basis of the many elaborate rituals that define our religious beliefs and practices. The messenger told our ancestors how to honor the Creator and give communal thanks for the many blessings of life by holding a series of gatherings inside our longhouses each lunar month. At these gatherings, one person was to recite the Thanksgiving Address, a prayer spoken on behalf of the people in which earth, water, sky, wind, insects, plants, and animals are specifically addressed with words of gratitude.

In addition, the messenger affirmed the ceremonies as a way of preserving the human-earth relationship through music and dance. These ceremonies brought much happiness to the Iroquois, but as the centuries passed the teachings became obscured as the Five Nations entered a time of fear and violence. It is said this era in Iroquois history was a terrible one during which the nations were controlled by merciless warlords and evil sorcerers, each of whom used terror to keep a firm grip upon the people. Each day brought new suffering, until the Iroquois began to doubt any goodness was left in the world.

It was then, when all hope had been abandoned, another messenger was sent by the Creator to the Iroquois. This prophet was conceived of a virgin woman among refugees who had fled the Iroquois homelands to seek sanctuary north of Lake Ontario. The messenger came in the form of a male child whose life mission was to bring peace to the world by forming a World League of Nations with the power to banish warfare as a means of resolving human disputes.

Called Skennenrahawi, or the Peacemaker, his greatest challenge was to convert the Iroquois to the ways of peace, no simple task given their notoriety for cruelty. Nonetheless, Skennenrahawi left his place of refuge, crossing Lake Ontario in a gleaming white canoe made of stone. He crossed the waters as rapidly as an arrow fired from a bow. Arriving on the far shore, he met a group of Mohawk hunters. He told them peace was coming to the Iroquois and they should go about and tell the people of the new way.

Skennenrahawi traveled throughout Iroquois territory teaching those who would listen about the rules that would bring peace. These rules, referred to as the Great Law of Peace, were to serve as the guiding regulations for all the Iroquois.

In time, Skennenrahawi met Jikonsasay, a female leader from the Neutral Nation west of the Senecas. Jikonsasay took great delight in provoking disputes from which she profited by supplying all sides with food and arms. However, she was persuaded to abandon her evil ways once she listened to Skennenrahawi explain how the Great Law would work.

In exchange for her assistance in spreading the Law, Skennenrahawi decided all Iroquois women would have a decisive role in selecting male leaders and would serve as clan leaders in their own right, as well as holding the power to participate actively in the political and spiritual lives of their respective nations.

Skennenrahawi also met Aiionwatha, a Mohawk-Onondaga man who was searching for an alternative to the chaos within Iroquois society. Aiionwatha (also referred to as Hiawatha) was articulate and courageous in his determination to bring Skennenrahawi's ideas to fruition. He met considerable resistance to his efforts. When his seven daughters were killed at Onondaga, he experienced such great despair that he wandered throughout the land, inconsolable.

It was Aiionwatha who devised the powerful condolence prayer recited before the elevation of a clan leader, words that were marked by the use of wampum, a device invented by him to record important events in Iroquois history.

The Onondaga wizard Tadodaho, a grossly deformed man whose head was capped by a nest of writhing snakes, opposed the work of Skennenrahawi, Jikonsasay, and Aiionwatha to establish a great league of peace. Tadodaho's refusal to relinquish his control of the Onondagas prevented the creation of the League. He was finally persuaded to change his mind when confronted by the other Iroquois nations at a great assembly on the southern shore of Onondaga Lake. Tadodaho was also given the position of chairman of the Haudenosaunee Confederacy, and his successors have continued to carry his name as their title of office.

The initial Grand Council of the Confederacy established a permanent format for all subsequent sessions. Fifty male leaders, called *rotiiane* (pronounced lo-di-ya-ne), sat in council as representatives of their respective nations. Every rotiiane carried a title name, which was passed on from one generation to the next.

Every one of the 50 rotiiane was chosen by the female clan leaders (clanmothers), approved by their individual clans, sanctioned by the national councils, and finally acknowledged by the Grand Council of the Confederacy.

The Founding Date of the Haudenosaunee Confederacy

The precise date for the founding of the Haudenosaunee Confederacy has been a matter of speculation for many years. Historians, anthropologists, archaeologists, theologians, and amateur sleuths have placed the raising of the Great Tree of Peace anywhere from the early 1600s to the middle decades of the fifteenth century.

Most of these "experts" point to various factors that, they argue, compelled the Iroquois to join forces in the face of external threats ranging from European-borne diseases to fierce competition over the fur trade. Some have gone so far as to excavate ancient Iroquois village sites to examine physical clues that might indicate when the Iroquois abandoned their palisaded hilltop communities to build new towns closer to the natural trade routes along rivers and lakes.

Few of these professionals have taken the time to listen to the oral traditions of the Haudenosaunee, but it is these stories that might offer the best evidence as to the date when the Grand Council was first summoned by the Peacemaker and his disciples Jikonsaseh and Aiionwatha.

Like all Native people in the Americas, the Iroquois have endured academic paternalism, which discounts as quasi-fantasy our history as passed across the generations by word of mouth. Yet it is these same social scientists who aggressively seek out Native "informants" to enlighten them as to the spiritual and social practices that define Iroquois life.

These professionals grudgingly acknowledge the Haudenosaunee were the most influential indigenous people in North America, yet they dig in their heels at the thought that the Iroquois might have sparked the democratic ideals of the founders of the infant United States. They seem determined to debunk any notion that the Haudenosaunee actually created and sustained complex, sophisticated nation-states capable of exercising active jurisdiction over a territory stretching from the Hudson River to the Mississippi.

Some of the Iroquois critics will go so far as to argue that the founding of the Confederacy was heavily influenced by the Europeans, inferring that such a political system was beyond the intellectual capacity of a primitive, warlike, and stone age people. After all, how smart can a people be if they don't have gunpowder, professional armies, or the religious heritage that placed European man at the center of the universe?

Fortunately there are scientists capable of marrying hard physical data with Iroquois oral history in determining an actual day when the Great League of Peace was established. Dr. Barbara Mann, Ph.D., an American Studies instructor at the University of Toledo, and Jerry Fields, an astronomer-mathematician at the same institution, examined evidence from a number of sources, the results of which were published in the *American Indian Culture and Research Journal* (Mann and Fields 1997).

Because there have been 144 Tadodahos since the founding of the League, they estimated an average number of years that a person would have been in office and subtracted that from the present date. Through oral history, they also knew the League was created during the month when the corn was ripe and the grass was knee high, clearly indicating the month of August. The scholars realized that the League and the introduction of corn to the Iroquois took place at the same period, which is, according to the physical evidence, around the year 1100. Corn had been brought into Iroquois territory from the Southwest and quickly became the Iroquois' most important source of food. With corn as a staple and in great abundance, the Iroquois population increased, along with its political and economic influence throughout the Northeast.

Fields and Mann were aware there was a solar eclipse during the Confederacy's birth that took place directly above the Seneca town of Ganondagan. They calculated there were eight eclipses in that region within nine hundred years, but only one that took place directly above central New York, during the time of day stated in the oral histories and in the corn-harvesting moon.

That day, according to Fields and Mann, corresponds to both physical data and Iroquois traditions. Given what the two scholars describe as "an unprecedented mass of evidence," we may safely set the ratification of the Haudenosaunee Confederacy as having taken place during the afternoon of August 31 in the year 1142.

Iroquois Sacred Places in New York

For those planning to spend vacation time in New York State, there are a number of places to consider that have special significance to the Iroquois. These sites are not known to most people and are rarely marked by plaques, yet to this day the informed Iroquois will stop for a few moments to reflect and remember.

North of Albany in the town of Colonie, where the Mohawk River meets the Hudson, is the Cohoes waterfall. The Iroquois believe this is the place where the prophet we call the Peacemaker performed one of his miracles some 800 years ago.

The Peacemaker was sent by the Creator to put an end to war by joining all nations in a league of peace. The Mohawks liked his plan but they had their doubts. In order to test the Peacemaker's powers, they had him climb a tall pine tree, which grew above Cohoes Falls. While he was perched near its top, they chopped it down and watched it tumble into the churning waters far below. When the Peacemaker did not immediately appear, they believed he had drowned and they sadly returned home. When they got to their village, they found the Peacemaker calmly sitting next to a fire, smoking his pipe, completely dry. It was then the Mohawks agreed to become the first nation in what was to become the Haudenosaunee Confederacy.

All along the Mohawk River are the ancient village sites of the Mohawk Nation. Such contemporary towns as Schoharie, Ft. Hunter, Fonda, and Canajoharie were originally Native communities. A visit to the Jesuit shrine at Auriesville is also of interest to learn about the Catholic experience among the Mohawks.

Just east of the city of Oneida is the hamlet of Oneida Castle, so called because the old-time Iroquois towns were surrounded by palisades that from a distance looked like castles. The Oneidas lived in Oneida Castle until the 1820s, when most of them moved to Wisconsin.

South of Canastota, near the junction of Oxbow and Alene Corners Roads, is a seldom-visited county park called Nichols Pond. At this site the Oneidas constructed a large town that was attacked in 1615 by Samuel De Champlain. The park is a most pleasant corner of Madison County and has a large sacred turtle rock upon which the Oneidas would meet and pray.

An important place for the Onondagas is the south shore of Onondaga Lake. Here the Peacemaker joined forces with the chiefs, clanmothers, and faithkeepers of the Confederacy to confront the sorcerer Tadodaho. Using the power of the good mind, they persuaded him to join the League as its chairman. Also important to the

Onondagas is their old town located just north of Nedrow on South Salina Street. At this meeting place, the Onondagas greeted ambassadors and dignitaries from many nations.

No visit to central New York would be complete without a tour of St. Marie Among the Iroquois, a museum on the eastern shores of Onondaga Lake just north of Syracuse, in the town of Liverpool. The museum is connected with a recreated fort, similar to the one constructed by the Jesuit priests in the seventeenth century. Reenactors dressed in the clothing of that era provide instruction as to the lives of the mission residents, while the museum has admirable displays on Iroquois life and culture of 300 years ago.

A drive along Cayuga Lake gives the tourist an idea of why the people of the Cayuga Nation fought so valiantly to keep their land. Its gently rolling hills, sheltered valleys, and pure waters provided the Cayugas with an abundance of food, while the area that is now the Montezuma Wildlife Refuge, with its plants and herbs, served as a pharmacy for the Iroquois.

South of Canandaigua Lake, just off State Route 364, is a prominent hill that has great meaning to the Senecas. They call it simply "the Great Hill" because they believe they sprang from the earth at this magical place.

Finally, there is Ganondagan, at the junction of State Routes 41 and 3 south of Victor. Upon this site lived Jikonsasay, the first Iroquois clanmother. It served as the capital of the Seneca Nation and currently has a nature trail, small museum, and learning center. A 60-foot longhouse in the ancient Seneca style, opened in 1997, provides Ganondagan's visitors with an opportunity to walk through the traditional domestic dwelling of the Iroquois.

There are, of course, many other sites of significance, but these few serve as an appropriate introduction to the sacred geography of the Haudenosaunee.

Legend of Two Serpents

There are many Iroquois stories passed down over the generations concerning the anticipated coming of the Europeans to North America and the attendant social, environmental, and political changes. When the Haudenosaunee (Iroquois) Confederacy was formed many generations before 1492, the Peacemaker, teacher of the Great Law of Peace, gave the people predictions as to what would happen once he was gone.

He told the assembled Five Nations a story they were to tell their children across the generations. It was of events he said would come to pass. This epic would begin with the Kaiienkehaka people, called by some the Mohawks.

It was said two young men had left the territory of the Mohawk Nation on a hunting expedition far to the east where the salt water meets the land. For some unknown reason famine had struck the villages of the Mohawk people. The crops were few and poor in quality, while the deer and moose had disappeared. The many rivers that flowed through Mohawk territory were empty of fish, while the skies were strangely void of birds.

Hunger compelled the hunters to search in all directions for food to feed the people. These two men spent many days paddling down one river after another in hopes of finding game, but their luck was very bad. No animals were to be found.

Finally, they reached the ocean. Not having been in this region before, they were amazed at the many different types of wildlife in the area. But when they looked to the eastern skies toward the rising sun, they saw something glowing in the distance. Curious, they decided to paddle their canoe into the swelling sea to find out what this shimmering light might be.

They were far from shore before they reached the light, which turned out to be two small snake-like creatures, one a pulsating silver and the other a luminous gold. Fascinated by the serpents, the hunters took them from the water, placed them in their canoe, and headed back to the shore.

Believing the Mohawk people would find the serpents to be of great value, the two men abandoned their hunt and headed directly toward home. When they arrived back in the Mohawk territory, it was just as they had expected. The people were quickly enchanted by the serpents. They prepared a special cage for them on the edge of the village and would sit for hours watching the bright colors emanating from the snakes.

Soon they discovered that the serpents had great appetites. To keep them satisfied, the Mohawks had to feed them all the time. They ate everything—corn, meat, fish, grass, roots, leaves. Everyone was busy trying to find enough food for the snakes, and soon stripped the village bare of anything edible.

As they ate, the creatures grew ever larger, causing the Mohawks to build bigger cages. Finally, when there was no more food left, the serpents rose in anger, broke free from their cage, and attacked the people. The snakes ate many of them before the people managed to flee in terror into the forest.

Brave hunters decided to kill the beasts and attacked them with spears, clubs, and arrows. But the animals were by then too large and too strong. The Mohawks were beaten back and defeated.

As the serpents searched for more food, they devastated the surrounding area. Soon very few animals were left alive to feed the Mohawks. Almost all had been consumed by the serpents. Driven by their insatiable hunger, the serpents left Mohawk territory, slithering their way west.

The Mohawks discovered that wherever the serpents went they left behind polluted waters, desolate lands, and millions of destroyed trees. No Iroquois nation could stand up to the serpents. As they searched for new hunting grounds, the golden snake went south while the silver crawled north. The Iroquois could tell where they were by the loud noises they made as they tore at the land and drove everything before them.

By this time, they had grown so large they could knock down trees whenever they passed. They were powerful enough to bore through mountains and drink up entire lakes. They had also grown to love the act of killing and would slay any living thing in their path.

After many generations had passed, the Mohawks felt safe since the serpents were said to be far to the west of Turtle Island. However, while on a hunting journey in that direction, a Mohawk man saw the golden serpent, now taller than a mountain. It was heading back to Iroquois territory.

In great fear the hunter raced back to Iroquois lands, shouting warnings as he went. As he paddled his canoe east, he learned the silver serpent was also making its way back to Mohawk territory.

What were the people to do? Faced with this crisis, they could not decide. Heated arguments confused and consumed the Mohawks. Some wanted to stand and fight, others to run and hide. Still more thought the only way to survive would be to try to feed the serpents as they had done hundreds of years before. So bitter was the debate that fighting broke out among the Mohawks, causing some to be killed.

Some remembered the old stories about how the great snakes had eaten Mohawk children. Rather than have this happen once again, they tried to warn the people, but only a few listened. It was just as they feared. The serpents struck the Mohawks with hatred and fury, scattering the people and hunting them down one by one. Only those who had fled the village to a safe place near a certain mountain survived. The serpents, however, knew their hiding place and continued to attack.

It was at this time, when it appeared the Mohawks had no chance of defeating the serpents, a Mohawk boy stood forth. He said he had a strange dream, one that told him how the snakes might be destroyed.

The Mohawks followed the instructions the boy had received in his dream. A very special bow was made from a willow tree with a string woven from the hair of the clanmothers. Arrows were carved and on their tips stones made of sharp white flint were placed. When the serpents appeared, the surviving Mohawk people gathered together around the boy as he pulled back on the bow and let the arrows fly. His aim was good, his heart strong. The arrows pierced the hides of the gigantic beasts, killing them.

Mohawk elders say the story has been handed down over the generations as a warning to the Iroquois about the great suffering they would endure at the hands of the Europeans. It is believed the gold serpent is the United States of America and the silver one is Canada.

It is said another grave threat to the Haudenosaunee would come from within, when the Iroquois would be torn apart by internal divisions caused by greed, spiritual differences, and the loss of our ancestral values. There may well be, it is told, a time when the Iroquois doubt they will survive until the next day, but if the people hold true to the Great Law of Peace and follow the teachings of Handsome Lake, they will prevail.

21 | Who Owns the Past?

G. PETER JEMISON

IN 1989, BEFORE NAGPRA became law, I organized a symposium entitled "Who Owns the Past?"[1] The symposium was held at the State University of New York (SUNY) at Buffalo during my graduate work in American Studies. Invited discussants included Native Americans and museum personnel from the Rochester Museum and Science Center, Rochester, New York. The Native Americans included Chief Irving Powless Jr., Onondaga Nation; John Mohawk, Seneca Nation of Indians, an assistant professor at SUNY Buffalo; and Geraldine Green, Seneca Nation of Indians, a Longhouse elder. Charles Hayes III, the director of research; Lorraine Saunders, a physical anthropologist and a research fellow; and Martha Sempowski, an archaeologist and a research fellow, all from the Rochester Museum and Science Center, represented the scientific and museum communities.

The symposium was organized to examine our differing views of human remains and sacred objects. Participants were each given 10 minutes to present a statement that outlined their points of view. They were then given an opportunity to interact and answer questions from fellow participants or audience members: a lively debate ensued.

---

1. "Who Owns the Past?" is the title of an unpublished manuscript edited by G. Peter Jemison and transcribed from a symposium with the same title. The symposium was supported in part by a grant from the New York State Council on the Humanities.

Previously published in *Native Americans and Archaeologists: Stepping Stones to Common Ground*, ed. N. Swidler, K. E. Dongoske, R. Anyon, and A.S. Downer (Walnut Creek, Calif.: AltaMira Press, 1997), 57–63. With permission by AltaMira Press. Swidler et al. introduced this essay as follows: "In discussions over the past 20 years or so between Native Americans and archaeologists, two issues have emerged as central: (1) Who owns the past? and (2) Who should control the disposition of Native American human remains? Over the years, many meetings have been held at the local, regional, and national levels. As anyone who attended those meetings can attest, they were characterized by discussions that were fairly stylized. The same questions were raised, and pretty much the same answers were offered.

"Here, Jemison summarizes one such meeting conducted in 1989, prior to the enactment of NAGPRA. The statements Jemison reports are very typical. This dialogue provides a basis for examining if, how, and to what degree NAGPRA has (or has not) altered the dialogue" (Swidler et al. 1997, 57).

I have excerpted portions of their statements to give an idea of each individual's point of view. For example, Charles Hayes made two initial points: "increasing sensitivity to the proper treatment of human remains from archaeological contexts, no matter what group is involved, appears to be gaining momentum and acceptance throughout the world. . . . Secondly, all of us are anxious to combat the ever-increasing looting and destruction of archaeological sites." Hayes further commented, "Those of us in museums in particular are vitally interested in documenting, preserving, and interpreting Native American heritage as part of our concern for the overall history of North America. Never has the general public been so enthused or better informed about Indians." Hayes was concerned that repatriation could have negative effects: "I do not believe any of us would want to have our descendants feel that we made irrational decisions with profound effects on human history."

John Mohawk looked at the history of Native American and white relations as it pertains to the display of human remains. He cited the case of Metacom, the Wampanoag chief (also known as King Philip) who was beheaded in 1676 in the town of Plymouth, Massachusetts, at the conclusion of King Philip's War.

> He [Metacom] was an Indian. His people were attacked by the New England colonists. He was killed. His head was cut off and it was placed on top of a pointed stake, to be left there on display for some nearly two decades. And at the time the way it was explained by the religious leaders of the Colony was that the Indians were the handmaidens of the devil, and they needed to be dealt with thus. So our first exhibits had what you might call a spiritual explanation for a political end.

In the nineteenth century, this type of exhibit and interpretation was replaced by the work of Lewis Henry Morgan, the father of modern anthropology. According to Professor Mohawk,

> Lewis Henry Morgan, who I believe had some Rochester connections, and some Iroquois connections, really made a call. He called for the study of disappearing peoples as a way of preserving for all time what I would best describe as man's price to civilization, as it were—the Social-Darwinist theory that people started out in extreme primitivism and then from primitivism they evolved socially through stages. He called for more study of people who were at that hour in some stage of this evolution. And what arose during this period in the nineteenth century was a lot of stuff that was at that time supposed to be science; it was going to be the science of how peoples were distributed along a curve or a graph of worthiness, if you will, arising from primitive peoples to the people who were going to do the study, to civilized peoples . . . a period that was called the period of scientific racism, science was used to explain a political end.

Mohawk listed the negative results of this line of reasoning and concluded:

We want the sciences that are supposed to serve humanity to serve all of humanity equally, and to serve the dignity of all people equally. We can't have some people's heads stuck up on pikes outside the village, and we can't have some people's sacred objects stuck on display under glass when that's offensive to the people who hold those objects sacred. We can't have some people's remains in cardboard boxes in the bottom of brick buildings while other groups of people are not in cardboard boxes in the building—and we can't call it science; it's politics that does that.

Lorraine Saunders, a physical anthropologist, contended that her work, which involves the study of human osteology, provides direct testimony from deceased individuals about themselves and their lives. "There are written histories of the early days after the arrival of Europeans on this continent. But they were the observations of people of another culture who did not understand and often judged harshly the different and, to them, alien societies that they were seeing." Continuing, she stated, "The sort of study that I do involves direct contact with these people individual by individual. The information comes directly from each person. In that way, it seems to me that I am giving them the opportunity to have some say in what is known about them today." She concluded, "The insights gained from the research of today, and future improvements in methods and technology, will allow an increasingly better understanding of the lives of the earlier inhabitants of this continent. Therefore, reburial, the destruction of the only means they have to be the informants, would be silencing them forever before the whole story has been told."

Geraldine Green, Seneca, and a Longhouse elder, spoke next. She began,

> I'm not used to speaking in lecture halls, or in front of students. As a matter of fact, this is the first time I have gone out, so people know what is going on. All this museum stuff, archaeology, the digging up of human remains, or why we have to prove that they were, and who owns it, all this is strange for me and I have to do quite a bit of rethinking and examining of our way of life because there is more to us than what you see here, believe me. There has to be; otherwise, we wouldn't be here as survivors. And those ancestors who they want information from, I just don't understand that, and am not even going to begin to address that for that is not our way of life. . . .
>
> In our way of life when a person dies, there is a certain funeral address which tells us what to do. We leave them alone, they are through. They have given what information they want. They have done their jobs; we need not bother them anymore. That is why they go to their rest; they have finished their job here, and it is very important to us that we do not disturb them anymore.

Martha Sempowski, an archaeologist, offered this explanation:

> Archaeology, then, from my point of view, offers you and your descendants the hope of more accurate treatment in history through its potential for more objective documentation of specific events and interactions that took place during that criti-

cal interaction between Europeans and Native Americans.... Oral traditions are a very important source of information, but can you be certain that oral traditions will meet all the needs of your children? Your grandchildren? Or generations that will follow them? Can you really be certain? Can you be sure that they won't have new questions about the past that none of us here today has even conceived of? Questions so specific as to time and place that really the best way to answer them is through the archaeological record, if not the only way.... If effected on a national scale, the reburial program that's being proposed, however nobly intended and emotionally satisfying it is, would destroy a very substantial portion of this record of the past for Native Americans.

Sempowski made a second point:

Right now there happen to be two large Seneca sites that are under threat from modern development. In both cases we were asked by Native Americans and by local planning boards to make representations concerning the significance or importance of those particular sites. What allowed us to make those statements and recommendations was reference to existing collections of archaeological materials. Finally, one of my greatest fears about the proposed mass reburial of museum collections is that it would unwittingly contribute to further site looting by making the artifacts existing in private collections extremely rare, and thus inflate their monetary value.

The last presenter was Chief Irving Powless. Speaking of sacred objects in museum collections, he said:

We are the ones that know how to use them, how to utilize them, and the purpose of these sacred objects. You do not know what their purpose is. You don't know the songs that go with these sacred objects. You don't know the speeches that go with these sacred objects. You don't know the purpose of these sacred objects. Those sacred objects obviously are for our people. They do not belong in a box in a museum or some art show. There is a definite purpose for these sacred objects, and these sacred objects should be in our possession, not in the possession of some anthropologist, archaeologist, or some museum or private collector.

Chief Powless gave examples of sacred objects and their power. One involved Hopi Kachinas in a plastic bag stored in a drawer at a museum in Washington, D.C., and the apparent consequences of their release from this insensitive treatment. He reflected on the inherent power that sacred objects have and the general lack of recognition or the disbelief with which most museologists and anthropologists approach them.

During the session that followed, the participants raised issues with one another, and then the audience got into the act. Typical of that discussion were the following exchanges. John Mohawk stated, "First I am personally in favor of more archaeological research and not less. In fact, there's not enough money being spent on serious research. What I'm opposed to is the continuation of museums as monuments to ethnocentrism in our culture." Later he added,

> Where is the Seneca country? Crazy Horse, when they asked him about that, he pointed to the east and he said, '[My land . . . Oglala Teton land . . . is] There where lie the bones of my ancestors. That is our land.' And the Seneca country, where lie the bones of our ancestors, that's our land. Now somebody else got this land, and after they got this land, they claimed these were nonconsecrated graves. You can dig a nonconsecrated grave like you dig up the grave of a dog or cat. They're not sacred; they weren't sacred to the first people that came after they got the land.

John continued,

> It's not about graves and bones and studying bones. It's about respect for the living. It's about respect for other people. . . . When you argue that the bones that our people left there are useful, more useful for scientific purposes than they are necessary for reburial to maintain the heart and essence of the culture, the continuity of the generations, you're making an ethnocentric argument. . . . I haven't been able to get an accurate count, but there looks like there might be millions of skeletons, two million skeletons, in museum. Who's studying these?

Lorraine Saunders responded,

> As far as ethnocentrism goes, in the study of human remains I can give a specific example to show that that is hardly true anymore. In 1984 I was codirector of an excavation in Rochester called the Highland Park excavation. It was a cemetery for several public institutions. When I first became involved, all they knew was that human bones had been found. They were asking what the demography was. In other words, were there males and females? Were there children? . . . Then the real question finally came up. What race are they? Okay. And I said they were white and the engineers went oh, great, thanks. They were afraid they were going to be Native American but since it was an abandoned white cemetery, there are laws that cover that. . . . In fact, you can take out these burials with a backhoe, with heavy equipment, if it's classified as an abandoned cemetery, which this was.

In the end, the archaeologists did excavate the remains, but Saunders wanted to illustrate a point. She continued, "We are interested in all people. That's what anthropology is, the study of mankind, not just of one group over another group. And when there is missing information, if there is more that we can learn, that's what we want to do. And we do that by studying human remains."

Charles Hayes asked this question,

> I'm talking about the sacred objects in the collections; if all these are taken out of our current museums, and the volume as just alluded to is tremendous, we can realistically think that this material is, or should it be all reburied? Some of the greatest art will be lost forever except for pictures, and this is what bothers me as a museologist as well. . . . is the Native American community prepared to lose this material?

Irving Powless spoke of Art Gerber (an "ethnographic art dealer") and his views of Native American art: "I am preserving the art of the Native American people, and I sell these objects for five hundred, six hundred, depending on how much I can get for them." Again quoting Gerber he said, "I think we should be able to continue to go into these 'art farms' [grave sites] and get these objects from the Native Americans." Chief Powless questioned how we reach this point when an individual like Gerber refers to Native American burial grounds as art farms. "Where do we come to when we, in the study of man, put these objects that come out of these 'art farms' on display, either in the museum or in collections, private or otherwise?"

Early in the presentations Martha Sempowski had stated, "I'm not talking about the excavation of graves, the digging of burial grounds. Archaeologists do not any longer in New York dig human graves." I shared the following:

> In the spring of 1988 we attended the annual meeting of the New York Archaeological Association (avocational and professional archaeologists), which is also a conference for the New York Archaeological Council (professional archaeologists). The meeting was held in Norwich, New York. Geraldine Green and I attended the meeting and heard the statement made that, in fact, the moratorium was something that the individual archaeologist could choose to follow and abide by or choose to ignore, but it really was up to the individual—it's voluntary. This statement was made by a well-known, professional archaeologist, and I might be overstating the concern I have, but not one individual at the conference rebuked him publicly when he made the statement, and it is that code of silence which still protects avocational and professional archaeologists who excavate human remains.

Recently, the Haudenosaunee Standing Committee on Burial Rules and Regulations, a committee of representatives from the Six Nations Iroquois Confederacy, of which I am the chairman, visited the Rochester Museum and Science Center. The meeting was a preliminary response to a full visit on NAGPRA-related matters. We were pleased to learn from Richard Shultz, director of the museum, that they did not intend to block our request for the return of our ancestors' human remains. They listened carefully to our concerns about contract archaeology that the museum carries out and our concerns that Senecas not be left out of, or barred from, on-site observance when there is a potential for the disturbance of human remains. They promised to look at their contractual agreements and add language to allow for Native American observers. With regard to removing sacred objects from exhibits at the museum, they promised to revisit the question. I have heard, although I can't confirm it, that our medicine masks will be removed from display cases in the museum.

Perhaps a new era has begun with this one institution that has major Seneca and other Haudenosaunee holdings—we earnestly hope so. However, I recently received a letter from a staff person at the Rochester Museum looking for a letter of support for a NAGPRA grant application to fund the museum to study the human remains in the collection. I found this ironic, considering that the museum needed an extension of the November 1995 deadline to complete the inventory of human remains in their collection.

The question of who owns the past, in this case, may have been decided by the federal government because NAGPRA mandates that museums must study our remains to be able to return them to us for reburial and their final resting place, a bitter irony in the 200-year-old history between American Indians and the imposition of United States Indian Law on sovereign Nations.

22 | Regenerating Identity
Repatriation and the Indian Frame of Mind

RICHARD W. HILL, SR.

ABOUT 40 GENERATIONS AGO, the Iroquois of upstate New York received a message of peace, power, and unity that formed the basis of what is called The Great Law of Peace. This Great Law served as the founding constitution for the Six Nations Iroquois confederacy. The oral tradition surrounding the formation of this confederacy and its procedural requirements were encoded in a series of sacred belts and strings of tubular shell wampum beads assembled about 1,000 years ago. Messages, beliefs, and hopes were spoken into these belts as a way to preserve their power for future generations. Through this wampum, the Iroquois were connected to previous generations and acted as a cultural bridge to future ones.

Unfortunately, this continuity was ruptured through the coercive sale, theft, and removal of many of these belts during the nineteenth century. The wampum documents have since become the center of strained relations between the 45,000-strong Iroquois nation and several major museums that hold these sacred items. In this paper, I focus on the struggle of the Iroquois to recover these wampum belts as a way of illustrating the cultural issues behind the politics of repatriation.

It has been 25 years since I first heard of the sacred wampum. Even growing up as an Iroquois, though, I never saw any of these pieces in our communities. Most of the known wampum belts were locked away in museums. As a young man, I learned of their fate and was part of a movement to recover the wampums. It seemed to many Native people that the glorious beauty of the past, as well as the spiritual legacy of the future, was imprisoned in museums. I felt strongly that if we were to survive as a people, we needed to hear the messages from the past and be empowered to carry this knowledge forward.

Previously published in *The Future of the Past: Archaeologists, Native Americans, and Repatriation*, ed. Tamara L. Bray (New York: Garland Publishing, 2001), 127–38. Reproduced by permission of Routledge/Taylor and Francis Group, LLC. Copyright © 2001.

Culture is, indeed, more than objects, but for many Native American nations, there are certain objects that are essential to manifesting that culture. Most Native American children were growing up without ever having seen the treasures of their cultural heritage. To me and many Native Americans of my generation, it seemed that the sanctioned institutions of culture in our society were actually contributing to our cultural decline, and this became intolerable.

The Changing Political Landscape

It is important to remember that the Native American Graves Protection and Repatriation Act (NAGPRA) was preceded by decades of confrontations between museums and Native Americans over the issues of cultural patrimony, representation, religious rights, and human rights. During the 1960s, a period of intense political unrest, the federal government had begun to redefine its relationship to Native Americans. An era of forced relocation and assimilation was coming to an end and a new age of self-determination loomed on the horizon. Native Americans were growing stronger in their own sense of identity, and consequently became more vocal and aggressive in addressing social inequities. Museums were just one sector of American society to come under scrutiny as part of the associated spiritual revitalization movements, and repatriation needs to be understood as one component of these larger social reforms.

It is difficult to explain how deeply these movements affected Native Americans. Generations of poverty, oppression, and self-doubt had to be overcome. Leaders came to see the restoration of traditional cultural values as one of the most important avenues for enabling change. A stronger cultural base, it was thought, would provide Native people with a stronger sense of self, a stronger sense of place, and a stronger sense of destiny. But as more college-aged Native Americans began to seek out their spiritual heritage in order to reconnect with traditional values, they found many of the paths blocked because the objects needed to perform necessary ceremonies and rites were in the possession of museums. When those same Indian students began to visit these institutions, they found the material component of their cultural heritage behind glass and strangely silent, the objects of non-Natives' gawking stares. Freeing the objects from their ethnological fate came to be equated with the struggle for the liberation of the Native American mind and spirit.

Around this same time, museums and the field of anthropology were undergoing their own kind of reformation. Various policies, programs, and practices were being questioned with regard to standards of fairness and equity. African Americans, Asian Americans, Hispanic Americans, women, and the alternative arts were all demanding more attention from museums. Museum trustees were just beginning to address inconsistencies in standards of conduct on issues of accessioning and deaccessioning. The mishandling and outright illegal activities of some museums caused administrators to take a hard look at their practices and to critically examine whether they were in fact upholding the public trust with which they were charged.

With demands for the reburial of human remains, the removal of sacred objects from public display, and the repatriation of cultural patrimony, Native Americans forced standard museum policies and practices onto the public stage. I cannot say which museum was the first to return human remains or which was the first to formally recognize the rights of Native Americans to their own cultural patrimony. Some museums, mainly smaller ones, responded immediately to the claims of Native peoples without requiring the force of law to compel them. But the Native American Graves Protection and Repatriation Act came about because many of the major museums would not address our concerns. While NAGPRA was the final resort for Native Americans at the time, we now see it as a new beginning.

The Iroquois Wampum Case

In 1970, the New York State Assembly Subcommittee on Indian Affairs recommended that the century-old Wampum Law be amended to allow the return of five wampum belts to the Onondaga Nation. The amendment was proposed in recognition of the Onondaga's traditional role as the wampum keepers of the Iroquois Confederacy, an alliance that also includes the Seneca, Cayuga, Oneida, Mohawk, and Tuscarora Nations. When we learned of the proposed amendment, it came as a surprise to many of us that the Wampum Law even existed. How had New York State become the wampum keeper for the Iroquois? How had wampum, one of the Iroquois' most sacred objects of cultural patrimony, ever left our possession?

In many ways, the Iroquois experience is similar to that of other Native nations. Many Native Americans of my generation were born into communities rent asunder by the divergent beliefs of their own members. Differing views of religion, governance, education, economy, and culture tore at the very fabric of our common identities. We had become confused about who we were, what we were supposed to do, and how well our traditional culture served our needs in cold war America.

Visits to museums exacerbated this cultural disorientation. Museums were painful because Native bones, as well as objects we believed to be sources of power for our communities, were on display. Many of these items were trophies, collected by soldiers, priests, teachers, and government bureaucrats, that had once belonged to our ancestors. Native Americans felt profoundly disconnected from those sources of power. Repatriation became the process through which we sought to reconnect with the ideals represented in those objects and to reclaim authority over them.

Like many young Indians in the 1970s, I was able to learn of the significance of these objects from two sources: the scholarly literature produced by non-Natives and the stories that were still known by the old people in our communities. As the Iroquois pushed an agenda of cultural and political renewal, museums, anthropologists, educators, and movie-makers were targeted as obstacles to Iroquois progress. My own search for information led me to the campus of the State University of New York at Buffalo, where I now teach and the place where I first met the leading proponent of repatriation, Oren Lyons, an Onondaga artist, college professor, and representative on the Onondaga Council of Chiefs. It was a meeting that changed my life.

Lyons and several other chiefs, together with the New York State Council on the Arts, had convinced the State of New York to pass legislation to return the major belts from the State Museum to the Iroquois Confederacy. However, an aggressive campaign to block that move was launched by the Committee on Anthropological Research in Museums under the aegis of the American Anthropological Association (Sturtevant et al. 1970). The scholars on this committee were able to convince then-governor Nelson Rockefeller to veto the proposed legislation. The "Iroquoianists" subsequently became embroiled in a very public controversy with the traditional Iroquois chiefs over the primacy of cultural and religious rights versus scientific and academic rights (e.g., J. Henry 1970). The wampum case set the general tone for negotiations over repatriation that eventually would affect all museums with Indian materials in their collections. In many ways, the issues raised in New York are still at the forefront of the debate over repatriation.

During this battle, the Iroquois used the media effectively to create public sympathy for their cause and public opinion came to favor the return of the wampums. In addition, the Iroquois challenged the anthropologists and historians at every turn. Essays written by scholars were critiqued by the Native press. Confrontations with scholars became standard operating procedure. Academic conferences could no longer just be about Native Americans; they had to include Native Americans.

Relationships between the Iroquois and scholars reached an all-time low in 1976 as America turned its attention to the celebration of its 200th birthday. To the Iroquois, the dispute over the wampum was symbolic of racist policies that continued to subject Native peoples to cultural oppression. The Iroquois argued that the belts were illegally removed without the consent of the traditional chiefs, and that they were essential to the cultural and spiritual continuity of the Iroquois. They argued that for one culture group to assert that its scientific interests took precedence over the religious rights of another was itself evidence of how deeply entrenched racial bias was in the social sciences.

The scholars responded that museums "owned" the sacred objects and that these items were essential for future studies of the Iroquois. They felt that by studying Native people, American society at large could learn more about human cultures in general. Their position hinged on the argument that the public had a right to know the cultural heritage of their homeland and a right to view and enjoy these objects. To the scholars, it was an issue of academic freedom, which, for them, entailed the right to study anything, secular or religious, in the pursuit of truth. They might have won more support if they had stuck to that argument.

Instead they turned to character assassination and this lost support for their cause among many museum professionals. The anthropologists argued that the contemporary Iroquois were acculturated and no longer understood their own traditions. The scholars reasoned that they knew more about Iroquois traditions than the Iroquois themselves and that the wampums would be best left in the care of the non-Native professionals (Fenton 1971; Sturtevant et al. 1970). They tried to discredit the Iroquois by labeling them as "Red Power militants." In a letter written in 1970 to the governor, the scholars argued that "state property should not be legislated away lightly in the illusion of religiosity or as capital in the civil rights movement" (Sturtevant et al. 1970, 14).

Not to be outdone, the Iroquois painted the scholars as egomaniacal racists who were more concerned with their research, grants, and publications than with the cultural preservation of their "subjects." They made it difficult for archaeologists to continue excavating Native American grave sites without publicly justifying their actions. They also forced museums to address the issue of repatriation and obliged them to publicly refute accusations of racism and political sabotage. The situation reached a boiling point in 1979 when the New York State Senate, for the ninth year in a row, failed to amend the Indian Law relating to the custody of the wampums. The scholars thought they had defeated the Iroquois once and for all, but this was not to be the end.

The Function of Wampum

Wampum undergirds the entire cultural worldview of the Iroquois. It is sacred by virtue of the shell from which it is made and because it was chosen by the Creator as the medium through which the Iroquois would retain and transmit information from generation to generation (cf. Hewitt 1892; Noon 1949; Tooker 1978). This sacredness is why the Iroquois felt so strongly about the need to have the wampum returned. Turmoil had become a way of life in the 13 Iroquois communities spread across New York, Ontario, and Quebec. Elective governments had replaced the traditional systems in all but three of the communities. Most of the Iroquois people, who now attended Christian churches, no longer visited the longhouses where traditional ceremonies took place. The legendary Grand Council, once respected and feared by Dutch, French, English, and colonial American leaders, was but a shadow of its former self. The Great Law was suffering and the hope was that it could be revitalized with the return of the wampum belts, the repositories of the original messages.

The term *wampum* refers to the small, tubular beads that are drilled through their long axis and range in color from white to blue to purple (Abrams 1994; Beauchamp 1901). The word derives from the Algonquian *wampumpeag*, which, during the fur trade era, came to refer to any type of shell bead and took on specifically monetary connotations. But originally, among Native American cultures of the Northeast, *wampum* had numerous meanings, functioning as it did within the social, cultural, political, and spiritual realms of the Iroquois, Huron, Ojibwa, and Algonquian nations (Hewitt 1907–10). In the Iroquoian language, the word for wampum is *gatgoa*, while the word for a string of wampum is *sgadgoad*. Each different wampum belt originally would have had its own specific name. For instance, the wampum belt used in the Iroquois condolence ceremony was called *henodosetha gatgoa*.

Wampum had been used in many ways in the past. Wampum beads could be offered to a grieving family to atone for the death of a loved one. They could be used to ransom a captive relative. In 1622, for instance, a Dutch trader received 140 6-foot-long strings of wampum in exchange for a chief whom he was holding hostage. Wampum strings were given to chiefs and clan mothers as confirmation of their title and oath of office, the strands of tiny shell beads representing their pledge to uphold the Great Law. Wampum strings with notched sticks attached were used to announce upcoming council meetings, the wampum serving both as the credentials for the messenger and to prove that the delegates attending would be the official representatives of their community. The symbolic designs woven into wampum belts recorded the terms of treaties between nations. Wampum strings also recorded the order of ceremonial speeches. As an item of ritual exchange between different groups, wampum served to confirm agreements or requests. It was, for instance, the appropriate gift to offer a bride's family, and newly married couples were given wampum to verify their marriage oath. The beads also functioned as articles of personal adornment among the Iroquois and were worn as headbands, necklaces, armbands, belts, shoulder sashes, earrings, chokers, cuffs, or kilts (Abrams 1994; Tooker 1978).

The importance of wampum among Native American nations was quickly recognized by Euroamerican officials and settlers. In one account of a Native conference in Montreal in 1756, the significance of the shell beads is reported as follows:

> These belts and strings of wampum are a universal agent among Indians, serving as money, jewelry, ornaments, annals, and registers; [they are] the bond of nations and individuals, [recognized as] an inviolable and sacred pledge which guarantees messages, promises and treaties. As writing is not in use among them [the Indians], they make a local memoir by means of these belts, each of which signifies a particular affair or circumstance of affairs. The chiefs of the village are the depositories of [these belts], and communicate them to the young people, who thus learn the history and engagements of their nation. (O'Callaghan 1968 [1756], 556)

It is also interesting to note how quickly wampum came to figure in intercultural protocols. Both the French and the English adopted aspects of the Native system to convince the Iroquois of the earnestness of their intentions. The French, who referred to wampum as "porcelain collars," recognized its importance as an element of ritual protocol early on. In 1636, for example, Father Le Jeune noted that "as the Porcelain that takes the place of gold and silver in this country is all-powerful, I presented in this Assembly a collar of twelve hundred beads of Porcelain, telling them [the Iroquois] that it was given to smooth the difficulties of the road to Paradise." George Washington, as a military officer and later as president, used wampum both to petition the Iroquois and to confirm agreements made between his government and the Iroquois Confederacy. Wampum was regularly exchanged at treaty councils and at nearly every other official function.

The Loss of the Wampum

Once Native Americans were no longer considered a military threat, the era of treaty-making was over. Iroquois were isolated on small reservations, and wampum lost its political significance. But the belts, which verified the original treaties, remained a visible and problematic reminder of promises unkept as the federal government attempted to discontinue its relations with the Confederacy. As the Iroquois became objects of study in the emerging field of ethnology in the mid-nineteenth century, scholars began to report on the cultural and spiritual significance of wampum in the past tense. While some wampum remained actively in use within the internal spheres of Iroquoian life, many belts began to slip away.

By the late nineteenth century, the Iroquois were embroiled in great debates about modernization. Reformers wanted the Iroquois to give up their old ways, including the Council of Chiefs. As a result of these conflicts, the Onondaga came to have two political bodies, the traditional chiefs who sat in council in the longhouse and a dissident government that had been elected under the terms of the Bureau of Indian Affairs. The old wampums, descended from the time of the founding of the Iroquois Confederacy, symbolized the ongoing power of the Council of Chiefs. Many modern-day Iroquois believe that the removal of the wampum that ensued was an attempt to destroy the traditional form of government.

In 1891, Onondaga Chief Thomas Webster, a member of the rival BIA-backed government, sold all the wampums in his possession to Major Carrington, a U.S. Indian census agent (Carrington 1892). Webster may have felt that by dislocating the wampums, the traditional chiefs would lose their source of power and authority. But many Iroquois leaders of today believe that he was coerced into selling the belts. It was well known among members of Iroquoian society that no individual had the authority to give, trade, or sell the wampum belts. These items were only held in trust by the Onondaga for the member nations of the Confederacy. The belts were understood to belong to all Iroquois people and were recognized as part of the cultural patrimony of the Iroquois Nation. It is this idea of shared communal property that lies behind much of the repatriation movement. If a collector or a museum were to have purchased wampum from individuals without the sanction of the collective, the sale would, by definition, be invalid.

Between 1900 and 1940, many of the old wampums were obtained by scholars (Fenton 1989). It is hard to understand why some Iroquois, many of them traditionalists, gave up the wampum to anthropologists, but the results were devastating. Some Iroquois feel that the scholars tricked the people into giving up their sacred materials. Some say that times were hard financially and ritualists sold the only possessions they had in order to feed their families. Other say that some longhouse people truly believed that their traditions were coming to an end and wanted museums to preserve the sacred wampums. Whatever the motivation, the modern generation of Iroquois wanted their wampum back.

The First Wampum Comes Home

In 1963, a wampum belt in the collections of the Buffalo Historical Society turned up missing after becoming a primary object of interest in a lawsuit. This wampum belt had been given by the Tuscarora nation to the Holland Land Company in 1799 to document the transfer of 1 square mile of land to the Tuscarora people. This land today constitutes the core of the Tuscarora reservation. This particular wampum belt subsequently became the focus of a legal battle between the Tuscarora Nation and the New York State Power Authority, which was seeking to condemn part of the Tuscarora reservation to build a giant hydroelectric plant at Niagara Falls. The belt was removed from the Historical Society and supposedly sent to a laboratory for authentication. It disappeared at this point and was never seen again. Many Iroquois suspected foul play on the part of the State. The Tuscarora lost their case and one-third of their reservation (Landy 1978, 523–24).

In 1975, as a research assistant at the Buffalo and Erie County Historical Society, I helped to arrange the return of several thousand wampum beads to the Onondaga Nation. It was an important occasion because the traditional leaders had to develop unified statements on cultural patrimony and the way in which the repatriation of the sacred objects was to proceed. They were also meeting to negotiate the display and handling of human remains with the museum officials. Dr. Walter Dunn, then director of the Historical Society, was open-minded and committed to a respectful resolution of the Iroquois' concerns. He and I subsequently traveled to the Onondaga reservation to return the wampum beads. For the first time in nearly a century, wampum flowed back into Iroquois hands.

The Iroquois who resided on the Canadian side of the border were also pursuing wampum missing from their territory. Their story is similar to that of the

Onondaga. One of their longhouse leaders, unbeknownst to the Council of Chiefs, had sold several belts to a collector. In 1975, the Council officially declared that the belts, which were now housed in the Heye Foundation's Museum of the American Indian in New York City, had been improperly sold. The chiefs hired Paul Williams, a young lawyer and the director of treaty research for the Union of Ontario Indians, to pursue their case in 1977. The Onondaga on the American side also put pressure on the museum. But the museum's Board of Trustees, which included both William Fenton and William Sturtevant, two scholars who had strenuously fought the repatriation of the wampum in the New York State Museum, resisted the Onondaga claims.

The Iroquois consequently changed their tactics. Rather than pressing the Heye Foundation to respect the religious rights of the traditional people, they sought to show that the wampums had been illegally removed and that the museum was in the possession of stolen property. Museum records clearly show that George Heye, the founder of the Museum of the American Indian, was aware of the questionable legal status of these items, and that one of the trustees actually suggested the museum sell the wampums before the Iroquois could recover them.

In the end, the Iroquois lawyers and the traditional chiefs were able to convince then-president of the Board of Trustees, Barber Conable, of the integrity of their position, and the trustees subsequently moved to return the belts that could be shown to have been illegally removed. In 1988, the Museum of the American Indian returned 11 wampum belts to the Council of Chiefs at the Grand River Reserve near Brantford, Ontario. It was one of the first examples of the repatriation of sacred objects from an American institution to a Native nation in Canada. The return involved only the belts that could be shown to have been unethically acquired, however. There are still a number of sacred wampums that remain part of the museum's collections.

The Onondaga Wampum Repatriation

On the American side of the border, a similar effort was under way to recover the wampum belts of the Onondaga Nation, by the traditional "Wampum Keepers" of the Iroquois Confederacy. Late in the nineteenth century, Onondaga Chief Thomas Webster had sold four of these belts to Henry B. Carrington, U.S. Indian census agent, for $75. Carrington subsequently offered them to a Dr. Oliver Crane, who sold them in 1893 to the mayor of Albany, John B. Thatcher, for $500. Thatcher wanted the belts to be displayed as unique cultural treasures of great antiquity. In 1893 they were shown at the World's Columbian Exposition in Chicago where they were included in a larger display on "American Indians." The following year the belts were loaned to the Onondaga Historical Association for display during the Onondaga County Centennial celebration. People displayed a genuine respect for what the wampum belts represented, but they were construed as relics of the glorious Iroquoian past. The Iroquois themselves were generally understood to be a "vanishing race" with little hope of surviving through the next century.

Chief Webster was removed from office in 1897 by the traditional chiefs for his actions. The Iroquois wanted their wampums back even then, but the collectors, who had a bill of sale, ignored the chiefs. To strengthen their position, the chiefs sought the assistance of anthropologists. The scholars convinced them that they needed the State University of New York to help them recover the wampum from the private collectors. In one of the strangest events in Iroquois history, the Regents of the State University of New York were appointed the Keepers of the Wampum in 1898 by a group of Onondaga. In the past, a traditional Onondaga chief had always been the holder of that title. The university, with the implied endorsement of the Onondaga, began to acquire most of the remaining wampums in order to make a case for the cultural integrity of the belts.

Section 27 of the New York State Indian Law, passed in 1899, conferred the title of Wampum Keeper upon the University of the State of New York. The State then took possession of several wampums they had acquired from private collectors on behalf of the Iroquois. The University held that by virtue of its title of Wampum Keeper, all wampums fell under its authority. In 1900, the Onondaga Nation and the University of the State of New York combined forces to file suit against John Thatcher, the "owner" of the wampums sold by Chief Webster, seeking their return. In this important early legal case for repatriation, the Iroquois lost. Judge Frank Hiscock ruled that the wampums "are curiosities and relics of time, a condition, and a confederation that has ceased to exist," and that the Onondaga claim could not be upheld. Thatcher was allowed to keep the wampum. Ironically, the University of the State of New York later decided to bequeath the wampum it had collected to the New York State Museum, rather than return it to the Onondaga.

The chiefs were not ready to give up. In 1907 another lawsuit was filed to obtain the return of the four wampum belts held by Thatcher. But this suit, too, was dismissed by a New York State judge who ruled, in effect, that the Confederacy no longer existed, that Thomas Webster did not hold the wampum in trust, and that he had a legal right to sell the belts. In 1909, the New York State Legislature passed another Wampum Law that bestowed upon itself the title of Wampum Keeper and claimed rights over any wampum in the possession of any Iroquois, past, present, or future. Having legislated away the rights of the Iroquois, the rush was on to collect wampum with anthropologists leading the charge.

Years later, Thatcher's widow decided to end the unwanted attention that had plagued her family by donating the four wampum belts originally obtained from Chief Webster to the New York State Museum. There they rested quietly from 1927 until the 1970s when the Onondaga raised the issue of return again. Deeming repatriation one of their highest priorities, the Iroquois began to track down the museums holding wampum. They knew that the old Heye Foundation, since renamed the Museum of the American Indian, and the Smithsonian Institution had wampum in their collections, but a survey conducted between 1978 and 1982 uncovered over 200 additional wampum belts and dozens of wampum strings in numerous other museums around the country.

In the mid-1980s, Martin Sullivan, director of the New York State Museum, and Ray Gonyea, cultural specialist for the Onondaga Nation, crafted a plan to circumvent the racist and unethical Wampum Laws of New York State. It involved transferring control of the wampum in the museum's collection to the State Board of Regents, a body independent of the State Legislature. Previous attempts to have the wampum repatriated had been repeatedly voted down by the State Legislature. Once control over the belts was transferred to the regents, the consent of the State Legislature was no longer required and the regents were free to return these important items of Iroquoian cultural patrimony. The principal wampum belts in the State Museum's collection were returned to the Onondaga Nation on 21 October 1989.

Wampum and the Seventh Generation

What will the return of the wampums mean to the coming generations of Iroquois? Will the reading of the wampum affect the way the Iroquois live in the future? Will the current generation be able to interpret and transmit the messages contained in the ancient wampums? These questions remain unanswered at present. The fact is that the wampums carry a significant part of our cultural history. It remains to be seen just how much of an impact they will have in the functioning of the Great Law and in dealing with the issues faced by this generation of Iroquois. The long delay in the recovery of the wampums has taken its toll. There are only two or three people left who have enough cultural memory and linguistic fluency to interpret the meaning of these belts for the next generation. Hundreds of longhouse elders have passed away as museums and scholars argued over their rights to our heritage. With the passing of each elder, some knowledge is lost. It is as if we are burying a cultural library in the ground at each funeral.

As Iroquois, we are told to think of the seventh generation to come when we deliberate on our future. In making our decisions and choosing our paths, we are to consider not our needs or the needs of our own children but the welfare of the generations to come. If Thomas Webster and the other Iroquois who sold the wampum entrusted to them had thought about the seventh generation, we might not be in the mess we find ourselves in today.

Many of my museum colleagues question the sincerity of the repatriation requests coming from Native tribes. They ask whether Native Americans might not simply turn around and resell the objects that they are recovering from the museums. I cannot speak for other Native nations, but the Iroquois have learned an expensive lesson. It has taken us 100 years to undo a cultural crime committed against our people. As long as we remember our cultural mandate, to consider the seventh generation to come, those wampums will never leave our possession again. Our very future as a people rests within those tiny shell beads.

But if the promise of repatriation is to be achieved, all museums need to cooperate. We need to recover all the wampums, as well as our other sacred objects. Museums need to consider new kinds of partnerships with Natives, ones that go beyond the object. Museums can help insure that cultural and religious beliefs continue and thrive. They can share their archival information, their photographs, and their recordings. They can play an important role in the Native American future. Repatriation is not an end; it is, in many ways, a new beginning. Through the processes and relations it engenders, museums will come to understand that cultural preservation is not only about keeping objects from decaying but also about keeping ideas, values, and beliefs viable for the many generations to come.

23 | Made in Akwesasne

SALLI M. KAWENNOTAKIE BENEDICT

Introduction

THE MOHAWK COUNCIL of Akwesasne Aboriginal Rights and Research Office welcomed the opportunity to provide a paper for the "Pendergast Volume." We believed this to be an appropriate occasion to present the chronology of Akwesasne's experience and add it to the record of greater archaeological experiences that most Aboriginal peoples on this continent have had to contend with. Another motive in our presentation is to emerge from the grieving process caused by what we regard as archaeological colonialism and to activate a reconciliation process between Aboriginal and non-Aboriginal cultures.

That said, we took this as an opportunity to provide our evolving view of the discipline and the possibility of building a new approach to archaeology that would suit Akwesasne's current needs for cultural resource management. Our "Made-in-Akwesasne"[1] approach to cultural resource management proposes some ideas on the possibility of Akwesasne's forming new and equitable relationships with institutions and agencies charged with archaeological responsibility and the protection of cultural resources. We believe that there can be substantial new energy dedicated to the promotion of reconciliation between Aboriginal peoples and the archaeological community.

Previously published (with modification) in *A Passion for the Past: Papers in Honour of James F. Pendergast,* ed. J. V. Wright and J.-L. Pilon, 435–53, Mercury Series, Archaeology Paper no. 164 (Gatineau, QC: Canadian Museum of Civilization, 2004), 435–53. Printed with permission by Salli M. Kawennotakie Benedict.

1. *Akwesasne* is a Mohawk word that means "Land where the Partridge Drums." Our oral history says that the loud roar of the rapids that once existed near Akwesasne, at what is now known as Long Sault, could be heard for great distances, far in advance of our approach to the area. It is said that the sound of the rapids under freezing ice sounded like the drumming sound that emanates from the chest of a partridge in its spring courtship rituals.

We look for those who have similar interests in assuring the preservation and perpetuation of Aboriginal cultural properties, to build a relationship with Aboriginal people and Akwesasronen as their *confrères*.

Lt. Col. James Pendergast crossed paths with Akwesasronen from time to time, in his pursuit of archaeological knowledge. His archaeological work took him throughout Akwesasne Aboriginal territory from the 1950s through the 1970s. Regarded as an archaeological and historical expert on this geographic area, he continued to provide expertise and consultation to his colleagues and to Mohawks of Akwesasne until he passed away in September 2000.

We remember his name and his work because he introduced himself to our people. That was an important step for us, given the number of archaeologists that had utilized our territory for study without our knowledge. We first met Mr. Pendergast when a reburial of human remains was necessary in the 1960s. He later developed some friendships, built over time, with some of our leadership and traditional faith-keepers. We used him as a sounding board and wellspring of information when we explored the relationship of our people today with our ancestors long-passed. Some of his information was useful to us, even though we still continue some well-warranted skepticism of most non-Native interpretations of "the past."

In May 2000, the Akwesasne community hosted the 8th North American Fur Trade Conference—the conference theme being "Aboriginal People in the Fur Trade." Breaking from the traditional format of earlier conferences, this conference welcomed oral and written presentations as well as demonstrations by Aboriginal and non-Aboriginal people who provided various perspectives on the role of Aboriginal people in the history of North America during the fur trade period. Mr. Pendergast delivered a paper on the fur trade on the Ottawa River, 1610–50, incorporating the great contribution of Aboriginal people to the history of the region.

History is not owned by Euro-North American cultures or by the culture that writes it down. This conference succeeded in respectfully bringing Aboriginal and Euro-North American perspectives together at one meeting. We are pleased that so many renowned scholars and academics also thought it was time to hear the Aboriginal voice in history. It is our hope that the voice of Aboriginal culture will become more audible in many disciplines. Aboriginal peoples will work to build their capacity in history, archaeology, and many other fields, as they have in many other avocations, as part of their nation-building efforts.

We expect that the voice of numerous Aboriginal nations will become more prominent in the critical review of archaeological and cultural resource management issues and in the formation of new practices, policies, standards, and laws that affect them.

Lt. Col. Pendergast had time in his final years to sit at our kitchen tables, to eat and to discuss our respective theories. We didn't always agree, but he did leave with a great respect for our determination, our cultural philosophies, and our concept of being part of an ongoing culture, built on ancient beginnings. He agreed that we have a right to preserve the continuity and relationships that we have with our ancestral predecessors. In his later years, we felt more comfortable with him when we talked of archaeology and history from our differing perspectives. It is too bad that this kind of dialogue didn't start years before. It's not too late. It is in this spirit that we bring our ideas to this volume (Wright and Pilon 2004).

All Is Relative

We introduce a variety of aspects of Akwesasne being, that we believe are essential and related to our view of cultural resource management and archaeology. It is our hope that others will learn to know us and how we feel about cultural resource management, by our description of our ourselves and our territory, our laws and protocols, our history with archaeologists, our responsibility to the territory, our deeply entrenched relationship to everything in Creation and to the place we call Akwesasne. We believe this approach will allow others to understand what we recommend for the future of archaeology at Akwesasne and perhaps elsewhere.

Akwesasne Aboriginal Territory

Akwesasne is Aboriginal territory utilized by Kanienkehaka/Mohawk people since time immemorial.[2] It is located along the Kaniatarowanenneh,[3] or St. Lawrence River, and encompasses mainland territory about 20 miles deep along the north and south shore of this great river, historically extending from around present-day Kingston, Ontario, to Montreal, Quebec. The Aboriginal territory at Akwesasne includes the great river and its tributaries, wetlands, and marshes; hundreds of islands and islets; and the diverse and abundant natural life that is part of this riverine ecosystem. Akwesasne also includes the people of Akwesasne, past, present, and future.

When we say "time immemorial," we assert that our use, occupation, and fundamental relationship with this area known as Akwesasne, as well as our memories of kinship lines, goes beyond our earliest collective memories. The long-time relationship that we have with this ancient region is one that we convey as kinship to the land and to the ancestors before us that were born of this land.

Our relationship with the land is fundamental to our cultural survival. We say that the land is our mother. We are born of her and are returned to her. We consider our relationship with the land to be a sacred one.

---

2. *Kanienkehaka* is a Mohawk word that means "People of the flint or crystal." It is the word that we use for describing the Mohawk people or the Mohawk Nation.

3. *Kaniatarowanenneh* is our Mohawk word for the St. Lawrence River. It means "Great River."

Today,[4] Akwesasne is the name of the contemporary community of Kanienkehaka/Mohawk people who live on islands and the mainland along the Kaniatarowanenneh, much diminished from its original expanse and character.

Even though our traditional territorial base has been diminished by historical use and taking by others, we have kept and continue to upkeep our historical ties, our oral tradition, and our traditional and naturalized knowledge of our ancient and contemporary homeland. The Kaniatarowanenneh region (and the Aboriginal territory that is part of it) has included Akwesasronen[5] as part of its environmental makeup, since people could inhabit the land.

Our Mohawk place names record our ancient sites, activities, and relationship with the environment here. Some of our Mohawk place names record the purposes and activities of ancient sites. Our oral traditions are maintained and often guarded from external review. Some of the stories that have been transferred generation after generation record the first human habitation of this region and record the retreat of the ice sheet and the succession of plant and animal life that reinhabited this area once the area rebounded from the weight of the ice. Our ancient songs still permeate the wood of the Longhouse where ceremonies are dedicated to our ancient relationships and responsibility to Creation. Our people maintain knowledge of the traditional territory and a strong bond with the place and people encompassed by Akwesasne in all phases of its existence.

Akwesasne is special and is not like any other. Perhaps that is the way that every responsible culture feels about their territory. Its unique character, its stories, its fruits, its inhabitants, its habitats, its cycles, and its other attributes are the knowledge of the people who are born of the land and entrusted with the responsibility of protecting, preserving, and perpetuating the knowledge of this territory, generation after generation.

Dr. Erica-Irene Daes (2000) illustrates the important connection that traditional

---

4. Mohawk Government at Akwesasne: Akwesasne preexists Canada and the United States of America, but the historical development of these two countries has made serious impacts upon the community here. One of the greatest impositions is the international boundary made by these two European-spawned nations that artificially dissects this ancient Mohawk territory. The interprovincial boundary between Canada's Quebec and Ontario provinces adds further jurisdictional complications to the community life of the people here.

Three Mohawk governments have sprung from this community. The ancient *Mohawk Nation Council of Chiefs* is the national and historic government of the Kanienkehaka people. Several Mohawk communities in Canada and the United States constitute the Mohawk Nation with Akwesasne being the "fire" or seat of the Mohawk Nation government.

By the late 1800s, the imposition of Canadian and U.S. laws at Akwesasne forced non-Aboriginal-style elected governments upon the people. The *St. Regis Tribal Council* is the community government for that portion of Akwesasne that is geographically situated on the "American" side. The *Mohawk Council of Akwesasne* is the community government for Akwesasronen and is situated on the "Canadian" portion of this community.

5. *Akwesasronen* is our Mohawk word for "People of Akwesasne."

peoples have to the land and the interrelatedness of all aspects of Creation to their survival. As to their tenacity and will to manage the land and all of its inclusions, she says:

> The old ceremonies, songs and names kept people tied to the land, and continually reminded people of their responsibilities. Strip away the ceremonies, symbols and knowledge from the land, or sell them off, and people will no longer feel responsible for the land. The heritage of a people is deeply rooted in their traditional territory. Heritage is not only a reflection and a celebration of a people's territory—it is a management system for the territory, and separating heritage from the land may have serious adverse ecological and social consequences.

When the environment has been severely impacted by forced manipulation and change, the Akwesasronen and all other elements of Creation also suffer and struggle to recover from its short- and long-term impacts. When ancestors or the goods of our ancestors are removed from the land, it takes away some of the sacred responsibilities that Akwesasronen have to the land. It is a grievous intrusion on our culture. We do not let the goods of the past be taken willingly. It causes us great sorrow. The loss of this responsibility is one that we grieve for a long time and surely has long-term effects on our society. We do not know all of the social impacts that this loss has on our people in the short and long term, but we have surely seen some of them. When cultural properties are removed from our responsibility we do not give up. We wait and we ponder a time of their recovery, sometimes passing the responsibility for waiting to successive generations of our people.

The Laws of the Land

Good laws and good people grow out of the land and the territory from which they are born. Man-made laws should support the natural laws of the land. That just makes sense. Haudenosaunee laws,[6] for example, reflect the interrelatedness of our people with the land. This encourages an ongoing connection with the land and evokes responsible behavior that is necessary to keep a perpetual relationship.

Kaianerakowa—Great Law of Peace

Akwesasne people are one of several communities comprising the Mohawk Nation. The Mohawk Nation is one of six independent nations who were brought

---

6. *Haudenosaunee* is the common name used among the Seneca, Tuscarora, Cayuga, Onondaga, Oneida, and Mohawk nations for the confederacy that was formed by the Peacemaker and accepted by our nations. The word means "People who make the Longhouse." The Mohawk word is similar and is *Rotinonsionni*.

together by a man of peace to form the Haudenosaunee Confederacy. The members of the Haudenosaunee Confederacy have accepted the Kaianerakowa or Great Law of Peace.[7]

Ohenten Kariwatekwen—Opening Address

The Kaianerakowa is a law that incorporates the management of our resources and within its articles. The Kaianerakowa incorporates the Ohenten Kariwatekwen or "words that come before all else," which has become to be known as the Thanksgiving Address.[8]

The Thanksgiving Address is the method by which we open and close each meeting, ceremony, or gathering of peoples. It is our thanksgiving to the Creator for all of the elements of Creation. We say that the Creator gave specific and individual instructions to every element within Creation. We thank them individually for carrying on those instructions and characteristics as part of the great circle of life. Not lost from this Address is a constant reminder of our enduring responsibility as people within this universe, and our interconnectedness with all elements of Creation.

Ohkwaho Kaionwi ne Akwesasne—Akwesasne Wolf Belt

The land and the people are one. Dr. Erica-Irene Daes (2000) writes that "[a] lawyer might refer to this concept as non-severability, which simply means that interrelated things should not be separated."

This is a concept that is reiterated in many ways throughout Kanienkehaka culture. The Akwesasne Wolf Belt is but one of the methods (fig. 23.1).[9] The Kaianerakowa and the Ohenten Kariwatekwen cited above reinforce the same concept.

Akwesasronen have a very special relationship with the territory they call Akwesasne. A belt known as the Akwesasne Wolf Belt, or Ohkwaho Kaionwi ne Akwesasne, was fashioned so that the people could record their ties to the land and give notice to others of the importance of Akwesasne to its people. We say that the Akwesasne Wolf Belt is like a charter, which was made to inform others about the new and unique character of the Akwesasne community. A written record of the meaning of the Akwesasne Wolf Belt has not been found. A description of a similar

---

7. *Kaianerakowa* is the Mohawk word that we use to mean the Constitution of the Haudenosaunee or Iroquois Nations. "The Great Law of Peace," is the common English translation that we use today.

8. *Ohenten Kariwatekwen* are Mohawk words that mean "the words that come before all else." We use words of thanksgiving to thank the Creator for all elements of Creation from the People to the Skyworld to the Creator. These words are used before every meeting, ceremony, or gathering of people. We say that it assists us to reach consensus or "one mind."

9. *Ohkwaho Kaionwi ne Akwesasne* are Mohawk words that mean "Akwesasne Wolf Belt." The Akwesasne Wolf Belt is the charter of the contemporary Akwesasne community.

Fig. 23.1. Akwesasne Wolf Belt.

belt survives for a Kanienkehaka community that is a sister to Akwesasne: Kahnesataka. This written record, combined with oral accounts, serves to outline our own thoughts about the meaning of the Akwesasne Wolf Belt.

Agneetha, the principle man of the Mohawk village at Kahnesataka, at the Lake of Two Mountains, addressed Sir John Johnson, the superintendent general of Indian Affairs, on February 8, 1788, with several wampum to emphasize his speech. Among them was one that was similar to the Akwesasne Wolf Belt. We draw from those words and our own oral history to extrapolate the charter of the people of Akwesasne.

Agneetha said, "and as was the custom of our forefathers, we immediately set about making a belt, which was delivered to you, by which our children would see that the lands was to be theirs forever, and as was customary with our ancestors, we placed the figure of a (wolf) at each end of the belt to guard our property and to give notice when an enemy approached and as soon as it was finished, we spread it on the ground and covered it with dirt, that no evil minded persons should find it, where it remained undisturbed . . ."

We offer the following interpretation of some of the symbolism used by Agneetha as it relates to Akwesasne's Belt:

> "And as was the custom of our forefathers, we immediately set about making a belt . . ." The first thing we speak of is the process of the community coming together. When Kanienkehaka people at Akwesasne felt that they were safe enough to use this part of Kanienkehaka territory for community-style living, they set about making a belt to record their interest in the territory, and to make special consideration about their new community.
>
> " . . . by which our children would see that the lands was to be theirs forever . . ." This speaks to our people's responsibility to the land, our children and our future. The land and a defined land base is essential for the survival of Kanienkehaka culture. The Akwesasne Wolf Belt assures the people that the land known as Akwesasne will be here for their present lifetimes and for the lifetimes of future generations. The Wolf Belt makes it known to others that certain territory has been marked for the exclusive use of the Akwesasne people, and that they expect others to respect these community boundaries. The Wolf Belt provides its people a sense of security and reminds them that they have the responsibility to protect and preserve what is within the boundary.

Because the land is to be theirs forever, they must make community plans and adopt methods and management systems that insure that the land is taken care of forever. Methods for long-range planning must be instilled in the mindset for every generation. Within Kanienkehaka culture we instill the responsibility in the present generation to make careful consideration of how their actions on the land will impact on the next seven successive generations. This is a responsibility that is handed to every generation and so it goes on "in perpetuity."

In effect the Akwesasne Wolf Belt becomes a declaration by the people that is part of their land management system. It is deeply rooted in their culture, and is a responsibility that is set in motion to last forever. "As soon as it was finished, we spread it on the ground and covered it with dirt." This speaks to the relationship of the people, to their laws, and to the land. They are inseparable. The Akwesasne Wolf Belt is covered with dirt to symbolize that the community, its laws, and the land are one. This is a very sacred concept. It means that the people and the land belong together. This is a bond as sacred as that of a mother to a child or as sacred as the connection we feel to our mother earth when we bury our dead.

Kaswentha—Two-Row Wampum

Traditionally, as Haudenosaunee people, we are taught to find the bridge between our cultures, so that we may have a relationship based on peace, friendship, and respect. For that, we have devised various methods by which European and Haudenosaunee cultures can interact as reasonable peoples.

We often offer the symbol of the Two-Row Wampum Belt, as the protocol which outlines the basis of an equitable relationship (fig. 23.2).[10]

The Two-Row Wampum Belt illustrates the concept of Haudenosaunee and European cultures traveling in separate vessels, down separate rivers, within the river of life. These are represented by two parallel rows of purple beads on a background of white.

We say that our vessel holds our culture, values, language, laws, practices, and all the things that we need to live as a people in this world. We say that the other vessel holds the culture, values, language, laws, practices, and entire way of living for Euro-North American people. We believe that both of these are valid ways of doing things, but that they must remain separate if each is to thrive and maintain a healthy relationship with one another.

The Two-Row Wampum Belt has three rows of white beads separating the two rivers of purple beads. Those beads keep us separate, but form a bridge between us. The three rows of white beads stand for peace, friendship, and respect. We believe that because we are reasonable peoples, that peace, friendship, and respect

---

10. *Kaswentha* is our Mohawk word for the Two-Row Wampum Belt.

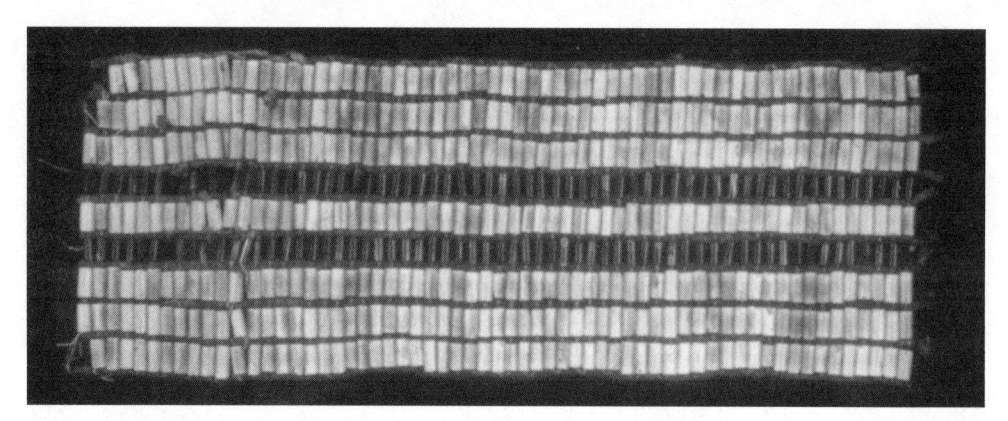

Fig. 23.2. Two-Row Wampum.

will insure our ability to maintain our distinct and separate characters, and also allow us to maintain our cultural strength that is essential in maintaining an ongoing relationship.

Archaeology as it has been practiced in North America has been justified by the values engrained in European culture. This system that was developed to search for knowledge of past cultures has overridden any cultural roadblocks placed on it by the Aboriginal nations who consider themselves the relatives of those whose history is in the ground.

This approach to gathering material culture for building a knowledge base contrasts greatly with the method in which our relationship with our people of the past is entrusted. When archaeology invades our territory or involves our culture, it crosses the line and imposes the values and reasoning of European culture upon ours. It is a very personal invasion. Euro-North American archaeology has represented an invasion of one culture upon another. Instead of building bridges, it creates great chasms of distrust. The value of the Two-Row Wampum protocol needs to be re-explored with archaeology in mind so that our two cultures can coexist in an environment of peace, friendship, and respect.

In Akwesasne, like some other Aboriginal communities, we recognize very few of the archaeologists that did work in our territory by name. That is because they never introduced themselves to us. As living people, and heirs of the cultures being studied, we have felt abstracted and inconsequential to the work of the archaeologists. The Canadian government laws and policies were not of any help to us because they did not obligate the archaeologists to communicate with us, let alone gain our permission. With no requirements for them to meet with us, they came to our territory and invaded the earth, taking cultural material to their museums, institutions, and storage facilities, backing up their reputations with voluminous records and published works.

Akwesasne is a community within the Mohawk Nation. Akwesasronen believe that Mohawk laws on Mohawk land are paramount. When dealing with Akwesasne cultural properties, Akwesasne culture, values, language, practices, and laws must apply. It is right that all respect and reciprocity should be given to the laws of the Aboriginal people of the land. It is time to review the Two-Row protocol so that each culture stays within the boundaries of its own vessel.

Sacred Trust Responsibility

Akwesasne holds the bones, the stones, and other evidence of our cultural existence and our continued being. Our recent relatives are buried here and so are the ancient relatives that we also know as our ancestors. Our people respect death and the journey that is taken by the deceased. Our responsibility is to all those before us to insure that their journey is uninterrupted. It is our responsibility to keep the people in the ground where they are becoming one with our mother the earth.

The people of Akwesasne recognize the importance of protecting and preserving the cultural legacy left to us by our ancestors and predecessors. This legacy and the gifts that they gave us insures that we will continue to survive as a people, strong in tradition, values, and culture. As a conscientious people, we understand that it is our responsibility and duty to care for the cultural objects of our ancestors and predecessors. We look on this responsibility as a Sacred Trust that will be carried by us and continually reinforced in our teachings for those yet to come.

The people of Akwesasne developed cultural resource management practices independently from those archaeological principles of Euro-North American design. We reject those principles of other cultures that impinge upon our Sacred Trust responsibility. Our cultural principles reiterate our responsibility for perpetual management of the cultural resources of the people who came before us and for taking responsibility, in each of our lifetimes, for protecting the remains and goods of the people of the past. We are born with a Sacred Trust Responsibility. We say that we have been practicing cultural resource management on our Aboriginal territory since the first of our ancestors were on this land.

Archaeologists have made a lasting impression at Akwesasne: The mysterious authority by which archaeologists have entered Akwesasne Territory, off and on, for almost 200 years has left an impression on us.

The reasons that we have heard from the archaeological community for unearthing the remains and goods of our ancestors and predecessors have left an impression on us. The manner in which the remains and goods are treated when they are removed from their ancient resting places has left an impression on us. The reports that we have heard in our conferences and meetings with other nations of Aboriginal people, over many years about their experiences and the treatment by the archaeological community to our cultural properties have left an impression upon us. The great ends to which Akwesasne and other Aboriginal nations must go, to have these goods returned, have also left a lasting impression on us.

The impressions made upon us do not easily disappear. Today we track the source of those impressions and follow them like footprints to their source, leading us to the records and repositories, and to agencies and institutions in Canada and the United States and elsewhere around the world. We are obliged to pursue the recovery of our cultural properties and have them returned to our care.

Archaeology at Akwesasne

Excavation, removal, collection, and display occurred at Akwesasne just as it did in other sites of Aboriginal occupation outside of Akwesasne. Cultural properties were stolen, graves were robbed, human remains were removed from their resting places, artifacts were traded and sold, and large collections of our cultural properties were held and continue to be held in private collections and museums.

The details of these stories shall remain safe from human consumption, because we believe it would only desecrate our ancestors and disturb the living.

We summarize by saying that archaeology at Akwesasne was well underway in the early 1800s, by those who had leased land in our community. Surface collecting became the "Sunday" occupation of pot-hunters and other curio collectors. By the late 1800s ancient mounds were excavated, unbeknownst to our people at the time, and removed to repositories that we still have not yet located. Some ancient burial places were utilized for recreational purposes without Mohawk consent. The Mohawk are currently pursuing negotiations to regain this land.

Those amateur and professional archaeologists who roamed the Akwesasne territory from the 1800s through the 1970s investigating particular sites were not invited by Akwesasronen or even introduced to our people. Oftentimes they carried out their work on remote islands or on the mainland within our territory, without our knowledge. Some of the collectors who were provided land leases approved by Indian Affairs resided on our islands and over the years they accumulated extensive collections. Some were farmers, who found artifacts when they ploughed the fields and later sold their collections as a "cash crop." Only now with investigation are we beginning to discover the extent to which archaeological excavation, collection, and removal was done at Akwesasne.

Affiliated with various universities in Canada, the United States, and elsewhere, anthropologists and archaeologists have flooded to our community and our sister communities seeking out our Elders, leaders, and traditional peoples, recording devices in hand. Sometimes the names are remembered, sometimes not. The products of their work rarely find their way back to us directly, but when by happenstance we come upon their published works, sometimes several years later, we have often been surprised and disappointed with the attributions and conclusions that are made from our interview sessions.

Sometimes archaeological work, on a grand scale, was authorized and permitted within our community by Canadian and American government departments and agencies. Those few times that we were notified that archaeological work was occurring gave us little comfort. Even though we were notified about the archaeology that was done during the construction of the St. Lawrence Seaway in the 1950s that ravaged numerous Akwesasne islands, it was done without our consent. The expediency of the Seaway gave license to archaeology to go to extraordinary means to extract and remove ancient objects and human remains to repository sites far away from Akwesasne.

The construction of the Seaway was devastating to our people on many levels. The ecosystem that we had depended on for survival was artificially altered. The great Kaniatarowanenneh that gave us life was muddied and the life habitat of the river was devastated. There were many fronts for our people to fight on all at once.

Some might ask why there were so few protests regarding archaeological excavation at the time that it happened. Most times our people were not aware of the situation at all. When they were, there was little that could be said. The late 1800s through to the 1950s was not a time of Indian[11] protest about such things. It was felt by some of our Elders that protests had the potential of bringing more attention to the matter and perhaps greater inhumanity to the situation. Our people remained quiet, unequipped at that time to wrest the problem.

Waiting for a Changing Attitude in Archaeology

Archaeology in the Akwesasne community does not have a historical relationship that is built on trust or mutual respect. That is too bad, but that is history.

Generally speaking of course, our image of archaeologists, whether stereotypical or not, are those academics who have worked to study ancient aboriginal cultures, ripping into the land collecting burial goods, human remains, and artifacts, building their own reputations without regard for the living aboriginal cultures who have a cultural bond with these goods. Some of our people have even wondered if they believed in the Creator.

At Akwesasne we found that our own people became more secretive and private about any information regarding cultural properties and sacred sites. The transmission of cultural information regarding the places of our ancestors to successive generations of our own people has therefore become more guarded. This is not a good thing, and it has caused our own people to have to salvage some aspects of cultural knowledge from the brink of being lost.

Archaeology must be counted among the list of oppressive acts that have been

---

11. "Indian" is the name that used to be a popular reference to the Aboriginal nations of North America. The Canadian Department responsible for Aboriginal people is still known as Indian and Northern Affairs Canada.

inflicted on Aboriginal cultures by Western civilization. Its effects are surely as oppressive and devastating to a culture as are relocation, confinement to reservations, or placement in residential schools. We believe that it is part of the process of cultural genocide. Akwesasronen facing oppressive situations firsthand have developed numerous coping and survival methods. Some have bought into the culture of the oppressor, some have lost their fighting spirit, and some have become angry and self-abusive. Unfortunately, sometimes, these traits are all we have to pass on to our children.

Fortunately, there are still some others who have waited and waited for more opportune times to make objections and to initiate change. Sometimes Akwesasronen have waited a whole lifetime, passing on the patience—for still more waiting—to our children. Akwesasronen wait for a new climate and new thinking in archaeological and cultural resource management. It is as slow as resolving land claims or as the resolution of residential school issues for its survivors, but it starts somewhere.

Roadblocks to Recovery

Archaeology, like other acts of subjugation, has made Akwesasronen feel oppressed, powerless, inadequate, and insecure about our knowledge of our own culture. Archaeologists historically have talked down to Akwesasronen when they are imparting their theories of the past. Their archaeological jargon prevails. Aboriginal people are largely part of the mysterious "prehistory" of North America, and "history" starts when European chroniclers take note of it. Sites are named after archaeologists or the non-Aboriginal persons who "discovered" the cultural properties and very little is solicited as the Aboriginal contribution to the knowledge base.

In the United States, after years of protest by Aboriginal people, a new law was enacted called the Native American Graves Protection and Repatriation Act (NAGPRA).[12] This law gave a new opportunity for Aboriginal peoples to learn the whereabouts of their cultural properties that were held by federally funded institutions and then to seek their recovery. The act is filled with flaws, but the legislation did put into motion a method whereby a reunion between Akwesasronen and other Aboriginal peoples and their ancestors could occur.

In Canada there is no law for the repatriation of cultural properties, human remains, or objects of cultural patrimony. There are policies and practices of various government departments, agencies, and museums. They are all different and act independently of one another. Repatriation is done on a case-by-case basis, after the remains or cultural objects are discovered by Akwesasronen. Negotiation can be a slow process and it may not be equitable. The process appears to be biased toward the possessor. After all, they have the goods.

12. H.R. 5237, Native American Graves Protection and Repatriation Act, October 1990.

We soon found out that there is no funding for the costs of the lengthy repatriation process for either the institution or the people who are seeking recovery. Searching for assistance to continue our own discovery, research, and repatriation efforts, we soon found out that there is no agency or federal department that is charged with repatriation as a specific responsibility. Somewhere between Heritage or Indian Affairs this subject needs to find a home. There is certainly no Canadian federal department advocating a systematic repatriation process. Aboriginal issues raised at Canadian federal roundtable discussions get a little more than lip service and the issues still go unattended. That's consultation for you.

Roadblocks always occur when Aboriginal peoples are seeking recovery of cultural properties. Some Canadian museums large and small and other agencies that have collected Aboriginal goods for many years had been hesitant about giving up cultural properties to Aboriginal peoples. In our earlier negotiations, some had even raised the issue of capacity, saying that Akwesasne and other Aboriginal communities do not have the expertise or proper facilities to care for the artifacts in the same way that they have. At Akwesasne, we have worked with various institutions to help them see that ours is a different capacity: knowledge and expertise. Cultural goods that are returned to us will not be treated in the same manner that they were treated within institutions because we are obliged to treat certain properties in prescribed ways and we are obliged to seek their return to our trust.

We should not be blindsided by the roadblocks. There are also some wonderful success stories. We can report that Akwesasronen have seen many successful repatriations in the last few years from very small museums to some of the larger museums and institutions in both the United States and Canada. It takes diligence and cooperation on both sides. It takes good people with good principles on both sides. We were fortunate to have dealt with archaeologists, museum curators, and personnel that truly made a difference and expedited the process in many ways. They are the ones that keep human dignity at the forefront of their thoughts. Our gratitude goes to these special people.

Archaeological principles and definitions are presently not harmonized with the cultures that are being studied. Maybe that is something that can change. Arbitrary archaeological definitions for cultural affiliation currently separate Aboriginal peoples from their ancestors and are among several of the hurdles that are thrown up as obstacles to recovery.

Within what we know as Akwesasne Aboriginal Territory, many non-Native definitions conclude that we are not related to certain Aboriginal people that inhabited this territory before us. We say that we are. Our ancestors and predecessors are all from Akwesasne and they are all part of this same territory. We all came from the land here and are made of the land. We are all part of the mother earth at Akwesasne. We are made of her and we go back to her. We are definitely related.

These roadblocks are not unfamiliar to us. They are the same roadblocks that appear when land claims or Aboriginal rights issues are being tested. The first thing that they try to break is our link to our ancestors, and our link to the land. At Akwesasne, one Canadian archaeologist was an expert witness in an Akwesasne Border Crossing case. His theory quickly hit the newspapers—"Mohawks Not Native to Canada"—and our natural response came the next day in "Mitchell says he's no immigrant."[13] To some, the assertion that we are recent interlopers, arriving not much earlier than Europeans to North America, is the argument that is thrown in to break down our unique tie to the land and to our claims to Aboriginal title.

Roadblocks always arise when there is fear of changing from an old system to a new one. We encourage all those pursuing cultural resource management of their own properties to find the methods to surpass these roadblocks so that the cultural resources of our people can be managed in the manner that they were intended.

Capacity Building

When you review some of the roadblocks, it is not difficult to see why all of those bright Akwesasronen who pursued higher education by the 1970s did not find any use for archaeology as a field of study. Until recently, it would be abhorrent for Akwesasronen to come home from university with archaeological training or to pursue archaeology as a career.

Archaeology, which may have been the farthest career from our minds in the 1970s, 1980s, and even 1990s, may now have a place in our community. Some of our own attitudes regarding its value are changing.

Our land base has been diminished and our population is growing. We have the technology at Akwesasne to utilize land in ways that we never did before. It has become apparent that we too could become responsible for the inadvertent destruction of cultural properties that we have criticized others so vocally for. We can't assume that the archaeologists came and took everything away from Akwesasne already. And we can't cover our eyes to the issues of responsibility that are before us.

Building our "capacity" in cultural resource management sets us out on our own journey. We need to look at what has been done in Western archaeology. We need to look at new models. We need to look at what other Aboriginal communities have done. And then, we need to work to build something "Made in Akwesasne."

Because we know that we must protect the cultural properties of our people and our land, it might mean taking a look at what Western archaeology has learned. With help from some archaeologists we can learn about the sites within our Aboriginal territory. We can learn how to delineate sites. We can learn about modern site protection. We can explore their theories about our ancestors. We can learn the

---

13. "Mohawks Not Native to Canada," *Standard Freeholder*, Cornwall, Ontario, 1 Oct. 1996. "Mitchell says he's no immigrant," *Standard Freeholder*, Cornwall, Ontario, 2 Oct. 1996.

methodologies that were used in the past and the entire history of archaeology if we need it. This is knowledge that we can use as modern tools when we are building our own approach to cultural resource management. We don't necessarily need all the tools in the toolbox. That will be our choice, once we have chosen the design of the system that we need to build.

Our "capacity" in the archaeological field is only now beginning to build, and it is only by designing a study of archaeology built more on our culture and community-appropriate protocols that this field of expertise can find a home within Akwesasne. For us it means building an approach to the protection of cultural resources that is compatible with our existing cultural management systems. It also means taking a look at our own integrated cultural management systems to insure that they can survive and provide the essential ingredients for long-term caregiving. These are our language, our values, our ceremonies, our commitment to the land and to the people of the past, present, and future. It may mean that we have to build up all of the components of our culture to assure that cultural resource management can be done now and for the future, in the manner that is acceptable to this community.

Some of our "capacity" needs to be reinvented to meet modern concerns. In our culture, ceremonies for reinterment are not part of normal ceremonial structure. When repatriation of the remains of our ancestors occurs today, we must build appropriate culturally acceptable methods that we believe are proper for their reburial. This is all new to us and some of our work in recovery of cultural properties takes long discussion among our Elders and faith-keepers in order to build an appropriate modern practice. This new practice may require the retrofit of ancient practices to meet our contemporary needs. That is for us to decide.

Dr. Daes (2000) says "that, as long as a few fragments of their heritage and history survived in the memories and hearts of their elders, there was still hope of recovering what seemed to be lost. Indeed, he tells us, the generation that re-discovers its history and spirituality will be even more powerful than its ancestors."

We believe that recovery of cultural properties will strengthen the contemporary traditional culture of our people. The return of objects of cultural significance has a great impact on our social and cultural structure. It gives us back some dignity and it revitalizes various responsibilities and purposes. We say that it gives us back our spiritual strength.

We believe that cultural resource management can also help us close the gap between generations. At Akwesasne, Elders within our community are well respected for their cultural knowledge. Sometimes we worry that our young people can lose the valuable transmission of culture between the older and younger generations.

Dr. Daes (2000) says that "a people can lose its heritage in a single generation. People who neither respect nor value their heritage can lose it—or sell it off—in no time at all. It is futile to hoard your heritage in museums and books if your children are ashamed of their parents and grandparents and only value what they see on television."

At Akwesasne, we have experienced losses in the transmission of culture from one generation to another. In the 1960s, we began to notice a severe loss in the strength of our Mohawk language, as external influences blocked our lines of transmission. What was nearly lost in one generation has taken us more than 40 years to begin to rebuild and we are not out of the woods yet. Because of that experience, we are mindful of the gap that grows between our youth and our Elders and we search for appropriate and successful adaptations that are surrogate infrastructures for the flow of cultural information from one generation to another. At Akwesasne, our museum and cultural centers have understood that culture is alive and must come out of the glass case and be part of the living and evolving culture of the land. These Akwesasne-based centers utilize methods that promote and perpetuate the culture. In this way they are cultural activists. That is the way to survival.

An approach to archaeology and cultural resource management has to be built so that it is accountable and subject to the scrutiny of the people whose ancestors are being studied. In Akwesasne's own community, we are accountable to ourselves and in our community governance initiatives we are obliged to build appropriate laws, policies, and best practices that instill the need for cultural resource management within our own administrative institutions. For instance, we have to reconcile protection of cultural properties with our need for land for housing, agriculture, and our own economic survival in a very limited land base. In our capacity building we need to take control and responsibility for the situation and take careful consideration of what we do today because of the impact it will have on our future.

In our "capacity building," we also need to take into consideration other issues within our own community. "Capacity building" means reinforcing a relationship between our contemporary elected community governments and our traditional cultural government based on common long-standing cultural principles and values. It means enacting contemporary enforceable laws and practices that are harmonized with traditional cultural principles and practices. And it means insuring that our young university graduates come home with the ability to blend their cultural knowledge with the technical skills and expertise that they bring to us from the outside.

We have different ways of saying things. We say that "Archaeology and the truth are not the same." Right now we do not hear our voice or truths in the archaeological story that is being told. Archaeological theories change all the time and our reasoning used to be more passive and we thought that sooner or later a theory will be developed that coincides more sensibly with our ancient stories, songs, place names, oral tradition, and other parts of the cultural archives that we utilize on a daily basis. We believe it is time to be a little more aggressive and offer our truths for examination. We believe that it is time to give recognition to other perceptions and other truths in our archaeological story and to recognize the values of each cultural perception. Perhaps this is something that we can work on together.

Looking externally, "capacity building" is expanding the relationship that we have with outside governments and agencies. We can begin by working together to build the proper protocols between us. Akwesasne needs to insure that Akwesasne's cultural resources are managed in a way that preserves human dignity. External governments may have other concerns. Somewhere there is a balance and a common place where we can work together on mutually agreeable principles, for the protection, preservation, and perpetuation of the cultural resources that we both believe are nonrenewable resources.

Some of the injuries of the past need to be healed and a method of reconciliation has to be found to address this issue. Reconciliation would be good for us all so that the new journeys that we take alongside each other in the river of life will be free from turbulence.

Made in Akwesasne

Made in Akwesasne is an appropriate name for a new cultural resource management strategy that will be developed within Akwesasne Territory. It comes from the people and territory whom it concerns. The artifacts were made in Akwesasne. Our ancestors are from Akwesasne. The archaeologists who came here received some reputation on their study of the cultural properties of Akwesasne. It is appropriate for our laws and protocols to apply to the properties of Akwesasne, whether they are still in our Aboriginal territory or removed to other locations.

Dr. Daes (2000) says that "[i]n international law, we refer to this as the principle of lex loci—that is 'the law of the place.' It is a very ancient principle among nations. It was recognized by the Roman Empire, and still applies to disputes over contracts, the ownership of private property, and family relationships, when the parties live in different countries."

One of our cultural ideologies is that "everything is related." It leads us to understand that the practice of archaeology or cultural resource management is part of an integrated management system. We need a strong language to carry out our ceremonies, and to address our ancestors. We need our ceremonies to insure our connection and respect for the natural world. We need our natural world to survive. We therefore cannot take our responsibility for cultural resource management lightly because of its potential ripple effect throughout our entire cultural system.

In reinventing a culturally appropriate type of archaeology, we have to insure that we challenge our reasons for the decisions that we make. We have to make sure that our reasons for excavating cultural goods are good reasons and that they stand up to cultural scrutiny. We need to deliberate with our Elders and cultural leaders and agree on the acceptable reasons for intrusion upon the resting places of the past.

At Akwesasne, we are working through our reasons. We have accepted certain tasks as the needs arise. When it is decided that work must be done on a sensitive area, our young people are trained in archaeological field methods that we have adapted to suit our community sensitivity. A great deal of preparation time is provided to our youth in order to meet our cultural obligation. Faith-keepers and traditional leaders spend time with them to insure that they understand the gravity of the work that must be done. The youth who participate do so knowing the great responsibility that is placed upon them. They pledge to stay away from drugs and alcohol, and to keep a good mind. They are taught to touch and walk softly on the land, and to have respect for the environment and the living things around them.

At the site, tools in hand, our youth open the day with the Ohenten Kariwatekwen, spoken in Mohawk. That sets the tone for each day. Throughout the day, Elders talk to them about their culture. When goods are uncovered, good notes and photographs are taken and the site is GPS'd[14] [located using a geographic positioning system]. The goods are carefully catalogued and then they are respectfully returned to the ground where they were found. At the end of each day a closing address is given in the Mohawk language.

Akwesasne Strategy

Akwesasne sees great value:
- in the organization of a roundtable between federal/provincial government departments/agencies and Aboriginal nations to discuss issues pertaining to protection of cultural properties, repatriation, and other related topics, with the view to developing appropriate enforceable mechanisms between our Nations' governments, leading to protocols, reciprocal arrangements, a repatriation law, and a responsible federal/provincial department/agency;
- in the development of a forum for the exchange of perspectives between Aboriginal people and non-Aboriginal cultural resource caregivers with a view to changing contentious policies and practices;
- in the reconciliation of Akwesasne and non-Akwesasne versions of human occupation within Akwesasne Aboriginal Territory;
- in the respect for Akwesasne's relationship with ancestors and predecessors;
- in making a place for Aboriginal perspectives in archaeology and history within the educational institutions of Canada utilizing Aboriginal educators;
- in placing a moratorium on the invasive analysis of human remains;

---

14. "GPS" stands for geographic positioning system in which an electronic tool provides geographic coordinates for the area located.

- in building protocols with provincial and federal governments for any future archaeological field work within Akwesasne's Aboriginal Territory;

- in developing an Akwesasne Historic Preservation Office that would oversee cultural resource management within its Aboriginal Territory and review applications and issue permits for archaeological work within Akwesasne's Aboriginal Territory;

- in designating and protecting certain archaeological sites and landscapes within Akwesasne Aboriginal Territory;

- in building the capacity of Akwesasne for cultural resource management;

- in instituting interim and long-term management agreements, as part of the ongoing relationship between Akwesasne and museums and other repositories;

- in insuring that some of Akwesasne's cultural properties are returned immediately and others allowed to remain within the institution as the needs be with provisions for input as to care and access of cultural properties;

- in the setting aside of provincial/federal funds for the ongoing repatriation processes and related issues with regard to cultural resource management that are inevitable in Akwesasne;

- in the setting aside of provincial/federal funds to assist Akwesasne to reinforce language and culture as part of the cultural management system for the care and maintenance of cultural properties;

- in sensitizing the public mindset to respect Akwesasne sacred sites and objects.

24 | Case Studies in Collaborative Archaeology
The Oneida Indian Nation of New York and Colgate University

JORDAN E. KERBER

WITH THE PASSAGE of the Native American Graves Protection and Repatriation Act (NAGPRA) in 1990 and the 1992 amendments to the National Historic Preservation Act of 1966, an increasing number of situations and projects across the United States have arisen in which archaeologists and American Indians have collaborated in the mutual pursuit of learning about the past. Several of these instances are well documented in Dongoske et al. (2000), Ferguson (1996), Klesert and Downer (1990), Swidler et al. (1997), Watkins (2000), and now Kerber (2006). Indeed the majority of Native American-archaeologist cooperative ventures are mandated by these two federal laws, which require, among several things, consultation with federally recognized Native American groups and tribal historic preservation officers in specific circumstances. There are other instances, however, that are not legislated. This article discusses two case studies in collaborative archaeology between the Oneida Indian Nation[1] and nearby Colgate University in central New York State. The first involves a summer workshop in archaeology for Oneida youth, and the second concerns the repatriation and curation of Oneida archaeo-

---

Previously published in *Cross-Cultural Collaboration: Native Peoples and Archaeology in the Northeastern United States*, ed. J. E. Kerber (Lincoln: Univ. of Nebraska Press, 2006), 233–49. Reprinted with permission by the University of Nebraska Press. © 2006 by the Board of Regents of the University of Nebraska Press.

1. The Oneidas call themselves *Onyota'a:ka*, which means "the People of the Standing Stone." They are members of the Six Nations Iroquois Confederacy (also known as the *Haudenosaunee*, an indigenous term meaning "the People of the Longhouse"). For purposes of this article, the terms *Oneida Indian Nation, the nation,* and *the Oneidas* refer only to the Oneida Indian Nation of New York (i.e., people of Oneida descent living in central New York State), and not to the Oneidas who live in Wisconsin or Ontario.

logical remains in Colgate's Longyear Museum of Anthropology. The former is the focus of the chapter, while the latter is discussed briefly.

Summer Workshop in Archaeology

Between 1995 and 2003, Colgate University, located in Hamilton, New York, has offered an annual workshop in archaeology to members of the Oneida Indian Nation (fig. 24.1). Held each summer for two weeks, the program has been directed by the author with assistance from several Colgate students and recent alumni, as

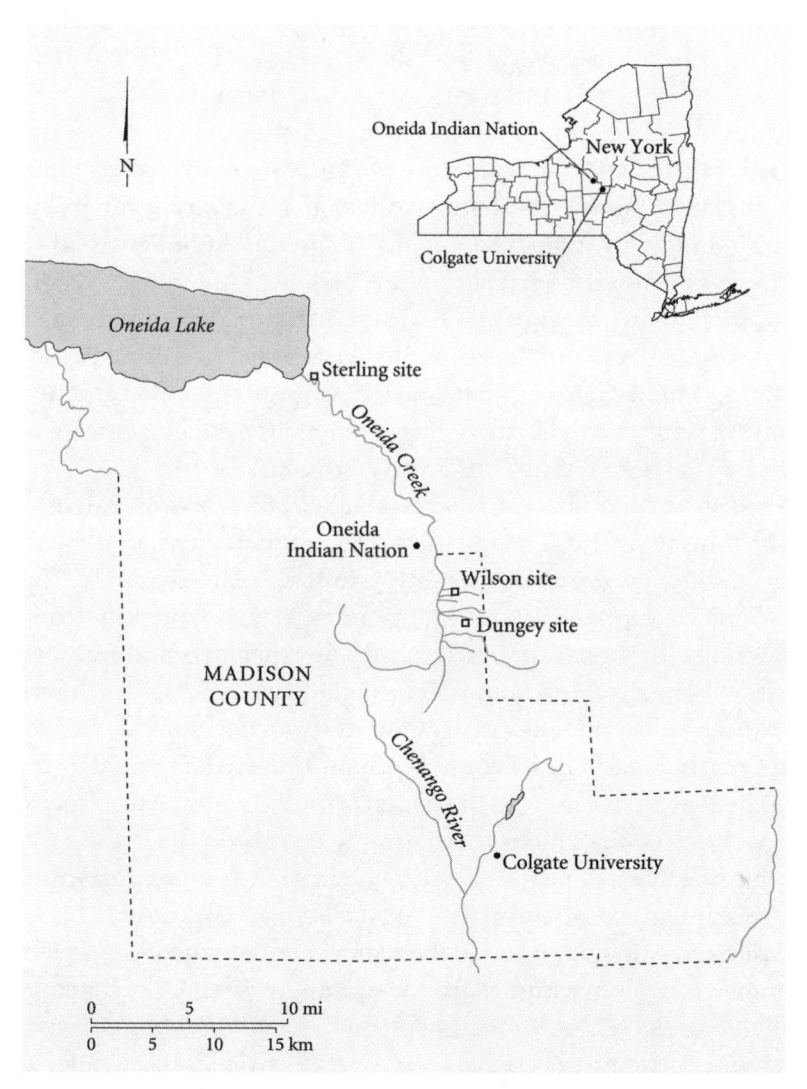

Fig. 24.1. New York State map, showing the location of Colgate University and the Sterling, Dungey, and Wilson sites.

well as other individuals. So far, more than 100 Oneida teenagers have participated in nine offerings of the workshop and have gained direct archaeological and laboratory experience in learning about their ancestors and other Native Americans who once occupied central New York.

The three primary goals of the workshop are (1) to strengthen the relationship between Colgate University and the Oneida Indian Nation by bringing together members of both communities in important educational experiences, (2) to provide a hands-on opportunity in archaeology for Oneida youth that involves the limited excavation and laboratory processing of prehistoric and historic nonhuman remains from nonsacred Native sites in the region, and (3) to identify, manage, and protect significant archaeological resources located in central New York.

The idea for the archaeological workshop developed in 1992 when I was director of the Native American Studies Program at Colgate. At that time, faculty in the program drafted a grant proposal for a three-year project to improve community relations between the university and neighboring Native American groups. One of the proposal's initiatives was a summer workshop in archaeology that I envisioned for Iroquois youth living in the vicinity of the campus. Although I had no experience working with American Indians in this manner, I am strongly committed to public education in archaeology and had successfully directed previous archaeological workshops for a lay audience in Rhode Island (see Kerber 1997). In 1994 the John Ben Snow Foundation awarded a matching grant to fund the summer workshop from 1995 until 1997. The university provided the match, which was viewed as "seed money" to help start this innovative project.

I selected the Oneida Indian Nation, a small but growing Native American community of just over 1,000 members, as the particular audience for this workshop because of its geographical proximity to the Colgate campus. Simply put, there is no other Native American group living closer to the university. In the process of writing the grant proposal, I called a few members and employees of the Oneida Indian Nation with whom I had previously developed an informal relationship to discuss the possibility of my offering an archaeological workshop to nation members. After receiving a favorable response, it was suggested by the Oneida Indian Nation that participants in the nation's Youth Work/Learn Program be the target group for the workshop if funding were obtained. The Youth Work/Learn Program employs Oneida Indian Nation teenagers in various summer projects, including landscaping and working in nation facilities and offices.

The emphasis of the program on the nation's young members seemed appropriate, because many American Indian communities have been concerned about their youth "losing touch" with their heritage. I hoped (perhaps naïvely or somewhat romantically, in retrospect) that by recovering artifacts used in the daily lives of their ancestors, especially on tribal land, the adolescents would feel a connection to their historic roots. For some workshop students, this was probably not the case, at least during their immediate involvement. But for others, as will be discussed below, I believe the workshop functioned in this way, despite the participants resembling more "generic" teenagers than Native Americans, listening to rap music and wearing the latest style clothing during the excavation. Several may not realize the positive effect of the program for years to come.

The workshop consisted of two five-day sessions during July and August, and each session involved between 3 and 15 participants; larger numbers of students participated in the first three summers than more recently, as the Youth Work/Learn Program has decreased somewhat in size. In the earlier workshops, two separate groups participated in both sessions, while later workshops involved the same group per session. Nevertheless, every workshop focused on the limited archaeological excavation of one or two nonsacred Native American sites and the laboratory processing of the recovered cultural remains. On the first day of a session, an orientation was held in order to introduce the students to the field of archaeology and to dispel some common misconceptions. As is typical of a lay public, most of the participants had no firsthand experience in an archaeological excavation. They knew about the subject primarily through films and television programs and erroneously believed that archaeologists excavate dinosaur fossils. Authentic historic and prehistoric cultural materials were presented during the orientation so that the participants could become familiar with the various types of objects they might later recover from the sites. Also, I emphasized that we would deliberately not excavate human burials or human skeletal remains during the workshop. I added that if any were to be accidentally discovered, the excavation would stop, and I would contact the Oneida Indian Nation for direction.

This point warrants further discussion, because I believe it is the principal reason why the Oneidas have permitted me to offer this program. Because I specify in each workshop proposal submitted to the Oneida Indian Nation's Men's Council and Clan Mothers that I will not knowingly excavate human skeletal remains during the project, a solid foundation of mutual trust and respect has developed between me and a number of members of the nation. It is no secret that relations between archaeologists and Native Americans are still often strained, largely owing to the excavation and analysis of Native American skeletal remains (see, e.g., Biolsi and Zimmerman 1997; Bray 2001; Mihesuah 2000). Since 1995 very few human skeletal remains have been accidentally discovered during the workshop. Only isolated human teeth and a few disarticulated bones from nonburial contexts were recovered at two sites. In both situations, following my notifying the Oneida Indian Nation about these remains, we stopped the excavation of the test units containing the human skeletal material, as instructed by the Oneidas, but the fieldwork continued elsewhere at the sites.

Fieldwork for each five-day workshop session lasted three days (weather permitting), followed by a day of laboratory work at Colgate University to clean the recovered archaeological materials. For every workshop, I received indispensable assistance in the field and the lab from two or three people with previous experience. Most of the assistants were Colgate undergraduates or recent alumni, including two who were of Iroquois descent. Some have pursued graduate work in anthropology and employment in contract archaeology. As I tell my assistants, it is rare, especially in the Northeast, to be able to supervise American Indian youth in archaeological projects on their own land. In addition, at least one staff member of the Oneida Youth Work/Learn Program was present throughout the entirety of each workshop session.

For the first three summers, from 1995 to 1997, under funding from the John Ben Snow Foundation and Colgate University, the workshop sessions were conducted near campus at three prehistoric sites situated on private property (not Oneida territory).[2] I had been conducting archaeological research with Colgate students in field methods classes at these sites for a few years before the first workshop session. The sites contain primarily stone tools and chipping debris, dating to between about 4,000 and 1,000 years ago. All archaeological materials recovered and cleaned by the participants in the 1995–97 workshop sessions were stored in the archaeology laboratory at the university for subsequent cataloguing, analysis, interpreting, and reporting by Colgate students in my field methods classes during the fall term (e.g., Kerber, Glennon, and Palmer 1996).

The completion of the 1997 workshop marked the end of the three-year matching grant from the Snow Foundation and Colgate. Because of the success of the program and what I believed to be its unrealized potential, I decided to approach the Oneidas for funding and permission to hold the workshop on their territory (as close as 24 km north of Colgate). It was not that the three prehistoric sites adjacent to campus were unimportant or unproductive, but rather that known sites on nation land were more recent. Many of these sites date to between the sixteenth and eighteenth centuries and were inhabited by the direct ancestors of the workshop participants, as opposed to some distant prehistoric Native American groups who may not be directly related to the Oneida people. It was (and still is) my hope that finding artifacts from these historic sites would ignite the interest and curiosity of Oneida youth in their heritage. In 1998 I submitted the proposal to the Oneida Indian Nation Men's Council and Clan Mothers. In addition to requesting nation funding for the 1998 summer workshop on Oneida territory, I stipulated that all recovered artifacts from this land would be curated at the nation's Shako:wi Cultural Center following their cataloging, analysis, and reporting at Colgate.[3]

2. *Oneida territory* and *Oneida land* here refer specifically to the more than 6,800 hectares of property in central New York State owned by the Oneida Indian Nation, as opposed to a much larger tract of about 101,000 hectares, representing the current land claim case.

3. Until recently, all the recovered remains from Oneida territory have been curated at the Shako:wi Cultural Center, in accordance with this proposal. Some of the objects also have been displayed there. The materials are now kept in a new archive storage facility in the nation's Children and Elders Center.

The Oneidas provided 100 percent funding of my 1998 proposal, and they permitted me to offer the workshop at the Sterling site, a multicomponent site dating between about 6,000 and 200 years ago, located on nation territory in Verona, New York (fig. 24.1).[4] Between 1998 and 2003, I submitted a similar proposal each year to the Oneida Indian Nation Men's Council and Clan Mothers, and each year they approved it. Beginning in 1999 and continuing until 2003, the Oneidas contributed the bulk of the financial support of the workshop, while Colgate provided a smaller portion of the funds. I intend to direct the workshop each summer for the foreseeable future, as long as joint funding is provided from the nation and the university and the workshop goals are met.

Between 1999 and 2001, the workshop sessions were held at the Dungey site in Stockbridge, New York, located to the south of the Sterling site (fig. 24.1). This village dates to about the 1660s–70s and was settled by the Oneida people, who lived in longhouses and practiced hunting, fishing, gathering, and horticulture, all the hallmarks of traditional Iroquois culture. Despite many years of previous collecting and excavating at the site by avocational archaeologists and other individuals, Oneida workshop participants and Colgate students recovered more than 4,000 historic remains from more than 100 test units completed between 1999 and 2001. The majority of the objects are Euroamerican in origin and represent trade goods (e.g., shell and glass trade beads, clay smoking-pipe fragments, cassock buttons, and metal objects). Other remains consist of stone tools and chipping debris, pottery, charcoal, animal bone, and a charred maize kernel.

In 2002 and 2003, the workshop shifted to the nearby Wilson site, just north of the Dungey site, also in Stockbridge (figs. 24.1 and 24.2). This site dates to approximately the 1590s to the 1620s and contains many of the same kinds of remains as found at the Dungey site, but with fewer artifacts of Euroamerican origin and more of indigenous manufacture (e.g., stone and pottery artifacts) and domesticated plant remains (e.g., maize, beans, and squash). Analysis and interpretation of the cultural materials recovered from the Sterling, Dungey, and Wilson sites are not discussed here but are presented in five unpublished reports, completed by Colgate students in my field methods classes, based on research that they and the workshop participants conducted at these Oneida sites (Kerber and Henry 1998; Kerber, Ochsner, and Saul 1999; Kerber, Benisch, and Zinn 2000; Kerber, Deegan, and Monk 2002; Kerber, Bidder, and Wild 2003). I have also given numerous presentations of this research, both with my Colgate students and separately, to members and employees of the Oneida Indian Nation and to members of the New York State Archaeological Association, among other groups. Further, former workshop assistants, both Colgate alumni, have used this work in the completion of a Ph.D.

---

4. It should be pointed out that the Oneida Indian Nation runs a lucrative casino (Turning Stone Casino), as well as other successful business enterprises.

Fig. 24.2. Oneida Youth Work/Learn Program participant rejoices at finding a seventeenth-century glass trade bead during the archaeological workshop at the Wilson site in August 2003 (Photo courtesy of Tim Sofranko).

dissertation (D. Henry 2001) and an undergraduate honors research paper (Danielson 2001).

    The success of the workshop can be evaluated on the basis of the more than 100 Oneida adolescents who have participated during the nine consecutive summers since 1995 and the fact that both the nation and the university have financially supported the program. In addition, several quotations from participants and nonparticipants alike reflect the importance of the experience. For instance, one workshop student commented that "it was interesting to learn about what archaeologists do, but the best thing was holding the materials used by my ancestors. I learned more about my culture and our past" (Malone and Hanks 1999/2000, 23). As a Youth Work/Learn Program staff member and schoolteacher stated, "You can't get a better history class than this. The kids are learning more than they'd ever learn in public school" (McCarroll 2001, 14). This person added, "These kids had hands-on discovery. They had a connection to history" (Walters 2003, 14). In a similar vein, an Oneida clan mother remarked, "Walking over the land where our ancestors walked

... thinking 'Our people were here' ... helps us to bring our ancestors back into our souls, into our hearts, and the artifacts are real. They add so much to the knowledge and understanding that we have of our very own people" (personal communication to Dixie Henry in 1999, cited in D. Henry 2001, 10).

Perhaps most telling is the statement from a member of the nation's Men's Council and Clan Mothers: "Everyone has studied our people, but not with cultural sensitivity. We revere those who have gone before us. We have our oral tradition, but to be able to provide our children with an actual hands-on experience with our past, that is invaluable" (Cronin 2001). Although this person admitted that "archaeology used to be a bad word among the Oneidas" (Corbett 2000), the workshop has changed this perception, while also helping to shape the identity of the participants. In his words, referring to the workshop, "It gives our people a connection with their past and a greater understanding of who they are. It is one thing to say 'I am Native American' and another to say 'I am Oneida and I know who I am.' That's one thing the nation and Colgate can provide" (Hubbard 1997).

There are other collaborative programs in archaeology with an emphasis on Native American youth that have been introduced in the United States and Canada. One that has had a similar effect on its young participants is the Red Earth Summer Archaeology Program for high school students, developed in cooperation with the Gila River Indian Community's Employment and Training Office in south-central Arizona (Ravesloot 1997, 177). The primary goal of the program, which lasts eight weeks, is to introduce high school students to archaeology. The parallels in expectations and outcomes between these two programs are clear:

> While it is our hope that one or more of the high school students who have participated in the Red Earth Archaeology Program will elect to pursue a career in archaeology, that result is not absolutely necessary for the program to be a success. More important is the fact that the program has provided Native American students with an opportunity to participate in the study of their past and that it has introduced some to higher education who most likely would not have had the experience. In the process of introducing Native American students to archaeology, I also believe we have managed to change some perceptions about archaeology and archaeologists. (Ravesloot 1997, 177)

Another indication of the success of the workshop came in 2000. Before the nation's planned removal of two small structures adjacent to the Dungey site, the Oneidas asked that this area be tested as part of the 2000 workshop. They wanted to determine whether any important archaeological remains existed at that location so that they could be protected from any impact from the removal. Fortunately, no significant cultural materials were encountered.

Over the past few summers in particular, there has been a substantial amount of favorable local, regional, and national media coverage by newspapers (including the *Christian Science Monitor*) and television and radio stations (including programs on the local PBS affiliate and interviews on a local NPR affiliate). This publicity has been mutually beneficial for both Colgate and the Oneidas, and it has helped to increase public awareness about archaeology, the Iroquois people, and the benefits of involving a Native American descendant community in archaeology. As a member of the nation's Men's Council and Clan Mothers stated, "The more people know about Oneidas, the more they will respect us" (Walters 2003, 14).

I often talked informally in the field and in the lab about the significance of the findings and asked the participants what the objects, as well as the workshop experience, meant to them. Occasionally, some individuals were willing to share their thoughts, while others remained silent, perhaps feeling uncomfortable about speaking to a group or to me as a person not of Oneida descent. One student, however, offered this personal insight during an interview with a newspaper reporter:

> I see this as an opening to many other things, not just archaeology. This is an opportunity that kids shouldn't overlook. It opens the door to religion and other issues around us. People need to get involved in our culture. We have lost a lot of people. . . . This makes me think about history and what's happened right here in Stockbridge, Munnsville, and Oneida. I think about how our people were separated when these lands were settled, and I dream about us (Oneidas) uniting again one day. When I'm out here, I can dream and think. When I find a bead, that is special to me . . . I still bead . . . when I find a bead, I feel good, and I feel a connection with my ancestors . . . and I feel hope for our future. I dream of my people coming together again. (Cronin 2001)

Thus, from various perspectives, the workshop has clearly been successful, even if, as with the Red Earth Summer Archaeology Program, no participants become archaeologists. The goals have been met, and important information and objects pertaining to Oneida heritage have been recovered. Further, mutual respect and trust have been fostered among those associated with this program at Colgate and the Oneida Indian Nation.

Repatriation and Curation

In addition to the workshop in archaeology, collaboration between the university and the Oneidas is ongoing in other ways. Since the mid-1990s, members of both communities have continued to work together in compliance with NAGPRA and in reaching agreements concerning the exhibition and curation of certain objects in Colgate's Longyear Museum of Anthropology. While the repatriation process is required by federal statute, decisions regarding the exhibition and curation of Oneida archaeological remains were reached voluntarily.

The Longyear Museum of Anthropology contains a relatively small archaeological and ethnographic collection of objects from around the world. The museum takes its name from John Longyear, an emeritus professor and Mesoamerican archaeologist who began to build the collection shortly after arriving at Colgate in 1948. Longyear continued to acquire materials for the collection until he retired in 1978, when the museum was named in his honor. Since its inception, the museum's collection has been used principally for teaching purposes, providing numerous opportunities over the years for students to work with professors in studying the materials and creating exhibits in the gallery.

The largest part of the collection consists of more than 7,000 objects of Iroquoian ancestry. The vast majority come from Oneida archaeological sites, dating to between about 1,000 and 300 years ago. These materials were excavated in the 1950s and 1960s by avocational archaeologists, who later sold or donated their extensive collections to the university while Longyear was curator. The Oneida objects in particular make up one of the largest extant repositories of this people's heritage, and it is safe to say that much of what is known about Oneida archaeology is based on these artifacts in the museum's collection (see Pratt 1976). Included among the objects were Oneida skeletal remains, which were also excavated by collectors and eventually obtained by the university. None of the sites from which the human and artifactual remains were excavated was owned at the time by the Oneida Indian Nation, although the nation has recently purchased property on which some of these sites are located.

In the mid-1990s Professor Gary Urton, then curator of collections at the museum, worked with Colgate students to inventory the Oneida remains and to add the collectors' provenience information to the newly created electronic database, which would store additional descriptive information (e.g., accession numbers, collectors' catalog numbers, object types, and raw materials). A student generated a summer research report and an undergraduate high honors research paper based on her experience in the museum (D. Henry 1995; 1996). The inventory included the Native American skeletal remains, representing at least six individuals, and more than 10 associated funerary objects that were removed from six archaeological sites by collectors in the 1950s and 1960s.

After the inventory was made, consultation was initiated with NAPGRA representatives of the Oneida Indian Nation, who were given a list of the skeletal remains and associated funerary objects. On 26 June 1995, all of these remains and objects were repatriated to the nation, and "the Oneida feasted their ancestors, burned tobacco to carry their thoughts and prayers, spoke words to the Creator then laid their people back to rest" (Hubbard 1997). One of the NAPGRA representatives spoke eloquently about the experience: "It helps to think these are my people, my ancestors housed in these institutions. To do the right thing, repatriations, can be strenuous and painstaking. It was quite straining, and quite rejuvenating at the same time. The nation is thankful for the approach the university has taken to correct a great wrong. Colgate has been very cooperative in working to resolve this sensitive issue" (Hubbard 1997).

When I became curator of collections in 2001, I continued to work with Colgate students on the laborious task of inventorying and updating the electronic database of the museum's entire holdings; this task has now been completed. As a result of this process, I have identified in the collection more than 1,000 unassociated funerary objects that were excavated from Oneida sites by the avocational archaeologists. The Oneida Indian Nation possesses this list of materials, along with the electronic database. At the time of this writing, they have not requested repatriation of these items, perhaps because of our relationship of mutual trust and respect. There may be another reason as well. For the past several years, the museum has no longer displayed artifacts in its collection that are known to have come from human burials. The grave objects curated in the museum may now be viewed only by appointment. These decisions were made voluntarily as a sign of good faith and out of respect for the sensitivity of the sacred objects.

It is possible, however, that future requests may be made to repatriate some or all of these unassociated funerary objects, in compliance with NAGPRA. In light of this possibility, three retired individuals with strong ties to the New York State Archaeological Association recently asked me whether they could volunteer to take digital photographs of the museum's objects that are subject to NAGPRA, in order to preserve images of these items before their possible repatriation. I thought this was a wonderful idea that would result in a significant and lasting contribution both to the museum's database and to the archaeology of the Iroquois.

After receiving a grant from the Lincoln Financial Group Foundation, the volunteers purchased a Nikon digital camera and other equipment to undertake the digital imaging project. Over the course of nearly four months, they took more than 1,000 digital photographs of over 1,500 objects in the museum; some of these items did not pertain to the Oneida Indian Nation but were photographed because of their potential for repatriation. With assistance from staff in Colgate's Collaboration for Enhanced Learning, the volunteers also created 39 QuickTime digital "movies" of pots (mostly Oneida), which provide 360-degree rotating views of the objects. All the digital photographs and movies were archived and also linked to the electronic database of the collection so that the images of certain items may be viewed. Other museums have made similar use of technology to document skeletal remains and artifacts subject to NAGPRA. At the University of Texas at Austin, for example, a scanning and replication project, begun in 1993, has utilized both a computerized tomography scanner to print high-resolution illustrations and to store detailed measurements of remains and another computer-controlled laser to sculpt precise nylon replicas of objects in advance of repatriation (Bower 1994, 186).

Shortly after the completion of the Longyear Museum digital imaging project in 2001, I met with a few members of the Oneida Indian Nation Men's Council and

Clan Mothers and nation employees to inform them of this accomplishment and to discuss ways they might use the digital images and the electronic database. We talked about the possibility of transferring this information to a computer for public viewing at the nation's Shako:wi Cultural Center, as well as the possibility of downloading some of the images onto the nation's Web site. I posed several questions at the meeting: Are the images themselves considered by the nation to be sacred, given that the objects that they represent are sacred? Should access to the images be restricted in any way, given that access to the sacred objects in the museum is restricted? Lastly, am I permitted by the nation to show these images in professional presentations and to my students? No one in the meeting responded to my questions, perhaps because they considered them to be rhetorical and thus not requiring a specific answer. These are new issues raised by technology, with very little discussion in the literature (e.g., Milun 2001).

My point in asking these questions was not only to demonstrate my sensitivity concerning the treatment of images of sacred Oneida objects but also to seek guidance from the nation as to the proper use of such images. Simply put, I was uncertain about what the Oneidas would deem inappropriate for viewing, and I did not want to use the images in a manner they would consider offensive. My questions remain unanswered, and I am still unclear whether these images are part of Oneida cultural property, in the manner that other indigenous peoples have redefined their heritage as a protected resource (see M. Brown 2003). I have shown the images at conferences and in classes but have not posted them or the electronic database on the museum's Web site. Also, I have incorporated the images in my Museum Studies course as the basis for student-designed electronic presentations of virtual exhibits, thereby avoiding displays of actual sacred objects.

Summary and Conclusion

In this chapter I have discussed two case studies in collaborative archaeology between the Oneida Indian Nation and Colgate University. The first case study consisted of a two-week summer workshop in archaeology that Colgate offered nine times between 1995 and 2003 to members of the nation's Youth Work/Learn Program. The workshop, directed by me and funded largely by the Oneidas, provided more than 100 Native American teenagers with hands-on experiences in the limited excavation and laboratory processing of prehistoric and historic nonhuman remains in central New York State. The other case study focused on ongoing collaboration between the nation and the university over the repatriation and curation of Oneida archaeological remains in Colgate's Longyear Museum of Anthropology. This cooperation stemmed from experiences in which both groups have continued to work together in compliance with NAGPRA and in voluntarily reaching agreements concerning the exhibition and curation of certain museum objects.

Such instances of cooperation and consultation over the past 10 years have created a strong relationship between the university and the Oneidas, built on mutual respect and trust. But like many relationships, it is fragile and requires nurturing and commitment. I am hopeful that with continued positive experiences this relationship will strengthen. Indeed collaborative archaeology can be a powerful tool for American Indians, while it may also bring together Native and non-Native communities in ways imagined and unimagined.

Acknowledgments

This chapter is a much expanded version of a previously published article (Kerber 2003). I wish to thank the Oneida Indian Nation Men's Council and Clan Mothers, particularly Richard Lynch, Brian Patterson, and Dale Rood, for permitting me to offer this archaeological workshop since 1995 and for providing the majority of funding since 1998. I am also grateful for the support of Randy Phillips, director of the Youth Work/Learn Program, and Anthony Wonderley, Oneida Indian Nation historian. I am indebted to Colgate University and the John Ben Snow Foundation for their financial support of the workshop, and to the Lincoln Financial Group Foundation for providing funding to complete the digital imaging project. I extend heartfelt gratitude to the more than 100 participants in nine years, as well as to Dixie Henry and all the other archaeological assistants who provided invaluable help. I thank Tim Sofranko for permission to use his photograph in figure 24.2. Lastly, I thank Barbara and Gordon DeAngelo and Vicky Jane, assisted by Ray Nardelli of Colgate's Collaboration for Enhanced Learning, for their monumental and voluntary effort for more than three months in taking more than 1,000 digital photographs of objects in Colgate's Longyear Museum of Anthropology; and Stenny Danielson and Seth Bidder for their long hours spent inventorying the museum's collection and updating its electronic database.

PART SIX

| *Research Sources*

25 | Research Sources

1. Origins

Beauchamp, William M. 1894. "The Origin of the Iroquois." *The American Antiquarian* 16, no. 2:61–69.

———. 1921. *The Founders of the New York Iroquois League and Its Probable Date.* Researches and Transactions of the N.Y.S. Archaeological Association 3, no. 1. Rochester, N.Y.

Bekerman, André, and Gary A. Warrick, eds. 1995. *Origins of the People of the Longhouse: Proceedings of the 21st Annual Symposium of the Ontario Archaeological Society.* Toronto: Ontario Archaeological Society.

Bursey, Jeffrey A. 1997. "Lessons from Burlington: A Re-consideration of the Pickering vs. Glen Meyer Debate." *Northeast Anthropology* 53:23–46.

Clermont, Norman. 1996. "The Origins of the Iroquoians." *The Review of Archaeology* 17, no. 1:59–62.

Crawford, Gary W., and David G. Smith. 1996. "Migration in Prehistory: Princess Point and the Northern Iroquoian Case." *American Antiquity* 61, no. 4:782–90.

Crawford, Gary W., David G. Smith, and Vandy E. Bowyer. 1997. "Dating the Entry of Corn *(Zea mays)* into the Lower Great Lakes Region." *American Antiquity* 62, no. 1:112–19.

D'Annibale, Cesare, and Brian D. Ross. 1994. "After Point Peninsula: Pickering vs. Owasco in the St. Lawrence Valley." *The Bulletin: Journal of the New York State Archaeological Association* 107:9–16.

Dieterman, Frank A. 2001. "Princess Point: The Landscape of Place." Ph.D. diss., Univ. of Toronto.

Dincauze, Dena F., and Robert J. Hasenstab. 1989. "Explaining the Iroquois: Tribalization on a Prehistoric Periphery." In *Centre and Periphery: Comparative Studies in Archaeology,* edited by T. C. Champion, 67–87. London: Unwin Hyman.

Emerson, J. Norman. 1961. "Problems of Huron Origins." *Anthropologica* 3, no. 2:181–201. Ottawa.

Hart, John P. 2001. "Maize, Matrilocality, Migration, and Northern Iroquoian Evolution." *Journal of Archaeological Method and Theory* 8, no. 2:151–82.

Hart, John P., and Hetty Jo Brumbach. 2003. "The Death of Owasco." *American Antiquity* 68, no. 4:737–52.

Hasenstab, Robert J. 1987. "Canoes, Caches, and Carrying Places: Territorial Boundaries and Tribalization in Late Woodland Western New York." *The Bulletin: Journal of the New York State Archaeological Association* 95:39–49.

Henige, David. 1999. "Can a Myth Be Astronomically Dated?" *American Indian Culture and Research Journal* 23, no. 4:127–57.

Jamieson, Susan M. 1992. "Regional Interaction and Ontario Iroquois Evolution." *Canadian Journal of Archaeology* 16:70–88.

Kapches, Mima. 1987. "The Auda Site: An Early Pickering Iroquois Component in Southeastern Ontario." *Archaeology of Eastern North America* 15:155–75.

Kuhn, Robert D., and Martha L. Sempowski. 2001. "A New Approach to Dating the League of the Iroquois." *American Antiquity* 66, no. 2:301–14.

Laccetti, Michael F. 1965. "The Round Top Site: A Postulated Early Owasco Component." *The Bulletin: Journal of the New York State Archaeological Association* 33:12–20.

———. 1974. "The Round Top Site: An Early Owasco Horticultural Stage." *The Bulletin: Journal of the New York State Archaeological Association* 62:4–26.

Lenig, Donald. 1965. *The Oak Hill Horizon and Its Relation to the Development of Five Nations Iroquois Culture*. Researches and Transactions of the New York State Archaeological Association 15, no 1. Buffalo.

Lenig, Wayne. 2000. "*In Situ* Thought in Eastern Iroquois Development: A History." *The Bulletin: Journal of the New York State Archaeological Association* 116:58–70.

Lucy, Charles L. 1991. "The Owasco Culture: An Update." *Journal of Middle Atlantic Archaeology* 7:169–88.

MacNeish, Richard S. 1976. "The *In Situ* Iroquois Revisited and Rethought." In *Culture Change and Continuity: Essays in Honor of James Bennett Griffin*, edited by C. E. Cleland, 79–98. New York: Academic Press.

Mann, Barbara A., and Jerry L. Fields. 1997. "A Sign in the Sky: Dating the League of the Haudenosaunee." *American Indian Culture and Research Journal* 21, no. 2:105–63.

Niemczycki, Mary Ann Palmer. 1984. *The Origin and Development of the Seneca and Cayuga Tribes of New York State*. Research Records no. 17. Rochester, N.Y.: Rochester Museum and Science Center.

———. 1986. "The Genesee Connection: The Origins of Iroquois Culture in West-Central New York." *North American Archaeologist* 7, no. 1:15–44.

———. 1987. "Late Woodland Settlement in the Genesee." *The Bulletin: Journal of the New York State Archaeological Association* 95:32–38.

———. 1991. "Cayuga Archaeology: Where Do We Go from Here?" *The Bulletin: Journal of the New York State Archaeological Association* 102:27–33.

Noble, William C. 1969. "Some Social Implications of the Iroquois 'In Situ' Theory." *Ontario Archaeology* 13:16–28.

———. 1975. "Van Besien (AfHd-2): A Study in Glen Meyer Development." *Ontario Archaeology* 24:3–96.

Noble, William C., and Ian T. Kenyon. 1972. "Porteous (AqHb-1): A Probable Early Glen Meyer Village in Brant County, Ontario." *Ontario Archaeology* 19:11–38.

Parker, Arthur C. 1916. "The Origin of the Iroquois as Suggested by Their Archaeology." *American Anthropologist* 18, no. 4:479–507.

Pendergast, James F. 1975. "An *In Situ* Hypothesis to Explain the Origin of the St. Lawrence Iroquoians." *Ontario Archaeology* 25:47–55.

Prezzano, Susan C. 1997. "Warfare, Women, and Households: The Development of Iroquois Culture." In *Women in Prehistory: North American and Mesoamerica*, edited by C. Claassen and R. A. Joyce, 88–99. Philadelphia: Univ. of Pennsylvania Press.

Ridley, Frank. 1958. "The Boys and Barrie Sites." *Ontario Archaeology* 4:18–40.

Ritchie, William A. 1934. *An Algonkin-Iroquois Site on Castle Creek, Broome County, N.Y.* Research Records no. 2. Rochester, N.Y.: Rochester Municipal Museum.

———. 1936. *A Fortified Village Site at Canandaigua, Ontario County, New York.* Research Records no. 3. Rochester, N.Y.: Rochester Museum of Arts and Sciences.

———. 1947. *Archaeological Evidence for Ceremonialism in Owasco Culture.* Researches and Transactions of the New York State Archaeological Association 11, no. 2. Rochester.

———. 1952. *The Chance Horizon: An Early Stage of Mohawk Iroquois Cultural Development.* Circular 29. Albany: New York State Museum and Science Service

Ritchie, William A., Donald Lenig, and P. Schuyler Miller. 1953. *An Early Owasco Sequence in Eastern New York.* Circular 32. Albany: New York State Museum and Science Service.

Schulenberg, Janet K. 2002a. "New Dates for Owasco Pots." In *Northeast Subsistence-Settlement Change A.D. 700–1300*, edited by J. P. Hart and C. B. Rieth, 153–65. New York State Museum Bulletin 496. Albany: State Univ. of New York, State Education Department.

———. 2002b. "The Point Peninsula to Owasco Transition in Central New York." Ph.D. diss., Pennsylvania State Univ.

Smith, David G., and Gary W. Crawford. 1997. "Recent Developments in the Archaeology of the Princess Point Complex in Southern Ontario." *Canadian Journal of Archaeology* 21, no. 1:9–32.

Snow, Dean R. 1984. "Iroquois Prehistory." In *Extending the Rafters: Interdisciplinary Approaches to Iroquoian Studies*, edited by M. K. Foster, J. Campisi, and M. Mithun, 241–57. Albany: State Univ. of New York Press.

———. 1991. "Dating the Emergence of the Iroquois League: A Reconsideration of the Documentary Evidence." In *A Beautiful and Fruitful Place: Selected Rensse-*

laerswijck Seminar Papers, edited by N.A.M. Zeller, 139–44. Albany: New Netherland Publishing.

———. 1994. "Paleoecology and the Prehistoric Incursion of Northern Iroquoians into the Lower Great Lakes Region." In *Great Lakes Archaeology and Paleoecology: Exploring Interdisciplinary Initiatives for the Nineties,* edited by R. I. MacDonald, 283–93. Ontario: Quaternary Sciences Institute, Univ. of Waterloo.

———. 1995. "Migration in Prehistory: The Northern Iroquoian Case." *American Antiquity* 60, no. 1:59–79.

———. 1996. "More on Migration in Prehistory: Accommodating New Evidence in the Northern Iroquoian Case." *American Antiquity* 61, no. 4:791–96.

Starna, William A., and Robert E. Funk. 1994. "The Place of the In Situ Hypothesis in Iroquoian Archaeology." *Northeast Anthropology* 47:45–54.

Stothers, David M. 1975. "The Emergence and Development of the Younge and Ontario Iroquois Traditions." *Ontario Archaeology* 25:21–30.

———. 1976. "The Princess Point Complex: A Regional Representative of an Early Late Woodland Horizon in the Great Lakes Area." In *The Late Prehistory of the Lake Erie Drainage Basin: A 1972 Symposium Revisited,* edited by D. S. Brose, 137–61. Cleveland: Cleveland Museum of Natural History.

———. 1977. *The Princess Point Complex.* National Museum of Man, Mercury Series, Archaeological Survey of Canada, Paper no. 58. Ottawa: National Museums of Canada.

———. 1995. "The 'Michigan Owasco' and the Iroquois Co-Tradition in Southern Michigan: Late Woodland Conflict, Conquest, and Cultural Realignment in the Western and Lower Great Lakes." *Northeast Anthropology* 49:5–41.

Trigger, Bruce G. 1978. "The Strategy of Iroquoian Prehistory." In *Archaeological Essays in Honor of Irving B. Rouse,* edited by R. C. Dunnell and E. S. Hall Jr., 275–310. The Hague: Mouton.

———. 1981. "Prehistoric Social and Political Organization: An Iroquoian Case Study." In *Foundations of Northeast Archaeology,* edited by D. R. Snow, 1–50. New York: Academic Press.

Tuck, James A. 1971. "The Iroquois Confederacy." *Scientific American* 224, no. 2:32–42.

White, Marian E. 1966. "The Owasco and Iroquois Cultures: A Review." *The Bulletin: Journal of the New York State Archaeological Association* 36:11–14.

Williamson, Ronald F. 1985. "Glen Meyer: People in Transition." Ph.D. diss., McGill Univ.

Witthoft, John. 1959. "Ancestry of the Susquehannocks." In *Susquehannock Miscellany,* edited by J. Witthoft and W. F. Kinsey III, 19–60. Harrisburg: Pennsylvania Historical and Museum Commission.

Wright, James V. 1984. "The Cultural Continuity of the Northern Iroquoian-Speaking Peoples." In *Extending the Rafters: Interdisciplinary Approaches to Iro-*

quoian Studies, edited by M. K. Foster, J. Campisi, and M. Mithun, 283–99. Albany: State Univ. of New York Press.

Wright, James V., and James E. Anderson. 1969. *The Bennett Site.* Bulletin 229. Ottawa: National Museum of Canada.

2. Precolumbian Dynamics

Abel, Timothy J. 2000. "The Plus Site: An Iroquoian Remote Camp in Upland Tompkins County, N.Y." *North American Archaeologist* 21, no. 3:181–215.

———. 2001. "The Clayton Cluster: Cultural Dynamics of a Late Prehistoric Village Sequence in the Upper St. Lawrence Valley." Ph.D. diss., State Univ. of New York at Albany.

———. 2002. "Recent Research on the Saint Lawrence Iroquoians of Northern New York." *Archaeology of Eastern North America* 30:137–54.

Abel, Timothy J., and David N. Fuerst. 1999. "The Prehistory of the Saint Lawrence Headwaters Region." *Archaeology of Eastern North America* 27:1–52.

Allen, Kathleen M. S. 1996. "Iroquoian Landscapes: People, Environments, and the GIS Context." In *New Methods, Old Problems: Geographic Information Systems in Modern Archaeological Research,* edited by H.D.G. Maschner, 198–222. Center for Archaeological Investigations, Occasional Paper no. 23. Carbondale: Southern Illinois Univ.

Anderson, James E. 1963. *The People of Fairty: An Osteological Analysis of an Iroquois Ossuary.* Bulletin 193, 28–129. Ottawa: National Museum of Canada.

Austin, Shaun J. 1994. "The Wilcox Lake Site (AlGu-17): Middle Iroquoian Exploitation of the Oak Ridges Moraine." *Ontario Archaeology* 58:49–84.

Bamann, Susan. 1993. "Settlement Nucleation in Mohawk Iroquois Prehistory: An Analysis of a Site Sequence in the Lower Otsquago Drainage of the Mohawk Valley." Ph.D. diss., State Univ. of New York at Albany.

Bamann, Susan E., Robert D. Kuhn, James Molnar, and Dean R. Snow. 1992. "Iroquoian Archaeology." *Annual Review of Anthropology* 21:435–60.

Beauchamp, William M. 1900. *Aboriginal Occupation of New York.* New York State Museum Bulletin 32(7). Albany: State Univ. of New York.

Bradley, James W. 1987. *Evolution of the Onondaga Iroquois: Accommodating Change, 1500–1655.* Syracuse, N.Y.: Syracuse Univ. Press.

Cadzow, Donald A. 1936. *Archaeological Studies of the Susquehannock Indians of Pennsylvania.* Vol. 3. Harrisburg: Publications of the Pennsylvania Historical Commission.

Campbell, Celina, and Ian D. Campbell. 1992. "Pre-Contact Settlement Pattern in Southern Ontario: Simulation Model for Maize-Based Village Horticulture." *Ontario Archaeology* 53:3–26.

Campbell, Ian D., and Celina Campbell. 1989. "The Little Ice Age and Neutral Faunal Assemblages." *Ontario Archaeology* 49:13–33.

Channen, E. R., and N. D. Clark. 1965. *The Copeland Site: A Pre-Contact Huron Site in Simcoe County, Ontario.* Anthropological Paper no. 8. Ottawa: National Museum of Canada.

Chapdelaine, Claude. 1990. "The Mandeville Site and the Definition of a New Regional Group Within the Saint Lawrence Iroquoian World." *Man in the Northeast* 39:53–63.

———. 1993a. "The Maritime Adaptation of the Saint Lawrence Iroquoians." *Man in the Northeast* 45:3–19.

———. 1993b. "The Sedentarization of the Prehistoric Iroquoians: A Slow or Rapid Transformation?" *Journal of Anthropological Archaeology* 12, no. 2:173–209.

Churcher, C. S., and Walter A. Kenyon. 1960. "The Tabor Hill Ossuaries: A Study in Iroquois Demography." *Human Biology* 32:249–73.

Clermont, Norman. 1990. "Why Did the Saint Lawrence Iroquoians Become Horticulturalists?" *Man in the Northeast* 40:75–79.

Dodd, Christine F. 1984. *Ontario Iroquois Tradition Longhouses.* National Museum of Man, Mercury Series, Archaeological Survey of Canada, Paper no. 124, 181–437. Ottawa: National Museums of Canada.

Dragoo, Don W. 1977. "Prehistoric Iroquoian Occupation in the Upper Ohio Valley." In *Current Perspectives in Northeastern Archaeology: Essays in Honor of William A. Ritchie,* edited by R. E. Funk and C. F. Hayes III, 41–47. Researches and Transactions of the New York State Archaeological Association 17, no. 1. Rochester.

Ellis, Chris J., and Neal Ferris, eds. 1990. *The Archaeology of Southern Ontario to A.D. 1650.* Occasional Publications of the London Chapter of the Ontario Archaeological Society no. 5. London, Ontario.

Emerson, J. Norman. 1954. "The Archaeology of the Ontario Iroquois." Ph.D. diss., Univ. of Chicago.

———. 1967. *The Payne Site: An Iroquoian Manifestation in Prince Edward County, Ontario.* Contributions to Anthropology no. 5. Bulletin 206, 126–257. Ottawa: National Museum of Canada.

Emerson, J. Norman, and Robert E. Popham. 1952. "Comments on the Huron and Lalonde Occupations of Ontario." *American Antiquity* 18, no. 2:162–64.

Engelbrecht, William E. 1974. "The Iroquois: Archaeological Patterning on the Tribal Level." *World Archaeology* 6, no. 1:52–65.

———. 1987. "Factors Maintaining Low Population Density among the Prehistoric New York Iroquois." *American Antiquity* 52, no. 1:13–27.

———. 1991. "Erie." *The Bulletin: Journal of the New York State Archaeological Association* 102:2–12.

———. 1994. "The Eaton Site: Preliminary Analysis of the Iroquoian Component." *The Bulletin: Journal of the New York State Archaeological Association* 107:1–8.

———. 2003. *Iroquoia: The Development of a Native World.* Syracuse, N.Y.: Syracuse Univ. Press.

Engelbrecht, William E., Earl Sidler, and Michael Walko. 1990. "The Jefferson County Iroquoians." *Man in the Northeast* 39:65–77.

Ferris, Neal. 1999. "Telling Tales: Interpretive Trends in Southern Ontario Late Woodland Archaeology." *Ontario Archaeology* 68:1–62.

Finlayson, William D. 1985. *The 1975 and 1978 Rescue Excavations at the Draper Site: Introduction and Settlement Patterns.* National Museum of Man, Mercury Series, Archaeological Survey of Canada, Paper no. 130. Ottawa: National Museums of Canada.

———. 1998. *Iroquoian Peoples of the Land of Rocks and Water, A.D. 1000–1650: A Study in Settlement Archaeology.* Vols. 1–4. Special Publication no. 1. London, ON: London Museum of Archaeology.

Finlayson, William D., and A. Roger Byrne. 1975. "Investigations of Iroquoian Settlement Patterns at Crawford Lake, Ontario—A Preliminary Report." *Ontario Archaeology* 25:31–36.

Finlayson, William D., and Robert J. Pearce. 1989. "Iroquoian Communities in Southern Ontario." In *Households and Communities,* edited by S. MacEachern, D.J.W. Archer, and R. D. Garvin, 301–6. Proceedings of the 21st Annual Chacmool Conference. Alberta: Archaeological Association of the Univ. of Calgary.

Fogt, Lisa M., and Peter G. Ramsden. 1996. "From Timepiece to Time Machine: Scale and Complexity in Iroquoian Archaeology." In *Debating Complexity,* edited by D. A. Meyer, P. C. Dawson, and D. T. Hanna, 39–45. Proceedings of the 26th Annual Chacmool Conference. Alberta: Archaeological Association of the Univ. of Calgary.

Foster, Gary A. M. 1990. *The Wolfe Creek Site, AcHm-3: A Prehistoric Neutral Frontier Community in Southwestern Ontario.* Monographs in Ontario Archaeology no. 3. Willowdale: Ontario Archaeological Society.

Fox, William A. 1976. "The Central North Erie Shore." In *The Late Prehistory of the Lake Erie Drainage Basin: A 1972 Symposium Revisited,* edited by D. S. Brose, 162–92. Cleveland: Cleveland Museum of Natural History.

———, ed. 1986. *Studies in Southwestern Ontario Archaeology.* Occasional Publications of the London Chapter of the Ontario Archaeological Society no. 1. London, Ontario.

Funk, Robert E. 1997. "An Introduction to the History of Prehistoric Archaeology in New York State." *The Bulletin: Journal of the New York State Archaeological Association* 113:4–59.

Funk, Robert E., and Robert D. Kuhn. 2003. *Three Sixteenth-Century Mohawk Iroquois Village Sites.* New York State Museum Bulletin 503. Albany: State Univ. of New York, State Education Department.

Griffin, James B. 1944. "The Iroquois in American Prehistory." *Papers of the Michigan Academy of Science, Arts, and Letters* 29:357–74.

Hart, John P. 2000a. "New Dates on Classic New York Sites: Just How Old Are Those Longhouses?" *Northeast Anthropology* 60:1–22.

———. 2000b. "New Dates from Old Collections: The Roundtop Site and Maize-Beans-Squash Agriculture in the Northeast." *North American Archaeologist* 20:7–17.

———. 2003. "Rethinking the Three Sisters." *Journal of Middle Atlantic Archaeology* 19:73–82.

———, ed. 1999. *Current Northeast Paleoethnobotany.* New York State Museum Bulletin 494. Albany: State Univ. of New York, State Education Department.

Hart, John P., and Christina B. Rieth, eds. 2002. *Northeast Subsistence-Settlement Change A.D. 700–1300.* New York State Museum Bulletin 496. Albany: State Univ. of New York, State Education Department.

Hart, John P., and C. Margaret Scarry. 1999. "The Age of Common Beans *(Phaseolus vulgaris)* in the Northeastern United States." *American Antiquity* 64, no. 4:653–58.

Hart, John P., and Nancy Asch Sidell. 1996. "Prehistoric Agricultural Systems in the West Branch of the Susquehanna River Basin, A.D. 800 to A.D. 1350." *Northeast Anthropology* 52:1–30.

———. 1997. "Additional Evidence for Early Cucurbit Use in the Northern Eastern Woodlands East of the Allegheny Front." *American Antiquity* 62, no. 3:523–37.

Hart, John P., Robert G. Thompson, and Hetty Jo Brumbach. 2003. "Phytolith Evidence for Early Maize *(Zea mays)* in the Northern Finger Lakes Region of New York." *American Antiquity* 68, no. 4:619–40.

Hasenstab, Robert J. 1990. "Agriculture, Warfare, and Tribalization in the Iroquois Homeland of New York: A G.I.S. Analysis of Late Woodland Settlement." Ph.D. diss., Univ. of Massachusetts, Amherst.

———. 1996a. "Aboriginal Settlement Patterns in Late Woodland Upper New York State." In *A Northeastern Millennium: History and Archaeology for Robert E. Funk*, edited by C. Lindner and E. V. Curtin. *Journal of Middle Atlantic Archaeology* 12:17–26.

———. 1996b. "Settlement as Adaptation: Variability in Iroquois Site Selections as Inferred through GIS." In *New Methods, Old Problems: Geographic Information Systems in Modern Archaeological Research,* edited by H.D.G. Maschner, 223–41. Occasional Paper no. 23. Carbondale: Center for Archaeological Investigations, Southern Illinois Univ.

Hatch, James W., and Gregory H. Bondar. 2001. "Late Woodland Palisaded Villages from Ontario to the Carolinas: Their Potential for Accurate Population Estimates." In *Archaeology of the Appalachian Highlands,* edited by L. P. Sullivan and S. C. Prezzano, 149–67. Knoxville: Univ. of Tennessee Press.

Hayden, Brian. 1982. "Recognizing Intact Iroquoian Domestic Refuse: The Draper Case." *Ontario Archaeology* 38:47–50.

———, ed. 1979. *Settlement Patterns of the Draper and White Sites: 1973 Excavations.* Publication no. 6. Burnaby, British Columbia: Department of Archaeology, Simon Fraser Univ.

Hayes, Charles F., III, and Betty Prisch. 1973. "A Prehistoric Iroquois Site on Farrell Farm." *The Bulletin: Journal of the New York State Archaeological Association* 59:19–28.

Houghton, Frederick. 1899. *On the Occurence [sic] on Iroquois Village Sites of Stone Scrapers and Perforators.* Buffalo, N.Y.: Reinecke and Zesch.

———. 1909a. "Indian Village, Camp and Burial Sites on the Niagara Frontier." *Bulletin of the Buffalo Society of Natural Sciences* 9, no. 3:261–375.

———. 1909b. "Report on Neuter Cemetery, Grand Island, N.Y." *Bulletin of the Buffalo Society of Natural Sciences* 9, no. 3:375–85.

———. 1916. "The Characteristics of Iroquoian Village Sites of Western New York." *American Anthropologist* 18, no. 4:508–20.

———. 1922. "The Archaeology of the Genesee Country." *Researches and Transactions of the New York State Archaeological Association* 3, no. 2:39–66. Rochester.

Hunt, Eleazer D. 1990. "A Consideration of Environmental, Physiographic, and Horticultural Systems as They Impact Late Woodland Settlement Patterns in Western New York State: A Geographic Information System (GIS) Analysis of Site Locations." Ph.D. diss., State Univ. of New York at Buffalo.

Hunter, Andrew F. 1902. "Notes on Sites of Huron Villages in the Township of Medonte." *Annual Archaeological Report for Ontario, 1901,* 56–100. Appendix to the Report of the Minister of Education for Ontario. Toronto.

———. 1907. Huron Village Sites. *Annual Archaeological Report for Ontario, 1906,* 1–56. Appendix to the Report of the Minister of Education for Ontario. Toronto.

Jamieson, James Bruce. 1983. "An Examination of Prisoner-Sacrifice and Cannibalism at the St. Lawrence Iroquoian Roebuck Site." *Canadian Journal of Archaeology* 7, no. 2:159–75.

Jamieson, Susan M. 1981. "Economics and Ontario Iroquoian Social Organization." *Canadian Journal of Archaeology* 5:19–30.

———. 1989. "Precepts and Percepts of Northern Iroquoian Households and Communities: The Changing Past." In *Households and Communities,* edited by S. MacEachern, D.J.W. Archer, and R. D. Garvin, 307–14. Proceedings of the 21st Annual Chacmool Conference. Alberta: Archaeological Association of the Univ. of Calgary.

Jury, Elsie McLeod Murray. 1974. *The Neutral Indians of South-Western Ontario.* Bulletin no. 13. London, ON: London Museum of Archaeology.

Kapches, Mima. 1976. "The Interments of Infants of the Ontario Iroquois." *Ontario Archaeology* 27:29–39.

———. 1979. "Intra-Longhouse Spatial Analysis." *Pennsylvania Archaeologist* 49, no. 4:24–29.

———. 1980. "Wall Trenches on Iroquoian Sites." *Archaeology of Eastern North America* 8:98–105.

———. 1981. "The Middleport Pattern in Ontario Iroquoian Prehistory." Ph.D. diss., Univ. of Toronto.

———. 1984. "Cabins on Ontario Iroquoian Sites." *North American Archaeologist* 5, no. 1:63–71.

———. 1990. "The Spatial Dynamics of Ontario Iroquoian Longhouses." *American Antiquity* 55, no. 1:49–67.

———. 1993. "The Identification of an Iroquoian Unit of Measurement: Architectural and Social/Cultural Implications for the Longhouse." *Archaeology of Eastern North America* 21:137–62.

———. 1994. "The Iroquoian Longhouse: Architectural and Cultural Identity." In *Meaningful Architecture: Social Interpretations of Buildings,* edited by M. Locock, 253–70. Worldwide Archaeology Series no. 9. Hampshire, UK: Avebury, Aldershot.

———. 2002. "The Internal Organization of Iroquoian Longhouses: A Response to Crowding?" *The Bulletin: Journal of the New York State Archaeological Association* 118:49–52.

Katzenberg, M. Anne. 1992. "Changing Diet and Health in Pre- and Protohistoric Ontario." In *Health and Lifestyle Change,* edited by R. Huss-Ashmore, J. Schall, and M. Hediger, 23–31. MASCA Research Papers in Science and Archaeology no. 9. Philadelphia: Univ. Museum of Archaeology and Anthropology, Univ. of Pennsylvania.

Katzenberg, M. Anne, and Henry P. Schwarcz. 1986. "Paleonutrition in Southern Ontario: Evidence from Strontium and Stable Isotopes." *Canadian Review of Physical Anthropology* 5, no. 2:15–21.

Katzenberg, M. Anne, Henry P. Schwarcz, Martin Knyf, and F. Jerry Melbye. 1995. "Stable Isotope Evidence for Maize Horticulture and Paleodiet in Southern Ontario, Canada." *American Antiquity* 60, no. 2:335–50.

Kent, Barry C. 1984. *Susquehanna's Indians.* Anthropological Series no. 6. Harrisburg: Pennsylvania Historical and Museum Commission.

Kidd, Kenneth E. 1952. "Sixty Years of Ontario Archaeology." In *Archaeology of Eastern United States,* edited by J. B. Griffin, 71–82. Chicago: Univ. of Chicago Press.

Knoerl, John J. 1988. "The Concept of Scale and Its Application to Prehistoric and Historic Iroquois Sites in the Lake Ontario Drainage Basin." Ph.D. diss., Binghamton Univ.

Knowles, Francis H. S. 1937. *The Physical Anthropology of the Roebuck Iroquois, with Comparative Data from Other Indian Tribes.* Bulletin 87, Anthropological Series no. 22. Ottawa: National Museum of Canada.

Kuhn, Robert D. 1994. "Recent CRM Contributions to Iroquoian Archaeology in New York State." *Archaeology of Eastern North America* 22:73–88.

Kuhn, Robert D., and Robert E. Funk. 2000. "Boning up on the Mohawk: An Overview of Mohawk Faunal Assemblages and Subsistence Patterns." *Archaeology of Eastern North America* 28:29–62.

Kuhn, Robert D., Robert E. Funk, and James F. Pendergast. 1993. "The Evidence for a Saint Lawrence Iroquoian Presence on Sixteenth-Century Mohawk Sites." *Man in the Northeast* 45:77–86.

Langdon, Stephen P. 1995. "Biological Relationships among the Iroquois." *Human Biology* 67, no. 3:355–74.

Latta, Martha A. 1991. "The Captive Bride Syndrome: Iroquoian Behavior or Archaeological Myth?" In *The Archaeology of Gender,* edited by D. Walde and N. D. Willows, 17–23. Proceedings of the 22nd Annual Chacmool Conference. Alberta: Archaeological Association of the Univ. of Calgary.

Lindner, Christopher, and Edward V. Curtin, eds. 1996. *A Northeastern Millennium: History and Archaeology for Robert E. Funk. Journal of Middle Atlantic Archaeology* 12.

MacDonald, Robert I. 1988. "Ontario Iroquoian Sweat Lodges." *Ontario Archaeology* 48:17–26.

———. 1992. "Ontario Iroquoian Semisubterranean Sweat Lodges." In *Ancient Images, Ancient Thought: The Archaeology of Ideology,* edited by A. S. Goldsmith, S. Garvie, D. Selin, and J. Smith, 323–30. Proceedings of the 23rd Annual Chacmool Conference. Alberta: Archaeological Association of the Univ. of Calgary.

Martijn, Charles A. 1990. "The Iroquoian Presence in the Estuary and Gulf of St. Lawrence River Valley." *Man in the Northeast* 40:45–63.

McCracken, Richard J. 1985. "Susquehannocks, Brule and Carantouannais: A Continuing Research Problem." *The Bulletin: Journal of the New York State Archaeological Association* 91:39–51.

Miroff, Laurie E., and Timothy D. Knapp, eds. 2007. *Tipping the Scale: Levels of Analysis in Iroquoian Archaeology.* Knoxville: Univ. of Tennessee Press.

Molto, Joseph Eldon. 1983. *Biological Relationships of Southern Ontario Woodland Peoples: The Evidence of Discontinuous Cranial Morphology.* National Museum of Man, Mercury Series, Archaeological Survey of Canada, Paper no. 117. Ottawa: National Museums of Canada.

Monckton, Stephen G. 1990. "Huron Paleothnobotany." Ph.D. diss., Univ. of Toronto.

———. 1992. *Huron Paleothnobotany.* Ontario Archaeological Reports no. 1. Toronto: Ontario Heritage Foundation.

———. 1994. "Reconstructing Local Paleoenvironments of Huron Villages: Potential and Problems of Archaeological Plant Macrofossils." In *Great Lakes Archaeology and Paleoecology: Exploring Interdisciplinary Initiatives for the Nineties,* edited by R. I. MacDonald, 209–18. Ontario: Quaternary Sciences Institute, Univ. of Waterloo.

Morin, Eugène. 2001. "Early Late Woodland Social Interaction in the St. Lawrence River Valley." *Archaeology of Eastern North America* 29:65–100.

Mullen, Grant J., and Robert D. Hoppa. 1992. "Rogers Ossuary (AgHb-131): An Early Ontario Iroquois Burial Feature from Brantford Township." *Canadian Journal of Archaeology* 16:32–47.

Niemczycki, Mary Ann Palmer. 1988. "Seneca Tribalization: An Adaptive Strategy." *Man in the Northeast* 36:77–87.

Noble, William C. 1968. "Iroquois Archaeology and the Development of Iroquois Social Organization (A.D. 1000–1650): A Study in Cultural Change Based on Archaeology, Ethnohistory, and Ethnology." Ph.D. diss., Univ. of Calgary.

———. 1975a. "Canadian Prehistory: The Lower Great Lakes-St. Lawrence Region." *Canadian Archaeological Association Bulletin* 7:96–121.

———. 1975b. "Corn and the Development of Village Life in Southern Ontario." *Ontario Archaeology* 25:37–46.

Norcliffe, Glen B., and Conrad E. Heidenreich. 1974. "The Preferred Orientation of Iroquoian Longhouses in Ontario." *Ontario Archaeology* 23:3–30.

Ounjian, Glenna L. 1997. "Glen Meyer and Neutral Palaeoethnobotany." Ph.D. diss., Univ. of Toronto.

Parker, Arthur C. 1907. *Excavations in an Erie Indian Village and Burial Site at Ripley, Chautauqua County, New York.* New York State Museum Bulletin 117. Albany: State Education Department.

———. 1918. *A Prehistoric Iroquoian Site on the Reed Farm, Richmond Mills, Ontario County, New York.* Researches and Transactions of the New York State Archaeological Association 1, no. 1. Rochester.

———. 1922. *The Archaeological History of New York.* Parts 1 and 2. New York State Museum Bulletins 235–38. Albany: State Univ. of New York.

———. 1929. "Aboriginal Cultures and Chronology of the Genesee County." *Proceedings of the Rochester Academy of Science* 6, no. 8:248–83.

Patterson, David Kingsnorth, Jr. 1984. *A Diachronic Study of Dental Palaeopathology and Attritional Status of Prehistoric Ontario Pre-Iroquois and Iroquois Populations.* Mercury Series, Archaeological Survey of Canada, Paper no. 122. Ottawa: National Museums of Canada.

———. 1986. "Changes in Oral Health among Prehistoric Ontario Populations." *Canadian Journal of Anthropology* 5:3–13.

Pearce, Robert J. 1996. *Mapping Middleport: A Case Study in Societal Archaeology.* Research Report no. 25. London, ON: London Museum of Archaeology.

Pendergast, James F. 1962. "The Crystal Rock Site: An Early Onondaga-Oneida Site in Eastern Ontario." *Pennsylvania Archaeologist* 32, no. 1:21–34.

———. 1963. *The Payne Site.* National Museum of Canada Bulletin 193, 1–27. Ottawa.

———. 1964. "Nine Small Sites on Lake St. Francis Representing an Early Iroquoian Horizon in the Upper St. Lawrence River Valley." *Anthropologica*, n.s., 6:183–221.

———. 1966a. *The Berry Site.* Bulletin 206, 26–53, Anthropological Series no. 72. Ottawa: National Museum of Canada.

———. 1966b. *Three Prehistoric Iroquois Components in Eastern Ontario: The Salem, Grays Creek, and Beckstead Sites.* Bulletin 208, Anthropological Series no. 73. Ottawa: National Museum of Canada.

———. 1981. *The Glenbrook Village Site—A Late St. Lawrence Iroquoian Component in Glengarry County, Ontario.* National Museum of Man, Mercury Series, Archaeological Survey of Canada, Paper no. 100. Ottawa: National Museums of Canada.

———. 1983. "St. Lawrence Iroquoian Burial Practices." *Ontario Archaeology* 40:49–56.

———. 1984. *The Beckstead Site—1977.* Mercury Series, Archaeological Survey of Canada, Paper no. 123. Ottawa: National Museums of Canada.

———. 1985. "Huron-St. Lawrence Iroquois Relations in the Terminal Prehistoric Period." *Ontario Archaeology* 44:23–39.

———. 1990. "Emerging Saint Lawrence Iroquoian Settlement Patterns." *Man in the Northeast* 40:17–30.

———. 1991. "The St. Lawrence Iroquoians: Their Past, Present, and Immediate Future." *The Bulletin: Journal of the New York State Archaeological Association* 102:47–74.

———. 1992. "Some Notes on Cross-Border Archaeology in This Region." *The Bulletin: Journal of the New York State Archaeological Association* 104:31–43.

———. 1993. "Some Comments on Calibrated Radiocarbon Dates for Saint Lawrence Iroquoian Sites." *Northeast Anthropology* 46:1–32.

———. 1996. "High Precision Calibration of the Radiocarbon Time Scale: CALIB 3.0.3 (Method 'A') in a St. Lawrence Iroquoian Context." *The Bulletin: Journal of the New York State Archaeological Association* 111–12:35–62.

———. 1999. "The Ottawa River Algonquin Bands in a St. Lawrence Iroquoian Context." *Canadian Journal of Archaeology* 23:63–136.

Pendergast, James F., and Claude Chapdelaine, eds. 1993. *Essays in St. Lawrence Iroquoian Archaeology.* Occasional Papers in Northeastern Archaeology no. 8. Dundas, ON: Copetown Press.

Perrelli, Douglas J. 2001. "Gender Roles and Seasonal Site Use in Western New York ca. A.D. 1500: Iroquoian Domestic and Ceremonial Production at the Piestrak and Spaulding Lake Sites." Ph.D. diss., State Univ. of New York at Buffalo.

Petersen, James B. 1990. "Evidence of the Saint Lawrence Iroquoians in Northern New England: Population Movement, Trade, or Stylistic Borrowing?" *Man in the Northeast* 40:31–39.

Pfeiffer, Susan. 1980. "Spatial Distribution of Human Skeletal Material Within an Iroquoian Ossuary." *Canadian Journal of Archaeology* 4:169–72.

———. 1983. "Demographic Parameters of the Uxbridge Ossuary Population." *Ontario Archaeology* 40:9–14.

———. 1984. "Paleopathology in an Iroquoian Ossuary, with Special Reference to Tuberculosis." *American Journal of Physical Anthropology* 65, no. 2:181–89.

———. 1986. "Morbidity and Mortality in the Uxbridge Ossuary." *Canadian Journal of Anthropology* 5, no. 2:23–31.

Pfeiffer, Susan, M. Anne Katzenberg, and Marc A. Kelley. 1985. "Congenital Abnormalities in a Prehistoric Iroquoian Village: The Uxbridge Ossuary." *Canadian Journal of Anthropology* 4, no. 2:83–92.

Pratt, Marjorie K. 1991. "The St. Lawrence Iroquois of Northern New York." *The Bulletin: Journal of the New York State Archaeological Association* 102:43–46.

Pratt, Peter P. 1961. "The Bigford Site: Late Prehistoric Oneida." *Pennsylvania Archaeologist* 31, no. 1:46–59.

———. 1963. "A Heavily Stockaded Late Prehistoric Oneida Iroquois Settlement." *Pennsylvania Archaeologist* 33, nos. 1–2:56–92.

———. 1976. *Archaeology of the Oneida Iroquois.* Vol. 1. Occasional Publications in Northeastern Anthropology no. 1. Rindge, N.H.: Man in the Northeast.

———. 1977. "A Perspective on Oneida Archaeology." In *Current Perspectives in Northeastern Archaeology: Essays in Honor of William A. Ritchie,* edited by R. E. Funk and C. F. Hayes III, 51–69. Researches and Transactions of the New York State Archaeological Association 17, no. 1. Rochester.

———. 1991. "Oneida Archaeology: The Last Quarter Century." *The Bulletin: Journal of the New York State Archaeological Association* 102:40–42.

Prezzano, Susan C. 1988. "Spatial Analysis of Post Mold Patterns at the Sackett Site, Ontario County, New York." *Man in the Northeast* 35:27–45.

———. 1993. "Longhouse, Village, and Palisade Community Patterns at the Iroquois Southern Door New York, Late Woodland." Ph.D. diss., Binghamton Univ.

Prezzano, Susan C., and Christina B. Rieth. 2001. "Late Prehistoric Cultures of the Upper Susquehanna Valley." In *Archaeology of the Appalachian Highlands,* edited by L. P. Sullivan and S. C. Prezzano, 168–76. Knoxville: Univ. of Tennessee Press.

Ramsden, Peter G. 1988. "Palisade Extension, Village Expansion and Immigration in Trent Valley Huron Villages." *Canadian Journal of Archaeology* 12:177–83.

———. 1990. "Saint Lawrence Iroquoians in the Upper Trent Valley." *Man in the Northeast* 39:87–95.

———. 1996. "The Current State of Huron Archaeology." *Northeast Anthropology* 51:101–12.

Rankin, Lisa K. 2000. *Interpreting Long-Term Trends in the Transition to Farming: Reconsidering the Nodwell Site, Ontario, Canada.* British Archaeological Reports International Series no. 830. Oxford, UK.

Reid, C. S. 1975a. *The Boys Site and the Early Ontario Iroquois Tradition.* National Museum of Man, Mercury Series, Archaeological Survey of Canada, Paper no. 42. Ottawa: National Museums of Canada.

———. 1975b. "New Trends in the Early Ontario Iroquois Tradition." *Ontario Archaeology* 25:7–20.

Ridley, Frank. 1952a. "The Fallis Site, Ontario." *American Antiquity* 18, no. 1:7–14.

———. 1952b. "The Huron and Lalonde Occupations of Ontario." *American Antiquity* 17, no. 3:197–210.

———. 1954. "The Frank Bay Site, Lake Nipissing, Ontario." *American Antiquity* 20, no. 1:40–50.

———. 1961. *Archaeology of the Neutral Indians.* Port Credit, ON: Etobicoke Historical Society.

Rieth, Christina B. 1997. "Culture Contact During the Carpenter Brook Phase: A Tripartite Approach to the Study of the Spatial and Temporal Movement of Early Iroquoian Groups Throughout the Upper Susquehanna River Valley." Ph.D. diss., State Univ. of New York at Albany.

Rippeteau, Bruce E. 1978. "The Upper Susquehanna Valley Iroquois: An Iroquoian Enigma." In *Essays in Northeastern Anthropology: In Memory of Marian E. White,* edited by W. E. Engelbrecht and D. K. Grayson, 123–51. Occasional Publications in Northeastern Anthropology no. 5. Rindge, N.H.

Ritchie, William A. 1961. "Iroquois Archaeology and Settlement Patterns." In *Symposium on Cherokee and Iroquois Culture,* edited by W. N. Fenton and J. Gulick, 25–38. Bulletin 180. Washington, D.C.: Bureau of American Ethnology.

———. 1980. *The Archaeology of New York State.* 2nd rev. ed. Harrison, N.Y.: Harbor Hill Books.

Ritchie, William A., and Robert E. Funk. 1973. *Aboriginal Settlement Patterns in the Northeast.* New York State Museum and Science Service Memoir 20. Albany: State Univ. of New York, State Education Department.

Rumrill, Donald A. 1985. "An Interpretation and Analysis of the Seventeenth Century Mohawk Nation: Its Chronology and Movements." *The Bulletin: Journal of the New York State Archaeological Association* 90:1–39.

Saunders, Lorraine P., and Martha L. Sempowski. 1991. "The Seneca Site Sequence and Chronology: The Baby or the Bathwater?" *The Bulletin: Journal of the New York State Archaeological Association* 102:13–26.

Saunders, Shelley R., and F. Jerry Melbye. 1990. "Subadult Mortality and Skeletal Indicators of Health in Late Woodland Ontario Iroquois." *Canadian Journal of Archaeology* 14:61–74.

Saunders, Shelley R., Peter G. Ramsden, and D. Ann Herring. 1992. "Transformation and Disease: Precontact Ontario Iroquoians." In *Disease and Demography in the Americas,* edited by J. W. Verano and D. H. Ubelaker, 117–26. Washington, D.C.: Smithsonian Institution Press.

Schoolcraft, Henry Rowe. 1975 [1846]. *Notes on the Iroquois: Or, Contributions to the Statistics, Aboriginal History, Antiquities, and General Ethnology of Western New York.* Millwood, N.Y.: Krauss Reprint.

Schwarcz, Henry P., F. Jerry Melbye, M. Anne Katzenberg, and Martin Knyf. 1985. "Stable Isotopes in Human Skeletons of Southern Ontario: Reconstructing Paleodiet." *Journal of Archaeological Science* 12:187–206.

Skinner, Alanson B. 1921. *Notes on Iroquois Archeology.* Indian Notes and Monographs no. 18. New York: Museum of the American Indian, Heye Foundation. 1978. Reprint. New York: AMS Press.

Smith, David G. 1997. "Radiocarbon Dating the Middle to Late Woodland Transition and Earliest Maize in Southern Ontario." *Northeast Anthropology* 54:37–73.

Snow, Dean R. 1985. *The Mohawk Valley Project: 1982 Field Season Report.* The Institute for Northeast Anthropology, State Univ. of New York at Albany.

———. 1995. *Mohawk Valley Archaeology.* Vol. 1, *The Sites.* Vol. 2, *The Collections.* Institute for Archaeological Studies, State Univ. of New York at Albany.

———. 1996. *The Iroquois.* Oxford, UK: Blackwell.

———. 1997. "The Architecture of Iroquois Longhouses." *Northeast Anthropology* 53:61–84.

———. 2001a. "Evolution of the Mohawk Iroquois." In *Societies in Eclipse: Archaeology of the Eastern Woodlands Indians, A.D. 1400–1700,* edited by D. S. Brose, C. W. Cowan, and R. C. Mainfort Jr., 19–25. Washington, D.C.: Smithsonian Institution Press.

———. 2001b. "The Lessons of Northern Iroquoian Demography." In *Archaeology of the Appalachian Highlands,* edited by L. P. Sullivan and S. C. Prezzano, 264–77. Knoxville: Univ. of Tennessee Press.

Spence, Michael W. 1994. "Mortuary Programmes of the Early Ontario Iroquoians." *Ontario Archaeology* 58:6–26.

Squier, Ephraim G. 1851. *Antiquities of the State of New York.* Buffalo, N.Y.: George H. Derby.

Stewart, Francis L. 1991. *The Faunal Remains from the Keffer Site (AkGv-14), a Southern Ontario Iroquoian Village.* Research Report no. 21. London, ON: London Museum of Archaeology.

Stopp, Marianne P. 1984. "An Archaeological Examination of the Baumann Site: A 15th Century Settlement in Simcoe County, Ontario." *Ontario Archaeology* 43:3–30.

Stothers, David M., and James R. Graves. 1983. "Cultural Continuity and Change: The Western Basin, Ontario Iroquois and Sandusky Traditions—A 1982 Perspective." *Archaeology of Eastern North America* 11:109–42.

Sutton, Richard E. 1988. "Palaeodemography and Late Iroquoian Ossuary Samples." *Ontario Archaeology* 48:42–50.

———. 1990. *Hidden Amidst the Hills: Middle and Late Iroquoian Occupations in the Middle Trent Valley.* Occasional Papers in Northeastern Archaeology no. 3. Dundas, ON: Copetown Press.

———. 1996. "The Middle Iroquoian Colonization of Huronia." Ph.D. diss., McMaster Univ.

Sykes, Clark M. 1980. "Swidden Horticulture and Iroquoian Settlement." *Archaeology of Eastern North America* 8:45–52.

———. 1981. "Northern Iroquoian Maize Remains." *Ontario Archaeology* 35:23–33.

Thompson, Robert G., John P. Hart, Hetty Jo Brumbach, and Robert Lusteck. 2004. "Phytolith Evidence for Twentieth-Century B.P. Maize in Northern Iroquoia." *Northeast Anthropology* 68:25–40.

Timmins, Peter A. 1985. *The Analysis and Interpretation of Radiocarbon Dates in Iroquoian Archaeology.* Research Report no. 19. London, ON: London Museum of Archaeology.

———. 1997. *The Calvert Site: An Interpretive Framework for the Early Iroquoian Village.* Mercury Series, Archaeological Survey of Canada, Paper no. 156. Quebec: Canadian Museum of Civilization, Hull.

Tooker, Elisabeth, ed. 1967. *Iroquois Culture, History, and Prehistory.* Proceedings of the 1965 Conference on Iroquois Research. New York State Museum and Science Service. Albany: State Univ. of New York, State Education Department.

Trigger, Bruce G. 1968. "Archaeological and Other Evidence: A Fresh Look at the 'Laurentian Iroquois.'" *American Antiquity* 33, no. 4:429–40.

———. 1970. "The Strategy of Iroquoian Prehistory." *Ontario Archaeology* 14:3–48.

———. 1978a. "Iroquoian Matriliny." *Pennsylvania Archaeologist* 48:55–65.

———. 1978b. "William J. Wintemberg: Iroquoian Archaeologist." In *Essays in Northeastern Anthropology: In Memory of Marian E. White,* edited by W. E. Engelbrecht and D. K. Grayson, 5–21. Occasional Publications in Northeastern Anthropology no. 5. Rindge, N.H.

———. 1990a. "Maintaining Economic Equality in Opposition to Complexity: An Iroquoian Case Study." In *the Evolution of Political Systems: Sociopolitics in Small-Scale Sedentary Societies,* edited by S. Upham, 119–45. New York: Cambridge Univ. Press.

———. 1990b. *The Huron: Farmers of the North.* New York: Holt, Rinehart, and Winston.

———, ed. 1978. *Handbook of North American Indians.* Vol. 15, *Northeast.* General Editor, W. C. Sturtevant. Washington, D.C.: Smithsonian Institution.

Tuck, James A. 1971. *Onondaga Prehistory: A Study in Settlement Archaeology.* Syracuse, N.Y.: Syracuse Univ. Press.

van der Merwe, Nikolaas J., Ronald F. Williamson, Susan Pfeiffer, Stephen Cox Thomas, and Kim Oakberg Allegretto. 2003. "The Moatfield Ossuary: Isotopic Dietary Analysis of an Iroquoian Community, Using Dental Tissue." *Journal of Anthropological Archaeology* 22, no. 3:245–61.

Vogel, J. C., and Nikolaas J. van der Merwe. 1977. "Isotopic Evidence for Early Maize Cultivation in New York State." *American Antiquity* 42, no. 2:238–42.

Warrick, Gary A. 1984. *Reconstructing Ontario Iroquoian Village Organization.* National Museum of Man, Mercury Series, Archaeological Survey of Canada, Paper no. 124, 1–180. Ottawa: National Museums of Canada.

———. 1988. "Estimating Ontario Iroquoian Village Duration." *Man in the Northeast* 36:21–60.

———. 1990. "A Population History of the Huron-Petun A.D. 900–1650." Ph.D. diss., McGill Univ.

———. 1996. "Evolution of the Iroquoian Longhouse." In *People Who Lived in Big Houses: Archaeological Perspectives on Large Domestic Structures,* edited by G. Coupland and E. B. Banning, 11–26. Monographs in World Archaeology no. 27. Madison, Wis.: Prehistory Press.

———. 2000. "The Precontact Iroquoian Occupation of Southern Ontario." *Journal of World Prehistory* 14, no. 4:415–66.

Webster, Gary S. 1983. "Northern Iroquoian Hunting: An Optimization Approach." Ph.D. diss., Pennsylvania State Univ.

———. 1984. "Susquehannock Animal Economy." *North American Archaeologist* 6, no. 1:41–62.

Whallon, Robert J. 1968. "Investigations of Late Prehistoric Social Organization in New York State." In *New Perspectives in Archaeology,* edited by S. R. Binford and L. R. Binford, 223–44. Chicago: Aldine.

White, Marian E. 1958a. "An Iroquois Sequence in New York's Niagara Frontier." *Pennsylvania Archaeologist* 28:145–50.

———. 1958b. "Dating the Niagara Frontier Iroquois Sequence." *The Bulletin: Journal of the New York State Archaeological Association* 14:4–9.

———. 1961. *Iroquois Culture History in the Niagara Frontier Area of New York State.* Univ. of Michigan Anthropological Papers no. 16. Ann Arbor.

———. 1963. "Settlement Pattern Change and the Development of Horticulture in the New York-Ontario Area." *Pennsylvania Archaeologist* 33, nos. 1–2:1–12.

———. 1972. "On Delineating the Neutral Iroquois of the Eastern Niagara Peninsula in Ontario." *Ontario Archaeology* 17:62–74.

———. 1976. "Late Woodland Archaeology in the Niagara Frontier of New York and Ontario." In *The Late Prehistory of the Lake Erie Drainage Basin: A 1972 Symposium Revisited,* edited by D. S. Brose, 110–36. Cleveland: Cleveland Museum of Natural History.

Whitthoft, John. 1951. "Iroquois Archaeology at the Mid-Century." *Proceedings of the American Philosophical Society* 95, no. 3:311–21.

Williamson, Ronald F. 1978. "Preliminary Report on Human Interment Patterns of the Draper Site." *Canadian Journal of Archaeology* 2:117–22.

———. 1983. *The Robin Hood Site: A Study in Functional Variability in Late Iroquoian Settlement Patterns.* Monographs in Ontario Archaeology no. 1. Toronto: Ontario Archaeological Society.

———, ed. 1998. *The Myers Road Site: Archaeology of the Early to Middle Iroquoian Transition.* Occasional Publications of the London Chapter of the Ontario Archaeological Society no. 7. London, ON.

Williamson, Ronald F., and Susan Pfeiffer, eds. 2003. *Bones of the Ancestors: The Archaeology and Osteobiography of the Moatfield Ossuary.* Mercury Series, Archaeology Paper no. 163. Gatineau, QC: Canadian Museum of Civilization.

Williamson, Ronald F., and David A. Robertson. 1994. "Peer Polities Beyond the Periphery: Early and Middle Iroquoian Regional Interaction." *Ontario Archaeology* 58:27–48.

Williamson, Ronald F., and Christopher M. Watts, eds. 1999. *Taming the Taxonomy: Toward a New Understanding of Great Lakes Archaeology.* Toronto: Eastendbooks.

Wintemberg, William J. 1928. *Uren Prehistoric Village Site, Oxford County, Ontario.* Bulletin 51, Anthropological Series no. 10. Ottawa: National Museum of Canada.

———. 1931. *Distinguishing Characteristics of Algonkian and Iroquoian Cultures.* Annual Report, 1929. Ottawa: National Museum of Canada.

———. 1936. *The Roebuck Prehistoric Village Site, Grenville County, Ontario.* Bulletin 83, Anthropological Series no. 19. Ottawa: National Museum of Canada.

———. 1939. *Lawson Prehistoric Village Site, Middlesex County, Ontario.* Bulletin 94, Anthropological Series no. 25. Ottawa: National Museum of Canada.

———. 1948. *The Middleport Prehistoric Village Site.* Bulletin 109, Anthropological Series no. 27. Ottawa: National Museum of Canada.

Winter, Joseph. 1971. "A Summary of Owasco and Iroquois Maize Remains." *Pennsylvania Archaeologist* 41, no. 3:1–11.

Wray, Charles F. 1973. *Manual for Seneca Iroquois Archaeology.* Honeoye Falls, N.Y.: Cultures Primitive.

Wray, Charles F., and Harry Schoff. 1953. "A Preliminary Report on the Seneca Sequence in Western New York—1550–1687." *Pennsylvania Archaeologist* 23, no. 2:53–63.

Wright, Dawn M. 1991. *An Archaeobotanical Report Based upon Flotation Analysis of Plant Materials from the Keffer Site, Vaughn, Ontario.* Research Report no. 22. London, ON: London Museum of Archaeology.

Wright, Gordon K. 1963. *The Neutral Indians.* Occasional Papers of the New York State Archaeological Association no. 4. Rochester.

Wright, James V. 1966. *The Ontario Iroquois Tradition.* Bulletin 210, Anthropological Series no. 75. Ottawa: National Museum of Canada.

———. 1972. *Ontario Prehistory: An Eleven-Thousand-Year Archaeological Outline.* Ottawa: National Museums of Canada.

———. 1974. *The Nodwell Site.* National Museum of Man, Mercury Series, Archaeological Survey of Canada, Paper no. 22. Ottawa: National Museums of Canada.

———. 1985. "The Comparative Radiocarbon Dating of Two Prehistoric Ontario Iroquoian Villages." *Canadian Journal of Archaeology* 9, no. 1:57–68.

———. 1992. "The Conquest Theory of the Ontario Iroquois Tradition: A Reassessment." *Ontario Archaeology* 54:3–16.

———. 1995. "Three Dimensional Reconstructions of Iroquoian Longhouses: A Comment." *Archaeology of Eastern North America* 23:9–21.

Wright, James V., and Jean-Luc Pilon, eds. 2004. *A Passion for the Past: Papers in Honour of James F. Pendergast.* Mercury Series, Archaeology Paper no. 164. Gatineau, QC: Canadian Museum of Civilization.

Wright, Milton J. 1986. *The Uren Site AfHd-3: An Analysis and Reappraisal of the Uren Substage Type Site.* Monographs in Ontario Archaeology no. 2. Toronto: Ontario Archaeological Society.

Wykoff, Milton William. 1988. "Iroquoian Prehistory and Climate Change: Notes for Empirical Studies of the Eastern Woodlands." Ph.D. diss., Cornell Univ.

———. 1991. "Black Walnut on Iroquoian Landscapes." *Northeast Indian Quarterly* 8, no. 2:4–17.

3. Postcolumbian Dynamics

Abler, Thomas S. 1970. "Longhouse and Palisade: Northeastern Iroquoian Villages of the Seventeenth Century." *Ontario History* 62:17–40.

———. 1989. "European Technology and the Art of War in Iroquoia." In *Cultures in Conflict: Current Archaeological Perspectives,* edited by D. C. Tkaczuk and B. C. Vivian, 273–82. Proceedings of 20th Annual Chacmool Conference. Alberta: Archaeological Association of the Univ. of Calgary.

Bradley, James W. 1987. "Native Exchange and European Trade: Cross-Cultural Dynamics in the Sixteenth Century." *Man in the Northeast* 33:31–46.

———. 2001. "Change and Survival among the Onondaga Iroquois since 1500." In *Societies in Eclipse: Archaeology of the Eastern Woodlands Indians, A.D. 1400–1700,* edited by D. S. Brose, C. W. Cowan, and R. C. Mainfort Jr., 27–36. Washington, D.C.: Smithsonian Institution Press.

Casselberry, Samuel E. 1971. "The Schultz-Funck Site (36LA7): Its Role in the Culture History of the Susquehannock and Shenk's Ferry Indians." Ph.D. diss., Pennsylvania State Univ.

Clark, Lynn. 2004. "Gender at an Early Seventeenth-Century Oneida Village." Ph.D. diss., Binghamton Univ.

Damkjar, Eric R. 1990. *The Coulter Site and Late Iroquoian Coalescence in the Upper Trent Valley.* Occasional Papers in Northeastern Archaeology no. 2. Dundas, ON: Copetown Press.

Engelbrecht, William E. 1985. "New York Iroquois Political Development." In *Cultures in Contact: The European Impact on Native Cultural Institutions in Eastern North America, A.D. 1000–1800,* edited by W. W. Fitzhugh, 163–83. Washington, D.C.: Smithsonian Institution Press.

———. 1995. "The Case of the Disappearing Iroquoians: Early Contact Period Superpower Politics." *Northeast Anthropology* 50:35–59.

Ferris, Neal. 2006. "In Their Time: Archaeological Histories of Native-Lived Contacts and Colonialisms, Southwestern Ontario A.D. 1400–1900." Ph.D. diss., McMaster Univ.

Fitzgerald, William R. 1979. "The Hood Site: Longhouse Burials in an Historic Neutral Village." *Ontario Archaeology* 32:43–60.

———. 1982a. "A Refinement of Historic Neutral Chronologies: Evidence from Shaver Hill, Christianson, and Dwyer." *Ontario Archaeology* 38:31–47.

———. 1982b. *Lest the Beaver Run Loose: The Early 17th Century Christianson Site and Trends in Historic Neutral Archaeology.* National Museum of Man, Mercury Series, Archaeological Survey of Canada, Paper no. 111. Ottawa: National Museums of Canada.

———. 1986. "Is the Warminster Site Champlain's Cahiague?" *Ontario Archaeology* 45:3–7.

———. 1990. "Chronology to Cultural Process: Lower Great Lakes Archaeology 1500–1650." Ph.D. diss., McGill Univ.

———. 2001. "Contact, Neutral Iroquoian Transformation, and the Little Ice Age." In *Societies in Eclipse: Archaeology of the Eastern Woodlands Indians, A.D. 1400–1700*, edited by D. S. Brose, C. W. Cowan, and R. C. Mainfort Jr., 37–47. Washington, D.C.: Smithsonian Institution Press.

Gramly, Richard M. 1996. *Two Early Historic Iroquoian Sites in Western New York.* Buffalo, N.Y.: Persimmon Press.

Guldenzopf, David B. 1984. "Frontier Demography and Settlement Patterns of the Mohawk Iroquois." *Man in the Northeast* 27:79–94.

———. 1986. "The Colonial Transformation of Mohawk Iroquois Society." Ph.D. diss., State Univ. of New York at Albany.

1986. "The Colonial Transformation of Mohawk Iroquois Society." Ph.D. diss., State Univ. of New York at Albany.

Hayes, Charles F., III, Connie Cox Bodner, and Lorraine P. Saunders, eds. 1994. *Proceedings of the 1992 People to People Conference: Selected Papers.* Research Records no. 23. Rochester, N.Y.: Rochester Museum and Science Center.

Heisey, Henry W., and J. Paul Witmer. 1962. "Of Historic Susquehannock Cemeteries." *Pennsylvania Archaeologist* 32, nos. 3–4:99–120.

Huey, Paul R. 1988. "Aspects of Continuity and Change at Fort Orange, 1624–1664." Ph.D. diss., Univ. of Pennsylvania.

Jackes, Mary K. 1977. "The Huron Spine: A Study Based on the Kleinburg Ossuary Vertebrae." Ph.D. diss., Univ. of Toronto.

———. 1983. "Osteological Evidence for Smallpox: A Possible Case from Seventeenth Century Ontario." *American Journal of Physical Anthropology* 60, no. 1:75–81.

———. 1986. "The Mortality of Ontario Archaeological Populations." *Canadian Journal of Anthropology* 5, no. 2:33–48.

———. 1996. "Complexity in Seventeenth Century Southern Ontario Burial Practices." In *Debating Complexity*, edited by D. A. Meyer, P. C. Dawson, and D. T. Hanna, 127–40. Proceedings of the 26th Annual Chacmool Conference. Alberta: Archaeological Association of the Univ. of Calgary.

Jamieson, James Bruce. 1990. "Trade and Warfare: The Disappearance of the Saint Lawrence Iroquoians." *Man in the Northeast* 39:79–86.

Jerkic, Sonja M. 1975. "An Analysis of Huron Skeletal Biology and Mortuary Practices: The Maurice Ossuary." Ph.D. diss., Univ. of Toronto.

Johnson, William C. 2001. "The Protohistoric Monongahela and the Case for an Iroquois Connection." In *Societies in Eclipse: Archaeology of the Eastern Woodlands Indians, A.D. 1400–1700*, edited by D. S. Brose, C. W. Cowan, and R. C. Mainfort Jr., 67–82. Washington, D.C.: Smithsonian Institution Press.

Johnston, Richard B., and L. J. Jackson. 1980. "Settlement Pattern at the Le Caron Site, a 17th Century Huron Village." *Journal of Field Archaeology* 7, no. 2:173–99.

Jordan, Kurt A. 2002. "The Archaeology of the Iroquois Restoration: Settlement, Housing, and Economy at a Dispersed Seneca Community, ca. A.D. 1715–1754." Ph.D. diss., Columbia Univ.

———. 2003. "An Eighteenth Century Seneca Iroquois Short Longhouse from the Townley-Read Site, c. A.D. 1715–1754." *The Bulletin: Journal of the New York State Archaeological Association* 119:49–63.

———. 2004. "Seneca Iroquois Settlement Pattern, Community Structure, and Housing, 1677–1779." *Northeast Anthropology* 67:23–60.

Jury, Wilfrid, and Elsie McLeod Murray Jury. 1954. *Sainte-Marie among the Hurons*. Toronto: Oxford Univ. Press.

———. 1955. *Saint Louis: Huron Indian Village and Jesuit Mission Site*. Bulletin no. 10. London, ON: London Museum of Archaeology.

Kapches, Mima. 2002. "Kidd's 'Chapel' and Its Longhouse Origins at Ste Marie among the Hurons." *The Bulletin: Journal of the New York State Archaeological Association* 118:41–48.

Kenyon, Walter A. 1982. *The Grimsby Site: A Historic Neutral Cemetery*. Toronto: Publications in Archaeology, Royal Ontario Museum.

Kidd, Kenneth E. 1949. *The Excavation of Ste. Marie I*. Toronto: Univ. of Toronto Press.

———. 1953. "The Excavation and Historical Identification of a Huron Ossuary." *American Antiquity* 18, no. 4:359–79.

———. 1969. *Historic Archaeology in Canada*. Anthropological Paper no. 22. Ottawa: National Museum of Canada.

Knight, Dean H. 1978. "The Ball Site: A Preliminary Statement." *Ontario Archaeology* 29:53–63.

———. 1987. "Settlement Patterns at the Ball Site: A 17th Century Huron Village." *Archaeology of Eastern North America* 15:177–88.

———. 1989. "Huron Houses: Structures from the Ball Site." In *Households and Com-

munities, edited by S. MacEachern, D. J. W. Archer, and R. D. Garvin, 287–92. Proceedings of the 21st Annual Chacmool Conference. Alberta: Archaeological Association of the Univ. of Calgary.

———. 2002. "The Function of Longhouses: An Example from the Ball Site." *The Bulletin: Journal of the New York State Archaeological Association* 118:27–40.

Knight, Dean H., and F. Jerry Melbye. 1983. "Burial Patterns at the Ball Site." *Ontario Archaeology* 40:37–48.

Kraus, Bertram S. 1944. "Acculturation: A New Approach to the Iroquoian Problem." *American Antiquity* 9, no. 3:302–18.

Lantz, Stanley W. 1980. "Seneca Cabin Site: Historic Component of the Venatta Site (30CA46)." *Pennsylvania Archaeologist* 50, nos. 1–2:9–41.

Latta, Martha A. 1976. "The Iroquoian Cultures of Huronia: A Study of Acculturation Through Archaeology." Ph.D. diss., Univ. of Toronto.

———. 1985a. "A 17th Century Attigneenongnahac Village: Settlement Patterns at the Auger Site (BdGw-3)." *Ontario Archaeology* 44:41–54.

———. 1985b. "Identification of 17th Century French Missions in Eastern Huronia." *Canadian Journal of Archaeology* 9:147–71.

Lenig, Donald. 1977. "Of Dutchmen, Beaver Hats and Iroquois." In *Current Perspectives in Northeastern Archaeology: Essays in Honor of William A. Ritchie*, edited by R. E. Funk and C. F. Hayes III, 71–84. Researches and Transactions of the New York State Archaeological Association 17, no 1. Rochester.

Lennox, Paul A. 1981. *The Hamilton Site: A Late Historic Neutral Town.* National Museum of Man, Mercury Series, Archaeological Survey of Canada, Paper no. 103, 211–403. Ottawa: National Museums of Canada.

———. 1984a. *The Hood Site: A Historic Neutral Town of 1640 A.D.* National Museum of Man, Mercury Series, Archaeological Survey of Canada, Paper no. 121, 1–183. Ottawa: National Museums of Canada.

———. 1984b. *The Bogle I and Bogle II Sites: Historic Neutral Hamlets of the Northern Tier.* National Museum of Man, Mercury Series, Archaeological Survey of Canada, Paper no. 121, 184–289. Ottawa: National Museums of Canada.

Mandzy, Adrian. 1990. "The Rogers Farm Site: A Seventeenth-Century Cayuga Site." *The Bulletin: Journal of the New York State Archaeological Association* 100:18–25.

Melbye, F. Jerry. 1983. "The People of the Ball Site." *Ontario Archaeology* 40:15–36.

Noble, William C. 1978. "The Neutral Indians." In *Essays in Northeastern Anthropology: In Memory of Marian E. White,* edited by W. E. Engelbrecht and D. K. Grayson, 152–64. Occasional Publications in Northeastern Anthropology no. 5. Rindge, N.H.

———. 1980. "Thorold: An Early Historic Niagara Neutral Town." In *Villages in the Niagara Peninsula,* edited by J. Burtniak and W. B. Turner, 43–55. St. Catharines, ON: Brock Univ.

———. 1984 "Historic Neutral Iroquois Settlement Patterns." *Canadian Journal of Archaeology* 8, no. 1:3–27.

———. 1985. "Tsouharissen's Chiefdom: An Early Historic 17th Century Neutral Iroquoian Ranked Society." *Canadian Journal of Archaeology* 9, no. 2:131–46.

———. 2002. "Historic Neutral Iroquois Settlement Structures." *The Bulletin, Journal of the New York State Archaeological Association* 118:19–26.

Parker, Arthur C. 1919. *A Contact Period Seneca Site Situated at Factory Hollow, Ontario County, N.Y.* Researches and Transactions of the New York State Archaeological Association 1, no. 2. Rochester.

Pendergast, James F., and Bruce G. Trigger, eds. 1972. *Cartier's Hochelaga and the Dawson Site.* Montreal: McGill-Queen's Univ. Press.

Pfeiffer, Susan. 1985. "Comparison of Adult Age Estimation Techniques, Using an Ossuary Sample." *Canadian Journal of Anthropology* 4, no. 2:13–17.

Pfeiffer, Susan, and Scott I. Fairgrieve. 1994. "Evidence from Ossuaries: The Effect of Contact on the Health of Iroquoians." In *In the Wake of Contact: Biological Responses to Conquest*, edited by C. S. Larsen and G. R. Milner, 47–61. New York: Wiley-Liss.

Pfeiffer, Susan, and Patricia King. 1983. "Cortical Bone Formation and Diet among Protohistoric Iroquoians." *American Journal of Physical Anthropology* 60:23–28.

Prevec, Rosemary, and William C. Noble. 1983. "Historic Neutral Iroquois Faunal Utilization." *Ontario Archaeology* 39:41–56.

Ramsden, Carol Naismith. 1989. *The Kirche Site: A 16th Century Huron Village in the Upper Trent Valley.* Occasional Papers in Northeastern Archaeology no. 1. Dundas, ON: Copetown Press.

Ramsden, Peter G. 1978. "An Hypothesis Concerning the Effects of Early European Trade among Some Ontario Iroquois." *Canadian Journal of Archaeology* 2:101–6.

Ritchie, William A. 1954. *Dutch Hollow, An Early Historic Period Seneca Site in Livingston County, New York.* Research Records no. 10. Rochester, N.Y.: Rochester Museum of Arts and Sciences.

Saunders, Lorraine P. 1986. "Biological Affinities among Historic Seneca Groups and Possible Precursive Populations." Ph.D. diss., Univ. of Texas.

Sempowski, Martha L. 1987. "Differential Mortuary Treatment of Seneca Women: Some Social Inferences." *The Bulletin: Journal of the New York State Archaeological Association* 95:50–57.

———. 1994. "Early Historic Exchange Between the Seneca and the Susquehannock." In *Proceedings of the 1992 People to People Conference: Selected Papers*, edited by C. F. Hayes III, C. C. Bodner, and L. P. Saunders, 51–64. Research Records no. 23. Rochester, N.Y.: Rochester Museum and Science Center.

Sempowski, Martha L., and Lorraine P. Saunders. 2001. *Dutch Hollow and Factory Hollow: The Advent of Dutch Trade among the Seneca.* Parts 1, 2, and 3. Charles F.

Wray Series in Seneca Archaeology. Vol. 3. Research Records no. 24. Rochester, N.Y.: Rochester Museum and Science Center.

Sempowski, Martha L., Lorraine P. Saunders, and Gian C. Cervone. 1988. "The Adams and Culbertson Sites: A Hypothesis for Village Formation." *Man in the Northeast* 35:95–108.

Smith, Ira F., III, and Jeffrey R. Graybill. 1977. "A Report on the Shenks Ferry and Susquehannock Components at the Funk Site, Lancaster County, Pennsylvania." *Man in the Northeast* 13:45–65.

Snow, Dean R. 1996. "Mohawk Demography and the Effects of Exogenous Epidemics on American Indian Population." *Journal of Anthropological Archaeology* 15, no. 2:160–82.

Snow, Dean R., and David B. Guldenzopf. 1998. "The Mohawk Upper Castle Historic District National Historic Landmark." *The Bulletin: Journal of the New York State Archaeological Association* 114:32–44.

Snow, Dean R., and Kim M. Lanphear. 1988. "European Contact and Indian Depopulation in the Northeast: The Timing of the First Epidemics." *Ethnohistory* 35, no. 1:15–33.

Snow, Dean R., and William A. Starna. 1989. "Sixteenth-Century Depopulation: A View from the Mohawk Valley." *American Anthropologist* 91:142–49.

Sohrweide, Gregory A. 2001. "Onondaga Longhouses in the Late Seventeenth Century on the Weston Site." *The Bulletin: Journal of the New York State Archaeological Association* 117:1–24.

Stewart, Marilyn C. 1973. "A Proto-Historic Susquehannock Cemetery Near Nichols, Tioga County, New York." *The Bulletin: Journal of the New York State Archaeological Association* 58:1–21.

Stothers, David. M. 1971. "The Shaver Hill Burial Complex: Reflections of a Neutral Indian Population." Ph.D. diss., Case Western Reserve Univ.

Sullivan, Norman C. 1997. "Contact Period Huron Demography." In *Integrating Archaeological Demography: Multidisciplinary Approaches to Prehistoric Population*, edited by R. R. Paine, 327–42. Occasional Paper no. 24. Carbondale: Center for Archaeological Investigations, Southern Illinois Univ.

Sykes, Clark M. 1983. "An Archaeological and Ethnohistorical Analysis of Huron Intra-Community Exchange Systems." Ph.D. diss., Univ. of Toronto.

Trigger, Bruce G. 1960. "The Destruction of Huronia: A Study in Economic and Cultural Change, 1609–1650." *Transactions of the Royal Canadian Institute* 33, no. 1:14–45. Toronto.

———. 1963. "Settlement as an Aspect of Iroquoian Adaptation at the Time of Contact." *American Anthropologist* 65, no. 1:86–101.

———. 1979. "Sixteenth Century Ontario: History, Ethnohistory, and Archaeology." *Ontario History* 71:205–23.

———. 1981. "Ontario Native People and the Epidemics of 1634–1640." In *Indians,*

Animals, and the Fur Trade: A Critique of 'Keepers of the Game,'" edited by S. Krech III, 19–38. Athens: Univ. of Georgia Press.

———. 1985. *Natives and Newcomers: Canada's "Heroic Age" Reconsidered.* Montreal: McGill-Queen's Univ. Press.

Tummon, Jeanie, and W. Barry Gray, eds. 1995. *Before and Beyond Sainte-Marie: 1987–1990 Excavations at the Sainte-Marie among the Hurons Site Complex.* Dundas, ON: Copetown Press.

Vandrei, Charles. 1987. "Observations on Seneca Settlement in the Early Historic Period." *The Bulletin: Journal of the New York State Archaeological Association* 95:8–17.

Warrick, Gary A. 2003. "European Infectious Disease and Depopulation of the Wendat-Tionontate (Huron-Petun)." *World Archaeology* 35, no. 2:258–75.

White, Marian E. 1967. "An Early Historic Niagara Frontier Iroquois Cemetery in Erie County, New York." *Researches and Transactions of the New York State Archaeological Association* 16, no. 1:1–36, 58–91. Rochester.

———. 1968. "A Re-examination of the Historic Iroquois Van Son Cemetery on Grand Island." *Bulletin of the Buffalo Society of Natural Sciences* 24:3–48.

Whitney, Theodore. 1970. "The Buyea Site, Ond 13–3." *The Bulletin: Journal of the New York State Archaeological Association* 50:1–14.

Wintemberg, William J. 1946. "The Sidey-Mackay Village Site." *American Antiquity* 11, no. 3:154–82.

Wray, Charles F., Martha L. Sempowski, and Lorraine P. Saunders. 1991. *Tram and Cameron: Two Early Contact Era Seneca Sites.* Charles F. Wray Series in Seneca Archaeology. Vol. 2. Research Records no. 21. Rochester, N.Y.: Rochester Museum and Science Center.

Wray, Charles F., Martha L. Sempowski, Lorraine P. Saunders, and Gian C. Cervone. 1987. *The Adams and Culbertson Sites.* Charles F. Wray Series in Seneca Archaeology. Vol. 1. Research Records no. 19. Rochester, N.Y.: Rochester Museum and Science Center.

Wright, Milton J. 1981. *The Walker Site.* National Museum of Man, Mercury Series, Archaeological Survey of Canada, Paper no. 103, 1–210. Ottawa: National Museums of Canada.

4. Material Culture Studies

Allen, Kathleen M. S. 1988. "Ceramic Style and Social Continuity in an Iroquoian Tribe." Ph.D. diss., State Univ. of New York at Buffalo.

———. 1992. "Iroquois Ceramic Production: A Case Study of Household-Level Organization." In *Ceramic Production and Distribution: An Integrated Approach*, edited by G. J. Bey III and C. A. Pool, 133–54. Boulder, Colo.: Westview Press.

Allen, Kathleen, and Ezra Zubrow. 1989. "Environmental Factors in Ceramic Production: The Iroquois." In *Ceramic Ecology, 1988: Current Research on Ceramic*

Materials, edited by C. C. Kolb, 61–95. British Archaeological Reports International Series no. 513. Oxford, UK.

Beauchamp, William M. 1882. "Indian Pipes." *American Antiquarian* 4, no. 4:326–29.

———. 1897. *Polished Stone Articles Used by the New York Aborigines Before and During European Occupation.* New York State Museum Bulletin 4, no. 18. Albany: State Univ. of New York.

———. 1898. *Earthenware of the New York Aborigines.* New York State Museum Bulletin 5, no. 22. Albany: State Univ. of New York.

———. 1901. *Wampum and Shell Articles Used by the New York Indians.* New York State Museum Bulletin 8, no. 41. Albany: State Univ. of New York.

———. 1902a. *Horn and Bone Implements of the New York Indians.* New York State Museum Bulletin 50. Albany: State Univ. of New York.

———. 1902b. *Metallic Implements of the New York Indians.* New York State Museum Bulletin 55. Albany: State Univ. of New York.

———. 1903. *Metallic Ornaments of New York Indians.* New York State Museum Bulletin 73. Albany: State Univ. of New York.

Boyle, David. 1898. "Clay and Stone Pipes." *Annual Archaeological Report for Ontario, 1897–98,* 17–22. Appendix to the Report of the Minister of Education for Ontario. Toronto.

———. 1901. "The Human Face in Clay." *Annual Archaeological Report for Ontario, 1900,* 18–21. Appendix to the Report of the Minister of Education for Ontario. Toronto.

———. 1904. "Stone and Brass Smoking Pipes." *Annual Archaeological Report for Ontario, 1903,* 57, 91. Appendix to the Report of the Minister of Education for Ontario. Toronto.

Bradley, James W. 1980a. "Dutch Bale Seals from 17th Century Onondaga Iroquois Sites in New York State." *Post-Medieval Archaeology* 14:197–200.

———. 1980b. "Ironwork in Onondaga, 1550–1650." In *Studies in Iroquoian Culture,* edited by N. Bonvillain, 109–18. Occasional Publications in Northeastern Anthropology no. 6. Rindge, N.H.

Bradley, James W., and Monte R. Bennett. 1984. "Two Occurrences of Weser Slipware from Early 17th Century Iroquois Sites in New York State." *Post-Medieval Archaeology* 18:301–5.

Bradley, James W., and S. Terry Childs. 1991. "Basque Earrings and Panther's Tails: The Form of Cross-Cultural Contact in Sixteenth Century Iroquoia." In *Metals in Society: Theory Beyond Analysis,* edited by R. M. Ehrenreich, 7–17. MASCA Research Papers in Science and Archaeology 8, no. 2. Philadelphia: Univ. Museum of Archaeology and Anthropology, Univ. of Pennsylvania.

Bradley, James W., and Gordon DeAngelo. 1981. "European Clay Pipe Marks from 17th Century Onondaga Iroquois Sites." *Archaeology of Eastern North America* 9:109–33.

Brasser, Ted J. 1980. "Self-Directed Pipe Effigies." *Man in the Northeast* 19:95–104.

Brumbach, Hetty Jo. 1975. " 'Iroquoian' Ceramics in 'Algonkian' Territory." *Man in the Northeast* 10:17–28.

———. 1985. "Ceramic Analysis and the Investigation of Matrilocality at the Smith Mohawk Site." *North American Archaeologist* 6, no. 4:341–55.

———. 1995. "Algonquian and Iroquoian Ceramics in the Upper Hudson River Drainage." *Northeast Anthropology* 49:55–66.

Carmody, Michael L. 2003. "Tools of Contact: A Functional Analysis of the Cameron Site Chipped-Stone Assemblage." In *Stone Tool Traditions in the Contact Era,* edited by C. R. Cobb, 59–77. Tuscaloosa: Univ. of Alabama Press.

Carpenter, Edmund S. 1942. "Iroquoian Figurines." *American Antiquity* 8, no. 1:105–13.

Cassedy, Daniel F., Paul A. Webb, and James W. Bradley. 1996. "The Vanderwerken Site: A Protohistoric Iroquois Occupation on Schoharie Creek." *The Bulletin: Journal of the New York State Archaeological Association* 111–12:21–34.

Ceci, Lynn. 1982. "The Value of Wampum among the New York Iroquois: A Case Study in Artifact Analysis." *Journal of Anthropological Research* 38, no. 1:97–107.

———. 1986. *The Origins of Wampum among the Seneca Iroquois.* Rochester, N.Y.: Rochester Museum and Science Center.

———. 1990. "Native Wampum as a Peripheral Resource in the Seventeenth-Century World-System." In *The Pequots in Southern New England: The Rise and Fall of an American Indian Nation,* edited by J. D. Wherry and L. Hauptman, 48–63. Norman: Univ. of Oklahoma Press.

Cervone, Gian C. 1987. "Seneca Pottery Analysis: Some Problems and Solutions in Refining the Potential of Attribute Analysis." *The Bulletin: Journal of the New York State Archaeological Association* 95:23–31.

Chapdelaine, Claude. 1992. "Mandeville Site: A Small Iroquoian Village and a Large Smoking-Pipe Collection—An Interpretation." In *Proceedings of the 1989 Smoking Pipe Conference: Selected Papers,* edited by C. F. Hayes III, C. C. Bodner, and M. L. Sempowski, 31–40. Research Records no. 22. Rochester, N.Y.: Rochester Museum and Science Center.

Chapdelaine, Claude, and Gregory G. Kennedy. 1990. "The Origin of the Iroquoian Rim Sherd from Red Bay." *Man in the Northeast* 40:41–44.

Chapdelaine, Claude, Laurier Turgeon, Gregory Kennedy, and D. Lalande. 1990. "The Origin of the Iroquoian Rim Sherd from Ile aux Basques." *Canadian Journal of Archaeology* 16:96–101.

Chilton, Elizabeth S. 1998. "The Cultural Origins of Technical Choice: Unraveling Algonquian and Iroquoian Ceramic Traditions in the Northeast." In *The Archaeology of Social Boundaries,* edited by M. T. Stark, 132–60. Washington, D.C.: Smithsonian Institution Press.

———. 1999. "One Size Fits All: Typology and Alternatives for Ceramic Research."

In *Material Meanings: Critical Approaches to the Interpretation of Material Culture,* edited by E. S. Chilton, 44–60. Salt Lake City: Univ. of Utah Press.

Cowin, Verna L. 2000. "Shell Ornaments from Cayuga County, New York." *Archaeology of Eastern North America* 28:1–13.

Crépeau, Robert R., and Gregory G. Kennedy. 1990. "Neutron Activation of St. Lawrence Iroquoian Pottery." *Man in the Northeast* 40:65–74.

Custer, Jay F. 1985. "Analysis of Grave Good Assemblages from the Strickler Site, a Contact Period Susquehannock Site in Lancaster County, Pennsylvania." *Journal of Middle Atlantic Archaeology* 1:33–42.

Dawson, Kenneth C. A. 1979. "Algonkian Huron-Petun Ceramics in Northern Ontario." *Man in the Northeast* 18:14–31.

Dunbar, Helene R., and Katharine C. Ruhl. 1974. "Copper Artifacts from the Engelbert Site." *The Bulletin: Journal of the New York State Archaeological Association* 61:1–10.

Emerson, J. Norman. 1968. *Understanding Iroquois Pottery in Ontario: A Rethinking.* Special Publication of the Ontario Archaeological Society no. 2. Toronto.

Engelbrecht, William E. 1971. "A Stylistic Analysis of New York Iroquois Pottery." Ph.D. diss., Univ. of Michigan.

———. 1972. "The Reflection of Pattern Behavior in Iroquois Pottery." *Pennsylvania Archaeologist* 42, no. 3:1–15.

———. 1974. "Cluster Analysis: A Method for the Study of Iroquois Prehistory." *Man in the Northeast* 7:57–70.

———. 1978. "Ceramic Patterning between New York Iroquois Sites." In *The Spatial Organisation of Culture,* edited by I. Hodder, 141–52. Pittsburgh, Pa.: Univ. of Pittsburgh Press.

———. 1984. "The Kleis Site Ceramics: An Interpretive Approach." In *Extending the Rafters: Interdisciplinary Approaches to Iroquoian Studies,* edited by M. K. Foster, J. Campisi, and M. Mithun, 325–42. Albany: State Univ. of New York Press.

Fitzgerald, William R., Dean H. Knight, and Allison Bain. 1995. "Untanglers of Matters Temporal and Cultural: Glass Beads and the Early Contact Period Huron Ball Site." *Canadian Journal of Archaeology* 19:117–38.

Fitzgerald, William R., and Peter G. Ramsden. 1988. "Copper Based Metal Testing as an Aid to Understanding Early European-Amerindian Interaction: Scratching the Surface." *Canadian Journal of Archaeology* 12:153–62.

Fitzgerald, William R., Laurier Turgeon, R. Holmes Whitehead, and James W. Bradley. 1993. "Late Sixteenth-Century Basque Banded Copper Kettles." *Historical Archaeology* 27, no. 1:44–57.

Fogelman, Gary L. 1991. *Glass Trade Beads in the Northeast and Including Aboriginal Bead Industries.* Turbotville, Pa.: Fogelman Publishing.

Fox, William A. 1979. "An Analysis of an Historic Huron Attignawantan Lithic Assemblage." *Ontario Archaeology* 32:61–88.

Garrad, Charles. 1969. "Iron Trade Knives on Historic Petun Sites." *Ontario Archaeology* 13:3–15.

Hagerty, Gilbert. 1963. "The Iron Trade-Knife in Oneida Territory." *Pennsylvania Archaeologist* 33, nos. 1–2:93–114.

———. 1985. *Wampum, War and Trade Goods West of the Hudson.* Interlaken, N.Y.: Heart of the Lakes Publishing.

Hamell, George R. 1992. "The Iroquois and the World's Rim: Speculations on Color, Culture, and Contact." *The American Indian Quarterly* 16:451–69.

———. 1996. "Wampum: Light, White, and Bright Things Are Good to Think." In *One Man's Trash Is Another Man's Treasure,* edited by A. van Dongen, 41–51. Williamsburg, Va.: Jamestown Settlement Museum.

———. 1998. "Long-Tail: The Panther in Huron-Wyandot and Seneca Myth, Ritual, and Material Culture." In *Icons of Power: Feline Symbolism in the Americas,* edited by N. J. Saunders, 258–91. London: Routledge.

Hancock, R. G. V., L. A. Pavlish, R. M. Farquar, R. Salloum, William A. Fox, and G. C. Wilson. 1991. "Distinguishing European Trade Copper and Northeastern North American Native Copper." *Archaeometry* 33, no. 1:69–86.

Harrington, Mark R. 1909. "Some Unusual Iroquois Specimens." *American Anthropologist* 11, no. 1:85–91.

Hayes, Charles F., III, Connie Cox Bodner, and Martha L. Sempowski, eds. 1992. *Proceedings of the 1989 Smoking Pipe Conference: Selected Papers.* Research Records no. 22. Rochester, N.Y.: Rochester Museum and Science Center.

Hayes, Charles F., III, Nancy Bolger, Karlis Karklins, and Charles F. Wray, eds. 1983. *Proceedings of the 1982 Glass Trade Bead Conference.* Research Records no. 16. Rochester, N.Y.: Rochester Museum and Science Center.

Hayes, Charles F., III, Lynn Ceci, and Connie Cox Bodner, eds. 1989. *Proceedings of the 1986 Shell Bead Conference: Selected Papers.* Research Records no. 20. Rochester, N.Y.: Rochester Museum and Science Center.

Hayes, Charles F., III, George R. Hamell, and Barbara M. Koenig, eds. 1980. *Proceedings of the 1979 Iroquois Pottery Conference.* Research Records no. 13. Rochester, N.Y.: Rochester Museum and Science Center.

Hayes, Charles F., III, and Jan Piet Puype, eds. 1985. *Proceedings of the 1984 Trade Gun Conference.* Part 1, "Dutch and Other Flintlocks from Seventeenth Century Iroquois Sites." Part 2, "Selected Papers." Research Records no. 18. Rochester, N.Y.: Rochester Museum and Science Center.

Hewitt, John N. B. 1907–10. "Wampum." In *Handbook of American Indians North of Mexico.* Part 2, edited by F. W. Hodge, 904–9. Bureau of American Ethnology Bulletin 30. Washington, D.C.: Smithsonian Institution.

Howes, William J. 1960. "Iroquoian-Mohawk Pottery of the Champlain Valley Area, Northern Vermont." *Bulletin of the Massachusetts Archaeological Society* 21, nos. 3–4:56–60.

Hunter, James R. 1986. "Summary of Huron Bead Sequence, A.D. 1590–1650." *The Bead Forum* 8.

Jamieson, Susan M. 1984. "Neutral Iroquois Lithics: Technological Process and Its Implications." Ph.D. diss., Washington State Univ.

Kapches, Mima. 1980. "Iroquois Effigy Rattle Pipes." *Ontario Archaeology* 33:59–68.

———. 1988. "The Analysis of Lithics from Four Markham Middleport Iroquoian Sites." *North American Archaeologist* 9, no. 1:1–16.

———. 1994. "The Hill Site: A Possible Late Early Iroquoian Ceramic Firing Site in South-Central Ontario." *Northeast Anthropology* 48:91–102.

Karklins, Karlis. 1974. "Seventeenth Century Dutch Beads." *Historical Archaeology* 8:64–82.

———. 1982. "Guide to the Description and Classification of Glass Beads." *History and Archaeology* 59:83–117. Ottawa: Parks Canada.

———. 1986. "A Note on the Neutron Activation Analysis of the 16th and 17th Century Blue Glass Trade Beads from the Eastern Great Lakes." *The Bead Forum* 9.

Karklins, Karlis, and Roderick Sprague. 1972. *Glass Trade Beads in North America: An Annotated Bibliography.* Historical Archaeology 6:87–101.

———. 1980. *A Bibliography of Glass Trade Beads in North America.* Moscow, Idaho: South Forks Press.

Kenyon, Ian T., and William R. Fitzgerald. 1986. "Dutch Glass Beads in the Northeast: An Ontario Perspective." *Man in the Northeast* 32:1–34.

Kidd, Kenneth E. 1954. "Fashions in Tobacco Pipes among the Iroquois Indians of Canada." *Royal Ontario Museum of Archaeology Bulletin* 22:15–21.

———. 1979. *Glass Bead-Making from the Middle Ages to the Early 19th Century.* History and Archaeology 30. National Historic Parks and Sites Branch. Ottawa: Parks Canada.

Kidd, Kenneth E., and Martha A. Kidd. 1970. "A Classification System for Glass Beads for the Use of Field Archaeologists." In *Canadian Historic Sites, Occasional Papers in Archaeology and History,* no. 1, 45–89. Ottawa.

Kist, Johannes B., Jan P. Puype, and R. B. F. van der Sloot. 1974. *Dutch Muskets and Pistols: An Illustrated History of Seventeenth Century Gunmaking in the Low Countries.* York, Pa.: George Shumway.

Kuhn, Robert D. 1985. "Trade and Exchange among the Mohawk-Iroquois: A Trace Element Analysis of Ceramic Smoking Pipes." Ph.D. diss., State Univ. of New York at Albany.

———. 1986. "Interaction Patterns in Eastern New York: A Trace Element Analysis of Iroquoian and Algonkian Ceramics." *The Bulletin: Journal of the New York State Archaeological Association* 92:9–21.

———. 1987. "Trade and Exchange among the Mohawk-Iroquois: A Trace Element Analysis of Ceramic Smoking Pipes." *North American Archaeologist* 8, no. 4:305–15.

———. 1989. "The Trace Element Analysis of Hudson Valley Clays and Ceramics." *The Bulletin: Journal of the New York State Archaeological Association* 99:25–30.

———. 1994a. "The Cromwell Site (NYSM 1121), Including a Brief Treatise on Early Seventeenth-Century Mohawk Pottery Trends." *The Bulletin: Journal of the New York State Archaeological Association* 108:29–38.

———. 1994b. "A Comparison of Human Face Effigy Pipes from the St. Lawrence Iroquoian Roebuck Site and the Mohawk Otstungo Site Using Trace Element Analysis." *The Ottawa Archaeologist* 21, no. 2:3–9.

———. 2004. "Reconstructing Patterns of Interaction and Warfare Between the Mohawk and Northern Iroquoians During the A.D. 1400–1700 Period." In *A Passion for the Past: Papers in Honour of James F. Pendergast*, edited by J. V. Wright and J.-L. Pilon, 145–66. Mercury Series, Archaeology Paper no. 164. Gatineau, QC: Canadian Museum of Civilization.

Kuhn, Robert D., and Susan E. Bamann. 1987. "A Preliminary Report on the Attribute Analysis of Mohawk Ceramics." *The Bulletin: Journal of the New York State Archaeological Association* 94:40–46.

Laidlaw, George E. 1902. "Effigy Pipes." *Annual Archaeological Report for Ontario, 1901*, 37–58. Appendix to the Report of the Minister of Education for Ontario. Toronto.

Latta, Martha A. 1987. "Iroquoian Stemware." *American Antiquity* 52, no. 4:717–24.

———. 1990. "The Stem of the Matter: Reply to Ramsden and Fitzgerald." *American Antiquity* 55, no. 1:162–65.

Lenig, Wayne. 1999. "Patterns of Material Culture in the First Quarter Century of New Netherlands Trade." *Northeast Anthropology* 58:47–74.

Lennox, Paul A., and Ian T. Kenyon. 1984. "Was That Middleport Necked or Pound Oblique? A Study in Iroquoian Ceramic Typology." *Ontario Archaeology* 42:13–26.

MacNeish, Richard S. 1952. *Iroquois Pottery Types: A Technique for the Study of Iroquois Prehistory*. Bulletin 124, Anthropological Series no. 31. Ottawa: National Museum of Canada.

Mathews, Zena Pearlstone. 1976. "Huron Pipes and Iroquoian Shamanism." *Man in the Northeast* 12:15–31.

———. 1978. *The Relation of Seneca False Face Masks to Seneca and Ontario Archaeology*. New York: Garland Publishing.

———. 1980a. "Of Man and Beast: The Chronology of Effigy Pipes among Ontario Iroquoians." *Ethnohistory* 27, no. 4:295–307.

———. 1980b. "Seneca Figurines: A Case Study of Misplaced Modesty." In *Studies in Iroquoian Culture*, edited by N. Bonvillain, 71–90. Occasional Publications in Northeastern Anthropology no. 6. Rindge, N.H.

———. 1981a. "The Identification of Animals on Ontario Iroquoian Pipes." *Canadian Journal of Archaeology* 5:31–47.

———. 1981b. "Janus and Other Multiple-Image Iroquoian Pipes." *Ontario Archaeology* 35:3–22.

———. 1982. "On Dreams and Journeys: Iroquoian Boat Pipes." *American Indian Art Magazine* 7, no. 3:46–51, 80.

Mayer, Joseph R. 1943. *Flintlocks of the Iroquois, 1620–1687*. Research Records no. 6. Rochester, N.Y.: Rochester Museum of Arts and Sciences.

McCashion, John H. 1975. "The Clay Tobacco Pipes of New York State (Part I: Caughnawaga 1667–1693)." *The Bulletin: Journal of the New York State Archaeological Association* 65:1–19.

———. 1979. "A Preliminary Chronology and Discussion of Seventeenth Century Clay Tobacco Pipes from New York State Sites." In *The Archaeology of the Clay Tobacco Pipe*, edited by P. Davey, 63–149. British Archaeological Reports International Series no. 60. Oxford, UK.

———. 1992. "The Clay Tobacco Pipes of New York State (Part IV)." *The Bulletin: Journal of the New York State Archaeological Association* 103:1–9.

Mitchell, Barry M. 1975. "Late Ceramics in Central Eastern Ontario: Iroquois or Algonquin?" *Ontario Archaeology* 25:61–77.

Motykova, Karla. 1969. "Seventeenth Century Huron Glass Beads." In *Palaeocology and Ontario Prehistory*, edited by W. M. Hurley and C. E. Heidrenreich, 88–104. Research Report. Toronto: Department of Anthropology, Univ. of Toronto.

Navias, R. A. 1995. "Iroquois Lanceolate Projectile Points." *The Bulletin: Journal of the New York State Archaeological Association* 109:28–33.

Niemczycki, Mary Ann Palmer. 1995. "Ceramics and Ethnicity in West-Central New York: Exploring Owasco-Iroquois Connections." *Northeast Anthropology* 49: 43–54.

Noble, William C. 1971. "The Sopher Celt: An Indicator of Early Protohistoric Trade in Huronia." *Ontario Archaeology* 16:42–47.

———. 1979. "Ontario Iroquois Effigy Pipes." *Canadian Journal of Archaeology* 3:69–89.

Pearce, Robert J. 1985a. *Draper Site Ground and Rough Stone Artifacts*. Research Report no. 17. London, ON: London Museum of Archaeology.

———. 1985b. *Draper Site Miscellaneous Ceramic Artifacts*. Research Report no. 18. London, ON: London Museum of Archaeology.

Peña, Elizabeth S. 1990. "Wampum Production in New Netherland and Colonial New York: The Historical and Archaeological Context." Ph.D. diss., Boston Univ.

Pendergast, James F. 1973. *The Roebuck Prehistoric Village Site Rim Sherds—An Attribute Analysis*. National Museum of Man, Mercury Series, Archaeological Survey of Canada, Paper no. 8. Ottawa: National Museums of Canada.

———. 1981. "Distribution of Iroquoian Discoidal Clay Beads." *Ontario Archaeology* 36:57–72.

Poulton, Dana R. 1985. *An Analysis of the Draper Site Chipped Lithic Artifacts.* Research Report no. 15. London, ON: London Museum of Archaeology.

Pratt, Peter P. 1960. "A Criticism of MacNeish's Iroquois Pottery Types." *Pennsylvania Archaeologist* 30:106–10.

———. 1961. *Oneida Iroquois Glass Trade Bead Sequence: 1585–1745.* Indian Glass Trade Beads, Color Guide Series no. 1. Fort Stanwix Museum, Rome, N.Y. Syracuse, N.Y.: Onondaga Printing.

Pretola, John P. 2002. "An Optical Mineralogy Approach to Northeastern Ceramics." In *A Lasting Impression: Coastal, Lithic, and Ceramic Research in New England Archaeology,* edited by J. E. Kerber, 179–205. Westport, Conn.: Praeger.

Prisch, Betty C. 1982. *Aspects of Change in Seneca Iroquois Ladles A.D. 1600–1900.* Research Records no. 15. Rochester, N.Y.: Rochester Museum and Science Center.

Ramsden, Peter G. 1977. *A Refinement of Some Aspects of Huron Ceramic Analysis.* National Museum of Man, Mercury Series, Archaeological Survey of Canada, Paper no. 63. Ottawa: National Museums of Canada.

———. 1990. "Death in Winter: Changing Symbolic Patterns in Southern Ontario Prehistory." *Anthropologica* 32:167–82.

Ramsden, Peter G., and William R. Fitzgerald. 1990. "More (or Less) on Iroquoian Stemware." *American Antiquity* 55, no. 1:159–61.

Richardson, James B. 1977. "The Impact of European Contact on Northeastern Iroquois and Algonkian Art Styles." In *Current Perspectives in Northeastern Archaeology: Essays in Honor of William A. Ritchie,* edited by R. E. Funk and C. F. Hayes III, 113–19. Researches and Transactions of the New York State Archaeological Association 17, no. 1. Rochester.

Rumrill, Donald A. 1991. "The Mohawk Glass Trade Bead Chronology: ca. 1560–1785." *Beads: Journal of the Society of Bead Researchers* 3:5–45.

Rutsch, Edward S. 1973. *Smoking Technology of the Aborigines of the Iroquois Area of New York State.* Rutherford, N.J.: Fairleigh Dickenson Univ. Press.

Shen, Chen. 1997. "Towards a Comprehensive Understanding of the Lithic Production System of the Princess Point Complex, Southwestern Ontario." Ph.D. diss., Univ. of Toronto.

———. 2000. "Tool Use-Patterning at the Grand Banks Site of the Princess Point Complex, Southwestern Ontario." *Northeast Anthropology* 60:63–87.

———. 2001. *The Lithic Production of the Princess Point Complex During the Transition to Agriculture in Southwestern Ontario.* British Archaeological Reports International Series no. 991. Oxford, UK.

Skinner, Alanson B. 1910. "Iroquois Material." In *Notes Concerning New Collections,* edited by R. H. Lowie, 271–329. Anthropological Papers of the American Museum of Natural History 4, no. 2. New York.

———. 1920. "An Iroquois Antler Figurine." *Indian Notes and Monographs* 2, no. 5:109–14. New York: Museum of the American Indian, Heye Foundation.

Slotkin, James S., and Karl Schmitt. 1949. "Studies of Wampum." *American Anthropologist* 51, no. 2:223–36.

Smith, David G. 1983. *An Analytical Approach to the Seriation of Iroquoian Pottery.* Research Report no. 12. London, ON: London Museum of Archaeology.

———. 1991. *Keffer Site (AkGv-14) Pottery and Ceramic Smoking Pipes.* Research Report no. 23. London, ON: London Museum of Archaeology.

———. 1997. *Archaeological Systematics and the Analysis of Iroquoian Ceramics: A Case Study from the Crawford Lake Area, Ontario.* Bulletin no. 15. London, ON: London Museum of Archaeology.

Snyder, Gary S. 1999. "Wampum: A Material Symbol of Cultural Value to the Iroquois Peoples of Northeastern North America." In *Material Symbols: Culture and Economy in Prehistory,* edited by J. E. Robb, 362–81. Center for Archaeological Investigations, Occasional Paper no. 26. Carbondale: Southern Illinois Univ.

Snyderman, George S. 1961. "The Function of Wampum in Iroquois Religion." *Proceedings of the American Philosophical Society* 105, no. 6:571–608.

Stark, Kathryn J. 1995. "European Glass Trade Beads and the Chronology of the Niagara Frontier Iroquois Sites." *Northeast Anthropology* 50:61–90.

Strauss, Alisa. 2000. "Iroquoian Food Techniques and Technologies: An Examination of Susquehannock Vessel Form and Function." Ph.D. diss., Pennsylvania State Univ.

Trigger, Bruce G., L. Yaffe, D. Dautet, H. Marshall, and Robert J. Pearce. 1984. "Parker Festooned Pottery at the Lawson Site: Trace-Element Analysis." *Ontario Archaeology* 42:3–11.

Trigger, Bruce G., L. Yaffe, M. Diksic, J.-L. Galinier, H. Marshall, and James F. Pendergast. 1980. "Trace-Element Analysis of Iroquoian Pottery." *Canadian Journal of Archaeology* 4:119–45.

van der Made, Herman. 1978. *Seventeenth Century Beads from Holland.* Archaeological Research Booklet no. 14. Lancaster, Pa.: G. B. Fenstermaker.

van der Sleen, W. G. N. 1963. "Bead-Making in Seventeenth-Century Amsterdam." *Archaeology* 16, no. 4:260–63.

von Gernet, Alexander D. 1982. "Interpreting Intrasite Spatial Distribution of Artifacts: The Draper Site Pipe Fragments." *Man in the Northeast* 23:49–60.

———. 1985. *Analysis of Intrasite Spatial Distribution: The Draper Site Smoking Pipes.* Research Report no. 16. London, ON: London Museum of Archaeology.

———. 1988. "The Transculturation of the Amerindian Pipe/Tobacco/Smoking Complex and Its Impact on the Intellectual Boundaries Between 'Savagery' and 'Civilization,' 1535–1935." Ph.D. diss., McGill Univ.

von Gernet, Alexander D., and Peter A. Timmins. 1987. "Pipes and Parakeets: Constructing Meaning in an Early Iroquoian Context." In *Archaeology as Long-Term History,* edited by I. Hodder, 31–42. Cambridge, UK: Cambridge Univ. Press.

Weber, Cynthia J. 1970. "Types and Attributes in the Study of Iroquois Pipes." Ph.D. diss., Harvard Univ.

———. 1971. "Types and Attributes in Iroquois Pipes." *Man in the Northeast* 2:51–65.

Wintemberg, William J. 1906. "Bone and Horn Harpoon Heads of the Ontario Indians." *Annual Archaeological Report for Ontario,* 1905, 33–56. Appendix to the Report of the Minister of Education for Ontario. Toronto.

———. 1908. "The Use of Shells by the Ontario Indians." *Annual Archaeological Report for Ontario,* 1907, 38–90. Appendix to the Report of the Minister of Education for Ontario. Toronto.

———. 1926. *Foreign Aboriginal Artifacts from Post-European Iroquoian Sites in Ontario.* Proceedings and Transactions of the Royal Society of Canada, 3rd ser., 22, no. 2. Ottawa.

———. 1935. "Archaeological Evidence of Algonkian Influences on Iroquoian Culture." *Transactions of the Royal Society of Canada,* 3rd ser., 29, no. 2, 231–42. Ottawa.

Witthoft, John, and W. Fred Kinsey, eds. 1969. *Susquehannock Miscellany.* Harrisburg: Pennsylvania Historical and Museum Commission.

Wonderley, Anthony. 2002. "Oneida Ceramic Effigies: A Question of Meaning." *Northeast Anthropology* 63:23–48.

———. 2005. "Effigy Pipes, Diplomacy, and Myth: Exploring Interaction Between St. Lawrence Iroquoians and Eastern Iroquois in New York State." *American Antiquity* 70, no 2:211–40.

Wood, Alice S. 1974. "A Catalogue of Jesuit and Ornamental Rings from Western New York State." *Historical Archaeology* 8:83–104.

Wray, Charles F. 1963. "Ornamental Hair Combs of the Seneca Iroquois." *Pennsylvania Archaeologist* 33, nos. 1–2:35–50.

———. 1964. "The Bird in Seneca Archaeology." *Proceedings of the Rochester Academy of Science* 11, no. 1:1–56.

———. 1969. "Stone Pipes of the New York State Indians." *Lapidary Journal* 23, no. 3:492–98.

———. 1985. "The Volume of Dutch Trade Goods Received by the Seneca Iroquois, 1600–1687 A.D." *New Netherland Studies Bulletin KNOB* 84, nos. 2–3:100–112.

Wright, Joyce M. 1999. *Numbers: A Message from the Past.* Bulletin no. 16. London, ON: London Museum of Archaeology.

5. Contemporary Iroquois Perspectives, Repatriation, and Collaborative Archaeology

Abrams, George H. J. 1994. "The Case for Wampum: Repatriation from the Museum of the American Indian to the Six Nations Confederacy, Brantford, Ontario, Canada." In *Museums and the Making of "Ourselves": The Role of Objects in*

National Identity, edited by F.E.S. Kaplan, 351–84. London: Leicester Univ. Press.

Benedict, Salli M. Kawennotakie. 2004. "Made in Akwesasne." In *A Passion for the Past: Papers in Honour of James F. Pendergast*, edited by J. V. Wright and J.-L. Pilon, 435–53. Mercury Series, Archaeology Paper no. 164. Gatineau, QC: Canadian Museum of Civilization.

Dean, Robert L., and Douglas J. Perrelli. 2006. "Highway Archaeology in Western New York: Archaeologists' Views of Cooperation between State and Tribal Review Agencies." In *Cross-Cultural Collaboration: Native Peoples and Archaeology in the Northeastern United States*, edited by J. E. Kerber, 131–49. Lincoln: Univ. of Nebraska Press.

Fenton, William N. 1989. "Return of Eleven Wampum Belts to the Six Nations Iroquois Confederacy on Grand River, Canada." *Ethnohistory* 36, no. 4:393–410.

George-Kanentiio, Doug. 2000. "Iroquois Roots." In *Iroquois Culture and Commentary*, by Doug George-Kanentiio, 17–34. Santa Fe: Clear Light Publishers.

Hill, Richard W., Sr. 1996. "Reflections of a Native Repatriator." In *Mending the Circle, A Native American Repatriation Guide*, edited by B. Meister, 81–96. New York: American Indian Ritual Object Repatriation Foundation.

———. 2001. "Regenerating Identity: Repatriation and the Indian Frame of Mind." In *The Future of the Past: Archaeologists, Native Americans, and Repatriation*, edited by T. L. Bray, 127–38. New York: Garland Publishing.

———. 2006. "Making a Final Resting Place Final: A History of the Repatriation Experience of the Haudenosaunee." In *Cross-Cultural Collaboration: Native Peoples and Archaeology in the Northeastern United States*, edited by J. E. Kerber, 3–17. Lincoln: Univ. of Nebraska Press.

Hill, Richard W., and Donald A. Grinde Jr. 1975. "Indian Historians Examine the Prehistory and History of the Iroquois: Problems in Methodology and Records." *Ontario Archaeology* 25:57–59.

Jemison, G. Peter. 1997. "Who Owns the Past?" In *Native Americans and Archaeologists: Stepping Stones to Common Ground*, edited by N. Swidler, K. E. Dongoske, R. Anyon, and A. S. Downer, 57–63. Walnut Creek, Calif.: AltaMira Press.

———. 2001. "Fur for Beads, Iron, Guns, and Alcohol." In *Aboriginal People and the Fur Trade: Proceedings of the 8th North American Fur Trade Conference, Akwesasne*, edited by L. Johnston, 91–96. Cornwall, ON, and Rooseveltown, N.Y.: Akwesasne Notes.

Kerber, Jordan E. 2006. "Case Studies in Collaborative Archaeology: The Oneida Indian Nation of New York and Colgate University." In *Cross-Cultural Collaboration: Native Peoples and Archaeology in the Northeastern United States*, edited by J. E. Kerber, 233–49. Lincoln: Univ. of Nebraska Press.

———. 2007. "Summer Workshops in Indigenous Archaeology: Voluntary Collaboration Between Colgate University and the Oneida Indian Nation of New

York." In *Collaborative Indigenous Archaeology at the Trowel's Edge: Explorations in Methodology, Education, and Ethics*, edited by S. W. Silliman. Tucson: Univ. of Arizona Press. In press.

Kroup, Ben A., Robert L. Dean, and Richard Hill, eds. 1986. *Art from Ganondagan: The Village of Peace*. Waterford: New York State Office of Parks, Recreation, and Historic Preservation.

Mt. Pleasant, Jane. 1989. "The Iroquois Sustainers: Practices of a Longterm Agriculture in the Northeast." *Northeast Indian Quarterly* 6, nos. 1–2:33–39. In *Indian Corn of the Americas: Gift to the World*, edited by J. Barreiro. Ithaca, N.Y.: Cornell Univ.

———. 2001. "The Three Sisters: Care for the Land and the People." In *Science and Native American Communities: Legacies of Pain, Visions of Promise*, edited by K. James, 126–34. Lincoln: Univ. of Nebraska Press.

Rossen, Jack. 2006. "New Vision Archaeology in the Cayuga Heartland of Central New York." In *Cross-Cultural Collaboration: Native Peoples and Archaeology in the Northeastern United States*, edited by J. E. Kerber, 250–64. Lincoln: Univ. of Nebraska Press.

———. 2007. "Field School Archaeology in the Changing Landscape of Central New York." In *Collaborative Indigenous Archaeology at the Trowel's Edge: Explorations in Methodology, Education, and Ethics*, edited by S. W. Silliman. Tucson: Univ. of Arizona Press. In press.

Snow, Dean R. 1989. "Wampum Belts Returned to the Onondaga Nation." *Man in the Northeast* 38:109–11.

Tooker, Elisabeth. 1998. "A Note on the Return of Eleven Wampum Belts to the Six Nations Iroquois Confederacy on Grand River, Canada." *Ethnohistory* 45, no. 2:219–36.

Versaggi, Nina M. 2006. "Tradition, Sovereignty, Recognition: NAGPRA Consultations with the Iroquois Confederacy of Sovereign Nations of New York." In *Cross-Cultural Collaboration: Native Peoples and Archaeology in the Northeastern United States*, edited by J. E. Kerber, 18–31. Lincoln: Univ. of Nebraska Press.

Wiles, Brian. 1991. "Sacred Wampums Returned to Haudenosaunee Confederacy." *Akwesasne Notes* 23, no. 2:11.

Works Cited

Index

| Works Cited

Abel, Timothy J. 2001. "The Clayton Cluster: Cultural Dynamics of a Late Prehistoric Village Sequence in the Upper St. Lawrence Valley." Ph.D. diss., State Univ. of New York at Albany.

Abler, Thomas S. 1980. "Iroquois Cannibalism: Fact Not Fiction." *Ethnohistory* 27, no. 4:309–16.

Abler, Thomas S., and Elisabeth Tooker. 1978. "Seneca." In *Handbook of North American Indians*. Vol. 15, *Northeast*, edited by B. G. Trigger, 505–17. Washington, D.C.: Smithsonian Institution.

Abrams, George H. J. 1976. *The Seneca People*. Phoenix, Ariz.: Indian Tribal Series.

———. 1994. "The Case for Wampum: Repatriation from the Museum of the American Indian to the Six Nations Confederacy, Brantford, Ontario, Canada." In *Museums and the Making of "Ourselves": The Role of Objects in National Identity*, edited by F.E.S. Kaplan, 351–84. London: Leicester Univ. Press.

Adams, Catherine F. 1975. *Nutritive Value of American Foods in Common Units*. Agriculture Handbook no. 456. Washington, D.C.: U.S. Dept. of Agriculture.

Adams, Francis M. 1973. "A Cross-Cultural Study of the Affective Meaning of Color." *Journal of Cross-Cultural Psychology* 4:135–56.

Aiken, S., P. Lee, D. Punter, and J. Stewart. 1988. *Wild Rice in Canada*. Toronto: NC Press.

Allen, Kathleen M. S. 1992. "Iroquois Ceramic Production: A Case Study of Household-Level Organization." In *Ceramic Production and Distribution: An Integrated Approach*, edited by G. J. Bey III and C. A. Pool, 133–54. Boulder, Colo.: Westview Press.

———. 1996. "Iroquoian Landscapes: People, Environments, and the GIS Context." In *New Methods, Old Problems: Geographic Information Systems in Modern Archaeological Research*, edited by H.D.G. Maschner, 198–222. Center for Archaeological Investigations, Occasional Paper no. 23. Carbondale: Southern Illinois Univ.

Ammerman, Albert J., and Luigi L. Cavalli-Sforza. 1973. "A Population Model for the Diffusion of Early Farming in Europe." In *The Explanation of Culture Change*, edited by C. Renfrew, 343–57. London: Duckworth.

———. 1979. "The Wave of Advance Model for the Spread of Agriculture in Europe." In *Transformations: Mathematical Approaches to Culture Change*, edited by C. Renfrew and K. L. Cooke, 275–93. New York: Academic Press.

Anderson, David A. 1995. "Susquehannock Longhouses and Culture Change During the Contact Period in Pennsylvania." M.A. thesis, Univ. of Pittsburgh.

Anderson, David G. 1991. "Examining Prehistoric Settlement Distribution in Eastern North America." *Archaeology of Eastern North America* 19:1–22.

———. 1994. *The Savannah River Chiefdoms: Political Change in the Late Prehistoric Southeast.* Tuscaloosa: Univ. of Alabama Press.

Andrefsky, William. 1980. "Implications of the Contextual/Structural Approach for Archaeology: An Iroquois Illustration." M.A. thesis, Binghamton Univ.

Anthony, David W. 1990. "Migration in Archaeology: The Baby and the Bathwater." *American Anthropologist* 92:895–914.

Aquila, Richard. 1983. *The Iroquois Restoration.* Detroit, Mich.: Wayne State Univ. Press.

Archaeological Services Inc. 1993. "An Archaeological Assessment of Proposed Pit Application (Varcoe Pit No. 2) Part of Lot 72, Concession 2, WPR, Township of Flos, Simcoe County, Ontario." On file, Ontario Ministry of Culture, Toronto.

Arès, Richard. 1970. "Les Relations des Jésuites et le Climat de la Nouvelle-France." *Memoires de la Societé Royale du Canada* 8:75–91.

Arzigian, Constance M. 2000. "Middle Woodland and Oneota Contexts for Wild Rice Exploitation in Southwestern Wisconsin." *Midcontinental Journal of Archaeology* 25:245–68.

Asch Sidell, Nancy. 2000. "Westheimer and Parlow Field Sites Tabular Summary." On file, New York State Museum, Albany.

———. 2002. "Paleoethnobotanical Indicators of Subsistence and Settlement Change in the Northeast." In *Northeast Subsistence-Settlement Change A.D. 700–1300,* edited by J. P. Hart and C. B. Rieth, 241–64. New York State Museum Bulletin 496. Albany: State Univ. of New York, State Education Department.

Aubin, George F. 1975. "Color Terms in Narragansett." In *Papers of the Seventh Algonquian Conference,* edited by W. Cowan, 105–14. Ottawa: Carleton Univ.

Austin, Shaun J. 1994. "The Wilcox Lake Site (AlGu-17): Middle Iroquoian Exploitation of the Oak Ridges Moraine." *Ontario Archaeology* 58:49–84.

Axtell, James. 1985. *The Invasion Within: The Contest of Cultures in Colonial North America.* New York: Oxford Univ. Press.

Bailey, Alfred Goldsworthy. 1937. *The Conflict of European and Eastern Algonkian Culture, 1504–1700. A Study in Canadian Civilization.* New Brunswick Museum Monograph Series no. 2. St. John, NB: New Brunswick Museum.

Bakker, Peter. 1990. "A Basque Etymology for the Word 'Iroquois.'" *Man in the Northeast* 40:89–93.

Ball, Terry D., and Jack D. Brotherson. 1992. "Effect of Varying Environmental Conditions on Phytolith Morphometries in Two Species of Grass *(Bouteloua curtipendula* and *Panicun virgatum)." Scanning Microscopy* 6:1163–81.

Bamann, Susan E. 1993. "Settlement Nucleation in Mohawk Iroquois Prehistory: An Analysis of a Site Sequence in the Lower Otsquago Drainage of the Mohawk Valley." Ph.D. diss., State Univ. of New York at Albany.

Bamann, Susan E., Robert D. Kuhn, James Molnar, and Dean R. Snow. 1992. "Iroquoian Archaeology." *Annual Review of Anthropology* 21:435–60.

Bartram, John. 1966 [1751]. *Observations on the Inhabitants, Climate, Soil, Rivers, Productions, Animals, and Other Matters Worthy of Notice made by Mr. John Bartram in his Travels from Pennsylvania to Onondago, Oswego, and the Lake Ontario, in Canada.* Reprint. March of America Series no. 41. Ann Arbor, Mich.: Univ. Microfilms.

Battarbee, Richard W. 1988. "The Use of Diatom Analysis in Archaeology: A Review." *Journal of Archaeological Science* 15:621–44.

Beauchamp, William M. 1892. *The Iroquois Trail, or Foot-Prints of the Six Nations, in Customs, Traditions, and History.* Fayetteville, N.Y.: H. C. Beauchamp.

———. 1895. "Mohawk Notes." *Journal of American Folklore* 8:217–21.

———. 1898. *Earthenware of the New York Aborigines.* New York State Museum Bulletin 5, no. 2. Albany: Univ. of the State of New York.

———. 1901. *Wampum and Shell Articles Used by the New York Indians.* New York State Museum Bulletin 8, no. 41. Albany: Univ. of the State of New York.

———. 1922. *Iroquois Folk Lore, Gathered from the Six Nations of New York.* Syracuse: Onondaga Historical Association.

Bekerman, André, and Gary A. Warrick, eds. 1995. *Origins of the People of the Longhouse: Proceedings of the 21st Annual Symposium of the Ontario Archaeological Society.* Toronto: Ontario Archaeological Society.

Benenson, Abram S., ed. 1975. *Control of Communicable Diseases in Man.* Washington, D.C.: American Public Health Association.

Bennett, Monte R. 1979. "The Blowers Site, Ond 1–4: An Early Historic Oneida Settlement." *Bulletin of the Chenango Chapter of the New York State Archaeological Association* 18, no. 2.

———. 1981. "A Longhouse Pattern on the Cameron Site (Ond 8–4)." *Bulletin of the Chenango Chapter of the New York State Archaeological Association* 19, no. 2.

———. 1983. "Glass Trade Beads from Central New York." In *Proceedings of the 1982 Glass Trade Bead Conference,* edited by C. F. Hayes III, N. Bolger, K. Karklins, and C. F. Wray, 51–58. Research Records no. 16. Rochester, N.Y.: Rochester Museum and Science Center.

———. 1984a. "Recent Findings in Oneida Indian Country." *Bulletin of the Chenango Chapter of the New York State Archaeological Association* 21, no. 1.

———. 1984b. "The Stone Quarry Site (Msv 4–2): A Mid-Seventeenth Century Oneida Iroquois Station in Central New York." *Bulletin of the Chenango Chapter of the New York State Archaeological Association* 21, no. 2.

———. 1988. "The Primes Hill Site, Msv 5–2: An Eighteenth Century Oneida Station." *Bulletin of the Chenango Chapter of the New York State Archaeological Association* 22, no. 4:1–21.

———. 1991. "Onneyutehage, Thurston, Msv 1: A Story of a Screened Sidehill Midden." *Bulletin of the Chenango Chapter of the New York State Archaeological Association* 24, no. 3.

Bennett, Monte R., and Reginald Bigford. 1968. "The Cameron Site." *Bulletin of the Chenango Chapter of the New York State Archaeological Association* 10, no. 2.

Bennett, Monte R., and Douglas Clark. 1978. "Recent Excavations on the Cameron Site (Ond 8–4)." *Bulletin of the Chenango Chapter of the New York State Archaeological Association* 17, no. 4.

Bennett, Monte R., and Richard Cole. 1976. "The Marshall Site, Msv 7–2." *Bulletin of the Chenango Chapter of the New York State Archaeological Association* 16, no. 3:8–14.

Bennett, Monte R., and Henry Hatton. 1988. "The Cameron Site (Ond 8–4) Revisited." *Bulletin of the Chenango Chapter of the New York State Archaeological Association* 23, no. 1:1–4.

Berlin, Andrea, Terry Ball, Robert Thompson, and Sharon Herbert. 2003. "Ptolemaic Agriculture, 'Syrian Wheat,' and *Triticum aestivum.*" *Journal of Archaeological Science* 30:115–21.

Berlin, Brent, and Paul Kay. 1969. *Basic Color Terms: Their Universality and Evolution.* Berkeley: Univ. of California Press.

Bierhorst, John. 1995. *Mythology of the Lenape: Guide and Texts.* Tucson: Univ. of Arizona Press.

Biggar, Henry P., ed. 1922–36. *The Works of Samuel de Champlain (1626).* 6 vols. Toronto: The Champlain Society.

———, ed. 1924. *The Voyages of Jacques Cartier: Published from the Originals with Translations, Notes and Appendices.* Publications of the Public Archives of Canada no. 11. Ottawa.

———, ed. 1929. *The Works of Samuel de Champlain (1626).* Vol. 3. Toronto: The Champlain Society.

Binford, Lewis R. 1965. "Archaeological Systematics and the Study of Cultural Process." *American Antiquity* 31, no. 2:203–10.

Biolsi, Thomas, and Larry J. Zimmerman, eds. 1997. *Indians and Anthropologists: Vine Deloria, Jr., and the Critique of Anthropology.* Tucson: Univ. of Arizona Press.

Blake, Leonard, and Hugh C. Cutler. 1983. "Plant Remains from the Gnagey Site." *Pennsylvania Archaeologist* 53:83–88.

Boas, Franz. 1940. *Race, Language, and Culture.* New York: MacMillan.

Bogucki, Peter. 1995. "Prelude to Agriculture in North-Central Europe." In *Before Farming: The Role of Plants and Animals in Early Societies,* edited by D. V Campana, 105–16. MASCA Research Papers in Science and Archaeology vol. 12 supplement. Philadelphia: Univ. Museum of Archaeology and Anthropology, Univ. of Pennsylvania.

———. 1996. "The Spread of Early Farming in Europe." *American Scientist* 84:242–53.

Bogucki, Peter, and Ryszard Grygiel. 1993. "The First Farmers of Central Europe: A Survey Article." *Journal of Field Archaeology* 20:399–426.

Bond, Stanley C., Jr. 1985. "The Relationship Between Soils and Settlement Patterns in the Mohawk Valley." In *The Mohawk Valley Project: 1982 Field Season Report,* edited by D. R. Snow, 17–40. Albany: Institute for Northeast Anthropology, State Univ. of New York.

Borstein, Marc H. 1975. "The Influence of Visual Perception on Culture." *American Anthropologist* 77, no. 4:774–98.

Boucher, Pierre. 1664. "True and Genuine Description of New France, Commonly called Canada, and of the Manners and Customs and Productions of that Country." In *Canada in the Seventeenth Century,* edited by E. L. Montizambert. 1883. Reprint. Montreal: G. E. Desbarats.

Bower, Bruce. 1994. "Fossils on File: Computerized Preservation May Give Reburied Bones Back to Science." *Science News* 145, no. 12:186–87.

Bowman, Irene. 1979. "The Draper Site: Historical Accounts of Vegetation in Pickering and Markham Townships with Special Reference to the Significance of a Large, Even-Aged Stand Adjacent to the Site." In *Settlement Patterns of the Draper and White Sites: 1973 Excavations,* edited by B. Hayden, 47–58. Department of Archaeology Publication 6. Burnaby, BC: Simon Fraser Univ.

Bowyer, Vandy E. 1995. "Palaeoethnobotanical Analysis of Two Princess Point Sites: Grand Banks (Affix-3) and Lone Pine (Affix-113) in the Grand River Area, Ontario." M.A. thesis, Univ. of Toronto.

Boyle, David. 1900. *Annual Archaeological Report for 1899.* Toronto: Ontario Ministry of Education.

Bozarth, Steven R. 1987. "Diagnostic Opal Phytoliths from Rinds of Selected *Cucurbita* Species." *American Antiquity* 52, no. 3:607–15.

Bradley, James W. 1979. "The Onondaga Iroquois: 1500–1655. A Study in Acculturation Change and Its Consequences." Ph.D. diss., Syracuse Univ.

———. 1983. "Blue Crystals and Other Trinkets: Glass Beads from 16th and Early 17th Century New England." In *Proceedings of the 1982 Glass Trade Bead Conference,* edited by C. F. Hayes III, N. Bolger, K. Karklins, and Charles F. Wray, 29–39. Research Records no. 16. Rochester, N.Y.: Rochester Museum and Science Center.

———. 1987a. *Evolution of the Onondaga Iroquois: Accommodating Change, 1500–1655.* Syracuse, N.Y.: Syracuse Univ. Press.

———. 1987b. "Native Exchange and European Trade: Cross-Cultural Dynamics in the Sixteenth Century." *Man in the Northeast* 33:31–46.

———. 1989. "Updating the Onondaga." Paper presented at the 73rd Annual Meeting of the New York State Archaeological Association, Norwich.

Bradley, James W., and S. Terry Childs. 1989. "Spirals and Rings: Analysis of Two 16th-Century Artifact Forms." Paper presented at the World Archaeology Conference, Baltimore.

———. 1991. "Basque Earrings and Panther's Tails: The Form of Cross-Cultural Contact in Sixteenth Century Iroquoia." In *Metals in Society: Theory Beyond Analysis,* edited by R. M. Ehrenreich, 7–17. MASCA Research Papers in Science and Archaeology 8, no. 2. Philadelphia: Univ. Museum of Archaeology and Anthropology, Univ. of Pennsylvania.

Braidwood, Robert J. 1964. *Prehistoric Men.* 7th ed. Glenview, Ill.: Scott, Foresman, and Company.

———. 1974. "The Iraq Jarmo Project." In *Archaeological Researches in Retrospect,* edited by G. R. Willey, 59–83. Cambridge, UK: Winthrop.

Brasser, Ted J. 1978a. "Mahican." In *Handbook of North American Indians.* Vol. 15, *Northeast,* edited by B. G. Trigger, 198–212. Washington, D.C.: Smithsonian Institution.

———. 1978b. "Early Indian-European Contacts." In *Handbook of North American Indians.* Vol. 15, *Northeast,* edited by B. G. Trigger, 78–88. Washington, D.C.: Smithsonian Institution.

———. 1980. "Self-Directed Pipe Effigies." *Man in the Northeast* 19:95–104.

Bray, Tamara L., ed. 2001. *The Future of the Past: Archaeologists, Native Americans, and Repatriation.* New York: Garland Publishing.

Bronson, Bennett. 1975. "The Earliest Farming: Demography as Cause and Consequence." In *Population, Ecology and Social Evolution,* edited by S. Polgar, 53–78. The Hague: Mouton.

Brose, David S., James A. Brown, and David W. Penney. 1985. *Ancient Art of the American Woodland Indians.* New York: Harry N. Abrams / Detroit Institute of Arts.

Brown, Donald M., G. A. McKay, and Lyman J. Chapman. 1980. *The Climate of Southern Ontario.* Climatological Studies no. 5. Toronto: Environment Canada, Atmospheric Environment Service.

Brown, James A. 1965. "The Prairie Peninsula: An Interaction Area in the Eastern United States." Ph.D. diss., Univ. of Chicago.

———. 1989. "On Style Divisions of the Southeastern Ceremonial Complex: A Revisionist Perspective." In *The Southeastern Ceremonial Complex: Artifacts and Analysis,* edited by P. Galloway, 183–204. Lincoln: Univ. of Nebraska Press.

Brown, Michael F. 2003. *Who Owns Native Culture?* Cambridge, Mass.: Harvard Univ. Press.

Brumbach, Hetty Jo. 1975. " 'Iroquoian' Ceramics in 'Algonkian' Territory." *Man in the Northeast* 10:17–28.

———. 1995. "Algonquian and Iroquoian Ceramics in the Upper Hudson River Drainage." *Northeast Anthropology* 49:55–66.

Brumbach, Hetty Jo, and Robert Jarvenpa. 1989. *Ethnoarchaeological and Cultural Frontiers: Athapaskan, Algonquian and European Adaptations in the Central Subarctic.* New York: Peter Lang Publishing.

Bryson, Reid A., and Wayne M. Wendland. 1967. "Tentative Climatic Patterns for Some Late Glacial and Post-Glacial Episodes in Central North America." In *Life, Land, and Water,* edited by W. J. Mayer-Oakes, 271–98. Occasional Papers no. 1. Winnipeg: Department of Anthropology, Univ. of Manitoba.

Bugler, Caroline. 1979. *Dutch Painting in the Seventeenth Century.* New York: Mayflower Books.

Burch, Wanda. 1990. "Sir William Johnson's Cabinet of Curiosities." *New York History* 71, no. 3:261–82.

Burnet, Macfarlane, and David O. White. 1972. *Natural History of Infectious Disease.* Cambridge, UK: Cambridge Univ. Press.

Bursey, Jeffrey A. 1995. "The Transition from the Middle to Late Woodland Periods: A Re-evaluation." In *Origins of the People of the Longhouse: Proceedings of the 21st Annual Symposium of the Ontario Archaeological Society,* edited by A. Bekerman and G. A. Warrick, 43–54. Toronto: Ontario Archaeological Society.

Bursey, Jeffrey A., and David G. Smith. 1999. "Report on the 1997 Excavations at the Forster Site (AgGx-134), Caledonia, Ontario." *Annual Archaeological Report for Ontario,* n.s., 9:95–97.

Cadzow, Donald A. 1936. *Archaeological Studies of the Susquehannock Indians of Pennsylvania.* Vol. 3. Harrisburg: Publications of the Pennsylvania Historical Commission.

Campbell, Celina, and Ian D. Campbell. 1992. "Pre-Contact Settlement Pattern in Southern Ontario: Simulation Model for Maize-Based Village Horticulture." *Ontario Archaeology* 53:3–26.

Campbell, Lyle, and Marianne Mithun, eds. 1979. *The Languages of Native America: Historical and Comparative Assessment.* Austin: Univ. of Texas Press.

Carlson, Catherine C., George J. Armelagos, and Ann L. Magennis. 1992. "Impact of Disease on the Precontact and Early Historic Populations of New England and the Maritimes." In *Disease and Demography in the Americas,* edited by J. W. Verano and D. H. Ubelaker, 141–54. Washington, D.C.: Smithsonian Institution Press.

Carpenter, Edmund, ed. 1986–88. *Materials for the Study of Social Symbolism in Ancient and Tribal Art: A Record of Tradition and Continuity; Based on the Researches and Writings of Carl Schuster.* 3 vols. New York: Rock Foundation.

Carrington, Henry. 1892. "Report on the Condition of the Six Nations of New York." In *Extra Census Bulletin: Indians,* edited by T. Donaldson, 19–83. Washington, D.C.: Bureau of the Census.

Cassedy, Daniel, and Paul Webb. 1999. "New Data on the Chronology of Maize Horticulture in Eastern New York and Southern New England." In *Current Northeast Paleoethnobotany,* edited by J. P. Hart, 85–100. New York State Museum Bulletin 494. Albany: State Univ. of New York, State Education Department.

Ceci, Lynn. 1979. "Maize Cultivation in Coastal New York: The Archaeological, Agronomical, and Documentary Evidence." *North American Archaeologist* 1:45–73.

———. 1985. "Shell Bead Evidence from Archaeological Sites in the Seneca Region of New York State." Paper presented at the Annual Conference on Iroquois Research, Rensselaerville, N.Y.

———. 1986. *The Origins of Wampum among the Seneca Iroquois.* Rochester, N.Y.: Rochester Museum and Science Center.

———. 1989. "Tracing Wampum's Origins: Shell Bead Evidence from Archaeological Sites in Western and Coastal New York." In *Proceedings of the 1986 Shell Bead Conference: Selected Papers,* edited by C. F. Hayes III, L. Ceci, and C. C. Bodner, 63–80. Research Records 20. Rochester, N.Y.: Rochester Museum and Science Center.

Cervone, Gian C. 1991. "Native Ceramic Vessels." In *Tram and Cameron: Two Early Contact Era Seneca Sites,* edited by C. F. Hayes III, M. L. Sempowski, and L. P. Saunders, 84–103 and 258–92. Charles F. Wray Series in Seneca Archaeology. Vol. 2. Research Records no. 21. Rochester, N.Y.: Rochester Museum and Science Center.

Chafe, Wallace L. 1961. *Seneca Thanksgiving Rituals.* Bureau of American Ethnology Bulletin 183. Washington, D.C.: Smithsonian Institution.

———. 1963. *Handbook of the Seneca Language.* Bulletin no. 388. Albany: New York State Museum and Science Service.

———. 1964. "Linguistic Evidence for the Relative Age of Iroquois Religious Practices." *Southwestern Journal of Anthropology* 20:278–85.

———. 1967. *Seneca Morphology and Dictionary.* Smithsonian Contributions to Anthropology no. 4. Washington, D.C.: Smithsonian Institution.

Champlain, Samuel de. 1907. *Voyages of Samuel de Champlain, 1604–1618.* New York: Barnes and Noble.

Chapdelaine, Claude. 1989. *Le Site Mandeville à Tracy, Variabilité Culturelle des Iroquoiens du Saint-Laurent.* Montreal: Recherches Amérindiennes au Québec.

———. 1993. "The Sedentarization of the Prehistoric Iroquoians: A Slow or Rapid Transformation?" *Journal of Anthropological Archaeology* 12, no. 2:173–209.

———. 1995. "Les Iroquoiens de l'est de la Vallée du Saint-Laurent." In *Archéologies Québécoises,* edited by A-M. Balac, C. Chapdelaine, N. Clermont, and F. Duguay, 161–84. Paléo-Québec 23. Montreal: Recherches Amérindiennes au Québec.

———, ed. 1992. "L'Origine des Iroquoiennes: Un Débat." *Recherches Amérindiennes au Québec* 22:3–36.

Chapman, Lyman J., and Donald F. Putnam. 1984. *The Physiography of Southern Ontario,* 3rd ed. Special vol. 2. Toronto: Ontario Geological Survey.

Charbonneau, Hubert, and Normand Robert. 1987. "The French Origins of the Canadian Population, 1608–1759." In *Historical Atlas of Canada.* Vol. 1, edited by R. C. Harris. Toronto: Univ. of Toronto Press.

Childe, V. Gordon. 1951. *Man Makes Himself.* New York: Mento Books.

Chilton, Elizabeth S. 1999. "One Size Fits All: Typology and Alternatives for Ceramic Research." In *Material Meanings: Critical Approaches to the Interpretation of Material Culture,* edited by E. S. Chilton, 44–60. Salt Lake City: Univ. of Utah Press.

Clermont, Norman. 1980. "L'Augmentation de la Population chez les Iroquoiens Préhistoriques." *Recherches Amérindiennes au Québec* 10:159–63.

———. 1990. "Why Did the Saint Lawrence Iroquoians Become Horticulturalists?" *Man in the Northeast* 40:75–79.

———. 1992. "L'Explosion Iroquoienne n'a pas eu Lieu." *Recherches Amérindiennes au Québec* 22, no. 4:14–17.

Clermont, Norman, Claude Chapdelaine, and Georges Barré. 1983. *Le Site Iroquoien de Lanoraie: Témoignage d'une Maison-Longue.* Montreal: Recherches Amérindiennes au Québec.

Coe, Michael, Dean R. Snow, and Elizabeth Benson. 1986. *Atlas of Ancient America.* New York: Facts on File.

Coleman, Derek, and Ronald F. Williamson. 1994. "Landscapes Past to Landscapes Future: Planning for Archaeological Resources." In *Great Lakes Archaeology and Paleoecology: Exploring Interdisciplinary Initiatives for the Nineties,* edited by R. I. MacDonald, 61–80. Waterloo, ON: Univ. of Waterloo, Quaternary Sciences Institute.

Conover, George S. C. 1889. *Kanadesaga and Geneva.* 3 vols. On file, Archives, Warren Hunting Smith Library, Hobart and William Smith Colleges, Geneva, N.Y.

———, ed. 1887. *Journals of the Military Expeditions of Major General John Sullivan against the Six Nations of Indians in 1779.* Auburn, N.Y.: Knapp, Peck, and Thompson.

Cook, Noble D. 1998. *Born to Die: Disease and New World Conquest, 1492 1650.* Cambridge, UK: Cambridge Univ. Press.

Cook, Sherburne F. 1973. "The Significance of Disease in the Extinction of the New England Indians." *Human Biology* 45:485–508.

Corbett, R. Patrick. 2000. "Nation Students Dig into Their Culture." *Utica Observer-Dispatch,* 1 Aug., 1C.

Coté, Marc, and Leila Inksetter. 2000. "Ceramics and Chronology of the Late Prehistoric Period: The Abitibi-Temiscamingue Case." Paper presented at the 33rd Annual Meeting of the Canadian Archaeological Association, Montreal.

Coult, Allan D., and Robert W. Haberstein. 1965. *Cross Tabulations of Murdock's World Ethnographic Sample.* Columbia: Univ. of Missouri Press.

Crawford, Gary W. 1992. "The Transitions to Agriculture in Japan." In *Transitions to Agriculture in Prehistory,* edited by A. B. Gebauer and T. D. Price, 117–32. Monographs in World Archaeology no. 4. Madison, Wis.: Prehistory Press.

Crawford, Gary W., and David G. Smith. 1996. "Migration in Prehistory: Princess Point and the Northern Iroquoian Case." *American Antiquity* 61, no. 4:782–90.

———. 2003. "Paleoethnobotany in the Northeast." In *People and Plants in Ancient Eastern North America,* edited by P. E. Minnis, 172–257. Washington. D.C.: Smithsonian Books.

Crawford, Gary W., David G. Smith, and Vandy E. Bowyer. 1997. "Dating the Entry of Corn *(Zea mays)* into the Lower Great Lakes Region." *American Antiquity* 62, no. 1:112–19.

Crawford, Gary W., David G. Smith, Joseph R. Desloges, and Anthony M. Davis. 1998. "Floodplains and Agricultural Origins: A Case Study in South-Central Ontario, Canada." *Journal of Field Archaeology* 25:123–37.

Crawford, Gary W., David G. Smith, Frank A. Dieterman, and Trevor L. Ormerod. 1999. "Lower Grand River Bars and Terraces: The 1997 Princess Point Project Field Season." *Annual Archaeological Report for Ontario,* n.s., 9:98–105.

Crawford, Gary W., and Hiroto Takamiya. 1990. "The Origins and Implications of Late Prehistoric Plant Husbandry in Northern Japan." *Antiquity* 64:899–911.

Crépeau, Robert R., and Gregory G. Kennedy. 1990. "Neutron Activation of St. Lawrence Iroquoian Pottery." *Man in the Northeast* 40:65–74.

Cronin, Michelle. 2001. "Local Archaeological Dig Continues to Unearth Artifacts." *Oneida Daily Dispatch*, 1 Aug., 14.

Crosby, Alfred W. 1976. "Virgin Soil Epidemics as a Factor in the Aboriginal Depopulation in America." *William and Mary Quarterly* 33:289–99.

———. 1986. *Ecological Imperialism: The Biological Expansion of Europe, 900–1900.* Cambridge, UK: Cambridge Univ. Press.

Crowe, Patrick. 1994. "Glottochronology and the Archaeological Record." Paper presented at the Annual Meeting of the Northeastern Anthropological Association, Geneseo, N.Y.

Daechsel, Hugh J., and Phillip J. Wright. 1988. "The Sandbanks Tradition—A Late Middle Woodland Manifestation in Eastern Ontario." Paper presented at the 21st Annual Meeting of the Canadian Archaeological Association, Whistler, BC.

Daes, Erica-Irene. 2000. *Protecting Knowledge: Traditional Resource Rights in the New Millenium.* Working Group on Indigenous Populations, United Nations Special Rapporteur on the Heritage of Indigenous Peoples. February.

Damkjar, Eric R. 1990. *The Coulter Site and Late Iroquoian Coalescence in the Upper Trent Valley.* Occasional Papers in Northeastern Archaeology no. 2. Dundas, ON: Copetown Press.

Danielson, Stentor. 2001. "Oneida-Archaeologist Relations: A Utilitarian Perspective on Cooperation Between American Indians and Archaeologists." Honors Research Paper, Colgate Univ., Hamilton, N.Y.

Dawson, Kenneth C. A. 1979. "Algonkian Huron-Petun Ceramics in Northern Ontario." *Man in the Northeast* 18:14–31.

Dean, Robert L., ed. 1984. "Archaeological Investigations at Gannagaro State Historic Site, Victor, Ontario County, New York, 1983–1984." On file, New York State Office of Parks, Recreation, and Historic Preservation, Waterford.

Deetz, James. 1965. *The Dynamics of Stylistic Change in Arikara Ceramics.* Series in Anthropology no. 4. Urbana: Univ. of Illinois.

Delage, Denys. 1993. *Bitter Feast: Amerindians and Europeans in Northeastern North America, 1600–64.* Translated by J. Brierly. Vancouver: Univ. of British Columbia Press.

Desloges, Joseph R., and I. J. Walker. 1995. "Fluvial Geomorphic Processes and Archaeological Site Integrity at the Grand Banks Site, Grand River, Ontario." Paper presented at the 60th Annual Meeting of the Society for American Archaeology, Minneapolis.

Dincauze, Dena F., and Robert J. Hasenstab. 1989. "Explaining the Iroquois: Tribalization on a Prehistoric Periphery." In *Centre and Periphery: Comparative Studies in Archaeology*, edited by T. C. Champion, 67–87. London: Unwin Hyman.

Divale, William. 1984. *Matrilocal Residence in Pre-Literate Society.* Ann Arbor, Mich.: UMI Research Press.

Division of Archives and History. 1929. *The Sullivan-Clinton Campaign in 1779.* Albany: State Univ. of New York.

Dobyns, Henry F. 1966. "Estimating Aboriginal American Population: An Appraisal of Techniques with a New Hemispheric Estimate." *Current Anthropology* 7:395–444.

———. 1983. *Their Number Become Thinned: Native American Population Dynamics in Eastern North America.* Knoxville: Univ. of Tennessee Press.

Dodd, Christine F. 1984. *Ontario Iroquois Tradition Longhouses*. National Museum of Man, Mercury Series, Archaeological Survey of Canada, Paper no. 124:181–437. Ottawa: National Museums of Canada.

Dodd, Christine F., D. Poulton, Paul A. Lennox, David G. Smith, and Gary A. Warrick. 1990. "The Middle Ontario Iroquoian Stage." In *The Archaeology of Southern Ontario to A.D. 1650*, edited by C. J. Ellis and N. Ferris, 321–59. Occasional Publications of the London Chapter of the Ontario Archaeological Society no. 5. London, Ontario.

Doebley, John F., Major M. Goodman, and Charles W. Stuber. 1986. "Exceptional Genetic Divergence of Northern Flint Corn." *American Journal of Botany* 73:64–69.

Dongoske, Kurt E., Mark Aldenderfer, and Karen Doehner, eds. 2000. *Working Together: Native Americans and Archaeologists*. Washington, D.C.: Society for American Archaeology.

Dorweiler Jane E., and John Doebley. 1997. "Developmental Analysis of *Teosinte* Glume Architecture: A Key Locus in the Evolution of Maize *(Poaceae)*." *American Journal of Botany* 84:1313–22.

Drake, Samuel G., ed. 1855. *Indian Captivities or Life in the Wigwam*. New York: Miller, Orton, and Mulligan.

Dunbar, Helene R., and Katharine C. Ruhl. 1974. "Copper Artifacts from the Engelbert Site." *The Bulletin: Journal of the New York State Archaeological Association* 61:1–10.

Dunnell, Robert C. 1971. *Systematics in Prehistory*. New York: Free Press.

———. 1982. "Science, Social Science, and Common Sense: The Agonizing Dilemma of Modem Archaeology." *Journal of Anthropological Research* 38:1–25.

Durbin, Marshall. 1972. "Basic Terms—Off-Color?" *Semiotica* 6, no. 3:257–78.

Echo-Hawk, Roger C. 2000. "Ancient History in the New World: Integrating Oral Traditions with the Archaeological Record." *American Antiquity* 65, no. 2:267–90.

Egan, Kathryn C. 2001. "Archaeobotanical Analysis." In *Stage III Archaeological Investigations at Zinselmeier No. 1 Site (ANR-222; A069–15–0026), Ontario Country, New York*, edited by D. J. Wier, 7–1–7–20. Jackson, Mich.: Commonwealth Cultural Resources Group.

Ellis, Chris J., and Neal Ferris, eds. 1990. *The Archaeology of Southern Ontario to A.D. 1650*. Occasional Publications of the London Chapter of the Ontario Archaeological Society no. 5. London, Ontario.

Ember, Melvin. 1978. "Size of Color Lexicon: Interaction of Cultural and Biological Factors." *American Anthropologist* 80, no. 2:364–67.

Emerson, J. Norman. 1961. "Problems of Huron Origins." *Anthropologica* 3, no. 2:181–201.

Engelbrecht, William E. 1971. "A Stylistic Analysis of New York Iroquois Pottery." Ph.D. diss., Univ. of Michigan.

———. 1974a. "Cluster Analysis: A Method for the Study of Iroquois Prehistory." *Man in the Northeast* 7:57–70.

———. 1974b. "The Iroquois: Archaeological Patterning on the Tribal Level." *World Archaeology* 6, no. 1:52–65.

———. 1978. "Ceramic Patterning Between New York Iroquois Sites." In *The Spatial Organisation of Culture*, edited by I. Hodder, 141–52. Pittsburgh, Pa.: Univ. of Pittsburgh Press.

———. 1984. "The Kleis Site Ceramics: An Interpretive Approach." In *Extending the Rafters: Interdisciplinary Approaches to Iroquoian Studies*, edited by M. K. Foster, J. Campisi, and M. Mithun, 325–42. Albany: State Univ. of New York Press.

———. 1985. "New York Iroquois Political Development." In *Cultures in Contact: The European Impact on Native Cultural Institutions in Eastern North America, A.D. 1000–1800,* edited by W. W. Fitzhugh, 163–83. Washington, D.C.: Smithsonian Institution Press.

———. 1987. "Factors Maintaining Low Population Density among the Prehistoric New York Iroquois." *American Antiquity* 52, no. 1:13–27.

———. 1991. "Erie." *The Bulletin: Journal of the New York State Archaeological Association* 102:2–12.

———. 1992. "Les Éventualités Démographiques chez les Iroquoiens." *Recherches Amérindiennes au Québec* 22, no. 4:17–19.

———. 1995. "The Case of the Disappearing Iroquoians: Early Contact Period Superpower Politics." *Northeast Anthropology* 50:35–59.

———. 1999. "Iroquoian Ethnicity and Archaeological Taxa." In *Taming the Taxonomy: Toward a New Understanding of Great Lakes Archaeology,* edited by R. F. Williamson and C. M. Watts, 51–59. Toronto: Eastendbooks.

———. 2003. *Iroquoia: The Development of a Native World.* Syracuse, N.Y.: Syracuse Univ. Press.

———. 2004. "Northern New York Revisited." In *A Passion for the Past: Papers in Honour of James F. Pendergast,* edited by J. V. Wright and J.-L. Pilon, 125–44. Mercury Series, Archaeology Paper no. 164. Gatineau, QC: Canadian Museum of Civilization.

Fecteau, Rudolphe D. 1985. "The Introduction and Diffusion of Cultivated Plants in Southern Ontario." M.A. thesis, York Univ.

Fecteau, Rudolphe D., James Molnar, and Gary A. Warrick. 1994. "Iroquoian Village Ecology." *Kewa* 94, no. 8:2–10.

Fenton, William N. 1940. "Problems Arising from the Northeastern Position of the Iroquois." *Smithsonian Miscellaneous Collections* 100:159–251.

———. 1962. "This Island, the World on the Turtle's Back." *Journal of American Folklore* 75:283–300.

———. 1967. "From Longhouse to Ranch-Type House: The Second Housing Revolution of the Seneca Nation." In *Iroquois Culture, History, and Prehistory: Proceedings of the 1965 Conference on Iroquois Research,* edited by E. Tooker, 7–22. Albany: New York State Museum and Science Service.

———. 1971. "The New York State Wampum Collection: The Case for the Integrity of Cultural Treasures." *Proceedings of the American Philosophical Society* 115, no. 6:437–61.

———. 1978. "Northern Iroquoian Cultural Patterns." In *Handbook of North American Indians.* Vol. 15, *Northeast,* edited by B. G. Trigger, 296–321. Washington, D.C.: Smithsonian Institution.

———. 1987. *The False Faces of the Iroquois.* Norman: Univ. of Oklahoma Press.

———. 1989. "Return of Eleven Wampum Belts to the Six Nations Iroquois Confederacy on Grand River, Canada." *Ethnohistory* 36, no. 4:393–410.

———. 1998 *The Great Law and the Longhouse: A Political History of the Iroquois Confederacy.* Norman: Univ. of Oklahoma Press.

Fenton, William N., and Elizabeth L. Moore, eds. and trans. 1977. *Customs of the American Indians Compared with the Customs of Primitive Times by Father Joseph François Lafitau (1724).* Vol. 2. Toronto: Champlain Society.

Ferguson, T. J. 1996. "Native Americans and the Practice of Archaeology." *Annual Review of Anthropology* 25:63–79.

Ferris, Neal. 1989. "Continuity Within Change: Settlement-Subsistence Strategies and Artifact Patterns of the Southwestern Ojibwa, A.D. 1750–1861." M.A. thesis, York Univ.

———. 1998. " 'I Don't Think We Are in Kansas Anymore': The Rise of the Archaeological Consulting Industry in Ontario." In *Bringing Back the Past: Historical Perspectives on Canadian Archaeology,* edited by P. J. Smith and D. Mitchell, 225–47. National Museum of Man, Mercury Series, Archaeological Survey of Canada, Paper no. 158. Ottawa: National Museums of Canada.

———. 1999. "Telling Tales: Interpretive Trends in Southern Ontario Late Woodland Archaeology." *Ontario Archaeology* 68:1–62.

Ferris, Neal, and Michael W. Spence. 1995. "The Woodland Traditions in Southern Ontario." *Revista de Arqueologia Americana* 9:83–138.

Fiedel, Stuart J. 1987. "Algonquian Origins: A Problem in Archaeological-Linguistic Correlation." *Archaeology of Eastern North America* 15:1–11.

———. 1991. "Correlating Archaeology and Linguistics: The Algonquian Case." *Man in the Northeast* 41:9–32.

———. 1999. "Algonquians and Iroquoians: Taxonomy, Chronology and Archaeological Implications." In *Taming the Taxonomy: Toward a New Understanding of Great Lakes Archaeology,* edited by R. F. Williamson and C. M. Watts, 193–204. Toronto: Eastendbooks.

Finlayson, William D. 1985. *The 1975 and 1978 Rescue Excavations at the Draper Site: Introduction and Settlement Patterns.* National Museum of Man, Mercury Series, Archaeological Survey of Canada, Paper no. 130. Ottawa: National Museums of Canada.

———. 1998. *Iroquoian Peoples of the Land of Rocks and Water, A.D. 1000–1650: A Study in Settlement Archaeology.* Vol. 1. Special Publication no. 1. London, ON: London Museum of Archaeology.

Fitzgerald, William R. 1982a. *Lest the Beaver Run Loose: The Early 17th Century Christianson Site and Trends in Historic Neutral Archaeology.* National Museum of Man, Mercury Series, Archaeological Survey of Canada, Paper no. 111. Ottawa: National Museums of Canada.

———. 1982b. *In the Shadow of the Great Beaver: Alterations in Burial Offerings in the Spencer Creek Area of Historic Neutralia.* On file, Ontario Heritage Foundation, Toronto.

———. 1986. "Is the Warminster Site Champlain's Cahiagué?" *Ontario Archaeology* 45:3–7.

———. 1988. "Some Preliminary Thoughts on Stylistic Changes to 16th and 17th Century Copper Alloy Kettles and Iron Axes." *Kewa* 88, no. 1:3–19.

———. 1990a. "Chronology to Cultural Process: Lower Great Lakes Archaeology 1500–1650." Ph.D. diss., McGill Univ.

———. 1990b. "Preliminary Observations on the Ivan Elliot (AiHa-16) Village and the Raymond Reid (AiHa-4) Hamlet, Wellington County, Ontario." *Kewa* 90, no. 6:2–16.

———. 1991a. *The Archaeology of the Sixteenth-Century Neutral Iroquoian MacPherson (AhHa-21) Village.* On file, Ministry of Culture and Communications, London, Ontario.

———. 1991b. "More (or Less) on Iroquoian Semi-Subterranean 'Sweat Lodges.' " *Arch Notes* 91, no. 2:8–11.

———. 1992. "Contact, Contraction, and the Little Ice Age: Neutral Iroquoian Transformation, A.D. 1450–1650." Paper presented at the 57th Annual Meeting of the Society for American Archaeology, Pittsburgh.

Fitzgerald, William R., and James Bruce Jamieson. 1985. "An Alternate Interpretation of Late Iroquoian Development." Paper presented at the 18th Annual Meeting of the Canadian Archaeological Association, Winnipeg.

Fitzgerald, William R., Dean H. Knight, and Allison Bain. 1994. "Untanglers of Matters Temporal and Cultural: Glass Beads and the Early Contact Period Huron Ball Site." On file, Wilfrid Laurier Univ., Waterloo, Ontario.

Fitzgerald, William R., Laurier Turgeon, R. Holmes Whitehead, and James W. Bradley. 1993. "Late Sixteenth-Century Basque Banded Copper Kettles." *Historical Archaeology* 27, no. 1:44–57.

Fogt, Lisa M., and Peter G. Ramsden. 1996. "From Timepiece to Time Machine: Scale and Complexity in Iroquoian Archaeology." In *Debating Complexity*, edited by D. A. Meyer, P. C. Dawson, and D. T. Hanna, 39–45. Proceedings of the 26th Annual Chacmool Conference. Alberta: Archaeological Association of the Univ. of Calgary.

Ford, Michael. 1982. *The Changing Climate: Responses of the Natural Flora and Fauna*. London: George Allen and Unwin.

Forge, Anthony. 1972. "Normative Factors in Settlement Size of Neolithic Cultivators." In *Man, Settlement and Urbanism*, edited by P. J. Ucko, R. Tringham, and G. W. Dimbleby, 363–76. London: Duckworth.

Foster, Michael K. 1987. "Linguistic Aspects of the In-Situ Hypothesis of Iroquoian Origins." Paper presented at the Annual Conference on Iroquois Research, Rensselaerville, New York.

Fox, William A. 1980a. "Pickering Chronology—The Uncooperative Dates." *Kewa* 80, no. 9:2–6.

———. 1980b. "Of Projectile Points and Politics." *Arch Notes* 80, no. 2:5–13.

———. 1986. "The Elliott Villages (AfHe-2)—An Introduction." *Kewa* 86, no. 1:11–17.

———. 1990a. "The Middle to Late Woodland Transition." In *The Archaeology of Southern Ontario to A.D. 1650*, edited by C. J. Ellis and N. Ferris, 171–88. Occasional Publications of the London Chapter of the Ontario Archaeological Society no. 5. London, Ontario.

———. 1990b. "The Odawa." In *The Archaeology of Southern Ontario to A.D. 1650*, edited by C. J. Ellis and N. Ferris, 457–73. Occasional Publications of the London Chapter of the Ontario Archaeological Society no. 5. London, Ontario.

———. 1995. "Concluding Remarks." In *Origins of the People of the Longhouse: Proceedings of the 21st Annual Symposium of the Ontario Archaeological Society*, edited by A. Bekerman and G. A. Warrick, 144–51. Toronto: Ontario Archaeological Society.

Fraser, Alexander, and Arthur E. Jones. 1909. *Old Huronia*. Fifth Report of the Bureau of Archives, Province of Ontario. Toronto: L. K. Cameroun.

Fritz, Gayle J., and Bruce D. Smith. 1988. "Old Collections and New Technology: Documenting the Domestication of *Chenopodium* in Eastern North America." *Midcontinental Journal of Archaeology* 13:3–27.

Fuller, Richard S., and Diane E. Silvia. 1984. "Ceramic Rim Effigies in Southwest Alabama." *Journal of Alabama Archaeology* 30, no. 1:1–48.

Funk, Robert E. 1993. *Archaeological Investigations in the Upper Susquehanna Valley, New York State*. Monographs in Archaeology. Buffalo, N.Y.: Persimmon Press.

Galinat, W. C. 1967. *Plant Habitat and Adaptation of Corn*. Bulletin no. 565. Amherst: Experimental Station, College of Agriculture, Univ. of Massachusetts.

Gardner, Paul S. 1992. "Identification of Some Plant Remains from the Binghamton Mall Site, New York." Public Archaeology Facility, Binghamton Univ., Binghamton, N.Y.

Garrad, Charles, and Conrad E. Heidenreich. 1978. "Khionontateronon (Petun)." In *Handbook of North American Indians.* Vol. 15, *Northeast,* edited by B. G. Trigger, 394–97. Washington, D.C.: Smithsonian Institution.

Gaskell, Ivan. 1990. *The Thyssen-Bornemisza Collection: Seventeenth-Century Dutch and Flemish Painting.* London: Philip Wilson.

Gates St-Pierre, Christian. 2001. "Two Sites, but Two Phases? Revisiting Kipp Island and Hunter's Home." *Northeast Anthropology* 62:31–53.

George-Kanentiio, Doug. 2000. *Iroquois Culture and Commentary.* Santa Fe: Clear Light Publishers.

Gibson, Stanford J. 1963. "Iroquois Pottery Faces and Effigies." *Bulletin of the Chenango Chapter of the New York State Archaeological Association* 5, no. 2:4–5.

———. 1968. "The Oran-Barnes Site." *Bulletin of the Chenango Chapter of the New York State Archaeological Association* 10, no. 1.

———. 1971. "An Elevation Comparison of Iroquois Sites in Three Valleys of Central New York State." *Bulletin of the Chenango Chapter of the New York State Archaeological Association* 12, no. 2:1–3.

———. 1991. "The Bean Pit, Msv 2, Diable Site." *Bulletin of the Chenango Chapter of the New York State Archaeological Association* 24, no. 1:1–7.

Gombrich, Ernst H. 1963. "Visual Metaphors of Value in Art." In *Meditations on a Hobby Horse and Other Essays on the Theory of Art,* edited by E. H. Gombrich, 12–29. London: Phaidon Press.

Gould, Stephen J. 1992. "Dinosaurs in the Haystack." *Natural History,* March, 2–13.

Gramly, Richard M. 1977. "Deerskins and Hunting Territories: Competition for a Scarce Resource of the Northeastern Woodlands." *American Antiquity* 42, no. 4:601–5.

Grant, W. L., and Henry P. Biggar. 1907–14. *The History of New France by Marc Lescarbot.* 8 vols. Toronto: The Champlain Society.

Grassman, Thomas. 1969. *The Mohawk Indians and Their Valley, Being a Chronological Documentary Record to the End of 1693.* Schenectady, N.Y.: Eric Hugo Photography and Printing.

Graybill, Jeffrey R. 1989. "The Shenks Ferry Complex Revisited." In *New Approaches to Other Pasts,* edited by W. F. Kinsey III and R. W. Moeller, 51–59. Bethlehem, Conn.: Archaeological Services.

Graymont, Barbara. 1972. *The Iroquois in the American Revolution.* Syracuse, N.Y.: Syracuse Univ. Press.

Grayson, Donald K. 1970. "Statistical Inference and Northeastern Adena." *American Antiquity* 35, no. 1:102–4.

Greber, N'omi B., and Katharine C. Ruhl. 1989. *The Hopewell Site: A Contemporary Analysis Based on the Work of Charles C. Willoughby.* Boulder, Colo.: Westview Press.

Gregg, Susan A. 1988. *Foragers and Farmers: Population Interaction and Agricultural Expansion in Prehistoric Europe.* Chicago: Univ. of Chicago Press.

———. 1991. "Indirect Food Production: Mutualism and the Archaeological Visibility of Cultivation." In *Between Bands and States,* edited by S. A. Gregg, 203–15. Center for Archaeological Investigations, Occasional Paper no. 9. Carbondale: Southern Illinois Univ.

Griffin, James B. 1944. "The Iroquois in American Prehistory." *Papers of the Michigan Academy of Science, Arts, and Letters* 29:357–74.

———. 1946. "Culture Change and Continuity in Eastern United States Archaeology." In *Man in Northeastern North America,* edited by F. Johnson, 37–95. Papers of the Robert S. Peabody Foundation for Archaeology, vol. 3. Andover, Mass.: Phillips Academy.

Grigg, David B. 1980. *Population Growth and Agrarian Change: An Historical Perspective.* Cambridge, UK: Cambridge Univ. Press.

Grove, Jean M. 1985. "The Timing of the Little Ice Age in Scandinavia." In *The Climatic Scene,* edited by M. J. Tooley and G. M. Sheail, 132–53. London: George Allen and Unwin.

———. 1988. *The Little Ice Age.* London: Methuen.

Grumet, Robert S. 1995. *Historic Contact: Indian People and Colonists in Today's Northeastern United States in the Sixteenth through Eighteenth Centuries.* Norman: Univ. of Oklahoma Press.

Guldenzopf, David. 1986. "The Colonial Transformation of Mohawk Iroquois Society." Ph.D. diss., State Univ. of New York at Albany.

Guthe, Alfred K. 1958. "A Possible Seneca House Site, A.D. 1600." *Pennsylvania Archaeologist* 28, no. 1:33–38.

Hall, Robert L. 1977. "An Anthropocentric Perspective for Eastern United States Prehistory." *American Antiquity* 42, no. 4:499–518.

Hamell, George R. 1979. "Of Hockers, Diamonds and Hourglasses: Some Interpretations of Seneca Archaeological Art." Paper presented at the Annual Conference on Iroquois Research, Albany.

———. 1980. "Gannagaro State Historic Site: A Current Perspective." In *Studies in Iroquoian Culture,* edited by N. Bonvillain, 91–107. Occasional Publications in Northeastern Anthropology no. 6. Rindge, N.H.

———. 1981. "Through the Great Black Door: Transformation at the Threshold. The World's Rim and the Woods'-edge in Northern Iroquoian Myth and Ritual." Paper presented at the Annual Conference on Iroquois Research, Rensselaerville, N.Y.

———. 1983. "Trading in Metaphors: The Magic of Beads. Another Perspective upon Indian-European Contact in Northeastern North America." In *Proceedings of the 1982 Glass Trade Bead Conference,* edited by C. F. Hayes III, N. Bolger, K. Karklins, and C. F. Wray, 5–28. Research Records no. 16. Rochester, N.Y.: Rochester Museum and Science Center.

———. 1986. "Life's Immortal Shell: Wampum among the Northern Iroquoians." Paper presented at the Shell Bead Conference, Rochester Museum and Science Center, Rochester, N.Y. Revised 1988.

———. 1987a. "Strawberries, Floating Islands, and Rabbit Captains: Mythical Realities and European Contact in the Northeast During the Sixteenth and Seventeenth Centuries." *Journal of Canadian Studies* 21, no. 4:72–94.

———. 1987b. "Mythical Realities and European Contact in the Northeast During the Sixteenth and Seventeenth Centuries." *Man in the Northeast* 33:63–87.

———. 1987c. "Mohawks Abroad: The 1764 Amsterdam Etching of Sychnecta." In *Indians and Europe: An Interdisciplinary Collection of Essays,* edited by C. F. Feest, 175–93. Aachen, Germany: Editions Herodot, Rader Verlag.

———. 1991. "Long-Tail: The Panther in Huron-Wyandot and Seneca Myth, Ritual, and Material Culture." In *Feline Symbolism in Pre-Columbian and Native America,* edited by N. J. Saunders. Southampton, England: Department of Anthropology, Univ. of Southampton.

———. 1998. "Long-Tail: The Panther in Huron-Wyandot and Seneca Myth, Ritual, and Material Culture." In *Icons of Power: Feline Symbolism in the Americas,* edited by N. J. Saunders, 258–91. London: Routledge.

Hamell, George R., and Hazel Dean John. 1987. "Ethnology, Archaeology, History and 'Seneca Origins.'" Paper presented at the Annual Conference on Iroquois Research, Rensselaerville, N.Y.

Hammer, C. U., H. B. Clausen, and W. Dansgaard. 1980. "Greenland Ice Sheet Evidence of Post-glacial Volcanism and Its Climatic Impact." *Nature* 288:230–35.

Hammer, Oyvind, David A. T. Harper, and Paul D. Ryan. 2001. "PAST: Paleontological Statistics Software Package for Education and Data Analysis." *Palaeontologia Electronica* 4, no. 1, <http://palaeoelectronica.org/2001-1/past/issue1_01.htm> (accessed Mar. 2002).

Harding, Anthony F. 1982. "Climatic Change and Archaeology in Piedmont Virginia." In *Middle and Late Late Woodland Research in Virginia,* edited by A. F. Harding, 1–10. Edinburgh: Edinburgh Univ. Press.

Harrington, M. R. 1908. "Some Seneca Corn-Foods and Their Preparation." *American Anthropologist* 10:575–90.

———. 1921. *Religion and Ceremonies of the Lenape.* Indian Notes and Monographs 19. New York: Museum of the American Indian, Heye Foundation.

Hart, John P. 1999a. "Maize Agriculture Evolution in the Eastern Woodlands of North America: A Darwinian Perspective." *Journal of Archaeological Method and Theory* 6:137–80.

———. 1999b. "Another Look at 'Clemson's Island.'" *Northeast Anthropology* 57:19–26.

———. 1999c. "Dating Roundtop's Domesticates: Implications for Northeastern Late Prehistory." In *Current Northeast Paleoethnobotany,* edited by J. P. Hart, 47–68. New York State Museum Bulletin 494. Albany: State Univ. of New York, State Education Department.

———. 2000a. "New Dates on Classic New York Sites: Just How Old Are Those Longhouses?" *Northeast Anthropology* 60:1–22.

———. 2000b. "New Dates from Old Collections: The Roundtop Site and Maize-Beans-Squash Agriculture in the Northeast." *North American Archaeologist* 20:7–17.

———. 2001. "Maize, Matrilocality, Migration, and Northern Iroquoian Evolution." *Journal of Archaeological Method and Theory* 8, no. 2:151–82.

Hart, John P., David L. Asch, C. Margaret Scarry, and Gary W. Crawford. 2002. "The Age of the Common Bean *(Phaseolus vulgaris* L.) in the Northern Eastern Woodlands of North America." *Antiquity* 76:377–85.

Hart, John P., and Hetty Jo Brumbach. 2003. "The Death of Owasco." *American Antiquity* 68, no. 4:737–52.

Hart, John P., and Bernard K. Means. 2002. "Maize and Villages: A Summary and Critical Assessment of Current Northeast Early Late Prehistoric Evidence." In *Northeast Subsistence-Settlement Change A.D. 700–1300,* edited by J. P. Hart and C. B. Rieth, 345–58. New York State Museum Bulletin 496. Albany: State Univ. of New York, State Education Department.

Hart, John P., and C. Margaret Scarry. 1999. "The Age of Common Beans *(Phaseolus vulgaris)* in the Northeastern United States." *American Antiquity* 64, no. 4:653–58.

Hart, John P., and Nancy Asch Sidell. 1996. "Prehistoric Agricultural Systems in the West Branch of the Susquehanna River Basin, A.D. 800 to A.D. 1350." *Northeast Anthropology* 52:1–30.

———. 1997. "Additional Evidence for Early Cucurbit Use in the Northern Eastern Woodlands East of the Allegheny Front." *American Antiquity* 62, no. 3:523–37.

Hart, John P., and John Edward Terrell, eds. 2002. *Darwin and Archaeology: A Handbook of Key Concepts*. Westport, Conn.: Bergin and Garvey.

Hart, John P., Robert G. Thompson, and Hetty Jo Brumbach. 2003. "Phytolith Evidence for Early Maize *(Zea mays)* in the Northern Finger Lakes Region of New York." *American Antiquity* 68, no. 4:619–40.

Hartney, Patrick C. 1981. "Tuberculous Lesions in a Prehistoric Population Sample from Southern Ontario." In *Prehistoric Tuberculosis in the Americas,* edited by J. E. Buikstra, 141–60. Northwestern University Archaeological Program Scientific Papers 5. Evanston, Ill.

Hasenstab, Robert J. 1978. "The Iroquois-Algonquian Border: An Ecological Explanation." Core program paper, Department of Anthropology, Univ. of Massachusetts, Amherst.

———. 1981. "Research Proposal: An Environmental Analysis of Iroquois Settlement in Central and Western New York State." On file, Rochester Museum and Science Center, Rochester, N.Y.

———. 1982. "Aboriginal Hilltop Occupations and Microclimate in the Appalachian Uplands." Paper presented at the 22nd Annual Meeting of the Northeastern Anthropological Association, Princeton, N.J.

———. 1986. "Northern Iroquoian Maize Horticulture: Extensive or Intensive Cultivation?" Statement of Field, Department of Anthropology, Univ. of Massachusetts, Amherst.

———. 1987. "Canoes, Caches, and Carrying Places: Territorial Boundaries and Tribalization in Late Woodland Western New York." *The Bulletin: Journal of the New York State Archaeological Association* 95:39–49.

———. 1990. "Agriculture, Warfare, and Tribalization in the Iroquois Homeland of New York: A G.I.S. Analysis of Late Woodland Settlement." Ph.D. diss., Univ. of Massachusetts, Amherst.

———. 1992. "In Situ but not in Vacuo: Iroquois Regional Interaction and the Development of Social Complexity in the Late Woodland Northeast." Ms. in possession of the author.

———. 1996. "Settlement as Adaptation: Variability in Iroquois Site Selections as Inferred through GIS." In *New Methods, Old Problems: Geographic Information Systems in Modern Archaeological Research,* edited by H.D.G. Maschner, 223–41. Center for Archaeological Investigations, Occasional Paper no. 23. Carbondale: Southern Illinois Univ.

Hassan, Fekri. 1981. *Demographic Archaeology*. New York: Academic Press.

Hastorf, Christine A., and Michael J. DeNiro. 1985. "Reconstruction of Prehistoric Plant Production and Cooking Practices by a New Isotope Method." *Nature* 315:489–91.

Hatch, James W., ed. 1980. *The Fisher Farm Site: A Late Woodland Hamlet in Context*. The Pennsylvania State Univ., Department of Anthropology, Occasional Papers no. 12. University Park, Pennsylvania.

Hay, Conran A., James W. Hatch, and Janet Sutton. 1987. *A Management Plan for Clemson Island Archaeological Resources in the Commonwealth of Pennsylvania.* Harrisburg: Pennsylvania Historical and Museum Commission, Bureau for Historic Preservation.

Hayden, Brian. 1978. "Bigger Is Better? Factors Determining Ontario Iroquois Site Sizes." *Canadian Journal of Archaeology* 2:107–16.

Hayden, Brian, and Aubrey Cannon. 1982. "The Corporate Group as an Archaeological Unit." *Journal of Anthropological Archaeology* 1:132–58.

Hayes, Charles F., III. 1967. "The Longhouse at the Cornish Site." In *Iroquois Culture, History, and Prehistory: Proceedings of the 1965 Conference on Iroquois Research,* edited by E. Tooker, 91–97. New York State Museum and Science Service. Albany: State Univ. of New York, State Education Department.

———. 1980. "An Overview of the Current Status of Seneca Ceramics." In *Proceedings of the 1979 Iroquois Pottery Conference,* edited by C. F. Hayes III, G. R. Hamell, and B. M. Koenig, 87–93. Research Records no. 13. Rochester, N.Y.: Rochester Museum and Science Center.

Hays, David G., Enid Margolis, Raoul Naroll, and Dale Revere Perkins. 1972. "Color Term Salience." *American Anthropologist* 74, no. 5: 1107–21.

Heidenreich, Conrad E. 1971. *Huronia: A History and Geography of the Huron Indians, 1600–1650.* Toronto: McClelland and Stewart.

———. 1978. "Huron." In *Handbook of North American Indians.* Vol. 15, *Northeast,* edited by B. G. Trigger, 368–88. Washington, D.C.: Smithsonian Institution.

———. 1990. "History of the St. Lawrence-Great Lakes Area to A.D. 1650." In *The Archaeology of Southern Ontario to A.D. 1650,* edited by C. J. Ellis and N. Ferris, 475–92. Occasional Publications of the London Chapter of the Ontario Archaeological Society no. 5. London, Ontario.

Henige, David. 1999. "Can a Myth Be Astronomically Dated?" *American Indian Culture and Research Journal* 23, no. 4:127–57.

Henry, Dixie L. 1995. *Bringing Our Ancestors Home . . . The Controversy over Repatriation.* Summer Research Report, Colgate Univ.

———. 1996. " 'The Tomb of the Red Man': Repatriation and Its Impact on the Role of the Museum." High Honors Research Paper, Colgate Univ.

———. 2001. *Cultural Change and Adaptation among the Oneida Iroquois, A.D. 1000–1700.* Ph.D. diss., Cornell Univ.

Henry, Jeannette. 1970. "A Rebuttal to the Five Anthropologists on the Issue of the Wampum Belts." *Indian Historian* 3, no. 2:15–17.

Hesse, Franklin J. 1975. "The Egli and Lord Sites: The Historic Component—'Unadilla' 1753–1778." *The Bulletin: Journal of the New York State Archaeological Association* 63:14–31.

Hewitt, John N. B. 1892. "Legend of the Founding of the Iroquois League." *American Anthropologist* 5:131–48.

———. 1907–10. "Wampum." In *Handbook of American Indians North of Mexico.* Part 2, edited by F. W. Hodge, 904–9. Bureau of American Ethnology Bulletin 30. Washington, D.C.: Smithsonian Institution.

———, ed. 1918. "Seneca Fiction, Legends, and Myths: Collected by Jeremiah Curtin and J. N. B. Hewitt." In *Thirty-Second Annual Report of the Bureau of American Ethnology to the*

Secretary of the Smithsonian Institution, 1910–1911, 37–819. Washington, D.C.: Government Printing Office.

———. 1928. *Iroquois Cosmology: Second Part with Introduction and Notes.* 43rd Annual Report of the Bureau of American Ethnology 1925–26. Washington, D.C.: Smithsonian Institution.

Hill, Richard W., Sr. 2001. "Regenerating Identity: Repatriation and the Indian Frame of Mind." In *The Future of the Past: Archaeologists, Native Americans, and Repatriation,* edited by T. L. Bray, 127–38. New York: Garland Publishing.

Hodder, Ian. 1986. *Reading the Past: Current Approaches to Interpretation in Archaeology.* Cambridge, UK: Cambridge Univ. Press.

———. 1987. "The Contextual Analysis of Symbolic Meanings." In *The Archaeology of Contextual Meanings,* edited by I. Hodder, 1–10. Cambridge, UK: Cambridge Univ. Press.

Horvath, Steven. 1977. "A Computerized Study of Princess Point Complex Ceramics: Some Implications of Late Prehistoric Social Organization in Ontario." In *The Princess Point Complex,* edited by D. M. Stothers, 309–17. National Museum of Man, Mercury Series, Archaeological Survey of Canada, Paper no. 58. Ottawa: National Museums of Canada.

Hubbard, John D. 1997. "An Ancient Wrong Righted." *The Colgate Scene,* May, 6.

Huey, Paul R. 1983. "Glass Beads from Fort Orange (1624–1676), Albany, New York." In *Proceedings of the 1982 Glass Trade Bead Conference,* edited by C. F. Hayes III, N. Bolger, K. Karklins, and C. F. Wray, 83–110. Research Records no. 16. Rochester, N.Y.: Rochester Museum and Science Center.

Hunt, Eleazer D. 1990. "A Consideration of Environmental, Physiographic, and Horticultural Systems as They Impact Late Woodland Settlement Patterns in Western New York State: A Geographic Information System (GIS) Analysis of Site Locations." Ph.D. diss., State Univ. of New York at Buffalo.

Hunter, William A. 1969 [1959]. "The Historic Role of the Susquehannock." In *Susquehannock Miscellany,* edited by J. Witthoft and W. F. Kinsey, 8–18. Harrisburg: Pennsylvania Historical and Museum Commission.

Ingram, M. J., G. Farmer, and T.M.L. Wigley. 1981. "Past Climates and Their Impact on Man: A Review." In *Climate and History: Studies in Past Climates and Their Impact on Man,* edited by T.M.L. Wigley, M. J. Ingram, and G. Farmer, 3–50. Cambridge, UK: Cambridge Univ. Press.

Jackes, Mary K. 1983. "Osteological Evidence for Smallpox: A Possible Case from Seventeenth Century Ontario." *American Journal of Physical Anthropology* 60:75–81.

———. 1986. "The Mortality of Ontario Archaeological Populations." *Canadian Journal of Anthropology* 5, no. 2:33–48.

Jackson, L. J. 1983. "Early Maize in South-Central Ontario." *Arch Notes* 83, no. 3:9–12.

Jacobs, Wilbur R. 1966. *Wilderness Politics and Indian Gifts, The Northern Colonial Frontier 1748–1763.* Lincoln: Univ. of Nebraska Press.

Jamieson, James Bruce. 1983. "An Examination of Prisoner-Sacrifice and Cannibalism at the St. Lawrence Iroquoian Roebuck Site." *Canadian Journal of Archaeology* 7, no. 2:159–75.

———. 1990a. "The Archaeology of the St. Lawrence Iroquoians." In *The Archaeology of Southern Ontario to A.D. 1650,* edited by C. J. Ellis and N. Ferris, 385–404. Occasional Publications of the London Chapter of the Ontario Archaeological Society no. 5. London, Ontario.

———. 1990b. "Trade and Warfare: The Disappearance of the Saint Lawrence Iroquoians." *Man in the Northeast* 39:79–86.
Jamieson, Susan M. 1986. "Late Middleport Catchment Areas and the Slack-Caswell Example." *Ontario Archaeology* 45:27–38.
———. 1991. "A Pickering Conquest?" *Kewa* 91, no. 5:2–18.
———. 1992. "Regional Interaction and Ontario Iroquois Evolution." *Canadian Journal of Archaeology* 16:70–88.
———. 1999. "A Brief History of Aboriginal Social Interactions in Southern Ontario and Their Taxonomic Implications." In *Taming the Taxonomy: Toward a New Understanding of Great Lakes Archaeology,* edited by R. F. Williamson and C. M. Watts, 175–92. Toronto: Eastendbooks.
Jennings, Francis P. 1968. "Glory, Death, and Transfiguration: The Susquehannock Indians in the Seventeenth Century." *Proceedings of the American Philosophical Society* 112, no. 1:15–33.
———. 1978. "Susquehannock." In *Handbook of North American Indians.* Vol. 15, *Northeast,* edited by B. G. Trigger, 362–67. Washington, D.C.: Smithsonian Institution.
Johnson, William C. 1990. "The Protohistoric Monongahela and the Case for an Iroquois Connection." Paper presented at the 57th Annual Meeting of the Eastern States Archaeological Federation, Columbus, Ohio.
———. 1992. "Ontario Iroquois and Monongahela Culture Contact During the Late Terminal Late Prehistoric and Protohistoric Periods: The Case for the Massowomeck Connection." Paper presented at the 25th Annual Meeting of the Canadian Archaeological Association, London, Ontario.
Johnston, Susan M. 1987. "Epidemics: The Forgotten Factor in Seventeenth Century Native Warfare in the St. Lawrence Region." In *Native People, Native Lands,* edited by B. Cox, 14–31. Ottawa: Carleton Univ. Press.
Jordan, Kurt A. 1997. "Pan-Iroquoian Trend or Mohawk Exceptionalism: A Reconsideration of the Longhouse to Loghouse Transition, 1687–1779." Paper presented at the Rochester Museum and Science Center Conference on the Iroquois Longhouse, Rochester, N.Y.
———. 2001a. "The Townley-Read/New Ganechstage Project: 1996–2000 Investigations of 18th Century and Prehistoric Components at the Townley-Read Site." In the author's possession.
———. 2001b. "Smiths and Senecas: Iron Tool Production and Use at the Townley-Read Site, ca. A.D. 1715–1754." On file, Early American Industries Association, Wilmington, Del.
———. 2002. "The Archaeology of the Iroquois Restoration: Settlement, Housing, and Economy at a Dispersed Seneca Community, ca. A.D. 1715–1754." Ph.D. diss., Columbia Univ.
Jordan, Terry G. 1985. *American Log Buildings: An Old World Heritage.* Chapel Hill: Univ. of North Carolina Press.
Jordan, Terry G., and Matti Kaups. 1989. *The American Backwoods Frontier: An Ethnic and Ecological Interpretation.* Baltimore: Johns Hopkins Univ. Press.
Justice, Noel D. 1987. *Stone Age Spear and Arrow Points of the Midcontinental and Eastern United States.* Bloomington: Indiana Univ. Press.
Kapches, Mima. 1981. "The Middleport Pattern in Ontario Iroquoian Prehistory." Ph.D. diss., Univ. of Toronto.

———. 1984. "Cabins on Ontario Iroquoian Sites." *North American Archaeologist* 5, no. 1:63–71.

———. 1987. "The Auda Site: An Early Pickering Iroquois Component in Southeastern Ontario." *Archaeology of Eastern North America* 15:155–75.

———. 1990. "The Spatial Dynamics of Ontario Iroquoian Longhouses." *American Antiquity* 55, no. 1:49–67.

———. 1992. "The Ontario Iroquoian Longhouse: A Study in Vernacular Architecture." Paper presented at the Architectural Conservancy of Ontario Conference, Brantford.

———. 1993. "The Identification of an Iroquoian Unit of Measurement: Architectural and Social/Cultural Implications for the Longhouse." *Archaeology of Eastern North America* 21:137–62.

———. 1995. "Chaos Theory and Social Movements: A Theoretical View of the Formation of the Northern Iroquoian Longhouse Cultural Pattern." In *Origins of the People of the Longhouse: Proceedings of the 21st Annual Symposium of the Ontario Archaeological Society*, edited by A. Bekerman and G. A. Warrick, 86–96. Toronto: Ontario Archaeological Society.

Karrow, Paul F., and Barry G. Warner. 1990. "The Geological and Biological Environment for Human Occupation in Southern Ontario." In *The Archaeology of Southern Ontario to A.D. 1650*, edited by C. J. Ellis and N. Ferris, 5–36. Occasional Publications of the London Chapter of the Ontario Archaeological Society no. 5. London, Ontario.

Katz, S. H., M. L. Hediger, and L. A. Valleroy. 1974. "Traditional Maize Processing Techniques in the New World." *Science* 184:765–73.

Katzenberg, M. Anne. 1993. "Applications of Elemental and Isotopic Analysis to Problems in Ontario Prehistory." In *Investigations of Ancient Human Tissue*, edited by M. K. Sandford, 335–60. New York: Gordon and Breach.

Katzenberg, M. Anne, Shelley R. Saunders, and William R. Fitzgerald. 1993. "Age Differences in Stable Carbon and Nitrogen Isotope Ratios in a Population of Prehistoric Maize Horticulturalists." *American Journal of Physical Anthropology* 90:267–81.

Katzenberg, M. Anne, and Henry P. Schwarcz. 1986. "Paleonutrition in Southern Ontario: Evidence from Strontium and Stable Isotopes." *Canadian Review of Physical Anthropology* 5, no. 2:15–21.

Katzenberg, M. Anne, Henry P. Schwarcz, Martin Knyf, and F. Jerry Melbye. 1995. "Stable Isotope Evidence for Maize Horticulture and Paleodiet in Southern Ontario, Canada." *American Antiquity* 60, no. 2:335–50.

Kent, Barry C. 1980. "An Update on Susquehanna Iroquoian Pottery." In *Proceedings of the 1979 Iroquois Pottery Conference*, edited by C. F. Hayes III, G. R. Hamell, and B. M. Koenig 99–103. Research Records no. 13. Rochester, N.Y.: Rochester Museum and Science Center.

———. 1993 [1984]. *Susquehanna's Indians*. Anthropological Series no. 6. Harrisburg: Pennsylvania Historical and Museum Commission.

Kenyon, Ian T. 1972. "The Neutral Sequence in the Hamilton Area." Paper presented at the 5th Annual Meeting of the Canadian Archaeological Association, St. John's, Newfoundland.

———. 1986. "Sagard's Rassade Rouge of 1624." In *Studies in Southwestern Ontario Archaeology*, edited by W. A. Fox, 53–59. Occasional Publications of the London Chapter of the Ontario Archaeological Society no. 1. London, Ontario.

Kenyon, Ian T., and William R. Fitzgerald. 1986. "Dutch Glass Beads in the Northeast: An Ontario Perspective." *Man in the Northeast* 32:1–34.

Kenyon, Ian T., and Thomas Kenyon. 1983. "Comments on 17th Century Glass Beads from Ontario." In *Proceedings of the 1982 Glass Trade Bead Conference,* edited by C. F. Hayes III, N. Bolger, K. Karklins, and C. F. Wray, 59–74. Research Records no. 16. Rochester, N.Y.: Rochester Museum and Science Center.

———. 1987. "The Iron Trade Axe in Ontario, ca. 1580–1650: Exploratory Data Analysis." *Kewa* 87, no. 7:10–20.

Kenyon, Walter A. 1968. *The Miller Site.* Art and Archaeololgy Occasional Paper no. 14. Toronto: Royal Ontario Museum.

Kerber, Jordan E. 1997. *Lambert Farm: Public Archaeology and Canine Burials along Narragansett Bay.* Case Studies in Archaeology. New York: Harcourt Brace College Publishers.

———. 2003. "Community-Based Archaeology in Central New York: Workshops Involving Native American Youth." *The Public Historian* 25, no. 1:83–90.

———, ed. 2006. *Cross-Cultural Collaboration: Native Peoples and Archaeology in the Northeastern United States.* Lincoln: Univ. of Nebraska Press.

Kerber, Jordan E., Bridget Benisch, and Terrence Zinn, eds. 2000. *Archaeological Investigations in Central New York: Colgate University Field Methods Project.* Vol. 3. Hamilton, N.Y.: Department of Sociology and Anthropology, Colgate Univ.

Kerber, Jordan E., Seth Bidder, and Michael Wild, eds. 2003. *Archaeological Investigations in Central New York: Colgate University Field Methods Project.* Vol. 5. Hamilton, N.Y.: Department of Sociology and Anthropology, Colgate Univ.

Kerber, Jordan E., Bryan Deegan, and Christen Monk, eds. 2002. *Archaeological Investigations in Central New York: Colgate University Field Methods Project.* Vol. 4. Hamilton, N.Y.: Department of Sociology and Anthropology, Colgate Univ.

Kerber, Jordan E., Megan Glennon, and Thomas Palmer, eds. 1996. *Archaeological Investigations in the Chenango Valley: Colgate University Field Methods Project.* Vol. 5. Hamilton, N.Y.: Department of Sociology and Anthropology, Colgate Univ.

Kerber, Jordan E., and Dixie L. Henry, eds. 1998. *Archaeological Investigations in Central New York: Colgate University Field Methods Project.* Vol. 1. Hamilton, N.Y.: Department of Sociology and Anthropology, Colgate Univ.

Kerber, Jordan E., Corrine Ochsner, and Helen Saul, eds. 1999. *Archaeological Investigations in Central New York: Colgate University Field Methods Project.* Vol. 2. Hamilton, N.Y.: Department of Sociology and Anthropology, Colgate Univ.

Keron, James. 2000. "The Dorchester Village Site (AfHg-24): A Large Uren Substage Village in Eastern Middlesex County." *Kewa* 100, no. 1/2:1–22.

Kidd, Kenneth E. 1953. "The Excavation and Historical Identification of a Huron Ossuary." *American Antiquity* 18, no. 4:359–79.

Kidd, Kenneth E., and Martha A. Kidd. 1983 [1970]. "Appendix: A Classification System for Glass Beads for the Use of Field Archaeologists." In *Proceedings of the 1982 Glass Trade Bead Conference,* edited by C. F. Hayes III, N. Bolger, K. Karklins, and C. F. Wray, 219–57. Research Records no. 16. Rochester, N.Y.: Rochester Museum and Science Center.

King, Frances B. 1992. "Floral Remains." In *The Prehistory of the Catawissa Bridge Replacement Site (36C09), Columbia County, Pennsylvania,* edited by T. C. East, J. A. Adovasio, W. C.

Johnson, and D. R. Pedler. Cultural Resource Management Program, Department of Anthropology, Univ. of Pittsburgh.

Klesert, Anthony L., and Alan S. Downer, eds. 1990. *Preservation on the Reservation: Native Americans, Native American Lands, and Archaeology.* Navajo Nation Papers in Anthropology no. 26. Window Rock, Ariz.: Navajo Nation Archaeology Department and the Navajo Nation Historic Preservation Department.

Knapp, Timothy D. 2002. "Pits, Plants, and Place: Recognizing Late Prehistoric Subsistence and Settlement Diversity in the Upper Susquehanna Drainage." In *Northeast Subsistence-Settlement Change A.D. 700–1300,* edited by J. P. Hart and C. B. Rieth, 167–92. New York State Museum Bulletin 496. Albany: State Univ. of New York, State Education Department.

Knight, Dean, and Sally Cameron. 1983. "The Ball Site, 1975–1982." On file, Wilfrid Laurier Univ., Waterloo, Ontario.

Knoerl, John J. 1988. "The Concept of Scale and Its Application to Prehistoric and Historic Iroquois Sites in the Lake Ontario Drainage Basin." Ph.D. diss., Binghamton Univ.

Kraft, Herbert C. 1972. "Archaeological Evidence for a Possible Masking Complex among the Prehistoric Lenape in Northwestern New Jersey." *The Bulletin: Journal of the New York State Archaeological Association* 56:1–11.

———. 1975. "The Late Woodland Pottery of the Upper Delaware Valley: A Survey and Reevaluation." *Archaeology of Eastern North America* 3:101–40.

Krech, Shepard, III. 1999. *The Ecological Indian: Myth and History.* New York: Norton.

Kuhn, Robert D. 1985. "Trade and Exchange among the Mohawk-Iroquois: A Trace Element Analysis of Ceramic Smoking Pipes." Ph.D. diss., State Univ. of New York at Albany.

———. 1986a. "Indications of Interaction and Acculturation Through Ceramic Analysis." In *The Mohawk Valley Project: 1983 Jackson-Everson Excavations,* edited by R. D. Kuhn and D. R. Snow, 75–92. Albany: Institute for Northeast Anthropology, State Univ. of New York.

———. 1986b. "Interaction Patterns in Eastern New York: A Trace Element Analysis of Iroquoian and Algonkian Ceramics." *The Bulletin: Journal of the New York State Archaeological Association* 92:9–21.

———. 1989. "The Trace Element Analysis of Hudson Valley Clays and Ceramics." *The Bulletin: Journal of the New York State Archaeological Association* 99:25–30.

———. 1994a. "The Cromwell Site (NYSM 1121), Including a Brief Treatise on Early Seventeenth-Century Mohawk Pottery Trends." *The Bulletin: Journal of the New York State Archaeological Association* 108:29–38.

———. 1994b. "A Comparison of Human Face Effigy Pipes from the St. Lawrence Iroquoian Roebuck Site and the Mohawk Otstungo Site Using Trace Element Analysis." *The Ottawa Archaeologist* 21, no. 2:3–9.

———. 2001. "The New York State Historic Preservation Office Archaeological Program, 1990 to 2000: A Ten-Year Retrospective." *The Bulletin: Journal of the New York State Archaeological Association* 117:25–35.

Kuhn, Robert D., and Robert E. Funk. 1994. "Mohawk Interaction Patterns During the Late Sixteenth Century." In *Proceedings of the 1992 People to People Conference: Selected Papers,* edited by C. F. Hayes III, C. C. Bodner, and L. P. Saunders, 77–84. Research Records no. 23. Rochester, N.Y.: Rochester Museum and Science Center.

———. 2000. "Boning up on the Mohawk: An Overview of Mohawk Faunal Assemblages and Subsistence Patterns." *Archaeology of Eastern North America* 28:29–62.

Kuhn, Robert D., Robert E. Funk, and James F. Pendergast. 1993. "The Evidence for a Saint Lawrence Iroquoian Presence on Sixteenth-Century Mohawk Sites." *Man in the Northeast* 45:77–86.

Kuhn, Robert D., and Martha L. Sempowski. 2001. "A New Approach to Dating the League of the Iroquois." *American Antiquity* 66, no. 2:301–14.

Kuhn, Robert D., and Dean R. Snow, eds. 1986. *The Mohawk Valley Project: 1983 Jackson-Everson Excavations.* Albany: Institute for Northeast Anthropology, State Univ. of New York.

Kurath, Gertrude P. 1968. *Dance and Song Rituals of Six Nations Reserve, Ontario.* Folklore Series 4, Bulletin 220. Ottawa: National Museum of Man.

Landy, David. 1978. "Tuscarora among the Iroquois." In *Handbook of North American Indians.* Vol. 15, *Northeast,* edited by B. G. Trigger, 518–34. Washington, D.C.: Smithsonian Institution.

Langdon, Stephen P. 1995. "Biological Relationships among the Iroquois." *Human Biology* 67, no. 3:355–74.

Langsner, Drew. 1982. *A Logbuilder's Handbook.* Emmaus, Pa.: Rodale Press.

Lantz, Stanley W. 1980. "Seneca Cabin Site: Historic Component of the Venatta Site (30CA46)." *Pennsylvania Archaeologist* 50, nos. 1–2:9–41.

Larson, Daniel O., and Joel Michaelson. 1990. "Impacts of Climatic Variability and Population Growth on Virgin Branch Anasazi Cultural Developments." *American Antiquity* 55, no. 2:227–49.

Latta, Martha A. 1991. "The Captive Bride Syndrome: Iroquoian Behavior or Archaeological Myth?" In *The Archaeology of Gender,* edited by D. Walde and N. D. Willows, 17–23. Proceedings of the 22nd Annual Chacmool Conference. Alberta: Archaeological Association of the Univ. of Calgary.

Le Roy Ladurie, Emmanuel. 1971. *Times of Feast, Times of Famine: A History of Climate since the Year 1000.* Garden City, N.Y.: Doubleday.

Leader, Jonathan M. 1988. "Technological Continuities and Specialization in Prehistoric Metalwork in the Eastern United States." Ph.D. diss., Univ. of Florida.

Lee, Thomas E. 1959. "An Archaeological Survey of Southwestern Ontario and Manitoulin Island." *Pennsylvania Archaeologist* 29, no. 2:80–92.

Lenig, Donald. 1965. *The Oak Hill Horizon and Its Relation to the Development of Five Nations Iroquois Culture.* Researches and Transactions of the New York State Archaeological Association 15, no 1. Buffalo.

Lennox, Paul A. 1981. *The Hamilton Site: A Late Historic Neutral Town.* National Museum of Man, Mercury Series, Archaeological Survey of Canada, Paper no. 103:211–403. Ottawa: National Museums of Canada.

———. 1984a. *The Bogle I and Bogle II Sites: Historic Neutral Hamlets of the Northern Tier.* National Museum of Man, Mercury Series, Archaeological Survey of Canada, Paper no. 121:184–289. Ottawa: National Museums of Canada.

———. 1984b. *The Hood Site: A Historic Neutral Town of 1640 A.D.* National Museum of Man, Mercury Series, Archaeological Survey of Canada, Paper no. 121:1–183. Ottawa: National Museums of Canada.

———, ed. 1995. *MTO Contributions to the Archaeology of the Late Woodland Period in Southwestern Ontario: Small Sites Investigations.* Research Report no. 24. London, ON: London Museum of Archaeology.

Lennox, Paul A., Christine F. Dodd, and Carl R. Murphy. 1986. *The Wiacek Site: A Late Middleport Component, Simcoe County, Ontario.* London: Ontario Ministry of Transportation.

Lennox, Paul A., and William R. Fitzgerald. 1990. "The Culture History and Archaeology of the Neutral Iroquoians." In *The Archaeology of Southern Ontario to A.D. 1650,* edited by C. J. Ellis and N. Ferris, 405–56. Occasional Publications of the London Chapter of the Ontario Archaeological Society no. 5. London, Ontario.

Lewis, Thomas M. N., and Madeline Kneberg. 1970. *Hiwassee Island: An Archaeological Account of Four Tennessee Indian Peoples.* Knoxville: Univ. of Tennessee Press.

Lightman, Alan, and Owen Gingerich. 1992. "When Do Anomalies Begin?" *Science* 255:690–95.

Little, Elizabeth A. 1999. "Maize Age and Isotope Values at the Goldkrest Site." In *Current Northeast Paleoethnobotany,* edited by J. P. Hart, 81–82. New York State Museum Bulletin 494. Albany: State Univ. of New York, State Education Department.

Livi-Bacci, Massimo. 1992. *A Concise History of World Population.* Translated by C. Ipsen. Cambridge, UK: Blackwell.

Lofstrom, Ted. 1987. "The Rise of Wild Rice Exploitation and Its Implication for Population Size and Social Organization in Minnesota Woodland Period Cultures." *The Minnesota Archaeologist* 46, no. 2:3–15.

Lopez, Julius, and Roy Latham. 1960. "Faces on Sebonac Pottery from Eastern Long Island, N.Y." *Pennsylvania Archaeologist* 30, no. 2:58–62.

Lopez, Julius, and Stanley Wisniewski. 1989. "The Ryders Pond Site II." In *The Coastal Archaeology Reader: Selections from the New York State Archaeological Association Bulletin, 1954–1977,* edited by G. S. Levine, 233–47. Readings in Long Island Archaeology and Ethnohistory. Vol. 2. Stony Brook, N.Y.: Suffolk County Archaeological Association.

Lounsbury, Floyd G. 1978. "Iroquoian Languages." In *Handbook of North American Indians.* Vol. 15, *Northeast,* edited by B. G. Trigger, 334–43. Washington, D.C.: Smithsonian Institution.

Lovis, William A. 1990. "Curational Considerations for Systematic Research Collections: AMS Dating of a Curated Ceramic Assemblage." *American Antiquity* 55, no. 2:382–87.

Lyman, R. Lee, and Michael J. O'Brien. 2002. "Classification." In *Darwin and Archaeology: A Handbook of Key Concepts,* edited by J. P. Hart and J. E. Terrell, 69–88. Westport, Conn.: Bergin and Garvey.

Lyman, R. Lee, Michel J. O'Brien, and Robert C. Dunnell. 1997. *The Rise and Fall of Culture History.* New York: Plenum Press.

MacDonald, Eva M., and Martin S. Cooper. 1992. "The Birch Site (BcGw-29): A Late Iroquoian Special Purpose Site in Simcoe County, Ontario." *Kewa* 92, no. 6:2–15.

MacDonald, John. 1986. "New Dates for Old Chronologies: Radiocarbon Dates for the Varden Site." *Kewa* 86, no. 9:8–22.

MacDonald, Robert I. 1986. "The Coleman Site (AiHd-7): A Late Prehistoric Iroquoian Village in the Waterloo Region." M.A. thesis, Trent Univ.

———. 1988. "Ontario Iroquoian Sweat Lodges." *Ontario Archaeology* 48:17–26.

MacDonald, Robert I., and Ronald F. Williamson. 1995. "The Hibou Site (Algo-50): Investigating Ontario Iroquoian Origins in the Central North Shore Area of Lake Ontario." In

Origins of the People of the Longhouse: Proceedings of the 21st Annual Symposium of the Ontario Archaeological Society, edited by A. Bekerman and G. A. Warrick, 9–42. Toronto: Ontario Archaeological Society.

MacNeish, Richard S. 1952. *Iroquois Pottery Types: A Technique for the Study of Iroquois Prehistory.* Bulletin 124, Anthropological Series no. 31. Ottawa: National Museum of Canada.

———. 1964. "The Food-Gathering and Incipient Agriculture Stage of Prehistoric Middle America." In *Natural Environments and Early Cultures.* Vol. 1 of *Handbook of Middle American Indians,* edited by R. C. West, 413–26. Austin: Univ. of Texas Press.

———. 1971. "Speculation about How and Why Food Production and Village Life Developed in the Tehuacan Valley, Mexico." *Archaeology* 24, no.4:307–15.

———. 1976. "The In Situ Iroquois Revisited and Rethought." In *Culture Change and Continuity: Essays in Honor of James Bennett Griffin,* edited by C. E. Cleland, 79–98. New York: Academic Press.

Malone, Jena, and Stephen Hanks. 1999/2000. "What I Dug on My Summer Vacation." *Dig: The Archaeology Magazine for Kids,* Dec./Jan., 22–23.

Mann, Barbara A., and Jerry L. Fields. 1997. "A Sign in the Sky: Dating the League of the Haudenosaunee." *American Indian Culture and Research Journal* 21, no. 2:105–63.

Martijn, Charles A. 1969. *Ile aux Basques and the Prehistoric Iroquois Occupation of Southern Quebec.* Trois-Rivières: Cahiers d'Achéologie Québecoise.

Mathews, Zena Pearlstone. 1976. "Huron Pipes and Iroquoian Shamanism." *Man in the Northeast* 12:15–31.

———. 1980. "Of Man and Beast: The Chronology of Effigy Pipes among Ontario Iroquoians." *Ethnohistory* 27, no. 4:295–307.

———. 1981a. "Janus and Other Multiple-Image Iroquoian Pipes." *Ontario Archaeology* 35:3–22.

———. 1981b. "The Identification of Animals on Ontario Iroquoian Pipes." *Canadian Journal of Archaeology* 5:31–47.

———. 1982. "On Dreams and Journeys: Iroquoian Boat Pipes." *American Indian Art Magazine* 7, no. 3:46–51, 80.

Matsuoka, Yoshihiro, Yves Vigouroux, Major M. Goodman, G. Jesus Sanchez, Edward Bukler, and John Doebley. 2002. "A Single Domestication for Maize Shown by Multilocus Microsatellite Genotyping." *Proceedings of the National Academy of Sciences* 99:6080–84.

Mayr, Ernst. 1982. *The Growth of Biological Thought.* Cambridge, Mass.: Harvard Univ. Press.

McAndrews, John H. 1988. "Human Disturbance of North American Forests and Grasslands: The Fossil Pollen Record." In *Vegetation History,* edited by B. Huntley and T. Webb, 673–97. Dordrecht, Netherlands: Kluwer Academic.

McCarroll, Christina. 2001. "Oneida Teens Unearth Layers of Their History." *Christian Science Monitor* 14 Aug., 14–15.

McGhee, Robert. 1997. "Presenting Indigenous History: The First Peoples Hall at the Canadian Museum of Civilization." In *At a Crossroads: Archaeology and First Peoples in Canada,* edited by G. P. Nicholas and T. D. Andrews, 235–39. Simon Fraser Univ., Burnaby, BC: Archaeology Press.

McKern, William C. 1939. "The Midwestern Taxonomic Method as an Aid to Archaeological Culture Study." *American Antiquity* 4, no. 4:301–13.

Megapolensis, Johannes, Jr. 1909. "A Short Account of the Mohawk Indians, by Reverend Johannes Megapolensis, Jr., 1644." In *Narratives of New Netherland, 1609–1664*, edited by J. F. Jameson, 168–80. Original Narratives of Early American History. New York: Charles Scribner's Sons.

Melville, Herman. 1851. *Moby-Dick; or, The Whale.* New York: Harper and Brother.

Mihesuah, Devon A., ed. 2000. *Repatriation Reader: Who Owns American Indian Remains?* Lincoln: Univ. of Nebraska Press.

Miller, Christopher L., and George R. Hamell. 1986. "A New Perspective on Indian-White Contact: Cultural Symbols and Colonial Trade." *Journal of American History* 73, no. 2:311–28.

Miller, Jay. 1997. "Old Religion among the Delawares: The Gamwing (Big House Rite)." *Ethnohistory* 44:113–34.

Milner, George R. 1992. "Disease and Sociopolitical Systems in Late Prehistoric Illinois." In *Disease and Demography in the Americas,* edited by J. W. Verano and D. H. Ubelaker, 103–16. Washington, D.C.: Smithsonian Institution Press.

———. 1999. "Warfare in Prehistoric and Early Historic Eastern North America." *Journal of Archaeological Research* 7, no. 2:105–51.

Milner, George R., David G. Anderson, and Marvin T. Smith. 1992. "The Distribution of Eastern Woodlands Peoples at the Prehistoric and Historic Interface." Paper presented at the 57th Annual Meeting of the Society for American Archaeology, Pittsburgh.

Milner, George R., and M. Anne Katzenberg. 1999. "Contributions of Skeletal Biology to Great Lakes Precontact History." In *Taming the Taxonomy: Toward a New Understanding of Great Lakes Archaeology,* edited by R. F. Williamson and C. M. Watts, 205–17. Toronto: Eastendbooks.

Milun, Kathryn. 2001. "Keeping-While-Giving-Back: Computer Imaging, Native American Repatriation, and an Argument for Cultural Harm." *PoLAR: Political and Legal Anthropology Review* 24, no. 2:39–57.

Miroff, Laurie E. 2002. "Upland Land Use Patterns During the Early Late Prehistoric (A.D. 700–1300)." In *Northeast Subsistence-Settlement Change, A.D. 700–1300,* edited by J. P. Hart and C. B. Rieth, 193–208. New York State Museum Bulletin 496. Albany: State Univ. of New York, State Education Department.

Mitchell, Richard S. 2003. "A Compendium of New York Plants, Their Habitats and Distributions and Uses." On file, New York State Museum, Albany.

Mitchell, Richard S., and Gordon C. Tucker. 1997. *Revised Checklist of New York State Plants.* New York State Museum Bulletin 490. Albany: State Univ. of New York, State Education Department.

Mithun, Marianne. 1984. "The Proto-Iroquoians: Cultural Reconstruction from Lexical Materials." In *Extending the Rafters: Interdisciplinary Approaches to Iroquoian Studies,* edited by M. K. Foster, J. Campisi, and M. Mithun, 259–81. Albany: State Univ. of New York Press.

Moffat, Charles R., and Constance M. Arzigian. 2000. "New Data on the Late Woodland Use of Wild Rice in Northern Wisconsin." *Midcontinental Journal of Archaeology* 25:49–81.

Molto, Joseph Eldon. 1983. *Biological Relationships of Southern Ontario Woodland Peoples: The Evidence of Discontinuous Cranial Morphology.* National Museum of Man, Mercury Series,

Archaeological Survey of Canada, Paper no. 117. Ottawa: National Museums of Canada.

Mooney, James, and Frans M. Olbrechts. 1932. *The Swimmer Manuscript: Cherokee Sacred Formulas and Medicinal Prescription.* Bureau of American Ethnology Bulletin 99. Washington, D.C.: Smithsonian Institution.

Moore, John H. 1987. *The Cheyenne Nation: A Social and Demographic History.* Lincoln: Univ. of Nebraska Press.

———. 1994. "Putting Anthropology Back Together Again: The Ethnogenetic Critique of Cladistic Theory." *American Anthropologist* 96:925–48.

Moorehead, Warren K., ed. 1938. *A Report of the Susquehanna River Expedition Sponsored in 1916 by the Museum of the American Indian, Heye Foundation.* Andover, Mass.: Andover Press.

Morgan, Lewis Henry. 1969 [1851]. *League of the Ho-dé-no-sau-nee, or Iroquois.* New York: Corinth Books.

———. 1962. *League of the Iroquois.* 1851. Reprint. Secaucus, N.J.: Citadel Press.

Morison, Samuel E. 1971. *The European Discovery of America: The Northern Voyages, A.D. 500–1600.* New York: Oxford Univ. Press.

Morris, William, ed. 1980. *The American Heritage Dictionary of the English Language.* Boston: Houghton Mifflin.

Mulholland, Susan C. 1993. "A Test of Phytolith Analysis at Big Hidatsa, North Dakota." In *Current Research in Phytolith Analysis: Applications in Archaeology and Paleoecology,* edited by D. M. Pearsall and D. R. Piperno, 131–45. Philadelphia: Univ. Museum of Archaeology and Anthropology, Univ. of Pennsylvania.

Mulholland, Susan C., and George Rapp Jr. 1992. "A Morphological Classification of Grass Silica Bodies." In *Phytolith Systematics: Emerging Issues,* edited by G. Rapp Jr. and S. C. Mulholland, 65–89. New York: Plenum Press.

Murphy, Carl, and Neal Ferris. 1990. "The Late Woodland Western Basin Tradition of Southwestern Ontario." In *The Archaeology of Southern Ontario to A.D. 1650,* edited by C. J. Ellis and N. Ferris, 189–278. Occasional Publications of the London Chapter of the Ontario Archaeological Society no. 5. London, Ontario.

Murray, Priscilla. 1980. "Discard Location: The Ethnographic Record." *American Antiquity* 45, no. 3:490–502.

Myers, Albert Cook, ed. 1912. *Narratives of Early Pennsylvania, West Jersey, and Delaware, 1630–1707.* Reprint. 1953, New York: Barnes and Noble.

Naroll, Raoul. 1970. "What Have We Learned from Cross-Cultural Surveys?" *American Anthropologist* 72:1227–88.

New York Archaeological Council. 1993–2001. *NYAC Abstracts.* Vols. 1–7. Albany.

Niemczycki, Mary Ann Palmer. 1983. "The Origin and Development of the Seneca and Cayuga Tribes of New York State." Ph.D. diss., State Univ. of New York at Buffalo.

———. 1984. *The Origin and Development of the Seneca and Cayuga Tribes of New York State.* Research Records no. 17. Rochester, N.Y.: Rochester Museum and Science Center.

———. 1986. "The Genesee Connection: The Origins of Iroquois Culture in West-Central New York." *North American Archaeologist* 7, no. 1:15–44.

---. 1988. "Seneca Tribalization: An Adaptive Strategy." *Man in the Northeast* 36:77–87.
---. 1991. "Cayuga Archaeology: Where Do We Go From Here?" *The Bulletin: Journal of the New York State Archaeological Association* 102:27–33.
Noble, William C. 1972. "The Cleveland Neutral Village (AhHb-7): A Preliminary Statement." On file, Department of Anthropology, McMaster Univ., Hamilton, Ontario.
---. 1975a. "Corn and the Development of Village Life in Southern Ontario." *Ontario Archaeology* 25:37–46.
---. 1975b. "Van Besien: A Study in Glen Meyer Development." *Ontario Archaeology* 24:3–83.
---. 1979. "Ontario Iroquois Effigy Pipes." *Canadian Journal of Archaeology* 3:69–89.
---. 1980. "Thorold: An Early Historic Niagara Neutral Town." In *Villages in the Niagara Peninsula*, edited by J. Burtniak and W. B. Turner, 43–55. St. Catharines, ON: Brock Univ.
Noble, William C., and Ian T. Kenyon. 1972. "Porteous (AgHb-1): A Probable Early Glen Meyer Village in Brant County, Ontario." *Ontario Archaeology* 19:11–38.
Noon, John. 1949. *Law and Government of the Grand River Iroquois*. Viking Fund Publications in Anthropology no. 12. New York: Viking.
O'Callaghan, Edmund B. 1968 [1756]. "A Calendar of Historical Manuscripts in the Office of the Secretary of State, Albany, State of New York, 1664–1776." Ridgewood, N.J.: Gregg Press.
Ollendorf, Amy L. 1992. "Towards a Classification Scheme of Sedge *(Cyperaceae)* Phytoliths." In *Phytolith Systematics: Emerging Issues*, edited by G. Rapp Jr. and S. C. Mulholland, 91–111. New York: Plenum Press.
Ontario Corn Committee. 1992. *Ontario Hybrid Corn Performance Trials*. Alliston: Ontario Ministry of Agriculture and Food.
Orser, Charles E., Jr. 1996. *A Historical Archaeology of the Modern World*. New York: Plenum Press.
Ortner, Donald J. 1992. "Skeletal Paleopathology: Probabilities, Possibilities, and Impossibilities." In *Disease and Demography in the Americas*, edited by J. W. Verano and D. H. Ubelaker, 5–14. Washington, D.C.: Smithsonian Institution Press.
Osgood, Charles E., William H. May, and Murray S. Miron. 1975. *Cross-Cultural Universals of Affective Meaning*. Urbana: Univ. of Illinois Press.
Otterbein, Keith F. 1968. "Internal War: A Cross-Cultural Study." *American Anthropologist* 70:277–89.
Overpeck, John T., Thompson Webb III, and I. C. Prentice. 1985. "Quantitative Interpretation of Fossil Pollen Spectra: Dissimilarity Coefficients and the Method of Modern Analogues." *Quaternary Research* 23:87–108.
Parker, Arthur C. 1910. *Iroquois Uses of Maize and Other Food Plants*. New York State Museum Bulletin 144, 5–133. Albany: Univ. of the State of New York.
---. 1916a. "The Origin of the Iroquois as Suggested by Their Archaeology." *American Anthropologist* 18:479–507.
---. 1916b. *The Constitution of the Five Nations or the Iroquois Book of The Great Law*. New York State Museum Bulletin 184. Albany: Univ. of the State of New York.
---. 1920. *The Archaeological History of New York*, Part 1. New York State Museum Bulletins 235–36. Albany: Univ. of the State of New York.

———. 1922. *The Archaeological History of New York.* Parts 1 and 2. New York State Museum Bulletins 235–38. Albany: Univ. of the State of New York.

———. 1989. *Seneca Myths and Folk Tales.* Reprint from 1923 original. Lincoln: Univ. of Nebraska Press.

Parry, M. L. 1981. "Climatic Change and the Agricultural Frontier: A Research Strategy." In *Climate and History: Studies in Past Climates and Their Impact on Man,* edited by T.M.L. Wigley, M. J. Ingram, and G. Farmer, 319–36. Cambridge, UK: Cambridge Univ. Press.

Patterson, David Kingsnorth, Jr. 1984. *A Diachronic Study of Dental Palaeopathology and Attritional Status of Prehistoric Ontario Pre-Iroquois and Iroquois Populations.* Mercury Series, Archaeological Survey of Canada, Paper no. 122. Ottawa: National Museums of Canada.

Pearce, Robert J. 1996. *Mapping Middleport: A Case Study in Societal Archaeology.* Research Report no. 25. London, ON: London Museum of Archaeology.

Pearce, Robert J., and Gary A. Warrick. 1999. "A Cluster of Pickering Sites in the Burlington Area, Halton Region." Paper presented at the 32nd Annual Meeting of the Canadian Archaeological Association, Whitehorse, Yukon.

Pearsall, Deborah M., and Dolores R. Piperno. 1993. "The Nature and Status of Phytolith Analysis." In *Current Research in Phytolith Analysis: Applications in Archaeology and Paleoecology,* edited by D. M. Pearsall and D. R. Piperno, 9–18. Philadelphia: Univ. Museum of Archaeology and Anthropology, Univ. of Pennsylvania.

Peebles, Christopher S. 1986. "Paradise Lost, Strayed, and Stolen: Prehistoric Social Devolution in the Southeast." In *The Burden of Being Civilized: An Anthropological Perspective on the Discontents of Civilization,* edited by M. B. Richardson and M. C. Webb, 24–40. Southern Anthropological Society Proceedings. Athens: Univ. of Georgia Press.

Pendergast, James F. 1966. *Three Prehistoric Iroquois Components in Eastern Ontario: The Salem, Grays Creek, and Beckstead Sites.* National Museum of Canada Bulletin 208, Anthropological Series no. 73. Ottawa: National Museums of Canada.

———. 1968. *The Summerstown Station Site.* Anthropology Paper no. 18. Ottawa: National Museums of Canada.

———. 1972. "An Analysis of the Dawson Site Archaeological Material." In *Cartier's Hochelaga and the Dawson Site,* edited by J. F. Pendergast and B. G. Trigger, 1–108. Montreal: McGill-Queen's Univ. Press.

———. 1975. "St. Lawrence Iroquoians." *Ontario Archaeology* 25:47–56.

———. 1981. *The Glenbrook Village Site—A Late St. Lawrence Iroquoian Component in Glengarry County, Ontario.* National Museum of Man, Mercury Series, Archaeological Survey of Canada, Paper no. 100. Ottawa: National Museums of Canada.

———. 1984. *The Beckstead Site—1977.* Mercury Series, Archaeological Survey of Canada, Paper no. 123. Ottawa: National Museums of Canada.

———. 1985. "Huron-St. Lawrence Iroquois Relations in the Terminal Prehistoric Period." *Ontario Archaeology* 44:23–39.

———. 1989. "The Significance of Some Marine Shell Excavated on Iroquoian Archaeological Sites in Ontario." In *Proceedings of the 1986 Shell Bead Conference: Selected Papers,* edited by C. F. Hayes III, L. Ceci, and C. C. Bodner, 97–112. Research Records 20. Rochester, N.Y.: Rochester Museum and Science Center.

———. 1991a. "The Massawomeck: Raiders and Traders into Chesapeake Bay in the Seventeenth Century." *Transactions of the American Philosophical Society* 81, no. 2. Philadelphia: American Philosophical Society.

———. 1991b. "The St. Lawrence Iroquoians: Their Past, Present, and Immediate Future." *The Bulletin: Journal of the New York State Archaeological Association* 102:47–74.

———. 1992. "Susquehannock Trade Northward to New France Prior to A.D. 1608: A Popular Misconception." *Pennsylvania Archaeologist* 62, no. 1:1–11.

———. 1993a. "Some Comments on Calibrated Radiocarbon Dates for Saint Lawrence Iroquoian Sites." *Northeast Anthropology* 46:1–32.

———. 1993b. "More on When and Why the St. Lawrence Iroquoians Disappeared." In *Essays in St. Lawrence Iroquoian Archaeology*, edited by J. F. Pendergast and C. Chapdelaine, 9–47. Occasional Papers in Northeastern Archaeology no. 8. Dundas, ON: Copetown Press.

———. 1997. "Hamlets Become Villages." In *Home Is Where the Hearth Is: The Contribution of Small Sites to Our Understanding of Ontario's Past*, edited by J.-L. Pilon and R. Perkins. Ottawa Chapter of the Ontario Archaeological Society.

Pendergast, James F., and Claude Chapdelaine, eds. 1993. *Essays in St. Lawrence Iroquoian Archaeology*. Occasional Papers in Northeastern Archaeology no. 8. Dundas, ON: Copetown Press.

Perry, Richard J. 1989. "Matrilineal Descent in a Hunting Context: The Athapaskan Case." *Ethnology* 28:33–51.

Petersen, James B., and Nancy Asch Sidell. 1996. "Mid-Holocene Evidence of *Cucurbita* sp. from Central Maine." *American Antiquity* 61, no. 4:685–98.

Peterson, Randolph L. 1966. *The Mammals of Eastern Canada.* Toronto: Oxford Univ. Press.

Pfeiffer, Susan. 1984. "Paleopathology in an Iroquoian Ossuary, with Special Reference to Tuberculosis." *American Journal of Physical Anthropology* 65, no. 2:181–89.

———. 1986. "Morbidity and Mortality in the Uxbridge Ossuary." *Canadian Journal of Anthropology* 5, no. 2:23–31.

Pfeiffer, Susan, and Scott I. Fairgrieve. 1994. "Evidence from Ossuaries: The Effect of Contact on the Health of Iroquoians." In *In the Wake of Contact: Biological Responses to Conquest*, edited by C. S. Larsen and G. R. Milner, 47–61. New York: Wiley-Liss.

Pfeiffer, Susan, and Patricia King. 1983. "Cortical Bone Formation and Diet among Protohistoric Iroquoians." *American Journal of Physical Anthropology* 60:23–28.

Pfeiffer, Susan, K. Stewart, and C. Alex. 1986. "Growth Arrest Lines among Uxbridge Ossuary Juveniles." *Ontario Archaeology* 46:27–32.

Pfister, Christian. 1981. "An Analysis of the Little Ice Age Climate in Switzerland and Its Consequences for Agricultural Production." In *Climate and History: Studies in Past Climates and Their Impact on Man*, edited by T.M.L. Wigley, M. J. Ingram, and G. Farmer, 214–48. Cambridge, UK: Cambridge Univ. Press.

Phelps, David S. 1983. "Archaeology of the North Carolina Coast and Coastal Plain: Problems and Hypotheses." In *The Prehistory of North Carolina: An Archaeological Symposium*, edited by M. A. Mathis and J. J. Crow, 1–51. Raleigh: North Carolina Department of Cultural Resources, Division of Archives and History.

Phillips, Ruth B. 1986. "Dreams and Designs: Iconographic Problems in Great Lakes Twined Bags." *Bulletin of the Detroit Institute of Arts* 62:27–37.

Pihl, Robert H., David A. Robertson, and Ronald F. Williamson. 1998. "Summary of 1996 Research by Archaeological Services Inc." *Annual Archaeological Report for Ontario,* n.s., 8:31–36.

Pihl, Robert H., and Ronald F. Williamson. 1999. "Turning the First Millennium: The Holmedale Site and Contributions to the Transitional Woodland along the Grand River in Southwestern Ontario." Paper presented at the Annual Symposium of the Canadian Archaeological Association, Whitehorse, Yukon.

Piperno, Dolores R., Thomas C. Andres, and Karen Stothert. 2000. "Phytoliths in *Cucurbita* and Other Neotropical Cucurbitacae and Their Occurrence in Early Archaeological Sites from the Lowland American Tropics." *Journal of Archaeological Science* 27:193–208.

Porter, Stephen C. 1981. "Recent Glacier Variations and Volcanic Eruptions." *Nature* 291:139–42.

Pratt, Peter P. 1961. "The Bigford Site: Late Prehistoric Oneida." *Pennsylvania Archaeologist* 31, no. 1:46–59.

———. 1963. "A Heavily Stockaded Late Prehistoric Oneida Iroquois Settlement." *Pennsylvania Archaeologist* 33, nos. 1–2:56–92.

———. 1976. *Archaeology of the Oneida Iroquois.* Vol. 1. Occasional Publications in Northeastern Anthropology no. 1. Rindge, N.H.: Man in the Northeast.

———. 1991. "Oneida Archaeology: The Last Quarter Century." *The Bulletin: Journal of the New York State Archaeological Association* 102:40–42.

Prezzano, Susan C. 1992. "Longhouse, Village, and Palisade: Community Patterns at the Iroquois Southern Door New York, Late Woodland." Ph.D. diss., Binghamton Univ.

Prezzano, Susan C., and Christina B. Rieth. 2001. "Late Prehistoric Cultures of the Upper Susquehanna Valley." In *Archaeology of the Appalachian Highlands,* edited by L. P. Sullivan and S. C. Prezzano, 168–76. Knoxville: Univ. of Tennessee Press.

Pringle, P. 1936. "Map of Lower Grand River." On file, Royal Ontario Museum, Toronto.

Ramenofsky, Ann F. 1987. *Vectors of Death: The Archaeology of European Contact.* Albuquerque: Univ. of New Mexico Press.

Ramsden, Carol Naismith, Ronald F. Williamson, Robert I. MacDonald, and C. Short. 1998. "Settlement Patterns." In *The Myers Road Site: Archaeology of the Early to Middle Iroquoian Transition,* edited by R. F. Williamson, 11–84. Occasional Publications of the London Chapter of the Ontario Archaeological Society no. 7. London, Ontario.

Ramsden, Peter G. 1977. *A Refinement of Some Aspects of Huron Ceramic Analysis.* National Museum of Man, Mercury Series, Archaeological Survey of Canada, Paper no. 63. Ottawa: National Museums of Canada.

———. 1978. "An Hypothesis Concerning the Effects of Early European Trade among Some Ontario Iroquois." *Canadian Journal of Archaeology* 2:101–6.

———. 1989. "Palisade Extension, Village Expansion and Immigration in Trent Valley Huron Prehistory." *Canadian Journal of Archaeology* 12:177–83.

———. 1990a. "The Hurons: Archaeology and Culture History." In *The Archaeology of Southern Ontario to A.D. 1650,* edited by C. J. Ellis and N. Ferris, 361–84. Occasional Publications of the London Chapter of the Ontario Archaeological Society no. 5. London, Ontario.

———. 1990b. "Saint Lawrence Iroquoians in the Upper Trent Valley." *Man in the Northeast* 39:87–95.

———. 1993. "The Huron-Petun: Current State of Knowledge." On file, Canadian Archaeological Association, Montreal.

———. 1996. "The Current State of Huron Archaeology." *Northeast Anthropology* 51:101–12.

Randle, Mandle C. 1953. "The Waugh Collection of Iroquois Folktales." *Proceedings of the American Philosophical Society* 97:611–33. Philadelphia.

Rankin, Lisa K. 2000. *Interpreting Long-Term Trends in the Transition to Farming: Reconsidering the Nodwell Site, Ontario, Canada.* British Archaeological Reports International Series no. 830. Oxford, UK.

Rapp, George, Eiler Henrickson, and James Allert. 1990. "Native Copper Sources of Artifact Copper in Pre-Columbian North America." In *Archaeological Geology of North America*, edited by N. P. Lasca and J. Donahue, 479–98. Centennial Special Vol. 4. Boulder, Colo.: Geological Society of America.

Rataul, Ralph C. 2001. "The Barker Site: Analysis of a Protohistoric Mohawk Ceramic Assemblage." Senior Honors Thesis, State Univ. of New York at Albany.

Ratcliff, Floyd. 1976. "On the Psychophysiological Bases of Universal Color Terms." *Proceedings of the American Philosophical Society* 120, no. 5:311–30.

Ravesloot, John C. 1997. "Changing Native American Perceptions of Archaeology and Archaeologists." In *Native Americans and Archaeologists: Stepping Stones to Common Ground*, edited by N. Swidler, K. E. Dongoske, R. Anyon, and A. S. Downer, 172–77. Walnut Creek, Calif.: AltaMira Press.

Reff, Daniel T. 1991. *Disease, Depopulation, and Culture Change in Northwestern New Spain, 1520–1764.* Salt Lake City: Univ. of Utah Press.

Reid, C. S., and Grace Rajnovich. 1991. "Laurel: A Re-evaluation of the Spatial, Social, and Temporal Paradigms." *Canadian Journal of Archaeology* 15:193–234.

Richter, Daniel K. 1992. *The Ordeal of the Longhouse: The Peoples of the Iroquois League in the Era of European Colonization.* Chapel Hill: Univ. of North Carolina Press.

Rickard, Lawrence V. 1973. *Stratigraphy and Structure of the Subsurface Cambrian and Ordovician Carbonates of New York.* Map and Chart Series no. 18. Albany: New York State Museum and Science Service.

Ricklis, Robert. 1967. "Excavation of a Probable Late Prehistoric Onondaga House Site." *The Bulletin: Journal of the New York State Archaeological Association* 39:15–17.

Ridley, Frank. 1954. "The Frank Bay Site, Lake Nipissing, Ontario." *American Antiquity* 20, no. 1:40–50.

Rieth, Christina B. 1997. "Culture Contact During the Carpenter Brook Phase: A Tripartite Approach to the Study of the Spatial and Temporal Movement of Early Iroquoian Groups Throughout the Upper Susquehanna River Valley." Ph.D. diss., State Univ. of New York at Albany.

———. 2002a. "Early Late Prehistoric Settlement: A View from Northcentral Pennsylvania." In *Northeast Subsistence-Settlement Change A.D. 700–1300*, edited by J. P. Hart and C. B. Rieth, 135–52. New York State Museum Bulletin 496. Albany: State Univ. of New York, State Education Department.

———. 2002b. "Early Late Prehistoric Settlement and Subsistence Diversity in the Southern Tier of New York." In *Northeast Subsistence-Settlement Change A.D. 700–1300*, edited by

J. P. Hart and C. B. Rieth, 209–26. New York State Museum Bulletin 496. Albany: State Univ. of New York, State Education Department.

Riley, Thomas J., Gregory R. Waltz, Charles J. Bareis, Andrew C. Fortier, and Kathryn E. Parker. 1994. "Accelerator Mass Spectrometry (AMS) Dates Confirm Early *Zea mays* in the Mississippi River Valley." *American Antiquity* 59, no. 3:490–97.

Ritchie, William A. 1928. *An Algonkian Village Site Near Levanna, N.Y.* Research Records no. 1. Rochester, N.Y.: Rochester Municipal Museum.

———. 1936. *A Prehistoric Fortified Village Site at Canandaigua, Ontario County, New York.* Research Records no. 3. Rochester, N.Y.: Rochester Museum of Arts and Sciences.

———. 1944. *The Pre-Iroquoian Occupations of New York State.* Rochester, N.Y.: Rochester Museum of Arts and Sciences.

———. 1946. *A Stratified Prehistoric Site at Brewerton, New York.* Research Records no. 5. Rochester, N.Y.: Rochester Museum of Arts and Sciences.

———. 1954. *Dutch Hollow, An Early Historic Period Seneca Site in Livingston County, New York.* Research Records no. 10. Rochester, N.Y.: Rochester Museum of Arts and Sciences.

———. 1961. "Iroquois Archaeology and Settlement Patterns." In *Symposium on Cherokee and Iroquois Culture,* edited by W. N. Fenton and J. Gulick, 25–38. Bulletin 180. Washington, D.C.: Bureau of American Ethnology.

———. 1965. *The Archaeology of New York State.* Garden City, N.Y.: Natural History Press.

———. 1969. *The Archaeology of New York State.* Rev. ed. Garden City, N.Y.: Natural History Press.

———. 1973. "The Kipp Island Site (Aub. 12–1, 13–1)." In *Aboriginal Settlement Patterns in the Northeast,* by William A. Ritchie and Robert E. Funk, 154–64. New York State Museum and Science Service Memoir 20. Albany: State Univ. of New York, State Education Department.

———. 1980. *The Archaeology of New York State.* Rev. ed. Harrison, N.Y.: Harbor Hill Books.

Ritchie, William A., and Robert E. Funk. 1973. *Aboriginal Settlement Patterns in the Northeast.* New York State Museum and Science Service Memoir 20. Albany: State Univ. of New York, State Education Department.

Ritchie, William A., Donald Lenig, and P. Schuyler Miller. 1953. *An Early Owasco Sequence in Eastern New York.* Circular 32. Albany: New York State Museum and Science Service.

Ritchie, William A., and Richard S. MacNeish. 1949. "The Pre-Iroquoian Pottery of New York State." *American Antiquity* 15, no. 2:97–124.

Robertson, David A., Stephen G. Monckton, and Ronald F. Williamson. 1995. "The Wiacek Site Revisited: The Results of the 1990 Excavations." *Ontario Archaeology* 60:40–91.

Rouse, Irving. 1958. "The Inference of Migrations from Anthropological Evidence." In *Migration in New World Culture History,* edited by R. H. Thompson. *University of Arizona Social Science Bulletin* 27:63–68.

Rovner, Irwin. 1983. "Plant Opal Phytolith Analysis: Major Advances in Archaeobotanical Research." In *Advances in Archaeological Method and Theory.* Vol. 6, edited by M. B. Schiffer, 225–66. New York: Academic Press.

Rozel, R. J. 1979. "The Gunby Site and Late Pickering Interactions." M.A. thesis, McMaster Univ.

Sagard-Théodat, Gabriel. 1939 [1632]. *The Long Journey to the Country of the Hurons,* edited by G. M. Wrong. Toronto: Champlain Society.

Sahlins, Marshall D. 1961. "The Segmentary Lineage: An Organization of Predatory Expansion." *American Anthropologist* 63:322–43.

———. 1976. "Colors and Cultures." *Semiotica* 16, no. 1:1–22.

Sauer, Carl O. 1971. *Sixteenth-Century North America.* Berkeley: Univ. of California Press.

Saunders, Shelley R. 1989. "The MacPherson Site Burials." On file, Department of Anthropology, McMaster Univ., Hamilton, Ontario.

Saunders, Shelley R., and F. Jerry Melbye. 1990. "Subadult Mortality and Skeletal Indicators of Health in Late Woodland Ontario Iroquois." *Canadian Journal of Archaeology* 14:61–74.

Saunders, Shelley R., Peter G. Ramsden, and D. Ann Herring. 1992. "Transformation and Disease: Precontact Ontario Iroquoians." In *Disease and Demography in the Americas*, edited by J. W. Verano and D. H. Ubelaker, 117–26. Washington, D.C.: Smithsonian Institution Press.

Schroeder, Sissel. 1999. "Maize Productivity in the Eastern Woodlands and Great Plains of North America." *American Antiquity* 64, no. 3:499–516.

Schulenberg, Janet K. 2002a. "The Point Peninsula to Owasco Transition in Central New York." Ph.D. diss., Pennsylvania State Univ.

———. 2002b. "New Dates for Owasco Pots." In *Northeast Subsistence-Settlement Change A.D. 700–1300*, edited by J. P. Hart and C. B. Rieth, 153–65. New York State Museum Bulletin 496. Albany: State Univ. of New York, State Education Department.

Schwarcz, Henry P., Jerry Melbye, M. Anne Katzenberg, and Martin Knyf. 1985. "Stable Isotopes in Human Skeletons of Southern Ontario: Reconstructing Paleodiet." *Journal of Archaeological Science* 12:187–206.

Sears, William H. 1961. "The Study of Social and Religious Systems in North American Archaeology." *Current Anthropology* 2, no. 3:223–31.

———. 1971. "Food Production and Village Life in the Southeastern United States." *Archaeology* 24, no. 4:322–29.

Seaver, James E. 1990. *A Narrative of the Life of Mrs. Mary Jemison.* 1824. Reprint. Syracuse, N.Y.: Syracuse Univ. Press.

Sempowski, Martha L. 1989. "Fluctuations Through Time in the Use of Marine Shell at Seneca Iroquois Sites." In *Proceedings of the 1986 Shell Bead Conference: Selected Papers*, edited by C. F. Hayes III, L. Ceci, and C. C. Bodner, 81–96. Research Records 20. Rochester, N.Y.: Rochester Museum and Science Center.

Service, Elman A. 1962. *Primitive Social Organization: An Evolutionary Perspective.* New York: Random House.

Shaul, David L. 1986. "Linguistic Adaptation and the Great Basin." *American Antiquity* 51, no. 2:415–16.

Shay, C. T. 1980. "Food Plants in Manitoba." In *Directions in Manitoba Prehistory, Papers in Honor of Chris Vickers*, edited by L. Pettipas, 233–90. Winnipeg: Manitoba Archaeological Society.

Shepard, Anna O. 1956. *Ceramics for the Archaeologist.* Publication 609. Washington, D.C.: Carnegie Institution of Washington.

Shimony, Annemarie Anrod. 1994. *Conservatism among the Iroquois at the Six Nations Reserve.* 1961. Reprint. Syracuse, N.Y.: Syracuse Univ. Press.

Silliman, Stephen W., ed. 2007. *Collaborative Indigenous Archaeology at the Trowel's Edge: Explorations in Methodology, Education, and Ethics.* Tucson: Univ. of Arizona Press. In press.

Simmons, William S. 1986. *Spirit of the New England Tribes.* Hanover, N.H.: Univ. Press of New England.

Sioui, Georges. 1992a. *For an Amerindian Autohistory.* Montreal: McGill-Queen's Univ. Press.

———. 1992b. "Les Nadoueks: Leur Histoire des Anneés 1000 à 1650 de Notre Ère." Paper presented at the Transferts Culturels en Amérique et Ailleurs Conference, Québec.

Skinner, Alanson B. 1921. *Notes on Iroquois Archeology.* Indian Notes and Monographs no. 18. New York: Museum of the American Indian, Heye Foundation.

Smith, Bruce D. 1989. "Origins of Agriculture in Eastern North America." *Science* 246:1566–71.

———. 1992. *Rivers of Change: Essays on Early Agriculture in Eastern North America.* Washington, D.C.: Smithsonian Institution Press.

Smith, David G. 1990. "Iroquoian Societies in Southern Ontario: Introduction and Historical Overview." In *The Archaeology of Southern Ontario to A.D. 1650,* edited by C. J. Ellis and N. Ferris, 279–90. Occasional Publications of the London Chapter of the Ontario Archaeological Society no. 5. London, Ontario.

———. 1995. "Cord-Marked Pottery and the Early Late Woodland in the Northeast." Paper presented at the 60th Annual Meeting of the Society for American Archaeology, Minneapolis.

———. 1997a. "Radiocarbon Dating the Middle to Late Woodland Transition and Earliest Maize in Southern Ontario." *Northeast Anthropology* 54:37–73.

———. 1997b. "Recent Investigations of Late Woodland Occupations at Cootes Paradise, Ontario." *Ontario Archaeology* 63:4–16.

———. 1997c. *Archaeological Systematics and the Analysis of Iroquoian Ceramics: A Case Study from the Crawford Lake Area, Ontario.* Bulletin no. 15. London, ON: London Museum of Archaeology.

Smith, David G., and Gary W. Crawford. 1995. "The Princess Point Complex and the Origins of Iroquoian Societies in Ontario." In *Origins of the People of the Longhouse: Proceedings of the 21st Annual Symposium of the Ontario Archaeological Society,* edited by A. Bekerman and G. A. Warrick, 55–70. Toronto: Ontario Archaeological Society.

———. 1997. "Recent Developments in the Archaeology of the Princess Point Complex in Southern Ontario." *Canadian Journal of Archaeology* 21, no. 1:9–32.

Smith, Ira F., III, and Jeffrey R. Graybill. 1977. "A Report on the Shenks Ferry and Susquehannock Components at the Funk Site, Lancaster County, Pennsylvania." *Man in the Northeast* 13:45–65.

Smith, John. 1910 [1608]. *A True Relation of Such Occurrences and Accidents of Note as Hath Happned in Virginia Since the First Planting of that Colony, in Travels and Works of Captain John Smith,* edited by E. Arber. Edinburgh: John Grant Co.

Smith, Marvin T. 1987. *Archaeology of Aboriginal Culture Change in the Interior Southeast: Depopulation During the Early Historic Period.* Ripley P. Bullen Monographs in Anthropology and History no. 6. Gainesville: Univ. Press of Florida / Florida State Museum.

Smith, Marvin T., and Julie Barnes Smith. 1989. "Engraved Shell Masks in North America." *Southeastern Archaeology* 8, no. 1:9–18.

Smith, Richard. 1989 [1906]. *A Tour of the Hudson, the Mohawk, the Susquehanna, and the Delaware in 1769,* edited by F. W. Halsey. Fleischmanns, N.Y.: Purple Mountain Press.

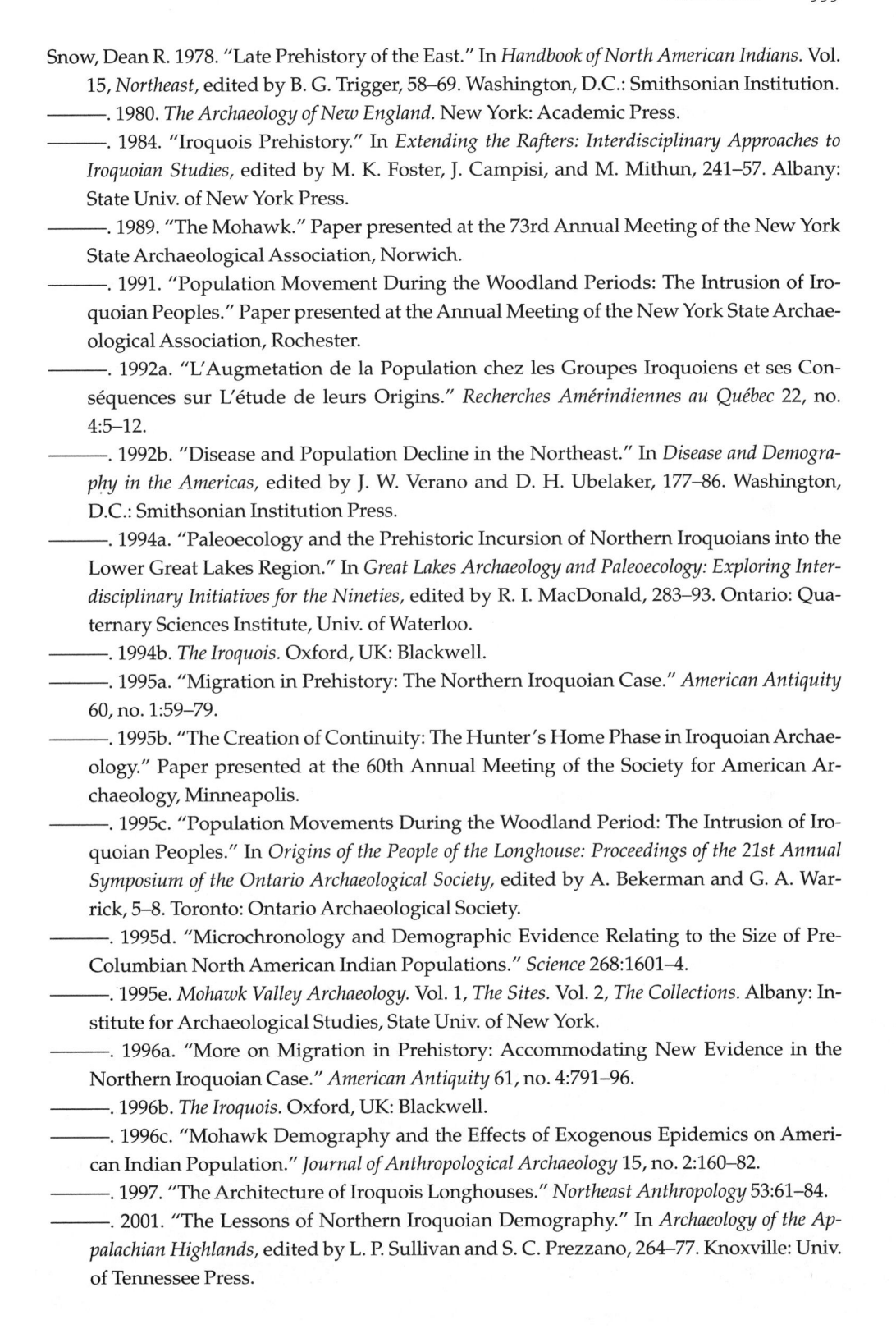

Snow, Dean R. 1978. "Late Prehistory of the East." In *Handbook of North American Indians*. Vol. 15, *Northeast*, edited by B. G. Trigger, 58–69. Washington, D.C.: Smithsonian Institution.

———. 1980. *The Archaeology of New England*. New York: Academic Press.

———. 1984. "Iroquois Prehistory." In *Extending the Rafters: Interdisciplinary Approaches to Iroquoian Studies*, edited by M. K. Foster, J. Campisi, and M. Mithun, 241–57. Albany: State Univ. of New York Press.

———. 1989. "The Mohawk." Paper presented at the 73rd Annual Meeting of the New York State Archaeological Association, Norwich.

———. 1991. "Population Movement During the Woodland Periods: The Intrusion of Iroquoian Peoples." Paper presented at the Annual Meeting of the New York State Archaeological Association, Rochester.

———. 1992a. "L'Augmetation de la Population chez les Groupes Iroquoiens et ses Conséquences sur L'étude de leurs Origins." *Recherches Amérindiennes au Québec* 22, no. 4:5–12.

———. 1992b. "Disease and Population Decline in the Northeast." In *Disease and Demography in the Americas*, edited by J. W. Verano and D. H. Ubelaker, 177–86. Washington, D.C.: Smithsonian Institution Press.

———. 1994a. "Paleoecology and the Prehistoric Incursion of Northern Iroquoians into the Lower Great Lakes Region." In *Great Lakes Archaeology and Paleoecology: Exploring Interdisciplinary Initiatives for the Nineties*, edited by R. I. MacDonald, 283–93. Ontario: Quaternary Sciences Institute, Univ. of Waterloo.

———. 1994b. *The Iroquois*. Oxford, UK: Blackwell.

———. 1995a. "Migration in Prehistory: The Northern Iroquoian Case." *American Antiquity* 60, no. 1:59–79.

———. 1995b. "The Creation of Continuity: The Hunter's Home Phase in Iroquoian Archaeology." Paper presented at the 60th Annual Meeting of the Society for American Archaeology, Minneapolis.

———. 1995c. "Population Movements During the Woodland Period: The Intrusion of Iroquoian Peoples." In *Origins of the People of the Longhouse: Proceedings of the 21st Annual Symposium of the Ontario Archaeological Society*, edited by A. Bekerman and G. A. Warrick, 5–8. Toronto: Ontario Archaeological Society.

———. 1995d. "Microchronology and Demographic Evidence Relating to the Size of Pre-Columbian North American Indian Populations." *Science* 268:1601–4.

———. 1995e. *Mohawk Valley Archaeology*. Vol. 1, *The Sites*. Vol. 2, *The Collections*. Albany: Institute for Archaeological Studies, State Univ. of New York.

———. 1996a. "More on Migration in Prehistory: Accommodating New Evidence in the Northern Iroquoian Case." *American Antiquity* 61, no. 4:791–96.

———. 1996b. *The Iroquois*. Oxford, UK: Blackwell.

———. 1996c. "Mohawk Demography and the Effects of Exogenous Epidemics on American Indian Population." *Journal of Anthropological Archaeology* 15, no. 2:160–82.

———. 1997. "The Architecture of Iroquois Longhouses." *Northeast Anthropology* 53:61–84.

———. 2001. "The Lessons of Northern Iroquoian Demography." In *Archaeology of the Appalachian Highlands*, edited by L. P. Sullivan and S. C. Prezzano, 264–77. Knoxville: Univ. of Tennessee Press.

Snow, Dean R., Charles T. Gehring, and William A. Starna, eds. 1996. *In Mohawk Country, Early Narratives about a Native People.* Syracuse, N.Y.: Syracuse Univ. Press.

Snow, Dean R., and Kim M. Lanphear. 1988. "European Contact and Indian Depopulation in the Northeast: The Timing of the First Epidemics." *Ethnohistory* 35:15–33.

Snow, Dean R., and William A. Starna. 1989. "Sixteenth Century Depopulation: A View from the Mohawk Valley." *American Anthropologist* 91:142–49.

Snyderman, George S. 1948. "Social and Political Patterns of Iroquois Society—Warfare." *Pennsylvania Archaeologist* 18, nos. 3–4.

Speck, Frank G. 1931. *A Study of the Delaware Indian Big House Ceremony.* Publications Vol. 2. Harrisburg: Pennsylvania Historical Commission.

———. 1937. *Oklahoma Delaware Ceremonies, Feasts and Dances.* Memoirs No. 7. Philadelphia: American Philosophical Society.

———. 1995. *Midwinter Rites of the Cayuga Long House.* 1949. Reprint. Lincoln: Univ. of Nebraska Press.

Spence, Michael W. 1992. "Three Burials from the Libby Site, Kent County, Ontario." On file, Department of Anthropology, Univ. of Western Ontario, London.

———. 1994. "Mortuary Programmes of the Early Ontario Iroquoians." *Ontario Archaeology* 58:6–26.

———. 1999. "Comments: The Social Foundations of Archaeological Taxonomy." In *Taming the Taxonomy: Toward a New Understanding of Great Lakes Archaeology,* edited by R. F. Williamson and C. M. Watts, 275–81. Toronto: Eastendbooks.

Spence, Michael W., and Robert H. Pihl. 1984. "The Early and Middle Woodland Occupations of Southern Ontario: Past, Present and Future Research." *Arch Notes* 84, no. 2:32–48.

Spence, Michael W., Robert H. Pihl, and Joseph Eldon Molto. 1984. "Hunter-Gatherer Social Group Identification: A Case Study from Middle Woodland Southern Ontario." In *Exploring the Limits: Frontiers and Boundaries in Prehistory,* edited by S. P. De Atley and F. J. Findlow, 117–42. British Archaeological Reports International Series no. 223. Oxford, UK.

Spence, Michael W., Robert H. Pihl, and Carl R. Murphy. 1990. "Cultural Complexes of the Early and Middle Woodland Periods." In *The Archaeology of Southern Ontario to A.D. 1650,* edited by C. J. Ellis and N. Ferris, 125–69. Occasional Publications of the London Chapter of the Ontario Archaeological Society no. 5. London, Ontario.

Spiess, Arthur E., and Bruce D. Spiess. 1987. "New England Pandemic of 1616–1622: Cause and Archaeological Implication." *Man in the Northeast* 34:71–83.

Squier, Ephraim G. 1851. *Antiquities of the State of New York.* Buffalo: George H Derby.

Staller, John E., and Robert G. Thompson. 2002. "A Multidisciplinary Approach to Understanding the Initial Introduction of Maize into Coastal Ecuador." *Journal of Archaeological Science* 29:33–50.

Starna, William A., and Robert E. Funk. 1994. "The Place of the In Situ Hypothesis in Iroquoian Archaeology." *Northeast Anthropology* 47:45–54.

Steward, Julian H. 1942. "The Direct Historical Approach to Archaeology." *American Antiquity* 7, no. 4:337–44.

———. 1955. *Theory of Culture Change.* Urbana: Univ. of Illinois Press.

Stewart, Michael. 1990. "Clemson's Island Studies in Pennsylvania: A Perspective." *Pennsylvania Archaeologist* 60, no. 1:79–107.

Stoltman, James B. 1978. "Temporal Models in Prehistory: An Example from Eastern North America." *Current Anthropology* 19, no. 4:703–46.

Stoltman, James B., and David A. Baerreis. 1983. "The Evolution of Human Ecosystems in the Eastern United States." In *Late Quaternary Environments of the United States.* Vol. 2, *The Holocene,* edited by H. E. Wright Jr., 252–68. Minneapolis: Univ. of Minnesota Press.

Stopp, Marianne P. 1984. "An Archaeological Examination of the Baumann Site: A 15th Century Settlement in Simcoe County, Ontario." *Ontario Archaeology* 43:3–30.

Stothers, David M. 1976. "The Princess Point Complex: A Regional Representative of an Early Late Woodland Horizon in the Great Lakes Area." In *The Late Prehistory of the Lake Erie Drainage Basin: A 1972 Symposium Revisited,* edited by D. S. Brose, 137–61. Cleveland: Cleveland Museum of Natural History.

———. 1977. *The Princess Point Complex.* National Museum of Man, Mercury Series, Archaeological Survey of Canada, Paper no. 58. Ottawa: National Museums of Canada.

———. 1981. "Indian Hills (33WO4): A Protohistoric Assistaeronon Village in the Maumee River Valley of Northwestern Ohio." *Ontario Archaeology* 36:47–56.

Stothers David M., and Richard A. Yarnell. 1977. "An Agricultural Revolution in the Lower Great Lakes." In *Geobotany,* edited by R. D. Romans, 209–32. New York: Plenum Press.

Stowe, Noel R. 1989. "The Pensacola Variant and the Southeastern Ceremonial Complex." In *The Southeastern Ceremonial Complex: Artifacts and Analysis,* edited by P. Galloway, 125–32. Lincoln: Univ. of Nebraska Press.

Strong, John A. 1989. "The Mississippian Bird-Man Theme in Cross-Cultural Perspective." In *The Southeastern Ceremonial Complex: Artifacts and Analysis,* edited by P. Galloway, 211–38. Lincoln: Univ. of Nebraska Press.

Struever, Stuart. 1971. *Prehistoric Agriculture.* Garden City, N.Y.: American Museum Sourcebooks in Anthropology.

Stuiver, Minze, and Paula J. Reimer. 1993. "Extended ^{14}C Data Base and Revised Calib 3.0 ^{14}C Calibration Program." *Radiocarbon* 35:215–30.

Stuiver, Minze, Paula J. Reimer, Edouard Bard, J. Warren Beck, G. S. Burr, Konrad A. Hughen, Bernd Kromer, Gerry McCormac, Johannes van der Plicht, and Marco Spark. 1998. "INTCAL98 Radiocarbon Age Calibration 24,000–0 cal B.P.." *Radiocarbon* 40:1041–83.

Sturtevant, William C., Donald Collier, Philip J. C. Dark, William N. Fenton, and Ernest S. Dodge. 1970. "An 'Illusion of Religiosity?' " *Indian Historian* 3, no. 2:13–14.

Sullivan, Norman C. 1997. "Contact Period Huron Demography." In *Integrating Archaeological Demography: Multidisciplinary Approaches to Prehistoric Population,* edited by R. R. Paine, 327–42. Occasional Paper no. 24. Carbondale: Center for Archaeological Investigations, Southern Illinois Univ.

Sulman, Felix G. 1982. *Short- and Long-Term Changes in Climate.* 2 vols. Boca Raton, Fla.: CRC Press.

Sutton, Richard E. 1995. "New Approaches for Identifying Prehistoric Iroquoian Migrations." In *Origins of the People of the Longhouse: Proceedings of the 21st Annual Symposium of the Ontario Archaeological Society,* edited by A. Bekerman and G. A. Warrick, 71–85. Toronto: Ontario Archaeological Society.

———. 1996. "The Middle Iroquoian Colonization of Huronia." Ph.D. diss., McMaster Univ.

Swidler, Nina, Kurt E. Dongoske, Roger Anyon, and Alan S. Downer, eds. 1997. *Native Americans and Archaeologists: Stepping Stones to Common Ground.* Walnut Creek, Calif.: AltaMira Press.

Taylor, Walter W. 1948. *A Study of Archaeology.* Memoir 69. Menasha, Wis.: American Anthropological Association.

Terrell, John E. 1986. *Prehistory in the Pacific Islands: A Study of Variation in Language, Customs, and Human Biology.* Cambridge, UK: Cambridge Univ. Press.

———, ed. 2001. *Archaeology, Language, and History: Essays on Culture and Ethnicity.* Westport, Conn.: Bergin and Garvey.

Terrell, John E., and John P. Hart. 2002. Introduction to *Darwin and Archaeology: A Handbook of Key Concepts,* edited by J. P. Hart and J. E. Terrell, 1–13. Westport, Conn.: Bergin and Garvey.

Terrell, John E., John P. Hart, Sibel Barut, Nicoletta Cellinese, Antonio Curet, Tim Denham, Chapurukha M. Kusimba, Kyle Latinis, Rabat Oka, Joel Palka, Mary E. D. Pohl, Kevin O. Pope, Patrick Ryan Williams, Helen Haines, and John E. Staller. 2003. "Domesticated Landscapes: The Subsistence Ecology of Plant and Animal Domestication." *Journal of Archaeological Method and Theory* 10, no. 4:323–68.

Thompson, Robert G. 1993. "Opal Phytolith Analysis Residues from the Mantaro Valley, Peru." Paper presented at the Northeast Andeanist Conference, Pittsburgh.

———. 2000. "Phytolith Analysis of Food Residues from Yutopian, Argentina." On file with Joan Gero, Department of Anthropology, American Univ., Washington, D.C.

Thompson, Robert G., and A. Umran Dogan. 1987. "The Identification of Maize in Food Residues on Utilized Ceramics at the Shea Site (32CS101)." *Phytolitharian Newsletter* 8:7–11.

Thompson, Robert G., John P. Hart, Hetty Jo Brumbach, and Robert Lusteck. 2004. "Phytolith Evidence for Twentieth-Century B.P. Maize in Northern Iroquoia." *Northeast Anthropology* 68:25–40.

Thompson, Robert G., Rose Kluth, and David Kluth. 1995. "Brainerd Ware Pottery Function Explored through Opal Phytolith Analysis of Food Residues." *Journal of Ethnobiology* 15:305.

Thompson, Robert G., and Susan C. Mulholland. 1994. "The Identification of Phytoliths in Food Residues on Utilized Ceramics." *Journal of Electron Microscopy Techniques* 7:146.

Thornton, Russell, Jonathan Warren, and Tim Miller. 1992. "Depopulation in the Southeast after 1492." In *Disease and Demography in the Americas,* edited by J. W. Verano and D. H. Ubelaker, 187–96. Washington, D.C.: Smithsonian Institution Press.

Thwaites, Reuben G., ed. 1896–1901. *The Jesuit Relations and Allied Documents, 1610–1791.* 73 vols. Cleveland: Burrows Brothers.

Tieszen, Larry L., and Tim Fagre. 1993. "Effect of Diet Quality and Composition on the Isotopic Composition of Respiratory CO_2, Bone Collagen, Bioapatite, and Soft Tissue." In *Prehistoric Human Bone—Archaeology at the Molecular Level,* edited by J. B. Lambert and G. Grupe, 121–55. Berlin: Springer-Verlag.

Timmins, Peter A. 1985. *The Analysis and Interpretation of Radiocarbon Dates in Iroquoian Archaeology.* Research Report no. 19. London, ON: London Museum of Archaeology.

———. 1989. "The Butler's Wood Site (AfHj-82) and the Middle Woodland Occupation of the Middle Thames River Drainage." *Kewa* 89, no. 8:2–18.

———. 1997a. *The Calvert Site: An Interpretive Framework for the Early Iroquoian Village.* Mercury Series, Archaeological Survey of Canada, Paper no. 156. Hull, QC: Canadian Museum of Civilization.

———. 1997b. "Born Glen Meyer, Growing up Uren: The Juvenile Ceramics from the Calvert Site." *Kewa* 97, no. 8:2–14.

Tooker, Elisabeth. 1963. "The Iroquois Defeat of the Huron: A Review of Causes." *Pennsylvania Archaeologist* 33, nos. 1–2:115–23.

———. 1964. *An Ethnography of the Huron Indians, 1615–1649.* Bulletin 190. Washington, D.C.: Bureau of American Ethnology.

———. 1970. *The Iroquois Ceremonial of Midwinter.* Syracuse, N.Y.: Syracuse Univ. Press.

———. 1971. "Clans and Moieties in North America." *Current Anthropology* 12, no. 3:357–76.

———. 1978. "The League of the Iroquois: Its History, Politics, and Ritual." In *Handbook of North American Indians.* Vol. 15, *Northeast*, edited by B. G. Trigger, 418–41. Washington, D.C.: Smithsonian Institution.

———. 1981. "Eighteenth Century Political Affairs and the Iroquois League." In *The Iroquois in the American Revolution: 1976 Conference Proceedings,* edited by C. F. Hayes III, 1–12. Research Records no. 14. Rochester, N.Y.: Rochester Museum and Science Center.

———. 1984. "The Demise of the Susquehannocks: A 17th Century Mystery." *Pennsylvania Archaeologist* 54, nos. 3–4:1–10.

———. 1991. *An Ethnography of the Huron Indians, 1615–1649.* 1964. Reprint. Syracuse, N.Y.: Syracuse Univ. Press.

Tremblay, Roland. 1999. "A Middle Phase for the Eastern St. Lawrence Iroquoian Sequence: Western Influences and Eastern Practices." In *Taming the Taxonomy: Toward a New Understanding of Great Lakes Archaeology,* edited by R. F. Williamson and C. M. Watts, 83–100. Toronto: Eastendbooks.

Trigger, Bruce G. 1970. "The Strategy of Iroquoian Prehistory." *Ontario Archaeology* 14:3–48.

———. 1972. "Hochelaga: History and Ethnohistory." In *Cartier's Hochelaga and the Dawson Site,* edited by J. F. Pendergast and B. G. Trigger, 1–108. Montreal: McGill-Queen's Univ. Press.

———. 1976. *The Children of Aataentsic I: A History of the Huron People to 1660.* 2 vols. Montreal: McGill-Queen's Univ. Press.

———. 1978a. "Iroquoian Matriliny." *Pennsylvania Archaeologist* 48:55–65.

———. 1978b. "William J. Wintemberg: Iroquoian Archaeologist." In *Essays in Northeastern Anthropology: In Memory of Marian E. White,* edited by W. E. Engelbrecht and D. K. Grayson, 5–21. Occasional Publications in Northeastern Anthropology no. 5. Rindge, N.H.

———. 1978c. "Early Iroquoian Contacts with Europeans." In *Handbook of North American Indians.* Vol. 15, *Northeast*, edited by B. G. Trigger, 344–56. Washington, D.C.: Smithsonian Institution.

---, ed. 1978d. *Handbook of North American Indians*. Vol. 15, *Northeast*. General Editor, W. C. Sturtevant. Washington, D.C.: Smithsonian Institution.

---. 1981a. "Prehistoric Social and Political Organization: An Iroquoian Case Study." In *Foundations of Northeast Archaeology*, edited by D. R. Snow, 1–50. New York: Academic Press.

---. 1981b. "Ontario Native People and the Epidemics of 1634–1640." In *Indians, Animals, and the Fur Trade: A Critique of "Keepers of the Game,"* edited by S. Krech III, 19–38. Athens: Univ. of Georgia Press.

---. 1985. *Natives and Newcomers: Canada's "Heroic Age" Reconsidered*. Montreal: McGill-Queen's Univ. Press.

---. 1989. *A History of Archaeological Thought*. Cambridge, UK: Cambridge Univ. Press.

---. 1990a [1969]. *The Huron: Farmers of the North*. New York: Holt, Rinehart, and Winston.

---. 1990b. "Maintaining Economic Equality in Opposition to Complexity: An Iroquoian Case Study." In *The Evolution of Political Systems: Sociopolitics in Small-Scale Sedentary Societies*, edited by S. Upham, 119–45. New York: Cambridge Univ. Press.

---. 1991a. "Early Native North American Responses to European Contact: Romantic versus Rationalistic Interpretations." *Journal of American History* 77, no.4:1195–215.

---. 1991b. "Distinguished Lecture in Archaeology: Constraint and Freedom—A New Synthesis for Archaeological Explanation." *American Anthropologist* 93, no. 3:551–69.

---. 1999. "Master and Servant: A Conference Overview." In *Taming the Taxonomy: Toward a New Understanding of Great Lakes Archaeology*, edited by R. F. Williamson and C. M. Watts, 303–22. Toronto: Eastendbooks.

Trigger, Bruce G., L. Yaffe, D. Dautet, H. Marshall, and R. Pearce. 1984. "Parker Festooned Pottery at the Lawson Site: Trace-Element Analysis." *Ontario Archaeology* 42:3–11.

Trigger, Bruce G., L. Yaffe, M. Diksic, J.-L. Galinier, H. Marshall, and James F. Pendergast. 1980. "Trace-Element Analysis of Iroquoian Pottery." *Canadian Journal of Archaeology* 4:119–45.

Trudel, Marcel. 1973. *The Beginnings of New France, 1524–1663*. Toronto: McClelland and Stewart.

Tuck, James A. 1971. *Onondaga Prehistory: A Study in Settlement Archaeology*. Syracuse, N.Y.: Syracuse Univ. Press.

---. 1978. "Northern Iroquoian Prehistory." In *Handbook of North American Indians*. Vol. 15, *Northeast*, edited by B. G. Trigger, 323–33. Washington, D.C.: Smithsonian Institution.

Turgeon, Laurier. 1990. "Basque-Amerindian Trade in the Saint Lawrence During the Sixteenth Century: New Documents, New Perspectives." *Man in the Northeast* 40:81–87.

---. 1997. "The Tale of the Kettle: Odyssey of an Intercultural Object." *Ethnohistory* 44, no. 1:1–29.

Turgeon, Laurier, and William R. Fitzgerald. 1992. "Les Objects des Échanges entre Français et Amérindiens au XVIe Siècle." *Recherches Amérindiennes au Québec* 22, nos. 2–3:152–67.

Turnbaugh, William A. 1977. *Man, Land and Time: The Cultural Prehistory and Demographic Patterns of North-Central Pennsylvania*. Williamsport, Pa.: Lycoming County Historical Society.

Turner, Victor W. 1967. "Color Classification in Ndembu Ritual: A Problem in Primitive Classification." In *The Forest of Symbols: Aspects of Ndembu Ritual,* edited by V. W. Turner, 59–92. Ithaca, N.Y.: Cornell Univ. Press.

———. 1973. "Symbols in African Ritual." *Science* 179:1100–1105.

Ubelaker, Douglas H. 1992. "North American Indian Population Size: Changing Perspectives." In *Disease and Demography in the Americas,* edited by J. W. Verano and D. H. Ubelaker, 169–76. Washington, D.C.: Smithsonian Institution Press.

Upham, Steadman. 1992. "Population and Spanish Contact in the Southwest." In *Disease and Demography in the Americas,* edited by J. W. Verano, and D. H. Ubelaker, 223–36. Washington. D.C.: Smithsonian Institution Press.

U.S. Department of Agriculture. 2002. "USDA Nutrient Database for Standard Reference," <http://www.nal.usda.gov/fnic/cgi-bin/nut_search.pl> (accessed Jan. 2002).

Vandrei, Charles. 1984. "An Overview of Seneca-European Economic Relations 1500 A.D.–1820 A.D." On file, Rochester Museum and Science Center, Rochester, N.Y.

Varley, Colin, and Aubrey Cannon. 1994. "Historical Inconsistencies: Huron Longhouse Length, Hearth Number, and Time." *Ontario Archaeology* 58:85–101.

Vennum, Thomas, Jr. 1988. *Wild Rice and the Ojibway People.* St. Paul: Minnesota Historical Society Press.

von Gernet, Alexander D. 1982. "Interpreting Intrasite Spatial Distribution of Artifacts: The Draper Site Pipe Fragments." *Man in the Northeast* 23:49–60.

———. 1988. "The Transculturation of the Amerindian Pipe/Tobacco/Smoking Complex and Its Impact on the Intellectual Boundaries Between 'Savagery' and 'Civilization,' 1535–1935." Ph.D. diss., McGill Univ.

———. 1993. "Archaeological Investigations at Highland Lake: 1991 Field Season." *Annual Archaeological Report for Ontario,* n.s., 3:74–79.

Wagner, Gail E. 1987. "Uses of Plants by Fort Ancient Indians." Ph.D. diss., Washington Univ.

Wagner, Norman E., Lawrence E. Toombs, and Eduard R. Riegert. 1973. *The Moyer Site: A Prehistoric Village in Waterloo County.* Waterloo, ON: Wilfrid Laurier Univ. Press.

Wallace, Anthony F. C. 1969. *The Death and Rebirth of the Seneca.* New York: Vintage Books.

———. 1978. "Origins of the Longhouse Religion." In *Handbook of North American Indians.* Vol. 15, *Northeast,* edited by B. G. Trigger, 442–48. Washington, D.C.: Smithsonian Institution.

Walters, Jolene. 2003. "Oneidas' History Unearthed." *Oneida Daily Dispatch,* 19 Feb., 1, 14.

Ward, G. K., and S. R. Wilson. 1978. "Procedures for Comparing and Combining Radiocarbon Age Determinations: A Critical Review." *Archaeometry* 20:19–31.

Warrick, Gary A. 1982. "The Long and the Short of Late Ontario Iroquoian House Size." Paper presented at the 15th Annual Meeting of the Canadian Archaeological Association, Hamilton, Ontario.

———. 1984. *Reconstructing Ontario Iroquoian Village Organization.* National Museum of Man, Mercury Series, Archaeological Survey of Canada, Paper no. 124:1–180. Ottawa: National Museums of Canada.

———. 1988. "Estimating Ontario Iroquoian Village Duration." *Man in the Northeast* 36:21–60.

———. 1990. "A Population History of the Huron-Petun, A.D. 900–1650." Ph.D. diss., McGill Univ.

———. 1992a. "Ministry of Transportation: Archaeological Investigations in the Central Region." *Annual Archaeological Report for Ontario*, n.s., 2:67–71.

———. 1992b. "Iroquoiens et taux de Croissance Préindustriels." *Recherches Amérindiennes au Québec* 22, no. 4:24–26.

———. 1996. "Evolution of the Iroquoian Longhouse." In *People Who Lived in Big Houses: Archaeological Perspectives on Large Domestic Structures*, edited by G. Coupland and E. B. Banning, 11–26. Monographs in World Archaeology no. 27. Madison, Wis.: Prehistory Press.

———. 2000. "The Precontact Iroquoian Occupation of Southern Ontario." *Journal of World Prehistory* 14, no. 4:415–66.

Warrick, Gary, James Bruce Jamieson, Jeffrey Bursey, and William A. Fox. 1987. "Sticks and Stones: A Re-evaluation of Prehistoric Iroquoian Warfare." Paper presented at the 20th Annual Chacmool Conference, Univ. of Calgary.

Warrick, Gary, and James Molnar. 1986. "An Iroquoian Site Sequence from Innisfil Township, Simcoe County." *Arch Notes* 86, no. 3:21–34.

Watkins, Joe E. 2000. *Indigenous Archaeology: American Indian Values and Scientific Practice*. Walnut Creek, Calif.: AltaMira Press.

Watson, Adam S. 2000. "Subsistence and Change at Townley-Read: A Faunal Analysis of a Historic Period Seneca Iroquois Site." Senior Honors Thesis, Cornell Univ.

Wattenwyl, Andre, and Heinrich Zollinger. 1979. "Color-Term Salience and Neurophysiology of Color Vision." *American Anthropologist* 81, no. 2:279–88.

Waugh, Frederick W. 1916. *Iroquois Foods and Food Preparation*. Anthropological Series no. 12, Memoir 86. Ottawa: Canada Department of Mines, Geological Survey.

Weber, Cynthia J. 1971. "Types and Attributes in Iroquois Pipes." *Man in the Northeast* 2:51–65.

Weinman, Paul L. 1969. *A Bibliography of the Iroquoian Literature*. New York State Museum Bulletin 411. Albany: State Univ. of New York.

Weslager, Clinton A. 1969. *The Log Cabin in America: From Pioneer Days to the Present*. New Brunswick, N.J.: Rutgers Univ. Press.

West, George A. 1934. *Tobacco, Pipes and Smoking Customs of the American Indians*. Bulletin of the Public Museum of the City of Milwaukee, 17. Reprinted in 1970. Westport, Conn.: Greenwood Press.

Whallon, Robert J. 1968. "Investigations of Late Prehistoric Social Organization in New York State." In *New Perspectives in Archaeology*, edited by S. R. Binford and L. R. Binford, 223–44. Chicago: Aldine.

White, Marian E. 1961. *Iroquois Culture History in the Niagara Frontier Area of New York State*. Anthropological Papers no. 16. Ann Arbor: Univ. of Michigan.

———. 1966. "The Owasco and Iroquois Cultures: A Review." *The Bulletin: Journal of the New York State Archaeological Association* 36:11–14.

———. 1976. "Late Woodland Archaeology in the Niagara Frontier of New York and Ontario." In *The Late Prehistory of the Lake Erie Drainage Basin: A 1972 Symposium Revisited*, edited by D. S. Brose, 110–36. Cleveland: Cleveland Museum of Natural History.

Whitney, Theodore. 1967. "The Bach Site." *Bulletin of the Chenango Chapter of the New York State Archaeological Association* 8, no. 4.

———. 1970. "The Buyea Site, Ond 13-3." *The Bulletin: Journal of the New York State Archaeological Association* 50:1–14.

———. 1971. "The Olcott Site, Msv-3." *Bulletin of the Chenango Chapter of the New York State Archaeological Association* 12, no. 3.

———. 1974. "Aboriginal Art and Ritual Objects." *Bulletin of the Chenango Chapter of the New York State Archaeological Association* 15, no. 1.

Willey, Gordon R. 1966. *An Introduction to American Archaeology: North and Middle America*. Vol. 1. Englewood Cliffs, N.J.: Prentice-Hall.

Willey, Gordon R., and Philip Phillips. 1958. *Method and Theory in American Archaeology*. Chicago: Univ. of Chicago Press.

Williamson, Ronald F. 1978. "Preliminary Report on Human Interment Patterns of the Draper Site." *Canadian Journal of Archaeology* 2:117–22.

———. 1985. "Glen Meyer: People in Transition." Ph.D. diss., McGill Univ.

———. 1990. "The Early Iroquoian Period of Southern Ontario." In *The Archaeology of Southern Ontario to A.D. 1650*, edited by C. J. Ellis and N. Ferris, 291–320. Occasional Publications of the London Chapter of the Ontario Archaeological Society no. 5. London, Ontario.

———. 1992. "Croissance Démographique et Continuité Culturelle dans le Nord-Est Américain." *Recherches Amérindiennes au Québec* 22, no.4: 26–28.

Williamson, Ronald F., and Carol Naismith Ramsden. 1998. "Summary and Conclusions" (chap. 6), "Settlement Patterns" (chap. 2). In *The Myers Road Site: Archaeology of the Early to Middle Iroquoian Transition*, edited by R. F. Williamson, 193–203. Occasional Publications no. 7. London, ON: London Chapter of the Ontario Archaeological Society.

Williamson, Ronald F., and David A. Robertson. 1994. "Peer Polities Beyond the Periphery: Early and Middle Iroquoian Regional Interaction." *Ontario Archaeology* 58:27–48.

———, eds. 1998. "The Archaeology of the Parsons Site: A Fifty Year Perspective." *Ontario Archaeology* 65/66:1–161.

Willoughby, Charles C. 1935. *Antiquities of the New England Indians*. Cambridge, Mass.: Peabody Museum of American Archaeology and Ethnology, Harvard Univ.

Wilson, Jim. 1991. "A Bad Analogy? Northern Algonquian Models and the Middle Woodland Occupations of Southwestern Ontario." *Kewa* 91, no. 4:9–22.

Winship, George Parker, ed. 1905. *Sailors Narratives of Voyages along the New England Coast, 1524–1624*. Boston: Houghton, Mifflin.

Wintemberg, William J. 1936. *The Roebuck Prehistoric Village Site, Grenville County, Ontario*. Bulletin 83, Anthropological Series no. 19. Ottawa: National Museum of Canada.

Witkowski, Stanley R., and Cecil H. Brown. 1977. "An Explanation of Color Nomenclature Universals." *American Anthropologist* 79, no. 1:50–57.

Witthoft, John. 1966. "Archaeology as a Key to the Colonial Fur Trade." *Minnesota History* 40:203–9.

———. 1969 [1959]. "Ancestry of the Susquehannocks." In *Susquehannock Miscellany*, edited by J. Witthoft and W. F. Kinsey III, 19–60. Harrisburg: Pennsylvania Historical and Museum Commission.

Woodley, Philip J. 1996. "The HH Site (AhGw-81), QEW Highway and Redhill Creek Expressway, Regional Municipality of Hamilton-Wentworth." On file, Ontario Ministry of Transportation, Downsview.

Woodley, Philip J., Rebecca Southern, and William R. Fitzgerald. 1992. "The Archaeological Assessment and Partial Mitigation of the Zamboni Cemetery (AgHb-144), Brantford." On file, Ministry of Culture and Communications, Toronto.

Wraxall, Peter. 1915. *An Abridgement of the Indian Affairs Contained in Four Folio Volumes, Transacted in the Colony of New York, from the Year 1678 to the Year 1751,* edited by C. H. McIlwain. Cambridge, Mass.: Harvard Univ. Press.

Wray, Charles F. 1973. *Manual for Seneca Iroquois Archaeology.* Honeoye Falls, N.Y.: Cultures Primitive.

———. 1979–82. "Field Notes: Townley-Read Site." On file, Research Division, Rochester Museum and Science Center, Rochester, N.Y.

———. 1982. "The Seneca Sequence." Talk presented at the Gannet School, Rochester Museum and Science Center.

———. 1983. "Seneca Glass Trade Beads c. A.D. 1550–1820." In *Proceedings of the 1982 Glass Trade Bead Conference,* edited by C. F. Hayes III, 41–49. Research Records no. 16. Rochester, N.Y.: Rochester Museum and Science Center.

———. 1985. "The Volume of Dutch Trade Goods Received by the Seneca Iroquois, 1600–1687 A.D." *New Netherland Studies Bulletin KNOB* 84, nos. 2–3:100–112.

Wray, Charles F., and Harry Schoff. 1953. "A Preliminary Report on the Seneca Sequence in Western New York—1550–1687." *Pennsylvania Archaeologist* 23, no. 2:53–63.

Wray, Charles F., Martha L. Sempowski, and Lorraine P. Saunders. 1991. *Tram and Cameron: Two Early Contact Era Seneca Sites.* Charles F. Wray Series in Seneca Archaeology. Vol. 2. Research Records no. 21. Rochester, N.Y.: Rochester Museum and Science Center.

Wray, Charles F., Martha L. Sempowski, Lorraine P. Saunders, and Gian C. Cervone. 1987. *The Adams and Culbertson Sites.* Charles F. Wray Series in Seneca Archaeology. Vol. 1. Research Records no. 19. Rochester, N.Y.: Rochester Museum and Science Center.

Wright, Gary A. 1974. *Archeology and Trade.* Addison-Wesley Module in Anthropology, no. 49. Reading, Mass.: Addison-Wesley.

Wright, James V. 1966. *The Ontario Iroquois Tradition.* Bulletin 210, Anthropological Series no. 75. Ottawa: National Museum of Canada.

———. 1972. *Ontario Prehistory: An Eleven-Thousand-Year Archaeological Outline.* Ottawa: National Museums of Canada.

———. 1974. *The Nodwell Site.* National Museum of Man, Mercury Series, Archaeological Survey of Canada, Paper no. 22. Ottawa: National Museums of Canada.

———. 1979. *Quebec Prehistory.* Toronto: Van Nostrand-Reinholt.

———. 1984. "The Cultural Continuity of the Northern Iroquoian-Speaking Peoples." In *Extending the Rafters: Interdisciplinary Approaches to Iroquoian Studies,* edited by M. K. Foster, J. Campisi, and M. Mithun, 283–99. Albany: State Univ. of New York Press.

———. 1987. "The Roebuck Site: A St. Lawrence Iroquois Prehistoric Village." In *Quaternary of the Ottawa Region and Guides for Day Excursions,* edited by R. J. Fulton, 55–58. 12th INQUA Congress, Ottawa.

———. 1990. "Archaeology of Southern Ontario to A.D. 1650: A Critique." In *The Archaeology of Southern Ontario to A.D. 1650,* edited by C. J. Ellis and N. Ferris, 493–503. Occasional Publications no. 5. London, ON: London Chapter of the Ontario Archaeological Society

———. 1992a. "Une Critique sur les Aspects Démographiques et la Migration Tardive des Iroquoiens." *Recherches Amérindiennes au Québec* 22, no. 4:29–32.

———. 1992b. "The Conquest Theory of the Ontario Iroquois Tradition: A Reassessment." *Ontario Archaeology* 54:3–16.

Wright, James V., and James E. Anderson. 1969. *The Bennett Site.* Bulletin 229. Ottawa: National Museum of Canada.

Wright, James V., and Rudolphe Fecteau. 1987. "Iroquoian Agricultural Settlement." In *Historical Atlas of Canada I: From the Beginning to 1800,* edited by R. C. Harris, plate 12. Toronto: Univ. of Toronto Press.

Wright, James V., and Jean-Luc Pilon, eds. 2004. *A Passion for the Past: Papers in Honour of James F. Pendergast.* Mercury Series, Archaeology Paper no. 164, 125–44. Gatineau, QC: Canadian Museum of Civilization.

Wright, Milton J. 1981. *The Walker Site.* National Museum of Man, Mercury Series, Archaeological Survey of Canada, Paper no. 103, 1–210. Ottawa: National Museums of Canada.

———. 1986. *The Uren Site AfHd-3: An Analysis and Reappraisal of the Uren Substage Type Site.* Monographs in Ontario Archaeology no. 2. Toronto: Ontario Archaeological Society.

Wrigley, Edward A. 1969. *Population and History.* Toronto: McGraw-Hill.

Wurst, LouAnn, and Nina M. Versaggi. 1993. "Under the Asphalt: The Archaeology of the Binghamton Mall Project." Binghamton, N.Y.: Public Archaeology Facility, Binghamton Univ.

Wykoff, Milton William. 1988. "Iroquoian Prehistory and Climate Change: Notes for Empirical Studies of the Eastern Woodlands." Ph.D. diss., Cornell Univ.

Yarnell, Richard A. 1993. "The Importance of Native Crops During the Late Archaic and Woodland Periods." In *Foraging and Farming in the Eastern Woodlands,* edited by C. M. Scarry, 13–26. Gainesville: Univ. Press of Florida.

Young, Susan A. 1995. "The Cobble Pit." *Bulletin of the Chenango Chapter of the New York State Archaeological Association* 25, no. 1.

Zvelebil, Marek. 1986. "Mesolithic Societies and the Transition to Farming: Problems of Time, Scale and Organisation." In *Hunters in Transition,* edited by M. Zvelebil, 167–88. Cambridge, UK: Cambridge Univ. Press.

Index

Abel, Timothy J., 327
Adams site, 224, 226, 297
Adirondacks, 394
Agneetha, 428
Aiionwatha (Hiawatha), 396
Akwesasne: archaeology at, 423–24, 432–34; capacity building for cultural resource management, 436–39; laws of the land, 426–27; "made in Akwesasne" strategy, 439–40; repatriation and roadblocks to recovery, 434–36; Sacred Trust responsibility of, 431–32; territory, 424–26; Two-Row Wampum Belt, 429–31; Wolf Belt, 427–29
Algonquians: cabins, 185; and gold, 320; Iroquois migration stopped by, 394; warfare with Neutral, 157, 261
Allegheny Valley/Ohio Valley/Ontario sphere of exchange, 196, 214, 216–18
Allen, Kathleen M. S., 169, 361
American Anthropological Association, 413
amino acid complementarity hypothesis, 121–22
Ammerman, Albert J., 26, 51
AMS dating, 36, 52–53, 57–66, 98–103
Andaste, 216
Anderson, David G., 43–44, 243
Anderson, James E., 25
Andrefsky, William, 232
Anthony, David W., 23
Appalachians, linguistic indicators of origins in, 46
art, sacred objects as, 408
Atironta, 187
Attignawantan, 230, 323
Attigneenongnahac, 230

Atwell site, 242
Auda site, 17
Ausable focus, 31, 135
availability model, 36–37

Bach site, 350, 354, 355
Bailey, Alfred Goldsworthy, 310n
Ball, Terry D., 109
Ball site, 183, 185–86
Bamann, Susan E., 169
Barker site, 329
"bark longhouses," 246
bark shingles, 180
Barrie site, 147
Bartram, John, 247
"Basque earrings," 303
Basque exchange network, 301
Bates site, 15, 227
bead study (Seneca and Susquehannock): background, 194–97; data analysis, 200–207; data sources, 197–200; discussion and conclusions, 211–18; method, 197; results, 207–11. *See also* shell, marine and freshwater; wampum
bean, common: amino acid complementarity hypothesis, 121–22; change in chronology of, 95; and marginal horticulture, 266; and Neutral cultural shifts, 258; nitrogen fixing, 170; as Owasco trait, 81–82; phytolith analysis, 118–19. *See also* maize-bean-squash cultivation
Beauchamp, William M., 225, 348
beaver pelt trade, 253–54
Beaver Wars, 323

545

Beecher site, 351
behavior: village movement and, 164–65
bench-support posts, 180
Bennett, Monte R., 350n
Bering Strait theory, 391–92
Berlin, Brent, 312n, 314n
Big House ceremony (Delaware), 367
black and black-ness, 313–14, 318. *See also* color
blue, 317, 318
Bogaert, Harmen Meyndertsz Van den, 231
Bogucki, Peter, 43, 66
Boland site, 81
Boyle, David, xxv, 252
Bozarth, Steven R., 111
bracelets, brass, 210, 211
Bradley, James W., 209, 222, 242, 328–29, 345
Braidwood, Robert J., 50
brass assemblages (Seneca and Susquehannock), 209–10, 211. *See also* spirals and hoops, copper and brass
Brébeuf, Jean de, 150, 178, 280
Breen collection, 55, 57
Bronson, Bennett, 138
Brotherson, Jack D., 109
Bruegel, Pieter the Elder, 264
Brûlé, Etienne, 197
Brumbach, Hetty Jo., 86
Bruyas, Jacques, 362
Bryson, Reid A., 263
Buffalo Historical Society, 417
bulk transport, 171
burials: "brutalized" remains, 255–56; clans and cemeteries, 228; and color, 314n, 315, 316; ossuaries, 149–50, 280–81; pots in, 362–63; repatriations, 403–9, 437; sacred responsibility to preserve, 431; spirals and hoops in, 209–10, 294–97. *See also* skeletal remains
Buyea site, 350, 351, 362

cabins, 183, 185, 186–87, 246–47
Cahiagué, 176, 185, 187
Calvert site, 142
Cameron site, 198, 199, 353, 356. *See also* bead study (Seneca and Susquehannock)
camps, 13, 16
Canandaigua phase, 13

canoe-navigable waterways, 170–71
capacity building, 436–39
"captive bride" explanation for exotic pottery, 322–25
Carantouanais, 216
carbohydrates and marginal horticulture, 266–67
carbon isotope studies, 112–17, 139, 144
cardinal direction, movement according to, 171
Carpenter Brook phase, 13
Carrington, Henry B., 418
Cartier, Jacques, 124, 191, 275, 311–12, 379
Cashie phase, 44
Castle Creek phase, 13
catlinite, 210–11
Caughnawaga site, 228
Cavalli-Sforza, Luigi L., 26, 51
Cayuga Lake, 399
Cayuga Nation, 28
cemeteries. *See* burials
census of Huron-Petun by Jesuits (1639–1640), 272, 279
ceramics: "captive bride" explanation for exotic pottery, 322–25; of Clemson's Island, 26; corn associated with, 361, 363; Early Iroquoian (southern Ontario), 149; and League formation, 230–32; manufacture, use, and social contexts, 360–64; migration hypothesis and discontinuities in, 25, 38; Mohawk rim sherd assemblages analysis, 326–31; Mohawk smoking pipes trace element analysis, 331–38, 340; Munsee Incised pottery, 365; Neutral, 258, 259, 260, 261; Oneida, 231–32; Ontario Iroquoian, 17; Point Peninsula and Owasco food residue AMS dating, 52–53, 57–66, 77–78, 79–80; of Point Peninsula Tradition, 12–13; pottery as women's domain, 360–61; Sandbanks, 135–36; Seneca, 231; in situ model anomalies, 22; size of pots, 361–62; social messages embodied in pots, 344n; St. Lawrence Iroquoian, 160; taxonomic bias in interpreting, 84–85; and tribal formation, 223–24, 225. *See also* effigies, ceramic
Cervone, Gian C., 359
Chamberlain site, 16
Champlain, Samuel de, 26, 127, 176, 185, 186–87, 197, 215–16, 247, 252, 258, 271, 276, 398

Chapdelaine, Claude, 50–52, 65
Chase site, 300
Chenango Point Binghamton Mall site, 36
Cheyenne case, 45–46
Childs, S. Terry, 209
Chilton, Elizabeth A., 344n
Christopher site, 224
chronologies. *See* dating and chronologies
CHUs (corn heat units), 265
clan affiliation, 226–29
Clausen, H. B., 263
clay sources and trace element analysis, 333–36
Clemson's Island Culture, 25–26, 28, 35, 38, 39, 42
Clermont, Norman, 27
clustered villages and tribal development, 220
Cohoes Falls, 398
Colgate University, 443–53
Colonie, N.Y., 398
colonization: and Middleport population growth, 151
color: and exchange of trade goods, 315–17; ideational values of light, bright, and white, 310–12, 315; preferences for, 317–20; semantics and ritual states-of-being, 312–15
Committee on Anthropological Research in Museums, 413
Conable, Barber, 418
Conestoga site, 242–43
Conover, George S., 236
contact. *See* European contact
cooking residues. *See* food residue analysis
Cootes Paradise site, 136–37
copper goods, 258, 301, 315–16. *See also* spirals and hoops, copper and brass
core-periphery hypothesis, 27
corn. *See* maize
corn harvest ceremony, 366, 368
corn heat units (CHUs), 265
Corn Mother, 366
Coulter site, 156
Covenant Chain, 320
Crane, Oliver, 418
Crawford, Gary W., 129, 136
creolized houses, 249
Cromwell site, 324
crowding and disease, 275
cultivating ecosystem type, 13

cultural development, 251
cultural ecology movement, 165–66
cultural resource management in Akwesasne, 422, 431, 436–40
culture, losses in transmission of, 438
culture-historic paradigm, 69, 82, 86–87

Daes, Erica-Irene, 425–26, 427, 437, 439
Dansgaard, W., 263
dating and chronologies: Early Iroquoian (southern Ontario), 144–45; food residue analyses, 52–53, 57–66, 98–103; Late Woodland Period, 13–15, 129; Ontario Iroquoian, 17–18, 128–30; Owasco, 13–15, 14, 44–45; Princess Point, 31–33, 129; Seneca and Susquehannock bead sites, 213, 217; and untested culture histories, 48–49; Woodland Period chronologies, xxvi. *See also* glottochronology
Dawson Creek site, 36
debris accumulation, 382–83
deer: and Neutral, 256, 258, 260, 266; and Uren, 147
defensibility of hilly terrain, 168, 338–39
Deganawidah, 230. *See also* Peacemaker (Skennenrahawi)
Delaware culture, 365–66, 367–68
DeNiro, Michael J., 97, 112, 115
depopulation from epidemic disease: archaeological estimate for Wendat-Tionontate, 279–80; overview, 269–70; St. Lawrence Iroquoians, 162; Wendat-Tionontate as ideal case study for, 270–71; Wendat-Tionontate bioarchaeology and analysis, 280–84; Wendat-Tionontate epidemics, 272–74, 283
Diable site, 350, 355
digital imaging, 452–53
Dincauze, Dena F., 27
discontinuities: in Cheyenne record, 46; and migration hypothesis, 24–25, 43; Princess Point and Ontario Iroquoian, 16–17, 131
disease, European: before 1634 in Northeastern North America, 274–76; and Algonquian traders, 275–76; and clan affiliation, 227; in Europe, 282–83; factors preventing early spread of, 282; Wendat-Tionontate

disease, European (*cont.*)
bioarchaeology and analysis, 280–84; Wendat-Tionontate epidemics, 272–74. *See also* depopulation from epidemic disease
Divale, William, 21–22, 35, 51, 133
Dobyns, Henry F., 162, 304
domesticate adoption, 51
Domestic Refuse Clusters (DRCs), 237
Draper site, 156, 181–83, 224, 377
Dunbar, Helene R., 302
Dungey site, 443, 447
Dunn, Walter, 417
Dunnell, Robert C., 70
Dunnville cluster, 137
Dutch Hollow site, 198, 199. *See also* bead study (Seneca and Susquehannock)
Dwyer site, 297

Eastern Eight-Row maize, 138, 139
eclipses, solar, 397–98
effigies, ceramic: archaeological approaches to, 344–46; areal distribution in Northeast, 346–48; and cornhusk people, 364–66; form and iconography (Oneida), 353–60; manufacture, use, and social contexts (Oneida), 360–64; mythic significance, 366–68; Oneida effigy sequence, 348–53; overview, 343–44; pipes, 345–46, 373–76, 378–79, 380–82
Egli site, 243–45
electron microprobe analysis, 297
Elwood site, 338–39
Emerson, J. Norman, 31, 252
end cubicle area of a longhouse, 180
Engelbrecht, William E., 4, 27, 84, 133, 322, 326, 329
England's Woods site, 329
epidemics. *See* depopulation from epidemic disease; disease, European
ethnographic systems vs. archaeological units, 84
Europe: disease in, 282–83; domesticate adoption in, 51; Little Ice Age in, 263–64; spread of agriculture into, 43
European contact: architectural influences, 185–87, 248–49; effects on cultural decline, 251; and Iroquoian warfare, 341; and redefinition of mythical realities, 306–8; and resurgence of goods exchange, 316–17; and World's edge, 309–10. *See also* disease, European
European goods: metals, 301–2; migration supposed as result of, 253–54; and Neutral, 260–61, 262
"European-style log cabins," 246–48
exchange networks: Allegheny Valley/Ohio Valley/Ontario sphere, 196, 214, 216–18; and color, 315–17; overview, 194–97; and smoking pipes, 333, 336–38. *See also* bead study (Seneca and Susquehannock)
exogamy, tribal, 231–32

Fairty, 280, 281
Farrell site, 223–24
Feast of the Dead, 364
Fecteau, Rudolphe D., 170, 264
Fenton, William N., xxv, 165, 363, 418
Ferris, Neal, 120
fertility rates, 158
Fiedel, Stuart J., 21, 133
Fields, Jerry L., 388, 397–98
Finlayson, William D., 129–30, 148
Fire Nation (Algonquian), 261
Fitzgerald, William R., 169, 185, 196, 198, 199n, 207–8, 209, 213, 213n
Five Nations Confederacy (League of the Iroquois): destruction of Ontario Iroquoians by, 176–77; disease among, 276; effigies among, 348; formation of, 229–32; founding of, 396–98, 410; Grand Council of the Confederacy, 396; longhouses of, 177; St. Lawrence Iroquoians, conflict with, 161. *See also* spirals and hoops
Follett, H. C., 57
food residue analysis—Hunter's Home, Kipp Island, and Wickham: AMS dates, 98–103; carbon isotope ratios, 112–17; discussion and conclusions, 117–22; importance of, 97; museum collections used for, 96–97; phytolith analysis, 103–12; sites, 97–98
food residue analysis—Point Peninsula and Owasco AMS dating, 52–53, 57–66, 77–78, 79–80
Footer site, 223–24
Forster site, 37

Fox, William A., 31
French dwellings among Huron, 186–87
Frontenac Axis, 10, 125
Funk, Robert E., 8, 13, 15, 20, 23, 45, 70, 71, 95, 164, 166, 228, 322, 336
fur trade, 253–54, 341
fusion model, 221–22, 224

Galinat, W. C., 95
Ganondagan site, 242–45, 399
Garoga site, 228, 329, 338–39, 341
Gates St-Pierre, Christian, 98
geographic information systems (GIS), 166–73
geology of Northern Iroquoia region, 10
Gerber, Art, 408
Getman site, 336, 337, 338–39
Gibson, Stanford J., 169
Gila River Indian Community, 449
GIS (geographic information systems), 166–73
glass beads. *See* bead study (Seneca and Susquehannock); color
Glen Meyer Tradition: chronology and dating, 14; and migration hypothesis, 26; and Pickering Conquest hypothesis, 148–49; and Princess Point, 37–38, 41–42; villages, 17
glottochronology: and homeland as Earth-Island, 307; and migration hypothesis, 6–7, 44, 132–33; and in situ model, 20. *See also* linguistic history
Gnagey site, 36
Goff site, 351, 362
gold, unappreciation of, 320
Gonyea, Ray, 420
Gould, Stephen J., 6
Grand Banks site, 33, 34, 36, 37–38
Grand Council of the Confederacy, 396, 414
Grand River focus, 31, 136, 137
Grand River valley sites, 136, 137–38
Graybill, Jeffrey R., 200
Great Hill, 399
Great Law of Peace, 394–96, 402, 410, 426–27
Great League of Peace. *See* Five Nations Confederacy
Great Tree of Peace, 396
Green, Geraldine, 403, 405, 408
Gregg, Susan A., 66
Griffin, James B., 10, 18–19, 48

Grimsby cemetery, 281
growing season, 168–69

Hamell, George R., 225, 303, 346, 360
Hamilton site, 183
Hammer, C. U., 263
Hart, John P., 78
Hasenstab, Robert J., 27
Hastorf, Christine A., 97, 112, 115
Haudenosaunee Confederacy. *See* Five Nations Confederacy
Haudenosaunee Standing Committee on Burial Rules and Regulations, 408
Hayden, Brian, 258
Hayes, Charles III, 403, 404, 407–8
health and disease. *See* depopulation from epidemic disease; disease, European
health and fertility rates, 158
hearth density and population estimates, 277–78, 279
hearths, 178
Heidenreich, Conrad E., 241, 266
Henige, David, 388
hepatitis, 276
Herbstritt, James, 198n
Hewitt, John N.B., 228
Heye, George, 418
Heye Foundation, 418, 420
Hiawatha (Aiionwatha), 396
Highland Park excavation, 407
hilltop occupation, 167–68, 338–39
Hiscock, Frank, 419
Hochelaga, 124
Holmedale site, 140
hoops. *See* spirals and hoops, copper and brass
Hopi, 393
horticulture: Little Ice Age and failure of, 254, 264–67; maize-bean-squash cultivation, 81–82, 94–96, 170; of Point Peninsula Tradition, 13; swidden, 307; and warfare intensification, 254–55. *See also* maize
house forms: cabins, 183, 185, 186–87, 246–47; classification of 18th-century forms, 246–49; at Levanna site, 56–57; Owasco vs. Point Peninsula, 15, 55; Princess Point, 137. *See also* longhouses
Hunt, Eleazer D., 169

Hunter, William A., 196
Hunter's Home phase, 13–14, 45, 55, 77
Hunter's Home site, 55–56, 57–65, 78–81. *See also* food residue analysis—Hunter's Home, Kipp Island, and Wickham
Huron, as term, 127
Huron confederacy, 230
Huron-Petun (Wendat-Tionontate): Algonquian relations, 158; archaeological estimates of population and depopulation, 276–80; bioarchaeology and analysis, 280–84; defined, 152; demographic stability, 152–53; epidemics recorded among, 272–74, 283; Feast of the Dead, 364; first contacts with French, 275; longhouses, 183; overview, 270–71; population estimates, 271–72; pottery styles found among Mohawk, 323–25, 327, 329–31; pot use, 360–61; villages, 155–56; villages and longhouse growth, 153–56
Husk Face Society, 364

Ibaugh site, 198n
Illinois State Geological Survey (SGS), 98
incursion model. *See* migration hypothesis
Indian Law (New York), 414, 419
influenza, 272–73
in situ model: anomalies in, 20–23, 42–43, 131; assumptions and overviews of, 7, 10, 18–20, 130; and continuity in archaeological data, 134; and Point Peninsula-Owasco sherd study, 65–66; punctuated vs. gradual model, 48, 49–52. *See also* migration hypothesis (incursion model)
intercultural houses, 249
Iroquoian (as term), xxiv, 126, 175
Iroquois (as term), xxiii–xxiv, 175
Iroquois Cosmology (Hewitt), 228

jacknife classification, 334
Jackowski, John, 326
Jackson-Everson site, 323
Jamieson, James Bruce, 161, 340
Jamieson, Susan M., 196, 213n, 217
Jamieson site, 158
Jarvenpa, Robert, 86
Jemison, Mary, 362

Jikonsasay, 395–96, 399
Johnson, John, 428
Johnson, William C., 196, 213n, 216–17

Kahnesataka, 428
Kanienkehaka ("People of the Flint"). *See* Mohawk Nation
Kapches, Mima, 17, 239–40, 245–46, 336, 337
Kay, Paul, 312n, 314n
Kent, Barry C., 196, 198, 212n, 216, 360
Kenyon, Ian T., 41, 198, 207–8, 213, 213n
kettles, copper, 301
Kidd and Kidd classification system, 200, 209
kinship and tribal formation, 307
Kipp Island phase, 97–98
Kipp Island site, 53–55, 57–65, 78–81. *See also* food residue analysis—Hunter's Home, Kipp Island, and Wickham
Kleinburg ossuary, 280–81
Knight, Dean H., 185
Koslow Corporation Metal Identification Set, 300
Kraft, Herbert C., 365–66, 367

Lafitau, Joseph-François, 361
lake effect, 169
lake plain sites, 171–72
Lakeshore Lodge, 135–36
Lalemant, Jerome, 283, 323
land, connection to, 425–26, 429
Larson, Daniel O., 257–58
Late Woodland Period: chronology and dating, xxvi, 13–15, 82–86, 129; as culture-historic construct, 69; GIS study of settlement patterns, 166–73; maize in, 95
Laudonniere, Goulaine de, 258
Laurentian Nadoueks. *See* St. Lawrence Iroquoian
The League (Morgan), 229
League of the Ho-de-no-sau-nee (Morgan and Parker), 388
League of the Iroquois. *See* Five Nations Confederacy
LeCaron, Father Joseph, 186
Legend of Two Serpents, 399–402
Le Jeune, Paul, 312n, 416
Lenig, Donald, 322

Lenig, Wayne, 329
Lescarbot, Marc, 258
Levanna site, 56–61, 63–65
light, ideational value of, 311, 315
linear stain features, 183
linguistic history: Appalachian origins, 46; material culture vs., 85–86; and migration hypothesis, 6–7, 35; oldest divergence from Proto-Northern-Iroquoian, 44; Proto-Algonquian, 133; proto-language reconstruction, 21; in situ model anomalies, 20–21. *See also* glottochronology; Proto-Northern-Iroquoian
Little Ice Age, 254, 263–64, 266–67
Little Water Medicine, 304
log cabins, 246–48
Lone Pine site, 33, 34, 37–38
longhouses: and clan affiliation, 227, 228; classic form of, 16; crowding and disease in, 275; debris accumulation in, 382–83; Huron-Petun and Neutral, 153–55, 257–58, 259–60; iron nails in, 244–45; and Mandeville pipe collection, 378, 382–83; and matrilocal residence, 133; orientation of, 228; Owasco, 15, 78; and population growth, 154–55; Princess Point, 137; raw materials and construction of, 177–78; significance and symbolism of, 174–75, 176–77; standard details, 179–81; structural variability, 181–87; Townley-Read Structure 1 (short longhouse), 234–46. *See also* house forms
Long Point site, 136–37
Longyear, John, 451
Longyear Museum of Anthropology, 450–53
Lovis, William A., 97, 98, 114, 122
Lower Grand River valley sites, 136, 137–38
Lyons, Oren, 413

Mackenzie-Woodbridge site, 185
MacNeish, Richard S.: on ceramics, 326, 328, 329; on culture development, 251; on effigies, 348–49, 348n, 351, 355, 357; on Neutral, 252; Ontario Iroquoian chronology, 128–29; on Owasco-Iroquois continuity, 3; on Owasco sherds, 58; and Owasco taxon construction, 73–74, 76–78, 82, 84–85; and in situ model, 18–19, 20, 31, 48–50, 130

maize: amino acid hypothesis on intensification of, 121–22; and Chapdelaine's model, 50, 51; cob chaff, 104; corn heat units (CHUs), 265; Eastern Eight-Row variety, 138, 139; and founding of League, 397; and marginal climate, 266–67; mythic and ritual aspects, 366; Northern Flint Corn complex, 104, 118; overview, 93–94; as Owasco trait, 81–82; pots associated with, 361, 363; Princess Point, 16, 33–34, 36–37, 42, 134, 138–40; and proto-language construction, 21; reasons for adoption of, 139–40; Southern Dent complex, 104; speculation on timing of, 95; and St. Lawrence Iroquoians, 160; wild rice compared to, 139. *See also* food residue analysis
maize-bean-squash cultivation, 81–82, 94–96, 170
Mandeville pipe collection: collection overview, 371; explanation for density of, 382–83; function of pipes, 378–82; morphology and style, 371–77; site description, 370–71; spatial relations at site, 377–78
Mann, Barbara A., 388, 397–98
marine shell. *See* shell, marine and freshwater; wampum
Marshall site, 351–52, 362
Martijn, Charles A., 254
Massawomeck, 196
material culture, social identity confused with, 84–86
Mathews, Zena Pearlstone, 378
matrilineage, 227–28, 344n, 395–96
matrilocal residence: as adaptive response, 24; and migration, 43, 130–31, 133; and pottery style differentiation, 337; in situ model anomalies, 21–22
McAndrews, John H., 264
measles, 272
Medieval warm epoch, 45
Megapolensis, Johannes, Jr., 320
Memorial Park site, 81
Metacom (King Philip), 404
metallographic analysis, 300
Meyer site, 136, 137
Michaelson, Joel, 257–58
microclimate and settlement patterns, 168–69
Middleport phase, 150–52

Middleport site, 37
Middle Woodland Period, 82–86
migration: and 14th-century social transformation, 336; archaeological problems, 23–24; Bering Strait theory, 391–92; and canoe-navigable waterways, 170–71; cardinal direction, movement according to, 171; European goods vs. horticultural distress as cause of, 253–54; spread of agriculture into Europe, 43; of St. Lawrence Iroquoians into Mohawk territory, 328–29; of war captives, 323–24. *See also* settlement patterns
migration hypothesis (incursion model): and AMS sherd study, 65–66; assumptions, 45–46; overview, 6–10, 130–34; and Princess Point, 35–39, 41–43; Snow's alternative hypothesis of incursion, 23–27, 41–47, 51–52. *See also* in situ model
Miller, Patricia L., 199
Milner, George R., 340
Minisink culture, 365
Mississippian influence, 149, 196
Mithun, Marianne, 25
Mohawk, John, 403, 404–5, 406–7
Mohawk Council of Akwesasne, 425n
Mohawk Council of Chiefs, 425n
Mohawk Nation: "captive bride" explanation for exotic pottery, 322–25; clan affiliation in, 228; effigies, 349; and gold, 320; and Huron, 323–24; laws, importance of, 430–31; Legend of Two Serpents, 399–402; origins of, 394; origins of warfare with Northern Iroquoians, 338–42; population, 278, 279; rim sherd assemblages analysis, 326–31; sacred sites, 398; settlement changes in response to warfare, 338–39; smoking pipe trace element analysis, 331–38, 340. *See also* Akwesasne
Mohawk River, 398
Molto, Joseph Eldon, 25
Monongahela, 196, 217
Montezuma Wildlife Refuge, 399
Morgan, Lewis Henry, xxv, 171, 229, 251, 388, 404
mortality rates and clan affiliation, 227, 228. *See also* depopulation from epidemic disease
Mt. Pleasant, Jane, 115
Mulholland, Susan C., 103, 104, 107

Munsee Incised pottery, 365
Murray, Priscilla, 383
museum collections: and crop history investigation, 96–97, 122; human remains and sacred objects in, 403–9, 452; of wampum, 411–14. *See also* repatriation
Museum of the American Indian, 418, 420
mutualist houses, 249
Myers Road site, 150
mythical realities and religion: and contact, 306–8; early teachings, 395; and effigies, 345–46, 364–68; World's Rim as cultural frontier, 308–10. *See also* oral traditions; ritual

NAGPRA. *See* Native American Graves Protection and Repatriation Act of 1990
nails, iron, 244–45
National Historic Preservation Act of 1966 (NHPA), 1992 amendments to, 387–88
nation development. *See* tribal formation
Native American Graves Protection and Repatriation Act of 1990 (NAGPRA): and Akwesasne, 434; confrontations preceding, 411; and Longyear Museum of Anthropology, 450–52; overview, 387–88; and "who owns the past," 403n, 409
Neo-Boreal. *See* Little Ice Age
Neutral Nation: cultural trends by century, 257–62; defined, 152, 252; demographic stability, 152–53; and European Contact, 262–63; history of archaeological research on, 252; Little Ice Age and horticultural failure, 263–67; longhouses, 183; territory and distribution, 252–56; villages and longhouse growth, 153–56
New York, sacred sites in, 398–99
New York State Archaeological Association, 408, 452
New York State Museum, 419, 420
Niagara Frontier, 231
Nichols Pond, 398
Niemczycki, Mary Ann Palmer, 225
Nipissing, 273
nitrogen fixing, 170
nitrogen isotope studies, 139
Noble, William C., 16, 41, 380

Nodwell site, 28, 151, 179–80
North American Fur Trade Conference, 423
Northern Flint Corn complex, 104, 111
Northern Iroquoians, as term, xxiv, 10
Nottoway Nation, 20

oak, 264
Oak Ridges Moraine, 146–47
O'Callaghan, Edmund B., 415
Olcott site, 352, 354
Oneida Castle, 398
Oneida Indian Nation Men's Council and Clan Mothers, 445, 446–47, 452–53
Oneida Indian Nation Youth Work/Learn Program, 444-50
Oneida Nation, 232, 443–54. *See also* effigies, ceramic
Onondaga Council of Chiefs, 413, 416
Onondaga Historical Association, 418
Onondaga Lake, 398–99
Onondaga Nation: clustering of sites, 221; effigies, 345, 348, 349; pottery, 328; sacred sites, 398–99; tribal formation, 222, 227; and wampum, 413, 416–20
Ontario, advantages of archaeology in, 127–28
Ontario Corn Committee, 265
oral traditions: archaeological record vs., 406; Great Law of Peace, 394–96; on League formation, 229–30; Legend of Two Serpents, 399–402; origins and migration from oral traditions, 392–94; tribal formation in, 224–25
origin myths, 225, 392–94
origins research and culture-historic taxa as unit of analysis, 67–70
Ossossane ossuary, 279, 280, 281
ossuary burials, 149–50, 280–81
osteology. *See* skeletal remains
Otstungo site, 328, 338–39, 341
Owasco Tradition: chronology and dating, 13–15, 44–45; and culture-historic paradigm, 67–70; definitions of, 15–16; as extensionally defined culture-historic taxon, 70–76, 82–87; food residue AMS dating studies, 52–66, 77–78, 79–80; and migration hypothesis, 25, 26; and in situ model, 19–20; traits used for taxonomy, 76–82

panthers, 304, 346
Parker, Arthur C., xxv, 3, 8–9, 18, 56–57, 68–78, 71–72, 75–76, 82, 363
Parker, Ely S., 229, 388
Parsons site, 156, 224
particle-induced X-ray emission (PIXE) spectrometry, 332
partitions in longhouses, 183
paternalism, academic, 397
Pawnee Nation, 393
Peacemaker (Skennenrahawi), 395–96, 398. *See also* Deganawidah
Pearsall, Deborah M., 104
Pendergast, James F., 161, 169, 196, 330, 382, 423–24
Pennsylvania Historical Museum Commission, 198
Petun, as term, 127. *See also* Huron-Petun (Wendat-Tionontate)
Phillips, Philip, 74
photography, digital, 452–53
phytolith analysis: and food residues, 103–4, 122; methods, techniques, and classification, 104, 107, 108; results, 107–12, 113, 114; samples, 104, 105, 106
Pickering Conquest hypothesis, 148–49
Pickering Tradition, 14, 17–18
Piperno, Delores R., 104
pipes. *See* smoking pipes
pits, defined, 178–79
PIXE (particle-induced X-ray emission) spectrometry, 332
pneumonia, 275
Point Pelee focus, 31, 135
Point Peninsula Tradition: chronology, 13–14; food residue AMS dating study, 52–53, 52–66, 77–78, 79–80; interpretation of ceramic types, 85; and migration hypothesis, 25; overview, 10–13; Owasco contrasted with, 15; and Proto-Northern-Iroquoian, 21; and in situ model, 19–20, 23
population density and community size: Early Iroquoian (southern Ontario), 145; Huron-Petun and Neutral, 153; St. Lawrence Iroquoian, 160–61; Uren, 146–47. *See also* depopulation
population estimates: 1492 North America, 269–70; and hearth density, 277–78;

population estimates (*cont.*)
  Wendat-Tionontate, 271–72, 276–80. *See also* depopulation
population growth: demographic stability of Huron-Petun and Neutral, 152–53; Early Iroquoian (southern Ontario), 143–44; and longhouse size, 154–55; and maize adoption, 140; and Middleport phase, 150–51; and migration hypothesis, 27
porcelaine, 311n
portages, 170–71
Porteous site: chronology, 16, 17; and migration model, 33, 39, 41
post molds, 178, 237–41, 243–44
post pits, 178, 181–82
pottery. *See* ceramics
Powless, Chief Irving, Jr., 403, 406, 408
Pratt, Peter P., 328, 350n, 351
precontact and prehistoric, as terms, 125–26
Primes Hill site, 243–45
Princess Point Complex: chronology, 31–33, 129; defined, 135; maize adoption and cultivation, 16, 33–34, 36–37, 42, 134, 138–40; and migration model, 35–39, 41–47; overview, 16, 31; pottery, 38–39; redefinitions of, 31–34; region map, 32; settlement patterns, 16, 34, 137–38; sites, 135–37; sociopolitical organization, 141
Princess Point type site, 37
protein, 121–22, 266–67
Proto-Algonquian, 133
Proto-Northern-Iroquoian: Appalachian origins, 46; and migration vs. in situ model, 21, 35, 133; oldest divergence from, 44

Quackenbush site, 158

racism, scientific, 404
Radisson, Pierre Esprit, 324
rainfall: and settlement patterns, 169
Ramsden, Peter G., 23, 131, 224
Rankin, Lisa K., 151
Rapp, George, Jr., 103, 107
Rataul, Ralph C., 329
Ravesloot, John C., 449
red and red-ness, 313–14, 318–19. *See also* color

Red Earth Summer Archaeology Program, 449, 450
religion. *See* mythical realities and religion
repatriation: and Akwesasne, 434–36; and Longyear Museum of Anthropology, 450–53; of Onondaga wampum, 417–20; symposium discussion on, 403–9
rice, wild. *See* wild rice
Richter, Daniel K., 345
Ritchie, William A.: on culture development, 251; and Dutch Hollow site, 198; on Hunter's Home A site, 56; and Kipp Island site, 53–55, 58, 103; on longhouse orientations, 228; and maize-bean-squash cultivation as defining trait, 94–95; Mohawk research, 322, 336; and Owasco chronology, 13; and Owasco taxon construction, 5, 15, 25, 26, 68–78, 82–86; on Point Peninsula, 10–11; and settlement patterns, 164, 166; in situ model, 8, 18–20, 49–52, 65
ritual: color and ritual states-of-being, 312–13; and European goods, 260–61; moral teachings and Great Law of Peace, 395; as social contract, 308; at Wood's-edge, 309n. *See also* mythical realities and religion
Riviere au Vase, 135
Robertson, David A., 337
Rochester Museum and Science Center, 408–9
Rockefeller, Nelson, 413
Roebuck site, 371, 381–82
rondel phytoliths. *See* phytolith analysis
Rothschild, Nan, 234
Roundtop site, 36, 78, 81, 96
Rouse, Irving, 24
Rovner, Irwin, 103
Ruhl, Katharine C., 302, 303
Rumrill, Donald, 326

Sackett site, 15
sacred places in New York, 398–99
sagamité (corn soup), 361
Sagard, Gabriel, 127, 186, 271, 276, 360–61, 362–63
Sahlins, Marshall D., 21–22, 226, 312n
Sandbanks Tradition, 135–36
Saunders, Lorraine, 403, 405, 407
Scanonaenrat, 279

scarlet fever, 273
Schoff, Harry, 200
Schoolcraft, Henry, 252
Schulenberg, Janet K., 97, 98, 99, 103, 116
Schultz site, 196, 198, 199, 217, 300. *See also* bead study (Seneca and Susquehannock)
scientific racism, 404
Sears, William H., 219
Seaver, James E., 225
Secor, Harold, 56
sedge, 111–12, 115, 120–21
Seely, Arthur, 56
Selden, G. B., 57
Sempowski, Martha, 403, 405–6, 408
Seneca Archaeology Research Project, 198, 200
Seneca Nation: clustering of sites, 221; and colors, 314n; effigies, 345, 348n, 349, 359; origin myth, 225; and resurgence of copper and shell trade, 316; sacred sites, 399; tribal formation, 223–26, 230, 307. *See also* bead study (Seneca and Susquehannock); spirals and hoops, copper and brass
Service, Elman A., 226
settlement patterns: and canoe-navigable waterways, 170–71; cardinal-direction movement, 171; cultural ecology studies (Late Woodland), 165–66; Early Iroquoian (southern Ontario), 141–45; GIS analysis (Late Woodland), 166–73; hilltop occupation, 167–68, 338–39; Huron-Petun and Neutral, 155–56, 158; maize inferred from, 95; and microclimate, 168–69; micro vs. macro, 164; and migration model, 37; nucleated villages, Owasco, 78–81; Owasco, 15–16; Point Peninsula, 15; Princess Point, 16, 34, 137–38; and rainfall, 169; in situ model anomalies, 23; social factors in, 171–72; and soils, 169–70; Uren, 146; village movement as correlate of behavior, 164–65; warfare and settlement size, 156–57
sexual division of labor: and ceramic effigies, 360–61; and ceramic styles, 324, 332–33, 337; and Mandeville pipes, 379–80
sexually specific features on effigies, 354
Shako:wi Cultural Center, 446, 453
shell, marine and freshwater: exchange of, 316; and Neutral, 258; and Seneca and Susquehannock, 210, 211, 215. *See also* wampum
sherds. *See* ceramics

Shultz, Richard, 408
Sidell, Asch, 119
silver, 320
Sioui, Georges, 127
skeletal remains: and Colgate summer workshop, 445; discussion on proper treatment and reburial of, 404–9; Point Peninsula vs. Owasco, 25; Wendat-Tionontate bioarchaeology, 280–81. *See also* burials; repatriation
Skennenrahawi (Peacemaker), 395–96, 398. *See also* Deganawidah
Sky Woman, 393
slash pits, 183
sleeping benches, 245–46
smallpox, 273–74, 276, 281, 283
Smith, Bruce D., 13
Smith, David G., 17, 129, 135–36
Smith, Ira F., 200
smoking pipes: density at Mandeville, 382–83; effigy pipes, 345–46, 373–76, 378–79, 380–82; function of, 378–82; Mandeville collection overview, 371; morphology, 371–72; size, 372–74; spatial relations of Mandeville collection, 377–78; styles, 374–77; trace element analysis (Mohawk), 331–38, 340. *See also* ceramics
Snow, Dean R., 50–52, 65, 103, 130–33, 241, 274, 276, 278, 392–93
Snow Foundation, 444, 446
social, asocial, and antisocial states-of-being, 313
social Darwinism, 404
social identity confused with material culture, 84–86
social order and ritual, 308
sociopolitical organization: and macrosettlement, 172; Middleport, 151–52; Princess Point, 141; Uren, 146
soils, 169–70
solar eclipses, 397–98
Southern Dent complex, 104
Southwest, American, 393
spatial dynamics, 174, 245–46
Speck, Frank G., 367, 368
Spence, Michael W., 324
Spencer-Bronte Neutral tribal grouping, 261
spirals and hoops, copper and brass: chronological and geographic distribution of, 211, 215, 292–94; description of, 290–92; interpretations of, 303–4; materials analysis,

spirals and hoops, copper and brass (cont.) 297–301; mortuary associations, 209–10, 294–97; Native fabrication of, 302–3; sources of European metals, 301–2
springs, 168
squash: change in chronology of, 95–96; as Owasco trait, 81; phytolith analysis, 111, 116, 118–19. See also maize-bean-squash cultivation
St. Lawrence Iroquoians: chronology, 129; as construct, 127; European contact and depopulation, 162, 275; overview, 159–62; pottery motifs at Mohawk sites, 325, 327–29, 330–31. See also Mandeville pipe collection
St. Lawrence Seaway, 433
St. Marie Among the Iroquois, 399
St. Regis Tribal Council, 425n
Starna, William A., 23
State University of New York, 419
Sterling site, 443, 447
Steward, Julian H., 85
Stewart, Michael, 25, 42
Stothers, David M., 16, 31, 34, 41, 130
straw men, 366
strep infection, 273
Sturtevant, William, 418
subsistence practices: Early Iroquoian (southern Ontario), 144; Neutral, 258, 260; of Point Peninsula Tradition, 13; Princess Point, 140; swidden incorporated into, 307. See also deer; horticulture; maize
Sullivan, Martin, 420
Sullivan-Clinton expedition (1779), 248
Sullivan site, 352
Sulman, Felix G., 263
summer workshop in archaeology (Colgate University), 443–50
Susquehannock Nation: effigies, 360; and migration hypothesis, 28. See also bead study (Seneca and Susquehannock); spirals and hoops, copper and brass
sweat lodges, 149–50
swidden horticulture, 307
Swidler, N., 403n

Tadodaho, 396, 398–99
Tahontaenrat, 230, 279

taxa, culture-historic, 67–70, 82–86
Taylor, Walter W., 74
Thanksgiving Address, 346, 395, 427, 440
Thatcher, John B., 418, 419
thermal belts, 168
Thompson site, 37
Thurston Horizontal pottery, 351, 357
Thurston site, 351–52, 362
Tionontate. See Huron-Petun (Wendat-Tionontate)
tobacco pipes. See smoking pipes
"Tory Houses," 248
Townley-Read/New Ganechstage Project, 234–36
Townley-Read Structure 1 (short longhouse): artifacts, 241–42; house plan and construction, 242–46; location, mapping, and excavations, 235–37; overview, 234–35; post mold patterns, 237–41
trace element analysis, 331–38, 340
trait assemblages as taxonomical criteria, 82–86
Transitional Woodland period, 129
treaty-making and wampum, 416
tribal formation: community fusion vs. alliances, 220–22; and contact, 307; Onondaga, 222; and political consolidation, 232; Seneca, 223–26, 230, 307; and village concentration, 158
Trigger, Bruce G., 15, 22, 23, 127, 133, 221, 228, 229, 309n, 335, 336
tuberculosis, 275
Tuck, James A., 8, 222, 224, 226, 227, 242
Turgeon, Laurier, 363–64
Turnbaugh, William A., 25
Tuscarora Nation, 20, 394, 417
Two-Row Wampum Belt, 429–31

Underwater Panther, 304
Union of Ontario Indians, 418
Uren phase, 145–50
Urton, Gary, 451
Uxbridge ossuary, 280, 281
uxorilocal residence, 130

Vaillancourt site, 350, 353, 354
Van Besien site, 17

Verrazzano, Giovanni da, 274, 320
Versaggi, Nina M., 45
villages. *See* settlement patterns
Vinette 2 series, 12

wall post density, 245
wall trenches, 182
wampum: Akwesasne Wolf Belt, 427–29; and future generations, 420–21; loss of, 416–17; meaning and function of, 311–12, 414–16; overview, 410–11; political battle over, 412–14; repatriations, 417–20; and revitalization movements, 411–12; Two-Row Wampum Belt, 429–31. *See also* shell, marine and freshwater
Wampum Laws (New York), 412, 419, 420
warfare: "captive bride" explanation for exotic pottery, 322–25; defensibility of hilly terrain, 168, 338–39; and dependence on horticulture, 254–55; disease interrupted by isolation from, 283; Huron-Petun, Neutral, and St. Lawrence, 156–57; League Iroquois vs. Ontario Iroquoians, 176–77; limitations of archaeological record on, 321–22; and matrilocality vs. patrilocality, 24; Mohawk vs. Northern Iroquoian, 327–30, 338–42; and settlement patterns, 171; traditional tribal vs. intensified territorial conflict, 340–41; and tribal formation, 225–26; and waterways, 170–71
Warfel, Steven, 198
Warrick, Gary A., 227, 245, 340–41, 361
Washington, George, 416
Washington Boro site, 198n, 212, 217
Waterloo cluster, 137
waterways, canoe-navigable, 170–71
Weber, Cynthia J., 336
Webster, Chief Thomas, 416, 418, 419, 420
weight distribution in house construction, 248
Weinman, Paul, xxv

Wendat-Tionontate. *See* Huron-Petun (Wendat-Tionontate)
Wendland, Wayne M., 263
Western Basin Tradition, 157
wetlands, movement away from, 168
Whallon, Robert J., 16, 22
White, Marian, 252
white and white-ness, 311, 313–15, 318. *See also* color
white pine, 264
white-tailed deer. *See* deer
Whitney, Theodore, 343, 350n, 354
"Who Owns the Past?" symposium, 403–9
Wickham site, 78–81. *See also* food residue analysis—Hunter's Home, Kipp Island, and Wickham
Wilcox Lake site, 147
wild rice: amino acid complementarity hypothesis, 121–22; maize compared to, 139; phytolith analysis, 104, 109, 111, 115–17, 119–20. *See also* food residue analysis
Willey, Gordon R., 7, 74
Williams, Paul, 418
Williamson, Ronald F., 17, 38, 43, 337
Wilson site, 443, 447
Wintemberg, William J., xxv, 20, 252
Witthoft, John, 303
Wolf Belt, Akwesasne, 427–29
woodchuck, 256, 258
World League of Nations, 395
World's Rim, 308–10
Wray, Charles F., 166, 168, 200, 223, 236, 359
Wright, James V., 16, 17, 18, 25, 31, 128–29, 130, 141–42, 148, 251, 252, 336
Wurst, LouAnn, 45
Wykoff, Milton William, 25, 169, 170

X-ray fluorescence (XRF) analysis, 332, 333–34

yellow as undesirable color, 319–20